WARRANTED CHRISTIAN BELIEF

WARRANTED CHRISTIAN BELIEF

Alvin Plantinga

New York   Oxford

Oxford University Press

2000

Oxford University Press

Oxford   New York
Athens   Auckland   Bangkok   Bogotá   Buenos Aires   Calcutta
Cape Town   Chennai   Dar es Salaam   Delhi   Florence   Hong Kong   Istanbul
Karachi   Kuala Lumpur   Madrid   Melbourne   Mexico City   Mumbai
Nairobi   Paris   São Paulo   Singapore   Taipei   Tokyo   Toronto   Warsaw

and associated companies in
Berlin   Ibadan

Copyright © 2000 by Alvin Plantinga

Published by Oxford University Press, Inc.
198 Madison Avenue, New York, New York 10016

Oxford is a registered trademark of Oxford University Press.

Library of Congress Cataloging-in-Publication Data
Plantinga, Alvin.
Warranted Christian belief / Alvin Plantinga.
p. cm.
Includes index.
ISBN 0-19-513193-2 (pbk.)—ISBN 0-19-513192-4
1. Apologetics.   2. Christianity—Philosophy.   3. Faith and reason—Christianity.
I. Title.
BT1102 .P57 1999
230'.01–dc21   98.054362

7 9 8

Printed in the United States of America
on acid-free paper

To

WILLIAM P. ALSTON

Mentor, Model, Friend

Preface

This book is about the intellectual or rational acceptability of Christian belief. When I speak here of Christian belief, I mean what is common to the great creeds of the main branches of the Christian church, what unites Calvin and Aquinas, Luther and Augustine, Menno Simons and Karl Barth, Mother Teresa and St. Maximus the Confessor, Billy Graham and St. Gregory Palamas—classical Christian belief, as we might call it.

Classical Christian belief includes, in the first place, the belief that there is such a person as God. God is a *person*: that is, a being with intellect and will. A person has (or can have) knowledge and belief, but also affections, loves, and hates; a person, furthermore, also has or can have intentions, and can act so as to fulfill them. God has all of these qualities and has some (knowledge, power, and love, for example) to the maximal degree. God is thus all-knowing and all-powerful; he is also perfectly good and wholly loving. Still further, he has created the universe and constantly upholds and providentially guides it. This is the *theistic* component of Christian belief. But there is also the uniquely Christian component: that we human beings are somehow mired in rebellion and sin, that we consequently require deliverance and salvation, and that God has arranged for that deliverance through the sacrificial suffering, death, and resurrection of Jesus Christ, who was both a man and also the second member of the Trinity, the uniquely divine son of God. I shall use the term 'Christian belief' to designate these two components taken together. Of course, I realize that others may use that term more narrowly or more broadly. There is no need to argue about words here: the beliefs I mentioned are the ones I shall discuss, however exactly we propose to use the term 'Christian'. I also recognize that there are partial approximations to Christian belief so understood, as well as borderline cases, beliefs such that it simply isn't clear whether they qualify as Christian belief. All of this is true, but as far as I can see, none of it compromises my project.

Accordingly, our question is this: is belief of this sort intellectually acceptable? In particular, is it intellectually acceptable for *us*, *now*? For educated and intelligent people living in the twenty-first century, with all that has happened over the last four or five hundred years? Some will concede that Christian belief was acceptable and even appropriate for our ancestors,[1] people who knew little of other religions, who knew nothing of evolution and our animal ancestry, nothing of contemporary subatomic physics and the strange, eerie, disquieting world it postulates, nothing of those great masters of suspicion, Nietzsche, Marx, and Freud, nothing of the acids of modern historical biblical criticism. But for us enlightened contemporary intellectuals (so the claim continues) things are wholly different; for people who know about those things (people of our rather impressive intellectual attainments), there is something naïve and foolish, or perhaps bullheaded and irresponsible, or even vaguely pathological in holding onto such belief.

But can't we be a little more precise about the objection? What, exactly, is the problem? The answer, I think, is that there are alleged to be *two* main problems. Western thought since the eighteenth-century Enlightenment has displayed at least two distinct styles of objection. First, there have been *de facto* objections: objections to the *truth* of Christian belief. Perhaps the most important *de facto* objection would be the argument from suffering and evil. This objection goes all the way back to Democritus in the ancient world but is also the most prominent contemporary *de facto* objection (see chapter 14). It has often been stated philosophically, but has also received powerful literary expression (for example, in Dostoevski's *The Brothers Karamazov*). The objection goes as follows: according to Christian belief, we human beings have been created by an all-powerful, all-knowing God who loves us enough to send his son, the second person of the divine Trinity, to suffer and die on our account; but given the devastating amount and variety of human suffering and evil in our sad world, this simply can't be true.

The argument from evil may be the most important *de facto* objection, but it isn't the only one. There are also the claims that crucial Christian doctrines—Trinity, Incarnation, or Atonement, for example—

---

1. And perhaps (as they may add) even for contemporaries who lead sheltered lives in cultural backwaters—for instance, the area between the east and west coasts of the United States.

are incoherent or necessarily false. Many have argued that the Christian doctrine of three divine persons with one nature cannot be coherently stated; many have claimed that it is not logically possible that a human being, Jesus of Nazareth, should also be the second person of the divine Trinity, and many have thought it impossible that one person's suffering—even if that person is divine—should atone for someone else's sins. Indeed, there are claims that the advance of science has somehow shown that there really isn't any supernatural realm at all—no God who has created us and governs our world, let alone a Trinity of divine persons, one of whom became a human being, died, and rose from the dead, thereby redeeming human beings from sin and suffering.

De facto objections, therefore, are many, and they enjoy a long and distinguished history in Western thought. Even more prevalent, however, have been *de jure* objections. These are arguments or claims to the effect that Christian belief, whether or not true, is at any rate unjustifiable, or rationally unjustified, or irrational, or not intellectually respectable, or contrary to sound morality, or without sufficient evidence, or in some other way rationally unacceptable, not up to snuff from an intellectual point of view. There is, for example, the Freudian claim that belief in God is really a result of wish fulfillment; there is the evidentialist claim that there isn't sufficient evidence for Christian belief; and there is the pluralist claim that there is something arbitrary and even arrogant in holding that Christian belief is true and anything incompatible with it false. *De facto* and *de jure* objections are separate species, but they sometimes coincide. Thus there is a *de jure* objection from suffering and evil as well as a *de facto*: it is often claimed that the existence of suffering and evil in the world makes it irrational to hold that Christian belief is, in fact, true.

De facto objections are relatively straightforward and initially uncomplicated: the claim is that Christian belief must be false (or at any rate improbable), given something or other we are alleged to know. Quite often the claim is that it is something we *now* know, something our ancestors allegedly did not know, as in Rudolf Bultmann's widely quoted remark that "it is impossible to use electrical light and the wireless and to avail ourselves of modern medical and surgical discoveries, and at the same time to believe in the New Testament world of spirits and miracles."[2] *De jure* objections, by contrast, while perhaps more widely urged than their *de facto* counterparts, are also much less straightforward. The conclusion of such an objection will be that there is something wrong with Christian belief—something other than falsehood—or else something wrong with the Christian believer:

2. *Kerygma and Myth* (New York: Harper and Row, 1961), p. 5.

it or she is unjustified, or irrational, or rationally unacceptable, in some way wanting. But *what* way, exactly? Just what is it to be unjustified or irrational? No doubt it is a bad thing to hold beliefs that are rationally unjustified: but what precisely is the problem? Wherein lies the badness? This is ordinarily not made clear. According to the evidentialist, for example, the evidence for Christian belief is *insufficient*: but insufficient for *what*? And suppose you believe something for which the evidence is insufficient: what, exactly, is the matter with you? Are you thereby subject to moral blame, or shown to be somehow incompetent, or unusually ignorant, or subject to some kind of pathology, or what? According to Freud and some of his followers, Christian and theistic belief is a product of wish fulfillment or some other projective mechanism. Well, suppose (contrary to fact, as I see it) that is true: just what is the problem? Is it that such a belief is likely to be false? Is it that if you accept a belief formed on the basis of wish fulfillment, you have done something that merits blame? Or are you, instead, a proper object of pity? What, precisely, is the problem?

These questions are much harder to answer than one might think. One project of this book is to try to answer them: I try to find a serious and viable *de jure* objection to Christian belief. That is, I try to find a *de jure* objection that is both a real objection and also at least plausibly attached to Christian belief. But there is a prior question: *is* there actually any such thing as Christian belief, conceived as Christians conceive it? Some thinkers (often citing the authority of the great eighteenth-century philosopher Immanuel Kant) argue that we couldn't so much as think about such a being as the Christian God, infinite and transcendent as he is supposed to be. That is because our all-too-human concepts could not apply to such a being; our concepts can apply only to finite beings, beings who are not transcendent in the way Christians take God to be. But if it is really true that our concepts cannot apply to an infinite and transcendent being, if we cannot so much as *think about* such a being, then we human beings also have no *beliefs* about such a being. Indeed, we *can't* have beliefs about such a being. And then the fact is there isn't any such thing as Christian belief: Christians *think* they have beliefs about an infinite and transcendent being, but in fact they are mistaken. In part I, "Is There a Question?" (chapters 1 and 2), I argue that there is no reason at all to accept this skeptical claim: Kant himself provides no reason, and those contemporaries who appeal to his authority certainly do no better.

That conclusion clears the deck for the main question of the book: is there a viable *de jure* objection to Christian belief? One that is independent of *de facto* objections and does not presuppose that Christian belief is false? There are, I believe, fundamentally three main candidates: that Christian belief is *unjustified*, that it is *irrational*, and that it is *unwarranted*. These candidates will be introduced in due course; for the moment, note just that three of the main characters of this drama, therefore, are justification, rationality, and warrant. In part II, "What Is the Question?" (chapters 3–4), I ask first whether a viable *de jure* criticism can be developed in terms of justification and rationality; I conclude that it cannot. Then I turn (chapter 5) to the objections offered by Freud, Marx, and Nietzsche; and here we finally find an initially promising candidate for a *de jure* objection. This complaint is in the vicinity of *warrant*. To see what warrant is, note that not all true beliefs constitute knowledge. You are an ardent Detroit Tigers fan; out of sheer bravado and misplaced loyalty, you believe that they will win the pennant, despite the fact that last year they finished last and during the off season dealt away their best pitcher. As it happens, the Tigers unaccountably do win the pennant, by virtue of an improbable series of amazing flukes. Your belief that they will, obviously, wasn't *knowledge*; it was more like an incredibly lucky guess. To count as knowledge, a belief, obviously enough, must have more going for it than truth. That extra something is what I call 'warrant.' As I see it, if there are any real *de jure* objections to Christian belief, they lie in the neighborhood of warrant.

That may not come as much of a surprise, given that this book is a sequel to *Warrant: The Current Debate* and *Warrant and Proper Function*.[3] In the first of those books I introduced the term 'warrant' as a name for that property—or better, *quantity*—enough of which is what makes the difference between knowledge and mere true belief. I went on to examine the various contemporary theories of warrant: what exactly *is* the property that distinguishes knowledge from mere true belief? I canvassed the contemporary theories on offer: is it justification? coherence? rationality? being produced by reliable belief-producing faculties or processes? The answer, I argued, is none of the above; none of these theories is right. In *Warrant and Proper Function* I went on to give what seems to me to be the correct answer: warrant is intimately connected with *proper function*. More fully, a belief has warrant just if it is produced by cognitive processes or faculties that are functioning properly, in a cognitive environment that is propitious for that exercise of cognitive powers, according to a design plan that is successfully aimed at the production of true belief. (For explanation of that perhaps baffling formula, see chapter 5.)

---

3. Both published by Oxford University Press (New York, 1993). This book is also, and in a slightly different direction, a sequel to *God and Other Minds* (Ithaca: Cornell University Press, 1967) and "Reason and Belief in God," in *Faith and Rationality*, ed. A. Plantinga and N. Wolterstorff (Notre Dame: University of Notre Dame Press, 1983).

According to Freud and Marx, therefore, the real problem with theistic (and hence Christian) belief is that it lacks warrant. In part III, "Warranted Christian Belief" (chapters 6–10), I address this objection. As it turns out, this *de jure* objection is really dependent on a *de facto* objection. That is because (as I argue) if Christian belief is true, then it is also warranted; the claim that theistic (and hence Christian) belief is unwarranted really presupposes that Christian belief is false. Freud and Marx, therefore, do not give us a *de jure* objection that is independent of the truth of Christian belief; their objection presupposes its falsehood. I go on (in chapter 6) to offer a model, the Aquinas/Calvin (A/C) model, for theistic belief's having warrant and argue that if theistic belief is in fact true, then something like this model is in fact correct.

In chapters 7 through 10, I extend the A/C model to cover full-blown Christian belief (as opposed to theistic belief *simpliciter*), beginning (in chapter 7) with an account of the place of *sin* in the model. Next (in chapters 8 and 9), I propose the extended A/C model; according to this model, Christian belief is warranted because it meets the conditions of warrant spelled out in *Warrant and Proper Function*. That is, Christian belief is produced by a cognitive process (the "internal instigation of the Holy Spirit" [Aquinas] or the "internal testimony of the Holy Spirit" [Calvin]) functioning properly in an appropriate epistemic environment according to a design plan successfully aimed at truth. Chapter 8, "The Extended A/C Model: Revealed to Our Minds," sets out the cognitive side of this process. The process involves the affections as well as reason, however (i.e., it involves will as well as intellect), and chapter 9, "The Testimonial Model: Sealed upon Our Hearts," explains some of the connections between reason and the affections. Chapter 10 concludes part III by considering various actual and possible objections to the model; none is successful. What I officially claim for the extended A/C model is not that it is *true* but, rather, that it is *epistemically possible* (i.e., nothing we know commits us to its falsehood); I add that if Christian belief is true, then very likely this model or something like it is also true. If I am right in these claims, there aren't any viable *de jure* criticisms that are compatible with the truth of Christian belief; that is, there aren't any viable *de jure* objections independent of *de facto* objections. And if *that* is so, then the attitude expressed in "Well, I don't know whether Christian belief is *true* (after all, who could know a thing like that?), but I do know that it is irrational (or intellectually unjustified or unreasonable or intellectually questionable)"—that attitude, if I am right, is indefensible.

Finally, in part IV, "Defeaters?" (chapters 11–14), I confront the following claim. Someone might concede that Christian belief could *in principle* be warranted in the way the model suggests; she might go on to insist, however, that in fact there are various *defeaters* for the warrant Christian belief might otherwise enjoy. A defeater for a belief *A* is another belief *B* such that once you come to accept *B*, you can no longer continue to accept *A* without falling into irrationality. In the present case, then, these alleged defeaters would be beliefs a knowledgeable Christian can be expected to have; they would also be beliefs such that one who accepts them cannot rationally continue in firmly accepting Christian belief. After exploring the nature of defeaters, I examine the chief candidates: first, the alleged abrasive results of historical biblical criticism; second, a recognition of the variety and importance of religions incompatible with Christian belief, together with certain related postmodern claims; and third, a deep recognition of the facts of suffering and evil. I argue that none of these succeeds as a defeater for classical Christian belief.

This book can be thought of in at least two quite different ways. On the one hand, it is an exercise in apologetics and philosophy of religion, an attempt to demonstrate the failure of a range of objections to Christian belief. *De jure* objections, so the argument goes, are either obviously implausible, like those based on the claim that Christian belief is not or cannot be justified, or else they presuppose that Christian belief is not true, as with those based on the claim that Christian belief lacks external rationality or lacks warrant. Hence there aren't any decent *de jure* objections that do not depend on *de facto* objections. Everything really depends on the *truth* of Christian belief; but that refutes the common suggestion that Christian belief, whether true or not, is intellectually unacceptable.

On the other hand, however, the book is an exercise in Christian philosophy: in the effort to consider and answer philosophical questions—the sorts of questions philosophers ask and answer—from a Christian perspective. What I claim for the extended A/C model of chapters 8 and 9 is twofold: first, it shows that and how Christian belief can perfectly well have warrant, thus refuting a range of *de jure* objections to Christian belief. But I also claim that the model provides a good way for Christians to think about the epistemology of Christian belief, in particular the question whether and how Christian belief has warrant. So there are two projects, or two arguments, going on simultaneously. The first is addressed to everyone, believer and nonbeliever alike; it is intended as a contribution to an ongoing public discussion of the epistemology of Christian belief; it does not appeal to specifically Christian premises or presuppositions. I shall argue that, from this public point of view, there isn't the faintest reason to think that Christian belief lacks justification, rationality, or warrant —at least no reason that does not presuppose the *falsehood* of Christian belief. The other project, however—the project of proposing an epistemological account of Christian belief from a Christian perspective —will be of special interest to Christians. Here the project is that of starting from an assumption of the truth of Christian belief and from that standpoint investigating its epistemology, asking whether and how such belief has warrant. We might think of this project as a mirror image of the philosophical naturalist's project, when he or she assumes the truth of naturalism and then tries to develop an epistemology that fits well with that naturalistic standpoint.

I hope Christians will find this second project appealing; I hope others as well may be interested—just as those who don't accept philosophical naturalism might nevertheless be interested to see what kind of epistemology would best go with naturalism. The centerpiece of each of the two projects—the apologetic project and the project in Christian philosophy—is the extended A /C model. Taken the first way, that model is a defense of the idea that Christian belief has warrant and an effort to show that if Christian belief is true, then (very likely) it does have warrant; taken the second, it is a recommendation as to how Christians can profitably understand and conceive of the warrant they take Christian belief to have.

The reader is owed an apology for the inordinate length of this book. All I can say by way of self-exculpation is that its length is due to a determination not to commit a tetralogy: a trilogy is perhaps unduly self-indulgent, but a tetralogy is unforgivable. (I suppose a cynic might question the difference between a tetralogy and a trilogy, the last member of which is twice as long as the preceding members.) In any event, not every reader need read every page. For example, those readers who are not tempted to think that our concepts could not apply to God can safely skip part I, and those readers who want to read only the central part of the story line can confine themselves to chapters 6 through 9. Furthermore, even though the book is long, I am aware that it covers a shameful amount of ground, and that in nearly every chapter (but in particular chapters 8 and 12) a really proper job would go into considerably more detail. My excuse is that it is important to see the forest as well as the trees; God may be in the details, but God is also in the whole sweeping vista of the epistemology of Christian belief.

Trained observers may note two styles of print: large and small. The main argument of the book goes on in the large print; the small print adds further analysis, argument, or other points the specialist may find of interest. This book is not written mainly for the specialist in philosophy. I hope and intend that it will be intelligible and useful to, for example, students who have taken a course in philosophy or apologetics, as well as the fabled general reader with an interest in its subject. Although it is the third member of a trilogy, the book is designed to be relatively independent of *Warrant: The Current Debate* and *Warrant and Proper Function* (and it therefore sometimes contains brief accounts of what goes on in them).

Most books, of course, are to one degree or another cooperative enterprises; every author is heavily indebted to others in a thousand profound ways. (This is, if anything, especially evident in those authors —one thinks of a long line of modern and contemporary philosophers, beginning perhaps with Descartes—who apparently believe that they have jettisoned all that has already been thought and written, starting the whole subject anew.) The present book is no exception; it is very much a cooperative enterprise. This is so for the usual reasons, but also for a special reason. At several junctures, I have simply appealed to the work of others—most often William P. Alston and Nicholas Wolterstorff—for a particular building block of the argument. This is especially so when I have little or nothing to add to what they have already said on the topic in question, but sometimes also when I might myself have a mildly different slant on the topic in question.

The book is also something of a cooperative enterprise by virtue of the advice, instruction, and criticism I have received from others —an embarrassingly large number of others (I am entirely sensible of the fact that with so much help, I should have done better). I'm grateful to all those who helped me with the first two volumes and also to Jonathan Kvanvig and the authors of the essays in his *Warrant in Contemporary Epistemology: Essays in Honor of Plantinga's Theory of Knowledge*. Among those to whom I am particularly grateful for help with this third volume are Karl Ameriks, Jim Beilby (who also kindly prepared the index), David Burrell, Kelly Clark, John Cooper, Kevin Corcoran, Andrew Cortens, Fred Crosson, Paul Draper, Steve Evans, Ronald Feenstra, Fred Freddoso, Richard Gale, Lee Hardy, John Hare, Van Harvey, David Hunt, Hugh McCann, Greg Mellema, Ric Otte, Neal Plantinga, Bill Prior, Tapio Puolimatka, Philip Quinn, Del Ratzsch, Dan Rieger, Robert Roberts, Bill Rowe, John Sanders, Henry Schuurman, James Sennett, Ernie Sosa, Michael Sudduth, Richard Swinburne, Bill Talbott, James VanderKam, Bas van Fraassen, Calvin Van Reken, Rene van Woudenberg, Steve Wykstra, and Henry Zwaanstra. (I've undoubtedly omitted people who belong on this list; to them, I express both my gratitude and my apologies.) William Alston, Dewey Hoitenga, Eleonore Stump, and Nicholas Wolterstorff read and commented on the entire manuscript; to them, I am especially grateful. One of my most significant debts is to a rotating cadre of Notre Dame graduate students who, as a group and over a period of several years, read the entire manuscript and submitted it to the sort of searching and detailed criticism that only aroused and contentious graduate students can muster. This group includes, among others, Mike Bergmann, Tom Crisp, Pat Kain, Andy Koehl, Kevin Meeker, Trenton Merricks, Marie Pannier, Mike Rea, Ray Van Arragon, and David VanderLaan. I am similarly indebted to Nicholas Wolterstorff's fall 1997 graduate seminar at Yale (especially Andrews Chignell and Dole), who (with their mentor) read the manuscript and provided illuminating and valuable comments. And once again

I thank Martha Detlefsen, whose valiant efforts to keep me and this manuscript properly organized have been ingenious and untiring.

These three volumes began life as Gifford Lectures at the University of Aberdeen in 1986 and 1987 and Wilde Lectures at Oxford in 1988. I am grateful to both sets of electors; I am equally grateful for the hospitality my wife and I enjoyed while visiting Aberdeen and Oxford. Thanks are also due to the University of Notre Dame for a sabbatical in 1995 and 1996 and to the National Endowment for the Humanities for a fellowship that same year. A couple of bits of this volume have already seen the light of publication: chapter 13 contains a few pages from "Pluralism: A Defense of Religious Exclusivism" in *The Rationality of Belief and the Plurality of Faith*, ed. Thomas Senor (Ithaca: Cornell University Press, 1995), and chapter 14 contains a few paragraphs from "On Being Evidentially Challenged," in *The Evidential Argument from Evil*, ed. Daniel Howard-Snyder (Bloomington: Indiana University Press, 1996).

Finally, I make special mention of William P. Alston. Bill was my teacher when I began graduate school in 1954 (if I wasn't able to understand Alfred Whitehead's *Process and Reality*, the subject of that first seminar, the fault was mine [or maybe Whitehead's], not Bill's.) I learned much from him then and much more from him since. His generosity in reading this entire manuscript was characteristic; so was the trenchancy and penetration of his comments. Alston's contributions to contemporary philosophy and philosophy of religion (his leadership in establishing the Society of Christian Philosophers and the journal *Faith and Philosophy*, his splendid works in epistemology and philosophy of religion) are, of course, well and widely known; there is no need to enumerate them here (and in any case they are nearly indenumerable). It is to him that I dedicate this book.

Notre Dame, Indiana   A. P.
September 1998

Contents

PART I

IS THERE A QUESTION?

1

Kant

"To whom will you liken me? Who is my equal? With what can you compare me? Where is my like?"

Isaiah 46:5

I. THE PROBLEM

Our interest, in this book, is the *de jure* question:[1] is it rational, reasonable, justifiable, warranted to accept Christian belief—Christian belief as outlined in the preface? Or is there something epistemically unacceptable in so doing, something foolish, or silly, or foolhardy, or stupid, or unjustified, or unreasonable, or in some other way epistemically deplorable? But there is a prior question: is the very idea of Christian belief coherent? Can there really be such a thing as Christian belief? Well, why should that be a question? Isn't it obvious that many people hold just those beliefs mentioned in the preface? Here is the problem. To accept Christian belief, I say, is to believe that there is an all-powerful, all-knowing, wholly good person (a person without a body) who has created us and our world, who loves us and was willing to send his son into the world to undergo suffering, humiliation, and death in order to redeem us. It is also to believe, of course, that no more than *one* being has these properties. And Christian belief involves not only that there *is* such a being but also that we are able to address him in prayer, *refer* to him, *think* and *talk* about him, and predicate properties of him. We have some kind of cogni-

---

1. For the contrast between *de jure* and *de facto* questions, see Preface, pp. viff.

tive access to and grasp of him. We can refer to him, for example, as
the all-powerful, all-knowing person who has created and upholds
the world, and we can predicate of him such properties as *being all-
powerful*, *being all-knowing*, and *having created the world*. We can use a
definite description like this to refer to this being, to pick him out, to
single him out for thought; and we can give a proper name to the
being thus singled out. For example, we can use the term 'God' as his
name.

Accordingly, Christians ordinarily take it for granted that it is
possible to refer to God by such descriptions as 'the all-powerful,
all-knowing creator of the universe', and possible, furthermore, to
predicate properties (wisdom, goodness) of the being thus referred
to. Of course, such a description succeeds in actually naming something only if there really *is* a being who is all-powerful and all-
knowing and created the universe. Furthermore, it must be possible, if I can think about God and predicate properties of him, not
only that there *be* such a being but also that *my concepts apply to it*. If
not, then I am not in a position to assert or believe or even entertain any of the propositions mentioned above, if indeed there *are*
any such propositions.

Now Christians also take it for granted that God is infinite, transcendent, and ultimate (however, precisely, we gloss those terms).
And just here is the alleged problem. It seems many theologians and
others believe that there is real difficulty with the idea that our concepts could apply to God—that is, could apply to a being with the
properties of being infinite, transcendent, and ultimate. The idea is
that if there is such a being, we couldn't speak about it, couldn't think
and talk about it, couldn't ascribe properties to it. If that is true, however, then, strictly speaking, Christian belief, at least as the Christian
understands it, is impossible. For Christians believe that there is an
infinite, transcendent, ultimate being about whom they hold beliefs;
but if our concepts cannot apply to a being of that sort, then there
cannot be beliefs about a being of that sort. This idea often sees the
light of publication; it is even more heavily present in the oral tradition. In the spirit of interdisciplinary ecumenism, therefore, I want to
begin by looking into this question.

Consider, for example, the theologian Gordon Kaufman:

> The central problem of theological discourse, not shared with any
> other "language game" is the meaning of the term "God." "God"
> raises special problems of meaning because it is a noun which by
> definition refers to a reality transcendent of, and thus not locatable
> within, experience.[2]

2. *God the Problem* (Cambridge: Harvard University Press, 1972), p. 8.

In particular, it seems to be widely accepted, among theologians, that Kant showed that reference to or thought about such a being (even if there is one) is impossible or at least deeply problematic,[3] or at any rate much more problematic than the idea that we can refer to and think about ourselves and other people, trees and mountains, planets and stars, and so on. Those theologians who think or suspect Kant showed this do not ordinarily develop the point in detail;[4] they ordinarily content themselves with a ritual bow in his direction. They do not explain *how* they think these things were shown or what the arguments establishing them are; perhaps they think (quite properly) that that is the job of philosophers. Some of these theologians then go on to suggest that language ostensibly about a transcendent God isn't what it looks like at all; it really serves some quite different purpose. Alternatively, perhaps, it really serves no useful purpose as it stands; what we have to do is *find* a useful purpose for it to serve. Perhaps it can be used, somehow, to further or promote human flourishing and humaneness,[5] or religious tolerance,[6] or liberating praxis, or the rights of women,[7] or the fight against oppression.

But what is important for my present purposes is not an exploration of the ways in which religious language might be reconstrued or restructured, once we see (as we think) that it cannot function the way ordinary believers think it does; I want, instead, to examine the prior claim that, indeed, it *cannot* function as ordinary believers assume it does. Is there really something especially problematic about referring to or thinking about God? Did Kant show that if there were such a person as God, we couldn't refer to or think about him? Or if 'show' is too strong a word, did he give us powerful or even decent reason to believe that our concepts couldn't apply to God, if there is such a being? Or if *he* didn't do that, do some of his contemporary followers—Gordon Kaufman, for example, or John Hick—give us a reason to think this is indeed true? And is the claim in question—that our concepts do not apply to God—a coherent one? (Or rather, is there a coherent claim somewhere in the nearby bushes, since clearly there are several *different* claims lurking in these bushes?)

---

3. The whole medieval tradition of negative theology also finds reference to God problematic. The difference is that the medievals took it for granted that, of course, we *can* refer to God; the problem is to explain just how this can be accomplished. For the contemporaries I am thinking of, however, the difficulties (whether apparent or real) lead them to doubt that we *can*, in fact, refer to and talk about a being that is ultimate and transcendent.

4. As we shall see in chapter 2, however, John Hick constitutes an exception.

5. As in Gordon Kaufman: see chapter 2, p. 41.

6. As in John Hick: see chapter 2, p. 60.

7. See Sallie McFague, *Models of God* (Philadelphia: Fortress Press, 1987).

Initially, the answer seems to be no; one who makes the claim seems to set up a certain subject for predication—God—and then declare that our concepts do not apply to this being. But if this is so, then, presumably, at least one of our concepts—*being such that our concepts don't apply to it*—does apply to this being. Either those who attempt to make this claim succeed in making an assertion or not. If they don't succeed, we have nothing to consider; if they do, however, they appear to be predicating a property of a being they have referred to, in which case at least some of our concepts do apply to it, contrary to the claim they make. So if they succeed in making a claim, they make a *false* claim.

Note how difficult it is, initially, to state the claim in question, the claim that if there is a being with the properties Christians ascribe to God, our concepts would not apply to that being. Consider the proposition

(1) If there were an infinite, transcendent, and ultimate being, our concepts could not apply to it.

But now suppose (1) were true. The idea, one takes it, is that we *do* have at least *some* grasp of the properties of being infinite, transcendent, and ultimate (else we shouldn't be able to understand the sentence or grasp the proposition it expresses). An infinite being, we might say, is an *unlimited* being—unlimited, that is, with respect to certain properties. Among these properties might be power, knowledge, goodness, love, and the like. (A being is unlimited with respect to power and (propositional) knowledge, for example, if there is a maximal degree of power and knowledge, and the being in question enjoys that maximal degree of those properties. It might be hard to say precisely what the maximal degree of these properties is; with respect to knowledge, we might begin by saying that a being displays that maximal degree if it knows all true propositions and believes no false proposition.) Perhaps we can also give an explanation of what it is for a being to be *transcendent*: such a being transcends the created universe; and a being transcends the created universe if it is not identical with any being *in* that universe (if it is not created) and if it depends on nothing at all for its existence. So we do have the ideas of transcendence and being infinite (and if not, then (1) makes no sense). And the idea behind (1) is that if there *is* such a being (i.e., if there is an infinite and transcendent being), then none of our concepts could apply to it. In particular, then, the concepts *being infinite* and *being transcendent* could not apply to it. But how could that be? How could it be that there is a being that is infinite and transcendent (i.e., falls under our concepts *infinity* and *transcendence*) but is nevertheless such that the concepts *infinity* and *transcendence* do not apply to it? Is the idea, perhaps, that these concepts are impossible, incoherent, like the concept of a round square, a concept such that we can just see *a priori* that it couldn't apply to anything, that there couldn't be a thing to which it applied?[8] That would make (1) trivially true, at least if a conditional with an impossible antecedent is thereby true. Of course, it would also make (1*) true:

> (1*) If there were an all-powerful, all-knowing being, our concepts *would* apply to it.

So presumably that is not the idea here. What, then, *is* the idea? I think the best we can do in trying to state such a view coherently is to say with John Hick (see below, pp. 47ff.) that there is a being to which none of our *positive, nonformal* concepts apply (a being that has none of the positive, nonformal properties of which we have concepts) and that this being, somehow, is the one with which Christians and others are in touch in religious practice. This is perhaps the best we can do; I shall argue below (pp. 59ff.), however, that it isn't good enough; it suffers from serious, indeed fatal difficulties.

So the suggestion is that Kant showed us, somehow, that there are real, perhaps insurmountable problems in the idea that there is a being like that acknowledged in traditional Christianity, to whom we can refer and to whom our concepts apply. This is a question of considerable import for our present project, for if this suggestion is right, then there really *isn't* any such question as the one I say I propose to discuss; then, the sentences Christians use to express (as they think) their beliefs, do not really express the kinds of propositions or thoughts Christians think they express. Indeed, perhaps, they don't express any propositions or thoughts at all but are a sort of disguised nonsense: they *look* as if they express propositions but in fact do not.

Before we explicitly turn to Kant, however, it is worth reminding ourselves that the claim in question is by no means a *new* claim in the present historical context. Beginning in the 1930s, the logical positivists were fond of insisting that the sentences Christians typically use—'God loves us' or 'The universe was created by God' or 'God was in Christ, reconciling the world to himself'—do not, as they are ordinarily used, say anything at all; they express no propositions at all; they are really disguised nonsense.[9] They *look* like they say something, and Christians and others *think* they say something; in fact, however, they altogether fail to express a proposition, just as does an obvious nonsense sentence like "'Twas brillig, and the slithy toves / did gyre and gimbol in the wabe." The positivists appealed to the

8. Thus some philosophers have claimed that the notion of *omnipotence* is incoherent; others have paid the same compliment to the notion of *omniscience* (see Patrick Grim and Alvin Plantinga, "Truth, Omniscience, and Cantorian Arguments: An Exchange," *Philosophical Studies* 70 [August 1993]); still others have argued the same point with respect to the idea that God is a person without a body.

9. See, e.g., A. J. Ayer, *Language, Truth and Logic* (New York: Dover Publications, 1946), pp. 115ff.

dreaded "Verifiability Criterion of Meaning," according to which a sentence makes sense, is literally significant, or is cognitively meaningful only if it is 'empirically verifiable' (or falsifiable)—only if, that is, its truth (or falsehood) can be established by something like the methods of natural and empirical science. Beginning in the 1940s or so, the main questions asked and answered by philosophers of religion in the English-speaking world were whether it is possible to refer to God at all and whether the sentences typically uttered by Christians and other believers in God really make sense or are, instead, nonsense, cognitively insignificant.[10] Of course it doesn't follow that such meaningless sentences are altogether useless; perhaps they serve some other function. Rudolf Carnap, for example, wondered whether the meaningless sentences of metaphysics and theology might not really be a form of *music*.[11] (It isn't known whether he expected them to supplant Mozart and Bach, or even Wagner. I myself doubt that metaphysics will ever replace Mozart, but perhaps we could see it as a peculiarly *avant-garde* form of *rock*.)

By now, logical positivism has retreated into the obscurity it so richly deserves.[12] There still persists, however, the widespread impression that reference to God is problematic; it is time to turn explicitly to Kant, the main source of this idea. Does his work offer cause for concern to those who propose to think about, refer to, pray to, or worship a being described the way Christians describe God— as a personal being who is transcendent and infinite?

10. See, e.g., *New Essays in Philosophical Theology*, ed. Antony Flew and Alasdair MacIntyre (London: SCM Press, 1955).

11. Perhaps metaphysics can have other aesthetic functions as well, as can Carnap's own work. Although, as far as I know, no one has ever used Carnap's writings as music (or even set them to music), in 1976 the Museum of Modern Art in Oxford displayed a page of Carnap's *Logical Syntax of Language* magnified about 20x and posted on the wall. No doubt a piece of metaphysics could serve the same purpose.

12. For an account of the harrowing vicissitudes of the Verifiability Criterion, see Carl Hempel, "Problems and Changes in the Empiricist Criterion of Meaning," in *Semantics and the Philosophy of Language*, ed. Leonard Linsky (Urbana: University of Illinois Press, 1952), and my *God and Other Minds* (Ithaca: Cornell University Press, 1967), chapter 7. Something like it lingers on, not only among some theologians who propose to reconstrue religious language in such a way that it no longer refers to God but also in the Wittgensteinian fideism of D. Z. Phillips and others, which is a sort of continuation of positivism by other means. Although some of this work is eminently worth discussing, I will not discuss it here, referring the reader instead to Nicholas Wolterstorff's perceptive "Philosophy of Religion after Foundationalism I: Wittgensteinian Fideism" (presently unpublished), to which I have little to add.

II. KANT

Immanuel Kant was a virtual titan of philosophy, with an absolutely enormous influence upon subsequent philosophy and theology. This is no doubt due to his great insight and raw philosophical power; it is perhaps also due to the grave hermeneutical difficulties that attend study of his work. The British philosopher David Hume writes with a certain surface clarity that disappointingly disappears on closer inspection. With Kant, there is good news and bad news: the good news is that we don't suffer that disappointment; the bad news is that it's because there isn't any surface clarity to begin with. We can't turn to a settled interpretation of Kant to see whether he showed or even held that our concepts don't apply to God; there is no settled interpretation.

The first thing to note, however, is that Kant often writes as if we *can* perfectly well refer to God. In the *Critique of Practical Reason* and elsewhere (*Religion within the Boundary of Pure Reason*; *Lectures on Philosophical Theology*), Kant regularly seems to refer to God and clearly takes himself to be doing exactly that. Even in the *Critique of Pure Reason*, his work most heavily influential in this skeptical direction, Kant often seems to suggest that we can indeed refer to and think about God. He often seems to suggest that the problem is not that we can't *think* about God but that we can't come to speculative or metaphysical *knowledge* of God. His aim in this *Critique*, he says, is to curb knowledge in order to make room for faith.[13] The faith in question, presumably, is like that expressed in the *Critique of Practical Reason* and elsewhere; it would certainly involve referring to God and taking his existence and attributes as a postulate of practical reason, a presupposition of the reality and seriousness of the moral life. Indeed, some who understand him this way believe that Kant was himself a theist, holding that the things in themselves are just things as they appear to God, that is, things as they really are.[14] Of course if this way of thinking about Kant is correct, then on his view it is perfectly possible to refer to God; if that is possible, it is also possible to ascribe properties and attributes to him; and if *that* is possible, then our concepts do, indeed, apply to him. For example, the negative concepts *not being in space and time* and *not being dependent on human beings for his existence* would thus apply to him. Further, on this understanding of

---

13. *Critique of Pure Reason*, tr. Norman Kemp Smith (New York: St. Martin's Press, 1965), Preface to second edition, Bxxx, p. 29: "I have therefore found it necessary to deny *knowledge* in order to make room for *faith*" (Kant's emphasis).

14. See Merold Westphal, "In Defense of the Thing in Itself," *Kant-Studien* 59/1 (1968), pp. 118ff.

Kant, such positive concepts as *having knowledge* and *having power* would apply to God, as would *having created the world*. On this understanding, it would be an error to suppose that Kant showed that our concepts can't apply to God—unless one were prepared to hold that Kant showed this but failed to notice that he did, thus mistakenly taking himself to be referring to that to which he himself showed it was not possible to refer. This latter is, of course, a possibility, although it would require an unusually high level of absentmindedness.

Still, the idea that according to Kant our concepts couldn't apply to God is no mere fabrication, no merely thoughtless misunderstanding—or, more exactly, if it is a misunderstanding, it is one with considerable basis in the Kantian text. There is much in the *Critique of Pure Reason* to suggest this or something like it; at any rate, there is much to suggest that the *categories of the understanding*, which are concepts of the first importance, do not apply to the things in themselves (and thus not to God). For example:

> If, therefore, we should attempt to apply the categories to objects which are not viewed as being appearances, we should have to postulate an intuition other than the sensible, and the object would thus be a noumenon in the *positive sense*. Since, however, such a type of intuition, intellectual intuition, forms no part whatsoever of our faculty of knowledge, it follows that the employment of the categories can never extend further than to the objects of experience. (A353, B309, Kant's emphasis)

Here and elsewhere, Kant suggests that the categories of the understanding do not apply beyond the realm of appearance, the world of phenomena. ("Suggests," I say; these passages, like all the others, contain more than a hint of possible ambiguity.) But if those categories do not apply to the noumena, the *Dinge an sich*, then perhaps the same goes for the rest of our concepts. And if our concepts do not apply beyond the world of experience, the world of appearance, then they do not apply to God, who, of course, would be a noumenon *in excelsis*. So the claim would be that Kant shows or believes (at any rate in the *Critique of Pure Reason*) that our concepts do not apply to God, in which case we cannot refer to or think about him.

A. Two Worlds or One?

What is to be said for this understanding of Kant? Hermeneutical obstacles of formidable proportions loom. First, how are we to think about this distinction between the noumena and the phenomena, the things in themselves and the things for us? Unfortunately, the commentators are not of one mind. There is a huge interpretative watershed, a continental divide, between two fundamentally different interpretations or basic pictures of what Kant had in mind, each with several variations when it comes to detail. According to the first and more traditional picture, Kant held that there are two realms of objects, two fundamentally different kinds of things. These are the phenomena, on the one hand, and the noumena, on the other; the things in themselves and the things *für uns*. (These two distinctions don't exactly coincide in Kant; the ways in which they don't aren't relevant to our present inquiry.) On the one hand, on this picture, there are tables and chairs, horses and cows, stars and planets, the oak tree in your backyard, just as we ordinarily think. These things really exist and are really there. They are *phenomenally real*, real parts of the world of experience. But they are also *transcendentally ideal*: that is, they are not part of the world as it is independent of human experience. On the other hand, there are the noumena, which are transcendentally real. These are the things as they are in themselves; they do not depend for their existence or character upon human beings or human experience. These two realms are disjoint: none of the phenomenal objects is a noumenon, and none of the noumenal objects is a phenomenon. Here are a couple of passages supporting this interpretation:

> Now we must bear in mind that the concept of appearances, as limited by the Transcendental Aesthetic, already of itself establishes the objective reality of *noumena* and justifies the division of objects into *phaenomena* and *noumena* and so of the world into a world of the sense and a world of the understanding (*mundus sensibilis et intelligibilis*) and indeed in such manner that the distinction does not refer merely to the logical form of our knowledge of one and the same thing, according as it is indistinct or distinct, but to the difference in the manner in which the two worlds can be first given to our knowledge, and in conformity with this difference, to the manner in which they are in themselves generically distinct from one another. (A 249, Kant's emphasis)

> Appearances are the sole objects which can be given to us immediately, and that in them which relates immediately to the object is called intuition. Appearances are not things in themselves; they are only representations, which in turn have their object—an object which cannot be intuited by us, and which may, therefore, be named the non-empirical, that is, transcendental object = x. (A109)

These phenomena are objects, objects that exist in space and time. The noumena, by contrast, are neither temporal nor spatial; space and time are forms of our intuition rather than realities that characterize the things in themselves. Noumena and phenomena, therefore, are distinct.

Still further, we have experience only of the phenomena, not of the noumena:

> We have sufficiently proved in the Transcendental Aesthetic that everything intuited in space or time, and therefore all objects of any experience possible to us, are nothing but appearances, that is, mere representations,

Further still, the phenomena, the world of stars and planets, trees and animals, depends on us for existence. The above passage continues:

> which in the manner in which they are represented, as extended beings, or as series of alternations have no independent existence outside our thoughts. (A491, B519)

Elsewhere:

> That nature should direct itself according to our subject ground of apperception, and should indeed depend upon it in respect of its conformity to law, sounds very strange and absurd. But when we consider that this nature is not a thing in itself but is merely an aggregate of appearances, so many representations of the mind, . . . (A114)

> Now to assert in this manner, that all these appearances, and consequently all objects with which we can occupy ourselves, are one and all in me, that is are determinations of my identical self, is only another way of saying that there must be a complete unity of them in one and the same apperception. (A129)

This is the more traditional way of understanding Kant, the way Kant was taken by his great successors. To put it briefly and all too baldly, there are two realms of objects; our experience is only of one realm, the realm of phenomena, which themselves depend on us for their existence; if we should go out of existence, so would they. That is because the phenomenal realm is somehow *constructed* by us out of the given, the data, the raw material of experience. The noumenal realm, however, is not thus dependent on us but is also such that we have no intuition, no direct experience of it. Finally, there is nevertheless a connection between the two worlds in that something like a causal transaction between the noumena and the transcendental ego (itself a noumenon) produces in us the given out of which we construct the phenomenal world.

Call the above *the two-world picture*; this has been the dominant interpretation. There has always been another basic interpretation of Kant, however, one that more recently has perhaps achieved majority status. According to this other picture, there really aren't *two* worlds after all, a world of phenomena and underlying it another world of noumena. There is only *one* world and only one kind of object, but there are (at least) two ways of thinking about or considering this one world. *All* objects are really noumenal objects, and talk about the phenomena is just a picturesque way of talking about how the noumena the only things there are, appear to us. The phenomena-noumena distinction is not between two kinds of objects but, rather, between how the things are in themselves and how they appear to us.

So, for example, Graham Bird:

Such phrases [e.g., 'transcendental objects and empirical objects'] should be understood to refer not to two different kinds of entity, but instead to two different ways of talking about one and the same thing.[15]

And Michael Devitt:

> It is tempting to equate an appearance with the foundationalist's sense datum, taking the thing-in-itself as the unknowable external cause of this mental entity. Kant's writing often encourages this temptation. Nevertheless, scholars seem generally agreed—and have convinced me—that this two-worlds interpretation is wrong. What Kant intends is the following influential, but rather mysterious, one world view.
>
> An Appearance is not a mental sense datum, but an external object *as we know it*. In contrast the thing-in-itself is the object independent of our knowledge of it; it is not a second object, and does not, indeed could not, cause an appearance. . . .[16]

Although this second picture is perhaps now the majority opinion, it seems a bit difficult to reconcile it with Kant's own view that his thought constituted a *revolution*—his famous second Copernican revolution.[17] After all, much of this second picture would be accepted even by such staunch prerevolutionaries as Aristotle and Aquinas. Both would agree that there is or can be a difference between the world (or any less impressive object) as it is in itself and the world as it appears to us; this is to admit no more than that we can be *mistaken* about the world or things in the world, and of course Aristotle and Aquinas would hardly deny that. Both would agree to something much stronger: that the world might have many properties of which we have no conception, so that our way of thinking about the world, the properties we ascribe to it, are not necessarily all and only the

15. *Kant's Theory of Knowledge* (New York: Humanities Press, 1962), p. 37.

16. *Realism and Truth* (Princeton: Princeton University Press, 1984), p. 59. See also D. P. Dryer, *Kant's Solution for Verification in Metaphysics* (Toronto: University of Toronto Press, 1966), chapter 11, section vi; H. E. Matthews, "Strawson on Transcendental Idealism," *Philosophical Quarterly* 19 (1969), pp. 204–220; Henry Allison, *Kant's Transcendental Idealism* (New Haven: Yale University Press, 1983). I am indebted, for these references, to Karl Ameriks ("Recent Work on Kant's Theoretical Philosophy," *American Philosophical Quarterly* 19 [1982], and "Kantian Idealism Today," *History of Philosophy Quarterly* 9 [1992]) and to James Van Cleve, *Problems from Kant* (New York: Oxford University Press, 1999).

17. "Hitherto it has been assumed that all our knowledge must conform to objects. But also attempts to extend our knowledge of objects by establishing something in regard to them *a priori*, by means of concepts, have, on this assumption, ended in failure. We must therefore make trial whether we may not have more success in the tasks of metaphysics, if we suppose that objects must conform to our knowledge. We should then be proceeding precisely on the lines of Copernicus' primary hypothesis." (Bxvii)

properties it has. For Aquinas or any other theist, this would be close
to a truism: God, obviously enough, has many properties we don't
know about, and presumably many of which we could not so much as
form a conception. The essential elements of the one-world view
seem perhaps a bit too uncontroversial, at least with respect to Kant's
predecessors, to constitute a revolution, Copernican or otherwise.

According to Merold Westphal:

> Finally, all twelve categories insofar as they constitute the
> world of human experience and are not merely formal fea-
> tures of judgment, are schematized with an essential refer-
> ence to time. Thus the object and property that would dis-
> appear from the world in the absence of human knowers
> are not object and property per se, but substance and acci-
> dent *as defined by human temporality*. Similarly, the truth and
> falsity that would disappear derive from the categories of
> reality and negation *as essentially linked to our experience of
> time*. Thus we are back to the tautology that in the absence
> of human cognition the world as apprehended by human
> minds would disappear.[18]

That does, indeed, seem to be a tautology, or at least a trivially necessary
truth; we could add that in the absence of bovine cognition, the world as
apprehended by bovine minds would disappear. But how could Kant
think of this as constituting a *revolution*, one according to which objects
must conform to our minds (rather than, as previously thought, our
minds to objects) if we are to have knowledge? Could a tautology constitute a revolution?

1. The One-World Picture and Reference to the Noumena

Our main interest here does not lie in trying to resolve the question
of what Kant intended: that is perhaps necessarily beyond our powers. Instead, we are looking to see if there is good reason, either
given by Kant or constructible from materials given by him, for the
conclusion that our concepts do not apply to God. And how does the
difference between these two interpretations of Kant bear on this
question? Consider the second picture first, and note that on this picture, if our concepts apply to *anything*, they apply to the *Dinge*, those
being the only things there are. Similarly, if we manage to refer to
and think about anything at all, we succeed in referring to and thinking about the *Dinge*, because they are all that there is. So how could
it be that the categories and our other concepts do not apply to
them?

18. "In Defense of the Thing in Itself," p. 170.

Well, what is it for a concept to apply to something, for something to fall under a concept? Consider the concept *being wise*. That concept applies to something (a thing falls under that concept) only if that thing is wise, only if, that is, it has the property of being wise. Properties and concepts are thus correlative. I have the concept *being wise* only if I grasp, ~~apprehend~~, understand the property *being wise*. I have the concept *being a prime number* if and only if I grasp or apprehend the property *being a prime number*. For each property or attribute of which I have a grasp, I have a concept. Of course there are properties of which I have no concept. Small children often lack the concept of being a philosopher; that is to say, they have no grasp of the property *being a philosopher*. Large philosophers often lack the concept of being a quark; that is to say, they have no grasp of the property *being a quark*. No doubt there are properties none of us human beings grasps.

One further familiar fact about properties and concepts: they have *negations* or *complements*. There is the property *being red*; there is also its complement, which, naturally enough, is *being unred*, *not being red*. There is the property of being wise but also the property of being unwise, failing to be wise. So if one of my concepts (e.g., *being wise*) does not apply to a thing, then the complement of that concept (*being nonwise*, *not being wise*) *does* apply to it.

> Perhaps you want to point out that this way of putting the matter presupposes that there are *negative* properties, such properties as *being nonred*, *being unwise*, and the like; you might object that in fact there are only positive properties, not negative ones. (You might also object to disjunctive and conjunctive properties.) This is no place to try to settle that issue. Clearly, there is the *concept* of a thing's failing to be wise (I know what it is for a thing not to be wise), even if there is no negative property *nonwisdom*. So if you object to negative properties, say that a thing falls under the concept *nonwisdom* just in case it does not fall under the concept *wisdom*; more generally, for any property *P*, a thing falls under the concept *P* if and only if it has the property *P*; it falls under the concept not-*P* if and only if it does not fall under the concept *P*.

Given this elementary lore about concepts and properties, how could it be that the categories and our other concepts do not apply to the *Dinge*? Take the categories first—the category of causality, for example. What would it mean to say that this category does not apply to the *Dinge*? So far as I can see, what this would mean is that the noumena do not stand in causal relations to each other or anything else. Consider the property *stands in causal relation to something*; if the category of causality does not apply to the noumena, then it must be that none of them has that property. So our concept *standing in causal relation to something* wouldn't apply to things as they are in themselves. It follows, however, that the complement of that category or concept *would* apply to things as they are in themselves: each of them would be such that it does not stand in a causal relation to anything else. The same would go for our other concepts. On this way of thinking of the matter, our 'positive' concepts, you might say, do not apply to things as they are in themselves, which is really to say that there is no positive property we grasp that characterizes a thing as it is in itself. As it stands, however, this needs more work: there are problems about this distinction between positive and negative properties. There are also problems of other sorts: what about such positive properties as *being self-identical*, for example? Are we to suppose the *Dinge* are not self-identical?

Well, perhaps these matters can be straightened out. (See chapter 2, p. 48.) For present purposes, what we need to see is that on this way of thinking, it would not really be the case that our concepts fail to apply to God in such a way that we cannot refer to and think about him. What *would* follow, given that he is a noumenon (of course, in this way of thinking, *everything* is a noumenon), is that God would not have any of the positive properties of which we have a grasp. It would not be the case that we couldn't refer to God and predicate properties of him: we could perfectly well do so, but we would be mistaken if we predicated of him a positive property of which we have a grasp. Thus we would make a mistake if we said that God is wise, or good, or powerful, or loving. That would be because *nothing* is wise, good, powerful, loving, and the like. (On the one-world picture, the *Dinge* are all there is; so if positive properties can't be ascribed to the *Dinge*, they can't be ascribed to anything.) Here there would be nothing at all special about *God*; what holds for him also holds for everything else. But those theologians who suggest that Kant showed we cannot refer to and think about God presumably believe that Kant showed there was a *special* problem about God; they don't think that what Kant really showed is that we can't talk or think about *anything*. As Kaufman puts it in the passage I quoted above (p. 4), "The central problem of theological discourse, not shared with any other 'language game,' is the meaning of the term 'God.' " So Kant, taken this way, doesn't fill this particular bill; it doesn't give us a relevant way of seeing that our concepts do not apply to God.

2. The Two-World Picture and Reference to the Noumena

Now suppose we consider the other main interpretation of Kant: the two-world picture. This is the more traditional way to understand Kant and still, perhaps, deserves the nod. (Here I am not interested in which picture most accurately represents Kant, but whether Kant, taken any plausible way, gives support to the idea that we cannot

refer to and think about God.[19]) On this picture, there are two disjoint realms: phenomena and noumena, the *Dinge* and the things of
experience. To add another quotation:

> Accordingly, that which is in space and time is an appearance; it is
> not anything in itself, but consists merely of representations, which,
> if not given in us—that is to say, in perception—are nowhere to be
> met with. (A494, B522)

Now when we think about the application of our concepts to the
noumena, we see that this two-world picture divides into two sub-
pictures.

(a) The Moderate Subpicture. On the one way of thinking,
(some of) our concepts *apply* to the things in themselves; we can
think about them and refer to them, all right, but we can't have
any *knowledge* of them. When we think about them, predicate
properties of them, what we have is just speculation, mere transcendental *schein*, and we deceive ourselves if we think we have
more. Our knowledge doesn't extend beyond experience; hence,
it does not extend to the realm of the things in themselves. This
would explain that bewildering variety and proliferation of metaphysical views Kant found so shocking. The reason, fundamentally, is really that all the metaphysicians have been just guessing,
whatever their pretensions to apodictic conclusions and conclusive certainty. Our reason can't operate in the rarefied atmosphere of the noumena, and the result of trying to do so is a mere
beating of wings against the void.

Of course Kant also represents his own work in the *Critique of
Pure Reason* as knowledge and as certain and conclusive. And in that
Critique he seems to tell us a fair amount about the *Dinge*: that they
are not in space and time, that the world of experience is (in part) a
result of a 'causal transaction'[20] between the *Dinge* and the transcendental ego, and that the latter has no intellectual intuition into the
former. So the picture isn't wholly coherent. Coherent or not, however, this picture doesn't even suggest that we cannot think about
and predicate properties of God. What it suggests, instead, is that
when we do, we are not on the sure path of knowledge but on some
much more hazardous climber's trail of mere opinion. So the mod-

---

19. Of course, I do not mean to suggest that the one- and two-world pictures as
I present them are the only possible (or actual) interpretations of Kant; clearly, there
are various complications and extensions of each. What I claim is that none of them
offers aid and comfort to the claim that our concepts do not apply to God.

20. We need the scare quotes because Kant's official view is that the concept of
causality doesn't apply to the *Dinge*.

erate subpicture, too, gives no aid and comfort to the claim that our concepts do not apply to God.

(b) The Radical Subpicture. There is a more striking version of the two-world picture, however, on which we do get the result that we can neither refer to God nor predicate properties of him (call it 'the radical subpicture'). On both versions of the two-world picture, the appearances are distinct from the things in themselves. The appearances are *objects*; they exist; they are empirically real. But they are also transcendentally ideal. And what this means, in part, is that they depend for their existence on us (on the transcendental ego[s]) and our cognitive activity. We ourselves are both noumena and phenomena: there is both a noumenal self and an empirical self. The things in themselves somehow impinge on us (taken as transcendental ego), causing *experience* in us; there is a productive interaction between the transcendental ego and the *Dinge* (the other *Dinge*, since the transcendental ego is itself a noumenon), the result of which is *experience*, the manifold of experience.

As it is initially given to us, this manifold of experience is a blooming, buzzing confusion with no structure. Perhaps it contains among other things what Kant calls 'representations' (*Vorstellungen*); these are of more than one kind, but among them might be phenomenal *qualia*, something like sense data, or Humean impressions and ideas. The manifold must be 'worked up' (Kant's term) and *synthesized* by the application of the categories and other concepts. Thus we impose structure and form on it, and in so doing we construct the phenomena, the appearances. So the phenomena, the things *für uns*, are constructed out of the manifold of experience.

Well, how do we do a thing like that? How do we construct a phenomenon (a horse, let's say) from the manifold of experience? At this point, the radical subpicture diverges from the more pedestrian version of the two-world picture, for on the radical subpicture, we construct objects by *applying concepts* (representations, *Vorstellungen*) to the manifold. The world of appearance gets constructed by virtue of our synthesizing the manifold, which proceeds by way of our applying concepts—both the categories and other concepts—to the manifold. We can't *perceive* or in some other way witness this construction; Kant says we are largely unconscious of the activity whereby we structure the manifold and construct the phenomena. Still, it proceeds by way of the application of concepts to the blooming buzzing manifold of experience.

This would require a way of thinking about concepts and their function that is very different from the way of thinking about them I outlined above (a way according to which a concept is fundamentally a grasp of a property). And Kant suggests a different way of thinking of concepts: he sometimes calls them *rules*. Kant says that the *understanding* is the faculty of concepts; it is the source of our concepts. But he also says of the understanding, "We may now characterize it as the *faculty of rules*. . . . Sensibility gives us forms (of intuition) but understanding gives us rules" (A126, Kant's emphasis). And he goes on to say,

> Rules, so far as they are objective . . . are called laws. Although we learn many laws through experience, they are only special determinations of still higher laws, and the highest of these, under which the others all stand, issue a priori from the understanding itself. They are not borrowed from experience; on the contrary, they have to confer upon appearances their conformity to law, and so to make experience possible. Thus the understanding is something more than a power of formulating rules through comparison of appearances; it is itself the lawgiver of nature. (A127)

I don't for a moment pretend that this passage or others that could be cited are easy to interpret. Still, the passage does seem to suggest that concepts are rules and rules are laws. What sort of rules and what sort of laws? Perhaps they are *rules for synthesizing the manifold, rules for constructing the phenomena*. This is the heart of the radical sub-picture. Again, I don't mean to suggest that this is Kant's view, but some of what he says suggests it. (Some of what he says also suggests that it is false; that is part of his charm.) For example: "What is first given to us is appearance. When combined with consciousness, it is called perception. . . . "

Interpretative difficulties abound; the basic idea, however, is that concepts are rules, rules for the synthesis of the manifold and the construction of phenomena. (They are also laws, laws whereby the phenomena are constructed from the manifold of experience.) These rules apply to portions or bits of experience and, by way of their application, the phenomena are constructed. A rule of this sort perhaps specifies that certain portions of the manifold are to be combined or 'thought together' as an object. So, for example, consider your concept of a horse: it instructs you to associate, think together a variety of representations, a variety of items of experience, thus unifying that bit of the manifold into an empirical object: a horse. It is a rule which would say something like: think *that* particular congeries of representations together as a unity.

Now again, I don't mean to claim that this is a coherent picture or a coherent way of thinking about concepts; on the contrary, I believe that it is not. But note that if it *is* coherent, then (at least if *all* of our concepts have this function[21] and *only* this function) our concepts will not apply to the noumena. Consider the concept *being a horse*.

---

21. As Karl Ameriks (private communication) reminded me, Kant's metaphysical deduction certainly *seems* intended to reveal concepts which are rules for judgments of *any* sort, whether limited to items of experience or not.

Understood this way, this concept is a rule for constructing phenomenal objects out of the manifold of experience. Of course it does not apply to the noumena: it cannot be used to construct an object out of *them*; they are not given to us (experience, the manifold, is what is given to us), and in any event they aren't the sorts of things out of which phenomenal objects *could* be constructed. So it isn't just that the concept *being a horse* does not apply to the *Dinge* in the sense that none of them, as it happens, is a horse (all are nonhorses), for then the complement of that concept—*being a nonhorse*—would apply. But *that* concept doesn't apply either: it, too, is a rule for constructing objects from the manifold. It is another way of unifying, synthesizing the manifold. So thought of, a concept could no more apply to the *Dinge* than a horse could be a number.

On the radical subpicture, therefore, our concepts surely wouldn't apply to God, if there were such a person. For God would be a noumenon. God would not be something we have constructed by applying concepts to the manifold of experience (God has created us; we have not constructed him.) So, on the radical subpicture, we can't refer to, think about, or predicate properties of God.

This way of thinking clearly displays a deep incoherence: on this picture, Kant holds that the *Dinge* stand in a causal or interactive relationship with us, taken as transcendental ego(s);[22] and he also says that they are not in space and time. But on the radical subpicture, Kant (at least if his intellectual equipment is like that of the rest of us) should not be able to refer to the *Dinge* at all, or even speculate that there might be such things. He certainly shouldn't be able to refer to them and attribute to them the properties of being atemporal and aspatial, or the property of affecting the transcendental ego(s), thereby producing experience in them. He shouldn't be able to refer to *us* (i.e., us transcendental egos), claiming that we don't have the sort of godlike intellectual intuition into reality that would be required if we were to have synthetic *a priori* knowledge of the world as it is in itself. (On this picture, we might say, Kant's thought founders on the fact that the picture requires that he have knowledge the picture denies him.) If this picture were really correct, the noumena would have to drop out altogether, so that all that there is is what has been structured or made by us. The idea that there might be reality beyond what we ourselves have constructed out of experience would not be so much as thinkable.[23]

---

22. How many of those transcendental egos are there, anyway? Like many questions of Kantian exegesis, this question is vexed. Indeed, on the radical subpicture, it is more than vexed. If the category of number doesn't apply to the noumena, then there is presumably no number n, finite or infinite, such that the right answer to the question "How many of those transcendental egos *are* there?" is n.

23. In addition, of course, there is the problem that it takes a great deal of effort to believe that we are really responsible for the existence of sun, moon, and

B. Arguments or Reasons?

Clearly, there are problems of coherence here. Suppose we ignore them for the moment: what kinds of reasons does Kant give for the contention that we can't think about, refer to, predicate properties of the *Dinge*? Or, if he gives no such reasons (perhaps because he thinks we *can* think about them), what sorts of reasons or arguments does his work suggest for that conclusion? This conclusion—that our concepts are really rules for synthesizing the manifold into phenomenal objects and that the only things we can think about are objects we ourselves have somehow constructed—is, to say the least, rather startling. Some pretty powerful arguments would be required.

Argument for this view is distressingly scarce. It is extremely difficult to find much that could pass muster as an argument, or even as one of those "considerations determining the intellect" John Stuart Mill sometimes gave when, as he conceded, he didn't have an argument. There is nothing here like the ontological or cosmological arguments for the existence of God, or Descartes' argument that a person is not identical with her body (but is, instead, an immaterial substance), or the argument for the conclusion that propositions, the things we believe and assert, are not contingent objects.[24] Perhaps one must think of the radical subpicture as a sort of hypothesis proposed as best explaining certain phenomena. More likely, those who urge it are simply overwhelmed by what they see as its sheer intellectual beauty and power; they don't feel the need of argument. Indeed, they find the picture so dazzling they are willing to put up with a strong dose of incoherence in addition to absence of argument. Well, if you find the radical subpicture overwhelmingly attractive, then (incoherence aside) I guess you'll have to go with it. Then again, that doesn't constitute much of a reason for the rest of us—those of us more impressed by the incoherence of the picture than its beauty—to accept it.

There is, however, a set of Kantian considerations that some might see as taking us partway to the conclusion. These are to be found in what he says about the *antinomies*: allegedly powerful arguments on both sides of a given question. Thus there is an allegedly compelling antinomical argument for the thesis that the world had a beginning in time, but an equally compelling argument for the antithesis that it did not. In the same way, there are compelling arguments for the theses that the world is composed of simples, that there is such a thing as agent causation (where an agent cause is a being that *freely* originates a new causal series), and that there is an ab-

---

stars, not to mention dinosaurs and other things, that (as we think) existed long before there were any human beings.

24. See my *Warrant and Proper Function* (WPF), pp. 117ff.

solutely necessary being; sadly enough, however, there are equally compelling arguments for the antitheses that the world is not composed of simples, that there is no such thing as agent causation, and that there is no absolutely necessary being. Here we seem to be in a nasty fix; we can prove four (everything in the *Critique* comes in fours) important theses, and for each of these four, we can also prove its denial.

Now Kant apparently intends these antinomies to constitute an essential part of the argument for his transcendental idealism, the doctrine that the things we deal with (stars and planets, trees, animals and other people) are transcendentally ideal (depend upon us for their reality and structure), even if empirically real. We fall into the problem posed by the antinomies, says Kant, only because we take ourselves to be thinking about things in themselves as opposed to the things for us, noumena as opposed to mere appearances:

> If in employing the principles of understanding we do not merely apply our reason to objects of experience, but venture to extend these principles beyond the limits of experience, there arise pseudo-rational doctrines which can neither hope for confirmation in experience nor fear refutation by it. Each of them is not only in itself free from contradiction, but finds conditions of its necessity in the very nature of reason—only that, unfortunately, the assertion of the opposite has, on its side, grounds that are just as valid and necessary. (A421, B449)

We solve the problem by recognizing our limitations, realizing that we can't think, or can't think to any good purpose, about the *Dinge*.

In presenting the antinomies, Kant does not explicitly argue for the radical subpicture. But suppose *we* try to find something like an argument there, either for the radical subpicture or for the conclusion we have been deriving from the radical subpicture, the conclusion that our concepts do not apply to the noumena, so that we cannot refer to and think about them. Perhaps the premises would be:

(2) If we are able to think about and refer to the *Dinge*, then the premises of the antinomical arguments (the premises of the arguments for the theses and for the antitheses) are about the *Dinge* and are all true,

and

(3) If those premises are all true, then the theses and antitheses would all be true, so that contradictions would be true.

Naturally enough, however,

(4) No contradictions are true.

Therefore:

(5) We cannot think about or refer to the *Dinge*.

We could perhaps weaken the first premise (2) to make it a bit more plausible:

(2*) If we can refer to and think about the *Dinge*, then each of the premises of the antinomical arguments will be about the *Dinge* and have overwhelming intuitive support.

(This is weaker, of course, because it says, not that the antinomical premises are true, if we can think about the *Dinge*, but that they strongly *seem* true to us.)

The second premise would then be:

(3*) If each of the premises has overwhelming intuitive support, we will have overwhelming reason to accept each of the theses and antitheses, and we see that each thesis is contradicted by its antithesis.

If, however, we weaken the first premise, we must strengthen one of the other two. Perhaps we could strengthen the third as follows:

(4*) It couldn't be that we should have overwhelming reason to accept a proposition p and also its contradictory not-p.

And the conclusion would be as before.

Is it really true that (as (4*) claims) we couldn't have overwhelming reason to accept both a proposition p and also its denial not-p?[25] This would be an interesting inquiry but would take us too far afield; in any event, it isn't necessary for our present purposes, for there are at least two impressive problems with these arguments, one debilitating and the other fatal. I shall briefly outline the first and then look into the second in more detail. The first, the debilitating objection, is that even if we are not able to think of the noumena, we *can* think of the phenomena; and if the first premises of these arguments are true for the *noumena*, what is to prevent their being true for the phenom-

---

25. It seems we *could* have good reason to accept each member of a set S of beliefs such that there is no possible world in which all the members of S are true (the conjunction of the members of S is impossible), as is shown by the paradox of the preface. I write a book, of course believing every proposition asserted therein. Past experience and self-knowledge, however, lead me to think that very likely the book contains at least one false statement. (All of my previous books, as I've discovered to my sorrow, contain false statements.) In the preface, therefore, I sadly concede that at least one statement in the book is false. The total set of my beliefs, therefore—the statements in the book plus the statement that at least one statement in the book is false—is such that it must contain at least one falsehood; nevertheless, I have good reason to accept each member.

ena as well? The two versions of the first premise ((2) and (2*)) of the argument claim the following: if it is true that we can think about the noumena, then the antinomical premises are about the noumena and either are true or have overwhelming intuitive support. Isn't it equally apparent that if we can think about the phenomena, then the antinomical premises are about the phenomena and are either true or have overwhelming support? If so, however, the argument would also prove that we can't refer to the appearances. What it would really prove, then, if it proved anything, is that we can't refer to or think about either noumena or phenomena. Because noumena and phenomena are all the things there are, the conclusion would be that we can't think about anything; and that seems a bit strong.

Much more should be said about this objection to the argument, but I want to turn to the fatal objection. That is just that the antinomical arguments are not, to put the best face on it, at all compelling. Here I will argue this only for the premises of the first antinomy; exactly similar comments would apply to the others. In the first antinomy, there is an argument for the conclusion that "The world had a beginning in time and is also limited as regards space" (A 426, B454); this is the thesis. There is also an argument for the antithesis: "The world has no beginning, and no limits in space; it is infinite as regards both time and space" (A426, B454). And the idea (in accordance with premises (2) and (2*)) is that if we can think about and refer to the *Dinge*, then both of these would be true or would have overwhelming intuitive support.

Well, what is the argument? I am sorry to say it is hard to take seriously. The argument for the thesis goes as follows:

> If we assume that the world had no beginning in time, then up to every given moment an eternity has elapsed, and there has passed away in the world an infinite series of successive states of things. Now the infinity of a series consists in the fact that it can never be completed through successive synthesis. It thus follows that it is impossible for an infinite world-series to have passed away, and that a beginning of the world is therefore a necessary condition of the world's existence. (A426, B454)

This argument proceeds by *reductio ad absurdum*: show that the denial of your conclusion leads to a contradiction, thereby proving your conclusion. The first premise is that if the world had no beginning in time, then at any point in time an infinite stretch of time would already have elapsed. This is dubious because it is at least abstractly possible that time and the world began together, some finitely many years (or seconds) ago. If so, then we should say that the world didn't have a beginning *in* time, although it did have a beginning *with* time. But let that pass. According to the second premise, "the infinity of a series consists in the fact that it can never be completed through successive synthesis"; that is, it is characteristic of an infinite series that it can't be completed by starting from the beginning (or, more generally, some point only finitely far from the beginning) and adding things (events, say) one at a time (or more generally, finitely many at a time). This is true, provided the things (events) in question are added at a constant rate. If you start with the first event (or the nth, for some finite n) and add another event every second, you will never complete the series: at any subsequent time only a finite number of events will have occurred. According to current lore about the infinite, however, there is no bar of this kind to completing the infinite series in a finite time if the time taken for each event diminishes appropriately. For example, the first event takes one second to happen; the second event takes half a second; the third a quarter, the fourth an eighth of a second, and so on. At that rate, it won't take long at all for an infinite number of events to have elapsed—only a couple of seconds.

But the real problem with the argument lies in a different direction. Kant points out that an infinite series can't be completed by starting from some point finitely far from the beginning and adding members finitely many at a time at a constant rate; fair enough. He then concludes, "It thus follows that it is impossible for an infinite world-series to have passed away, and that a beginning of the world is therefore a necessary condition of the world's existence." This doesn't follow at all. To claim that it does is to claim just what is to be proved: *that the series in question had a beginning*. The premise tells us that if you start from some finite point in a series—that is, some point finitely far from the *beginning* of the series—and add a finite number per unit time, then you will never complete the series. Fair enough; but if the world has existed for an infinite stretch of time, then there *was* no first moment, no first event, and no beginning either to the series of moments or the series of events; more generally, at any preceding moment an infinite time would *already* have elapsed. To conclude, as Kant does, that it is impossible that an infinite series of events has occurred is just to assume that the series in question had a beginning—that is, is finite—but that is precisely what was to be proved. So the argument really has no force at all. It is not as if it is an argument the premises of which have a certain limited amount of intuitive plausibility; it is rather that this transition to the conclusion completely begs the question by assuming what was to be proved: that the series in question has a beginning. The argument therefore fails to establish its conclusion; it merely assumes it. It therefore gives us no reason at all for accepting that conclusion.

The argument for the antithesis is no more promising. Here is how Kant puts it:

> Let us assume that it [the world] had a beginning. Since the beginning is an existence which is preceded by a time in which the thing is not, there must have been a preceding time in which the world

was not, i.e., an empty time. Now no coming to be of a thing is possible in an empty time, because no part of such a time possesses, as compared with any other, a distinguishing condition of existence rather than nonexistence. . . . (A427, B455)

Again, the argument is by *reductio*: assume the denial of your conclusion and show that it is impossible, thereby establishing the conclusion. Here the two premises are

> (6) The beginning of an event or a thing is always preceded by a time in which the thing is not, that is, a time at which the thing in question does not exist.

and

> (7) In an empty time (a time at which nothing exists) nothing could come to be, because there would be no more reason for it to come to be at one part of that empty time than at any other part of it.

Neither premise is at all compelling. As to the first, this is true only if it is not possible that time and the world (the first event) should come into existence *together, simultaneously*. Is it known that this isn't possible? Certainly not. Indeed, some of the most popular theories of time (relational theories) would assume, not merely that this is *possible*, but that it is *true*.

As for the second premise, it is equally unpromising. Suppose (in accord with the picture governing the argument) an infinity of time had elapsed before the first event of the world took place—before its creation, say. The objection is that there would have been no more reason for God to create the world at *one* moment than at any *other*; hence he wouldn't or couldn't have created it at any moment at all. Again, why believe this? If God proposed to create the world, and no time was more propitious than any other, why couldn't he just arbitrarily *select* a time?[26]

> This argument is like those arguments that start from the premise that God, if he created the world, would have created the best world he could have; they go on to add that for every world God could have created (weakly actualized,[27] say) there is an even better world he could have created or weakly actualized; therefore, they conclude, he wouldn't

26. Compare Augustine's answer to those who wanted to know what God was doing before he created the world in *The Confessions of St. Augustine*, tr. Rex Warner (New York: New American Library, 1963), book 11, chapter 12, pp. 265–66.

27. For the notion of weak actualization, see my *The Nature of Necessity* (Oxford: Clarendon Press, 1974), p. 173, and *Alvin Plantinga*, ed. James Tomberlin and Peter van Inwagen (Dordrecht: D. Reidel, 1985), p. 49.

have weakly actualized any world at all, and the actual world has not been weakly actualized by God. Again, there seems no reason to believe the first premise. If there were only *finitely* many worlds among which God was obliged to choose, then perhaps he would have been obliged, somehow, to choose the best (although even this is at best dubious).[28] But if there *is* no best world at all among those he could have chosen (if for every world he could have chosen, there is a better world he could have chosen), why think a world's failing to be the best is sufficient for God's being unable to actualize it? Suppose a man had the benefit of immortality and had a bottle of wine that would improve every day, no matter how long he waits to drink it. Would he be rationally obliged *never* to drink it, on the grounds that for any time he might be tempted to, it would be better yet the next day? Suppose a donkey were stranded exactly midway between two bales of hay: would it be rationally obliged to stay there and starve to death because there is no more reason to move to the one bale than to the other?

The arguments for the other antinomies don't fare any better. In no case is there anything like a conclusive argument (given the assumption that we are thinking about the *Dinge*) for either the thesis or the antithesis. In some cases, we may not *know* or *be able to tell* which (thesis or antithesis) is true: but that doesn't constitute much of an argument for the conclusion that we can't think about the noumena. What would be needed for the argument to work would be a really powerful argument for the thesis and an equally powerful argument for the antithesis. In none of these cases do we have something like that.

Suppose we think a bit further about antinomies and paradoxes in connection with this question of concluding that we simply can't think about a given area or topic. Consider the Russell paradoxes, in their simple set-theoretical guise. Like Frege, we are all initially inclined to think that for every condition or property, there exists the set of just those things that meet the condition or have the property. It is pointed out that there is such a property as *being non-self-membered*, the property a thing has just if it is not a member of itself; hence there must be a set *S* of non-self-membered sets, but then *S* is a member of itself if and only if it is not a member of itself, which is a contradiction. Here it would be unduly enthusiastic to conclude that we can't really think and talk about sets as they are in themselves and can instead think only about sets that we have ourselves constructed, sets as they appear to us. One takes the argument as proving only that there is no set of non-self-membered sets and that, contrary to appearances, it is not true that for every property or condition, there exists the set of just those things satisfying the condition or displaying the property.

28. See Robert Adams's "Must God Create the Best?" *Philosophical Review* 81 (1972), pp. 317–32.

Take, instead, the Russell paradox as specified to properties, rather than sets; in some ways, this is a more serious paradox. One is initially inclined to think that there are properties, that some properties (for example, the property of being a property) exemplify themselves, so that there is such a property as *self-exemplification*, and that every property has a complement. These together lead to trouble: they imply that there is such a property as *non-self-exemplification*, which inconsiderately both does and doesn't exemplify itself.[29] Once again, however, it hardly seems to follow that we simply can't think and talk about properties *an sich*. We needn't hold that if we can think about properties *an sich*, then there is a property that both does and doesn't exemplify itself. We can quite properly conclude, instead, that one of the group of propositions we are initially inclined to accept must be false, and we look for the one with the least intuitive warrant or support, the one we are least strongly inclined to believe. (We might be inclined to think, for example, that there really isn't such a property as *non-self-exemplification* [even though it seems as if there is] so that either there is no such property as *self-exemplification*, or it is false that every property has a complement.) This is mildly disquieting, and gives us reason for a bit of humility with respect to the deliverances of reason, but we certainly aren't forced into the position of holding that we can't refer to and think about properties *an sich*.

In what conditions *would* this drastic conclusion be right? Perhaps in none at all, and if in some, it is hard to say which. At the least, however, it would involve our being very strongly inclined to accept each member of a set of propositions about some subject matter, which set (by argument forms we are very strongly inclined to accept) entails a contradiction. It would also involve there being *several* such sets of propositions about the subject matter in question. *Each* of the premises and arguments involved would have to have very powerful, maximal or near maximal intuitive support; otherwise, we could more reasonably hold that a premise (or argument form) with only moderate intuitive support is false (or invalid). If there were several such sets of propositions— about properties, say—and each of these propositions and argument forms had the degree of intuitive support enjoyed by, say, *2 + 1 = 3* and *modus ponens*, then perhaps the right conclusion to draw would be that either there simply aren't any such things as the objects in the alleged realm, or that if there are, we are incapable of thinking about them.

Even here, however, there would be reason to doubt the success of the argument. It would involve as a premise something like:

(8) If there are several sets of premises about properties, each member of each set having maximal intuitive warrant, and the members of each set together entail a contradiction, then we cannot refer to and think about properties *an sich*.

---

29. If you balk at such properties as *self-exemplification* and *non-self-exemplification*, conduct the argument instead in terms of *conditions*; see Tomberlin and van Inwagen, *Alvin Plantinga*, p. 320.

The next premise would be the antecedent of (8), and the conclusion would be the consequent of (8)—that is, the proposition that we cannot refer to and think about properties *an sich*. But if that conclusion were true, how could we grasp (8), the first premise? That premise seems to be, among other things, about properties *an sich*, and if we grasp it, we are able to think about properties *an sich*. The argument appears to be self-referentially self-refuting: if it is a successful argument, its first premise is both about noumena and such that we can grasp it, in which case that premise must be false.

The sensible Kantian conclusion, so it seems to me, is that if, indeed, we can refer to and think about the *Dinge*, reason alone doesn't tell us such things as whether the world had a beginning in time or whether there are simple substances. It seems more likely than not, perhaps, that there are simple substances and that there are free agents who initiate new causal chains in the world, but the negations of these propositions are not demonstrably mistaken. Most certainly, it is not the case that both these propositions *and* their denials are demonstrable, so that each is both demonstrably true and, furthermore, demonstrably false.

We must also recall that the whole scheme, the whole radical sub-picture, seems incoherent in a familiar way. One who states and proposes this scheme makes several claims about the *Dinge*: that they are not in space and time, for example, and more poignantly, that our concepts don't apply to them (applying only to the phenomena), so that we cannot refer to or think about them. But if we really *can't* think the *Dinge*, then we can't think them (and can't whistle them either); if we can't think about them, we can't so much as entertain the thought that there *are* such things. The incoherence is patent.

Would it be possible to induce coherence by refusing to make the distinction between phenomena and noumena, speaking only of what, if we *did* make that distinction, would be the phenomena, and claiming that whatever there is, is either a bit of experience or an object constructed by us from bits of experience by way of concepts (i.e., rules for constructing things from experience)? That is extremely hard to believe: are the stars, for example, which, as far as we can tell, existed long before we did, either bits of human experience or objects constructed by us from bits of human experience? How are we supposed to make sense of that? On this view, furthermore, the objection to Christian belief would not be that serious Christians improperly take it that they can refer to God; the objection would be that there is no God. If there were such a person, he certainly wouldn't be either a bit of human experience or something we have constructed from it. Still further, on this picture we ourselves (because we are among the things there are) would either have constructed ourselves from bits of experience or we would just *be* bits of experience; but of course we couldn't have constructed ourselves before we existed, so we must have started off, at least, as bits of experience with the power to construct things. Not a pretty picture. And even if we could somehow induce coherence here, why should we feel obliged to believe it? What possible claim could such a bizarre scheme have on us?

By way of conclusion then: it doesn't look as if there is good reason in Kant or in the neighborhood of Kant for the conclusion that our concepts do not apply to God, so that we cannot think about him. Contemporary theologians and others sometimes complain that contemporary philosophers of religion often write as if they have never read their Kant. Perhaps the reason they write that way, however, is not that they have never read their Kant but rather that they *have* read him and remain unconvinced. They may be unconvinced that Kant actually claimed that our concepts do not apply to God. Alternatively, they may concede that Kant did claim this, but remain unconvinced that he was *right*; after all, it is not just a given of the intellectual life that Kant is right. Either way, they don't think Kant gives us reason to hold that we cannot think about God.

2

Kaufman and Hick

Our subject is the *de jure* question about Christian belief: the question whether it is rational, or reasonable, or rationally justifiable, or intellectually defensible to accept such belief. A previous question, as we saw in the last chapter, is the question whether there *is* any *de jure* question about Christian belief or, indeed, any *de facto* question either. Christian belief is belief, among other things, in the existence of God. And Christians believe that God is *infinite*: unlimited with respect to such important properties as knowledge, wisdom, goodness, and power. They also believe that God is *transcendent*: distinct from the created universe, in no way dependent on it, and such that it is dependent on him. Finally, they assume that it is possible to refer to God, talk and think about him, address him in prayer, and worship him. Many contemporary theologians, however, apparently believe that these ideas are excessively naive: they hold that there are profound problems in the very idea that we can refer to and think about a being characterized in the way Christians characterize God. In particular, they seem to believe that Immanuel Kant gave us excellent reason to be (at best) extremely suspicious of such naively realistic ways of thinking about God or religious language. As we saw in the last chapter, however, there is really nothing in Kant to suggest that in fact we can't think or talk about God. More generally, it is exceedingly hard to see how to construct an argument—an argument for the conclusion that we cannot refer to and think about God—from materials to be found in the work of Kant. Of course that doesn't show that no such argument can be found: but if one *can* be found, it is, I should say, up to those who think there is one to produce and develop it.

In this chapter, I shall pursue this question into the present: if Kant gives us no reason to accept this conceptual agnosticism, do contemporary theologians (or writers in religious studies) do so? I choose two representatives: Gordon Kaufman and John Hick.

I. KAUFMAN

A. The Real Referent and the Available Referent

According to Gordon Kaufman,

> The central problem of theological discourse, not shared
> with any other "language game," is the meaning of the term
> "God." "God" raises special problems of meaning because it is
> a noun which by definition refers to a reality transcendent of,
> and thus not locatable within, experience. A new convert may
> wish to refer the "warm feeling" in his heart to God, but God
> is hardly to be identified with this emotion; the biblicist may
> regard the Bible as God's Word; the moralist may believe God
> speaks through men's consciences; the churchman may be-
> lieve God is present among his people—but each of these
> would agree that God himself transcends the locus referred
> to. As the Creator or Source of all that is, God is not to be
> identified with any particular finite reality; as the proper ob-
> ject of ultimate loyalty or faith, God is to be distinguished
> from every proximate or penultimate value or being. But if
> absolutely nothing within our experience can be directly
> identified as that to which the term "God" properly refers,
> what meaning does or can the word have?[1]

So the claim is that God is not to be identified with any particular finite reality—on the grounds, presumably, that God is not in fact
identical with any particular finite reality. From the Christian perspective, this is, of course, no more than the sober truth: God is infinite and therefore not identical with any finite reality. So far, so good.
Kaufman apparently infers from this, however, that "absolutely nothing within our experience can be directly identified as that to which
the term 'God' properly refers"; he adds that if this is so, then there
is a real problem for the reference of our term 'God': if "nothing
within our experience can be directly identified as that to which the
term 'God' properly refers, then what meaning does or can the word
have?" I realize this last is a *question*, but it looks like a *rhetorical* question; the idea is that if nothing within our experience can be directly
identified as that to which the term 'God' properly refers, then the
term 'God' doesn't refer to anything, or at any rate there is a real
problem about its referring to something.

Here, therefore, we have two claims:

1. *God the Problem* (Cambridge: Harvard University Press, 1972), p. 7. Henceforth GP.

(a) if God is not a finite reality, then absolutely nothing within our experience can be directly identified as that to which the term 'God' properly refers.

and

(b) if nothing within our experience can be directly identified as that to which the term 'God' properly refers, then the term 'God' doesn't refer to anything, or at least it is problematic that it does.

These claims awaken Kantian echoes—echoes that get stronger as we move further into Kaufman's thought. And surely both are initially dubious. Consider (a). First, we must ask what it means to say that "nothing within our experience can be directly identified as that to which the term 'God' properly applies." What is it, as Kaufman is thinking of it, for something to be within our experience, and to be such that it can be directly identified as that to which a certain term properly applies? What about my friend's cat Maynard: is Maynard something within our experience which can be directly identified as that to which the term 'Maynard' properly applies? I should think so: else the problem is not merely with reference to God, but with reference to anything at all; Kaufman's suggestion, I think, is that the problem is specifically with respect to God. According to (a) it is because God is *infinite* that the term 'God' doesn't properly apply to anything within our experience. Now why, precisely, is that true? Maynard, I take it, is something within our experience, and this is because we can experience Maynard. We can perceive him: we can see, hear, touch, and sometimes smell him. The idea must be, then, that if God is not a finite reality, then we cannot experience him; we cannot perceive him (we cannot see, hear, or touch him) or in any other way experience him. An infinite being—one that is omnipotent and omniscient, for example—cannot be perceived or experienced in any way whatever.

Is that really true? How does the fact that God is infinite mean that we cannot experience him? Many Christians and Jews believe that God spoke to Moses from the burning bush; Moses heard him. He spoke to Abraham in a dream. He spoke to several people when he said, "This is my beloved Son in whom I am well pleased"; these people all heard him. Christians may also believe that the Holy Spirit works in their hearts, producing conviction and faith, as well as the religious affections of which Jonathan Edwards spoke; are they not then experiencing God? The term 'experience' (taken as either a noun or a verb) is notoriously slippery, but if these things do in fact happen, do not the people involved experience God? Christians may go still further and hold that in some circumstances some people *perceive* God, a theme that has received explicit and powerful treatment in William P. Alston's *Perceiving God*. If they are right, then in these

1

cases too they experience God. Now Kaufman apparently thinks the fact that God is infinite—unlimited along several dimensions— means that these people are mistaken: whatever they think, they do *not* experience God. Again, why so? God is infinite with respect to power, that is, omnipotent: how does that so much as slyly suggest that God cannot make himself heard or that he cannot be experienced? He is infinite with respect to knowledge, that is, omniscient; does that somehow show that he could not speak to Abraham or anyone else? Is it perhaps the combination of omnipotence and omniscience that shows this? It is certainly hard to see how.

If God is omnipotent, infinitely powerful, won't he be able to manifest himself in our experience, bring it about that we experience him? He will be unable to do so, presumably, under those conditions, only if it is logically impossible (impossible in the broadly logical sense) that an omniscient and omnipotent being should be able to make himself heard. But so far as I can see, there isn't even the slightest reason to think that; certainly Kaufman gives us none. I will go into the question of the nature of experience of God in more detail in chapters 6, 8, and 9; here I only want to point out that it seems initially implausible to declare that God, if he is infinite and omnipotent, could not bring it about that we experience him.

The second premise (b)—the claim that if nothing within our experience can be directly identified as that to which the term 'God' refers, then the term 'God' doesn't refer to anything (or it is at least problematic that it does)—also seems dubious. Cosmologists tell us of the Big Bang, an event that occurred several billion years ago in which an explosion of enormous energy caused an expansion from an initial configuration of enormous density. I suppose the Big Bang is not something within our experience, something that can be directly identified as that to which the term 'the Big Bang' correctly refers; does it follow that there is a profound problem with this term? Is the real problem with contemporary cosmology not just the speculative nature of those suggestions about many universes and what happened during Planck time, but rather the very idea that we can refer to and think about that initial Big Bang? It isn't easy to see why: at the least, a powerful argument would be required. And if there is no particular problem here, why is there a special problem in the case of God?[2]

---

2. One source of Kaufman's views here may be a sort of lingering allegiance to the "Verifiability Criterion of Meaning" mentioned above (pp. 7–8): "Since seemingly no clear experiential evidence can be cited for or against that to which the word 'God' allegedly refers, the question has been repeatedly raised whether all talk about him is not in the strict sense cognitively meaningless" (p. 8). As we saw in chapter 1, however, there is little to be said for the Verifiability Criterion.

Well, then, someone might say, if there is no problem about referring to an infinite being, how do we refer to God? In chapter 1, I suggested that we could do so, first, by way of definite descriptions such as 'the creator of the heavens and the earth', 'the omnipotent and omniscient creator of the world', 'the divine father of our lord and savior Jesus Christ', 'the divine person who spoke to Abraham', 'the divine person I am presently experiencing,' and so on. Each of these descriptions will refer to something if there is exactly one thing exemplifying the properties mentioned in the description; if not, then the description will not refer. (If Christian belief is true, of course, then each of these terms does refer to something, indeed, to the *same* thing.)

Furthermore, we can use the proper name 'God' to refer to the being denoted by those descriptions. That term can serve as a proper name, for me, of God, in several ways. For example, I might 'fix the reference' of the term 'God' by one of the above descriptions, such as 'the creator of heaven and earth'; if, indeed, just one person created the heavens and the earth, and if that person is also denoted by those other descriptions, then my name 'God' will be a proper name of the same being as that denoted by those descriptions. My name will be a proper name of a being who is omniscient, omnipotent, the creator of the world, the father of our lord and savior Jesus Christ, and the like. Under these conditions, my name 'God' will express an essence of that being.[3] Perhaps *my* name, introduced in that way, will not express the *same* essence of God as *your* name, introduced by way of a different description. Even so, however, they will express logically equivalent (even if epistemically inequivalent) essences of God.[4]

Alternatively, I might not get my proper name of God by using a definite description to fix the reference and then officially baptize the thing to which the description refers: I might instead just catch the name, so to speak, from others. In fact, this is the more usual way. Proper names, like colds, are ordinarily caught from our associates. As a child, I hear talk of God, talk in which the name 'God' occurs; I pick up the name, tacitly or implicitly intending to use it to refer to the same being to which those from whom I get the name refer. If they do indeed succeed in referring to God by using that name, then so will I. (Here is another way in which the success of my noetic ventures depends on the success of similar ventures on the parts of those around me: see *Warrant and Proper Function*, pp. 77–78.)

In any event, Kaufman holds that we can neither know nor experience what he calls 'the real referent' of the term 'God':

The real referent for "God" is never accessible to us or in any way open to our observation or experience. It must remain always an unknown X. . . . (GP 85)

3. See my *The Nature of Necessity* (Oxford: Oxford University Press, 1974), pp. 77ff.

4. See my "The Boethian Compromise," in *American Philosophical Quarterly* (1978).

When Christians use the term 'God', therefore, they do not refer to the real referent of that term (but then why call it "the real referent"?). To whom or what (if anything) *do* they refer when they say such things as that God was in Christ, reconciling the world to himself, or that God created the heavens and the earth, or that God is our faithful and loving father? The answer, says Kaufman, is that when they say these things they are referring to the "available referent" of the name 'God', and the available referent is an *imaginative construct*, something we have somehow created:

> For all practical purposes it is the *available referent* —a particular imaginative construct—that bears significantly on human life and thought. It is the "available God" whom we have in mind when we worship or pray . . . it is the available God in terms of which we speak and think whenever we use the word "God." In this sense "God" denotes for all practical purposes what is essentially a mental or imaginative construct. (GP 85–86)

> God is a symbol—an imaginative construct—that enables men to view the world and themselves in such a way as to make action and morality ultimately (metaphysically) meaningful. (GP 109)

So the available God, the God whom we have in mind when we worship and pray, the being to which we refer when we use the term 'God'—this being is a human creation, an imaginative construct, something we ourselves have created. The view seems to be initially that there is this available referent, but also a *real* referent of the term 'God', a being with whom we have no noetic contact and about whom we cannot speak. Or rather, the view is, I think, that there *might* be a real referent, and that *if* there is, it is a being we cannot think about:

> This fact, that the God actually available to people is an imaginative construct, does not necessarily mean that God is "unreal" or "merely imaginary" or something of that sort. That question remains open for further investigation. (GP 86)

> Does this mean, then, that the conclusion is, after all, that God really does not exist, that He is only a figment of our imaginations? If those words are intended to put the speculative question about the ultimate nature of things, then, as we have seen, there is no possible way to give an answer. (GP 111)

In essence, then, Kaufman's view in *God the Problem* appears to be the following. The term 'God' has an available referent: this is a human construction, something we have created; when we speak of God in worship or to him in prayer, it is this available referent about which (or to which) we are talking. Perhaps the term also has a real referent. If so, however, it transcends our experience and is hence something to which our concepts do not apply: a mere unknown X, to adopt Kaufman's Kantian terminology.

Now I've already argued that there seems no good reason to hold this position. Here I must go on to add that there is excellent reason *not* to hold it. As it stands, the view is incoherent. First, the 'available referent': the suggestion is that when Christians pray and worship and speak about God, they are talking about the available referent. When they say such things, for example, as 'God created the heavens and the earth', they are really attributing this property —the property of having created the heavens and the earth—to the available referent. But the available referent is a human construct, and hence presumably did not exist before there were human beings. How then did it manage to create the heavens and the earth? Could it somehow do this before it existed? In any event, an imaginative construct, a symbol, a structure of meanings of some kind is just not the sort of thing that *could* create the heavens and the earth or, indeed, anything else. A symbol, an imaginative construct, may have properties: *being a construct*, for example, or *being a symbol*, or *being appropriately used by human beings for such and such a purpose*; it certainly won't have such properties as *being omniscient* or *creating the world*. I suppose it could be that Christians are confused: they *think* they are referring to and talking about something that created them, but the fact is they are referring to something they themselves have created. Is it really plausible to think they are as confused as all that, however? Those who believe there is no such person as God will see Christians as mistaken in thinking there is, and perhaps it is at least sensible to think them mistaken in that way. Is it really sensible to think them mistaken in such a way that they predicate the properties of God of a mere construct? Well, perhaps that could happen; but surely a strong argument would be required to make this even reasonably plausible.

Say that a property *P entails* a property *Q* just if it is necessary in the broadly logical sense that everything that exemplifies *P* also exemplifies *Q*; and say that a concept *C contains* a property *P* if the property of which *C* is a grasp entails *P*. Then it is clear that a concept might *contain* such properties as *being omniscient* or *having created the world* (even if it couldn't *exemplify* them), and equally clear that the concept corresponding to the definite description 'the omniscient creator of the world' contains the properties *being omniscient* and *being the creator of the world*. Could it be that what Kaufman really means is not that Christians assert that the available referent—which is something like a concept containing salient properties of God—*exemplifies* those properties, but rather that it *contains* them? This too seems wrong. It is indeed true that certain concepts, including some associated with descriptions of God, contain those properties. When Christians make their characteristic claims, however, they are not merely saying such things as that the concept *being the omniscient creator of the heavens and earth* contains the properties *being omniscient* and *being the creator of the heavens and earth*. That would, of course, be true; it would also be wholly trivial. It wouldn't be at all distinctive of

Christians or theists: even the most hardened atheist would agree that this concept contains those properties. What Christians claim entails rather that these properties are *exemplified*, that there really exists a being who has them.

The above seems to be the literal construal of Kaufman's words; of course there are other possibilities in the neighborhood. Perhaps, for example, he thinks of the available referent not as a being with the properties Christians ascribe to God, but as something like a certain type with which those properties are associated.[5] This may seem a more sympathetic construal of Kaufman; I doubt that it really is. If Kaufman's claim is that Christians ordinarily worship that *type*, then his claim is outrageous in just the way I suggest. If his claim, however, is only that Christians *believe* they worship a being having the properties associated with the type but are possibly mistaken, then is his claim more than the uninteresting suggestion that Christians may be wrong about whether there is such a person as God?

Now consider the real referent. The idea is that our concepts do not apply to the real referent, if indeed there is such a thing. It follows that this being is not wise, almighty, or the creator of the heavens and the earth. For consider our concept of wisdom. This concept applies to a thing just if that thing is wise. So a being to which this concept did not apply would not be wise, whatever else it might be. If, therefore, our concepts do not apply to the real referent of the term 'God', then our concepts of being loving, almighty, wise, creator, and redeemer do not apply to it, in which case it is not loving, almighty, wise, a creator, or a redeemer. It wouldn't have any of the properties Christians ascribe to God. And of course so far this is in accord with Kaufman's intentions.

I suspect, however, that his official position has other consequences Kaufman does not intend. If this being, this real referent, is really such that *none* of our concepts applies to it, then it will also lack such properties as self-identity, existence, and *being either a material object or an immaterial object*, these being properties of which we have concepts. Indeed, it wouldn't have the property of being the real referent of the term 'God' or any other term; our concept *being the referent of a term* will not apply to it. The fact is this being won't have any properties at all because our concept of having at least one property does not apply to it. Kaufman's view seems to entail that there could be a being that had no properties, didn't exist, wasn't self-identical, wasn't either a material object or an immaterial object, and didn't have any properties.

Taken strictly, therefore, Kaufman's position is incoherent.

5. See Nicholas Wolterstorff's so-far-unpublished *From Presence to Practice; Mind, World, and Entitlement to Believe*, chapter 1.

B. The Function of Religious Language

Perhaps it is for reasons like these that in more recent work, in particular *The Theological Imagination*,[6] Kaufman seems to have given up the real referent. Instead, he claims that "it is an error to reify God into an independent being" (TI 38), that "To regard God as some kind of describable or knowable object over against us would be at once a degradation of God and a serious category error" (TI 244), and that

> It is a mistake, therefore, to regard qualities attributed to God (e.g., aseity, holiness, omnipotence, omniscience, providence, love, self-revelation) as though they were features or activities of such a particular being. Rather, in the mind's construction of the image/concept of God, the ordinary relation of subject and predicate is reversed. Instead of the subject (God) being a *given* to which the various predicate adjectives are then assigned, here the descriptive terms themselves are the building blocks which the imagination uses in putting together its conception. . . . Contemporary theological construction needs to recognize that these terms and concepts do not refer directly to "objects" or "realities" or their qualities and relations, but function rather as the building blocks or reference points which articulate the theistic world-picture or vision of life. (TI 244)

Why must we think these terms do not, in fact, denote an all-powerful, all-wise creator of the universe? As far as I can see, it is because Kaufman does not believe that there is any such thing: he thinks, so far as I can see, that the proper attitude toward this proposition is either disbelief or withholding, either atheism or agnosticism. Naturally enough, if there is no being of that sort, then none of our terms will denote a being of that sort. This is perhaps a surprising position for a theologian; a theologian who does not believe in God is like a mountaineer for whom it is an open question whether there are any mountains or a plumber agnostic about pipes: a beguiling spectacle, but hard to take seriously.[7]

And why does he think there is no such person? Again, there is precious little by way of argument. He cites first "the rise of a new con-

---

6. Subtitled *Constructing the Concept of God* (Philadelphia: Westminster Press, 1981; hereafter TI). See also his *Essay on Theological Method* (Missoula, Mont.: Scholars Press, 1975 and 1979).

7. Unhappily, this spectacle is not at present uncommon. Compare, for example, Don Cupitt, who has similar views sometimes expressed with a certain amiable dottiness: "It is spiritual vulgarity and immaturity to demand an extra-religious reality of God" (p. 10 of his *Taking Leave of God* [New York: Crossroad, 1981]); he adds, "The real external existence of God is of no religious interest" (p. 96).

sciousness of the significance of religious pluralism";[8] second, he says in the same article, "new theories about the ways in which cultural and linguistic symbolic or conceptual frames shape all our experiencing and thinking . . . have given rise in theologians to a new self-consciousness about the extraordinarily complex and problematic character of all so-called 'religious truth-claims,' including those that are made by Christian faith"; third, he refers to the traditional problem of evil but with a twist: Christians themselves are responsible for more of the evil the world displays than they would like to think. (This last, sadly enough, is true, and perhaps [to take just one example] part of the occasion for modern apostasy, in the West, was the unedifying spectacle of Christians at each other's throats in the sixteenth and seventeenth centuries.) It is an enormous leap, however, to the conclusion that probably there is no such person as God. In chapter 14, we'll examine the question whether evil constitutes a defeater for Christian belief, and in chapter 13 we'll do the same for the plurality of religions the world displays. As for the second suggestion—the claim that many now hold that "cultural and linguistic symbolic or conceptual frames shape all our experiencing and thinking"—perhaps this claim is true: but if it casts doubt on all of our experiencing and thinking, thus including Christianity, doesn't it do the same for every other way of thinking, including the thought that it casts doubt on what we think? If so, it would seem to leave everything as it was, not functioning as a reason for being doubtful specifically about theism (or, indeed, anything else).

One might expect someone who is atheist or agnostic about God to move away from religion altogether, viewing religious devotion and belief with something of a jaundiced or a pitying eye. This is not Kaufman's course. Instead, he argues that religious practice and devotion "still has an important function to play in life." This function, of course, is not that of putting us in touch with a being with the properties traditionally ascribed to God or that of enabling us to appropriate the salvation in Jesus Christ that God has promised us. Rather, this new function requires that theologians should *construct* or *reconstruct* the concept of God. Religious language is still important, but it should be recast so as no longer to involve a forlorn attempt to refer to a being who isn't there. Instead, it should be used to promote human flourishing, "human fulfillment and meaning" (TI 34). The word 'God' is to be associated with a symbol or image or concept theologians construct; it is their job to reconstruct the concept or symbol 'God' in a way that is appropriate to our present historical situation. (Thus in *Theology for a Nuclear Age*, he suggests that in this modern nuclear age we should think of God as "the historical

---

8. "Evidentialism: A Theologian's Response," *Faith and Philosophy* (January 1989), p. 30.

evolutionary force that has brought us all into being."[9]) The word 'God', therefore, should no longer be thought of as referring to the all-powerful, all-knowing, all-loving person who has created the world; it is not to be thought of as referring to a person at all. Instead, this word is to be seen as a sort of *symbol* of certain states of affairs. For example, Christians have thought of *transcendence* as a property of God; Kaufman recommends that, in constructing the new symbol, we retain transcendence:[10]

> What seems to be at stake here is a claim that human individuals and communities need a center of orientation and devotion outside themselves and their perceived desires and needs if they are to find genuine fulfillment. (TI 35–36)

> God symbolizes that in the ongoing evolutionary historical process which grounds our being as distinctively human and which draws (or drives) us on toward authentic human fulfillment (salvation). . . . And ritualized devotion to God in religious cult as well as in the private disciplines of prayer and meditation still has an important function to play in life. (TI 41)

More generally:

> "God" is the personifying symbol of that cosmic activity which has created our humanity and continues to press for its full realization. Such a personification has a considerable advantage for some purposes over abstract concepts such as "cosmic forces" or "foundation for our humanity in the ultimate nature of things": the symbol "God" is concrete and definite, a sharply defined image, and as such it can readily become the central focus for devotion and service. . . . "God" is a symbol that gathers up into itself and focuses for us all those cosmic forces working toward the fully humane existence for which we long. (TI 50)

> Speech about the Christian God as "real" or "existent" expresses symbolically this conviction that free and loving persons-in-community have a substantial metaphysical foundation, that there are cosmic forces working toward this sort of humanization. (TI 49)

> The Christian image/concept of God, as I have presented it here, is an imaginative construct which orients selves and communities so as to facilitate development toward loving and caring selfhood, and toward communities of openness, love, and freedom. (TI 48)

---

9. Manchester: Manchester University Press, 1985, p. 43.

10. How do properties such as transcendence or aseity get related to those symbols we construct? Do we just draw up a list of properties and declare them associated with the term 'God'? It is far from easy to see how this is supposed to work, and Kaufman doesn't say.

The idea, so far as I can grasp it, seems to be this. Perhaps there is no such person as theists have traditionally believed in. Nevertheless, it is a good idea to continue to use the term 'God' and, in fact, to continue to utter many of the very same words and phrases and sentences as do those who believe in God; done properly, this will promote human flourishing. How, exactly? Perhaps as follows. We realize, first, that there is probably no such person as God. We are then free to select a concept/image 'God' and associate with it certain properties—existence and transcendence, perhaps—and use that symbol to symbolize such things as that the world is hospitable, to at least some degree, to distinctively human aspirations, goals, needs, and desires. We are to say such things as 'God is real', meaning that in fact there are forces in the world that contribute to human flourishing. (We should add, I suppose, that the devil is also real, thereby symbolizing that there are forces working *against* human flourishing.) We are to say 'God is independent of us,' meaning thereby that a community or person needs a focus of interest outside itself to flourish. (Perhaps we should add that 'We are justified by the suffering and death of Jesus Christ,' thereby symbolizing the fact that we do not always feel guilty, or 'God was in Christ, reconciling the world to himself,' thereby meaning that things are now more propitious for human flourishing than they have been at some times in the past.) And saying these things will itself promote human flourishing.

Can we take any of this seriously? This is not a matter of pouring new wine into old wineskins: what we have here is nothing like the rich, powerful, fragrant wine of the great Christian truths; what we have is something wholly drab, trivial, and insipid. It is not even a matter of throwing out the baby with the bathwater; it is, instead, throwing out the baby and keeping the tepid bathwater, at best a bland, unappetizing potion that is neither hot nor cold and at worst a nauseating brew, fit for neither man nor beast. Furthermore, this rehashing of secularity under the guise of 'reconstructing' Christianity encourages dishonesty and hypocrisy; it results in a sort of private code whereby one utters the same phrases as those who accept Christian belief but means something wholly different by them. You thereby appear to concur with those who accept Christian belief; in fact, you wholly reject what they believe. You can thereby patronize the person in the pew (who has not reached your level of enlightenment) but without paying the cost of unduly disturbing her. The fact is such double-talk is at best confusing and deceptive, contributing only to misunderstanding, dishonesty, and hypocrisy. Wouldn't it be vastly more honest to follow the lead of, for example, Bertrand Russell, A. J. Ayer, Daniel Dennett, Richard Dawkins, or even Madalyn Murray O' Hair, declaring forthrightly that there is no God and that Christianity is an enormous mistake?

II. HICK

John Hick's work is interesting both intrinsically and with respect to our topic; he too holds a view heavily indebted to Kant, and his view too can be put (with considerable qualifications) as the view that our concepts do not apply to God or 'The Real'. There are evocative echoes of Kant and also evocative echoes of some of the trials and tribulations dogging an effort to find a coherent interpretation or understanding of Kant.

A. The Real

The traditional doctrine of *divine ineffability* is to be found in Christianity, as well as other religious traditions. Hick believes that this doctrine is really the recognition of a quasi-Kantian distinction between God (the Real, the Ultimate[11]) *as it is in itself* and *as it is for us* (as we know or experience it):

> In each of the great traditions a distinction has been drawn, though with varying degrees of emphasis, between the Real (thought of as God, Brahman, the Dharmakaya . . .) in itself and the Real as manifested within the intellectual and experiential purview of that tradition. (236)

So far, so good; this claim—that there is a distinction between the Real as it is in itself and as it is for us—is relatively weak. It requires only that the way we think of God does not completely match what God actually is; it would be satisfied if, for example, there are things about God that we didn't know or, more strongly, if there were things about him we *couldn't* know.

But Hick goes much further; the Real is such that we cannot say anything at all about it, in that none of our terms can be literally (and correctly) applied to it:

> Thus although we cannot speak of the Real *an sich* in literal terms, nevertheless we live inescapably in relation to it. (351)

> It is within the phenomenal or experienceable realm that language has developed and it is to this that it literally applies. Indeed the system of concepts embodied in human language has contributed reciprocally to the formation of the humanly perceived world. It is as much constructed as given. But our language can have no purchase on a postulated noumenal reality which is not even partly formed by human concepts. This lies outside the scope of our cognitive capacities. (350)

---

11. *An Interpretation of Religion* (New Haven: Yale University Press, 1989), pp. 236–39. Unless otherwise noted, page references to Hick's work will be to this book.

This sounds like the two-world interpretation of Kant (above, pp. 10ff.). There is the phenomenal realm, to which our language literally applies; this "humanly perceived world" is as much constructed as given, and it is constructed, in part, by virtue of our application of concepts. However, there is also a noumenal world ('The Real'), "which is not even partly formed by human concepts," and as a result it is outside the scope of our cognitive capacities. And here some of the same questions arise as with the two-world interpretation of Kant: why think something is within the scope of our cognitive capacities only if it is partly formed by human concepts? Are horses and dinosaurs (partly) formed by our concepts? (Which parts?) And if the noumena lie outside the scope of our cognitive capacities, how is it that we know something about them, or even that there are any such things?

More frequently, however, he adopts the one-world view:

> Kant distinguished between noumenon and phenomenon, or between a *Ding an sich* and that thing as it appears to human consciousness. . . . In this strand of Kant's thought—not the only strand, but the one which I am seeking to press into service in the epistemology of religion—the noumenal world exists independently of our perception of it and the phenomenal world is that same world as it appears to our human consciousness. . . . I want to say that the noumenal Real is experienced and thought by different human mentalities, forming and formed by different religious traditions, as the range of gods and absolutes which the phenomenology of religion reports. (241–42)

Further, it is unclear whether Hick thinks we can or can't, do or don't perceive this being or in some other way experience it. On the negative side, we have

> If the Real in itself is not and cannot be humanly experienced, why postulate such an unknown and unknowable *Ding as sich*? The answer is that the divine noumenon is a necessary postulate of the pluralistic religious life of humanity. (249)

On the positive side, we have, for example,

> Analogously, I want to say that the noumenal Real is experienced and thought by different human mentalities, forming and formed by different religious traditions, as the range of gods and absolutes which the phenomenology of religion reports. (242)

and

> The noumenal Real is such as to be authentically experienced as a range of both theistic and nontheistic phenomena. (246–47)

There are several more passages to quote on each side; clearly, Hick is ambivalent about the answer to this question. But perhaps this is not fatal; his answer, I should think, would be "In a way, yes, and in a way, no." The noumenal real makes a crucial causal contribution of some sort to our experience; perhaps it doesn't matter whether we say that we actually experience it or say, instead, only that it contributes to our experience.

Another ambiguity, however, is not so easily dismissed. In chapter 19, Hick seems to say that our concepts do not apply to the noumenon, or, as he puts it there, none of our terms applies literally to it. He quotes the Buddha as saying, with respect to where or in what sphere a Tathagata (a fully enlightened being) arises after death, that none of the terms 'arises', 'does not arise', 'both arises and does not arise,' and 'neither arises nor does not arise' applies to the condition of the Tathagata (346). Hick apparently approves of this suggestion and adds, "We have here the idea of realities and circumstances which transcend the categories available in our unillumined thought and language. Their total elusiveness is signaled by the Buddha's rejection not only of the straight positive and negative assertions but also of their combination and disjunction" (347). Hick also claims that "we cannot speak of the Real *an sich* in literal terms" (351). If Hick really means that none of our terms applies literally to the Real, then it isn't possible to make sense of what he says. I take it the term 'tricycle' does not apply to the Real; the Real is not a tricycle. But if the Real is not a tricycle, then 'is not a tricycle' applies literally to it; it is a nontricycle. It could hardly be neither a tricycle nor a nontricycle, nor do I think that Hick would want to suggest that it could.

In chapter 14, however, Hick makes a suggestion of quite a different kind. As he says, "it would not indeed make sense to say of X that *none* of our concepts apply to it" (p. 239); for example, at least our concept *being such that we can refer to it* would have to apply to any X of which we were properly prepared to say anything at all, including that our concepts do not apply to it. The idea is rather, says Hick, that among our concepts, only *formal* concepts and *negative* concepts apply to the Real. That is to say, of the properties of which we have a grasp, only those that are formal, such as *having some properties, being self-identical*, and *being such that 7 + 5 = 12*, and those that are negative, such as *not being a horse, not being a tricycle*, and *not being good*, would apply to it. Hick adds that there is a substantial tradition within Christianity and other religions, according to which we should distinguish

> between what we might call substantial properties, such as 'being good', 'being powerful', 'having knowledge', and purely formal and logically generated properties such as 'being a referent of a term' and 'being such that our substantial concepts do not apply'. What they wanted to affirm was that the substantial characterizations do not apply to God in God's self-existent being, beyond the range of human experience. They often expressed this by saying that we can only make negative statements about the Ultimate. . . . This *via neg-*

ativa (or *via remotionis*) consists in applying negative concepts to the Ultimate—the concept of not being finite, and so on—as a way of saying that it lies beyond the range of all our positive substantial characterizations. It is in this qualified sense that it makes perfectly good sense to say that our substantial concepts do not apply to the Ultimate. (239)

Here Hick is apparently *endorsing* what he sees these traditions as delivering. I am not sure there is any way of harmonizing chapter 14 with chapter 19; if not, I suggest we go with chapter 14.

At some points in characterizing these traditions he is historically incorrect. For example, he claims that "Calvin taught that we do not know God's essence but only God as revealed to us" (250), and he refers to Calvin's *Institutes*, I: xiii: 21. But Calvin doesn't teach that we can't know *anything* of God's essence. In this chapter, he begins by arguing that

> The scriptural teaching concerning God's infinite and spiritual essence ought to be enough, not only to banish popular delusions, but also to refute the subtleties of secular philosophy.[12]

He goes on to point out that we can't '*measure*' God '*by our own senses*' as he puts it:

> But even if God to keep us sober speaks sparingly of his essence, yet by those two titles that I have used ['infinite' and 'spiritual'], he both banishes stupid imaginings and restrains the boldness of the human mind. Surely his infinity ought to make us afraid to try to measure him by our own senses. (p. 121)

Calvin's next point is that because God is a spirit, we can't properly attribute corporeal characteristics to him. He concedes that Scripture does seem to attribute such characteristics (a mouth, an arm, ears, eyes, hands) to him, but those who therefore take it that he *has* such bodily characteristics fail to understand that "as nurses commonly do with infants, God is wont in a measure to 'lisp' in speaking to us" (p. 121). Here Calvin clearly thinks we know that God 'in himself' is infinite, spiritual, and incorporeal; his essence includes infinity and incorporeality. In the passage to which Hick refers, furthermore, Calvin's point is to caution us not to try to figure out God's essence by way just of the resources of reason; given its limitations, that is bound to prove futile:

> For how can the human mind measure off the measureless essence of God according to its own little measure, a mind as yet unable to establish for certain the nature of the sun's body, though men's eyes daily gaze upon it? . . . Let us then

12. Tr. Ford Lewis Battles and ed. John T. McNeill (Philadelphia: Westminster Press, 1960), I, xiii, 1, p. 120. (Page references to the *Institutes* are to this edition.)

> willingly leave to God the knowledge of himself. . . . But we
> shall be "leaving it to him" if we conceive him to be as he
> reveals himself to us, without inquiring about him else-
> where than from his Word. (I, xiii, 1, p. 146)

The point is that Scripture is a much better source of knowledge of God (including knowledge of his essence) than rational speculation. But Calvin didn't think for a moment that none of our positive substantial concepts applies to God; he clearly believed that God really is the creator of the heavens and the earth, that he really does love us, that he is incorporeal, wise, powerful, loving, and the like.

On this view, Hick's claim about the Real is not that none of our concepts applies to it or that none of our terms literally applies to it; that is clearly incoherent. His claim, instead, is that only our *formal* concepts and terms and our *negative* concepts and terms apply to it. That is to say, the only properties it has of which we have a grasp are formal properties and negative properties. Consider first those formal concepts. Included here would be, first of all, concepts of properties which are such that *everything* has them and furthermore has them *necessarily*.[13] Hick is thinking (I take it) of properties such that it is necessary that everything has them: such properties as *being self-identical, having properties, having essential properties, being either a horse or a nonhorse*, and *being such that 7 + 5 = 12*. These properties are necessarily had by everything.

> We might add that they are *essential* to everything, where a property is essential to an object if it is not possible that the object exist but lack the property: the property of being self-identical would be an example. We could add still further that each of these properties is such that it is *necessary* that everything has it essentially. So take any of the properties under consideration: everything has it, it is necessary that everything has it, everything has it essentially, and it is necessary that everything has it essentially. *Existence* is another of those formal properties: everything exists, existence is an essential property of everything, and it is a necessary truth that existence is essential to everything.

But these aren't the only properties that Hick means to include under the rubric 'formal'. Others are such properties as *being referred to by human beings* and *being thought of by John*. So the idea is not that we cannot talk or think about the being in question. On the contrary: we can think about it, refer to it, and say of it that it exists. We can say of it, furthermore, that we can refer to it.

---

13. A concept's meeting the first condition but not the second (i.e., being such that everything falls under it but not such that everything *necessarily* falls under it) is not sufficient for its being formal. For example, the concept *either not living on the moon or else not being human* applies to everything (there are no human beings who live on the moon), but it isn't a formal concept in the intended sense.

Second, in addition to formal properties, we can predicate *negative* properties of this being—that is, we can *correctly* predicate negative properties of it. This is implied by Hick's position as I have so far explained it. We can see this as follows. First, note that every property has a complement, where the complement of a property *P* is the property of not having *P*. Each of the properties of which we have a concept has a complement: the property of *not* having that property. Thus the complement of the property *wisdom* is the property of not being wise, a property enjoyed by everything that is not wise. And if we have a grasp, a conception, of the property in question (wisdom, for example) then we also have a grasp of its complement. Now consider any property *P* and its complement *-P*; the property *P or -P* is one of those formal properties every thing necessarily has. Of course, anything that has *that* property has either the property *P* or else has its complement *-P*. (For anything you pick, either it is wise or it is not wise.) According to Hick's position as so far explained, however, the Real doesn't have any positive nonformal property of which we have a grasp. It follows, then, that for all the positive properties *P* of which we have a grasp, the Real has *-P*.

> Here we are speaking of the properties the thing in question has, not about our abilities or lack thereof to *know* or *warrantedly believe* something or other about its properties. I say that every object has essentially the property of having *P or -P* for any property *P*; I say further that if a being has *that* property, then either it has *P* or it has *-P*. Still, a being might be *known* (or justifiably believed or warrantedly believed) to have *P or -P* without being known (justifiably believed, etc.) to have *P* and without being known to have *-P*. I do not know and have no view on the question whether Socrates ever owned a horse; nevertheless, either he did own a horse or he didn't. In developing Hick's view, then, I am taking for granted a sort of realism: the idea that things (some things) can be a certain way even if neither I nor any other human being knows whether they are that way or not. There is nothing in what Hick says to suggest that his position obliges him to take issue with this truism.

So the idea is that we can predicate negative properties of this being. Furthermore, the idea is that we can *correctly* predicate negative properties of it: it *has* negative properties. Indeed, for each of the nonformal positive properties we grasp, the Real has the *complement* of that property (which is a negative property). Among our positive concepts, only the purely formal ones apply to this being; as for the rest of our concepts, only the negative ones apply to it. The Real doesn't have wisdom: therefore it has nonwisdom; it does not have love: therefore it has nonlove; and so on for all the other positive nonformal properties we grasp. But, you say: it is not possible that there be a being that has only formal and negative properties. No doubt that's true; still, it is neither here nor there, so far as Hick's claim goes. The being in question may very well *have* positive properties in addition to the formal properties; it is only required by Hick's position that those be positive properties *of which we have no concept*, properties of which we have no grasp. And we certainly don't know that there aren't any positive properties like that.

We must ask two questions here: first, is this Hickian position coherent? And second, is there any reason to accept it?

B. Coherent?

1. *Can There Be a Being with Only Formal and Negative Properties?*

This being, says Hick, has no positive, nonformal properties of which we have a concept; the only positive properties it has are those of which we have no grasp. This is not clearly incoherent. We can't just see, I think, that there couldn't be a being like that; that is because we have a very slim grasp of those properties we don't grasp. We just don't know enough about them to know that it isn't possible that there be a being like that. Of course, we also have no reason to think that there *can be* such a being: the fact that we *can't* see that there *can't be* a being like that is little or no reason for thinking we *can* see that there *can be*. (It is one thing to fail to see that something is impossible; it is quite another to see that it is possible.) In this case, so it seems, we don't know enough to be able to tell whether it is possible that there be such a being. So suppose we provisionally concede, at least for purposes of argument, that it is possible that there be such a being.

But if there is such a being, how is it that we are able to refer to it, have some way of singling it out as a subject of predication? How can that be done? Not, to be sure, by way of the definite descriptions whereby Christians believe they can pick out God—such descriptions, say, as 'the all-powerful, all-knowing creator of the world'; such descriptions involve positive, nonformal properties of which we have a conception. Could we instead use the description: 'the being that has no positive, substantial properties of which we have a grasp'? No; for if there is *one* such being, then maybe there are several more, none with any positive, nonformal properties we can grasp but differing from each other in positive, nonformal properties we *can't* grasp. So we have no reason to think that *that* description will work either. (Of course once again we don't know that it doesn't work; for all we know or can tell, there is exactly one being with no positive nonformal properties of which we have a grasp.)

Now Hick's idea, I think, is that those who practice the great religions really refer to *this* being (the Real, which has no positive nonformal properties of which we have a grasp) when (as it seems to them) they refer to God, Allah, Brahman, Shiva, Vishnu, the Dharmakaya, or whatever. So Christians *think* they refer to a being who is personal, loving, knowledgeable, and the like; the fact is, however, they do *not* refer to such a being, but to a being who doesn't have any of these properties or, indeed, any other positive properties of which we have a grasp. Is this really possible? Is it possible that we refer to a being, thinking it has properties $P_1, \ldots, P_n$, when, in fact, it *doesn't* have any of those properties or any other positive properties of which we have a conception? This too is not at any rate clearly impossible. It can certainly happen that we refer to a being when we are very much mistaken about the properties it has. I have never met you; in a letter, I tell you that I am a world-class tennis player and an athlete of enviable talents; the fact is that I am a complete duffer at tennis and at every similar activity. I go on to claim that I have a tenor voice to rival Pavarotti's, have a Nobel prize in economics, am strikingly handsome, and write splendid poetry; all of this is whoppingly false. (In fact, I am unable even to appreciate any poetry above the level of William E. McGonagall, poet and tragedian,[14] know absolutely nothing about economics, can't sing a note, and am very plain.) Then I have few of the properties you ascribe to me; still, you can refer to me.

Of course, there must be *some* kind of connection between us. You can't pick me out as that handsome tenor-cum-poet-cum-economist who lives in (say) Jamestown, North Dakota; that description doesn't apply to me.[15] However you *can* refer to me as the one who wrote you a letter claiming to be all these things (supposing you received only one such letter). And perhaps something similar would be so for the Real. How is the reference supposed to go? Well, presumably Hick's idea is that we can refer to the Real as the being that the practitioners of the great religions refer to when they think they are referring to beings with the properties ascribed to God, Allah, Brahman, Vishnu, and the like. Obviously, that just pushes the problem back a step: how do *they* refer to it? How does it happen that when Christians use the term 'God' they are, in fact, referring to this being that has no positive properties they grasp, despite the fact that

14. See McGonagall's *Poetic Gems* (Dundee: David Winter and Son; London: Gerald Duckworth, first published in two parts in 1890 and first published as one volume in 1934). See also his *More Poetic Gems*, *Still More Poetic Gems*, *Yet More Poetic Gems*, and *Poetic Gems Once Again*.

15. But even this might be possible; if I have some other way of referring to you but also think that this description applies to you, then perhaps when I use that description, thinking it applies to you, I do, in fact, refer to you. Suppose God doesn't have some of the properties we think he has: suppose, for example, he isn't simple, in the classical sense, but composite, with a distinction to be made between him and his properties, between him and his existence, and so on. Even so, if a creed like the Belgic Confession refers to him as the spiritual, simple, creator of the universe, it still refers to him by that description, even if the description doesn't apply.

they *think* they are referring to a being with a lot of positive properties of that sort? Again, there would have to be some connection between them and the Real. (It isn't the case, of course, that the practitioners of Christianity, say, *hypothesize* that there is a being with no positive properties of which we have a grasp to whom they refer when they think they are referring to an omnipotent, omniscient, and wholly good creator of the universe; that would make no sense.) So how *do* they refer to this being? Well, presumably this could happen only if they had some kind of *experiential contact* with it, experienced this being in one way or another (whatever precisely it means to say that one being experiences another). They *think* they are in contact with a being with the properties ascribed to God; they are mistaken, however—not in thinking they are in contact with *something*, but in thinking the something with which they are in contact has the properties they ascribe to God.

Now perhaps this is possible: still, it does require a modification —and a significant modification—of Hick's position. If this is the way the wind blows, then the Real enjoys at least one positive nonformal property of which we have a conception: the property *being experienced by us*. It stands in at least one positive nonformal relation of which we have a conception: the relation *being experienced by*. (So the ambiguity we noted above, pp. 44–45, must be resolved in favor of the alternative according to which we *do* experience the Real.) And that may lead to more, for what is involved in something's being *experienced* by us or by the practitioners of the great religions? What is it for something to be experienced by us? Here there are several views. One is that the thing in question *appears to* us, in a way that defies further analysis. Another is that it *causes* us to be appeared to in a certain way, or causes some other kind of experience in us (and meets certain other conditions). What these have in common is at the least the idea that in order to experience the Real, we must be in causal contact with it, stand in a *causal relation* with it.

There is perhaps one alternative to be found in the history of philosophy: that would be the idea that we could experience something, perhaps in an analogically extended sense of 'experience', if there were a *preestablished harmony* between experiential states of ours and states of the thing in question.[16] But that, too, would involve the thing in question's

16. Kant's objection to this Leibnizian suggestion is that any such preestablished harmony would not be a *cognitive* relation; it couldn't support our having knowledge of the things in question. But it is very difficult to see why that should be so. Suppose God brings it about that our cognitive states appropriately match those of the world around us, and suppose the other conditions for warrant are met (as outlined, e.g., in *Warrant and Proper Function*): why wouldn't that be sufficient for our having knowledge of those things?

being in a causal relation to the thing or person (in Leibniz's thought, God) who arranges the preestablished harmony. Here, too, therefore, a causal relation would be required between the thing experienced and something else, so that here, too, that thing stands in causal relations and (perhaps at one or more removes) in causal relations to the experiencing subject.

And this means that Hick or a Hickian (for perhaps we are going beyond Hick's position here) must also ascribe another positive nonformal property to the Real: the property of being causally connected with us human beings. This is not a merely formal property, and it is also not a negative property. Still further, it may involve additional properties: whatever properties are necessarily connected with standing in a causal relation to human beings. The thing in question could not, for example, be like numbers and propositions are ordinarily thought to be: abstract objects that are incapable of standing in causal relations. So the being in question must have the property of being a concrete object, as opposed to an abstract object. The property of being a concrete object is also a nonformal property (many things lack it); as we shall see below, it isn't easy to tell whether it is a positive or a negative property. And of course there may be still more properties necessarily connected with the property of standing in a causal relation with us human beings.

2. *Positive versus Negative Properties*

Should we perhaps say that this last property—being a concrete object—is really a *negative* property? Why can't we think of the property *being concrete* as simply the complement of the property *being abstract*, with the latter positive and the former negative? Perhaps *being concrete* is really just *not being abstract*. But this leads to a real difficulty: why go *that* way? Can't we just as well take the property *being abstract* as the property *not being concrete*, so that *being concrete* is the positive property and *being abstract* the negative? How do we determine which of the two properties really is positive, and which is really negative?

Indeed, are we guaranteed that this distinction between positive and negative properties really applies to properties at all? Is there really such a distinction for properties? Of course, there is a distinction between positive and negative *predicates*, linguistic items or phrases such as 'is a horse', 'is not a cat,' and the like. (Both 'not being abstract' and 'not being concrete' are negative predicates; both 'is concrete' and 'is abstract' are positive predicates.) But do we know that this distinction between positive and negative extends beyond predicates to properties? What makes a predicate (in English) negative is the presence in it of some negative particle, such as 'not' or 'non' or 'un' (as in 'unlimited') or 'a' (as in 'asymmetrical') or 'dis' or 'anti' (as in 'antidisestablishmentarianism'). But properties presumably don't contain particles or other bits of language. What would distinguish positive *properties* from negative *properties*? *Is* there really such a distinction?

This is not an easy question to answer. Can the Hickian perhaps claim that he really owes us no further answer? There is a distinction between positivity and negativity for properties, he says, and there is no way of getting behind this distinction, to say what it consists in, what it is that makes a property positive, or anything of that sort. This distinction is rock bottom and cannot be explained in terms of anything else. There are clear examples: wisdom is a positive property, and its complement, unwisdom (enjoyed both by those things capable of but lacking wisdom and by those not capable of it), is clearly a negative property; the distinction itself is ultimate and can't be explained in other terms.

Well, maybe so, but can we say anything general about which properties are positive and which negative? Presumably the idea is that (1) every property is either positive or negative, (2) every property has a complement, (3) the complement of a property P has the opposite sense from P (that is, the complement of a positive property is negative and the complement of a negative property is positive), (4) a property equivalent[17] to a given property has the same sense as that property, and (5) the Real has no positive properties of which we have a conception. (We have already seen that there must be exceptions to this last principle, but let that pass.) Furthermore, (6) no negative property of which we have a conception entails[18] a positive property of which we have a conception; else the Real would have those positive properties entailed by those negative properties of which we have a conception. What about conjunctive and disjunctive properties? A conjunctive property $P \& Q$ is negative if and only if both P and Q are negative. (If $P \& Q$ were negative and either P or Q were positive, the negative $P \& Q$ would entail a positive property, in which case the Real would have that positive property.) What about disjunctive properties? A disjunction $P v Q$ of properties of which we have a conception could not be positive if either P or Q were negative: else the positive $P v Q$ would be entailed by the negative P or the negative Q.

So far as I can see, there is nothing problematic about (1)–(6) at the level of logic alone. Indeed, note that we can give a 'truth table' (actually, a 'positivity table') for the complement of a property and for disjunction and conjunction among properties, and note further that the positivity table for conjunction is the truth table for disjunction and the positivity table for disjunction the truth table for conjunction. Mapping disjunction for properties onto conjunction for propositions, and conjunction for properties onto disjunction for propositions, we can help ourselves to some results from propositional logic and see that the logic of properties generated by (1)–(6) is consistent, complete, decidable, and so on.

17. Where P is equivalent to Q if and only if it is necessary in the broadly logical sense that whatever exemplifies either P or Q exemplifies both P and Q.
18. Where a property A entails a property B if (and only if) it is necessary that any object that has A also has B.

Nevertheless, there still remains a problem with coherence. It appears, initially at least, that some nonformal positive properties are entailed by negative properties (given that there is such a distinction for properties). For example, according to Hick, the Real is both ultimate and infinite:

> Unlimitedness, or infinity, is a negative concept, the denial of limitation. That this denial must be made of the Ultimate is a basic assumption of all the great traditions. It is a natural and reasonable assumption: for an ultimate that is limited in some mode would be limited by something other than itself; and this would entail its nonultimacy. (237–38)

But what about this property of being ultimate? First, what is it to be ultimate? Well, at the least it is to be independent of all other beings, not depending on any other beings for existence or for intrinsic properties. And that sounds appropriately negative. Nevertheless, it entails the property of being self-sufficient; and *that* sounds positive. So it looks as if the negative property *being independent of all others* entails the positive property *being self-sufficient*. Of course, it is perhaps possible to bite the bullet and maintain that the property of being self-sufficient, contrary to appearances, is really negative. Well, perhaps we can live with that. But what about infinity?

According to Hick, the property of being unlimited, being infinite, is a negative property: it is the complement of the positive property of being limited or being finite. (Here is another case where it is far from obvious, initially, which of the pair in question is positive and which negative; let's just concede for purposes of argument that *being limited* is a positive property.) Here we run into a real problem. What is this property of being unlimited? It is the negative property *not being limited*. Well, what is it to be limited? In the spatial analogue from which the notion is taken, it is to have limits or borders. A country that is unlimited, therefore, would have no borders and occupy all of space. (Again, *having no borders* sounds negative while *occupying all of space* sounds positive.)

Now of course the idea is not that the Real is *spatially* unlimited and occupies all of space. But then how does the analogy apply? In the spatial analogue, there are two features: an unlimited country is unlimited in a certain respect or along a certain dimension: space. It is also unlimited by any other country or space-occupying entity. In the same way, then, the Real, if it is unlimited, is unlimited along certain dimensions and is unlimited by any other being. Christians have traditionally thought of God as unlimited, infinite, in both these ways. To take the second first, God is unlimited by any other being: that is, he is unlimited in power or with respect to his being able to accomplish his will; no being can obstruct him, none can prevent him from doing what he wills. Clearly, this property, even if we think of it as negative, entails positive properties. If God is unlimited with respect to power, then he has power, which is certainly a positive property. If he is unlimited with respect to being able to accomplish his will, then he has the positive property of being able to accomplish his will. And if nothing can prevent him from doing what he wills, then he has the positive property of being able to do what he wills.

Being unlimited along certain dimensions or in certain important respects is similar. God is not unlimited in every respect: that could presumably be so only if he had every property to the maximal degree, which is impossible. If, for example, he has the property of being a spirit, then he does not also have the property of being a material object—a tree, for instance. Rather, the traditional idea has been that God has every *great-making* property to the maximal degree.[19] So God is unlimited with respect, for example, to *knowledge*. And a being that is not limited with respect to knowledge has the maximal degree of knowledge, is omniscient, all-knowing. Such a being, of course, would have the positive property *being a knower*.[20]

Is there a way out of this difficulty for the Hickian? Perhaps. He might try saying that this being is ultimate and unlimited, all right, but only with respect to properties of which we have no grasp. With respect to all the properties of which we do have a grasp, it is indeed limited, limited in the limiting sense of not exemplifying the property at all. It has the complement of every property we have a grasp of; it has other properties we have no grasp of; and the way in which it is infinite is that it has to the maximal degree some properties of which we have no grasp.

Well, this sounds a little bizarre, but perhaps it avoids incoherence (and anyway, who promised us that reality would not be bizarre?). The idea is that there is a being that has no positive properties of which we have a conception, except for being involved in human experience and any properties that entails. This being is also unlimited in that it has to the maximal degree properties of which we have no conception.

19. This idea is what drives the ontological argument; see my *The Nature of Necessity*, chapter 10.

20. Indeed, the being in question would have at least uncountably many such properties: for each proposition P, the being in question would have the property of knowing whether P is true. Here I assume that there are at least uncountably many distinct propositions. This seems relatively uncontroversial in view of the fact that for each distinct real number r, there is the distinct proposition r *is not identical with the Taj Mahal*.

C. Religiously Relevant?

Even if the view is not incoherent, it pays another price. For suppose we believe there is a being of that sort. It is for us an empty idea; still, that is not to say that there couldn't be such a being. I don't know whether it *is* possible that there be a being like this, and have no grounds for making a judgment either way as to whether it is possible. Suppose we concede for the moment that it is. The basic question here is this: what reason is there for thinking such a being, if indeed there could be and is such a being, is in any special way connected with *religion*? According to Hick, "we can say of the postulated Real *an sich* that it is the noumenal ground of the encountered gods and experienced absolutes witnessed to by the religious traditions" (246). Why should we think so? What reason is there for thinking this being is connected in some way with Christianity or with any other religion? Why say that Christians are in fact referring to or witnessing to this being? Maybe it is, instead, connected with warfare, prostitution, family violence, bigotry, or racism. And why think this being, or contact with it, has anything to do with "transformation of human existence from self-centredness to Reality-centredness" (355)? Perhaps it is especially when human beings are in the grip of self-aggrandizement, hate, selfishness, and the like that they are most in contact with this being. If it has no positive properties of which we have a conception, why is the one assumption the least bit better than the other? The basic problem, here, is that if the Real has no positive properties of which we have a conception, then we have no reason at all to think that it is *in religion* that human beings get in experiential contact with this being, rather than in any other human activity: war or oppression, for example. This being has none of the properties ascribed by the practitioners of most of the great religions to the beings they worship: it is not good, or loving, or concerned with human beings, or wise, or powerful; it has not created the universe, does not uphold it, and does not pay attention to the universe or the creatures it contains. It is an unknown and unknowable X. But then why associate this unknowable X with religion, as opposed to warfare, violence, bigotry, and the horrifying things human beings often do to each other?

We can put this question another way. Hick suggests that when Christians make their characteristic utterances, saying, for instance, "In Christ, God was reconciling the world to himself," what they say cannot be literally true but can be *mythologically* true. By 'literal' truth, he just means truth, ordinary truth: "The literal truth or falsity of a factual assertion . . . consists in its conformity or lack of conformity to fact: 'it is raining here now' is literally true if and only if it is raining here now" (348). The mythological truth of a statement is a horse of quite another color: "A statement or set of statements about X is mythologically true if it is not literally true but nevertheless tends to evoke an appropriate dispositional attitude to X" (348). So some dispositional attitudes toward the Real are appropriate and others (presumably) are not; some ways of responding to it are appropriate and others (presumably) not:

> Thus although we cannot speak of the Real *an sich* in literal terms,[21] nevertheless we live inescapably in relation to it, and in all that we do and undergo we are having to do with it as well as, and in terms of, our more proximate situations. Our actions are appropriate or inappropriate not only in relation to our physical and social environments but also in relation to our ultimate environment, the Real. True religious myths are accordingly those that evoke in us attitudes and modes of behaviour which are appropriate to our situation *vis-à-vis* the Real. (351)

And now our question can be put in terms of this suggestion. Why think that "we live in relation to . . . the Real" at all? Either the relation *living in relation to* is merely formal or it is not. If it is, then it would have no connection with religion. So it isn't. But if it isn't, then (1) we have still another positive property had by the Real: the property of being such that we live in relation to it. And (2) (and more poignantly) why think we live in relation to the Real at all? After all, we don't live in relation to just any old thing—the highest mountain on Mars, for example, or the meanest shark in the Indian Ocean. If the Real has no positive properties of which we have a grasp, what is the reason for thinking we live in relation to it?

Second, why think some ways of behavior are appropriate to the Real and others are not? Again, unless this is a purely formal relationship, not just anything is such that some ways of behaving are appropriate or, for that matter, inappropriate with respect to it. None of my behavior, I think, is either appropriate or inappropriate with respect to the highest mountain on Mars or the meanest shark in the Indian Ocean. If the Real has no positive properties of which we have a grasp, how could we possibly know or have grounds for believing that some ways of behaving with respect to it are more appropriate than others?

Hick, of course, thinks that some ways of behaving with respect to the Real *are* more appropriate than others, and goes on to specify what those ways are: we are behaving appropriately with respect to the Real when we learn to turn away from self-centeredness and

---

21. Recall that we are amending this claim from chapter 19 in the light of chapter 14; we *can* speak literally of the Real, but only to predicate negative and purely formal properties of it, together with those positive properties entailed by its being such that we human beings are in experiential contact with it.

selfishness ("the transformation of human existence from self-centredness to Reality-centredness"). But why think that? This would, indeed, make sense if the Real had the attributes of God: if it were, in fact, a person who loves us, and wills that we turn from loving only ourselves to loving him above all and our neighbor as ourselves, and has so designed us that we attain our end and happiness when we do so. But the Real doesn't have any of *those* properties (they being positive properties of which we have a conception). And if it has no positive properties of which we have a grasp, why not suppose that hateful and selfish behavior are appropriate with respect to it? Or behaving in that weak, sniveling, envious way that Nietzsche thought characteristic of real Christians? We can't have it both ways. If this being is really such that we literally know nothing positive about it (if it has no positive properties of which we have a grasp), then there is no reason to think self-centered behavior is less appropriate with respect to it (granting, indeed, that some modes of behavior *are* more appropriate with respect to it than others) than living a life of love.

We can put the question in still another way. Hick apparently thinks that some religious conceptions or ideas are *authentic* manifestations ("personae" or "impersonae") of the Real:

> And to the extent that 'the God and Father of our Lord Jesus Christ' is indeed an authentic *persona* of the Real, constituting the form in which the Real is validly thought and experienced from within the Christian strand of religious history, to that extent the dispositional response appropriate to this *persona* constitutes an appropriate response to the Real. . . .

and of the eternal Buddha nature, he says

> And to the extent that this is an authentic *impersona* of the Real, validly thought and experienced from within the Buddhist tradition, life in accordance with the Dharma is likewise an appropriate response to the Real. (353)

Again, the main question here is obvious: if the Real has no positive, nonformal properties of which we have a grasp, how could we possibly know or have reason to believe that any such *personae* or *impersonae* are authentic or, for that matter, inauthentic? Authenticity implies a certain fit between the *(im)persona* in question and the Real; but if we have no positive idea what the Real is like, we have no reason to think some *personae* or *impersonae* fit it better than others. Again, Hick thinks not only that some *do* fit better than others but also that we have some idea what they are: the God and Father of our Lord Jesus Christ, for example, and also others from other traditions. But how could we have reason to think a thing like that? If all we know about the Real is what Hick says we know, then for all we can tell, God, Vishnu and the Buddha are inauthentic and it is, for example, Ares, the god of war, Lucifer, and Stalin (or, for that matter, Uriah Heep or

Beavis and Butthead) that are the authentic *personae* of the Real. Again, we can't have it both ways. If we know nothing about the Real, we have no reason to pick the *personae* Hick picks as authentic manifestations of it. The main point is that if the Real has no positive nonformal properties of which we have a grasp, then, for all we can see, any department of human life is as revelatory of the Real as any other. We don't have any way to pick and choose among them, thinking, for example, that the great world religions are where the Real manifests itself or where human beings experience it. For all we know, on this showing, it is in living like a thugee or like a member of the Ku Klux Klan that one is most authentically in touch with the Real.

D. Is There Such a Thing?

So the view seems to be of dubious coherence. Stated carefully, it isn't initially incoherent. From Hick's point of view, however, the most important feature of this alleged being is that it is in some special way associated with religion; this being is what those who serve God, Brahman, and so on are really referring to; in the great world religions, people get into a special relationship to it. And that seems wholly gratuitous; perhaps the Real is really connected with those who serve themselves, or power, or white supremacy. But I come now, finally, to the question what reason Hick has for postulating such a being: why does he think there *is* a being with no positive properties of which we have a grasp? Hick's answer:

> The Real *an sich* is postulated by us as a pre-supposition, not of the moral life, but of religious experience and the religious life, whilst the gods, as also the mystically known Brahman, Sunyata and so on, are phenomenal manifestations of the Real occurring within the realm of religious experience. Conflating these two theses one can say that the Real is experienced by human beings, but experienced in a manner analogous to that in which, according to Kant, we experience the world: namely by informational input from external reality being interpreted by the mind in terms of its own categorial scheme and thus coming to consciousness as meaningful phenomenal experience. (243)

Why should we want to postulate such a thing, a thing with no positive properties of which we have any grasp, but which is experienced by human beings in the great religions? More to the point, why does *Hick* postulate such a being?

The answer, I think, must be explained dialectically. Hick began his spiritual odyssey as a traditional, orthodox Christian, accepting what I have been calling 'Christian belief'. He was then struck by the fact that there are other religions in which the claims of orthodox Christianity—trinity, incarnation, atonement—are rejected. Furthermore, so far as one can tell from the outside, so to speak, the claims of these other religions, taken literally, are as respectable, epistemically speaking, as the claims of Christianity. Still further, according to Jesus himself, "By their fruits you shall know them." The most important fruits, Hick thinks, are *practical*: turning away from a life of selfishness to a life of service; on this point, these other religions, he thinks, seem to do as well as Christianity. The conclusion he draws is that where Christianity differs from the others, we can't properly hold that it is literally true and the others literally false; that would be, he thinks, a sort of intellectual arrogance, a sort of spiritual imperialism, a matter of exalting ourselves and our beliefs at the expense of others. Instead, we must hold that the great religions are all equally valuable and equally true. How do we do this? Here is Hick's response:

> But if the Real in itself is not and cannot be humanly experienced, why postulate such an unknown and unknowable *Ding an sich*? The answer is that the divine noumenon is a necessary postulate of the pluralistic religious life of humanity. For within each tradition we regard as real the object of our worship or contemplation. If, as I have already argued, it is also proper to regard as real the objects of worship or contemplation within the other traditions, we are led to postulate the Real *an sich* as the presupposition of the veridical character of this range of forms of religious experience. Without this postulate we should be left with a plurality of *personae* and *impersonae* each of which is claimed to be the Ultimate, but no one of which alone can be. We should have either to regard all the reported experiences as illusory or else return to the confessional position in which we affirm the authenticity of our own stream of religious experience whilst dismissing as illusory those occurring within other traditions. But for those to whom neither of these options seems realistic the pluralistic affirmation becomes inevitable, and with it the postulation of the Real *an sich*, which is variously experienced and thought. . . . (249)

Now this passage is apparently an *argument* of some kind, an argument for the conclusion that there is a being (the Real) of the sort Hick says there is. The argument seems to proceed from two premises: (1) all the great religions are "veridical," and (2) none of them is more veridical than the others. How does the argument go? The idea, I think, is that if we suppose there is a being of the sort Hick says there is, then, according to Hick, we can see how (1) and (2) could be true. I'm not sure I see just how that is supposed to go, but let that pass. What isn't as easily ignored, however, is a sort of incoherence. "Within each tradition," he says, "we regard as real the object of our worship or contemplation." So within the Christian tradition, we regard God as real; it is also "proper to regard as real the objects of worship or contemplation within the other traditions." This, of course, leads to a problem; for some of the *personae* and *impersonae* are such that if they are real, and have the properties ascribed to them, then *other (im)per-*

sonae are either unreal or do not have the properties ascribed to *them*. Well, perhaps the idea, as Hick seems to suggest elsewhere, is that we are to regard each of the *(im)personae* as *empirically* real, not *transcendentally* real (not really real); and perhaps we are to understand *that* as meaning that each being is such that by way of it, the practitioners of the religion in question somehow get in touch with the Real. The essential point, however, is that we are not to think of one or some of these as more valuable or closer to the truth than the others; that would be arbitrary and unwarranted. We should no longer regard as *really* real (or rather real *simpliciter*) the objects of worship of our own tradition. We must treat all traditions alike.

Now the way Hick proposes to do this is to declare that all the traditions are actually mistaken; the beliefs in each tradition are mostly false. ("Literally" false, he says; but literal truth and falsehood, as Hick conceives them, are just truth and falsehood.) Still, there is something right or valid in religion—the recognition that there is something beyond the natural world, and the encouragement to live a life in which self-centeredness is overcome. So really, the bottom line is that Hick cannot find it in himself to think one religion— Christianity, say—is true and the others false, or that one is closer to the truth than the others. At bottom, there is a generous desire to avoid the self-aggrandizement and self-exaltation he sees as attaching to the declaration that one's own religious beliefs are true and those of others false.

Here there are three comments or questions. First, is this posture in fact possible for a human being: can a person accept it, and accept it authentically, without bad faith or doublethink? I am to remain a Christian, to take part in Christian worship, to accept the splendid and powerful doctrines of traditional Christianity. However, I am also to take it that these doctrines are only *mythologically* true: they are literally false, although accepting them (i.e., accepting them as true, as literally true) puts or tends to put one into the right relation with the Real. And how can I possibly accept them, adopt *that* attitude toward them, if I think they are only mythologically true—that is, really false? I could, indeed, believe that they are mythologically true; believing *that*, however, doesn't move one toward the right kind of life; it is only believing the teachings *themselves* that allegedly has that salutary effect. Once I am sufficiently enlightened, once I see that those doctrines are not true, I can no longer take the stance with respect to them that leads to the hoped-for practical result. I am left, instead, in the position of a sad and disillusioned Gnostic. I no longer hold Christian belief; I recognize, as I think, that it is in fact false. I also see, of course, that those who *do* accept it as true are mistaken, deluded; but at any rate they are in the fortunate position of enjoying the comfort and strength and consolation these false beliefs bring; they are also being moved closer to the right kind of life by virtue of accepting them. Neither the comfort[22] and consolation nor the practical efficacy is available to me.

Second, there is something wholly self-defeating, so it seems to me, in Hick's posture. If we take this position, then we can't say, for example, that Christianity is right and Buddhism wrong; as Christians, we don't disagree with the Buddhists; and we take this stance in an effort to avoid self-exultation and imperialism. But we do something from the point of view of intellectual imperialism and self-exaltation that is much worse: we now declare that *everyone* is mistaken here, everyone except for ourselves and a few other enlightened souls. We and our graduate students know the truth; everyone else is sadly mistaken. Isn't this to exalt ourselves at the expense of nearly everyone else? Those who think there really is such a person as God are benighted, unsophisticated, unaware of the real truth of the matter, which is that there isn't any such person (even if thinking there is can lead to practical fruits). We see Christians as deeply mistaken; of course we pay the same compliment to the practitioners of the other great religions; we are equal-opportunity animadverters. We benevolently regard the rest of humanity as misguided; no doubt their hearts are in the right place; still, they are sadly mistaken about what they take to be most important and precious. I find it hard to see how this attitude is a manifestation of tolerance or intellectual humility: it looks more like patronizing condescension.

The basic problem is that, given our actual intellectual and spiritual situation, it simply isn't possible to avoid serious disagreement with others. If some people believe p and others believe something q incompatible with p, there is no way in which we can avoid serious disagreement. If we affirm p, we disagree with those who affirm q; if we affirm q, we disagree with those who affirm p; if we propose a higher resolution, saying that neither p nor q is true (though perhaps each is 'mythologically true'), then we disagree with both groups.[23] But if it is imperialistic or somehow out of order to affirm p, thus disrespecting the partisans of q, why is it better to disrespect them all by pronouncing them all wrong?

Third, Hick doesn't, of course, produce an *argument* for the conclusion that no religion could be closer to the truth than others; it is more like a practical postulate, a benevolent and charitable resolu-

22. According to the Heidelberg Catechism (Q. 1), "My only comfort in life and in death is that I am not my own, but belong—body and soul, in life and in death—to my faithful Savior Jesus Christ." According to Hick, however, my only comfort in life and in death is that I know the sad truth: believing the great teachings of Christianity has beneficial effects, but those teachings are, in fact, false.

23. The same goes if we propose to remain agnostic about p and q; see below, chapter 13.

tion to avoid imperialism and self-aggrandizement. But is this the way to do it? Clearly, in most areas of life, some people *are* closer to the truth than others. If the nominalists are right, all of us realists are wrong; if the modal skeptics are right, we modal true believers are mistaken; if the white supremacists are right, many of the rest of us, bent as we are on toleration, are wrong, and seriously wrong. Why should it be different in religion? The idea that in religion we must all be equally right and all equally wrong seems no more compelling than the idea that in thinking *about* religion we must all be equally right and equally wrong. Hick's reason for thinking all religions equally right seems to be a desire to avoid self-aggrandizement; shouldn't the same desire lead him to hold that his views *about* religion—his view, for example, that they are all equally right and equally wrong—really have no more claim to truth than any other view here (for example, the view that Christianity alone, say, is correct)? He doesn't do that, and rightly so. We can't properly do so in religious belief either. In religious belief as elsewhere, we must take our chances, recognizing that we could be wrong, dreadfully wrong. There are no guarantees; the religious life is a venture; foolish and debilitating error is a permanent possibility. (If we can be wrong, however, we can also be right.)

Our topic, in this book, is the *de jure* question with respect to Christian belief—not the question whether Christian belief is *true* (although, of course, that is the more important question) but whether it is *reasonable* or *rational* or *rationally justifiable* to accept it. We have been examining a preliminary matter: *is* there really such a question? Is there really such a thing as Christian belief? Or is it rather the case that even if there were such a person as God, we couldn't refer to and think about him, or predicate positive, nonformal properties of him? Our results, so far, have been that there isn't the slightest reason to think so. There is no reason at all to think it isn't possible to think about God; there is no reason at all to think that we cannot predicate such positive, nonformal properties of him as wisdom, knowledge, love, and all the rest. Obviously, there is enormously more to be said; this topic deserves a book in itself. There isn't room for that in *this* book; so we shall have to content ourselves with what we have. At any rate, we can rest in the assurance that if there is reason to think our question ill-formed or somehow logically out of order, it is at the least exceedingly well concealed. We can therefore go in reasonable confidence to the next question: what, precisely, *is* this *de jure* question?

PART II

WHAT IS THE QUESTION?

3

Justification and the Classical Picture

In part I, I considered a certain kind of objection to the *de jure* question with respect to Christian belief—the question, that is, whether it is rational or reasonable or intellectually respectable to accept Christian belief. This objection was that the *de jure* question is, to say the least, premature: strictly speaking, it isn't really possible to hold a belief of the sort traditional Christians think they hold. That is because Christians think of God as ultimate and infinite, and there is something conceptually out of order with the very idea that it is possible to have a belief about a being that is ultimate and infinite. I concluded that this objection isn't cogent; there is here no obstacle to raising the *de jure* question.

But the next thing to see is that it is far from obvious just what that *de jure* question or objection is supposed to be; precisely what question (or questions) *is* it that critics mean to press when they ask whether Christian and theistic belief is rational, or rationally defensible, or rationally justifiable, or whatever? Critics claim that Christian belief is not rationally justified or justifiable: what, precisely, is the infirmity or defect they are ascribing to the Christian believer? What, exactly, is the question? Call this question the 'metaquestion'. One problem with contemporary discussions of the justification of Christian belief is that the metaquestion is almost never asked. People ask whether Christian belief is rational or reasonable or rationally justifiable; they turn immediately to *answering* that question, without first considering just what the question is. What *is* it? That is not easy to say; nevertheless, it is our subject in part II.

This chapter is devoted to examining a certain answer to the metaquestion: that the *de jure* question is whether Christian belief is *justified*. That question is one that originates in *classical foundationalism*, a way of thinking about these topics that has historically been extremely influential and is still very much with us now. According to the classical foundationalist, the *de jure* question is really the question whether Christian belief is justified; but how is this term to be understood? I shall examine the seventeenth-century roots of classical foundationalism, explore the connection between justification and evidentialism that the classical foundationalist sees, and briefly outline some of its contemporary descendants. Then in the second half of the chapter, I'll argue both that classical foundationalism faces insuperable problems, and that the notion of justification does not offer a satisfying version of the *de jure* question.

We must begin with some history—first, a look back into the relatively recent past and then a deeper look into the more remote past. With respect to the first, I can make my point most easily by referring to some earlier work of my own; please forgive the personal reference. The present book, as I said in the preface, is a sequel to *Warrant: The Current Debate* (hereafter WCD) and *Warranted Proper Function* (hereafter WPF); it is also and perhaps more important a sequel to *God and Other Minds*[1] and "Reason and Belief in God."[2] The chief topic of *God and Other Minds*, as I put it then, is the "rational justification" of belief in God. I set out to address the *de jure* question; like everyone else, however, I didn't so much as raise the metaquestion. Following my elders and betters, I initially took it for granted that this question of the rational justification of theistic belief is identical with, or intimately connected with, the question whether there are *proofs*, or at least *good arguments*, for or against the existence of God. You discuss this question of the rationality of belief in God by consulting the evidence: does it on balance support theistic belief? (If it does [and does so strongly enough], such belief is rational; otherwise it is irrational.)

And *that* question, in turn, was so taken that the way to answer it is by considering the *arguments* for and against the existence of God. On the pro side, there were the traditional theistic proofs, the cosmological, teleological, and ontological arguments, to follow Kant's classification. On the con side, there was, first of all, the problem of evil (construed as the claim that the existence of evil is logically inconsistent with the existence of a wholly good, all-powerful, and all-knowing God). Then there were also some rather opaque claims to the effect that the progress of modern science, or the attitudes necessary to its proper pursuits, or perhaps something similar lurking in the nearby bushes, or maybe something else that had been learned by "man come of age"—the idea was that something in this general neighborhood also offers evidence against the existence of God. And

1. Ithaca: Cornell University Press, 1967.

2. In *Faith and Rationality*, ed. Alvin Plantinga and Nicholas Wolterstorff (Notre Dame: University of Notre Dame Press, 1983).

it was also clearly assumed that belief in God was rational and proper only if on balance the evidence, so construed, favored it. So here is a possible answer to the metaquestion and a candidate for the post of being the *de jure* question: does the evidence support Christian belief? In this chapter I want to think about this answer to the metaquestion. Does it give us a serious question for Christian believers or a serious criticism of Christian belief?

In *God and Other Minds*, I argued first that the theistic proofs or arguments do not succeed. In evaluating these arguments, I employed a traditional but wholly improper standard: I took it that these arguments are successful only if they start from propositions that compel assent from every honest and intelligent person and proceed majestically to their conclusion by way of forms of argument that can be rejected only on pain of insincerity or irrationality. Naturally enough, I joined the contemporary chorus in holding that none of the traditional arguments was successful. (I failed to note that no philosophical arguments of any consequence meet *that* standard; hence the fact that theistic arguments do not is of less significance than I thought.) I then argued that the objections to theistic belief are equally unimpressive; in particular, the deductive argument from evil (the argument that there is a contradiction between the existence of God and the existence of evil), I said, is entirely unsuccessful. So I saw, as I thought, that neither the arguments *for* the existence of God nor the arguments *against* it are conclusive; but then where does that leave us with respect to the question of the rationality or rational justifiability of belief in God? Does it follow, as seemed to be the prevailing opinion, that *agnosticism* was the right response and that belief in God, under these conditions, is irrational, contrary to reason, not rationally justifiable? That seemed to me wrong, but where could we go to pursue this question? How could we carry the inquiry further?

Faced with this impasse, I decided to compare belief in God with other beliefs, in particular, our belief in other minds. There is allegedly a traditional philosophical problem of other minds: since we can't perceive the thoughts and feelings of other people, do we know and how do we know they really *have* thoughts and feelings? More poignantly, how do we know that what we take to be persons (beings with thoughts, feelings, and intentions) really *are* persons and not, for example, cunningly constructed robots?[3] I noted that the dialectical structure uncovered in the case of theistic arguments is recapitulated in the case of other minds: the objections to belief in other minds

3. Actually, this is not a traditional philosophical problem in the sense that it is a problem for *all* philosophers or *all* positions in philosophy; you will find it pressing only if you accept some version of classical foundationalism.

don't seem at all formidable, but unhappily there also aren't any good arguments *for* other minds—particularly if we employ the same high standards of goodness as were ordinarily applied to theistic arguments. I claimed that the strongest argument for the existence of God and the strongest argument for other minds are similar and that they fail in similar ways. Hence my "tentative conclusion": "if my belief in other minds is rational, so is my belief in God. But obviously the former is rational; so, therefore, is the latter."

Here two things are noteworthy. First, I was somehow both accepting but also questioning what was then axiomatic: that belief in God, if it is to be rationally acceptable, must be such that there is *good evidence* for it. This evidence would be *propositional* evidence: evidence from other propositions you believe, and it would have to come in the form of arguments. This claim wasn't itself argued for: it was simply asserted, or better, just assumed as self-evident or at least utterly obvious. What was then taken for granted has now come to be called '*evidentialism*' (a better title would be 'evidentialism with respect to belief in God', but that's a bit unwieldy). Evidentialism is the view that belief in God is rationally justifiable or acceptable only if there is *good evidence* for it, where good evidence would be arguments from other propositions one knows. If it is accepted apart from such evidence or arguments, then it is at best intellectually third-rate: irrational, or unreasonable, or contrary to one's intellectual obligations.

Second, I failed to ask why this question of rational justifiability is important or, indeed, what the question *is*. I didn't give *that* question—namely, the question what *is* this rational justifiability of which I am speaking?—so much as a passing glance. Further, why would rational justification, whatever precisely it is, require *evidence*? What is the connection between evidence and justification? And if the latter *does* require evidence, why would that evidence have to take the form of arguments (deductive or probabilistic), evidence from other propositions one already believes? And what sorts of propositions could properly function as the premises of these arguments? I didn't raise these questions. It wasn't, however, because their answers were well-known, so that further inquiry would be carrying coals to Newcastle. On the contrary: no one else asked or answered these questions either; instead, people turned directly to the arguments for and against theistic belief, taking it utterly for granted that this was the way to investigate its rational justification.[4] Taking evidentialism for granted was *de rigueur* then and is still popular now. But what *is*

---

4. The exception was William James, whose "The Will to Believe," in *The Will to Believe and Other Essays in Popular Philosophy* (New York: Longmans, Green, 1897), was widely anthologized and took the radical line (as it was then perceived) that if religious belief is a *live* option for you, and a *forced* option, then believing even without evidence is excusable. See below, p. 89.

this rational justification? And why *does* it require evidence, propositional evidence? And how does it happen that everyone just took for granted this connection between justification and propositional evidence? These are some of the questions we must ask.

I. JOHN LOCKE

Here what we need is another bit of history, some more of that archaeology of which Foucault speaks (although again [see WCD, p. 11] I doubt that we will uncover a hidden political agenda or a subterranean bid for power). This question as to the rational justifiability of Christian belief goes back to the Enlightenment response to the spiritual and intellectual ferment generated (in part) by the Reformation; the characteristically modern response to this ferment can be seen as getting its start in the works of René Descartes and John Locke. Both Descartes and Locke were impressed by the enormous disagreement in religious and philosophical matters; this means, of course, that error pervades our belief in these areas. They were also impressed (along with their successors) with the meager progress made in philosophical matters. Philosophy, said Descartes, "has been cultivated for many centuries by the best minds that have ever lived, and nevertheless no single thing is to be found in it which is not a subject of dispute, and in consequence which is not dubious."[5] Descartes has his remedy (a characteristically modern remedy): start over. Discard anything that isn't certain, and rebuild your noetic structure on the basis of what *is* certain. Recall those famous words in the introduction to the *Meditations*:

> It is now some years since I detected how many are the false beliefs that I had from my earliest youth admitted as true, and how doubtful was everything I had since constructed on this basis, and from that time I was convinced that I must once for all seriously undertake to rid myself of all the opinions which I formerly accepted, and commence to build anew from the foundation. . . .[6]

It is John Locke, however, not Descartes, who is probably most crucial for our understanding of the *de jure* question and the modern compulsion to ask it.[7] In the "Epistle to the Reader" prefacing his long, rambling *An Essay concerning Human Understanding*, Locke re-

---

5. Part I of the *Discourse on the Method of Rightly Conducting the Reason and Seeking Truth in the Sciences*, in *The Philosophical Works of Descartes*, tr. and ed. Elizabeth S. Haldane and G. R. T. Ross (New York: Dover, 1955 [originally published by Cambridge University Press in 1931]), pp. 85–86.

6. *The Philosophical Works of Descartes*, p. 144.

7. See Nicholas Wolterstorff's luminous and illuminating essay on Locke in *John Locke and the Ethics of Belief* (Cambridge: Cambridge University Press, 1996).

counts a meeting with "five or six friends," in which they discussed a
certain subject that Locke doesn't there identify:

> [They] found themselves quickly at a stand, by the difficulties that
> rose on every side. After we had awhile puzzled ourselves, without
> coming any nearer a resolution of those doubts which perplexed us,
> it came into my thoughts that we took a wrong course; and that be-
> fore we set ourselves upon inquiries of that nature, it was necessary
> to examine our own abilities, and see what *objects* our understand-
> ings were, or were not, fitted to deal with. This I proposed to the
> company, who all readily assented; and thereupon it was agreed
> that this should be our first inquiry.[8]

That discussion was the genesis of the *Essay*; it probably took place in
the winter of 1670–71,[9] and a momentous meeting it was. The book
itself wasn't finished (or at least published) for another eighteen years
or so, which accounts in part for its length and rather disorganized,
repetitious character.

Locke doesn't tell us what the topic of discussion was, but James
Tyrell, one of the five or six friends at the gathering, noted in the
margin of his copy of the *Essay* (now in the British Museum) that the
topic of discussion was "the principles of morality and revealed religion."[10] And Locke's *Essay* has been immensely influential in modern
thought on this topic; it is perhaps not too much to say that his seminal work is the single most important source of the way of thinking
on these topics that has dominated Western thought for the last three
centuries. This book ushers in epistemology in the West. It is not, of
course, that previous philosophers had nothing to say about epistemology. After all, Plato's *Theaetetus* asks one of the main questions in
the theory of knowledge: what is it that must be added to mere true
belief to get knowledge? What is that quality or quantity, enough of
which makes the difference between true belief and knowledge?
Aristotle and Aquinas, furthermore, had much to say about *scientia*,
scientific knowledge, and also much to say about how the process of
intellection works, what goes on when someone knows or believes
something. Still, the questions Locke asked and the answers he gave
have a peculiarly modern ring; we resonate to them, because his way
of thinking about them became the modern way of thinking about
them; and despite postmodern proclamations of the death or end of

---

8. *An Essay concerning Human Understanding,* ed. with "Prolegomena" by Alexander Fraser (New York: Dover, 1959 [first published by Oxford University Press in
1894]), vol. 1, p. 9. Subsequent page references to Locke's essay are to this edition.

9. Fraser's footnote 1, p. 9.

10. Fraser's "Prolegomena," p. xvii.

epistemology, this is still, for the most part, our way of thinking about these matters.

Locke lived through one of the most turbulent periods of British intellectual and spiritual history; it was, in particular, the religious ferment and diversity, the enormous variety of religious opinion, that caught his attention. Of course he knew that in parts of the world other than Europe there were religions quite different from Christianity, but he was particularly impressed by the diversity of religious opinion in his own country. There was the Catholic-Protestant debate, and within Protestantism there were countless sects, countless disagreements and controversies; it was a time when every man thought what was right in his own eyes. Locke proposes to inquire into

> the grounds of those persuasions which are to be found amongst men, so various, different, and wholly contradictory; and yet asserted somewhere or other with such assurance and confidence, that he that shall take a view of the opinions of mankind, observe their opposition, and at the same time consider the fondness and devotion wherewith they are embraced, the resolution and eagerness wherewith they are maintained, may perhaps have reason to suspect, that either there is no such thing as truth at all, or that mankind hath no sufficient means to attain a certain knowledge of it. (Locke's Introduction to the *Essay*, para. 2, p. 27)

One problem here, says Locke, is *fideism*; many oppose faith to reason, declaring both that faith prescribes what reason proscribes, and that it is faith that is to be accepted and followed:

> For, to this crying up of faith in *opposition* [his emphasis] to reason, we may, I think, in good measure ascribe those absurdities that fill almost all the religions which possess and divide mankind. For men having been principled with an opinion, that they must not consult reason in the things of religion, however apparently contradictory to common sense and the very principles of all their knowledge, have let loose their fancies and natural superstition; and have been by them led into so strange opinions, and extravagant practices in religion, that a considerate man cannot but stand amazed at their follies, and judge them so far from being acceptable to the great and wise God, that he cannot avoid thinking them ridiculous and offensive to a sober good man. So that, in effect, religion, which should most distinguish us from beasts, and ought most peculiarly to elevate us, as rational creatures, above brutes, is that wherein men often appear most irrational, and more senseless than beasts themselves (bk. IV, chap. xviii, para. 11, p. 426)

Another source of riotous error and confusion in religion is *tradition*, believing a proposition just because you have been taught it or because those around you believe it:

> The great obstinacy that is to be found in men firmly believing quite contrary opinions, though many times equally absurd, in the various religions of mankind, are as evident a proof as they are an unavoidable consequence of this way of reasoning from received traditional principles. So that men will disbelieve their own eyes, renounce the evidence of their senses, and give their own experience the lie, rather than admit of anything disagreeing with these sacred tenets. (IV, xx, 10, p. 450)

Tradition, he says (in characteristic Enlightenment disparagement),

> keeps in ignorance or error more people than all the other [the other sources of error] together . . . I mean the giving up our assent to the common received opinions, either of our friends or party, neighbourhood or country. How many men have no other ground for their tenets, than the supposed honesty, or learning, or number of those of the same profession? (IV, xx, 17, pp. 456–57)

Appeals to tradition to settle disagreement had become ineffective; there were just too many. One had to choose which of these many conflicting traditions to endorse. Locke thought this disorderly pluralism quite scandalous; it was even more scandalous that there seemed no rational way to put an end to the contentious disputes.

The *Essay* was Locke's attempt to do what he could to put matters right. Book IV, "Of Knowledge and Probability," is the end of the book—both in comprising the last three hundred pages or so and in dealing with the question whose resolution is Locke's goal; and even in book IV he spends another two hundred pages before explicitly addressing it. That main question is: *how should we regulate our opinion with respect to belief in general? In particular, how shall we regulate our opinion with respect to religious belief?* As A. D. Woozley[11] says, this is the principal topic of the *Essay*. As he also says, readers often don't get to it, being a bit disheartened by having to wade through what amounts to a six-hundred-page preface. Still, it is what he says on this head that is most crucial to an understanding of Locke's enterprise, as well as to our metaquestion.

---

11. Introduction to his abridgment of the *Essay* (New York: NAL Penguin, 1974 [originally published Collins, 1964]), p. 15. The *Essay* is long and confusing; it was composed over many years and didn't receive anything like the final editing it needed. As a result, it has been published in abridged editions going all the way back to 1694 (Boston: Printed by Manning & Loring, for J. White, Thomas & Andrews, D. West, E. Larkin, J. West and the proprietor of the Boston bookstore) four years or so after its publication and ten years before Locke's death. These abridgments sometimes delete some of the passages most important to a proper understanding of the *Essay*; for example, A. D. Woozley's omits the absolutely crucial passage quoted on pp. 86–87, below.

A. Living by Reason

The initial problem, of course, is that disorderly crowd of opinions: "men, extending their inquiries beyond their capacities, and letting their thought wander into those depths where they can find no sure footing, it is no wonder that they raise questions and multiply disputes, which, never coming to any clear resolution, are proper only to continue and increase their doubts, and to confirm them at last in perfect skepticism" (Locke's Introduction to the *Essay*, para. 7, p. 31). Like Hume and Kant after him, Locke thinks the remedy requires that we first make a juster and more accurate appraisal of our intellectual capacities and capabilities:

> Whereas were the capacities of our understandings well considered, the extent of our knowledge once discovered, and the horizon found which sets the bounds between the enlightened and dark parts of things; between what is and what is not comprehensible by us, men would perhaps with less scruple acquiesce in the avowed ignorance of the one, and employ their thoughts and discourse with more advantage and satisfaction in the other. (Locke's Introduction to the *Essay*, para. 7, p. 31)

The aim is not to achieve Cartesian certainty (about which he makes several disparaging remarks). Rather, "If we can find out those measures, whereby a rational creature, put in that state in which man is in this world, may and ought to govern his opinions, and actions depending thereon, we need not to be troubled that some other things escape our knowledge" (Introduction, para. 6, p. 31). What we need to find out is how we *may* and *ought to* govern and regulate our opinion, or assent. And his answer, in prototypical Enlightenment fashion, is that we ought to govern our opinion by *following reason*. But what does that mean? What is opinion and what is reason, and how can we govern the former by following the latter?

1. Opinion

If we are to have any hope of overcoming the contentious and disputatious horde of conflicting opinion with which we are beset, says Locke, we must all learn to govern opinion and assent properly. Following Plato, Locke thinks of *opinion* as contrasting with *knowledge*; to see what he thinks opinion is, we must therefore look to his views about knowledge. He thinks we have four kinds of knowledge, all of them involving certainty. First, there is what he regards as the paradigm of knowledge: perceiving the "agreement or disagreement of our ideas." It isn't easy to see precisely what he had in mind here, but the principal sort of knowledge involved here is the knowledge of

self-evident propositions, such propositions as $2 + 1 = 3$.[12] A properly functioning human being can simply see that these propositions
are true (and further, that they couldn't possibly be false). There is no
issue of *regulating* this kind of belief, says Locke, because a properly
formed human being simply can't withhold belief from self-evident
propositions: "This part of knowledge is irresistible, and like bright
sunshine, forces itself immediately to be perceived, as soon as ever
the mind turns its view that way; and leaves no room for hesitation,
doubt, or examination, but the mind is presently filled with the clear
light of it" (IV, ii, 1, p. 177). Such knowledge is *certain*; it is "beyond
all doubt, and needs no probation, nor can have any; this being the
highest of all human certainty" (IV, xvii, 14, p. 407).

Second, there is knowledge of propositions about the contents of
your own mind, that is, propositions about the ideas of which you are
the subject. An example would be your knowledge that you have a
mild pain in your left elbow, or that you seem to see something white
(i.e., things look to you the way they look when you are in fact seeing
something white). This knowledge, says Locke, is *infallible* (IV, i, 4, p.
169, and elsewhere). This means at least that you cannot mistakenly
believe such a proposition; if you believe that you seem to see something white, it follows that you *do* seem to see something white
(though, of course, you may be mistaken in thinking there really is
something white there). Following later custom, let's say that propositions of this sort about my own mental states are *incorrigible* for me.

Third, there is also a kind of knowledge of "other things," of external objects around you:

> And of this, the greatest assurance I can possibly have, and to which
> my faculties can attain, is the testimony of my eyes, which are the
> proper and sole judges of this thing; whose testimony I have reason
> to rely on as so certain, that I can no more doubt, whilst I write this,
> that I see white and black, and that something really exists that
> causes that sensation in me, than that I write or move my hand;
> which is a certainty as great as human nature is capable of, con-
> cerning the existence of anything, but a man's self alone, and of
> God. (IV, xi, 2, pp. 326–27; see also IV, ii, 14, p. 186)

It isn't wholly clear just what it is I know here: do I know that the
piece of paper is white, that my hand is moving, and that the ink is
black? Locke vacillates. Sometimes (for example, when commenting
on the relation between faith and reason) he speaks as if our knowledge of external objects includes the sort of everyday knowledge we
get from perception: that my hand is moving, that the trees in the
backyard are budding, and so on. Other times, and perhaps when

12. For an account of self-evidence, see WPF, chapter 6.

he's being more careful or at least more official, he suggests that what we know of the external world is much sparser, more like *My current ideas of treehood and green are caused by something external to me*. I may not know what these external objects are like (I don't know that they include trees, or buds, or objects that are green), but I do know that there is *something* external causing me to have these ideas.

And fourth, there is *demonstrative* knowledge. I can come to know a proposition by deducing it from or seeing that it is entailed by propositions of the above three sorts (where a proposition *p entails* a proposition *q* just if it is not possible, in the broadly logical sense, that *p* be true and *q* false.[13] Accordingly, some propositions that you can deduce from propositions that are self-evident, incorrigible, or evident to the senses are also certain for you; among these propositions, Locke thinks, is the existence of God (IV, x, 1–6, pp. 306–10). Indeed, he adds, "From what has been said, it is plain to me we have a more certain knowledge of the existence of a God, than of anything our senses have not immediately discovered to us."

When it comes to *knowledge*, therefore, we have no control over our giving assent; assent is elicited willy-nilly, and the question of how we should regulate assent in this area therefore does not arise. (We can't regulate it at all, anymore than I could regulate the direction in which I fall, if I fell off a cliff.) Of course, knowledge forms only a *part* of the beliefs to be found in a human noetic structure and, according to Locke, a relatively *small* part ("Our knowledge, as has been shown, being very narrow," IV, xv, 2, p. 364). It is *opinion* that includes the bulk of what we ordinarily believe; and it is with respect to opinion—that which we believe but do not know—that the question of regulation *does* arise.

2. Reason

Locke's crucial claim is that we must be guided, in the formation of opinion, by reason. Well, what is reason? First, it is "a faculty in man, that faculty whereby man is supposed to be distinguished from beasts, and wherein it is evident he much surpasses them" (IV, xvii, 1, p. 386). Second, reason is the power whereby we can discern broadly logical relations among propositions (IV, xviii, 3, p. 417), which, of course, are the candidates for our assent, the things we believe. In particular, by virtue of employment of reason, we distinguish two kinds of relations among propositions:

13. I do not and cannot know *all* propositions entailed by those of the above sort, of course; some might be much too complicated and difficult for me to grasp, and others might be such that I simply can't see the connection between them and propositions of the above three sorts. For still others, the argument for them is so long and complicated that I lack the certainty required by knowledge.

The greatest part of our knowledge depends upon deductions and intermediate ideas: and in those cases where we are fain to substitute assent instead of knowledge, and take propositions for true, without being certain they are so, we have need to find out, examine, and compare the grounds of their probability. In both these cases, the faculty which finds out the means, and rightly applies them, to discover certainty in the one, and probability in the other, is that which we call *reason*. For, as reason perceives the necessary and indubitable connexion of all the ideas or proofs one to another, in each step of any demonstration that produces knowledge; so it likewise perceives the probable connexion of all the ideas or proofs one to another, in every step of a discourse, to which it will think assent due. (IV, xvii, 2, p. 387)

It is by reason, therefore, that we perceive deductive and probabilistic relations among propositions. We needn't say anything here about deductive relations between propositions; and while much needs to be said about probability, Locke doesn't say it. He does say a little, however, beginning rather inauspiciously by declaring, "Probability is likeliness to be true" (IV, xv, 3, p. 365). The uninformative character of this, however, is ameliorated by his pointing out[14] that probability has to do with what occurs 'for the most part' in our experience; and he adds that testimony from others also establishes probability (IV, xv, 4, pp. 365–66). Locke seems to think of probability as an objective relation among propositions; he probably also thinks that it is a quasi-logical relationship among them; his views, therefore, may be precursors of those of J. M. Keynes, Rudolf Carnap, and others.[15] Probability, furthermore, comes in degrees: "Upon these grounds depends the probability of any proposition: and as the conformity of our knowledge, as the certainty of observations, as the frequency and constancy of experience, and the number and credibility of testimonies do more or less agree or disagree with it, so is any proposition in itself more or less probable" (IV, xv, 6, p. 367). Here he seems to suggest that a proposition is probable to some degree "in itself"; he is better understood, I think, as holding that probability is a relation between propositions. A proposition has a certain degree of probability 'for me' (i.e., relative to those propositions that are certain for me); what counts with respect to the formation of my opinion is the probability of the candidate in question with respect to what is certain for me.

14. As Aristotle also did; see WPF, p. 159.

15. What he says is consistent with other views, however, including the one proposed in chapter 9 of WPF.

3. Regulating Opinion by Reason

Locke's claim is that we should regulate our opinion or assent by reason; but what does this mean? How do you do a thing like that? His answer, fundamentally, is that I must regulate my opinion in such a way that I opine only that which is *probable* with respect to that which is *certain* for me. I have no control over my assent when it comes to knowledge, what is certain for me; however, I do have control over my assent when it comes to opinion, what isn't certain. And the rule here is that I must not assent to a proposition unless it is probable with respect to what is certain for me. Assent, furthermore, comes in degrees[16] (IV, xvi, 1, p. 369). More exactly, then, the rule is that I should *proportion my degree of assent to the probability of the proposition in question*: "The grounds of probability we have laid down in the foregoing chapter: as they are the foundations on which our *assent* is built, so are they also the measure whereby its several degrees are, or ought to be regulated" (IV, xvi, 1, p. 369). More specifically, for any proposition that comes to my attention, I should proportion my degree of assent to it to the degree to which that proposition is probable with respect to what is certain for me. Proper procedure here is "not entertaining any proposition with greater assurance than the proofs [deductive or inductive] it is built upon will warrant" (IV, xix, 1, p. 429) (probabilistic proofs as well as deductive proofs). Another way to put this: I should proportion degree of assent to the evidence; that is, I should believe a proposition *p* with a firmness that is proportional to the degree to which *p* is probable with respect to what is certain for me. This is what it is to regulate or govern opinion according to reason.

B. Revelation

The question that started off the whole discussion issuing in the nine hundred pages of the *Essay* was on "the principles of morality and revealed religion." But now we see that we are to regulate our opinion by reason, that is, proportion our belief in a proposition to the degree to which it is probable with respect to what is certain for us. Does this mean, then, that divine revelation, "revealed religion," is to play no

---

16. Here I think he means to point to two phenomena: first, that one believes some propositions more firmly than others, and second, that we judge some propositions more probable than others. To illustrate the first, I believe that $7 + 5 = 12$ more firmly than I believe that Glasgow is west of Aberdeen, but I do believe both of these propositions. As for the second, I believe it is reasonably probable that all the continents of Earth once formed a supercontinent; I also believe that it is more probable that the works attributed to Shakespeare were really written by Shakespeare, not by Bacon.

role in the right regulation of opinion? If that regulation demands that we proportion degree of assent to the evidence, what room is there for assenting to "the great things of the Gospel," as Jonathan Edwards calls them, the incarnation, atonement, and other central features of Christianity? Must we conclude that God could not reveal to us propositions unavailable by the use of our natural faculties? Surely not: "God, in giving us the light of reason, has not thereby tied up his own hands from affording us, when he thinks fit, the light of revelation" (IV, xviii, 8, p. 423). Even if he does afford us the light of revelation, however, must we not regulate assent in such a way as to believe what he reveals, only if the latter is probable with respect to what is certain for us? If so, how can we accept what he teaches by way of revelation? Incarnation, atonement, and trinity don't seem particularly probable with respect to what is self-evident or about my own mental states.

Locke answers, first, that God indeed can and does reveal such truths to us, and that what he reveals should certainly be believed: "we may as well doubt of our own being, as we can whether any revelation from God be true" (IV, xvi, 14, p. 383); "Whatever God hath revealed is certainly true: no doubt can be made of it" (IV, xviii, 10, p. 425). But then does he think these great truths are probable with respect to what is certain for us? First, he declares repeatedly that we can't properly believe what goes against reason in the sense of going contrary to the principles of knowledge:

> a man can never have so certain a knowledge, that a proposition which contradicts the clear principles and evidence of his own knowledge was divinely revealed, or that he understands the words rightly wherein it is delivered, as he has that the contrary is true, and so is bound to consider and judge of it as a matter of reason, and not swallow it. . . . (IV, xviii, 8, p. 424)

However, it is not required that to be worthy of assent, such a teaching must be probable with respect to what is certain for me. Rather, what has to be probable, in this way, is that the doctrine in question *is indeed revealed*, really is proposed for our assent by the Lord:

> So that faith is a settled and sure principle of assent and assurance, and leaves no manner of room for doubt or hesitation. *Only we must be sure that it be a divine revelation, and that we understand it right:* else we shall expose ourselves to all the extravagancy of enthusiasm . . . (IV, xvi, 14, p. 383)

and

> Whatever God hath revealed is certainly true: no doubt can be made of it. This is the proper object of faith: but whether it be a *divine* revelation or no, reason must judge. (IV, xviii, 10, p. 425)

Locke's constant question is 'how do you know that this is from God?' "How do I know that God is the revealer of this to me; that this impression is made upon my mind by his Holy Spirit; and that therefore I ought to obey it? If I know not this, how great soever the assurance is that I am possessed with, it is groundless; whatever light I pretend to, it is but *enthusiasm*" (IV, xix, 10, p. 435). "*Reason*," he says, "*must be our last judge and guide in everything*" (IV, xix, 14, p. 438, his emphasis). He goes on:

> I do not mean that we must consult reason, and examine whether a proposition revealed from God can be made out by natural principles, and if it cannot, that then we may reject it: but consult it we must, and by it examine whether it be a revelation from God or no: and if reason finds it to be revealed from God, reason then declares for it as much as for any other truth, and makes it one of her dictates. (IV, xix, 14, p. 439)

Overall, then, the view is this: God can certainly reveal truths to us. We are not obliged to accept as revealed, however, anything that would go contrary to what we would otherwise know, even with respect to the lowest level of knowledge. Furthermore, a given candidate *p* for revelation, if it doesn't have evidence from what is certain, cannot have any more epistemic probability than is enjoyed by the proposition that *p* is indeed a revelation from God (IV, xvi, 14, p. 383). So we are to follow reason, in the formation of religious opinion, but so doing does not preclude accepting certain propositions as specially revealed by God, and accepting them on that basis.

II. CLASSICAL EVIDENTIALISM, DEONTOLOGISM, AND FOUNDATIONALISM

In *God and Other Minds*, I took for granted what was then axiomatic: that belief in God is rationally justifiable only if there are good arguments for it, and only if the arguments in favor of it are stronger than the arguments against it. The origin—at least the proximate origin—of this idea is to be found in the work of Locke I've been outlining. A belief is acceptable, he says, only if it is either itself certain or else probable (i.e., more probable than not) with respect to propositions that are certain for me. Christian belief, clearly enough, is not certain for me: it is not self-evident, incorrigible, or a deliverance of the senses. Hence, if it is to be acceptable, it must be probable with respect to propositions of these sorts. Locke doesn't, so far as I know, explicitly raise the question whether I must *know* or *believe* that the belief is thus probable, if it is to be acceptable for me; I think he assumes that it must be. He thinks of the matter in terms of *applying a*

test: a certain belief *p* comes within your purview; you are to determine whether it is probable with respect to what is certain for you in
order to determine whether it is acceptable for you. But then you will
acceptthe belief only if you see or believe that it does pass this test.

Evidentialism is the claim that religious belief is rationally acceptable only if there are good arguments for it; Locke is both a paradigm evidentialist and the proximate source of the entire evidentialist tradition,[17] from him through Hume and Reid and Kant and the
nineteenth century to the present. Locke's *classical evidentialism* is one
element of a larger whole that also includes classical *foundationalism*
and classical *deontologism*. This connected complex of theses and attitudes has been enormously influential in epistemology since the
Enlightenment, and enormously influential especially with respect to
our question, the question of the rational justifiability of religious belief: call it *the classical package*. The classical package includes ways of
thinking about faith, reason, rationality, justification, knowledge, the
nature of belief, and other related topics. It is hard to overemphasize
the importance of these ways of thinking for the *de jure* question. We
have seen how Locke is the fountainhead of the evidentialist tradition, one of the elements in the classical package; but he is also a
main source, for us moderns (and postmoderns), of the other two elements: classical foundationalism and classical deontologism. I now
turn to them.[18]

A. Classical Foundationalism

First, classical foundationalism is *foundationalism*. Here the crucial notion is that of believing one proposition *on the evidential basis* of others.
Like any important philosophical notion, this one has its problems,
complications, and perplexities. Let's ignore them. The notion is ser-
viceable even if it is less than wholly clear, and at any rate there are
clear examples. I believe that 32×94 is 3008 (I've just calculated it);
I believe this proposition on the evidential basis of others, such as
$4 \times 2 = 8, 4 \times 3 = 12, 8 + 2 = 10$, and so on. However I don't believe

17. In "Reason and Belief in God," I suggested that Aquinas was also an evidentialist in this sense; various people (Alfred Freddoso, Norman Kretzmann,
Eleonore Stump, Linda Zagzebski, and John Zeis in "Natural Theology: Reformed?"
in *Rational Faith: Catholic Responses to Reformed Epistemology*, ed. Linda Zagzebski
[Notre Dame: University of Notre Dame Press, 1993], p. 72) remonstrated with me,
pointing out that things were much more complicated than I thought. The fact is
that Aquinas is an evidentialist with respect to *scientia*, scientific knowledge. But it
doesn't follow that he thought a person could properly accept belief in God, say, only
if he had (or there are) good theistic arguments. On the contrary, Aquinas thought
it perfectly sensible and reasonable to accept this belief on faith.

18. I examine classical foundationalism in detail in WCD and "Reason and
Belief in God"; here I shall be brief and schematic.

those latter on the evidential basis of any other propositions at all; instead, they are 'basic' for me. I simply see that they are true, and accept them. I accept many propositions in this basic way: that there is snow in my backyard, for example, and that it is still white. I also believe, in the basic way, that it seems to me that I am seeing something white (I am being appeared to whitely), that I had cornflakes for breakfast, and a thousand other things. The propositions I accept in the basic way are, so to say, starting points for my thought. (This is not to say, of course, that what you take as basic doesn't depend on what else you know or believe. I believe in the basic way that what I see coming toward me is a truck; someone with no acquaintance with trucks or motor vehicles couldn't form that belief at all, let alone hold it in the basic way.)

The propositions that I accept in this basic way are the *foundations* of my structure of beliefs—my 'noetic structure', as I shall call it for ease of reference.[19] And according to the foundationalist, in an acceptable, properly formed noetic structure, every proposition is either in the foundations or believed on the evidential basis of other propositions. Indeed, this much is trivially true; a proposition is in the foundations of my noetic structure if and only if it is basic for me, and it is basic for me if and only if I don't accept it on the evidential basis of other propositions. This much of foundationalism should be uncontroversial and accepted by all.[20] Further (and still properly uncontroversial), for every proposition in my noetic structure that is not in the foundations, there is an evidential path terminating in the foundations: that is, if A is nonbasic for me, then I believe it on the basis of some other proposition B, which I believe on the basis of some other proposition C, and so on down to a foundational proposition or propositions.[21]

Now Locke clearly accepts this much; but he also accepts more. A foundationalist will also typically claim that not just any belief is *properly* basic; some propositions are such that if I accept them in the basic way, there is something wrong, something skewed, something unjustified about my noetic structure. Imagine, for example, that because of an inordinate admiration for Picasso, I suddenly find myself with the belief that he didn't die; like Elijah, he was directly transported to heaven (in a peculiarly warped sort of chariot with a great misshapen eye in the middle of its side). If I don't believe this proposition on the evidential basis of any others, it is basic for me. But there is something defective, wrong, unhappy in my believing this proposition in the basic way; this proposition is not *properly* basic. Noting that only *some* propositions seem to be properly basic, a foundationalist may go

19. For an account of noetic structures, see WCD, pp. 72ff.
20. Even by coherentists: see WCD, pp. 78ff.
21. See "Reason and Belief in God," p. 54.

on to lay down conditions of proper basicality, admitting some kinds of propositions to this exalted condition and rejecting others. And the classical foundationalist holds that the only propositions that are properly basic for me are the ones that are *certain* for me.

Certainty is another difficult and much contested notion; again, let us ignore the difficulties and contests, noting that classical foundationalists don't always agree as to which propositions are indeed certain in this way. Descartes admits only propositions that are self-evident or incorrigible. Locke accepts these as properly basic; he also adds, as I said earlier, propositions that are 'evident to the senses'—at least such propositions as *something is causing me to have the ideas I do in fact have*, and possibly also more robust propositions, such as that *the ground is showing through the snow in my backyard*. Let's say, a bit vaguely, that according to classical foundationalists, a proposition is properly basic, for a person S, if and only if it is self-evident for S, or incorrigible for S, or evident to the senses for S.

Further, according to the classical foundationalists (and everyone else), you can't properly believe just any proposition on the basis of just any other. I can't properly believe, for example, the proposition that Abraham lived around 1800 B.C. on the basis of the proposition that Brutus stabbed Julius Caesar; the latter has nothing to do, evidentially speaking, with the former. Rather, I properly believe A on the basis of B only if B *supports* A, is in fact evidence for A. Again, this notion of evidential support is difficult and controversial;[22] once more, let us ignore the difficulties and controversies and note that different classical foundationalists propose different evidential relationships as being what is required if my belief of A on the basis of belief B is to be proper. Descartes seems to suggest that a proposition is acceptable in the superstructure of my noetic structure only if I have *deduced it from* or *seen it to be entailed by* those in the foundations. This is an extremely strenuous standard (and in fact very few of our beliefs turn out to be acceptable on this standard.) Locke admitted *probabilistic* support or evidence, and he also admitted *testimony*. Later on, Charles Sanders Peirce and others went further still and admitted also what he sometimes called 'abduction'—something like the relationship between a scientific theory and the evidence on which it is based. Stating classical foundationalism at its most capacious, therefore, suppose we put it as follows:

> (CF) A belief is acceptable for a person if (and only if) it is either properly basic (i.e., self-evident, incorrigible, or evident to the senses for that person), or believed on the evidential

22. See WCD, pp. 69ff.

basis of propositions that are acceptable and that support it deductively, inductively, or abductively.

In a properly run noetic structure, therefore, if you take any belief *B* that is not basic (not in the foundations), *B* will be accepted on the basis of other beliefs that are acceptable and that support *B* (either deductively, inductively, or abductively); if those others are not in the foundations, they will be accepted on the basis of still others that are acceptable and that support them, and so on, down to the foundations—that is, down to propositions that are self-evident, incorrigible, or evident to the senses for you.

Classical foundationalism, as I say, has been enormously influential from the Enlightenment to the present. For many philosophers and others (for myself earlier on), it has amounted to a sort of unquestioned assumption, unquestioned because it isn't seen clearly enough even to recognize as an assumption. Locke's views here, particularly with respect to religion, have achieved the status of orthodoxy, and most discussions of the rational justification of religious belief have been and still are conducted in the unthinking acceptance of that framework. There may be modifications of one sort or another, analogical extensions of the original framework, departures of one sort or another; there may be a sort of unease with it, a dimly felt sense that not all is well with it; still, for most of us, the basic framework remains in the near neighborhood of classical foundationalism.

B. Classical Deontologism

We must now ask a question that has been clamoring for attention all along. Suppose your beliefs *don't* correspond to the standards the classical foundationalist or evidentialist holds before you: so what? Exactly what is the matter with you? You will be told that your belief structure is unacceptable and not rationally justified, and that you yourself are irrational; but again, so what? What is wrong with being irrational or with holding beliefs that are not rationally justified? It certainly sounds reprehensible, but what, exactly, is the problem? That is what we must know if we are to understand our *de jure* question. Consider, for example, John Mackie in *The Miracle of Theism*.[23] He believes he has shown that the central doctrines of theism are not rational or "rationally defensible" because (as he thinks) he has shown that they are not probable with respect to what he takes to be the relevant evidence. What does he mean here by "rational"? How is he using this protean term? Suppose he is right in thinking that it would be irrational to be a theist if theistic belief is not probable with

23. Oxford: Oxford University Press, 1982.

respect to the evidence (whatever precisely that is): what is this property of irrationality that would then afflict theism or theists? Mackie
doesn't say. And Mackie is not alone in failing to say. Many evidentialist objectors argue that theistic belief is irrational because there is
insufficient evidence for it; they clearly think being irrational is a bad
business; but they seldom say what's bad about it. Instead, they move
immediately to the task of showing, as they think, that there *is* insufficient evidence for belief in God. This prior question, nevertheless,
remains crucial: insufficient for *what*? What is supposed to be bad
about believing in the absence of evidence?

Contemporary evidentialist objectors don't (for the most part)
explicitly say; their progenitor Locke, however, *does* say. His question,
you recall, is how "a rational creature, put in that state in which man
is in this world, may and ought to govern his opinions, and actions
depending thereon." And his answer, as we have seen, is that a rational creature in our circumstances ought to govern his opinions by
reason—that is, proportion his belief to what is certain for him. But
how are we to understand the 'may' and 'ought' and 'should' that
Locke employs in stating his project?

At first sight, his words have a *deontological* ring; they are redolent
of duty, obligation, permission, being within your rights and the rest
of the deontological stable. Closer inspection reveals that this is, indeed, how they are to be taken. It is Locke's idea that we have a *duty*,
an *obligation* to regulate opinion in the way he suggests. We enjoy
high standing as rational creatures, creatures capable of belief and
knowledge. *Noblesse oblige*, however; privilege has its obligations, and
we are obliged to conduct our intellectual or cognitive life in a certain
way. Our exalted station as rational creatures, creatures with reason,
carries with it duties and requirements:

> faith is nothing but a firm assent of the mind: which, if it be regu-
> lated, as is our duty, cannot be afforded to anything but upon good
> reason; and so cannot be opposite to it. He that believes without
> having any reason for believing, may be in love with his own fan-
> cies; but neither seeks truth as he ought, nor pays the obedience
> due to his Maker, who would have him use those discerning facul-
> ties he has given him, to keep him out of mistake and error. He that
> does not this to the best of his power, however he sometimes lights
> on truth, is in the right but by chance; and I know not whether the
> luckiness of the accident will excuse the irregularity of his proceed-
> ing. This at least is certain, that he must be accountable for what-
> ever mistakes he runs into: whereas he that makes use of the light
> and faculties God has given him, and seeks sincerely to discover
> truth by those helps and abilities he has, may have this satisfaction
> in doing his duty as a rational creature, that, though he should miss
> truth, he will not miss the reward of it. For he governs his assent
> right, and places it as he should, who, in any case or matter what-
> soever, believes or disbelieves according as reason directs him. He

that doth otherwise, transgresses against his own light, and misuses those faculties which were given him to no other end, but to search and follow the clearer evidence and greater probability. (IV, xvii, 24, pp. 413–14)

Here Locke isn't speaking about specifically religious faith (faith as contrasted with reason, say), but about assent or opinion generally; and his central claim here is that there are duties and obligations with respect to its management or regulation. In particular, you are obliged to give assent only to that for which you have good reasons, good evidence: you are to accept a proposition only if it is probable with respect to what is certain for you. Someone who doesn't regulate opinion in this way "neither seeks truth as he *ought*, nor pays the *obedience* due to his Maker" (emphasis added); God commands us to seek truth in this way and to regulate opinion in this way. Someone who does seek truth in this way, even if he should happen to miss it, still "may have this satisfaction in doing his duty as a rational creature." You govern your assent "right," he says, and you place it as you "should" if you believe or disbelieve as reason directs you. And if you don't do that, then you transgress against your own lights. One who governs his opinion thus is acting in accord with duty, is within his rights, is flouting no obligation, is not blameworthy, is, in a word, *justified*.

The English terms 'justified', 'justification', and the like, go back at least to the King James version of the Bible. We are justified, in this use, if Christ's atoning sacrifice for sin has applied to us, so that we are now no longer blameworthy and our sin has been covered, removed, obliterated, taken away; we are no longer guilty; it is as if (so far as guilt is concerned) our sin had never existed. As a matter of fact, the term taken in that sense goes back to Wycliffe's 1382 translation of the Bible; the *Oxford English Dictionary* cites especially Romans 5:16. And Locke is really claiming that you are justified in this sense (guiltless, conforming to your obligations and duties) in believing a proposition *p* only if *p* is either certain for you or such that it is probable with respect to propositions that are certain for you. More precisely, your assent to *p* is justified only if the degree of your assent to *p* is proportional to the degree to which *p* is probable with respect to what is certain for you. If you believe in some other way, then you are going contrary to your epistemic obligations; you are guilty; you are flouting epistemic duty. This is the aboriginal and basic idea of the justificationist tradition, the palimpsest in terms of which other justificationist notions are to be understood by way of analogical extensions. And of course there are analogical extensions. For example, if you follow Locke in thinking we have such a duty, then you will be inclined to transfer the term 'justified' from the believer to the believed and speak, as in fact we do speak, of a *proposition's* being justified, or justified for someone, meaning that the person in question has a good bit of evidence for the proposition in question. You will also say, no doubt, that there is a good deal of *justification or rational justification* for a given proposition, meaning thereby that there is a good deal of evidence for it.[24]

III. BACK TO THE PRESENT

Locke's thought initiates the classical package: evidentialism, deontologism, and classical foundationalism. It is according to the first two that Christian belief requires evidence; that is, Christian believers are within their intellectual rights and conforming to intellectual duty, only if they have evidence for that belief. It is according to the third that the evidence must trace back, finally, to what is certain for them: what is self-evident or incorrigible or evident to the senses. This connection between justification and evidence has been at the center of the whole justificationist tradition in Western epistemology; it has been of particular importance for subsequent thought about the *de jure* question for Christian belief. According to this tradition, the *de jure* question is really the question whether Christian belief is rationally justified—that is, whether believers are justified in holding these beliefs, and whether they are conforming to intellectual duty in holding them. The main intellectual duty, however, is that of proportioning belief to the evidence, to what is certain. Hence the first version of the *de jure* question gets transformed into a second: do believers have sufficient evidence for their beliefs? We now see the connection between these two forms of the *de jure* question: the first is the basic question, but if we add (with Locke and the classical tradition) that the main duty here is that of proportioning belief to evidence, then we get the second question.

I say Locke's influence—and that of the classical package—has been paramount in discussions of the *de jure* question. If I am right, we should expect at least two things. We should expect, first, that those who raise the *de jure* question would put it in terms of evidence, argument, propositional evidence, evidence from other things one thinks. And we should expect, second, that they would also put it in terms of justification—justification construed deontologically or in terms of some analogical extension of deontology. Both of these expectations are amply fulfilled. Of course I don't expect you just to take my word for it, and I don't have the space for extensive documentation; I shall instead just give a bit of corroborating evidence.

24. There are many other analogical extensions or retrenchments of this original notion of justification, and many other analogically extended uses of the term; see WCD, chapter 1.

For the last hundred years, W. K. Clifford's essay "The Ethics of Belief" has been cited in discussions of the *de jure* question; Clifford (that "delicious *enfant terrible*," as William James called him) claimed (with charming and restrained understatement) that "it is wrong, always, everywhere, and for anyone to believe anything upon insufficient evidence."[25] Here we have the combination of deontologism and evidentialism. This passage doesn't display classical foundationalism as well (it doesn't say what the evidence must consist in), but no doubt Clifford was a classical foundationalist; at least he thought that belief in God requires evidence. William James's essay "The Will to Believe"[26] has been a sort of companion piece to Clifford's; it has been cited for almost as long in discussions of our question, and because James comments on and criticizes Clifford, the two essays have often been anthologized in tandem. James titled his essay "The Will to Believe"; "The *Right* to Believe" would have been more accurate. His central claim is that under certain conditions it is not contrary to duty to believe a proposition (a proposition that isn't certain) even if one has no evidence for it. If believing this proposition is a *forced* option and a *live* option, for you, and if there is no evidence *against* it, then you have a right to believe it, even though you don't have evidence *for* it. In this way James tries to make room for belief in God (even if not full Christian belief) by inserting it in the gaps of the evidence. The evidentialism and deontologism, again, are evident.[27]

James and Clifford wrote a hundred years ago and more; but the last half-century has seen a host of evidentialist objectors to Christian belief, thinkers who hold both that this sort of belief, if it is to be rational, must be accepted on the basis of propositional evidence, and that the evidence is insufficient. (Among them would be Brand Blanshard,[28] Bertrand Russell,[29] Michael Scriven,[30] Antony Flew,[31]

25. *Lectures and Essays* (London: Macmillan, 1901), p. 183.

26. In *The Will to Believe, and Other Essays in Popular Philosophy* (New York: Longmans, Green, 1897).

27. "It's not exactly emphasized any longer, but one of James's original purposes in promoting pragmatism was not to get rid of empirically unverifiable beliefs, but to make room, in a scientist world view, for faith and God. . . . This was explicitly the context for the 1898 lecture" (Louis Menand, "An American Prodigy," *New York Review of Books* [December 2, 1993], p. 33). The "1898 lecture" is "The Will to Believe."

28. *Reason and Belief* (London: Allen and Unwin, 1974), pp. 400ff.

29. "Why I Am Not a Christian" in his *Why I Am Not a Christian* (New York: Simon and Schuster, 1957), pp. 3ff.

30. *Primary Philosophy* (New York: McGraw-Hill, 1966), pp. 87ff.

31. *The Presumption of Atheism* (London: Pemberton, 1976), pp. 22ff.

Wesley Salmon,[32] J. C. A. Gaskin,[33] Anthony O'Hear,[34] to some degree Richard Gale,[35] and John Mackie in his posthumous book, *The Miracle of Theism*.[36]) Although the deontological component in these positions is often more muted than the evidentialism, it is clearly present and sometimes wholly explicit. Thus Blanshard:

> everywhere and always belief has an ethical aspect. There is such
> a thing as a general ethic of the intellect. The main principle
> of that ethic I hold to be the same inside and outside religion.
> That principle is simple and sweeping: equate your assent to the
> evidence.[37]

Of course it isn't only evidentialist objectors to theistic belief who embrace evidentialism. John Locke himself was an evidentialist, but no evidentialist objector. Locke thought that religious belief is 'evidence essential'[38] in the sense that it can be rationally accepted only if believed on the basis of good evidence; he also thought the requisite good evidence was available. Several contemporary writers follow in his footsteps: they accept evidentialism, but believe the evidence is forthcoming (or at least aren't sure that it *isn't*). Among them would be, for example, Basil Mitchell[39] and William Abraham;[40] Stephen Wykstra defends a "more sensible" evidentialism.[41] Anthony Kenny displays some sympathy for evidentialism;[42] as does Richard Swinburne: "the use of symbols . . . enables me to bring out the close

32. "Religion and Science: A New Look at Hume's Dialogues," *Philosophical Studies* 33 (1978), pp. 176ff.

33. *The Quest for Eternity: An Outline of the Philosophy of Religion* (New York: Penguin, 1984).

34. *Experience, Explanation, and Faith: An Introduction to the Philosophy of Religion* (London, Boston: Routledge and Kegan Paul, 1984).

35. *On the Nature and Existence of God* (Cambridge: Cambridge University Press, 1991).

36. Oxford: Oxford University Press, 1982.

37. *Reason and Belief,* p. 401. More evidence for the pervasive influence of the deontological component of the classical package can be found in chapter 1 of WCD. There I argue that both the prevalence of *internalism* in contemporary epistemology and the multifarious and confusing array of concepts of justification among contemporary epistemologists can be understood in terms of their relation to deontology.

38. To use Stephen Wykstra's term; see his "Towards a Sensible Evidentialism: On the Notion of 'Needing Evidence,'" in *Philosophy of Religion: Selected Readings*, 2d ed., ed. William Rowe and William Wainwright (New York: Harcourt Brace Jovanovich, 1989).

39. See his *The Existence of God* (New York: Oxford University Press, l981).

40. *An Introduction to the Philosophy of Religion* (Englewood Cliffs, N.J.: Prentice Hall, 1985).

41. "Towards a Sensible Evidentialism."

42. See his *Faith and Reason* (New York: Columbia University Press, 1983), especially chapters 3 and 4.

similarities which exist between religious theories and large scale hypotheses."[43] Terence Penelhum is no evidentialist, but evidential considerations play a large role in his *God and Skepticism*;[44] the same can be said for Gary Gutting's *Religious Belief and Religious Skepticism*.[45]

Still, it is the evidentialist objectors that most clearly display evidentialism. John Mackie's *The Miracle of Theism* is evidentialism at its most formidable; by way of conclusion, then, suppose we briefly note the form evidentialism takes in that book. Mackie proposes to "examine the arguments for and against the existence of God carefully and in some detail, taking account both of the traditional concept of God and of the traditional proofs of his existence and of more recent interpretations and approaches." He goes on:

> If it is agreed that the central assertions of theism are literally meaningful, it must also be admitted that they are not directly verified or directly verifiable. It follows that any rational consideration of whether they are true or not will involve arguments. . . . it [whether God exists] must be examined either by deductive or inductive reasoning or, if that yields no decision, by arguments to the best explanation; for in such a context nothing else can have any coherent bearing on the issue. (pp. 4, 6)

Mackie assumes that the rational acceptability of theistic belief depends on the outcome of this examination: if, on balance, the evidence favors theism, then theistic belief is rationally acceptable; if the evidence favors atheism, then theism is not rationally acceptable. The evidentialism, of course, is palpable.

Now Mackie takes it that theism is a *hypothesis*, something like a very large-scale scientific hypothesis (the theory of evolution, perhaps, or general relativity). He assumes further that its rational acceptability depends upon its success as a hypothesis. Speaking of religious experience, he makes the following characteristic remark: "Here, as elsewhere, the supernaturalist hypothesis fails because there is an adequate and much more economical naturalistic alternative" (p. 198). Clearly, this remark is relevant only if we think of belief in God as or as like a scientific hypothesis, a theory designed to explain some body of evidence, and acceptable to the degree that it succeeds in explaining that evidence. On this way of looking at the matter, there is a relevant body of evidence shared by believer and

---

43. See his *The Existence of God* (Oxford: Clarendon Press, 1979). Swinburne, however, can't be considered an evidentialist in view of his "Principle of Credulity": "that (in the absence of special considerations) if it seems (epistemically) to a subject that *x* is present, then probably *x* is present" (p. 254).

44. Dordrecht: D. Reidel, 1983.

45. Notre Dame: University of Notre Dame Press, 1982.

unbeliever alike; theism is a hypothesis designed to explain that body
of evidence; and theism is rationally defensible only to the extent that
it is a good explanation thereof.

Now Mackie thinks it is *not* a good explanation: he concludes, "In
the end, therefore, we can agree with what Laplace said about God:
we have no need of that hypothesis" (p. 253); he goes on to claim,
"The balance of probabilities, therefore, comes out strongly against
the existence of a god." He clearly takes it for granted, furthermore,
that if the balance of probabilities comes out as he says it does, then
there is no case for theism, and the theist stands revealed as somehow
irrational or intellectually deficient or perhaps intellectually out of
line; as he puts it, "It would appear from our discussion so far that
the central doctrines of theism, literally interpreted, cannot be rationally defended."[46]

But why make assumptions like that? Why think that theism is
rationally acceptable only if there are good arguments for it? Why
think that it is, or is significantly like, a scientific hypothesis? Of
course these assumptions form part of the classical package: well,
why should we accept that package? Clearly there are sensible alternatives. Consider our memory beliefs, for example: obviously, one
could take a Mackie-like view here as well. I believe that I had a ba-
nana for breakfast; one could hold that a belief like this (and indeed
even the belief that there has been such a thing as the past) is best
thought of as like a scientific hypothesis, designed to explain such
present phenomena as (among other things) apparent memories; if
there were a more "economical" explanation of these phenomena
that did not postulate, say, the existence of the past or of past facts,
then our usual beliefs in the past "could not be rationally defended."
But here this seems clearly mistaken; the availability of such an "explanation" wouldn't in any way tell against our ordinary belief that
there has really been a past. Why couldn't the same hold for theism
or, more broadly, for Christian belief? What is to be said for (and
against) the classical package, taken in particular with respect to
Christian belief ?

---

46. Indeed, Mackie takes the title of his book from Hume's ironic suggestion
that

> upon the whole, we may conclude that the *Christian Religion* not only was at
> first attended with miracles, but even at this day cannot be believed by any
> reasonable person without one. . . . Whoever is moved by *Faith* to assent to
> it, is conscious of a continued miracle in his own person, which subverts all
> the principles of his understanding, and gives him a determination to be-
> lieve what is most contrary to custom and experience. *An Enquiry*
> *Concerning Human Understanding* (LaSalle, Ill.: Open Court, 1966), p. 145.

IV. PROBLEMS WITH THE CLASSICAL PICTURE

The classical picture has been enormously influential in guiding thought about the *de jure* question; its near relatives still dominate discussion of it; in particular, the evidentialism of the classical picture persists. This picture, however, like some other big pictures, doesn't survive close examination; it is subject to powerful, indeed, fatal objections. After pointing out some of the problems, I'll consider contemporary analogical extensions of the various elements of the classical picture to see whether any of them supports the evidentialism that is still widely popular and finds such a comfortable home in the classical picture. I'll conclude that in fact there is no reason at all to think that Christian belief requires argument or propositional evidence, if it is to be justified. Christians—indeed, well-educated, contemporary, and culturally aware Christians—can be justified, so I shall argue, even if they don't hold their beliefs on the basis of arguments or evidence, even if they aren't aware of any good arguments for their beliefs, and even if, indeed, there aren't any. Indeed, it is *obvious* that they can be justified in this way; as I shall argue, that suggests that the *de jure* question we seek is not this question of justification; that question is too easy to answer.

So, first, what are these problems attaching to the classical picture? Recent philosophy has not been kind to classical foundationalism; many objections have been raised, many problems pointed out. I shall confine my attention to two objections, both fatal. First, as I've argued elsewhere,[47] classical foundationalism appears to be self-referentially incoherent: it lays down a standard for justified belief that it doesn't itself meet. More exactly, the classical foundationalist, in asserting (and presumably believing) his classical foundationalism, lays down a standard for being justified, blameless, within one's intellectual rights: a standard which his own belief in the classical picture doesn't meet. Stated at slightly greater length, what he claims is that

> (CP) A person *S* is justified in accepting a belief *p* if and only if *either* (1) *p* is properly basic for *S*, that is self-evident, incorrigible, or Lockeanly evident to the senses for *S*,[48] *or*

47. "Reason and Belief in God," pp. 61ff.
48. Here I am reading Locke (see above, pp. 76–77) as claiming that what I know immediately is only that my sensations are caused by external objects of some kind or other, not that those objects have the properties of trees, horses, or the other sorts of objects we think there are.

(2) *S* believes *p* on the evidential basis of propositions that are
    properly basic and that evidentially support *p* deductively, in-
    ductively, or abductively.

Here I ignore the fact that the 'believes on the basis of' relation is
not transitive. The classical picture doesn't really require that all of one's
nonbasic beliefs be believed on the evidential basis of basic beliefs; some
nonbasic beliefs may be believed on the basis of other nonbasic beliefs
that support them, provided those others are believed on the basis of
still other beliefs that support them, provided those others. . . . To put
this more accurately, say that a nonbasic belief is *properly based* if and only
if it is believed on the evidential basis of beliefs that are either properly
basic or properly based. Then, according to the classical picture, every
nonbasic belief must be properly based.

Further, I ignore another condition that is really part of the classical picture. Suppose I believe *p* on the basis of propositions $q_1, q_2 \ldots q_n$
where the q_i in fact support *p*, but I can't see that they do. (Perhaps I believe that there is no greatest cardinal on the basis of ordinary axioms
for set theory, but don't know, can't see, and have no reason to believe
that the latter support the former.) Then, presumably, on the classical
picture I am not justified in this belief. My duty is to believe a nonbasic
proposition on the basis of propositions that I can *see* support it, not just
any old propositions that happen to support it, whether or not I can see
it. Hence perhaps we should add what Locke and Descartes take for
granted here: if *S* is justified in believing *p* on the basis of other propositions, it must be that those other propositions support *p*, of course; further, *S* must also *recognize* that they do so.

A. Self-Referential Problems

Now consider (CP) itself. First, it isn't properly basic according to the
classical foundationalist's lights. To be properly basic, it would have to
be self-evident, incorrigible, or Lockeanly evident to the senses. But
first, it isn't self-evident for the foundationalist (or for the rest of us).
Even if someone claims it has *some* intuitive support, one couldn't
with a straight face claim that it has enough intuitive support to be
self-evident. For if it were self-evident, it would be such that it isn't
even possible for a properly functioning human being to understand
it without seeing that it is true.[49] Clearly (CP) isn't like that at all; for
example, *I* understand it, and I don't see that it is true; and I'll bet
the same goes for you. In this regard (CP) is wholly unlike *2 + 1 = 3*
or *If all cats are animals and Maynard is a cat, then Maynard is an animal.*
Second, it isn't about anyone's mental states and therefore isn't incorrigible for the foundationalist (or any of the rest of us). And third,
it obviously isn't evident to the senses.

---

49. See WPF, p. 109.

According to (CP) itself, therefore, (CP) is not properly basic. That means that if (CP) is true, those who are within their rights in believing (CP) must believe it on the evidential basis of other propositions—propositions that *are* properly basic and that evidentially support it. And if they do, in fact, believe it in that way, then there will be good inductive, deductive, or abductive arguments to (CP) from propositions that are properly basic according to (CP). As far as I know, there aren't any such arguments. As far as I know, no classical foundationalist has produced any such arguments or proposed some properly basic propositions that support (CP). It is of course possible that there *are* such arguments, even if so far no one has produced them; but the probabilities seem to be against it. So probably one who accepts (CP) does so in a way that violates (CP); (CP) lays down a condition for being justified, dutiful, which is such that one who accepts it probably violates it. If it is true, therefore, the devotee of (CP) is probably going contrary to duty in believing it. So it is either false or such that one goes contrary to duty in accepting it; either way, one shouldn't accept it.

But couldn't one who accepts (CP) perhaps find a sort of *inductive* argument for it?[50] Perhaps the defender of (CP) ('the classicist', as I'll call her) reads Roderick Chisholm[51] and embraces 'particularism'; she proposes to develop a criterion of justified belief by assembling samples of justified and samples of unjustified belief and finding a criterion that best fits them. She assembles a reasonably large and representative sample *J* of cases of beliefs that, as she thinks, are justified, such that the believer is dutiful in accepting them, and another such sample *U* of beliefs that she takes to be unjustified, accepted in such a way as to flout intellectual duty. Then perhaps she notes that all of the beliefs in *J* but none in *U* conform to (CP); she conjectures that a belief is justified if and only if it conforms to (CP). This would be an inductive argument, of sorts, for (CP).

Here is the question, however: are its premises properly basic according to the classical picture? The premises include, crucially, the propositions with respect to each member of *J* that it is justified and of each member of *U* that it is not justified. What form do such beliefs take? Well, presumably the sample classes would include such proposi-

50. See Philip Quinn's "In Search of the Foundations of Theism," *Faith and Philosophy* 2 (1985), pp. 474ff.; my response, "The Foundations of Theism: A Reply," *Faith and Philosophy* 3 (1986), p. 298; and Quinn's rejoinder, "The Foundations of Theism Again," in *Rational Faith: Catholic Responses to Reformed Epistemology*, ed. Linda Zagzebski (Notre Dame: University of Notre Dame Press, 1993), pp. 22ff. I am grateful to Quinn for showing that this possibility needs to be taken much more seriously than I had been taking it.

51. *Theory of Knowledge*, 3d ed. (Englewood Cliffs, N.J.: Prentice Hall, 1989), p. 7. See also "Reason and Belief in God," pp. 75ff.

tions as S_1 *is justified in believing* B_1 *in circumstances* C_1, *and* S_2 *is not justified in believing* P_2 *in circumstances* C_2. (The sample classes need not include only actual beliefs, so to speak; they should also include clear cases of beliefs that *would be* justified in certain circumstances, whether or not anyone has ever actually held such beliefs in those circumstances.) And presumably these are beliefs she accepts in the basic way. (She can't, of course, use (CP) to arrive at them; that would be blatantly circular.) Clearly, beliefs of these sorts aren't either incorrigible or evident to the senses for her; so if they are properly basic, then, according to (CP), they would have to be self-evident.

Now here the classicist will be told that she has a really nasty problem: she will be told that there aren't any cases *at all* where it is self-evident that a belief is unjustified, such that the believer has gone contrary to duty and in fact warrants disapproval and blame. The alleged reason is that our beliefs are not within our direct control; one can't just *decide* to hold or withhold a belief. If you offer me $1,000,000 to believe that I am under 30, or even to stop believing that I am over 30, there is no way (short of mind-altering drugs, say) I can collect. Still, this is by no means the whole story. A full examination of this question would take us too far afield, but first some of my beliefs are *indirectly* within my control (in the way in which, for example, my weight is), even if I can't simply decide what to believe and what not to. I can train myself not to assume automatically that people in white coats know what they are talking about; I can train myself to pay more attention to the evidence, to be less credulous and gullible (or less cynical and skeptical), and so on.

Furthermore, some of my beliefs or belief states *are*, in a way, within my direct control. I don't at the moment have a belief on the question of the year of George Washington's birth; a quick look at my encyclopedia or a call to my eighth-grade history teacher would remedy this deficiency. It is therefore directly within my power to bring it about that I have a belief on that topic. We might even go on to say that there is a belief on that topic (the one the encyclopedia reports) such that it is directly within my power to bring it about that I have *that* belief. Still further, I can be in a state of epistemic sin by virtue of failing to have a certain belief. If it is my responsibility to care for a child and I see her playing with a suspicious looking bottle but don't take the trouble to examine its label, I can't expect to deflect blame by claiming that I didn't know the bottle contained poison. I *should* have known. ("I didn't know the gun was loaded" doesn't always suffice for self-exculpation; it might be my responsibility to know.) And there are plenty of other ways to be in epistemic sin by virtue of the beliefs you hold or don't hold. I believe that you failed to pay your income taxes last year because X, whom I would have known to be irresponsible had I made any inquiries, said so; and I was in the wrong not to make further inquiries.) I am malicious and wish you ill; the speaker says your thought is deep and rigorous; by virtue of my ill will, I form the belief that what she said is that your thought is weak and frivolous. Out of vanity and pride, I may form the belief that my work is unduly neglected when the fact is it gets more attention than it deserves. And so on. Further, in these cases it is perhaps self-evident that the beliefs in question are unjustified, formed in a way contrary to duty; at any rate I am not prepared to dispute the claim.

So suppose we accommodate the classical foundationalist by stipulating that at any rate there are *some* cases of self-evidently unjustified belief: there still remains a real problem for the classicist. That is because these cases, at least the ones I can think of, lend no support to the claim that it is unjustified to form a belief that is neither properly basic (according to classical standards) nor believed on the basis of such propositions. More important, aren't there cases where a belief *is* formed according to (CP), but is nevertheless unjustified? I shouldn't form the belief that you failed to pay your taxes last year on the basis of merely casual inquiry; the stakes are too high. But suppose I do just that: your false friend Myrtle tells me you didn't pay them; I believe this in the usual way, a way, let us assume, that conforms to (CP); I am nevertheless unjustified in that belief.

And on the other side, aren't there any number of cases where it is self-evident that a belief *not* formed in accord with (CP) *is* justified? Someone asks you what you had for breakfast; you reply that it was an orange and some cornflakes. You can't really think of any propositions that are properly basic according to (CP) and support your memory belief; but isn't it self-evident that you are not guilty, not worthy of reproof or blame, in so believing? And of course there will be an enormous number of examples of this sort. And the relevance of this is as follows: if the samples are chosen in any responsible and plausible way (if they are appropriately 'random'), they will not support that conjecture that a person is conforming to intellectual duty if and only if her beliefs conform to (CP). Hence, I can't see how a devotee of (CP) could responsibly argue for it by way of such an inductive, particularist procedure; and hence I conclude that there is probably no way in which the classicist can argue for (CP). If so, however, then (because she also holds that (CP) is not properly basic) she will be unjustified in believing (CP) if it is true; it is therefore self-referentially incoherent for her.

B. Most of Our Beliefs Unjustified?

In his controversies with David Hume, Thomas Reid pointed out that the vast majority of our beliefs do not seem to conform to (CP): at least as far as justification is concerned, they are none the worse for that. This sentiment was echoed in the nineteenth century by others, in particular, Cardinal Newman. Says Newman:

> Nor is the assent which we give to facts limited to the range of self-consciousness. We are sure beyond all hazard of a mistake, that our own self is not the only being existing; that there is an external world; that it is a system with parts and a whole, a universe carried on by laws; and that the future is affected by the past. We accept and hold with an unqualified assent, that the earth, considered as a phe-

nomenon, is a globe; that all its regions see the sun by turns; that there are vast tracts on it of land and water; that there are really existing cities on definite sites, which go by the names of London, Paris, Florence and Madrid.[52]

But how much of this can be seen to be probable with respect to what is certain for us? How much meets the classical conditions for being properly basic? Not much, if any. I believe that I had cornflakes for breakfast, that my wife was amused at some little stupidity of mine, that there really are such 'external objects' as trees and squirrels, and that the world was not created ten minutes ago with all its dusty books, apparent memories, crumbling mountains, and deeply carved canyons. These things, according to classical foundationalism, are not properly basic; they must be believed on the evidential basis of propositions that are self-evident or evident to the senses (in Locke's restricted sense) or incorrigible for me. Furthermore, they must be probable and seen to be probable with respect to propositions of that sort: there must be good arguments, deductive, inductive, or abductive to these conclusions from those kinds of propositions.

If there is any lesson at all to be learned from the history of modern philosophy from Descartes through Hume (and Reid), it is that such beliefs *cannot* be seen to be supported by, to be probable with respect to beliefs that meet the classical conditions for being properly basic. So either most of our beliefs are such that we are going contrary to epistemic obligations in holding them, or (CP) is false. It certainly doesn't *seem* that we must be flouting duty in holding these beliefs in the way we do. I believe in the basic way that there is a lot of snow in the backyard just now and that I met my class yesterday; I don't believe either of these things on the basis of propositions that meet the classical conditions for proper basicality; I do not believe there *are* any propositions of that sort with respect to which they are probable. Of course I realize I could be mistaken; but am I flouting duty in so believing? I reflect on the matter as carefully as I can; I simply see no duty here—and not because I doubt the existence of duties generally, or of epistemic duties specifically. Indeed there are duties of that sort: but is there a duty to conform belief to (CP)? I don't think so. But then how can I be guilty, blameworthy, for believing in this way?

> Could it be that I escape blame only because of ignorance? As we saw in WCD (pp. 15ff.), there is a distinction to be drawn between subjective and objective duty, a distinction that goes all the way back to the New Testament. The apostle Paul takes up the question whether it is

52. *A Grammar of Assent* (Notre Dame: University of Notre Dame Press, 1979), p. 149.

wrong to eat meat sacrificed to idols. Paul holds that this isn't *really* wrong; however, if someone *thinks* (mistakenly) that it is wrong, then it is wrong for him to do so: "I am absolutely convinced, as a Christian, that nothing is impure in itself; only, if a man considers a particular thing impure, then to him it is impure" (Romans 14:14). Certain kinds of actions (e.g., eating meat sacrificed to idols) are objectively permissible: if what makes an action wrong is that God has prohibited it, then these actions have not been prohibited by God. But if I *believe* they are wrong—say I mistakenly believe they *have* been prohibited by God—then I am blameworthy if I perform them. Conversely, certain actions in certain situations are objectively wrong; they are not to be done. Still, if I don't know that they are not to be done and justifiably believe that they are permissible, then I am not blameworthy if I do one of them. My objective duty is what I objectively ought to do; my subjective duty is what I (nonculpably) take to be my objective duty.

And perhaps the classical foundationalist can take advantage of this distinction as follows: "True," he says, "you are not blameworthy in failing to conform your beliefs to (CP). But that is only because of ignorance. Fortunately for you, you nonculpably can't see that you have a duty to conform your beliefs to (CP); that protects you from blame and guilt; nevertheless, you really do have an objective duty to regulate belief in the fashion I have described, even if you can't see that you do." Here discussion seems to come to an end. All I can do is ask my interlocutor why he thinks there is such an objective duty and how he came to the knowledge, as he thinks, that there is any such thing. Can he do more than to simply repeat that as a matter of fact we all have this duty? But why should we believe that? What reason is there for thinking it true? Further, *I* can't properly accept (CP), even if by some wild chance it happens to be true. For if it is true, then to do my duty with respect to accepting it, I must believe it only on the basis of properly basic propositions, and ones such that I can see that they evidentially support (CP). But I *don't* see that any such propositions support it (and the evidentialist apparently can't help me by, e.g., giving me an appropriate argument). So if it is true and I accept it, I will be going contrary to objective duty; but if I accept it, I will (naturally enough) think it is true, and will therefore *believe* I am going contrary to my objective duty; hence if it is true and I believe it, I will be going contrary both to objective and subjective duty.

V. CHRISTIAN BELIEF JUSTIFIED

The classical package taken neat, so to speak, can't be right: there simply doesn't seem to be a duty to form belief in accordance with (CP). Of course there may be other sorts of intellectual duties. There is a duty to the truth of some kind. It may be hard to state this duty exactly;[53] perhaps it is in the neighborhood of a requirement to do

53. See WCD, p. 33.

your best to believe as many important truths as possible and avoid as
many important falsehoods as possible. Whatever precisely our duties to the truth, I want to argue next that Christian belief can certainly be justified and can certainly be justified when taken in the
basic way. We are construing justification in a broadly deontological
way, so that it includes being within one's epistemic rights and also includes being epistemically responsible with respect to belief formation. (Perhaps you will think the second follows from the first.) This
is a perfectly reasonable requirement; if Christian belief cannot be
held in such a way as to satisfy it, then there is something wrong with
Christian belief. But it isn't at all difficult for a Christian—even a sophisticated and knowledgeable contemporary believer aware of all
the criticisms and contrary currents of opinion—to be justified, in
this sense, in her belief; and this whether or not she believes in God
or in more specific Christian doctrines on the basis of propositional
evidence. Consider such a believer: as far as we can see, her cognitive
faculties are functioning properly; she displays no noticeable dysfunction. She is aware of the objections people have made to Christian belief; she has read and reflected on Freud, Marx, and Nietzsche
(not to mention Flew, Mackie, and Nielsen) and the other critics of
Christian or theistic belief; she knows that the world contains many
who do not believe as she does. She doesn't believe on the basis of
propositional evidence; she therefore believes in the basic way. Can
she be justified (in this broadly deontological sense) in believing in
God in this way?

The answer seems to be pretty easy. She reads Nietzsche, but remains unmoved by his complaint that Christianity fosters a weak,
whining, whimpering, and generally disgusting kind of person: most
of the Christians she knows or knows of—Mother Teresa, for instance—don't fit that mold. She finds Freud's contemptuous attitude
toward Christianity and theistic belief backed by little more than implausible fantasies about the origin of belief in God[54] (patricide in the
primal horde? Can he be serious?); and she finds little more of substance in Marx. She thinks as carefully as she can about these objections and others, but finds them wholly uncompelling.

On the other side, although she is aware of theistic arguments
and thinks some of them not without value, she doesn't believe on
the basis of them. Rather, she has a rich inner spiritual life, the sort
described in the early pages of Jonathan Edwards's *Religious Affections;*[55] it seems to her that she is sometimes made aware, catches a

54. See below, chapter 5, pp. 137ff.
55. Ed. John Smith (New Haven: Yale University Press, 1959, first published
1746), p. 271.

glimpse, of something of the overwhelming beauty and loveliness of the Lord; she is often aware, as it strongly seems to her, of the work of the Holy Spirit in her heart, comforting, encouraging, teaching, leading her to accept the "great things of the gospel" (as Edwards calls them), helping her see that the magnificent scheme of salvation devised by the Lord himself is not only for others but for her as well. After long, hard, conscientious reflection, this all seems to her enormously more convincing than the complaints of the critics. Is she then going contrary to duty in believing as she does? Is she being irresponsible? Clearly not. There could be something *defective* about her, some malfunction not apparent on the surface. She could be *mistaken*, a victim of illusion or wishful thinking, despite her best efforts. She could be wrong, desperately wrong, pitiably wrong, in thinking these things; nevertheless, she isn't flouting any discernible duty. She is fulfilling her epistemic responsibilities; she is doing her level best; she is justified.

And this is not only true, but *obviously* true. We may feel in some subterranean way that without evidence she isn't justified; if so, this must be because we are importing some other conception of justification. But if it is justification in the deontological sense, the sense involving responsibility, being within one's intellectual rights, she is surely justified. How could she possibly be blameworthy or irresponsible, if she thinks about the matter as hard as she can, in the most responsible way she can, and she still comes to these conclusions? Indeed, no matter *what* conclusions she arrived at, wouldn't she be justified if she arrived at them in this way? Even if they are wholly unreasonable, in some clear sense? An inmate of Pine Rest Christian Psychiatric Hospital once complained that he wasn't getting the credit he deserved for inventing a new form of human reproduction, "rotational reproduction," as he called it. This kind of reproduction doesn't involve sex. Instead, you suspend a woman from the ceiling with a rope and get her rotating at a high rate of speed; the result is a large number of children, enough to populate a city the size of Chicago. As a matter of fact, he claimed, this is precisely how Chicago *was* populated. He realized, he said, that there is something churlish about insisting on getting all the credit due him, but he did think he really hadn't gotten enough recognition for this important discovery. After all, where would Chicago be without it?

Now there is no reason to think this unfortunate man was flouting epistemic duty, or derelict with respect to cognitive requirement, or careless about his epistemic obligations, or cognitively irresponsible. Perhaps he was doing his level best to satisfy these obligations. Indeed, we can imagine that his main goal in life is satisfying his intellectual obligations and carrying out his cognitive duties. Perhaps he was dutiful *in excelsis*. If so, he was *justified* in these mad beliefs, even if they are mad, and even though they result from cognitive dysfunction.[56]

Our main quarry, of course, is the *de jure* objection or question. One prominent candidate is the question whether the Christian believer can be epistemically *justified* in believing as she does. Take that term in its original and basic deontological sense. Then the question is: can the Christian believer be within her epistemic rights and epistemically responsible in forming belief as she does? Can she be justified even if she doesn't believe on the basis of propositional evidence and even if there is no good propositional evidence? The answer to *this* question is obvious—*too* obvious, in fact, for it to be the *de jure* question, at least if that question is to be worthy of serious disagreement and discussion. *Of course* she can be justified, and my guess would be that many or most contemporary Christians *are* justified in holding their characteristically Christian beliefs. We must therefore look elsewhere for the *de jure* question.

VI. ANALOGICAL VARIATIONS

A. Variations on Classical Foundationalism

The classical picture taken neat, therefore, is subject to devastating difficulty. Nowadays, however, it is seldom taken neat. Instead, there are many analogical extensions or analogically related alternatives for each of the three main components of the classical package: the evidentialism, the classical foundationalism, and the deontology. For example, John Mackie[57] retains the evidentialist component, claiming that Christian belief requires evidence on the part of the believer. But Mackie apparently construes *evidence* much more broadly than the classicist. In his view as in the classical picture, there is a body of knowledge—my evidence—with respect to which a belief must be probable, if it is to be justified; however, this evidence includes much more for Mackie than it does in the classical picture. It includes what is self-evident and incorrigible, of course, but it also includes ordinary perceptual judgments, memory beliefs, some basic science, some of the maxims of probability theory, and so on. Alternatively, we might follow Stephen Wykstra, who concedes that an *individual* Christian believer doesn't need evidence to be justified; still, Christian belief,

---

56. Again, what I've really argued is that this believer is subjectively justified. Can the classical foundationalist concede this but claim that he is not objectively justified, that there really is a duty, whether he knows it or not, to believe only on the basis of evidence? But is there even the slightest reason to think there *is* any such duty? Here at the least the classicist owes us an argument.

57. *The Miracle of Theism.*

he suggests, is evidence-essential in the sense that there must be propositional evidence for it *in the Christian community.*[58] Or we might go still further, following Norman Kretzmann[59] and broadening the classical requirement in such a way that what is required is only that the believer have evidence of *some* sort, even if the evidence in question isn't propositional. Sensuous experience might then be evidence for perceptual belief; other sorts of experience, perhaps some of the kinds of experience that go under the rubric 'religious experience', could also be evidence for Christian belief. These variations are all variations on the classical foundationalist component of the classical picture: according to Mackie and Kretzmann, the believer must have evidence, but *evidence* is more broadly construed; according to Wykstra, on the other hand, evidence is required, but it need not be possessed by the individual believer, so long as it resides somewhere in the believer's community. Mackie, Kretzmann, and Wykstra retain the evidentialism (with respect to Christian belief) of the classical picture, but modify the foundationalism.

It isn't clear whether they accept the deontological component of the classical picture; suppose for the moment we keep that component fixed, modifying only the evidential requirement. It is then obvious, I think, that the believer can be justified even if there aren't good arguments from Mackie-style evidence, even if there isn't good propositional evidence in the community, and even if there isn't evidence in the broad Kretzmann sense. If it seems to me very strongly that the great things of the gospel are true, if upon reading the Scriptures I find myself convinced, and if after considerable reflection—on all the objections, for example—I still find myself convinced, how could I be properly blamed for believing as I do? Again, I could be wrong, deluded, a victim of wishful thinking, subject to some kind of cognitive disorder: nevertheless, there is no duty I am flouting. If the *de jure* question is whether the believer can be justified, or justified without evidence, the answer is still too easy: of course she can.

B. Variations on the Deontology

The above involved extensions of the *classical foundationalist* ingredient of the classical picture. Note that we can also ring the analogical changes on the deontological component, and we can mix and match the extensions in a dazzling variety of combinations. I can't possibly examine all these multifarious versions of evidentialism in all their

58. See above, footnote 38.
59. In *Our Knowledge of God: Essays on Natural and Philosophical Theology*, ed. Kelly Clark (Dordrecht: Kluwer, 1992).

permutations and combinations,[60] but I do wish to examine one particularly salient variety: *Alston* justification, which is *believing on the basis of a reliable ground or indicator*. Alston puts it as follows:

> to be justified in believing that p is to be in a *strong position* for realizing the epistemic aim of getting the truth. . . . I will begin by making the plausible assumption that to be in an epistemically strong position in believing that p is to have an adequate ground or basis for believing that p. Where the justification is mediate, this ground will consist in other things one knows or justifiably believes. Where it is immediate, it will consist typically of some experience. . . .[61]

A belief is justified, therefore, if and only if it is formed on the basis of an adequate ground. Clearly, Alston justification differs radically from the original deontological notion. That is because it doesn't contain so much as a hint of the deontology of the classical picture: "I reject all versions of a deontological concept [of justification] on the grounds that they either make unrealistic assumptions of the voluntary control of belief or they radically fail to provide what we expect of a concept of justification."[62] Well then, why does he call what he proposes 'justification'? Or better, why do I consider it under the rubric 'justification'? How is it an analogical extension of that notion? The answer is that what it requires—that the belief in question be based on a truth-conducive ground—is an analogical extension of what, according to the classical picture, *is* the relevant duty. There is a complex and interesting relation between justification taken deontologically, as in the classical picture, and Alston justification (justification as truth-conducive evidence or ground). The latter discards the deontology of the former, but takes the term 'justification' to denote the condition which, according to the former, is sufficient for satisfying the duty that, according to the former but not the latter, is in fact laid on us human beings. (I'll leave as homework the problem of figuring out how to state this more intelligibly.)

Now what sort of animal is a ground of belief? A *mediate* ground of a belief, according to Alston, is another *belief*, on the basis of which the belief in question is formed; an *immediate* ground of a belief is an *experience*, on the basis of which the belief is formed. And what is it for the ground of a belief to be *adequate*? "The ground of a belief will suffice to justify it only if it is sufficiently indicative of the truth of the belief. If the ground is to be adequate to the task, it must be the case that the belief is very probably true, given that it was formed on that basis."[63] The idea, therefore, is that the ground G of a belief B is ade-

---

60. For some of them, see WCD, chapter 1. I leave as homework the problem of showing that Christian belief can indeed be justified on these construals.
61. *Perceiving God* (Ithaca: Cornell University Press, 1991), p. 73.
62. Ibid.
63. Ibid., p. 75.

quate just if a certain conditional probability is high: the probability that B is true *given that* it has been formed on G. And here the probability in question is an *objective* probability[64] of some sort; if a belief B is justified, then it was formed on the basis of a ground G, such that the objective conditional probability of B on G ($P(B/G)$) is high. I form the belief that the largest oak in my backyard is now losing its leaves. I form this belief on the basis of experience of some kind—as Alston might state the matter, it seems to me that the tree is presenting itself to me as losing its leaves. Then that belief is justified if and only if it is objectively probable that the tree *is* losing its leaves, given that I undergo that experience. Putting these elements together, we can say that a belief B is justified—actually, *prima facie* justified—for S if and only if it is formed on the basis of a truth-conducive ground G—if and only if, that is, it is formed on the basis of some ground G, such that the objective probability that B is true, given that it has been formed on G, is high.

C. Is This the *de Jure* Question?

Have we found the (or a) relevant *de jure* question? Is the right question to ask the question whether Christian belief is *Alston* justified? More specifically, the question, for a given Christian belief B I hold—the belief, say, that in Christ, God was reconciling the world to himself—is whether there is some truth-conducive ground G such that I hold the belief in question on the basis of that ground. But is this really a viable *de jure* question? I want to suggest that it is not. When we ask the *de jure* question about Christian belief, we are asking whether Christian belief is acceptable, OK, such that a sensible, intelligent, rational, informed person in something like our epistemic circumstances could or would hold such beliefs. The question as to whether such belief sometimes or typically has a truth-conducive *ground*, however, seems to be a very different question. I have two reasons for thinking so.

In the first place, several important sorts of beliefs—*a priori* belief and memory belief in particular—do not seem to *have* a ground in Alston's sense at all, but are nonetheless perfectly in order from an epistemic point of view. Consider memory. You remember what you had for lunch: lentil soup and a doughnut. This belief isn't based on propositional evidence. You don't infer it from other things you know or believe, such things, perhaps, as your knowledge that you always have a doughnut and lentil soup for lunch, or your knowledge that it is now shortly after lunchtime and there are doughnut crumbs on your desk and an empty plastic soup dish in your trash. So it doesn't have a mediate ground. But it also isn't based on an experience. At any rate, it is clear that memory beliefs are not based on anything like *sensuous* experience or phenomenal imagery.[65] There may *be* a bit of such imagery present (a fragmentary and partial image of a doughnut or a bowl, perhaps), but you certainly don't form the belief *on the basis of* that image. It is clear that you could remember without having that imagery—or, indeed, any other imagery; some people report that they have no phenomenal imagery associated with memory at all. So the imagery isn't necessary. It is also insufficient; you could also have that imagery without remembering. The reason is that the imagery that goes with *imagining* that you had a doughnut and lentil soup for lunch, or *entertaining the proposition* that you did, is indistinguishable (at least in my own case) from the imagery that goes with *remembering* that you had a doughnut and lentil soup for lunch. And even if you do have fairly explicit phenomenal imagery in connection with this memory, you surely don't know that it was *lentil* soup on the basis of that imagery; the image isn't nearly clear, detailed, and explicit enough to enable you to distinguish it from, for example, imagery of pea soup, or bean soup, or many other kinds of soup.[66]

Accordingly, it isn't that you know it was lentil soup *on the basis of* this experience; you don't form the belief that it was lentil soup with that experience as ground. (The image seems to be more like a disposable decoration.) Instead, you simply remember, simply form that belief. Or, perhaps more accurately, that belief is formed in you: you don't yourself, so to speak, take much of a hand in forming it.

The same goes (though perhaps more controversially) for *a priori* belief.[67] I believe the proposition *Necessarily, if all men are mortal and Socrates is a man, then Socrates is mortal*. Now there is, indeed, a sort of imagery connected with this belief when I entertain it—perhaps something like a fragmentary image of the relevant English sentence written on a blackboard as in a logic class. But surely the belief isn't formed on the *basis* of that imagery; that imagery isn't anything like a *ground* for it; it doesn't stand to that imagery in anything like the way in which my belief that the snow in my backyard is melting stands to the visual imagery I now enjoy. Indeed, the imagery accompanying that proposition is the same, so far as I can tell, as that which accompanies entertaining *Necessarily, if all men are mortal and Socrates is mortal, then Socrates is a man*.

So many memory and *a priori* beliefs are not formed on the basis of a ground in Alston's sense, either mediate or immediate. But of course many memory and *a priori* beliefs are eminently sensible, reasonable, rational, and the like. It therefore follows that a belief need

65. See WPF, pp. 58ff.
66. See WPF, pp. 57ff.
67. See WPF, pp. 104ff.

not have a truth-conducive ground to be reasonable, sensible, or rational.

Second, there are also beliefs that *do* have a truth-conducive ground (explained as Alston explains it) but are nonetheless not sensible or reasonable. A belief is based on an adequate ground, says Alston, if and only if it is based on a ground such that it is objectively probable that it is true, given that it is based on that ground. Note that (if objective probability conforms to the probability calculus) a *necessary* truth will have an objective probability of 1 on any other proposition whatever. Consider therefore the proposition *29 × 38 = 1102*: the probability of this proposition is 1 on any condition whatever. Any belief in this proposition on *any* ground, therefore, is automatically a belief on the basis of an adequate ground. More generally, any grounded belief in any necessary proposition *p* is justified on this account; for the objective conditional probability that *p* on any proposition will be 1. So suppose I am extraordinarily gullible when it comes to set theory and believe, say, Cantor's Theorem (according to which the cardinality of any set is always less than that of its power set), not because I have understood a proof or been told by someone competent that it is true, but just because I picked up a comic book on the sidewalk and found therein a character who claims it is his favorite theorem. Then this belief of mine has a truth-conducive ground, but isn't rational or reasonable.

Further and closer to current concerns, according to the bulk of the theistic tradition, God is a necessary being who has his most important attributes essentially: there is no possible world in which he does not exist, and none in which he lacks such attributes as omniscience, goodness, love, and the like. If this is true, then the proposition that there is such a being as God (or that he is omniscient, or loving) will have an unconditional objective probability of 1, and consequently an objective conditional probability of 1 on any other proposition. Hence for any ground at all, the probability that one of those beliefs is true, given that it is formed on the basis of that ground, is 1. In asking the *de jure* question about belief in God, however, we presumably do not mean to ask a question to which an affirmative answer follows just from the fact that God is a necessary being who has his primary attributes essentially. Suppose God is indeed a necessary being; then if I believe in God just to please my friends, or because I am brainwashed or hypnotized, or because I am part of an evil social system, I will be justified in the Alston sense. If so, however, it is too easy to achieve justification in this sense.

No doubt there are variations on Alston justification, and in a complete treatment we should have to deal with them. But *vita brevis est*, even if *philosophia longa est*. I tentatively conclude, therefore, that the *de jure* question is not the question of whether Christian belief is Alston justified. The *de jure* question is still elusive.

4

Rationality

We have seen that the relevant *de jure* question—the question whether Christian belief is justified, or rational, or reasonable, or intellectually respectable—can't be the question of justification strictly so called. That is, it can't be the Lockean, deontological question whether Christian believers are or can be epistemically responsible, within their epistemic rights, flouting no epistemic duties, in believing as they do. That question, we saw, is much too easy to answer: obviously, a believer—even an intelligent, well-educated, contemporary believer who has heard and considered all the objections—can be justified in this original sense. We saw also that there are analogically extended senses of the term 'justification'; but none of them is such that it is clear that a Christian believer can't be justified, in that sense, in holding Christian belief. Believers may be *mistaken*; they may be *deluded*; they may be *foolish*; they may be insufficiently *critical* (in a way that doesn't involve blameworthiness); but there is no reason to think either that they are inevitably derelict in their epistemic duties or that they are unjustified in one of those analogical extensions of the term.

I. SOME ASSORTED VERSIONS OF RATIONALITY

Of course there are other questions lurking in the nearby bushes, other ways to construe the *de jure* question. In particular, we can ask whether the believer is *rational* in believing as she does. Many who put the *de jure* question or urge a *de jure* criticism put it in terms of rationality, not justification. (More often, they put it *both* ways, sometimes just using the one as a synonym for the other.) So suppose we look into this matter: could it be that the appropriate *de jure* question is whether Christian belief (with or without evidence) is rational?

But what is it for a belief to be *rational*? The first thing to note is that this term is multifarious, indeed, polyphonous, as our postmodern compatriots like to say. There are several importantly different ideas of rationality floating around, and the first thing we have to do is to specify the concept of rationality involved in our question. What *are* the main conceptions of rationality? In *Warrant: The Current Debate* (hereafter WCD), I specified some different but analogically related senses of the term. The basic sense is (1) Aristotelian rationality, the sense in which, as Aristotle said, "Man is a rational animal." Related to it in various ways are (2) rationality as proper function; (3) rationality as within or conforming to the deliverances of reason; (4) means-ends rationality, where the question is whether a particular means someone chooses is, in fact, a good means to her ends; and (5) deontological rationality. We must look briefly at these; after that, we shall turn at slightly greater length to William Alston's *practical* rationality. Our task will be lightened, however, by the fact that we have already dealt with (5) in the last chapter.[1]

A. Aristotelian Rationality

According to Aristotle, man is a rational animal. Fair enough—on this point as on others, Aristotle is no doubt right: but what specifically did he have in mind? Here the term 'rational' apparently points to or expresses a property that distinguishes human beings from other animals. As Aristotle saw it, this property is the possession of *ratio*, the power of reason. The idea is that human beings, unlike at least some other animals, have concepts and can hold beliefs; they can reason, reflect, and think about things, even things far removed in space or time; human beings are (or, at any rate, can be) *knowers*. This is what it is to be a rational creature; and this is what Aristotle saw as distinctive about human beings. Of course rational powers can come in degrees. We ordinarily think of ourselves (no doubt in a burst of specific chauvinism) as much more talented, along these lines, than other terrestrial animals, although perhaps we are prepared to concede that some of them display at least rudimentary powers of reason. We also realize there may be other creatures, perhaps in other parts of the universe, that put us absolutely in the shade when it comes to intellectual power. Now is the *de jure* question the question whether a creature rational in this sense can accept Christian belief? Presumably not: given the many millions of rational animals who *do* accept it, that question, like the question of justification, has much too easy an answer.

---

1. Deontological rationality is really *justification*; see above, chapter 3, p. 87. It is worth noting the analogical connection between justification and rationality.

B. Rationality as Proper Function

If we agree that rational creatures do and therefore can accept Christian belief, we might ask whether it is only *malfunctioning* rational creatures that do so, creatures whose rational faculties are in some way dysfunctional. A person who suffers from pathological confusion, or flight of ideas, or the manic stage of bipolar disorder, or delusions (perhaps thinking the Martians are out to get him) is said to be irrational. Here the problem is dysfunction, malfunction of the rational faculties. The paranoid doesn't form beliefs in the way a normal, properly functioning human being does; some part of the cognitive apparatus fails to function properly. Pathologically confused people may not know what day it is or where they live. Such dysfunction can be long-term or episodic; if it is the latter, then after the episode is over, we say rationality is *restored*. This sense of rationality, therefore, has to do with *proper function*, the absence of dysfunction or pathology: you are rational if not subject to such pathology. Correlatively, irrationality, in this sense, is a matter of malfunction of (some of) the rational faculties, the faculties by virtue of which we are rational animals. So there is an analogical connection between Aristotelian rationality and rationality construed as proper function.

We must distinguish two forms of rationality as proper function. On the one hand, there is what we might call *internal* rationality. We can initially characterize internal rationality as a matter of proper function of all belief-producing processes 'downstream from experience'. How can we explain this metaphor? We may begin by noting that experience comes in several varieties. First, there is *sensuous imagery*, the kind of experience you have most prominently in vision but in hearing, smelling, tasting, and touching as well. To use Roderick Chisholm's terminology, in this kind of experience one is *appeared to* in such and such a way. Sensuous imagery plays an enormously significant role in perception; perceptual beliefs are formed *in response to* sensuous imagery and *on the basis of* such imagery.

Still, this isn't the only kind of experience that goes with belief formation. In chapter 3 (p. 106) and in *Warrant and Proper Function* (188–93, hereafter WPF), I pointed out that the formation of *memory* beliefs is often unaccompanied by phenomenal experience, or else accompanied only by fragmentary, fleeting, indistinct, hard-to-focus sensuous imagery. You remember that you went to a party in Novosibirsk; there is a bit of imagery, all right, although it is fleeting, partial, indistinct, and such that when you try to focus your attention on it, it disappears. But there is another kind of experience present: the belief that it was *Novosibirsk* (and not, say, Cleveland) seems *right*, *acceptable*, *natural*; it forces itself upon you; it seems somehow inevitable (the right words are hard to find). The belief *feels* right, acceptable, and natural; it feels different from what you think is a false belief. The same goes for *a priori* belief. You believe that no dogs are sets. This belief, too, involves little by way of sensuous imagery. When you consider that proposition, perhaps it is as if you catch a momentary and fleeting glimpse of part of a sentence expressing the proposition, or perhaps a fragmentary glimpse of a dog, or perhaps of a dog enclosed within braces; this imagery seems unimportant, however, more like mere decoration than something on the basis of which the belief in question is formed. And here, too, there is also this other sort of experience: it's just seeming *true* and indeed *necessarily* true that no dogs are sets. Thinking about this proposition *feels* different from thinking about the proposition that some dogs (your dog Tietje, for example) *are* sets. Still a third kind of example, also discussed in more detail in WPF (48ff.): the knowledge that it is *you* (as opposed to someone else) who is now perceiving the page in front of you. This too is not a matter of sensuous imagery: it is not on the basis of sensuous imagery that you believe it is *you* who are perceiving that page, rather than your cousin in Cleveland. Here too there is that *other* sort of phenomenal experience, that feeling that the proposition in question is the *right* one.

Suppose we call this second kind of phenomenal experience *doxastic* experience because it always goes with the formation of belief.[2] Internal rationality includes, in the first place, forming or holding the appropriate beliefs in response to experience, including both phenomenal imagery and doxastic experience. With respect to the first, I will form beliefs appropriate to the phenomenal imagery I enjoy: for example, when appeared to in the way that goes with seeing a gray elephant, I will not form the belief that I am perceiving an orange flamingo. That sort of response is precluded by internal rationality. But perhaps the second—forming the right beliefs in response to doxastic experience—is more interesting. A pathological skeptic, for example, might have the same sort of doxastic experience as the rest of us, but still be unable to form the appropriate beliefs. I might be appeared to in the way that goes with seeing that Peter is running toward me; out of pathological caution, however, I am unable to believe that he is really running toward me (after all, it could be a cunningly contrived robot, or I could be dreaming, or a brain in a vat, or a victim of some other kind of illusion; and can I be certain that it is really *me* that he is running toward?). This sort of response is also precluded by internal rationality. By contrast, René Descartes notes that there are people "whose cerebella are so troubled and clouded by the violent vapours of black bile, that they . . . imagine

2. From δοξα, the Greek word for belief. In WPF I called this kind of experience 'impulsional evidence'.

that they have an earthenware head or are nothing but pumpkins or are made of glass."[3] That sort of response is *not* (necessarily) precluded by internal rationality. Perhaps these madmen are subjected to overwhelming doxastic experience here. Perhaps this proposition —that their heads are made of glass—seems utterly obvious to them, as obvious as that $3 + 1 = 4$. Then the problem lies with this *seeming*, with their having this kind of doxastic experience. *Given* this doxastic experience, what proper function requires (all else being equal) is forming this belief; and that they do. They display *external* irrationality, but not internal irrationality.

There is more that internal rationality requires; we can deal with it briefly. A person is internally rational only if her beliefs are *coherent*, or at any rate are sufficiently coherent to satisfy proper function. If she is internally rational, then if she believes that her head is made of earthenware, she will not also believe that it is made of flesh and blood—or at least won't believe these both within the confines of the same thought, so to speak. Much more ought to be said about the coherence required by proper function; it will have to await another occasion. Further, an internally rational person will draw the right inferences when the occasion arises: for example, someone who is internally rational but believes that her head is made of earthenware will probably believe that playing football (at any rate without a really good helmet) is very dangerous. Still further, given the beliefs she has, she will make the right decisions with respect to her courses of action—that is, the decisions required by proper function. Given that you *do* believe you are made of glass, for example, the rational thing to do is to avoid bumps. And finally, if she is internally rational, she will do what proper function requires with respect to such things as preferring to believe what is true, looking for further evidence when that is appropriate, and in general being epistemically responsible.

And now that we have internal rationality in hand, external rationality is easy to explain. It requires, first, proper function with respect to the formation of the sensuous experience on which perceptual belief is based. And it consists second in the formation of the right kind of doxastic experience—that is, the sort of doxastic experience required by proper function.

I suppose it would be widely conceded that Christian belief can be held by people whose rational faculties are not malfunctioning, or at any rate not malfunctioning in a way that involves clinical psychoses.[4] The fact is many Christian believers are able to hold jobs,

---

3. *Meditations*, Meditation I.
4. Although Richard Rorty somewhere suggests that in the new liberal society, those who think there is such a thing as the chief end of man will have to be consid-

some even as academics. (Of course, you may think this latter guarantees little by way of cognitive proper function.) So presumably the *de jure* question is also not the question of whether Christian belief can be held by people whose cognitive or rational faculties are functioning properly, at least in this clinical sense. But this by no means settles the issue; there are subtler forms of cognitive malfunction, and impedance of cognitive proper function. As a matter of fact, the (or a) sensible version of the *de jure* question does lie in the neighborhood of one of these subtler forms. We'll return to the notion of proper function in more depth and detail in the next chapter, where we explore the notion of warrant. In the meantime, however, suppose we turn to still another kind of rationality.

C. The Deliverances of Reason

First, what *are* the deliverances of reason? Here we have to take the term 'reason' a bit more narrowly than we did in thinking about Aristotelian rationality. Among the things we know, some are *self-evident*. It isn't entirely easy to see what it is for a proposition to be self-evident;[5] the rough idea, however, is that a proposition is self-evident if it is so utterly obvious that we can't even understand it without seeing that it is true. Examples would be propositions like *7 + 5 = 12*; *if all men are mortal and Socrates is a man, then Socrates is mortal*; and *if Tom is taller than Sam, and Sam is taller than George, then Tom is taller than George*. And the idea is that reason, taken in this narrower sense, is the faculty or power whereby we see the truth of self-evident propositions. Of course it is also reason whereby we see that one proposition entails or implies another: if I learn from the bartender that everyone at the party was drunk, and from you that Paul was at the party, I can conclude that Paul was drunk. The deliverances of reason, therefore, will be self-evident propositions, together with propositions that are self-evident consequences of deliverances of reason. (We might put this by saying that self-evidence is closed under self-evident consequence.) And then we might say that a proposition is *rational* if it is among the deliverances of reason, and *irrational* if its *denial* is among the deliverances of reason. Note that many propositions—for example, the proposition that Caesar crossed the Rubicon—will then be neither rational nor irrational: neither

---

ered insane. See also Daniel Dennett, *Darwin's Dangerous Idea* (New York: Simon and Schuster, 1995), p. 516, where he suggests that perhaps Baptists should be kept in zoos and preserved as interesting cultural relics, but only if they refrain from telling their children such patent untruths as that "'man' is not a product of evolution by natural selection" (519).

5. See WPF, pp. 108ff.

they nor their denials are among the deliverances of reason.[6] And again, the connection with Aristotelian rationality is easy to see: reason taken in this narrow sense is one of the faculties the possession of which distinguishes us from other animals, and when it is functioning properly, what it yields are the deliverances of reason.

There is a problem here. The deliverances of reason obviously come in degrees: some seem much more compelling than others, and only some have the overwhelmingly obvious nature of the propositions mentioned above. So, for example, it is obvious, I think, that there aren't any things that do not exist, although this has been disputed, and although it is not as obvious as the propositions mentioned in the above paragraph. Another example is serious actualism: the proposition that an object has properties only in worlds in which it exists.[7] This proposition has intuitive warrant, intuitive support, and can be deduced from actualism, together with other obvious principles; but it isn't just self-evident. You can understand it and nevertheless reject it, and indeed some philosophers do exactly that.[8] Should we admit these propositions that have at least some intuitive warrant to the august company of deliverances of reason, even if they are not self-evident? Indeed we should; if we do, however, we can no longer say that the deliverances of reason are closed under self-evident entailment. That is because of Russell-like paradoxes. It is a deliverance of reason that there are properties, that there is such a property as self-exemplification, and that every property has a complement, so that there is also such a property as non-self-exemplification. The rest of the sad story is well known.

Is Christian belief rational in this sense? No; the central truths of Christianity are certainly not self-evident, nor, so far as anyone can see, are they such that they can be deduced from what is self-evident. Of course, that is nothing whatever against Christian belief; the same holds for, for example, what we are taught by historians, physicists, and evolutionary biologists. So the *de jure* question can't be the question whether Christian belief is rational in this sense. That is because a negative answer to the question is supposed to be a serious criticism of Christian belief; but it is no criticism of Christian belief (or the theory of evolution, or the belief that you live in Cleveland) that it is not a deliverance of reason in this sense.

---

6. Alternatively, we might say that a proposition is irrational if its *denial* is among the deliverances of reason, and rational if it is not irrational: then, of course, every proposition will be either rational or irrational.

7. See "Replies," in *Alvin Plantinga*, ed. James Tomberlin and Peter van Inwagen (Dordrecht: D. Reidel, 1985), pp. 316ff.

8. See John Pollock, "Plantinga on Possible Worlds," in *Alvin Plantinga*, pp. 126ff., and also Nathan Salmon, "Nonexistence," *Noûs* (September 1998), p. 290.

Well, is Christian belief *irrational*, in this sense? That is, are the denials of some of the propositions falling within Christian belief either self-evident or deducible from propositions that are self-evident? Could *that* be the *de jure* question? If Christian beliefs were irrational in this sense, that would certainly be something against them. Some have certainly argued that characteristic Christian belief is inconsistent. For example, it has often been claimed that the existence of God is incompatible with the existence of evil; Christian doctrine, however, embraces both. I believe it is clear, however, that there is no inconsistency here;[9] in fact those contemporaries who press the problem of evil against Christian or theistic belief no longer make that claim of inconsistency.

Some atheologians have also urged that certain Christian doctrines (e.g., the doctrine of the trinity or the doctrine of the incarnation) are self-contradictory and hence inconsistent with the deliverances of reason. But these claims are at best inconclusive; everything depends on which precise formulation of these doctrines we consider. Some of these formulations may perhaps be inconsistent, although it is very hard to find any formulations of these doctrines that are both clearly inconsistent and also widely accepted. (In particular, the formulations to be found in the great creeds of the Christian church are not clearly inconsistent.) Other formulations clearly are not inconsistent. Further, Christians who come to realize that they have accepted an inconsistent version of one of these doctrines can easily replace that version by one that is not inconsistent. So if this were the *de jure* question, then even if some formulations of central Christian doctrine are contrary to the deliverances of reason, the unhappy condition of believing such a thing could be easily avoided: just move to a formulation that is not inconsistent. But those who urge the *de jure* question with respect to Christian belief do not, presumably, mean to claim just that Christian belief is inconsistent: even if it is perfectly consistent, they think, there is still something seriously wrong with it. We can't mollify them merely by pointing out that there are consistent versions of Christian belief. This, too, it seems, is not the *de jure* question.

D. Means-End Rationality

What about means-end rationality, what our continental cousins sometimes call *Zweckrationalität*? This is the sort of rationality displayed by the actions of someone who aims to achieve a certain goal

---

9. See chapter 9 of my *The Nature of Necessity* (Oxford: Oxford University Press, 1974).

and chooses means that are effective for attaining that goal. Perhaps, more exactly, we should say that this kind of rationality characterizes the actions of a rational creature—one rational in the Aristotelian and proper function sense—who is aiming to achieve a certain goal; so once again we see the connection with the basic Aristotelian sense. Means-end rationality is a matter of knowing how to get what you want; we might think of it as the cunning of reason.[10] If I want to get to Los Angeles as quickly as possible, it would be irrational to take the bus or ride my bicycle: the rational thing to do would be to take the plane.

Is the *de jure* question about *this* kind of rationality? Means-end rationality is a property of actions; hence it isn't initially obvious that belief is the sort of thing that *can* be rational and irrational in this sense, because it isn't initially obvious that beliefs are actions. In fact it seems initially obvious that beliefs (believings) are *not* actions. You don't ordinarily form a given belief because you think holding that belief would be a good means to some end or other. Still, suppose we did think of belief as a sort of action (perhaps in a limiting sense); then presumably the end in view would be believing or knowing the truth. And then Christian belief would be rational in this sense if and only if a rational person, one whose cognitive faculties were functioning properly, would or could choose this means to the end of believing the truth. But there is something very peculiar about this suggestion. What you rationally choose as a means to an end depends on what you believe—for example, on what you believe about the likelihood that a given course of action will yield the result you are aiming at. But what if your aim is to believe truth? Then (pretending for the moment that what you believe is within your power in the appropriate way) you will, of course, believe a proposition if you think it is true: for if it is true, then, naturally enough, believing it is a good way to believe truth. So taking the action of believing Christian teaching will be rational for you, if, in fact, you do believe Christian teaching. (This oddness brings out the way in which belief really isn't action or, if it is, at least isn't much like other forms of action.) The real question, then, will be whether a rational person can believe the claims of Christianity, whether a rational person can accept Christian belief. And that means that the question whether Christian belief is means-end rational really reduces to the question whether it is rational in some other sense: the Aristotelian sense or, more likely, the proper function sense. So we don't have here an independent sense of rationality; because we have already dealt with that sense, what we really see is that the *de jure* question can't be this question of means-end rationality either.

10. Of course there are many variations on this notion of rationality. The ratio-

II. ALSTONIAN PRACTICAL RATIONALITY

None of the varieties of rationality I have so far mentioned offers the resources for a sensible *de jure* question. In his magisterial book, *Perceiving God,*[11] William Alston proposes still another way to construe rationality (and the *de jure* question). Given the power and depth of Alston's account, this one merits a more careful look.

A. The Initial Question

The conclusion of Alston's book is really that it is *rational—practically* rational, as he says—for at least many of us to engage in what he calls 'Christian Mystical Practice' (CMP, for short): the practice of forming beliefs about God (or the Ultimate) on the basis of experience of God, or more exactly (putative) *perception* of God (or the Ultimate):

> My main thesis in this chapter, and indeed in the whole book, is that CMP is *rationally engaged in* [my emphasis] since it is a socially established doxastic practice that is not demonstrably unreliable or otherwise disqualified for rational acceptance. (194)

The sort of rationality at issue here is 'practical' rationality; we shall therefore consider whether the *de jure* question might be the question whether Christian belief is practically rational in his sense. Now Alston himself does not really address specifically Christian belief—trinity, incarnation, atonement, and resurrection, for example. He is instead concerned with the sorts of beliefs that are produced by (putative) perception of God. These include such beliefs as that God is glorious, delightful, holy, majestic, all-powerful, loving, and the like, as well as such beliefs as that he is strengthening, supporting or comforting one. These are not specifically Christian beliefs, and, of course, our *de jure* question is about the rationality of specifically Christian beliefs. Nevertheless, perceptual beliefs about God could contribute support to Christian beliefs about God; in any event, it will be of interest to ask whether Christian belief is rational in the sense of rationality Alston identifies, even if he himself does not address that issue. Further, the question whether Christian belief is practically rational seems to me at any rate *closer* to the *de jure* question we seek than the candidates we have already canvassed. But what is this 'practical rationality'? How does Alston understand this protean notion, and how does he argue for the practical rationality of CMP and the beliefs it produces?

---

nal action might be the one that would *in fact* lead to the achievement of your goal, or the one you *think* would, or the one you *would* think would, if your cognitive faculties were functioning properly, or the one you would think would if your cognitive faculties were functioning properly and you reflected long enough, or the one you would think would if . . . and you were sufficiently acute, or . . . and you were not distracted by lust, greed, or ambition, and so on.

11. Ithaca: Cornell University Press, 1991. Subsequent page references will be to this book.

B. Doxastic Practices

Here we need a bit of stage setting. A distinctive feature of Alston's entire epistemology is its emphasis upon *social doxastic practices*—socially established ways of forming belief. (It makes a certain rough sense to think of Alston as judiciously blending Reid with Wittgenstein.[12]) For example, there is sense perception (hereafter SP), the social practice of forming beliefs on the basis of perception of objects in our environment; there is also the practice of forming beliefs by way of reasoning, both deductive and nondeductive, as well as the practice of forming beliefs on the basis of memory. Together these three form what Alston calls "the standard package," perhaps because they are shared by all properly functioning human beings. Further, there is the practice of attributing beliefs, desires, pains and pleasures, affective states, spiritual gifts, and the like to our fellow human beings. Thomas Reid calls this practice (or, rather, the faculty or power that underlies it) 'sympathy'; we may think of sympathy as part of SP or, if we prefer, as a practice intimately linked with SP, but nonetheless separate and semiautonomous. (If we think of it the latter way, we should consider it part of the standard package.)

These are *doxastic* practices: they issue in the formation of beliefs. They are also *social* practices in that they contain a considerable component contributed by our social environment. SP, for example, involves a substantial social component in that what we learn from others by way of teaching and testimony becomes part of the practice. For example, what we learn from others is involved in the society of checks and tests whereby we determine whether a putative perception is a real perception; I had to learn from others (parents, for example) what it *is* that I perceive when I perceive a tree or house or star. The contributions of nature and nurture may vary over these different practices; the contribution of nurture is perhaps maximal with respect to SP and perhaps minimal with respect to our grasp of elementary arithmetic and logic.

In addition to these universally shared practices, there is also what Alston calls MP, 'mystical practice', the practice whereby many but not all of us form beliefs about God (or the Ultimate) on the basis of experience or perception of God (or the Ultimate). CMP is a specific variant of mystical practice, where the beliefs formed are the specifically Christian beliefs held by Christians of all stripes in many different parts of the world and at all times since the beginning of the Christian era.

C. Epistemic Circularity

Clearly, we can raise many questions about these practices: in particular, we can ask whether they are reliable. We can also ask whether we can *show* that they are reliable. If we ask this latter question about SP, then we are asking whether we can show or successfully argue that the beliefs

---

12. See Alston's "A Doxastic Practice Approach to Epistemology," *Knowledge and Skepticism,* ed. M. Clay and K. Lehrer (Boulder, Colo.: Westview Press, 1988).

formed in this practice are for the most part true or, at any rate, *close* to the truth, or *likely* to be true or close to the truth. Our main target, of course, is CMP; but because Alston thinks of CMP as essentially involving *perception* of God, he attacks the question of the reliability of CMP in tandem with the counterpart question about SP.

Alston concedes that we can't give a good noncircular argument for the claim that CMP is in fact reliable. He pays the same compliment to SP, however: we can't give a good noncircular argument for *its* reliability either. So that distressing fact about CMP is balanced by a complementary distressing fact about SP. The problem with arguments for the reliability of SP is typically what he calls *epistemic circularity*, a malady from which an argument for the reliability of a faculty or source of belief suffers when one of its premises is such that my acceptance of that premise originates in the operation of the very faculty or source of belief in question. If you give an epistemically circular argument for the reliability of a faculty, then you rely on that very faculty for the truth of one of your premises. An obvious example would be arguing that your intuitive arithmetical faculties are reliable by pointing out that your arithmetic intuitions seem to you to be intuitively sound. A less obviously circular project would be that of trying to determine if human cognitive faculties (including your own) are reliable by doing some science: you find out what human beings think, and then check to see whether what they think is true. Clearly enough, this procedure is epistemically circular, for you rely on human cognitive faculties—yours—in finding out what human beings think and also checking to see if what they think is true. Alston detects many examples of epistemic circularity (more than you might have thought), some obvious and some not so obvious. I believe he succeeds in establishing the important conclusion that it is not possible to show in a noncircular fashion that SP is reliable—at any rate he gets as close to establishing this conclusion as philosophers ever get to establishing any important conclusion.[13]

So according to Alston, SP and CMP are in the same leaky epistemological boat. Indeed, the fact is, he argues, all of our basic doxastic practices are in the same epistemological boat; none of them can be shown in noncircular fashion to be reliable.

D. The Argument for Practical Rationality

The unhappy developments just explained, says Alston, present us with a "crisis of rationality" and a "desperate situation": "The course of the argument led us to the conclusion that with respect to even those sources of belief of which we are normally the most confident we have no sufficient noncircular reason for taking them to be reliable" (146). What are we to do? Well, we are obliged to settle for second best: although we can't show that any of these practices is *reliable*, perhaps we can show that *we* are rational—*practically* rational—to engage in them.

---

13. The argument is given at even greater depth and explicitness in his *The Reliability of Sense Perception* (Ithaca: Cornell University Press, 1993).

Alston offers two connected arguments for supposing that it is practically rational to engage in these practices. According to the first, in essence, it is perfectly sensible or rational to continue to form beliefs in the SP and CMP ways, because (1) those ways do not lead to massive inconsistencies, (2) there is no reason to think them unreliable, (3) we know of no alternative doxastic practices whose reliability we *could* demonstrate in an epistemically noncircular fashion, and (4) changing to some other practice would be massively difficult and disruptive. According to the second argument, any socially and psychologically established doxastic practice that meets certain other plausible conditions is *prima facie* rational (i.e., such that it is *prima facie* rational to engage in it); such a practice will be all-things-considered rational if, as far as we can see, there is no reason to abandon it. These two arguments are connected, as I shall argue below; it is only the second that he explicitly employs with respect to CMP.

Suppose we begin by examining the second argument; as we shall see, this argument leads back to the first. Here is how Alston puts the matter:

> My main thesis . . . is that CMP is rationally engaged in since it is a socially established doxastic practice that is not demonstrably unreliable or otherwise disqualified for rational acceptance. If CMP is, indeed, a socially established doxastic practice, it follows from the position defended in Chapter 4 that it is prima facie worthy of rational participation. And this means that it is prima facie rational to regard it as reliable, sufficiently reliable to be a source of prima facie justification of the beliefs it engenders. And if, furthermore, it is not discredited by being shown to be unreliable or deficient in some other way that will cancel its prima facie rationality, then we may conclude that it is unqualifiedly rational to regard it as sufficiently reliable to use in belief formation. (194)

> The basic contention is that it is prima facie rational to engage in CMP . . . because it is a socially established doxastic practice; and that it is unqualifiedly rational to engage in it . . . because we lack sufficient reason for regarding it as unreliable or otherwise disqualified for rational participation. (223)

The main premise of this argument, then, is:

> It is *prima facie* rational (practically rational) to engage in a socially established doxastic practice, and unqualifiedly rational (rational all things considered) to engage in a socially established practice that doesn't encounter severe internal or external incompatibilities.

And in chapters 5 through 7 Alston goes on to argue that CMP is indeed a socially established doxastic practice, and that it does not encounter severe internal or external incompatibilities.

E. Practical Rationality Initially Characterized

Turn now to the main premise. First, I don't know precisely how to state the second part, the part about 'rationality all things considered', but while this is mildly annoying, it isn't really serious, because I intend to comment only on the first part. How exactly are we to understand this proposition, and what is the sense of 'rational' in which it is *prima facie* rational to engage in a socially established doxastic practice? As to the second, we are talking about the rationality or lack thereof of *taking a course of action*, of *doing* something or other, of *acting* in a certain way. (That is why we're talking *practical* rationality.) Whether an action is rational for me will obviously have something to do with what it is I am *aiming at* in taking that action, what I am trying to accomplish, what my *purpose, end, goal* is. So the kind of rationality at issue is that *means-ends* rationality, that *Zweckrationalität* we came across above (p. 115). The rational action, for me, is the one that will contribute to the realization of my goal, or contribute more to it than any other action open to me. But is it the action that will *in fact* contribute to my goal that is rational for me, or the one *I believe* will so contribute? Presumably the second: I am not irrational, in taking a given line of action, if I make a perfectly sensible mistake about what the best means to my end is.[14] If I am thirsty and what I want is a drink of water, it will be rational for me to open the faucet and hold a glass under it; I believe that is a fine way to get a glass of water. It would be irrational for me, under these circumstances, to go (instead) for a walk in the desert; I know that water is hard to find in the desert. On the other hand, if I believed that the faucet isn't connected to any source of water, then the action of opening the faucet wouldn't be a rational way for me to get a drink; and if I believed the nearest water is in the Sonoran Desert just outside Tucson, the action of going for a walk in the desert would be rational.

Now the case under consideration, of course, is the case of those doxastic practices; we are to ask whether it is rational to form beliefs by engaging in SP, CMP, or both. Here our relevant aim or goal, says Alston, is that of getting in the right relation to the truth, achieving some appropriate balance between avoiding error and believing truth. And now the question for us is whether a rational way to try to achieve that goal is to form beliefs as we always have, by employing SP, CMP, or both. Of course, this question has about it a certain air of unreality. It is up to me whether I open the faucet to get a drink of water, but it isn't really up to me whether I will form beliefs in accord with SP. I don't have any choice in the matter. And that means that the question of the practical rationality of continuing in SP is a little peculiar. I might as well ask whether it is rational for me to continue to be such that the earth attracts my body with a force that is inversely proportional to the square of the distance between us: this really isn't up to me. The same goes with respect to my

14. As we saw above in footnote 10, there are important distinctions within this category.

major ways of forming belief: it isn't up to me whether I form beliefs in those ways. I can try as hard as I like, but (apart from such draconian measures as mind-altering drugs) I doubt that I could seriously alter my basic belief-forming proclivities. Offer me a million dollars to believe that I live in Wyoming or that I am really the president of the United States: I can strain my utmost, but I won't be able to collect.[15]

Alston is perfectly well aware of the problem here, and what he suggests is that the interesting question is whether it would be rational to continue to engage in the practice in question *if it were within my power to continue and within my power to refrain* (168). The question is what it *would* be rational for me to do, if I were in a certain position: a position in which one of the things I believe, and believe truly, is that it is within my power to continue to form beliefs in the ways I have (by using the standard package and CMP), and also within my power to refrain from forming beliefs in those ways—either forming no beliefs at all of those sorts, or perhaps using some quite different belief-forming practice.

F. The Original Position

Suppose (with an apologetic bow to John Rawls) we call this position the 'original position'. Our question, specified to the standard package, is something like this. Suppose I am in the original position: I know (or at any rate believe truly) that it is within my power to stop forming beliefs in the ordinary way, via SP, memory, and reasoning (the standard package). Perhaps I also know that it is within my power to choose some other way of forming belief. Then what would be the rational thing to do: continue to form beliefs as I have all along, try some other way, or give up on this whole belief-forming enterprise?

The answer, as we have seen, depends at least in part on my aims, ends, and goals. If my aim is psychological comfort, feeling really good about myself, perhaps I should choose some belief-forming mechanisms that lead me to think I am a really fine fellow. Perhaps I should choose a way that will bring it about that I believe I have just won the Nobel Prize in chemistry, heroically overcoming such serious obstacles as that I have no training in the subject and know next to nothing about it. Naturally I should carefully avoid any belief-forming practices on the basis of which I would come to see the true extent of my failures and ineptness, my sins and miseries, as the Heidelberg Catechism puts it. In the present context, of course, my aim, according to Alston, is not personal comfort, or happiness, or psychological well-being, but getting properly in touch with the truth.

The rational course depends on my aims and goals; it also depends on what I believe—that is, what I believe at the time I take the decision in question. If my aim is to feel good about myself, it would be irrational to choose belief-forming mechanisms that, as I believe, would lead to a

---

15. Well, perhaps I do have a *bit* more control over my belief-forming proclivities than over whether my body is attracted by the earth. The fact is there are rather standard ways in which I can influence, mold, or form my belief-producing tendencies.

proper knowledge of my sins and miseries. To make the rational choice, I must figure out which course is most likely to lead to the accomplishment of my goal(s), and then act on that belief by taking that course. And this leads to an important question about the main premise. As you recall, it begins thus: It is *prima facie* rational (practically rational) to engage in a socially established doxastic practice. . . . But why this emphasis on *socially established* doxastic practices? True, if in the original position I think socially established practices are *especially likely* to yield true beliefs, then the rational thing for me to do, in that position, is to choose socially established doxastic practices. But what if I *don't* think that? I unwisely read Nietzsche, becoming convinced that the common herd is commonly wrong; I develop a lordly Nietzschean disdain for the ways in which the generality of humankind form their belief. Then presumably the rational thing would be to choose practices that are *not* socially established. I should, instead, choose practices that are enjoyed only by the fortunate few whose Promethean efforts have taken them far beyond *hoi polloi*. Why is social establishment important or relevant? What counts, for practical rationality, is what I think will achieve my goal; in the original position, it may or may not be the case that I think socially established practices are especially likely to achieve my goal of believing the truth.

Here we see the connection between the first and second of Alston's arguments for the practical rationality of SP and CMP. The main premise of the second argument, we might say, takes it for granted that in the original position I believe that socially established practices *are* as likely to lead us to the right relationship to the truth as any alternative; and indeed I suppose most of us do in fact believe that. The main premise of the first argument is different; it is that I don't know that SP (or CMP) is subject to any massive unreliability, and I also don't know of any alternative practice I could adopt which is such that I could show with respect to it that it is reliable. In the original position (the first argument continues), I would have this belief (I would believe that I know of no better alternative practice); therefore, the rational thing to do is to stick with what I've got. (Or if that seems a bit strong, it is at any rate true that sticking with my present practices is *a* rational thing to do.) The first argument is the basic one; the second argument takes for granted the main premise of the first argument and then incorporates something else most of us are in fact inclined to believe, namely, that *socially established* doxastic practices have a good chance of being reliable, perhaps a better chance than idiosyncratic doxastic practices.

G. The Wide Original Position

These thoughts lead to a crucial question: precisely what *is* it that I believe in the original position? In particular, what do I believe *about the reliability of SP and CMP* in that position? Is the idea that my beliefs, in the original position, are as much as possible like the beliefs I do in fact have, given that (in that position) I know or truly believe that it is within my power to give up SP, CMP, or both? (Call this the wide original position.) Perhaps that is the way to think of the original position. But this doesn't take us very far. The fact is that I now believe that both SP and

CMP are reliable. Therefore, if my beliefs in the original position are the ones I do in fact have, the question as to the rational course is easily answered: obviously, I should continue to form beliefs in the way I have *been* forming them. My aim is to be in the right relationship to the truth; I propose to attain as good a mixture of achieving the truth and avoiding error as possible; but in fact I believe that SP and CMP offer a vastly better chance to achieve that goal than any alternative I can think of; therefore, the rational choice for me to make, obviously enough, is to continue both in SP and in CMP.

Here there is a strong odor of triviality. I do *in fact* think both SP and CMP are reliable; so if, in the original position, I have the beliefs about SP and CMP that in fact I *do* have, then in that position, naturally enough, the rational choice would be to continue with SP and CMP. Given what I do believe about them, that would be the rational thing to do. This conclusion, while no doubt true, is pretty weak tea. *Of course*, if I knew I could refrain from forming beliefs in the SP and CMP way, and also believed that those ways were reliable, more reliable than any alternative way open to me, I would choose to continue to form beliefs that way. True, but not very interesting: how would this fact show or tend to show that my SP and CMP beliefs are in fact rational, in some interesting sense? We are told that if we knew it was within our power to continue to form beliefs in this way, and also within our power to abstain from so doing, then if we believed that SP and CMP are reliable, the rational thing to do would be to choose to continue to form beliefs in those ways. No doubt: nothing of interest follows. The same would go for any beliefs I have, no matter how crazy. The same would go, for example, for the insane beliefs of Descartes's madmen, who believed that they themselves were gourds—zucchini, perhaps, or summer squash—and that their heads were made of pottery. If I really do believe that I am a summer squash, then the rational thing for me to do, if offered the chance, is to continue to form beliefs in a way that yields (as I see it) this true belief. Still, that doesn't show that this belief itself is rational. We haven't yet located the *de jure* question.

However we do have to consider another facet of the dialectical situation, one that so far I have been slighting: *I am aware, in the original position, of the fact that neither SP, nor CMP, nor any other major doxastic practice can be noncircularly shown to be reliable.* That, after all, is what, according to Alston, precipitated the crisis of rationality and called forth the question of rationality in the first place. It is after we realize *this*, he thinks, that we are in the desperate situation of which he speaks. So we must add that in the original position I am aware of the fact that we can't noncircularly establish that the practices in question are reliable. (We must also add, perhaps, that I have devoted some attention to this fact, have thought about it at least a bit; perhaps we should say that I am *acutely* aware of it.)

This changes very little. In the original position as now conceived (the wide original position), I know that it is within my power to withhold perceptual and Christian belief; I also know that it isn't possible to give a good noncircular argument for the reliability of these sources of belief; but otherwise my beliefs are as much as possible like they are in fact. And our question remains: what would be the rational thing to do: continue with SP and CMP, or stop forming beliefs in those ways? Again, however, the answer is too easy: *of course* the rational thing would be to continue with SP and CMP. Once more, this is because I am in fact convinced that these sources of belief are reliable. True enough: I realize that I can't give a good noncircular argument for their reliability, but this gives me no pause. I can't see that this puts us in a desperate situation or that it should lead to a crisis of rationality: for this situation is a necessary feature of *any* doxastic condition. Not even God himself, necessarily omniscient as he is, can give a noncircular argument for the reliability of his ways of forming beliefs.[16] God himself is trapped inside the circle of his own ideas. About all we can say about God's ways of forming beliefs is that it is necessary, in the broadly logical sense, that a proposition p is true if and only if God believes p.[17] Of course God knows that and knows, therefore, that all of his beliefs are true. However (naturally enough), he knows this only by virtue of relying on his ways of forming beliefs. If, *per impossible*, he became a bit apprehensive about the reliability of those ways of forming beliefs, he would be in the same boat as we are about that question. He couldn't give an epistemically noncircular argument for the reliability of his ways of forming beliefs; for the beliefs constituting the premises of any such argument would themselves have been formed in those ways. But any epistemic debility that afflicts a necessarily omniscient being is hardly worth worrying about.

In the wide original position, therefore, I would be convinced that SP and CMP are reliable sources of belief, despite the fact that I realize it isn't possible to give a good noncircular argument for their reliability; hence, in the wide original position, the rational thing to do, obviously, would be to continue with them. We are still mired in triviality. We still don't have either the *de jure* question or the original position quite right. The problem is that if, in the original position, we have the beliefs we *actually* have with respect to SP and CMP, then it is trivially obvious that the rational decision would be to continue to form beliefs in those ways. Unfortunately, the fact that this is the rational decision, given those beliefs, does nothing to show that the beliefs we form on the basis of SP and CMP are rational in any interesting sense. In particular, the atheologian who raises the *de jure* question with respect to Christian belief will not be mollified if told that it would be rational, given that you thought CMP reliable, to decide to continue to form beliefs in the CMP way.

16. Here I assume what Alston disputes: that God has beliefs. (Of course, on Alston's view, there would be something *like* beliefs in God.) But this is really irrelevant to the point I make here, which is that it is a necessary truth that no *doxastic* agent, no matter how exalted, could give a good, epistemically noncircular argument for the reliability of his doxastic faculties.

17. See my "Divine Knowledge," in *Christian Perspectives on Religious Knowledge*, ed. C. Stephen Evans and Merold Westphal (Grand Rapids: Eerdmans, 1993).

H. A Narrow Original Position?

In any event, there would be something very peculiar about supposing that the original position includes the beliefs I actually have about the reliability of SP and CMP (as well as the beliefs I actually form on the basis of those practices). The whole question of the rationality or sensibleness of CMP and SP arises, after all, because we realize we can't successfully argue that those sources of belief are reliable. (It is this realization that precipitates the "crisis of rationality.") We need a term for those beliefs which are such that we can't successfully argue that the sources that produce them are reliable: say that such beliefs are *uncredentialed.* Then the crisis of rationality, with respect to SP and CMP beliefs, arises because we realize that they are uncredentialed. What to do? Alston suggests that at any rate we can argue that it is *practically* rational to form belief in the CMP and SP ways. That will give us *something*, even if it is settling for second best. So the idea is to show that there is something rational or reasonable about beliefs formed the SP and CMP ways, by showing that it would be rational to choose to form beliefs that way in the original position. But then presumably there would be something at best very peculiar about relying on the belief that CMP and SP are reliable; that belief itself, of course, is uncredentialed.

And, in fact, Alston's idea, in *Perceiving God*, is that these beliefs are *not* to be included in the original position:

> But I was also thinking of this subject [the person in the original position] as realizing that s/he is unable to show that any of these practices are reliable, and believing that this implies that s/he is unable to use beliefs in that reliability, or beliefs that presuppose that reliability, to determine the most rational course to take *vis-à-vis* belief formation.[18]

The suggestion is, I think, that in the original position we *bracket* our confidence in the practices in question; better, we simply don't *have* any beliefs of this sort in that position. In making this decision, we languish (or flourish) behind a veil of ignorance. This is a *narrow original position.* We are to engage in the following thought experiment: try to see what it would be rational to do if you didn't already believe in the reliability of SP or CMP, knew that there are no good noncircular arguments for their reliability, and (correctly) believed that it is up to you whether you engage in those practices: under those conditions, would it be rational to continue in forming beliefs the SP or CMP way? The idea here seems to be that the original position wouldn't include the belief that SP or CMP is reliable, or even any of the beliefs formed on the basis of SP and CMP; for presumably *those* beliefs presuppose the reliability of SP and CMP (at least if I understand what Alston means here by 'presuppose').[19]

---

18. Alston's reply to comments on *Perceiving God* at a meeting of the Society of Christian Philosophers (concurrent with the meeting of the Eastern Division of the American Philosophical Association) in Atlanta, December, 1993 (a published version can be found in *The Journal of Philosophical Research* 20 (1995), pp. 67ff.

19. Another reason for supposing SP and CMP beliefs are not to be included in

Well then, what beliefs *are* included in this narrow original position? Which of my beliefs could I sensibly use, in coming to a decision as to whether to continue with CMP, SP, or both? Alston holds, of course, that I can properly use the premises of his arguments for the practical rationality of CMP and SP; these are included in the original position. As you recall, the premises of the first argument include something like

(1) SP and CMP do not lead to massive inconsistencies; there is no reason to think them unreliable; we know of no alternative doxastic practices whose reliability we *could* demonstrate in an epistemically noncircular fashion; and it would be disruptive to stop forming belief in these ways;

the premises of the second include

(2) SP and CMP are socially established practices that are not demonstrably unreliable or otherwise disqualified; and it would be disruptive to stop forming belief in these ways.

Here (1) would be teamed with another premise according to which it is practically rational to decide to continue a practice that meets the conditions (1) says SP and CMP meet; there would be a similar premise to go with (2). And Alston's idea is that at any rate we can use *these* premises in coming to a decision as to whether to continue in SP and CMP. So even though the original position is narrow, it would still include the premises of his arguments.

But why so? Why would it be appropriate to rely on these premises, in the original position? The problem with relying on the beliefs that CMP and SP are reliable and on the beliefs that are formed by way of CMP and SP, of course, is that it is these very beliefs that are uncredentialed. Doesn't the same go, however, for the doxastic practices that yield (1) and (2)? Can we do any better with respect to them? For example, both (1) and (2) include the belief that *we have been engaging in CMP and SP*, forming beliefs in the CMP and SP ways. But how do I know that *we* have been doing this for some time? Presumably, it is only by way, in part, of perception itself: I perceive other people (or, to be really finicky, their bodies), and that perception is necessary to my knowledge that they use CMP, SP, or both. But perceptual beliefs are also uncredentialed: so these beliefs of mine are uncredentialed.[20] And how do I know that we *have* been doing this for some time? Presumably by way of mem-

---

the narrow original position: if they were, then, of course, in that position we would think them *true*, and we would know that they were delivered by SP and CMP. But then, obviously, we would have excellent reason to think SP and CMP are reliable, and it would be obvious that the rational thing to do would be to continue forming beliefs the SP and CMP way; we would be back at the previous condition of triviality.

20. Does the fact that the argument takes as a premise a belief that is a deliverance of the very practice under consideration show that the argument is epistemically circular? Not obviously: the conclusion of *this* argument is not that SP is reliable, but that it is practically rational to engage in it.

ory. Memory beliefs too, sadly enough, are uncredentialed; there is no way, as far as I can see anyway, in which one can show, in an epistemically noncircular way, that memory is reliable. And how do we know that it would be disruptive to stop forming beliefs in these ways? Presumably on the basis of our general knowledge of human beings and human nature, at least part of which comes by way of perception. And how do I know the truth of those additional premises, according to which it would be practically rational to continue with doxastic practices that meet the conditions laid down in (1) and (2)? Here presumably the idea is that these beliefs are *self-evident*, or obvious, or at any rate have a good deal of intuitive support. Therefore these premises would be among the deliverances of *reason*. Therefore they too are uncredentialed; we can't give an epistemically noncircular argument for the reliability of reason, for in giving such an argument, obviously enough, we would be obliged to rely upon reason. So (1) and (2) are no better off than the beliefs that SP and CMP are reliable: if the latter can't properly be used in the original position because they are uncredentialed, then the same is true of the former.

Indeed, as Alston himself points out (146–47), it is easy to see that *none* of our beliefs is credentialed. Even if we could give an argument to show that a given source of belief was, in fact, reliable, in making that argument we would be obliged to rely on *other* sources of beliefs. In particular, we would have to rely on reason; but clearly we can't establish that reason is reliable without relying on reason itself; so beliefs that are produced by reason are uncredentialed. Hence, if we insist that the original position must include only credentialed beliefs, it won't include any beliefs at all. And if it doesn't contain any beliefs at all, then in the original position you wouldn't have the faintest idea what to do, whether to continue with SP and CMP or not. You might as well flip a coin; more likely, the rational thing to do would be to withhold judgment altogether. But why would that matter with respect to the question of the rationality of forming beliefs in the SP or CMP way? Obviously, if you had no beliefs to go on, you couldn't come to a sensible decision as to whether to continue with SP or CMP; why would *that* fact show that there is something irrational in forming belief in accord with SP and CMP? If you had no beliefs at all on the subject, you couldn't come to a sensible decision as to whether to continue with SP and CMP: but that fact is quite irrelevant to the question whether there is something wrong with forming beliefs in the SP and CMP ways. If so, however, the *de jure* question would not be the question whether it would be rational to continue with CMP (or SP) if I were in the narrow original position.[21]

21. Do I know, however (in the narrow original position), that I have been forming beliefs all along in the SP and CMP way, and that it would therefore be inconvenient to *change* my way of forming beliefs, whether or not other people are involved? I think this leads to a puzzle, illustrating the limitations of this kind of counterfactual thought experiment. I am to imagine myself in the narrow original position, one in which I don't have any SP and CMP beliefs; but then, of course, I would have a

Should we perhaps consider a different possible narrow original position for SP and CMP? As for the first, take the original position to include the standard package *minus perception*: reason, memory, and introspection, the faculty (or means) whereby we know what our experience is (for example, how we are appeared to). Of course it would include only part of memory: in the original position thus conceived, I wouldn't have any memory belief that depends upon perceptual belief. (For example, I wouldn't have the memory belief that I saw a cat yesterday, but only the belief that it *seems to me* that I saw a cat.) What I would have to go on, therefore, would be just introspection, reason, and some fragment of memory. Then the original position with respect to SP includes (1) my knowing that it is within my power to form beliefs in the SP way and also within my power to withhold SP beliefs, (2) my knowing that it is not possible to give a good noncircular argument for the reliability of SP, (3) my having no views as to the reliability or unreliability of this practice, and (4) my not having SP beliefs or beliefs dependent on perceptual beliefs. My aim or purpose, of course, is to believe truth and avoid error. And now the question is: what would it be rational for me to do, if in fact I were in that position? Decide to continue to form beliefs the SP way? Or reject them?

Again, however, the real question, it seems to me, is this: why is *that* question relevant? That is, why would the answer to the question what it would be rational to do in *that* position have anything to do with whether it is rational, or whatever, for me to form beliefs in the SP way in the position I am actually in? I doubt that anything epistemically interesting hangs on the answer to it. What we have left isn't much to go on, and I really can't see where the probabilities would lie.[22] Well, suppose the answer is that those probabilities lie with agnosticism. All things considered, from the perspective of the narrow original position with respect to SP, it looks as if the course most likely to produce the most favorable position with respect to the truth is *agnosticism* about the deliv-

---

different way of forming beliefs from the way in which I actually do form them. If I were in that position, it would not be true that if I were not to employ SP and CMP, then I would be changing my ways of forming beliefs; for in the narrow original position I don't form beliefs in those ways! What this shows, I think, is that this counterfactual way of trying to get at the *de jure* question, either about SP or about CMP, suffers from substantial limitations. For example, perhaps you endorse conservatism: all else being equal, you say, the sensible thing to do is to continue with the way you've *been* doing things. But in the narrow original position, the conservative thing would be to continue in the agnosticism that is part of that position; so if, in that position, you accept conservatism, then the rational thing to do would be to remain agnostic.

22. Another possibility is that in the narrow original position with respect to SP, I continue to form beliefs the CMP way (so that the narrow position with respect to SP includes the beliefs I actually form on the basis of CMP). In that case, I think the probabilities would be with SP, at least if one thing I know in that position is that I have an enormously powerful tendency or natural inclination to form beliefs the SP way. God, as Descartes insisted, is no deceiver.

erances of SP; the rational thing to do would be to withhold these beliefs.
How would that be relevant to the question whether it is *in fact* (in the
situation in which in fact I find myself) rational, in some interesting
sense of 'rational', to form belief the SP way? If we decide this question
by asking whether it would be practically rational to do so *in this narrow
original position*, we are entirely ignoring *perception* as a source of warrant.
We are treating it as if it had no authority or credentials of its own, even
with respect to the very area to which it seems to be addressed. We are
treating it in the way Thomas Reid thinks Hume treats it.

As Reid also asks, however, why should I trust reason (and that
smidgin of memory) more than SP?[23] Why should SP have to prove itself before the bar of reason?[24] To descend from the level of metaphor:
why is it rational (in the relevant sense of 'rational', whatever precisely
that is) for me to form belief in the SP way only if it is more likely than
not *from the perspective just of reason, that fragment of memory, and introspection* that SP is reliable? Perhaps, from that impoverished point of view,
it is *not* more likely than not that SP is reliable; does that show anything
of interest? I doubt it. Suppose our battery of ways of forming beliefs,
our belief-forming faculties, are in fact reliable; suppose, indeed, that we
have been created by God, who intended that we be able to know the
sorts of things we think we know by virtue of just such a battery of faculties: reason, memory, sense perception, introspection, sympathy, the
sensus divinitatis and the internal instigation of the Holy Spirit (see
below, chapter 8), if there are such sources of belief, and all the rest.
What reason is there to think that if these faculties *are* reliable, then it
would *appear* that they are from the perspective just of reason, that bit of
memory, and introspection? Maybe those three simply aren't able to give
much of an answer: would that matter with respect to the rationality of
forming perceptual beliefs? I can't see that it would. So it isn't clear to
me that, in the case of SP, it matters much which answer we get here.
The question was: would it be practically rational, in the narrow original
position, to decide to engage in SP, to form beliefs in the SP way? The
answer to *that* question, however, doesn't really matter with respect to
the question whether it is rational for us to engage in SP; we don't have
here a sensible *de jure* question about SP.

23. "The sceptic asks me, Why do you believe the existence of the external object which you perceive? This belief, sir, is none of my manufacture; it came from the
mint of Nature; it bears her image and superscription; and, if it is not right, the fault
is not mine; I ever took it upon trust, and without suspicion. Reason, says the sceptic, is the only judge of truth, and you ought to throw off every opinion and every belief that is not grounded on reason. Why, sir, should I believe the faculty of reason
more than that of perception? They came both out of the same shop, and were made
by the same artist; and if he puts one piece of false ware into my hands, what should
hinder him from putting another?" (*An Inquiry into the Human Mind*, in *Thomas Reid's
Inquiry and Essays*, ed. Ronald Beanblossom and Keith Lehrer [Indianapolis: Hackett
Publishing, 1983], pp. 84–85).

24. See WCD, pp. 97ff. Of course I don't mean to suggest that Alston thinks SP
does have to prove itself before the bar of reason; I am exploring various answers to
the question 'what do we know or believe in the original position?'

The situation is a bit different with CMP. First, the narrow original position is different. It includes introspection, memory, and reason, as in the previous case, but it also includes perception and sympathy. So the narrow original position with respect to CMP includes my aiming at the truth, believing what I do, in fact, believe on the basis of the standard package; it also includes having no beliefs one way or the other about the reliability of CMP. I am to try to decide which among the courses open to me is the most likely to get me in the right relation to the truth. One option is to accept CMP. Another is to reject it in favor of some other systematic practice of forming beliefs on the questions to which CMP is addressed: for example, I could accept philosophical naturalism, or perhaps some non-Christian religious practice. Still another option, presumably, would be to continue in the agnosticism that is part of the original position, and yet another is to adopt a sort of ironic Rortian double-mindedness, a frame of mind as difficult to describe as it is intriguing, one in which at one level I believe these things; at another, I maintain a certain delicate distance, sheepishly conceding that I do in a way believe these things, but adding that officially I don't take these beliefs at all seriously, instead adopting toward them an attitude of irony and condescension. (In my study, when I reflect on it, I can see things straight; but in church, with all that liturgy, those hymns, those people I love and admire, that Bible reading and powerful preaching. . . .) And the question is, if I were in this situation, what would be the rational thing for me to do: adopt CMP, adopt some alternative to it, or remain agnostic?

Here, it seems to me, agnosticism should probably get the nod. All things considered, the best road to avoiding error and believing truth on the topics of CMP *as judged from this narrow original position* is agnosticism. To establish this, of course, would require a lot of work—first, a canvass of all the rational arguments for and against the existence of God, and then an examination of the arguments for and against the thought that we human beings do, in fact, perceive God (given that there is such a person). From the point of view of the standard package,[25] I think, it is somewhat more likely than not that there is such a person as God. Although the standard arguments don't have anything like the probative force some have claimed for them, they do have (I think) *some* force; there are, in addition, a great number of other theistic arguments, all with at least a bit of force.[26] On the other side is the problem of evil, of course; on balance, however, it seems to me that the nod goes to theism. But what about the claim that we human beings do in fact *perceive* God? Here I think the appropriate attitude would be agnosticism: from the point of view of the resources included in the narrow original position, one simply can't determine whether we human

25. Eliminating, of course, Calvin's *sensus divinitatis*, even if, as Calvin thought, that belief-forming power or mechanism is part of the original epistemic equipment of humankind generally.

26. As outlined in my so-far-unpublished "Two Dozen or So Good Theistic Arguments."

beings perceive God. But to discuss this matter in proper detail would take us too far afield—particularly in view of the fact that the question put this way is, in any event, the wrong question.

For why suppose that if CMP is sensible or rational (in some important sense of that multifarious term), then *from the point of view of the standard package* it must be more likely than not that CMP is reliable? Consider memory, and consider its credentials from the point of view of the rest of the standard package. Suppose you don't know that there's been a past; you know only what reason, perception, and introspection tell you. How likely is it, from that perspective, that the deliverances of memory are mostly true? Not very likely, I'd say. Would that be a reason for mistrusting it, regarding it as suspect, or believing that it was less than wholly rational to rely on it? Would it so much as slyly suggest that it isn't rational to form beliefs in the memory way? I don't see how. But then presumably the same thing goes for CMP. Suppose there is such a thing as perception of God; suppose that CMP is in fact reliable. Would it follow that it is more probable than not, *just given the deliverances of the standard package*, that CMP is reliable? I don't think so.

So there is no reason to hold that it is rational to take part in CMP only if its reliability is more likely than not with respect to the standard package. To think otherwise is to arbitrarily assume in advance that if CMP is a source of warranted belief, it must be likely with respect to the standard package that it is reliable; but there is no reason to accept this assumption. Here things stand with CMP just as with SP. It seems entirely arbitrary to insist that it is rational to engage in SP only if the reliability of SP is more likely than not with respect to the deliverances of some group of epistemic powers that doesn't include SP; in the same way, it is not sensible to conclude that CMP is rational only if its reliability is more likely than not from the perspective of the standard package. Suppose God has created us with a battery of faculties aimed at our being able to acquire truth in different areas: it doesn't follow that the reliability of any of these faculties would be more probable than not with respect to the deliverances of some package of faculties that does not include the one in question.

By way of summary, then: either the original position with respect to CMP is wide or it is narrow. If it is wide, then it will include my belief that CMP is reliable; in that case, the rational decision, clearly enough, would be to continue with CMP. But this does nothing to relieve any anxieties someone might have about the rationality or reasonability of CMP. If the original position is narrow, however, then it really doesn't matter whether from *that* position it would be rational to continue with CMP.

Now suppose we return to specifically Christian belief. Our quarry is the *de jure* question: what is this rationality or rational justification Christian belief is alleged by its detractors not to have? Our current suggestion is that perhaps it is practical rationality. Perhaps the *de jure* question is the question whether Christian belief is in fact practically rational and the *de jure* objection is that it is not. But the same dialectic applies here as in the case of CMP. If we are thinking of the original position with respect to Christian belief as wide, then it will include Christian belief itself. From that point of view, obviously, the rational decision would be to continue to form and maintain belief in the way in which I do, in fact, form and maintain it (i.e., to form and maintain Christian belief); but that does little to show that Christian belief is rational in any interesting sense. So suppose, by contrast, that the appropriate original position is narrow. Then, to be sure, it will include only the standard package and it won't include Christian belief. Now perhaps from that perspective it isn't at all clear that the rational decision would be to endorse Christian belief; perhaps the rational decision would be to give it up. So what? Why should the truth of Christian belief (or the reliability of the sources producing it) have to be more likely than not from *that* standpoint for it to be rational? Why think that the rationality, in some interesting sense, of Christian beliefs requires that it be more likely than not *from the standpoint of the standard package* that it is reliably produced? No reason; hence we still haven't located the *de jure* question.

So what *is* the question? Surely there is a sensible *de jure* question lurking somewhere in this neighborhood: what might it be? Where shall we look for it? Perhaps in the following locality. Go back to the wide original position, and recall that if, in that position, I accept SP and CMP beliefs, then, trivially, the rational thing to do is to decide to continue to form beliefs in those ways. Of course this would be true for other beliefs as well. In fact it would be true even for beliefs that are in some clear sense *ir*rational. René Descartes notes that there are people "whose cerebella are so troubled and clouded by the violent vapours of black bile, that they . . . imagine that they have an earthenware head or are nothing but pumpkins or are made of glass."[27] No doubt these people avoided bumps like the plague. Given that you *do* believe you are made of glass, the rational thing to do *is* to avoid bumps. In the same way, given that you *do* believe you are made of glass, the rational thing to do in the service of truth is (if you are given the choice) to continue in that belief. After all, you think the belief is *true*; so if your aim is to believe truth and avoid falsehood, you will continue to hold it.

Fair enough: *given* that you think your head is made of glass, it is rational to wear your football helmet wherever you go, and rational to decide, if presented with the choice, to continue in that belief. But is it rational to hold that belief in the *first* place? Given that you hold the beliefs produced by SP or CMP and you don't know of any epistemically superior practice, it is indeed rational to continue to form beliefs in that way: is it or was it rational, reasonable, sensible to hold those beliefs in the first place?

It is in this neighborhood, I suggest, that we must look for the *de jure* question with respect to Christian belief. What is it that determines whether a given way of acting or believing, given that your circumstances are thus-and-so, is rational or reasonable, in the relevant sense? Here is my suggestion: what determines this is what a creature of our kind with *properly functioning* reason (*ratio*) would do or believe, given that she was in those circumstances. Or perhaps it is what someone with

27. *Meditations*, Meditation I.

ideal *ratio*—*ratio* ideal for our kind of creature—would do or think in the circumstances. The question is really about the human design plan; it has to do with what that design plan, or perhaps a slightly idealized version of it, dictates for the situation in question. The question is about the sorts of beliefs a properly functioning human being would have in the relevant circumstances. What kind of question is *this*? It isn't a question of *practical* rationality. The question is not: given that I am in circumstances C, have aims and beliefs A and B, and have raised the question whether or not to do X, how likely is it that doing X will contribute to my aims and goals? (How sensible would it be to do X?) It's a different kind of question altogether. In the next chapter we shall have to try to specify this question and get a closer look at it.

5

Warrant and the Freud-and-Marx Complaint

The genius of a man capable of explaining religion seems to me to be of a higher order than that of a founder of religion. And that is the glory to which I aspire.

Charles DuPuis

What we have seen so far is what the *de jure* question and criticism are *not*: it is not the complaint that the believer is not within her intellectual rights in believing as she does; it is not the complaint that she has no good argument from propositions that are self-evident, about her own mental states, or evident to the senses for her; it is not the complaint that she has no good argument of some *other* sort; it is not the complaint that her Christian belief lacks Alstonian justification, or means-end rationality; and it is not the complaint that it isn't practically rational to decide to continue to form belief on the basis of experience. None of these criticisms has much of a leg to stand on.

So the *de jure* criticism has proven elusive. In the last chapter, however, we did finally catch a glimpse of our quarry—no more than a glimpse, though—and in this chapter I want to look further into the nature of this style of criticism, in part by trying to come to an understanding of the rejection of religious belief associated with Freud and Marx. Then I will point out the connection between the *de jure* question, properly understood, and *warrant*, the subject of the two preceding books in this series. In the next few chapters, I will consider more explicitly the question whether Christian belief can have warrant even if it doesn't receive it by way of argument or propositional evidence. This is really the question (as I might have put it in

"Reason and Belief in God"[1]) whether belief in God and Christian belief more generally can be properly basic—properly basic with respect to warrant. (It is also the question I was raising [rather inchoately] in *God and Other Minds*.[2]) Perhaps another way to put this question is to ask whether Christian belief can get warrant, not by argument but by virtue of (broadly construed) religious experience.

I. THE F&M COMPLAINT

As we have seen, atheologians (those who argue against Christian belief) have often claimed that Christian belief is *irrational*; so far, we have failed to find a sensible version of this claim. But perhaps we can make progress by exploring the animadversions on Christian belief proposed by Freud, Marx, and the whole cadre of their nineteenth- and twentieth-century followers.[3] We could also examine here Nietzsche's similar complaint: that religion originates in slave morality, in the *ressentiment* of the oppressed. As Nietzsche sees it, Christianity both fosters and arises from a sort of sniveling, cowardly, servile, evasive, duplicitous, and all-around contemptible sort of character, which is at the same time envious, self-righteous, and full of hate disguised as charitable kindness. (Not a pretty picture.) I've chosen not to consider Nietzsche for two reasons: first, he really has little to add to what Marx and Freud say; second, he is harder to take seriously. He writes with a fine coruscating brilliance, his outrageous rhetoric is sometimes entertaining, and no doubt much of the extravagance is meant as overstatement to make a point. Taken overall, however, the violence and exaggeration seem pathological; for a candidate for the sober truth, we shall certainly have to look elsewhere.[4]

1. In *Faith and Rationality*, ed. Alvin Plantinga and Nicholas Wolsterstorff (Notre Dame: University of Notre Dame Press, 1983).

2. Ithaca: Cornell University Press, 1967.

3. Of course, it wasn't only *Christian* belief that drew their fire: Freud and Marx were equal-opportunity animadverters, attacking religion generally and without discrimination.

4. I don't mean for a moment to dispute Merold Westphal's contention (in *Suspicion and Faith: The Religious Uses of Modern Atheism* [Grand Rapids: W. B. Eerdmans, 1993]) that Christians have something to learn from Nietzsche (as from Freud and Marx). Of course they do, but the same lessons can be learned at a much subtler level from, for example, the Bible—where, as Westphal points out, Nietzsche's criticisms, insofar as they are on the mark, are anticipated. Taken as a serious account of the origin of Christianity, however, Nietzsche's intemperate scoldings can't really be seen as a serious contribution to the subject.

Now Freud, Marx, and their many epigoni (and anticipators) *criticize* religious belief; they purport to find something *wrong* with it; they are 'masters of suspicion' and (at any rate in their own view) *unmask* it. And in examining their critical comments on religious belief, I think we can finally locate a proper *de jure* question: one that is distinct from the *de facto* question, is such that the answer is nontrivial, and is relevant in the sense that a negative answer to it would be a serious point against Christian belief. The first order of business, therefore, is to try to get clear as to what the Freud-Marx critical project ('the F&M complaint', as I shall call it) really *is*.

A. Freud

There are several sides to Freud's critique of religion. For example, he was fascinated by what he saw as the Darwinian picture of early human beings coming together in packs or herds (like wolves or elk), all the females belonging to one powerful, dominant, jealous male, and he tells a dramatic story about how religion arose out of an extraordinary interaction among the members of that primal horde:

> The father of the primal horde, since he was an unlimited despot, had seized all the women for himself; his sons, being dangerous to him as rivals, had been killed or driven away. One day, however, the sons came together and united to overwhelm, kill, and devour their father, who had been their enemy but also their ideal. After the deed they were unable to take over their heritage since they stood in one another's way. Under the influence of failure and remorse they learned to come to an agreement among themselves; they banded themselves into a clan of brothers by the help of the ordinances of totemism, which aimed at preventing a repetition of such a deed, and they jointly undertook to forgo the possession of the women on whose account they had killed their father. They were then driven to finding strange women, and this was the origin of the exogamy which is so closely bound up with totemism. The Totem meal was the festival commemorating the fearful deed from which sprang man's sense of guilt (or 'original sin'). . . .
>   . . . This view of religion throws a particularly clear light upon the psychological basis of Christianity, in which, as we know, the ceremony of the totem meal still survives, with but little distortion, in the form of Communion.[5]

5. "An Autobiographical Study," in volume 20 of the *Standard Edition of the Complete Psychological Works of Sigmund Freud* (London: Hogarth Press and the Institute of Psychoanalysis, 1953–74), p. 68. See also *Totem and Taboo*, authorized translation by James Strachey (New York: W. W. Norton, 1950 [originally published in 1913]), pp. 140ff.

Strong stuff, this, displaying Freud's redoubtable imaginative powers and his ability to tell a sensational story;[6] all the elements— sex, murder, cannibalism, remorse—of a dandy Hollywood spectacular are here. Taken as a serious attempt at a historical account of the origin of religion, though, it has little to recommend it and is at best a wild guess, much less science than science fiction.[7] But perhaps Freud didn't intend it as sober and literal truth. (He himself calls it a 'vision'.) Perhaps it is something like a parable, maybe something like how some Christians understand early *Genesis* or *Job*, meant to illustrate and present a truth in graphic but nonliteral form. (Maybe here as elsewhere Freud is under the spell of biblical ways of writing and thinking.) And just as it isn't always easy to draw the right moral from a biblical parable, so it isn't easy to see what Freud intends us to gather from this gripping if grisly little tale.

In any event, Freud offers quite a different account of the psychological origins of religious (theistic) belief:

> These [religious beliefs], which are given out as teachings, are not precipitates of experience or end-results of thinking: they are illusions, fulfillments of the oldest, strongest and most urgent wishes of

---

6. Freud tells a similarly fantastic story about how we human beings tamed fire—"a quite extraordinary and unexampled achievement," he says—and turned it to our use:

> Psychoanalytic material, incomplete as it is and not susceptible to clear interpretation, nevertheless admits of a conjecture—a fantastic-sounding one—about the origin of this human feat. It is as though primal man had the habit, when he came in contact with fire, of satisfying an infantile desire connected with it, by putting it out with a stream of his urine. The legends that we possess leave no doubt about the originally phallic view taken of tongues of flame as they shoot upwards. Putting out fire by micturating— a theme to which modern giants, Gulliver in Lilliput and Rabelais' Gargantua, still hark back—was therefore a kind of a sexual act with a male, an enjoyment of sexual potency in a homosexual competition. The first person to renounce this desire and spare the fire was able to carry it off with him and subdue it to his own use. By damping down the fire of his own sexual excitation, he had tamed the natural force of fire. This great cultural conquest was thus the reward for his renunciation of instinct. Further, it is as though woman had been appointed guardian of the fire which was held captive on the domestic hearth, because her anatomy made it impossible for her to yield to the temptation of this desire. (*Civilization and Its Discontents*, tr. and ed. James Strachey [New York: W. W. Norton, 1961 (originally published in 1930 as *Das Unbehagen in der Kultur*)], p. 37)

7. Here see, e.g., Wilhelm Schmidt, *The Origin and Growth of Religion: Facts and Theories*, tr. H. J. Rose (New York: L. MacVeagh, Dial Press, 1931), p. 114, who makes an attempt to evaluate this story as serious science; see also Evan Fales, "Scientific Explanations of Mystical Experiences, Part I: The Case of St. Teresa," *Religious Studies* 32, no. 1 (June 1996), p. 148.

mankind. The secret of their strength lies in the strength of those wishes. As we already know, the terrifying impressions of helplessness in childhood aroused the need for protection—for protection through love—which was provided by the father; and the recognition that this helplessness lasts throughout life made it necessary to cling to the existence of a father, but this time a more powerful one. Thus the benevolent rule of a divine Providence allays our fear of the dangers of life; the establishment of a moral world-order ensures the fulfillment of the demands of justice, which have so often remained unfulfilled in human civilization; and the prolongation of earthly existence in a future life provides the local and temporal framework in which these wish-fulfillments shall take place.[8]

As we see, there is more to Freud's critique than phantasmagoric fables about the primal horde. The idea is that theistic belief arises from a psychological mechanism Freud calls 'wish-fulfillment'; the wish in this case is father, not to the deed, but to the belief. Nature rises up against us, cold, pitiless, implacable, blind to our needs and desires. She delivers hurt, fear, and pain; in the end, she demands our death. Paralyzed and appalled, we invent (unconsciously, of course) a Father in Heaven who exceeds our earthly fathers as much in power and knowledge as in goodness and benevolence; the alternative would be to sink into depression, stupor, paralysis, and finally death. According to Freud, belief in God is an *illusion* in a semitechnical use of the term: a belief that arises from the mechanism of wish-fulfillment. This illusion somehow becomes internalized.[9]

An illusion (as opposed to a delusion), says Freud, is not necessarily false; and he goes on to add that it isn't possible to prove that theistic belief is mistaken. Nevertheless, there is more here than a mere antiseptic comment on the origin of religion. Although religion originates in the cognitive mechanism of wish-fulfillment, Freud apparently believes that it is within our power to resist this illusion, and that there is something condemnable, something intellectually irresponsible, in failing to do so:

> If ever there was a case of a lame excuse we have it here. Ignorance is ignorance; no right to believe anything can be derived from it. In other matters no sensible person will behave so irresponsibly or rest content with such feeble grounds for his opinions and for the line he takes. . . . Where questions of religion are concerned, people are

8. *The Future of an Illusion*, tr. and ed. James Strachey (New York: W. W. Norton, 1961), p. 30. This work was originally published as *Die Zukunft einer Illusion* (Leipzig: Internationaler Psychoanalytischer Verlag, 1927).

9. And in such a way that it (or its deliverances) rather resembles Calvin's *sensus divinitatis* (chapter 6, below); see *Moses and Monotheism* (New York: Vintage, 1967), pp. 167ff.

guilty of every possible sort of dishonesty and intellectual mis-demeanour.[10]

Psychoanalysis, furthermore, provides arguments against the truth of religious belief: "If the application of the psycho-analytic method makes it possible to find a new argument against the truths [*sic*] of religion, *tant pis* for religion . . ." (p. 37). Once we see that reli-gious belief takes its origin in wishful thinking, we will presumably no longer find it attractive; perhaps this will also induce in us a certain pity for those benighted souls who will never rise to our enlightened heights:

> The whole thing is so patently infantile, so incongruous with reality, that to one whose attitude to humanity is friendly, it is painful to think that the great majority of mortals will never be able to rise above this view of life.[11]

Freud hopes and expects that we human beings will eventually give up religious belief, once we are clear about its origin, in favor of a view of the world that is closer to the actual facts of the matter:

> I am reminded of one of my children who was distinguished at an early age by a peculiarly marked matter-of-factness. When the chil-dren were being told a fairy story and were listening to it with rapt attention, he would come up and ask: "Is that a true story?" When he was told it was not, he would turn away with a look of disdain. We may expect that people will soon behave in the same way to-wards the fairy tales of religion. . . .[12]

The fundamental theme here, therefore, is that religious belief arises from wish-fulfillment. We shall have to try to see more exactly what this amounts to and what bearing, if any, it has on the rationality of Christian belief; first, however, we should briefly note Marx's rather similar criticism.

B. Marx

Marx's most famous pronouncement on religion:

> The basis of irreligious criticism is *man makes religion*, religion does not make man. In other words, religion is the self-consciousness and the self-feeling of the man who has either not yet found him-self, or else (having found himself) has lost himself once more. But

---

10. *The Future of an Illusion*, p. 32.
11. *Civilization and Its Discontents*, p. 21.
12. *The Future of an Illusion*, p. 29. Freud isn't unambiguously sanguine on this point; he thinks there are three powers (religion, art, and philosophy) that challenge the claims of science to cognitive supremacy, and of these three only religion "is to be taken seriously as an enemy" (22:160).

man is no abstract being squatting outside the world. Man is the *world of man*, the state, society. This state, this society, produce religion, a *perverted world consciousness*, because they are a *perverted* world. . . .

Religious distress is at the same time the *expression* of real distress and the *protest* against real distress. Religion is the sigh of the oppressed creature, the heart of a heartless world, just as it is the spirit of a spiritless situation. It is the *opium* of the people.

The abolition of religion as the *illusory* happiness of the people is required for their *real* happiness. The demand to give up the illusions about its condition is the *demand to give up a condition which requires illusions*. The criticism of religion is therefore *in embryo the criticism of the vale of woe*, the *halo* of which is religion [Marx's emphasis].[13]

Marx suggests that religion arises from *perverted* world consciousness—perverted from a correct, or right, or natural condition. Religion involves a cognitive dysfunction, a disorder or perversion that is apparently brought about, somehow, by an unhealthy and perverted social order. Religious belief, according to Marx, is a result of cognitive dysfunction, of a lack of mental and emotional health. The believer is therefore in an etymological sense insane. Because of

---

13. "Contribution to the Critique of Hegel's Philosophy of Right, Introduction," in *On Religion*, by Karl Marx and Friedrich Engels, tr. Reinhold Niebuhr (Chico, Calif.: Scholar's Press, 1964), pp. 41–42. Engels echoes Marx:

All religion, however, is nothing but the fantastic reflection in men's minds of those external forces which control their daily life, a reflection in which the terrestrial forces assume the form of supernatural forces. In the beginnings of history it was the forces of nature which were first so reflected and which in the course of further evolution underwent the most manifold and varied personifications among the various peoples. . . . But it is not long before, side by side with the forces of nature, social forces begin to be active—forces which confront man as equally alien and at first inexplicable, dominating him with the same apparent natural necessity as the forces of nature themselves. . . . At a still further stage of evolution, all the natural and social attributes of the numerous gods are transferred to *one* almighty god, who is but a reflection of the abstract man. Such was the origin of monotheism. . . . It is still true that man proposes and God (that is, the alien domination of the capitalist mode of production) disposes. . . . What is above all necessary for this is a social *act*. And when this act has been accomplished, when society, by taking possession of all means of production and using them on a planned basis, has freed itself and all its members from the bondage in which they are now held by these means of production which they themselves have produced but which confront them as an irresistible alien force; when, therefore man not only proposes, but also disposes—only then will the last alien force which is still reflected in religion vanish; and with it will also vanish the religious reflection itself, for the simple reason that then there will be nothing left to reflect. (*Anti-Dühring*, pp. 147–49 in *On Religion*)

a dysfunctional, perverse social environment, the believer's cognitive equipment isn't working properly. If his cognitive equipment *were* working properly—if, for example, it were working more like Marx's—he would not be under the spell of this illusion. He would instead face the world and our place in it with the clear-eyed apprehension that we are alone, and that any comfort and help we get will have to be of our own devising.[14]

And here we can see an initial difference between Freud and Marx: Freud doesn't necessarily think religious belief is produced by cognitive faculties that are malfunctioning. Religious belief—specifically belief in God—is, indeed, produced by wish-fulfillment; it is the product of illusion; still, illusion and wish-fulfillment have their functions. In this case, their function is to enable us to get along in this cold and heartless world into which we find ourselves thrown. How then is this a *criticism* of religious belief? Freud speaks elsewhere of a "reality principle." Beliefs produced by wish-fulfillment aren't oriented toward reality; their function is not to produce *true* belief, but belief with some other property (psychological comfort, for example). So we could initially put it like this: religious belief is produced by cognitive processes whose function is not that of producing true beliefs, but rather that of producing beliefs conducive to psychological well-being. We will look into this in more detail below; for the moment, perhaps what we can say is that the Marxist criticism of religious belief is that it is produced by disordered cognitive processes, while the Freudian criticism is that it is produced by processes that are not aimed at the production of true beliefs.

C. Others

We must take a deeper look at these claims. First, however, we should note that although Freud and Marx often get the credit for this alleged unmasking (perhaps with a crumb thrown in the direction of Nietzsche), its essence is to be found much earlier. Jean-Jacques Rousseau (1712–78) thought Christian belief was a product of corrupt society, and that the natural spirituality of our souls has been damaged by a Christianized civilization; he thus anticipates Marx in seeing Christian belief as a result of cognitive malfunction resulting from social malfunction. David Hume, a British contemporary of Rousseau, anticipates Freud:

> It must necessarily, indeed, be allowed, that, in order to carry men's intention beyond the present course of things, or lead them into any inference concerning invisible intelligent power, they must be actuated by some passion, which prompts their thought and reflection; some motive, which urges their first enquiry. But what passion shall we here have recourse to, for explaining an effect of such

mighty consequences? Not speculative curiosity, surely, or the pure love of truth. That motive is too refined for such gross apprehensions; and would lead men into enquiries concerning the frame of nature, a subject too large and comprehensive for their narrow capacities. No passions, therefore, can be supposed to work upon such barbarians, but the ordinary affections of human life; the anxious concern for happiness, the dread of future misery, the terror of death, the thirst of revenge, the appetite for food and other necessaries. Agitated by hopes and fears of this nature, especially the latter, men scrutinize with a trembling curiosity, the course of future causes, and examine the various and contrary events of human life. And in this disordered scene, with eyes still more disordered and astonished, they see the first obscure traces of divinity.[15]

What is crucial here is the claim that religious belief does not arise from 'the pure love of truth', but from other sources: desire for happiness, fear of death, and the like. In fact Hume ironically suggests that Christian belief is so contrary to experience and to the "principles of understanding" (i.e., the deliverances of reason) that a reasonable person can accept it only by virtue of a miracle:

> upon the whole, we may conclude that the *Christian Religion* not only was at first attended with miracles, but even at this day cannot be believed by any reasonable person without one. . . . Whoever is moved by *Faith* to assent to it, is conscious of a continued miracle in his own person, which subverts all the principles of his understanding, and gives him a determination to believe what is most contrary to custom and experience.[16]

So the fundamental thrust of Hume's suggestion, as of Freud's, is that religious belief doesn't emerge from the segment of our whole cognitive economy that is, as we might put it, aimed at the production of *true belief*; it comes, instead, from a desire for security or a fear of death or whatever. And of course what underlies Hume's ironic jape is the idea that Christian belief goes directly contrary to the deliverances of reason and experience.

Many of our contemporaries also see religious beliefs in these terms. Thus Northrop Frye weighs in on Marx's side, but employs Freudian or semi-Freudian categories: speaking of "the curious aberration of 'believing the Bible'," he says:

---

14. There is another possibility as to how to understand Marx here: see below, p. 162.

15. *David Hume: The Natural History of Religion*, ed. H. E. Root (Stanford, Ca.: Stanford University Press, 1957), p. 166.

16. *An Enquiry Concerning Human Understanding* (La Salle, Ill.: Open Court, 1956), p. 145.

such belief is really a voluntarily induced schizophrenia, and probably a fruitful source of the infantilism and hysterical anxieties about belief which are so frequently found in the neighborhood of religion, at least in its more uncritical areas.[17]

In the same vein, we have Don Cupitt: "Theological realism can only be actually *true* for [i. e. thought to be true by] a heteronomous consciousness such as no normal person ought now to have."[18] Those who claim that they really are 'theological realists' (i.e., claim that they really do believe in God), he says, are hypocrites[19] or have succumbed to "a kind of madness."[20] Cupitt seems to think that (perhaps, as they say, 'given what we now know') you would have to be psychotic to actually *be* a theological realist (one who believes that there really is such a person as God); if you are not psychotic but nonetheless *profess* theistic belief, then you must be one of those hypocrites Christian churches are supposed to be full of.

A final witness. Charles Daniels agrees with Freud in finding the origin of religious belief in wishful thinking:

> we must begin to entertain suspicions that the explanation for these [religious] experiences does not lie in any perceived religious reality, but is rather the effect of some other cause — perhaps excessive emotion and fervor. . . .
>
> It is not at all difficult, however, to construct a plausible explanation not consisting of mere possibilities like the machinations of demons, why people should come very strongly to believe there to be a divinely populated religious reality which is perceived in religious experience even when there is none . . . we very much *want* there to be an understandable order to the universe, we very much *want* our lives to be of consequence, and we very much *want* to know in practical detail what's right and wrong. Religion addresses what we very much want. The universe has an intelligible order because there is an intelligent powerful God who made it. We are important because God made us (as Christians say, "in his image") and gave us the faculties of understanding and free, intelligent action.[21]

---

17. Speaking of infantilism, Frye's intemperate comments call to mind schoolyard debating styles (perhaps about fifth grade): "Oh Yeah? Well, the trouble with you is you're crazy, and so's your whole dumb family!"

18. *Taking Leave of God* (New York: Crossroad, 1980), p. 12. One gathers that Cupitt thinks it is "our modern form of consciousness" that makes this obligatory.

19. Ibid., p. 21.

20. *The World to Come* (London: SCM Press, 1982), p. 83.

21. "Experiencing God," *Philosophy and Phenomenological Research* (1989), pp. 497, 499.

D. How Shall We Understand the F&M Complaint?

Now the F&M (Freud-and-Marx) complaint is, naturally enough, a *complaint*, a (negative) criticism of religious belief, including Christian belief. But the general project under which the efforts of Freud and Marx fall is that of giving *naturalistic explanations* of religious belief, explanations that don't involve the truth of the beliefs in question or the truth of any other supernaturalistic beliefs or hypotheses. Many (in addition to those cited above) have joined them in this effort, and by now there is quite a variety of naturalistic explanations of religious belief.[22] But of course giving a naturalistic account of a kind of belief isn't automatically a criticism of that kind of belief.

> Consider *a priori* belief, belief in such propositions as the laws of logic, perhaps, or the basic truths of arithmetic, or the proposition that if all cats are animals, and Maynard is a cat, then Maynard is an animal. Perhaps it is possible to give a 'naturalistic' account of our knowledge of these truths: an account, that is, that stands in the same relation to them as a naturalistic account of religious belief stands to it. Such an account would not invoke the truth of these *a priori* beliefs as part of the explanation; it would proceed instead by outlining certain salient features of the causal genesis or antecedents of these beliefs, perhaps pointing to events of some kind in the nervous system. The existence of a causal explanation, of this sort, of *a priori* belief would not show or tend to show that such beliefs are unreliable.
>
> The same would go for religious belief. To show that there are natural processes that produce religious belief does nothing, so far, to discredit it; perhaps God designed us in such a way that it is by virtue of those processes that we come to have knowledge of him. Suppose it could be demonstrated that a certain kind of complex neural stimulation could produce theistic belief. This would have no tendency to discredit religious belief—just as memory is not discredited by the fact that one can produce memory beliefs by stimulating the right part of the brain. Clearly, it is possible both that there is an explanation in terms of natural processes of religious belief (perhaps a brain physiological account of what happens when someone holds religious beliefs), and that these beliefs have a perfectly respectable epistemic status.

If we are to have a *criticism* of religion by way of a naturalistic explanation, what we need is something that in some way *discredits* religious belief, casts doubt on it, shows that it is not epistemically respectable—in a word, shows that there is something wrong with it. And the criticism, of course, is that religious belief (including

---

22. See, for example, J. Samuel Preus, *Explaining Religion* (New Haven: Yale University Press, 1987).

Christian belief) is *irrational*. But irrational in just what way? What exactly is wrong with religious belief, according to the F&M complaint? How, exactly, shall we understand the F&M complaint?

First, an assumption underlying it. Going all the way back to Plato and Aristotle, it has been assumed that there are intellectual or cognitive or rational *powers* or *faculties*, or (possibly) *virtues*: for example, perception and memory. Joining the computer craze, we might say that these faculties have inputs and outputs; their outputs are beliefs. It is these processes that produce in us the myriad beliefs we hold. These faculties are also something like *instruments*; and, like instruments, they have a *function* or *purpose*. If we thought of ourselves as created and designed either by a Master Craftsman or by evolution, these cognitive faculties would be the parts of our total cognitive establishment or total cognitive design whose purpose it is to produce *beliefs* in us. Their overall purpose, furthermore, is presumably to produce *true* beliefs in us; to put it a bit less passively, they are designed in such a way that by using them properly we can come to true belief. Our cognitive faculties work over a surprisingly large area to deliver beliefs of many different topics: beliefs about our immediate environment; about the external world at large; about the past; about numbers, propositions, and other abstract objects and the relations between them; about other people and what they are thinking and feeling; about what the future will be like; about right and wrong; about God.

These faculties and processes are the instruments or organs, as we might put it, whereby we come to have knowledge. They are aimed at the truth in the sense that their purpose or function is to furnish us with true belief. Like any other instruments or organs, they can *work properly or improperly*; they can function well or malfunction. A wart or a tumor doesn't either malfunction (although it might be by virtue of malfunction in some system that the tumor is present) or function properly: it doesn't *have* a function or purpose. But an organ—your heart, for example, or liver or pancreas—does have a function, and does either work properly or malfunction. And the same goes for cognitive faculties or capacities: they too can function well or ill. The condition in which they function really badly is insanity; of course there are much milder, less intrusive forms of cognitive malfunction.

Now among these faculties one of the most important is *reason*. Taken *narrowly*, reason is the faculty or power whereby we form *a priori* beliefs, beliefs that are *prior* to experience or, better, independent, in some way, of experience.[23] These beliefs include what in chapter 4

---

23. See my *Warrant and Proper Function* (hereafter WPF), chapter 6.

we called the deliverances of reason: first of all, simple truths of arithmetic and logic, such as *2 + 1 = 3* and *if all men are mortal and Socrates
is a man, then Socrates is mortal*. They also include such beliefs as that
nothing can be red all over and also green all over and that to be a
person you must at least be potentially capable of forming beliefs and
having ends or aims. Still further, they include more controversial
items, such as the belief that there are properties, states of affairs,
propositions, and other abstract objects, and the belief that no object
has a property in a possible world in which it doesn't exist. (So I say,
anyway; there are those who disagree.) The deliverances of reason
also include beliefs that obviously follow from deliverances of reason.[24] And still further, reason is the power or capacity whereby we
see or detect logical relationships among propositions.

There are other faculties or rational powers that have as their
purpose the production of true beliefs in us;[25] for example, there
are perception and memory, which, along with reason, constitute
the standard package of chapter 4. Further, there are *introspection*,
by which I learn such things about myself as that I am appeared to
a certain way, and believe this or that; *induction*, whereby (in a way
that defies explicit statement) we come to expect the future to be
like the past in certain respects, thereby being able to learn from experience;[26] and Thomas Reid's *sympathy*, whereby we come to be
aware of what other people are thinking, feeling, and believing.
Still further, there is *testimony* or *credulity*, whereby we learn from
others, by believing what they tell us. By sympathy I learn that you
are telling me that your name is Archibald; for me to *believe* you,
however, something further is required. (Thus by perception, I see
that you are in such and such a bodily state; by sympathy, I learn
that you are claiming that your name is Archibald; and by testimony, I believe you.)

The Enlightenment looked askance at testimony and tradition;
Locke saw them as a preeminent source of error. The Enlightenment
idea is that perhaps we *start* by learning from others—our parents,
for example. Properly mature and independent adults, however, will
have passed beyond all that and believe what they do on the basis of
the evidence. But this is a mistake; you can't know so much as your
name or what city you live in without relying on testimony. (Will you
produce your birth certificate for the first, or consult a handy map
for the second? In each case you are of course relying on testimony.)
As Thomas Reid puts it:

24. But see above, chapter 4, p. 114.
25. For more detail, see WPF, chapters 3–9.
26. See WPF, pp. 122ff.

I believed by instinct whatever they [my "parents and tutors"] told me, long before I had the idea of a lie, or a thought of the possibility of their deceiving me. Afterwards, upon reflection, I found they had acted like fair and honest people, who wished me well. I found that, if I had not believed what they told me, before I could give a reason for my belief, I had to this day been little better than a changeling. And although this natural credulity hath sometimes occasioned my being imposed upon by deceivers, yet it hath been of infinite advantage to me upon the whole; therefore, I consider it as another good gift of Nature.[27]

In addition to the cognitive powers or rational faculties mentioned so far there may be others that are more controversial. For example, we seem to have a moral sense: certain kinds of behavior and certain kinds of character seem wrong, bad, to be avoided; others seem right, good, fitting, to be promoted. It is obviously wrong (all else being equal) to hurt young children or to refuse to care for your aging parents; perhaps we see this by way of a sort of moral sense. (It is no doubt because this moral sense can malfunction, or atrophy, that inability to tell right from wrong is a legal defense.) My point here is not to argue that indeed there *is* a moral sense, although I believe that there is, but rather to note that there could well be truth-aimed faculties in addition to the ones mentioned so far. Similarly a believer in God might think that there is such a thing as Calvin's *sensus divinitatis*,[28] a natural, inborn sense of God, or of divinity, that is the origin and source of the world's religions; perhaps there is also such a thing as the inward invitation or instigation of the Holy Spirit (to anticipate chapter 8) whereby the believer comes to accept the central truths of the Christian faith.

As we have seen, these rational faculties can function either properly or improperly. We ordinarily take it for granted that when our cognitive faculties are functioning properly, when they are not subject to dysfunction or malfunction, then, for the most part, the beliefs they produce are true, or close to the truth. If your perceptual faculties are functioning properly, what you think you see is probably what you do see. (If you are suffering from delirium tremens, all bets are off.) There is, we might say, *a presumption of reliability* for properly functioning faculties; we are inclined (rightly or wrongly) to take it that properly functioning cognitive faculties for the most part deliver true belief. Of course there will be mistakes and disagreements, and we may be inclined to skepticism about various areas of belief: polit-

---

27. *Essays on the Intellectual Powers of Man*, in *Thomas Reid's Inquiry and Essays*, ed. R. Beanblossom and K. Lehrer (Indianapolis: Hackett, 1983), VI, 5, pp. 281–82; see also WPF, pp. 77ff.

28. See below, chapter 6.

ical beliefs, for example, as well as beliefs formed at the limits of our ability, as in particle physics and cosmology; but the bulk of the everyday beliefs delivered by our rational faculties, so we think, are true. At any rate, the deliverances of our rational faculties, taken broadly, comprise our best bet for achieving truth.

Returning finally to the F&M complaint, it's clear that it has to do with the deliverances of our rational faculties. Freud and Marx acquiesce in the presumption of reliability; they assume (as do we all) that when our rational faculties are functioning properly and are used properly, then for the most part their deliverances are true, or at any rate close to the truth. Of course, as we saw, it is possible for cognitive faculties to function well or ill. The insane beliefs of Descartes's madmen[29] were due to cognitive malfunction of some sort. There are more subtle ways, however, in which nonrational or irrational beliefs can be formed in us. First of all, there are belief-forming processes or mechanisms that are aimed, not at the formation of true belief, but at the formation of belief with some other property—the property of contributing to survival, perhaps, or to peace of mind or psychological well-being in this sometimes dangerous and threatening world of ours.[30] Those with a lethal disease may believe their chances for recovery much higher than the statistics in their possession would warrant; again, the function of the relevant process would not be that of furnishing true beliefs but of furnishing beliefs that make it more likely that the believer will recover. A mountaineer whose survival depends on his ability to leap a crevasse may form an extremely optimistic estimate of his powers as a long-jumper; it is more likely that he will be able to leap the crevasse (or at least give it a try) if he thinks he can than if he thinks he can't. Most of us form estimates of our intelligence, wisdom, and moral fiber that are considerably higher than an objective estimate would warrant; no doubt 90 percent of us think ourselves well above average along these lines.[31]

---

29. Above, p. 133.
30. See WPF, pp. 11ff.
31. I can't resist repeating (from WPF, p. 12) a couple of passages from Locke:

> Would it not be an insufferable thing for a learned professor, and that which his scarlet would blush at, to have his authority of forty years standing wrought out of hard rock Greek and Latin, with no small expence of time and candle, and confirmed by general tradition, and a reverent beard, in an instant overturned by an upstart novelist? Can any one expect that he should be made to confess, that what he taught his scholars thirty years ago, was all errour and mistake; and that he sold them hard words and ignorance at a very dear rate? (*An Essay concerning Human Understanding*, ed. A. D. Woozley [New York: World Publishing, 1963], IV, xx, 11)

A person may be blinded (as we say) by ambition, failing to see that a certain course of action is wrong or stupid, even though it is obvious to everyone else. Our idea, here, is that inordinately ambitious people fail to recognize something they would otherwise recognize; the normal functioning of some aspect of their cognitive powers is inhibited or overridden or impeded by that excessive ambition. You may be blinded also by loyalty, continuing to believe in the honesty of your friend long after an objective look at the evidence would have dictated a reluctant change of mind. You can also be blinded by covetousness, love, fear, lust, anger, pride, grief, social pressure, and a thousand other things. In polemic, it is common to attack someone's views by claiming that the denial of what they think is patently obvious (i.e., such that any right-thinking, properly functioning person can immediately see that it is so); we then attribute their opposing this obvious truth either to dishonesty (they don't really believe what they say; after all, who could?) or to their being blinded by something or other—maybe a reluctance to change, an aversion to new ideas, personal ambition, sexism, racism, or homophobia. Thus according to Judith Plaskow, "If the Rabbinical Assembly Law Committee cannot see that it is reflecting and supporting a long history of religious homophobia (Jewish and otherwise), then it is either willfully blind or patently dishonest."[32] In a similar vein, Richard Dawkins insists (in a recent review in the *New York Times*), "It is absolutely safe to say that if you meet someone who claims not to believe in evolution, that person is ignorant, stupid or insane (or wicked, but I'd rather not consider that)."[33] Dawkins apparently thinks the truth of evolution is utterly clear and obvious to anyone

---

And

> Let never so much probability land on one side of a covetous man's reasoning, and money on the other, it is easy to foresee which will outweigh. Tell a man, passionately in love, that he is jilted; bring a score of witnesses of the falsehood of his mistress, 'tis ten to one but three kind words of hers, shall invalidate all their testimonies . . . and though men cannot always openly gain-say, or resist the force of manifest probabilities, that make against them; yet yield they not to the argument. (Ibid., IV, xx, 12)

32. "Burning in Hell, Conservative Movement Style," *Tikkun* (May–June 1993), pp. 49–50. Recall in this connection Don Cupitt's charge that those who claim to accept "theological realism" (i.e., those who claim to believe that there really is such a person as God) are "hypocrites or psychotics"—the former, presumably, if they merely *claim* to be theological realists, and the latter if they really are.

33. *New York Times*, April 9, 1989, sec. 7, p. 34. Daniel Dennett goes Dawkins one (or two) better, claiming that one who so much as harbors doubts about evolution is "inexcusably ignorant" (*Darwin's Dangerous Idea* [New York: Simon and Schuster, 1995], p. 46)—thus displaying *both* ignorance *and* wrongdoing.

who is not unduly ignorant, is not too stupid to follow the arguments, and is sane (i.e., with rational faculties that are functioning properly); it is therefore obvious that all who aren't just (wickedly) lying through their teeth would have to admit that they believe in evolution. What are appealed to in all these cases are mechanisms that can override or cancel what our rational faculties would ordinarily deliver, substituting a belief that is either *contrary* to what unimpeded rational faculties would deliver, or at any rate *distinct* from what reason would deliver.

What we see, therefore, is that there are at least three ways in which a belief can fail to be a proper deliverance of our rational faculties: it may be produced by malfunctioning faculties, by cognitive processes aimed at something other than the truth, or by faculties whose function has been impeded and overridden by lust, ambition, greed, selfishness, grief, fear, low self-esteem, and other emotional conditions.[34] Accordingly, a belief can fail to be a proper deliverance of our rational faculties by way of malfunction and by way of being produced by a process that is not aimed at the production of true belief.

And here we come to the heart of the F&M objection: when F&M say that Christian belief, or theistic belief, or even perhaps religious belief in general is *irrational*, the basic idea is that belief of this sort is not among the proper deliverances of our rational faculties. It is not produced by properly functioning truth-aimed cognitive faculties or processes. It is not produced by belief-producing processes that are free of dysfunction and whose purpose it is to furnish us with true belief. And this means that the presumption of the reliability of properly functioning cognitive faculties does not apply to the processes that yield belief in God or Christian belief more broadly. The fundamental idea is that religious belief has a source distinct from those of our faculties that are aimed at the truth. Alternatively, if religious belief *does* somehow issue from those truth-aimed faculties, their operation, when they function in such a way as to produce religious belief, is overridden and impeded by something else: a need for security, or for feeling important in the whole scheme of things, or for psychological comfort in the face of this pitiless, intimidating, and implacable world we face.

Just what sort of deviation from the norm does religious belief present? Here Freud and Marx seem to diverge. Although Marx has relatively little to say about religion, there is of course that famous passage I quoted above (pp. 140–41); he seems to hold that what our rational faculties teach us (when they are unimpeded by that cogni-

---

34. This last (perhaps we can call it 'impedance') is not strictly a case of malfunction, but for present purposes I shall include it under malfunction.

tive dysfunction produced by a perverted social order) is that there is no God and no religious meaning to life. There is no Father in Heaven to turn to and no prospect of anything, after death, but dissolution. The fundamental idea is that religious belief is irrational in a double sense: first, it is a product of cognitive faculties that are malfunctioning in response to social and political disorder; second, what these faculties produce when malfunctioning in this way is contrary to the deliverances of our rational faculties—that is, contrary to what they deliver when they function properly. For Freud, too, the main point is that theistic and religious belief, or theistic belief insofar as it is religious, does not arise from the proper function of truth-aimed cognitive processes or faculties, but rather from wishful thinking.[35] This is the force of Freud's claim that religious belief is an *illusion*. Of course, illusions have their functions, and a place in the human cognitive design plan; they may serve important ends, such as the end Freud thinks religious belief serves. Nevertheless, such cognitive processes as wishful thinking are not aimed at the production of true beliefs. Beliefs produced by wishful thinking are therefore irrational or nonrational in the sense that they are not produced by our rational faculties; they are not produced by truth-aimed cognitive processes. Like Marx, however, Freud thinks religious belief is also irrational in a stronger sense. Such belief runs *contrary* to the deliverances of our rational powers; they are "patently infantile" and "foreign to reality."

The F&M criticism, then, is that religious belief is not produced by cognitive faculties that are functioning properly and aimed at the truth. And this, I think, leads us finally to a viable *de jure* question. Those who raise this question are not interested first of all in the *truth* of Christian belief: their claim is that there is something wrong with believing it. Christian belief may be true, and it may be false; but at any rate it is irrational to accept it. They are best construed, I think, as complaining that Christian belief is not produced by cognitive faculties functioning properly and aimed at the truth. Now what this suggests (at least to anyone who has taken a look at the first two volumes in this series) is *warrant*. Freud and Marx, from the perspective

---

35. Freud thinks of *reason* as the aggregate of those faculties (and he thinks of them as the ones involved in the pursuit of science); his idea, furthermore, is that reason taken this way is the only means we have for achieving the truth. Displaying that touching confidence in science characteristic of the Enlightenment, Freud assumes that scientific reason will enable us to achieve the truth in areas where for centuries we wandered in darkness; more modestly, perhaps reason so taken gives us our best shot at the truth. Ironically enough, there is excellent reason to doubt that Freud's characteristic contributions themselves constitute science in any sensible sense; see Adolf Grünbaum's *The Foundations of Psychoanalysis* (Berkeley: University of California Press, 1984).

of those volumes, are really complaining that theistic belief and religious belief generally *lack warrant*. And the *de jure* criticism, so it seems to me, is best construed as the claim that Christian belief, whether true or false, is at any rate without warrant.

II. WARRANT: THE SOBER TRUTH

I've said most[36] of what I have to say about the nature of warrant in *Warrant: The Current Debate* (WCD) and WPF. To spare the reader a trip to the library, however, I will briefly recapitulate; readers who want more depth and detail should consult those volumes (although on pp. 156ff. below I make a correction to what is said in WCD and WPF). The question is as old as Plato's *Theaetetus*: what is it that distinguishes knowledge from mere true belief? What further quality or quantity must a true belief have, if it is to constitute knowledge? This is one of the main questions of epistemology. (No doubt that is why it is called 'theory of knowledge'.) Along with nearly all subsequent thinkers, Plato takes it for granted that knowledge is at least true belief: you know a proposition *p* only if you believe it, and only if it is true. But Plato goes on to point out that true belief, while necessary for knowledge, is clearly not sufficient: it is entirely possible to believe something that is true without knowing it. You are congenitally given to pessimism; you believe that the stock market will plunge tomorrow, even though you have no evidence; even if you turn out to be right, you didn't know. You have traveled two thousand miles to the North Cascades for a climbing trip; you are desperately eager to climb. Being an incurable optimist, you believe it will be bright, sunny, and warm tomorrow, despite the forecast, which calls for high winds and a nasty mixture of rain, sleet, and snow. As it turns out, the forecasters were wrong, and tomorrow turns out sunny and beautiful: your belief was true, but didn't constitute knowledge.

Suppose we use the term 'warrant' to denote that further quality or quantity (perhaps it comes in degrees), whatever precisely it may be, enough of which distinguishes knowledge from mere true belief. Then our question (the subject of WPF): what is warrant? My suggestion (WPF, chapters 1 and 2) begins with the idea that a belief has warrant only if it is produced by cognitive faculties that are functioning properly, subject to no disorder or dysfunction—construed as

---

36. The rest is to be found in my reply to Alston, Ginet, Steup, Swinburne, and Taylor in "Reliabilism, Analyses and Defeaters," *Philosophy and Phenomenological Research* 55/2 (1995), pp. 427ff.; "Respondeo," in *Warrant in Contemporary Epistemology: Essays in Honor of Plantinga's Theory of Knowledge*, ed. J. Kvanvig (Lanham, Md.: Rowman and Littlefield, 1996); "Warrant and Accidentally True Belief," *Analysis* 57, n. 2 (April 1, 1997), p. 140; and pp. 156ff., below.

including absence of impedance as well as pathology. The notion of proper function is fundamental to our central ways of thinking about knowledge.

But that notion is inextricably bound with another: that of a *design plan*.[37] Human beings and their organs are so constructed that there is a way they *should* work, a way they are *supposed* to work, a way they work when they work right; this is the way they work when there is no malfunction. There is a way in which your heart is supposed to work: for example, your pulse rate should be about 50 to 80 beats per minute when you are at rest and (if you are under age forty) achieve a maximum rate of some 180 to 200 beats per minute when you are exercising really hard. If your resting pulse is 160, or if you can't get your pulse above 60 beats per minute no matter how hard you work, then your heart isn't functioning properly. (Then again, a *bird* whose resting heart rate is 160 might be perfectly healthy.) We needn't initially take the notions of *design plan* and *way in which a thing is supposed to work* to entail *conscious* design or purpose. I don't here mean to claim that organisms are created by a conscious agent (God) according to a design plan, in something like the way in which human artifacts are constructed and designed (although in fact I think something like that is true). I am not supposing, initially at least, that having a design plan implies having been created by God or some other conscious agent; it is perhaps possible that evolution (undirected by God or anyone else) has somehow furnished us with our design plans.[38] I mean, instead, to point to something nearly all of us, theists or not, believe: there is a way in which a human organ or system works when it works properly, works as it is supposed to work; and this way of working is given by its design or design plan.

Proper function and design go hand in hand with the notion of *purpose* or *function*. The various organs and systems of the body (and the ways in which they work) have their functions, their purposes: the function or purpose of the heart is to pump the blood; of the immune system, to fight off disease; of the lungs to provide oxygen; of peristalsis, to move nutrients along the intestinal tract, and so on. If the design is a *good* design, then when the organ or system functions properly (i.e., according to its design plan), that purpose will be achieved. The design plan specifies a particular way of working that subserves that purpose. Of course, the design plan for human beings will include specifications for our *cognitive* system or faculties, as well as for noncognitive systems and organs. Like the rest of our organs and systems, our cognitive faculties can work well or ill; they can mal-

37. See WPF, pp. 11ff.
38. Although in WPF, chapter 11, I argue that there is no viable naturalistic account of proper function.

function or function properly. They too work in a certain way when they are functioning properly—and work in a certain way to accomplish their purpose. Accordingly, the first element in our conception of warrant (so I say) is that a belief has warrant for someone only if her faculties are functioning properly, are subject to no dysfunction, in producing that belief.[39]

But that's not enough. Many systems of your body, obviously, are designed to work *in a certain kind of environment*. You can't breathe under water; your muscles atrophy in zero gravity; you can't get enough oxygen at the top of Mount Everest. Clearly, the same goes for your cognitive faculties; they too will achieve their purpose only if functioning in an environment much like the one for which they were designed (by God or evolution). Thus they won't work well in an environment (on some other planet, for example) in which a certain subtle radiation impedes the function of memory.

And this is still not enough. It is clearly possible that a belief be produced by cognitive faculties that are functioning properly in an environment for which they were designed, but nonetheless lack warrant; the above two conditions are not sufficient. We think that the purpose or function of our belief-producing faculties is to furnish us with true (or verisimilitudinous) belief. As we saw above in connection with the F&M complaint, however, it is clearly possible that the purpose or function of *some* belief-producing faculties or mechanisms is the production of beliefs with some other virtue—perhaps that of enabling us to get along in this cold, cruel, threatening world, or of enabling us to survive a dangerous situation or a life-threatening disease. So we must add that the belief in question is produced by cognitive faculties such that the purpose of those faculties is that of producing true belief. More exactly, we must add that the portion of the design plan governing the production of the belief in question is aimed at the production of true belief (rather than survival, or psychological comfort, or the possibility of loyalty, or something else).

Even this isn't sufficient. We can see why by reflecting on a fantasy of David Hume's:

> This world, for aught he knows, is very faulty and imperfect, compared to a superior standard; and was only the first rude essay of some infant Deity, who afterwards abandoned it, ashamed of his lame performance; it is the work only of some dependent, inferior Deity; and is the object of derision to his superiors; it is the production of old age and dotage in some superannuated Deity; and ever since his death, has run on at adventures, from the first impulse and active force, which it received from him.[40]

---

39. For necessary qualifications, see WPF, pp. 9ff. and 22–42.

40. *Dialogues Concerning Natural Religion*, ed. Nelson Pike (Indianapolis and New York: Bobbs-Merrill, 1970), p. 53.

So imagine that a young and untutored apprentice deity sets out to build cognitive beings, beings capable of belief and knowledge. Immaturity and incompetence triumph; the design contains serious glitches. In fact, in some areas of the design, when the faculties work just as they were designed to, the result is ludicrously false belief: thus when the cognitive faculties of these beings are working according to their design plan, they constantly confuse horses and hearses, forming the odd beliefs that cowboys in the old West rode hearses and that corpses are usually transported in horses. These beliefs are then produced by cognitive faculties working properly in the right sort of environment according to a design plan aimed at truth, but they still lack warrant. What is missing? Clearly enough, what must be added is that the design plan in question is a *good* one, one that is *successfully* aimed at truth, one such that there is a high (objective) probability that a belief produced according to that plan will be true (or nearly true).

Put in a nutshell, then, a belief has warrant for a person *S* only if that belief is produced in *S* by cognitive faculties functioning properly (subject to no dysfunction) in a cognitive environment that is appropriate for *S*'s kind of cognitive faculties, according to a design plan that is successfully aimed at truth. We must add, furthermore, that when a belief meets these conditions and does enjoy warrant, the *degree* of warrant it enjoys depends on the strength of the belief, the firmness with which S holds it. This is intended as an account of the central *core* of our concept of warrant; there is a penumbral area surrounding the central core where there are many analogical extensions of that central core; and beyond the penumbral area, still another belt of vagueness and imprecision, a host of possible cases and circumstances where there is really no answer to the question whether a given case is or isn't a case of warrant.[41] This means that the sort of classical analysis in which necessary and sufficient conditions are set out in a stylishly austere clause or two is of limited value here. What we need, instead, is an explanation and description of how the account works in the main areas of our cognitive life; that was the task of WPF.

> Responses to the above account of warrant have made it abundantly clear that it needs a certain kind of supplementation and fine tuning.[42] To see this, consider the following kind of Gettier example. I own a Chevrolet van, drive to Notre Dame on a football Saturday, and unthinkingly park in one of the many spaces reserved for the football coach. Naturally, his minions tow my van away and, as befits such *lèse-majesté*, destroy it. By a splendid piece of good luck, however, I have won the

41. As I argue in WPF, pp. 212–13.
42. By Robert Shope in "Gettier Problems," in *Routledge Encyclopedia of Phil-*

Varsity Club's Win-a-Chevrolet-Van contest, although I haven't yet heard the good news. You ask me what sort of automobile I own; I reply, both honestly and truthfully, "A Chevrolet van." My belief that I own such a van is true, but 'just by accident' (more accurately, it is only by accident that I happen to form a true belief); hence it does not constitute knowledge. All of the nonenvironmental conditions for warrant, furthermore, are met. It also looks as if the environmental condition is met: after all, isn't the cognitive environment here on earth and in South Bend just the one for which our faculties were designed? What is important about the example is this: it is clear that if the coach's minions had been a bit less zealous and had *not* destroyed my van, the conditions for warrant outlined above would have obtained and I would have known that I owned a Chevrolet van. In the actual situation, however, the one in which the van is destroyed, my belief is produced by the very same processes functioning the very same way in (apparently) the same cognitive environment. Hence, on my account, either both of these situations are ones in which I know that I own a Chevrolet van, or neither is. But clearly one is, and the other isn't. Therefore my account is apparently defective.[43]

Consider another Gettier example, this one antedating Gettier's birth (it was proposed by Bertrand Russell). I glance at a clock, forming the opinion that it is 3:43 P.M.; as luck would have it, the clock stopped precisely twenty-four hours ago. The belief I form is indeed true; again, however, it is true 'just by accident' (the clock could just as well have stopped an hour earlier or later); it does not constitute knowledge. As in the previous case, if the clock had been running properly and I had formed the same belief by the same exercise of cognitive powers, I would have known; here, therefore, we have another example that apparently refutes my account. Still another example: I am not aware that Paul's look-alike brother Peter is staying at his house; if I'm across the street, take a quick look, and form the belief that Paul is emerging from his house, I don't know that it's Paul, even if in fact it is (it could just as well have been Peter emerging); again, if Peter hadn't been in the neighborhood, I would have known.

What is crucial, in each of these cases, is that my cognitive faculties display a certain *lack of resolution*. I am unable, by a quick glance, to distinguish the state of affairs in which the clock is running properly and

osophy, ed. Edward Craig (London: Routledge, 1998), and his forthcoming book *Knowledge as Power*; Richard Feldman in "Plantinga, Gettier, and Warrant," in *Warrant in Contemporary Epistemology: Essays in Honor of Plantinga's Theory of Knowledge*, ed. Jonathan Kvanvig (New York: Rowman and Littlefield, 1996), p. 216; and Peter Klein, "Warrant, Proper Function, Reliabilism, and Defeasibility," in *Warrant in Contemporary Epistemology*, p. 105. I am grateful to all three for instruction and enlightenment. For my reply and an effort at repair, see "Respondeo," in *Warrant in Contemporary Epistemology*.

43. For fuller development here, see "Respondeo," in *Warrant in Contemporary Epistemology*, pp. 314ff.

telling the right time from a state of affairs in which it stopped just twelve or twenty-four hours earlier. I cannot distinguish Paul from Peter just by a quick look from across the street. Of course, this lack of resolution is in each case relative to the particular exercise of cognitive powers in question. If I had watched the clock for ten minutes, say, I would have known that it isn't running, and if I had walked across the street and taken a good look, I'd have known that it wasn't Paul but Peter at the door.

What I can't distinguish by those exercises of my epistemic powers are different *cognitive minienvironments*. In "Respondeo," there is a fuller development of the distinction between cognitive maxienvironments and cognitive minienvironments; here the following will suffice. First, a cognitive maxienvironment is more general and more global than a cognitive minienvironment. Our cognitive maxienvironment here on earth would include such macroscopic features as the presence and properties of light and air, the presence of visible objects, of other objects detectable by cognitive systems of our kind, of some objects not so detectable, of the regularities of nature, of the existence and general nature of other people, and so on. Our cognitive faculties are designed (by God or evolution) to function in *this* maxienvironment, or one like it. They are not designed for a maxienvironment in which, for example, there is constant darkness, or where everything is in a state of constant random flux, or where the only food available contains a substance that destroys short-term memory, or where there aren't any distinguishable objects, or no regularities of a kind we can detect; in such an environment, our faculties will not fulfill their function of providing us with true beliefs. Now a given cognitive maxienvironment can contain many different minienvironments—for example, the one where the clock stops, but also one where it doesn't; the one where Peter is visiting Paul, but also one where he isn't; the one where the coach's minions destroy my van, but also one where they magnanimously temper the punishment I so richly deserve, contenting themselves with painting the windshield black.

And now here's the point: some cognitive minienvironments—such as those of the Notre Dame van case, the clock that stopped, Peter's visit to Paul—are *misleading* for some exercises of cognitive faculties, even when those faculties are functioning properly and even when the maxienvironment is favorable. The maxienvironment is right, but the minienvironment isn't; in those minienvironments the cognitive faculties in question (more exactly, particular exercises of the cognitive faculties in question) can't be counted on to produce true beliefs. The basic idea is this: our cognitive faculties have been designed for a certain kind of maxienvironment. Even within that maxienvironment, however, they don't function perfectly (they sometimes produce false belief), although they do function reliably. (Perhaps perfectly functioning cognitive faculties would require too much brain size, thus interfering with the achievement of other desiderata.) In some minienvironments, therefore, they can't be counted on to produce a true belief: if they do, it is just by accident and does not constitute knowledge. So even if the maxienvironment is favorable and the other conditions of warrant are met, a belief could still be true 'just by accident', thus not constituting knowledge.

It is clear, therefore, that S knows p, on a given occasion, only if S's cognitive minienvironment, on that occasion, is not misleading—more exactly, not misleading with respect to the particular exercise of cognitive powers producing the belief that p. So the conditions of warrant (i.e., for the degree of warrant sufficient for knowledge[44]) need an addition: the maxienvironment must, indeed, be favorable or appropriate, but so must the cognitive minienvironment. What must then be added to the other conditions of warrant is the *resolution condition*:

> (RC) A belief B produced by an exercise E of cognitive powers has warrant sufficient for knowledge only if MBE (the minienvironment with respect to B and E) is favorable for E.

What does 'appropriateness' or 'favorability', or 'nonmisleadingness', for a cognitive minienvironment, consist in: can we say anything more definite? Intuitively, a minienvironment is favorable, for an exercise of cognitive powers, if that exercise *can be counted on* to produce a true belief in that minienvironment. Perhaps this is as specific as we can sensibly get; in "Respondeo," however, I went on to make a tentative suggestion as to how we could say a bit more precisely what this favorability consists in. Where B is a belief, E the exercise of cognitive powers that produces B, and MBE a minienvironment with respect to B and E, say that

> (F) MBE is *favorable* for E if and only if, if S were to form a belief by way of E in MBE, S would form a true belief.[45]

Sadly enough, though, (F) won't do the trick at all; the relevant counterfactual itself can be true 'just by accident'—that is, by accident from the point of view of the design plan.[46] There are plenty of possible cases to demonstrate this: here is one. Return to those impecunious Wisconsinites trying to put the best face on things by erecting a lot of fake barns.[47] Suppose I am driving through the area on an early September morning when there is a good deal of mist and fog. I glance to the right and see a real barn; as it happens, all the nearby fake barns (which outnumber the real ones) are obscured by the morning mist; I

---

44. The thought is not that a belief produced in an unfavorable minienvironment has no warrant at all, but only that it doesn't have a degree of warrant sufficient for *knowledge*. See Trenton Merricks's "Warrant Entails Truth," *Philosophy and Phenomenological Research*, 55, no. 4 (December 1995), p. 841; see also Sharon Ryan's reply, "Does Warrant Entail Truth?" *Philosophy and Phenomenological Research* 56, no. 1 (March 1996), p. 183, and Merricks's rejoinder, "More on Warrant's Entailing Truth," *Philosophy and Phenomenological Research* 57, no. 3 (September 1997), p. 627.

45. Here I am assuming (contrary to the usual semantics for counterfactuals) that truth of antecedent and consequent is not sufficient for truth of the counterfactual (a counterfactual can be false even if it has a true antecedent and a true consequent). What is also required is that there be no sufficiently close possible world in which the counterfactual has a true antecedent and false consequent.

46. As was pointed out to me by Thomas Crisp.

47. See WPF, pp. 32–33.

say to myself, "Now that is a fine barn!" The belief I form is true; the relevant counterfactual is also true because of the way the fake barns are
obscured by mist; but the belief does not have warrant sufficient for
knowledge.

What to do? Here is another (also tentative) suggestion. Recall that
the resolution problem arises because I can't (for example) distinguish
Paul from Peter from across the street just by looking; this particular exercise of cognitive powers displays insufficient resolution for that. So
consider a given exercise of cognitive powers E, the belief B formed on
that occasion, and a relevant cognitive minienvironment MBE. If the
conditions of warrant have been met, B will be probable (ordinarily very
probable) with respect to MBE. Of course, MBE is a state of affairs.
Among the states of affairs it includes are some that E is competent to
detect, that are cognitively accessible to E. Thus in the twin case the appearance of a person, of a man, of someone across the road, and the
like, are all detectable by E—that is, just by taking a look. On the other
hand, it's being Paul rather than Peter who appears in the doorway is
not thus detectable; they look just alike at this distance, and I know
nothing entailing that Peter isn't there. So consider the conjunction of
circumstances C contained in MBE such that C is detectable by E; call
this conjunctive state of affairs $DMBE$. In the case in question, these circumstances will be observable, and observable by way of taking a look
from across the road. In the typical case, furthermore (assuming that
the general conditions of warrant are met), B will also be probable with
respect to $DMBE$. And now we can say what it is for a minienvironment
to be favorable:

> MBE is favorable just if there is no state of affairs S included in MBE
> but not in $DMBE$ such that the objective probabilityof B with respect
> to the conjunction of $DMBE$ and S falls below r,

where r is some real number representing a reasonably high probability.
In the twin case, for example, a state of affairs S such that B is not probable enough with respect to the conjunction of $DMBE$ and S would be
Peter's being in the house as well as Paul, and being indistinguishable
from him from across the street. In the case of the impecunious Wisconsinites, it is that there are more fake barns than real barns in the
neighborhood. Also, of course, I don't specify the requisite level of probability r, which in any case will display a certain contextual character,
differing from case to case.

This suggestion seems promising, although induction leads me to
be less than wholly confident that it is right. It may be that in the long
run we can't say more than that the minienvironment must be favorable.
The overall picture, then, is as follows. Our faculties are designed for a
certain kind of cognitive maxienvironment, one that sufficiently resembles the one in which we do, in fact, find ourselves. And when a belief is
formed by properly functioning faculties in an environment of that sort
(and the bit of the design plan that governs its production is successfully
aimed at truth), then the belief in question has *some* degree of warrant,
even if it happens to be false. But our cognitive faculties are not maximally effective—not only in that there is much we aren't capable of com-

ing to know but also in that we are sometimes prone to err, even when the maxienvironment is right and the relevant faculties are functioning properly. Another way to put the same point: within a favorable cognitive maxienvironment, there can be minienvironments for a given exercise of our faculties, in which it is just by accident, dumb luck, that a true belief is formed, if one is indeed formed. A true belief formed in such a minienvironment doesn't have warrant sufficient for knowledge, even if it has some degree of warrant. To achieve that more exalted degree of warrant, the belief must be formed in a minienvironment such that the exercise of the cognitive powers producing it can be counted on to produce a true belief. Hence the resolution condition. Beliefs that meet all of the conditions will then constitute knowledge (provided they are accepted with sufficient firmness).

I have neglected several important components of our epistemic establishment. First, I have said nothing here about *defeaters*; in chapter 11, I'll address this topic. Another very important topic ignored here[48] is that of epistemic probability. Further, knowledge or warrant seems to have a *contextual* character; the degree of warrant necessary for knowledge seems to depend, to some extent, on circumstances and context. I don't have the space to go into these matters here.

III. THE F&M COMPLAINT AGAIN

Now we are ready to return to the F&M complaint. What we see is a clear if surprising connection between the topic of warrrant and the F&M complaint: the latter is really the claim that theistic belief *lacks warrant*. According to Freud, theistic belief is produced by cognitive faculties that are functioning properly, but the process that produces it—wishful thinking—does not have the production of true belief as its purpose; it is aimed, instead, at something like enabling us to carry on in the grim and threatening world in which we find ourselves. Therefore, theistic belief does not meet the third condition of warrant; as a result, the presumption of reliability that goes with warranted beliefs does not apply to it. Theistic belief is no more respectable, epistemically speaking, than propositions selected entirely at random. Suppose I have a random generator of English declarative sentences (sentences that express propositions); it randomly chooses one of a stockpile of a million sentences and their negations, flashing its selection on a big screen. I use the machine, recommending the resulting proposition to you for belief. You quite properly demur, pointing out that there isn't the slightest reason to think the belief in question true. Theistic belief, thinks Freud, has no better epistemic credentials, for the believer, than the propositions expressed

---

48. But treated in WPF, chapter 9.

by those sentences would have for someone for whom they have no source of warrant in addition to their appearing on the screen. It is baseless superstition.

Still further, Freud thinks, once we see that theistic and religious belief has its origin in wishful thinking, we will also see that it is very probably false. There is no good argument from this fact about its origin to the conclusion that it is false; nor is it that someone who recognizes its origin in wishful thinking will simply see that it is false. It is rather just that people of sense who know something about how the world works will take it to be probably false. They will take the same attitude toward theistic and Christian belief that they take toward the stories in Greek or Aztec or Persian mythology: we can't really prove that these stories are false, but their chances of being true are pretty slim. So the proper intellectual attitude toward these beliefs isn't merely agnosticism; it is that the beliefs in question are unwarranted and furthermore are very probably false.

Marx's views are similar. He thinks first that theistic and religious belief is produced by cognitive faculties that are not functioning properly. Those faculties are, to the extent that they produce such belief, dysfunctional; the dysfunction is due to a sort of perversion in social structure, a sort of social malfunction. Religious belief therefore doesn't meet the first condition of warrant; it is therefore without warrant, and an intellectually healthy person will reject it. Further, Marx also thinks that a person whose cognitive faculties are functioning properly and who knows what was known by the middle of the nineteenth century will see that materialism is very probably true, in which case Christian and theistic belief is very likely false. So he would join Freud in the contention that Christian and theistic belief is without warrant, a baseless superstition, and very probably false.

> We could see the matter slightly differently. Perhaps the problem with religious belief, according to Marx, is not that it is produced by *malfunctioning* faculties, but rather that capitalist society constitutes a hostile environment for the operation of human cognitive faculties; then the problem would be the second condition rather than the first. Still another possibility: perhaps the production of theistic or religious belief is like a damage-control mechanism. When people are subjected to the nasty conditions of capitalism, they come to believe these tales of a God and another world as a means of coping with their otherwise intolerable situation. Then Marx's view would be more like Freud's, and religious belief could be seen as an illusion in the Freudian sense. There would remain the following difference. According to Freud, the inclination to form religious belief arises out of our nature and is therefore to be expected, no matter what the social structure. According to this version of Marx, however, religious belief is a response to the very special social circumstances of misery and injustice generated by capitalist society, so that there need be no inclination toward it among people in a society

that doesn't display that or a similar perversion. Of course Marx actually says little about religion, not enough to make it possible to distinguish one of these possibilities as the one he had in mind.

The F&M complaint, therefore, is that theistic belief and religious belief in general lack warrant. So say Freud and Marx—but are they right? In the next chapter, we shall turn to a model for the possession of warrant by Christian belief. Model in hand, we shall then evaluate the F&M complaint.

PART III

WARRANTED CHRISTIAN BELIEF

6

Warranted Belief in God

To know in a general and confused way that God exists is implanted in us by nature. . . .

Thomas Aquinas

for since the creation of the world God's invisible qualities—his eternal power and divine nature—have been clearly seen, being understood from what has been made. . . .

St. Paul

The *de jure* challenge to Christian (or theistic) belief, as we have seen, is the claim that such belief is irrational or unreasonable or unjustified or in some other way properly subject to invidious epistemic criticism; it contrasts with the *de facto* challenge, according to which the belief in question is false. Put just like that, the *de jure* rebuke is pretty vague and general; we can't do much by way of evaluating the proposed complaint without achieving a clearer and more specific formulation of it. As we have seen, clear and sensible formulation of the *de jure* criticism—at any rate of one that isn't just obviously mistaken—has proven elusive. In the last chapter, however, we were able to make progress by considering the F&M (Freud and Marx) complaint. What we saw is that this complaint is really the claim that Christian and other theistic belief is *irrational* in the sense that it originates in cognitive malfunction (Marx) or in cognitive proper function that is aimed at something other than the truth (Freud)—comfort, perhaps, or the ability to soldier on in this appalling world in which we find ourselves. To put it another way, the claim is that such belief doesn't originate in the proper function of cognitive faculties successfully aimed at producing true beliefs. To put it in still another way, the charge is that theistic and Christian belief *lacks warrant*.

By way of response, in this chapter I shall first offer a model— a model based on a claim made jointly by Thomas Aquinas and John Calvin—for a way in which theistic belief could have warrant. Once we see how theistic belief might have warrant, we can also see the futility of the F&M complaint and its contemporary successors. In the remaining chapters of part III, I shall extend the model to cover specifically Christian belief. Chapter 7 will deal with sin and its noetic results. The extended model crucially involves the notion of *faith*. Following Aquinas and Calvin, I shall argue that faith has both an intellectual and an affective component: chapter 8 will therefore examine the way in which, as Calvin says, the great truths of the gospel are "revealed to our minds," and chapter 9 will examine the way in which, as he also says, they are "sealed unto our hearts." Then in chapter 10, I'll consider and reply to objections to the original and extended models.

I. THE AQUINAS/CALVIN MODEL

A. Models

I say I propose in this chapter to give a *model* of theistic belief's having warrant; but what sort of animal is a model, and what would it be good for? There are models of many different kinds: model airplanes, artists' models, models in the sense of exemplars, models of a modern major general. There is also the logician's sense of model in which, for example, any consistent first-order theory has a model in the natural numbers. My use of the term here is more abstract than the first and more concrete than the second. The rough idea is this: to give a model of a proposition or state of affairs S is to show *how it could be* that S is true or actual. The model itself will be *another* proposition (or state of affairs), one such that it is clear (1) that it is possible and (2) that if it is *true*, then so is the target proposition. From these two, of course, it follows that the target proposition is possible. In this chapter, I shall give a model of theistic belief's having warrant: the Aquinas/Calvin (A/C) model. Then in chapters 7, 8, and 9, I will extend the A/C model to a model in which specific and full-blooded Christian belief has warrant.

I claim four things for these two models. First, they are possible, and thus show it is possible that theistic and Christian belief have warrant. The sense of possibility here, however, isn't just broadly logical possibility—after all, such obvious falsehoods as *the population of China is less than a thousand* are possible in *that* sense—but something much stronger. I claim that these models are *epistemically* possible:

they are consistent with what we know, where "what we know" is what all (or most) of the participants in the discussion agree on.[1]

Second, and related to the first assertion, I claim that there aren't any cogent objections to the model—that is, to the proposition that the model is in fact true or actual. More exactly, there are no cogent objections of a philosophic or scientific kind (or indeed any other kind) to the model that are not *also* cogent objections to theism or Christian belief. Another way to put it: any cogent objection to the *model's* truth will also have to be a cogent objection to the truth of *theistic or Christian belief*. I shall go on to argue that if Christian belief is indeed true, then the model in question or one very like it is also true. If I am successful, therefore, the upshot will be that there is no viable *de jure* (as opposed to *de facto*) challenge either to theistic or to Christian belief. There is no sensible challenge to the rationality or rational justification or warrant of Christian belief that is not also a challenge to its *truth*. That is, there is no *de jure* challenge that is independent of a *de facto* challenge. That means that a particularly popular way of criticizing Christian belief—to be found in the evidentialist objection, in the F&M complaint, in many versions of the argument from evil, and in still other objections—is not viable. This is the sort of challenge that goes as follows: "I don't know whether Christian (or theistic) belief is *true*—how could anyone know a thing like that? But I do know that it is irrational, or rationally unacceptable or unjustified or without warrant (or in some other way epistemically challenged)." If my argument is right, no objection of this sort has any force.

Third, I believe that the models I shall present are not only possible and beyond philosophical challenge but also *true*, or at least verisimilitudinous, close to the truth. Still, I don't claim to *show* that they are true. That is because the A/C model entails the truth of the-

---

1. Epistemic possibility is stronger than broadly logical possibility, but also weaker. There are propositions that are epistemically possible, but not possible in the broadly logical sense—true for all we know, but nonetheless impossible. Of course I can hardly be required to produce one; but I *can* produce a pair one or the other of which enjoys this distinction. Thus consider *existentialism*: the proposition that singular states of affairs and propositions are not necessarily existent but are ontologically dependent upon the objects with respect to which they are singular. For example, according to existentialism, no proposition singular with respect to Socrates—*Socrates was wise*, for example—could have existed if Socrates had not. I believe existentialism is false (see my "On Existentialism," *Philosophical Studies* [July 1983]), but I could scarcely claim to *know* that it is false, and, I believe, the same goes for everyone else. Existentialism is therefore epistemically possible. The same goes, naturally enough, for its denial. Each of these propositions, however, is necessarily true if true at all; hence one or the other is necessarily false, in the broadly logical sense, even if epistemically possible.

ism and the extended A/C model the truth of classical Christianity. To show that these models are true, therefore, would also be to show that theism and Christianity are true; and I don't know how to do something one could sensibly call 'showing' that either of these *is* true. I believe there are a large number (at least a couple dozen) good arguments for the existence of God; none, however, can really be thought of as a *showing* or *demonstration*. As for classical Christianity, there is even less prospect of demonstrating its truth.[2] Of course this is nothing against either their truth or their warrant; very little of what we believe can be 'demonstrated' or 'shown'.

Fourth, there is a whole range of models for the warrant of Christian belief, all different but similar to the A/C and extended A/C models. (In claiming that models I present are close to the truth, what I am claiming is that they belong to that range.) And the fourth thing to say here is that if classical Christian belief *is* indeed true, then one of these models is very likely also true. Alternatively, for one who thinks Christian belief true, one or more of these models (or their disjunction) is a good way in which to conceive the warrant of Christian belief.

B. Presentation of the Model

Thomas Aquinas and John Calvin concur on the claim that there is a kind of natural knowledge of God (and anything on which Calvin and Aquinas are in accord is something to which we had better pay careful attention). Here I want to propose a model based on Calvin's version of the suggestion, not because I think Calvin should be the cynosure of all eyes theological, but because he presents an interesting development of the particular thought in question. And here, as in several other areas, we can usefully see Calvin's suggestion as a kind of meditation on and development of a theme suggested by Aquinas. According to the latter, "To know in a general and confused way that God exists is implanted in us by nature."[3] In the opening chapters of the *Institutes of the Christian Religion*,[4] Calvin concurs: there is a sort of natural knowledge of God. Calvin expands this theme into a suggestion as to the way in which beliefs about God can have warrant; he has a suggestion as to the nature of the faculty or mechanism whereby we acquire true beliefs about God. His idea here

---

2. As I shall argue below, p. 271.

3. *Summa Theologiae* I, q. 2, a.1, ad 1. In *Summa contra Gentiles* Aquinas adds, "There is a certain general and confused knowledge of God, which is in almost all men . . ." (Bk. III, ch. 38).

4. Tr. Ford Lewis Battles and ed. John T. McNeill (Philadelphia: Westminster Press, 1960 [originally published in 1555]). Page references to the *Institutes* are to this edition.

can also be seen as a development of what the apostle Paul says in Romans 1:

> For the wrath of God is revealed from heaven against all ungodliness and wickedness of men who by their wickedness suppress the truth. For what can be known about God is plain to them, because God has shown it to them. Ever since the creation of the world his invisible nature, namely, his eternal power and deity, has been clearly perceived in the things that have been made. So they are without excuse. . . . (Romans 1:18–20)[5]

For our purposes, Calvin's basic claim is that there is a sort of instinct, a natural human tendency, a disposition, a nisus to form beliefs about God under a variety of conditions and in a variety of situations. Thus in his commentary on the above passage:

> By saying, that God has made it manifest, he means, that man was created to be a spectator of this formed world, and that eyes were given him, that he might, by looking on so beautiful a picture, be led up to the Author himself.[6]

In the *Institutes,* he develops this thought:

> There is within the human mind, and indeed by natural instinct, an awareness of divinity. This we take to be beyond controversy. To prevent anyone from taking refuge in the pretense of ignorance, God himself has implanted in all men a certain understanding of his divine majesty. . . . Since, therefore, men one and all perceive that there is a God and that he is their maker, they are condemned by their own testimony because they have failed to honor him and to consecrate their lives to his will . . . there is, as the eminent pagan says, no nation so barbarous, no people so savage, that they have not a deep seated conviction that there is a God. . . . Therefore, since from the beginning of the world there has been no region, no city, in short, no household, that could do without religion, there lies in this a tacit confession of a sense of deity inscribed in the hearts of all. (*Institutes* I, iii, 1, p. 44)[7]

---

5. As Etienne Gilson says, very many medieval and later thinkers have found in this passage a charter for natural theology, construed as the effort to present proofs or arguments for the existence of God. But is Paul really talking here about proofs or arguments? Natural theology, as Aquinas says, is pretty difficult for most of us; most of us have neither the leisure, ability, inclination, nor education to follow those theistic proofs. But here Paul seems to be speaking of *all* of us human beings; what can be known about God is *plain*, he says. It is true that this knowledge comes by way of what God has made, but it doesn't follow that it comes by way of *argument*, the arguments of natural theology, for example. See below, p. 175.

6. *Commentaries on the Epistle of Paul the Apostle to the Romans*, volume XIX of *Calvin's Commentaries* (Grand Rapids: Baker Book House, 1979; originally printed for the Calvin Translation Society of Edinburgh, Scotland), p. 70.

7. The "eminent pagan" is Cicero. John Beversluis suggests that these passages

Calvin goes on to claim that many rejections of God, or attempts to do without him, are really further testimonies to this natural inclination:

> Men of sound judgment will always be sure that a sense of divinity which can never be effaced is engraved upon men's minds. Indeed, the perversity of the impious, who though they struggle furiously are unable to extricate themselves from the fear of God, is abundant testimony that this conviction, namely that there is some God, is naturally inborn in all, and is fixed deep within, as it were in the very marrow. . . . From this we conclude that it is not a doctrine that must first be learned in school, but one of which each of us is master from his mother's womb and which nature itself permits no one to forget, although many strive with every nerve to this end. (I, iii, 3, p. 46)

Separated from the extravagance of expression that sometimes characterizes Calvin, the basic idea, I think, is that there is a kind of faculty or a cognitive mechanism, what Calvin calls a *sensus divinitatis* or sense of divinity, which in a wide variety of circumstances produces in us beliefs about God. These circumstances, we might say, trigger the disposition to form the beliefs in question; they form the occasion on which those beliefs arise. Under these circumstances, we develop or form theistic beliefs—or, rather, these beliefs are formed in us; in the typical case we don't consciously choose to have those beliefs. Instead, we find ourselves with them, just as we find ourselves

---

from the *Institutes* are really directed to human knowledge *before the fall*, and that, according to Calvin, "*fallen* human beings lack both the direct and immediate knowledge of God with which they were originally created and the capacity to achieve it. In Plantinga's language, the 'innate tendency, or nisus, or disposition' to believe in God with which human beings were originally created is no longer operative in fallen humanity" ("Reforming the Reformed Objection to Natural Theology," *Faith and Philosophy* 12, no. 2 (April 1995), p. 193; see also p. 197. Of course Calvin interpretation is not my project here; still, Calvin is pretty clearly teaching that all people, fallen as well as unfallen, have this knowledge ("naturally inborn in all"; "each of us is master from his mother's womb"). Furthermore, as Beversluis points out, according to Calvin (following Romans 1) this knowledge renders those who have "failed to honor him" condemned by their own words (guilty); but of course that isn't possible unless the *sensus divinitatis* is working in them, even if it is not in its pristine state.

There is an additional subtlety here: Beversluis speaks of a tendency "to believe in God." There is obviously an important difference between believing in God and believing that God exists (that there is such a person as God); chapter 9 is devoted in part to that difference. Perhaps in unfallen humanity, according to Calvin, the *sensus divinitatis* is a disposition to believe *in* God (to love him, trust him, see his beauty and glory and loveliness), but in fallen humanity only a tendency to believe *that there is* such a person, just as (according to the book of James) the devils do. See chapter 7 on the noetic effects of sin.

with perceptual and memory beliefs. (You don't and can't simply *decide* to have this belief, thereby acquiring it.)[8] These passages suggest that awareness of God is natural, widespread, and not easy to forget, ignore, or destroy. Seventy years of determined but unsuccessful Marxist efforts to uproot Christianity in the former Soviet Union tend to confirm this claim.[9]

Second, it also sounds as if Calvin thinks knowledge of God is *innate*, such that one has it from birth, "from his mother's womb." Still, perhaps Calvin doesn't really mean to endorse either of these suggestions. The *capacity* for such knowledge is indeed innate, like the capacity for arithmetical knowledge. Still, it doesn't follow that we know elementary arithmetic from our mother's womb; it takes a little maturity. My guess is Calvin thinks the same with respect to this knowledge of God; what one has from one's mother's womb is not this knowledge of God, but a capacity for it. Whatever Calvin thinks, however, it's our model; and according to the model the development of the *sensus divinitatis* requires a certain maturity (although it is often manifested by very young children).

The *sensus divinitatis* is a disposition or set of dispositions to form theistic beliefs in various circumstances, in response to the sorts of conditions or stimuli that trigger the working of this sense of divinity. Calvin thinks in particular of some of nature's grand spectacles. Like Kant, he was especially impressed, in this connection, by the marvelous compages of the starry heavens above:

> Even the common folk and the most untutored, who have been taught only by the aid of the eyes, cannot be unaware of the excellence of divine art, for it reveals itself in this innumerable and yet distinct and well-ordered variety of the heavenly host. It is, accordingly, clear that there is no one to whom the Lord does not abundantly show his wisdom. (I, v, 2, p. 53)

You see the blazing glory of the heavens from a mountainside at 13,000 feet; you think about those unimaginable distances; you find yourself filled with awe and wonder, and you form the belief that God must be great to have created this magnificent heavenly host. But it isn't only the variety of the heavenly host that catches his eye here:

8. See my "Reason and Belief in God," in *Faith and Rationality*, ed. Alvin Plantinga and Nicholas Wolterstorff (Notre Dame: University of Notre Dame Press, 1983), pp. 34ff.

9. It is no part of the model, however, to hold that the *sensus divinitatis* is never subject to malfunction; perhaps it is sometimes diseased or even inoperative. It can also be impeded in the usual ways, and its deliverances can perhaps sometimes be extinguished by the wrong kind of nurture.

Lest anyone, then, be excluded from access to happiness, he not only sowed in men's minds that seed of religion of which we have spoken, but revealed himself and daily discloses himself in the whole workmanship of the universe. As a consequence, men cannot open their eyes without being compelled to see him. . . . But upon his individual works he has engraved unmistakable marks of his glory . . . wherever you cast your eyes, there is no spot in the universe wherein you cannot discern at least some sparks of his glory. (I, v, 1, p. 52)[10]

Calvin's idea is that the workings of the *sensus divinitatis* is triggered or occasioned by a wide variety of circumstances, including in particular some of the glories of nature: the marvelous, impressive beauty of the night sky; the timeless crash and roar of the surf that resonates deep within us; the majestic grandeur of the mountains (the North Cascades, say, as viewed from Whatcom Pass); the ancient, brooding presence of the Australian outback; the thunder of a great waterfall. But it isn't only grandeur and majesty that counts; he would say the same for the subtle play of sunlight on a field in spring, or the dainty, articulate beauty of a tiny flower, or aspen leaves shimmering and dancing in the breeze. "There is no spot in the universe," he says, "wherein you cannot discern at least some sparks of his glory." Calvin could have added other sorts of circumstances: there is something like an awareness of divine disapproval upon having done what is wrong, or cheap, and something like a perception of divine forgiveness upon confession and repentance. People in grave danger instinctively turn to the Lord to ask for succor and support, having formed the belief that he can hear and help if he sees fit. (They say there are no atheists in foxholes.) On a beautiful spring morning (the birds singing, heaven and earth alight and alive with glory, the air fresh and cool, the treetops gleaming in the sun), a spontaneous hymn of thanks to the Lord—thanks for your circumstances and your very existence—may arise in your soul. According to the model, therefore, there are many circumstances, and circumstances of many kinds, that call forth or occasion theistic belief. Here the *sensus divinitatis* resembles other belief-producing faculties or mechanisms. If we wish to think in terms of the overworked functional analogy, we can think of the *sensus divinitatis*, too, as an input-output device: it takes

---

10. Compare Charles Sanders Peirce:

A man looks upon nature, sees its sublimity and beauty, and his spirit gradually rises to the idea of God. He does not see the Divinity, nor does nature prove to him the existence of that Being, but it does excite his mind and imagination until the idea becomes rooted in his heart.

Quoted by Edward T. Oakes, "Discovering the American Aristotle," *First Things* (December 1993), p. 27.

the circumstances mentioned above as input and issues as output theistic beliefs, beliefs about God. We must note six further features of the model.

1. Basicality

According to the A/C model, this natural knowledge of God is not arrived at by inference or argument (for example, the famous theistic proofs of natural theology) but in a much more immediate way. The deliverances of the *sensus divinitatis* are not quick and *sotto voce* inferences from the circumstances that trigger its operation. It isn't that one beholds the night sky, notes that it is grand, and concludes that there must be such a person as God: an argument like that would be ridiculously weak. It isn't that one notes some feature of the Australian outback—that it is ancient and brooding, for example—and draws the conclusion that God exists. It is rather that, upon the perception of the night sky or the mountain vista or the tiny flower, these beliefs just arise within us. They are *occasioned* by the circumstances; they are not conclusions from them. The heavens declare the glory of God and the skies proclaim the work of his hands: but not by way of serving as premises for an argument. Awareness of guilt may lead me to God; but it is not that in this awareness I have the material for a quick theistic argument: I am guilty, so there must be a God. This argument isn't nearly as silly as it looks; but when the operation of the *sensus divinitatis* is triggered by perception of my guilt, it doesn't work by way of an argument. I don't take my guilt as *evidence* for the existence of God, or for the proposition that he is displeased with me. It is rather that in that circumstance—the circumstance of my clearly seeing my guilt—I simply find myself with the belief that God is disapproving or disappointed.

In this regard, the *sensus divinitatis* resembles perception, memory, and *a priori* belief. Consider the first. I look out into the backyard; I see that the coral tiger lilies are in bloom. I don't note that I am being appeared to a certain complicated way (that my experience is of a certain complicated character) and then make an argument from my being appeared to in that way to the conclusion that in fact there are coral tiger lilies in bloom there. (The whole history of modern philosophy up to Hume and Reid shows that such an argument would be thoroughly inconclusive.) It is rather that upon being appeared to in that way (and given my previous training), the belief that the coral tiger lilies are in bloom spontaneously arises in me. This belief will ordinarily be *basic*, in the sense that it is not accepted on the evidential basis of other propositions. The same goes for memory. You ask me what I had for breakfast; I think for a moment and then remember: pancakes with blueberries. I don't argue from the fact that it *seems* to me that I remember having pancakes for breakfast to the conclusion that I did; rather, you ask me what I had for breakfast, and the answer simply comes to mind. Or consider *a priori* belief. I don't infer from other things that, for example, *modus ponens* is a valid form of argument: I just see that it is so and, in fact, *must* be so. All of these, we might say, are starting points for thought. But (on the model) the same goes for the sense of divinity. It isn't a matter of making a quick and dirty inference from the grandeur of the mountains or the beauty of the flower or the sun on the treetops to the existence of God; instead, a belief about God spontaneously arises in those circumstances, the circumstances that trigger the operation of the *sensus divinitatis*. This belief is another of those starting points for thought; it too is basic in the sense that the beliefs in question are not accepted on the evidential basis of other beliefs.[11]

Of course there are options here. The model could be developed in such a way that the role of the *sensus divinitatis* is to enable one to see the truth of the crucial premise for a quick theistic argument—such as *the heavens can be gloriously beautiful only if God has created them*. This proposition is a consequence of theism in any event; what the present suggestion would add is that it plays a crucial role in the genesis of theistic belief.[12] In the *Summa Theologiae* passage quoted above in footnote 3, Aquinas goes on to make a suggestion like this: he suggests that this natural knowledge of God is "immediate," but also by way of inference:

this is due either to the fact that it is self-evident that God exists, just as other principles of demonstration are—a view held by some people, as we said in Book One—or, what seems indeed to be true, that man can immediately reach some sort of knowledge of God by natural reason. For, when men see that things in nature run according to a definite order, and that ordering does not occur without an orderer, they perceive in most cases that there is some orderer of the things that we see.

Here two things are noteworthy. First, what Aquinas says here suggests that this knowledge (the second variety) is by way of inference, so that, strictly speaking, this knowledge of God would not be basic. The inference, however, would be very quick, elementary, and obvious, so that perhaps believing by way of this kind of inference isn't easily distinguished from believing in the basic way.

Second, note that this knowledge of God can indeed be very confused:

---

11. It is worth noting that even if I believe something in the basic way, it doesn't follow that I wouldn't cite various other propositions in response to your question, "Why do you believe *p*? What is your reason for believing *p*?" See "Reason and Belief in God," p. 51.

12. For suggestions as to how the model could be developed in this direction, see Michael Sudduth, "Prospects for 'Mediate' Natural Theology in John Calvin," *Religious Studies* 31, no. 1 (March 1995), p. 53.

But this knowledge admits of a mixture of many errors. Some people have believed that there is no other orderer of worldly things than the celestial bodies, and so they said that the celestial bodies are gods. Other people pushed it farther, to the very elements and the things generated from them, thinking that motion and the natural function which these elements have are not present in them as the effect of some other orderer, but that other things are ordered by them.

Contemporary naturalists such as Daniel Dennett and Richard Dawkins[13] would presumably concur with those who think that "motion and the natural function which these elements have are not present in them as the effect of some other orderer." Aquinas would apparently include them among those who have a natural knowledge of God—at least if they also believe that there is *something* (if only, e.g., natural laws) that orders the things we see. Apparently this kind of knowledge of God, oddly enough, does not preclude being an atheist or a naturalist.

Perhaps we can understand Aquinas as follows. Consider the description *that which orders what we see*. This description in fact applies to God. One who believes that it does indeed apply to something or other can therefore have *de re* knowledge of God; for example, she can believe of *that which orders what we see* that it has one or another properties—that it exists, is powerful, and indeed orders what we see. This would be to believe *de re* of God that he exists, is powerful, and orders what we see. But this knowledge also "admits of many errors": for example, the naturalist thinks that what orders what we see is, in fact, the ensemble of natural laws; she therefore believes *de re* of God that he is the ensemble of natural laws.

Calvin's view of natural knowledge of God would be a bit different. Following Paul in Romans 1, he holds that the natural knowledge in question is sufficient to render human beings *guilty*—guilty of failing to worship, obey, and commit ourselves to God. Hence this knowledge includes that God is to be worshiped and obeyed, so that God couldn't be, for example, the ensemble of natural laws. (Of course there is a sense in which one *does* obey natural laws—if there are any[14]—but in this sense you can't fail to obey them, and wouldn't necessarily be guilty if you could and did.)

2. Proper Basicality with Respect to Justification

On the A/C model, then, theistic belief as produced by the *sensus divinitatis* is basic. It is also *properly* basic, and that in at least two senses. On the one hand, a belief can be properly basic for a person in the

---

13. See the former's *Darwin's Dangerous Idea* (New York: Simon and Schuster, 1995) and the latter's *The Blind Watchmaker* (New York: W. W. Norton, 1986).

14. For arguments casting doubt on the existence of natural laws, see Bas van Fraassen's *Laws and Symmetry* (Oxford: Clarendon Press, 1989), pp. 17ff.

sense that it is indeed basic for him (he doesn't accept it on the evidential basis of other propositions) and, furthermore, he is *justified* in holding it in the basic way: he is within his epistemic rights, is not irresponsible, is violating no epistemic or other duties in holding that belief in that way. This is the sense of proper basicality that was foremost in "Reason and Belief in God." That sense was foremost there because there I was contesting the views of the evidentialist objectors to theistic belief. They didn't ordinarily say precisely what they think the problem is with believing in God in the basic way (without propositional evidence), but as far as I can see, they were claiming that belief in God taken that way is *unjustified*. Further, they apparently understood justification and lack of justification in deontological terms: to be unjustified is to be epistemically irresponsible, to flout an epistemic duty or requirement of some sort. As I argued above in chapter 3, however, it is really pretty obvious that a believer in God is or can be deontologically justified. You think about the matter carefully and at length, considering the F&M complaint and all the rest, but it still seems clear or obvious (perhaps even overwhelmingly so) that there is such a person as God: how could someone sensibly claim that you were being irresponsible or derelict with respect to some epistemic duty? That would be a hard saying indeed.

3. Proper Basicality with Respect to Warrant

There is another sense in which a belief can be properly or improperly basic: *p* is properly basic for *S* in *this* sense if and only if *S* accepts *p* in the basic way, and furthermore *p* has *warrant* for *S*, accepted in that way. Perceptual beliefs are properly basic in this sense: such beliefs are typically accepted in the basic way, and they often have warrant. (They are often produced by cognitive faculties functioning properly in a congenial epistemic environment according to a design plan successfully aimed at truth.) The same goes for memory beliefs, some *a priori* beliefs, and many other beliefs. I suppose the fact is most of our beliefs that have warrant, have it in this basic way; it is only in a smallish area of our cognitive life that the warrant a belief has for us derives from the fact that it is accepted on the evidential basis of other beliefs. Of course, sometimes beliefs are accepted in the basic way but do not have warrant. As we saw in chapter 4, this can be due to cognitive malfunction, or to a cognitive faculty's being impeded by such conditions as rage, lust, ambition, grief, and the like; it can also be because the bit of the design plan governing the production of the belief is aimed not at truth but at something else (survival, e.g.), or because something in the testimonial chain has gone wrong (one of your friends has lied to you), or for still other reasons.

According to the A/C model I am presenting here, theistic belief produced by the *sensus divinitatis* can also be *properly basic with respect to warrant.*[15] It isn't just that the believer in God is within her epistemic rights in accepting theistic belief in the basic way. That is indeed so; more than that, however, this belief can have warrant for the person in question, warrant that is often sufficient for knowledge. The *sensus divinitatis* is a belief-producing faculty (or power, or mechanism) that under the right conditions produces belief that isn't evidentially based on other beliefs. On this model, our cognitive faculties have been designed and created by God; the design plan, therefore, is a design plan in the literal and paradigmatic sense. It is a blueprint or plan for our ways of functioning, and it has been developed and instituted by a conscious, intelligent agent. The purpose of the *sensus divinitatis* is to enable us to have true beliefs about God; when it functions properly, it ordinarily *does* produce true beliefs about God. These beliefs therefore meet the conditions for warrant; if the beliefs produced are strong enough, then they constitute knowledge.[16]

There will be a complicated and many-sided interplay between the deliverances of the *sensus divinitatis* and the deliverances of other sources of belief, just as there is a complicated interplay between the deliverances of perception, which are accepted in the basic way, and other sources of belief. It is not the case, of course, that a person who acquires belief by way of the *sensus divinitatis* need have any well-formed ideas about the source or origin of the belief, or any idea that there is such a faculty as the *sensus divinitatis*. (Just as most of us don't have well-developed ideas as to the source and origin of our *a priori* beliefs.) Nor would such a person accept the belief in question on the basis of the following sort of argument: this belief seems to be a deliverance of the *sensus divinitatis*; the *sensus divinitatis* is a reliable belief-producing mechanism; therefore, probably this belief is true. Of course not; here, as in the case of other original sources of belief (memory, perception, *a priori* belief, etc.), the belief in question isn't typically accepted on the basis of any argument at all, and the belief can have warrant even if the believer has no second-level beliefs at all about the belief in question.

15. And since a belief has warrant only if it is produced by properly functioning processes or faculties, a belief properly basic with respect to warrant is also properly basic with respect to rationality (that is, rationality as proper function; see above, p. 110).

16. Of course it doesn't follow that theistic belief can't get warrant by way of argument from other beliefs; nor does it follow that natural theology and more informal theistic argument is of no worth in the believer's intellectual and spiritual life. Note further that, according to the model, *sin* damages the *sensus divinitatis* and compromises its operation; see below, p. 184 and chapter 7.

4. Natural *Knowledge of God*

This capacity for knowledge of God is part of our original cognitive equipment, part of the fundamental epistemic establishment with which we have been created by God. In this, it contrasts with one of the subjects of chapter 8, the internal instigation of the Holy Spirit. As we shall see there, the latter is an element in the divine response to human sin and the human predicament, a predicament in which we human beings require healing, restoration, and salvation. According to fundamental Christian teaching, the central divine response to our predicament is the incarnation and atonement: the life, sacrificial death, and resurrection of Jesus Christ, the divine son of God. By virtue of this divine response, we human beings can be put right with God and live triumphantly with him in this life and the next. Another part of God's response to our condition, however, is Scripture and the testimony of the Holy Spirit. God speaks to us in Scripture, teaching us his response to our fallen condition and the way in which this response is to be appropriated by us. By virtue of the inward instigation of the Holy Spirit, we see that the teachings of Scripture are true. This work of the Holy Spirit, therefore, is a very special kind of cognitive instrument or agency; it is a belief-producing process, all right, but one that is very much out of the ordinary. It is not part of our original noetic equipment (not part of our constitution as we came from the hand of the Maker), but instead part of a special divine response to our (unnatural) sinful condition. Later, we will look at these notions in more detail; here, the thing to see is the contrast between the activity of the Holy Spirit in our cognitive lives, on the one hand, and the *sensus divinitatis* on the other. The former is part of a special response to the fallen condition into which humankind has precipitated itself; the latter is part of our original epistemic endowment. The former is a special divine response to sin; presumably it would not have taken place had there been no sin. The latter would no doubt have been part of our epistemic establishment even if humanity had not fallen into sin.

5. Perceptual *or* Experiential *Knowledge?*

Suppose something like the A/C model is in fact correct: knowledge of God ordinarily comes not through inference from other things one believes, but from a *sensus divinitatis*, as characterized above. Would it follow that our knowledge of God comes by way of *perception*? That is, would it follow that the warrant enjoyed by theistic belief is perceptual warrant? Not necessarily. This is not because there is any real question about the possibility or, indeed, the actuality of perception of God. I believe William Alston has shown that if there is such a person as God, there could certainly be perception of him, and indeed *is* perception of him. Alston's powerful discussion shows that the usual objections to perception of God (no independent way of checking, disagreement as to what God is like, differences from sense perception, apparent relativity to the theological beliefs of the alleged perceiver, and so on) have very little to be said for them.[17]

Of course it isn't wholly clear just what perception *is* (there is as much dispute about that as about any other philosophical topic); conceivably, the way to think of perception strictly so-called is such that it essentially involves specifically sensuous imagery. This imagery need not be of the sort that goes with *our* sense perception; other kinds are certainly possible. (Perhaps sensuous imagery goes with the bat's echolocation, a kind of imagery wholly foreign to us.) But sensuous imagery of *some* kind may be necessary for perception, and perhaps it is also required that this imagery plays a certain specific (and hard to specify) causal role in the genesis of the candidates for perceptual belief in question.

What Alston thinks of as putative perception of God, however, often appears not to involve sensuous imagery.[18] If so, then, strictly speaking, there wouldn't be *perception* of God; what Alston's discussion would then show is that (given the existence of God) there could certainly be and probably is something very *like* perception of God (something that is epistemically on all fours with perception in that it, like the latter, can be a source of warrant). This something, therefore, can properly be called 'perception' in an analogically extended sense of that term. To the believer, the presence of God is often *palpable*. A surprising number of people report that at one time or another, they *feel* the presence of God, or at any rate it *seems* to them that they feel the presence of God—where the 'feeling' also doesn't seem to go by way of sensuous imagery. Many others (by no means for the most part spiritual heroes or even serious believers) report hearing God speak to them. And among these cases, cases where it seems right or nearly right to speak of *perceiving* God (feeling his presence, perhaps hearing his voice), there is great variation. There are the shattering, overwhelming sorts of experiences had by Paul (then 'Saul') on the road to Damascus and reported by mystics and other masters of the interior life. In these cases there may be vivid sensuous imagery of more than one kind. Still, there is also a sort of awareness of God where it seems right to say one feels his presence, but where there is little or none of

17. *Perceiving God; The Epistemology of Religious Experience* (Ithaca: Cornell University Press, 1991), chapters 1, 2, 5, and 6 (hereafter PG).

18. "Although mystical perception may or may not involve sensory content, I will be focusing on the non-sensory variety, since, in my judgment, it has a better claim to be a genuine direct perception of God" (PG, p. 36).

the sort of sensuous imagery that typically goes with perception; it is more like a nonsensuous impression of a brooding presence. And (apparently) there are all sorts of examples between these two extremes.

So I have no doubt that perception of God or something very much like it does occur, and occur rather widely. But would beliefs gained by way of the *sensus divinitatis* of the A/C model be *perceptual* belief—that is, would the knowledge of God afforded (in the A/C model) by the *sensus divinitatis* be by way of perception? I'm inclined to think not. There are different accounts of what is essential to perception; Alston's, I think, is as good as any. As he puts it,

> what I take to be definitive of perceptual consciousness is that something (or so it seems to the subject) *presents* itself to the subject's awareness as so-and-so—as red, round, loving, or whatever. When I stand before my desk with my eyes closed and then open them, the most striking difference in my consciousness is that items that I was previously merely thinking about or remembering, if conscious of them in any way, are now *present* to me. (PG, p. 36)

Of course it isn't easy to say, in every sort of case, when the object seems to present itself to the subject; let's suppose we have something of a grasp of this notion and can tell within reasonable limits when it applies. Then I think it is clear that in some of the experiences that are, on the model, operations of the *sensus divinitatis*, there is a sense of God's actually being presented to, present to, one's awareness, but in others not. In the sorts of cases Calvin speaks of (the night sky, the mountains, the ocean), it is sometimes as if one feels, perceives the very presence of God. This would be what Alston calls (p. 21) indirect perception of God—the perception of God mediated by the perception of something else (the night sky, the mountains). In other cases of this sort, however, God doesn't seem exactly *present*, or *presented*, even though various beliefs about him—that he is powerful, glorious, to be worshiped, obeyed, thanked—arise. And in some of the other sorts of manifestations of the *sensus divinitatis*—situations of guilt, danger, gratitude—the sense that God is actually present to one, as Alston is thinking of it, seems rarer. So according to the model, the operation of the *sensus divinitatis* doesn't necessarily involve perception of God.

Well, even if this sort of knowledge of God isn't perceptual, can we at any rate say that it is by way of *religious experience*? Can we say that the warrant it gets comes from experience? The first thing to see is that this term 'religious experience' is construed in a thousand different ways to cover a vast and confusing variety of cases; the question as it stands is multiply ambiguous and, in fact, we are probably better off boycotting the term.[19] Still, perhaps we can say at least the

---

19. As Alston (PG, p. 34) suggests.

following: the operation of the *sensus divinitatis* will always involve the presence of experience of some kind or other, even if sensuous imagery isn't always present. Sometimes there is sensuous imagery; sometimes there is something like feeling the presence of God, where there seems to be no sensuous imagery present, but perhaps something (necessarily hard to describe) *like* it; often there is also the sort of experience that goes with being frightened, feeling grateful, delighted, foolish, angry, pleased, and the like. A common component is a sort of awe, a sense of the numinous;[20] a sense of being in the presence of a being of overwhelming majesty and greatness. None of these is inevitably connected with the operation of the *sensus divinitatis*, although perhaps no occasion of its operation fails to display one or another of these varieties of experience. But there is another sort of experience that is always present in the operation of the *sensus divinitatis*. Recall the distinction made a couple of chapters back between sensuous imagery and what I called above *doxastic experience*, the sort of experience one has when entertaining any proposition one believes. Entertaining, for instance, the proposition that $3 + 2 = 5$ or that Mount Everest is higher than Mount Blanc *feels* different from entertaining one you think is clearly false—$3 + 2 = 6$, for example, or *Mount Blanc is higher than Mount Everest*. The first two feel natural, right, acceptable; the second two feel objectionable, wrong, eminently rejectable.[21] As I say, this experience is always connected with operations of the *sensus divinitatis*, because always connected with the formation or sustenance of any belief.

So all of these varieties of experience can be found in the operation of the *sensus divinitatis*; doxastic experience accompanies any beliefs formed by its operation, as it does the formation of any other belief. So back to our question: shall we therefore say that knowledge by way of the *sensus divinitatis* comes by way of religious experience, that it is *experiential* knowledge? Shall we say that (on the model) the warrant it has comes from experience? I don't propose to answer the question. An answer would involve a long and essentially irrelevant effort to answer *another* question: "What does it mean to say that the warrant of a belief comes from (or comes by way of) experience, religious or otherwise?" This is an interesting question, and a tough question (doxastic experience always accompanies the formation of *a priori* belief, and scraps of sensuous imagery typically accompany it; does the warrant of *a priori* belief therefore come from experience?). But we don't need an answer to that question for our purposes. We

---

20. See Rudolf Otto, *The Idea of the Holy* (New York: Oxford University Press, 1958).

21. For more on doxastic evidence, see *Warrant and Proper Function* (hereafter WPF), pp. 190ff.

can be satisfied with an account of how (on the model) the *sensus divinitatis* does in fact work; given that account, the answer to the question whether this is by way of experience is unimportant and optional.

6. Sin and Natural Knowledge of God

Finally, according to the A/C model this natural knowledge of God has been compromised, weakened, reduced, smothered, overlaid, or impeded by sin and its consequences. In the next chapter, we shall explore the noetic effects of sin in more detail, and in chapter 8 we shall see that (on the model) the *sensus divinitatis* is restored to proper function by regeneration and the operation of the Holy Spirit. For now, we note only that the knowledge of God provided by the *sensus divinitatis*, prior to faith and regeneration, is both narrowed in scope and partially suppressed. Due to one cause or another, the faculty itself may be *diseased* and thus partly or wholly disabled. There is such a thing as cognitive disease; there is blindness, deafness, inability to tell right from wrong, insanity; and there are analogues of these conditions with respect to the operation of the *sensus divinitatis*. According to Marx and Marxists, of course, it is belief in God that is a result of cognitive disease, of dysfunction. In an etymological sense, Marx thinks, the believer is insane. A milder, more conciliatory way to put it is that the believer, from those perspectives, is irrational; rational faculties fail to work as they should. But here the A/C model stands Freud and Marx on their heads (more accurately, what we see here is part of F&M's extensive borrowing from Christian and Jewish ways of thinking); according to the model, it is really the *unbeliever* who displays epistemic malfunction; failing to believe in God is a result of some kind of dysfunction of the *sensus divinitatis*.

And here we should note that the notion of warrant can be usefully generalized. So far, we have thought of warrant as a property or characteristic of beliefs; the basic idea is that a belief enjoys warrant when it is formed by properly functioning cognitive faculties in a congenial epistemic environment according to a design plan successfully aimed at truth—which includes, we should note, the avoidance of error. But *withholdings*, failures to believe, can also be dictated by a design plan successfully aimed at truth and the avoidance of error. You have conflicting evidence for the proposition that there is intelligent life in other parts of the universe: some of those you trust say yes, some say no, and some say there is little evidence either way. You therefore withhold that belief, believing neither that there is nor that there isn't life elsewhere in the universe. Your friends with the rocky marriage tell you conflicting stories about the latest quarrel: by virtue of past experience in similar situations you have learned to believe neither story without further corroboration. Your young son asks you how high the highest mountain in Antarctica is; you have a dim impression of having heard that it is in the neighborhood of 16,000 feet, but don't really know; you form no belief on the subject. In all of these cases, withholding is what the design plan dictates. Thus withholding displays a sort of analogue of warrant: it too can in certain circumstances be dictated by the proper function of cognitive faculties operating in a congenial epistemic environment according to a design plan successfully aimed at truth and the avoidance of error.

By contrast, if you call and ask what I am doing at the moment and I don't form the belief that I am sitting at my computer trying to work on my book, there is something wrong somewhere in my noetic establishment. I am introduced to someone at a party; although I have no reason to do so, I withhold the belief that what I see before me is a person, motivated by nothing more than the broadly logical possibility that what I see is really an extraordinarily clever hologram with sound effects attached. I read Bertrand Russell and see that it is possible (in the broadly logical sense) and compatible with appearances that the world popped into existence just five minutes ago, complete with all those apparent memories, crumbling mountains, and dusty books; as a result, I withhold the belief that I am more than five minutes old. In these cases, my failure to believe is a sign, not of exemplary epistemic caution, but of cognitive malfunction; these withholdings *lack* the analogue of warrant. Of course I might, in a frenzy due to philosophical error, come to the conclusion that in some way I *ought* not to believe in other people; I might come to the conclusion that such belief is unjustified, somehow; and I might try not to believe in other people. I might even succeed for brief periods in my study. But it is exceedingly hard to maintain this attitude, as is demonstrated by the famous lady who dropped Bertrand Russell a postcard on which she wrote something like "I agree entirely with you that solipsism is the correct and most reasonable position: so why aren't there more of us solipsists?" As Hume notoriously noted, it is exceedingly hard to maintain this attitude for long, or outside your study. The fact is that someone who consistently believes that she is the only person in the universe is suffering from a serious mental disorder, and the same is true for the person who is merely agnostic about the existence of other persons.

We could put the same point by saying that some withholdings are rational and some irrational. An important sense of the term 'rational'[22] is one in which a belief is rational if it is produced by cognitive faculties functioning properly. But the same can be said for withholdings: they can be produced by cognitive faculties function-

---

22. As we saw above, p. 110.

ing properly, as in the first three examples above, but also by cognitive faculties functioning improperly, as in the next three examples. According to the model, the same thing can happen with respect to belief in God. Failure to believe can be due to a sort of blindness or deafness, to improper function of the *sensus divinitatis*. On the present model, such failure to believe is irrational, and such withholdings lack the analogue of warrant. It doesn't follow that failure to believe is *unjustified*—if it is due solely to cognitive malfunction, then there is no dereliction of epistemic duty—but it is nonetheless irrational. Contrary to a sort of ethos induced by classical foundationalism, it is not the case that the way to demonstrate rationality is to believe as little as possible; withholding, failure to believe, agnosticism, is not always, from the point of view of rationality, the safest and best path. In some contexts it is instead a sign of serious irrationality.

According to the present model, then, the *sensus divinitatis* has been damaged and corrupted by sin. Further, according to the extended model I mean to propose in chapter 8, the *sensus divinitatis* is partly healed and restored to proper function by *faith* and the concomitant work of the Holy Spirit in one's heart. So the model as so far outlined is incomplete; the rest will come in chapters 8 and 9. Even if incomplete, however, the model as so far outlined will suffice for present purposes. For it shows us a sufficiently detailed way in which a properly functioning *sensus divinitatis* can produce theistic belief which is (1) taken in the basic way and (2), so taken, can indeed have warrant, and warrant sufficient for knowledge.

II. *IS* BELIEF IN GOD WARRANT-BASIC?

A. If False, Probably Not

As we saw above, Freud doesn't really *argue* that theistic belief has no warrant if taken in the basic way: he seems to assume that such belief is false, and then infers in rather quick and casual fashion that it is produced by wish-fulfillment and hence doesn't have warrant. Here (despite the appearance of carelessness) perhaps Freud's instincts are right: I shall argue that if theistic belief is false, but taken in the basic way,[23] then it probably has no warrant. First, as we saw above, no false belief has warrant sufficient for knowledge; therefore, if theistic belief is false, it doesn't have *that* degree of warrant. Still, couldn't it nonetheless have *some* warrant? There are at least two reasons for

---

23. And, let's add, not taken on testimony. That is because testimony, like inference, is not an ultimate source of warrant; a belief taken on testimony has warrant for someone only if that belief has warrant for the testifier. See WPF, p. 83.

thinking not. First, when does a false belief have warrant? Typically, in a case where the faculty that produces the belief is working at the limit of its capability. You see a mountain goat on a distant crag and mistakenly think you see that it has horns; as a matter of fact, it is just too far away for you to see clearly that it doesn't have horns. You are a particle physicist and mistakenly believe that a certain subatomic model is close to the truth: working as you are at the outer limits of the cognitive domain for which our faculties are designed, your belief is false but not without warrant. If there is no such person as God, of course, then there is no such thing as a *sensus divinitatis*; and what truth-aimed faculty would be such that it is working at the limit of its ability in producing the belief that there *is* such a person as God, if that latter belief is false? It is exceedingly hard to think of decent candidates. Further, if your faculties are functioning properly and are unimpeded by desire for fame, ambition, lust, and the like, then if they are working at the limit of their capability, you will not ordinarily believe the proposition in question with great firmness— you will not believe it with anything like the degree of firmness often displayed by theistic belief. Thus you won't be sure that you see horns on that goat: you will instead think to yourself, "Well, it *looks* as if it has horns, but it's too far away to be sure." You won't insist that your physical model is correct; if you believe it is, it will be with a certain tentativeness. These considerations suggest that if theistic belief is false, it is not produced by cognitive processes successfully aimed at the truth, and hence does not have warrant.

There is another and more important consideration, which we can approach indirectly as follows. A belief has warrant only if the cognitive process that produces it is successfully aimed at the truth— that is, only if there is a high objective probability that a belief produced by this process is true (given that the process is functioning properly in the sort of epistemic environment for which it is designed). Now from the fact that a belief is false, it doesn't follow that it is not produced by a process or faculty successfully aimed at truth. It could be that on a given occasion a process issues a false belief, even though there is a substantial objective probability that any belief it produces will be true (given the satisfaction of the other conditions of warrant). For example, a reliable barometer may give a false reading because of an unusual and improbable confluence of circumstances. Physicists tell us that it is possible (though extremely unlikely) that, for just a moment, all the air molecules in the room should congregate in the upper northwest corner of the room. Suppose this happens; at that moment, the air pressure in the vicinity of the barometer in the lower southeast corner of the room is zero; the barometer, however, still registers 29.72, because there hasn't been a long enough time for it to react to the change. The fact that it issues a false reading under these circumstances doesn't mean it is not a reliable instrument. Similarly for a cognitive process: there might in fact be a high probability that a belief it produces is true, despite the fact that on a given occasion (even though the other conditions of warrant are satisfied) it issues a false belief. Couldn't something similar hold for the processes that produce belief in God? Might it not be that belief in God is produced by cognitive processes successfully aimed at the truth, even if that belief is, as a matter of fact, false?

I think not. A proposition is objectively probable, with respect to some condition C, only if that proposition is true in most of the nearby possible worlds that display C.[24] But now consider the process that produces theistic belief: if it is successfully aimed at truth, then in most of the nearby possible worlds it produces a true belief. Assuming that in those nearby possible worlds it produces the same belief as it does in fact (i.e., belief in God) it follows that in most of the nearby possible worlds that belief is in fact true: in most of the nearby possible worlds there is such a person as God. However, that can't be, if the fact is there is no such person as God. For if in fact (in the actual world) there is no such person as God, then a world in which there *is* such a person—an omniscient, omnipotent, wholly good person who has created the world—would be enormously, unimaginably different from the actual world, and enormously dissimilar from it. So if there is no such person as God, it is probably not the case that the process that produces theistic belief produces a true belief in most of the nearby possible worlds. Therefore, it is unlikely that belief in God is produced by a process that is functioning properly in a congenial epistemic environment according to a design plan successfully aimed at the production of true belief. So if theistic belief is false, it probably has no warrant. Freud is right: if theistic belief is false, then it is at the least very likely that it has little or no warrant.

B. If True, Probably So

On the other hand, if theistic belief is *true*, then it seems likely that it *does* have warrant. If it is true, then there is, indeed, such a person as God, a person who has created us in his image (so that we resemble him, among other things, in having the capacity for knowledge), who loves us, who desires that we know and love him, and who is such that it is our end and good to know and love him. But if these things are so, then he would of course intend that we be able to be aware of his presence and to know something about him. And if that is so, the natural thing to think is that he created us in such a way that we would come to hold such true beliefs as that there is such a person as

24. For an account of the connection between possible worlds and objective probability, see WPF, p. 162.

God, that he is our creator, that we owe him obedience and worship, that he is worthy of worship, that he loves us, and so on. And if *that* is so, then the natural thing to think is that the cognitive processes that *do* produce belief in God are aimed by their designer at producing that belief. But then the belief in question will be produced by cognitive faculties functioning properly according to a design plan successfully aimed at truth: it will therefore have warrant. Again, this isn't certain; the argument is not deductively valid. It is abstractly possible, I suppose, that God has created us with a certain faculty *f* for knowing him; for one reason or another, *f* always malfunctions, and some other faculty *f'* created to produce some *other* beliefs, often malfunctions in such a way that *it* produces belief in God. Then our belief in God wouldn't have warrant, despite the fact that it is true. (This would be something like a sort of complex and peculiar theological Gettier problem.) And the abstract character of this possibility is perhaps strengthened when we think of the fact that human beings, according to Christian belief, have fallen into sin, which has noetic effects as well as effects of other sorts. Nevertheless, the more probable thing, at least so far as I can see, is that if in fact theism is true, then theistic belief has warrant.

Suppose we try to take a deeper look. How could we make sense of the idea that theism is true but belief in God doesn't have warrant?

We'd have to suppose (1) that there is such a person as God, who has created us in his image and has created us in such a way that our chief end and good is knowledge of him, and (2) that belief in God (i.e., *our* belief in God, human belief in God) has no warrant: is not produced by cognitive processes successfully aimed at giving us true beliefs about God, functioning properly in a congenial epistemic environment. That is, we'd have to think that belief in God is produced by cognitive processes that either (1) are not functioning properly (because of disease or impedance), (2) are not aimed at producing true beliefs about God, or (3) are so aimed but not *successfully* aimed, or (4) the cognitive environment is uncongenial, not one for which our faculties are designed. With respect to (4), however, we are supposing God has created us; there seems no reason at all to think our epistemic environment is not the one for which he created us. (We have no reason, for example, to think that our ancestors originated on some other planet and made a long, hazardous journey to Earth.) With respect to (3), because, by hypothesis, theistic belief is true, it seems that if the cognitive process that produces it *is* aimed at the truth, it is successfully aimed at the truth. That leaves us with (1) and (2). Given that God would certainly *want* us to be able to know him, the chances are excellent that he would create us with faculties enabling us to do just that. So the natural thing to think is that those faculties that produce theistic belief were indeed designed to produce that sort of belief and are functioning properly in so doing. Of course it is possible, in the broadly logical sense, that the faculties designed to produce theistic belief don't work for one reason or another, and some other faculties not aimed at producing theistic belief malfunction, thus producing it. The same, I suppose, is abstractly possible with respect to perception: the original faculties whereby we knew our environment began to malfunction, and by some serendipitous happenstance, *other* faculties began to malfunction in just such a way as to produce our perceptual beliefs. Possible, but not likely. This is an abstract possibility, but not much more. And suppose, improbably, that something like this did happen with the original *sensus divinitatis*: it stopped working (perhaps as a result of sin), and some other faculty began to malfunction and leapt into the breach, by serendipitous happenstance producing the very sorts of beliefs the original *sensus divinitatis* did: then it would seem likely that God has *adopted* this other way of working as our design plan, so that theistic belief does indeed have warrant, but via a sort of circuitous route. The conclusion to draw, I think, is that the epistemic probability of theistic belief's being warranted, given that theism is true, is very high.[25]

III. THE *DE JURE* QUESTION IS NOT INDEPENDENT OF THE *DE FACTO* QUESTION

And here we see the ontological or metaphysical or ultimately religious roots of the question as to the rationality or warrant or lack thereof for belief in God. What you properly take to be rational, at least in the sense of warranted, depends on what sort of metaphysical and religious stance you adopt. It depends on what kind of beings you think human beings are, what sorts of beliefs you think their noetic faculties will produce when they are functioning properly, and which of their faculties or cognitive mechanisms are aimed at the truth. Your view as to what sort of creature a human being is will determine or at any rate heavily influence your views as to whether theistic belief is warranted or not warranted, rational or irrational for human beings. And so the dispute as to whether theistic belief is rational (warranted) can't be settled just by attending to epistemological considerations; it is at bottom not merely an epistemological dispute, but an ontological or theological dispute.

You may think humankind is created by God in the image of God—and created both with a natural tendency to see God's hand in

---

25. Here we must also suppose, in accord with the conclusion of part IV of this book, that it is not the case that those who believe in God for the most part have *defeaters* for that belief.

the world about us and with a natural tendency to recognize that we have indeed been created and are beholden to our creator, owing him worship and allegiance. Then, of course, you will not think of belief in God as in the typical case a manifestation of any kind of intellectual defect. Nor will you think it is a manifestation of a belief-producing power or mechanism that is not aimed at the truth. It is instead a cognitive mechanism whereby we are put in touch with part of reality—indeed, by far the most important part of reality. It is in this regard like a deliverance of sense perception, or memory, or reason, the faculty responsible for *a priori* knowledge. On the other hand, you may think we human beings are the product of blind evolutionary forces; you may think there is no God and that we are part of a godless universe. Then you will be inclined to accept the sort of view according to which belief in God is an illusion of some sort, properly traced to wishful thinking or some other cognitive mechanism not aimed at the truth (Freud) or to a sort of disease or dysfunction on the part of the individual or society (Marx).

And this dependence of the question of warrant or rationality on the truth or falsehood of theism leads to a very interesting conclusion. If the *warrant* enjoyed by belief in God is related in this way to the *truth* of that belief, then the question whether theistic belief has *warrant* is not, after all, independent of the question whether theistic belief is *true*. So the *de jure* question we have finally found is not, after all, really independent of the *de facto* question; to answer the former we must answer the latter. This is important: what it shows is that a successful atheological objection will have to be to the *truth* of theism, not to its rationality, justification, intellectual respectability, rational justification, or whatever. Atheologians who wish to attack theistic belief will have to restrict themselves to objections like the argument from evil, the claim that theism is incoherent, or the idea that in some other way there is strong evidence against theistic belief. They can't any longer adopt the following stance: "Well, I certainly don't know whether theistic belief is *true*—who could know a thing like that?—but I do know this: it is irrational, or unjustified, or not rationally justified, or contrary to reason or intellectually irresponsible or . . ." There isn't a sensible *de jure* question or criticism that is independent of the *de facto* question. There aren't any *de jure* criticisms that are sensible when conjoined with the *truth* of theistic belief; all of them either fail right from the start (as with the claim that it is unjustified to accept theistic belief) or else really presuppose that theism is false. This fact by itself invalidates an enormous amount of recent and contemporary atheology; for much of that atheology is devoted to *de jure* complaints that are allegedly independent of the *de facto* question. If my argument so far is right, though, there *aren't* any sensible complaints of that sort. (More modestly, none have been so far proposed; it is always possible, I suppose, that someone will come up with one.)

IV. THE F&M COMPLAINT REVISITED

Now that we have the A/C model before us, we can deal with the
F&M complaint in summary fashion. As we saw in the last chapter,
Marx's complaint about religion is that it is produced by cognitive faculties that are malfunctioning; this cognitive dysfunction is due to *social* dysfunction and dislocation. Besides that famous "Religion is the
opium of the people" passage, however, Marx doesn't have a lot to
say about religious belief—except, of course, for a number of semi-
journalistic gibes and japes and other expressions of hostility.[26] I shall
therefore concentrate on Freud, who holds (as we saw in the last
chapter) not that theistic belief originates in cognitive malfunction,
but that it is an *illusion*, in his technical sense. It finds its origin in
wish-fulfillment, which, although it is a cognitive process with an important role to play in the total economy of our intellectual life, is
nevertheless not aimed at the production of true beliefs. On Freud's
view, then, theistic belief, given that it is produced by wish-fulfillment,
does not have warrant; it fails to satisfy the condition of being produced by cognitive faculties whose purpose it is to produce true belief. He goes on to characterize religious belief as "neurosis," "illusion," "poison," "intoxicant," and "childishness to be overcome," all
on one page of *The Future of an Illusion*.[27]

Not to be outdone, a substantial number of subsequent psychol-
ogists, sociologists, and anthropologists have followed his lead. Thus
Albert Ellis:

> Religiosity is in many respects equivalent to irrational thinking and
> emotional disturbance. . . . The elegant therapeutic solution to
> emotional problems is to be quite unreligious . . . the less religious
> they are, the more emotionally healthy they will be.[28]

Sometimes these suggestions take rather bizarre forms, worthy, almost to be compared with Freud's own highly imaginative stories
about the origin of religion and the taming of fire.[29] According to
Michael P. Carroll, for example, praying the rosary is "a disguised
gratification of repressed anal-erotic desires"—a substitute for "playing with one's feces."[30] Perhaps this isn't up to Freud's standard when

26. See *On Religion* by Karl Marx and Frederick Engels, ed. Reinhold Niebuhr
(Chico, Calif.: Scholars Press, 1964). This is a collection of bits of various writings on
religion by Marx and Engels.

27. New York: W. W. Norton, 1961 (originally published 1927), p. 49.

28. "Psychotherapy and Atheistic Values," *Journal of Consulting and Clinical
Psychology* 48, no. 5 (October 1980), pp. 635–39.

29. See above, pp. 137–38.

30. "Praying the Rosary: The Anal-Erotic Origins of a Popular Catholic
Devotion," *Journal for the Scientific Study of Religion* 26, no. 4 (December 1987), p. 491.

it comes to evoking that mist-enshrouded world of our distant ancestors, but it does match Freud for implausibility. A rather common view has been that religious belief is not so much a matter of illusion or cognitive malfunction as of simple stupidity. This view has sometimes been expressed rather colorfully; thus Warren Wilson blamed the growth of evangelical Protestant groups in rural America on the fact that "among country people there are many inferior minds." He went on to explain that revivalism was bound to persist in these regions "until we can lift the administration of popular institutions that are governed by public opinion out of the hand of the weak brother and the silly sister."[31] This kind of opinion is still widely popular among those who propose to study religion scientifically,[32] although (given current sensibilities) ordinarily not expressed with quite the same reckless enthusiasm.

Following Voltaire, Rousseau, and others, furthermore, people in these fields regularly declare that (in this modern, scientific age) the death of religion is at hand[33]—about as often, perhaps, as others predict that the return of Jesus Christ is at hand. Of course previous predictions of the former kind (like previous predictions of the latter) have failed; as a result, these forecasts of the demise of religion (if not of the world) now tend to be more circumspect. For example:

> the evolutionary future of religion is extinction. Belief in supernatural beings and in supernatural forces that affect nature without obeying nature's laws will erode and become only an interesting historical memory. To be sure, this event is not likely to occur in the next generation; the process will very likely take several hundred years, and there will probably always remain individuals, or even occasional small cult groups who respond to hallucination, trance, and obsession with supernaturalist interpretation. But as a cultural trait, belief in supernatural powers is doomed to die out, all over the world, as a result of the increasing adequacy and diffusion of scientific knowledge . . . the process is inevitable.[34]

31. *The Farmer's Church* (New York: Century, 1925), p. 58.

32. See, for example, Herbert Simon's recent article, "A Mechanism for Social Selection and Successful Altruism," *Science* 250 (December 1990), pp. 1665ff, in which he argues that the behavior of people like Mother Teresa, who are prepared to sacrifice their own interests for those of other people, is to be explained in terms of "docility" and "bounded rationality."

33. Freud himself was often more careful on this point; see footnote 12, above, p. 140.

34. Anthony F. C. Wallace, *Religion: An Anthropological View* (New York: Random House, 1966), pp. 264–65. Like the last three quoted passages, this one is quoted in Rodney Stark, Laurence Iannaccone, and Roger Finke, "Rationality and the 'Religious' Mind," *Economic Inquiry* 36, no. 3 (July 1998). This very interesting paper takes an innovative approach to serious religious belief, swimming against the stream of sociological analyses that see such belief as a manifestation of one or another kind of irrationality.

Is there any reason to believe these things? Is there any evidence for the F&M complaint? Why should anyone believe it? First, however, it is only fair to defend this complaint against a fairly common objection. The F&M style of criticizing religious (or other) belief is often improperly dismissed as an instance of the 'genetic fallacy'. The question, so the claim goes, is whether the theistic beliefs in question are *true*; the question is not how it is that someone comes to hold them or what the origin of the belief might be. Furthermore (so the claim continues), questions of origin are ordinarily irrelevant to questions of truth. ("Ordinarily"—of course we can think of silly exceptions. For example, we might know that Sam came to believe a proposition by accepting the testimony of someone who, on the subject of the belief in question, asserts nothing but falsehoods; in that case the origin of the belief is obviously relevant to its truth.)

This criticism of the F&M complaint is mistaken. True, questions of origin are ordinarily not relevant to the question of the *truth* of a belief; but they can be crucially relevant to the question of the *warrant* a belief enjoys. The objector fails to note that there are *de jure* questions and criticisms as well as *de facto*; his objection is relevant only if it is the *latter* sort that is at issue. But the F&M complaint is that theistic belief is not *rational* and lacks *warrant*. Unlike memory beliefs, *a priori* beliefs, or perceptual belief, theistic belief does not originate in the proper function of cognitive processes successfully aimed at the production of true belief. And if the problem, according to F&M, is that such beliefs have no *warrant*, then questions of origin may be intensely relevant; on many accounts of warrant, including the one I defend in WPF, the genesis of a belief *is* intimately connected with the degree of warrant, if any, it enjoys.

Furthermore, there is an indirect connection with truth. Return to the random generator of p. 161, above: I use the machine, proposing the selected proposition to you for belief. You demur, citing the origin of the proposed belief, whereupon I accuse you of committing the genetic fallacy. Surely I am wrong; the fact is you haven't committed a fallacy at all, and your real complaint is that you haven't the faintest reason to think the proposition in question true. It is the same with beliefs that have no warrant for anyone. We ordinarily assume that propositions with warrant have something going for them: it is likely, or at least more likely than not, that they will be true. If I have reason to think your belief that your name is 'Sam' has warrant (you're pretty likely to know what your name is), then I have a reason to accept this belief. If I know that a belief has no warrant for anyone, however, then I have no reason at all to think that belief true, no reason at all to *rely* on that proposition. Once I see this, I see that the proposition in question has no claim whatever on my belief.

But is Freud right: *does* theistic belief arise from wish-fulfillment, thereby failing to have warrant? Is there any reason to believe this?

Does he offer argument or evidence for this claim, or (in Mill's phrase) other considerations to determine the intellect? Or is it mere assertion? Note that if the F&M complaint is to be a successful criticism, if it is to show that theistic belief lacks warrant, it must meet two conditions. First, it must show that theistic belief really *does* arise from the mechanism of wish-fulfillment; second (as I'll explain below), it must show that this *particular* operation of that mechanism is not aimed at the production of true beliefs. Consider the first. Freud offers no more than the most perfunctory argument here, and one can see why: it isn't easy to see how to argue the point. How would one argue that it is *that* mechanism, wish-fulfillment, rather than some other, that produces religious belief? Much of religious belief, after all, is not something that, on the face of it, fulfills your wildest dreams. Thus Christianity (as well as other theistic religions) includes the belief that human beings have sinned, that they merit divine wrath and even damnation, and that they are broken, wretched, in need of salvation; according to the Heidelberg Catechism, the first thing I have to know is my sins and miseries. This isn't precisely a fulfillment of one's wildest dreams. A follower of Freud might say: "Well, at any rate *theistic* belief, the belief that there is such a person as God, arises from wish-fulfillment." But this also is far from clear: many people thoroughly dislike the idea of an omnipotent, omniscient being monitoring their every activity, privy to their every thought, and passing judgment on all they do or think. Others dislike the lack of human autonomy consequent upon there being a Someone by comparison with whom we are as dust and ashes, and to whom we owe worship and obedience.

And in any event where is the evidence (empirical or otherwise) for the Freudian claim? A survey wouldn't be of much use. Hardly anyone reports believing in God out of wish-fulfillment; the usual reports are, instead, of being seized, compelled, or overwhelmed, or its just seeming right after considerable thought and agony, or its having always seemed clearly true, or its suddenly becoming obvious that it is really so. It certainly doesn't *seem* to those of us who believe in God that we do so out of wish-fulfillment. Of course that won't be taken as relevant; the beauty of Freudian explanations is that the postulated mechanisms all operate unconsciously, unavailable to inspection. The claim is that you subconsciously recognize the miserable and frightening condition we human beings face, subconsciously see that the alternatives are paralyzing despair or belief in God, and subconsciously opt for the latter. Even after careful introspection and reflection, you can't see that the proffered explanation is true: that fact won't be taken as even the slightest reason for doubting the explanation. (Just as with your indignant denial that you hate your father because you see him as a rival for your mother's sexual favors. In fact your indignation may be taken as confirmation; you are *resist-*

ing what at some level you know or suspect is the proper diagnosis.)
So suppose you subject yourself to a decade or so of psychoanalysis,
but still can't see that this is the origin of your belief; well (so you'll
be told), psychoanalysis isn't always successful. (In fact its cure rate, as
far as scientific study can demonstrate, is about the same as no treatment at all.) Now things *could* be like this; and in the nature of the
case maybe this sort of thing can't be demonstrated. Still, why should
we believe it?

As far as I can see, the only evidence Freud actually offers is the
claim that we see a lot of young people, nowadays, who give up religion when their father's authority breaks down:

> Psycho-analysis has made us familiar with the intimate connection
> between the father-complex and belief in God: it has shown us that
> a personal God is, psychologically, nothing other than an exalted fa-
> ther, and it brings us evidence every day of how young people lose
> their religious beliefs as soon as their father's authority breaks down.
> Thus we recognize that the roots of the need for religion are in the
> parental complex: the almighty and just God, and kindly Nature,
> appear to us as grand sublimations of father and mother. . . .[35]

No doubt Freud saw a good bit of that in his day (and perhaps
even in his own case: his relationship with his father, according to
E. M. Jones,[36] seems to have left much to be desired). But how is this
alleged evidence supposed to confirm the thesis that theistic belief results from wish-fulfillment? The claim is that when the father's authority (Freud doesn't say whether he means specifically with respect
to religious belief or more generally) breaks down, young people
often lose their religious beliefs. How is that fact, supposing that it is
a fact, supposed to be evidence for the thesis that theistic belief results from wish-fulfillment? That's not at all obvious. Suppose theistic
belief did result from wish-fulfillment: then wouldn't we expect some
kind of correlation between serious belief and a recognition of the
pitiless, indifferent character of nature? On Freud's thesis, we would
expect that a young person would start evincing belief in God perhaps fairly soon after he comes to see that this is in fact the way the
world is. But (given the thesis) why would we expect someone whose
father's authority had suffered a breakdown to give up belief in God?

35. Memoir of Leonardo da Vinci in *The Standard Edition of the Complete
Psychological Works of Sigmund Freud*, ed. J. Strachey (London: Hogarth Press, 1957),
vol. 11, p. 123.

36. *Degenerate Moderns* (San Francisco: Ignatius Press, 1993), p. 191. According
to Jones, Freud thought of his father as weak and "a pervert." Jeffrey Masson, *The
Complete Letters of Sigmund Freud to Wilhelm Fliess, 1887–1904* (Cambridge: Harvard
University Press, 1985), p. 222. See also Paul Vitz's *Sigmund Freud's Christian Unconscious* (New York: Guilford, 1988).

The fact is someone who had a warm, loving, respectful relation with his father would be less likely to see the cold and indifferent face of nature than someone whose father had lost authority. As far as I can see, therefore, this alleged evidence doesn't fit well with the main Freudian thesis about the origin of theistic belief and certainly doesn't serve as evidence for it. Perhaps it shows instead that some young people like to display their maturity and independence by rejecting the religious stance of their parents, whatever that stance might be. (Thus at present we find many cases of children rejecting the *unbelief* of their parents.) But it certainly doesn't tend to show that religious or theistic belief arises out of wish-fulfillment.

Of course the thesis isn't stated exactly, or with enough detail to enable us to see just what *would* be evidence for it. One naturally thinks that there must be a deeper, more precise statement of the theory somewhere; sadly enough, one can't find any such thing. The evidence for the theory would perhaps have to be something like the way it fits or explains all the data, all the phenomena of religious or theistic belief. But before we could seriously assess its fit with the evidence, the theory would have to be stated much more precisely; we should have to be able to see what it does and doesn't predict much more clearly than, in fact, we can. Freudian explanations have never been strong along these lines.[37]

Even if it were established that wish-fulfillment *is* the source of theistic belief, however, that wouldn't be enough to establish that the latter has no warrant. It must also be established that wish-fulfillment *in this particular manifestation* is not aimed at true belief. The cognitive design plan of human beings is subtle and complicated; a source of belief might be such that *in general* it isn't aimed at the formation of true belief, but in some special cases it is. So perhaps this is true of wish-fulfillment; in general, its purpose is not that of producing true belief, but in this special case precisely that *is* its purpose. Perhaps human beings have been created by God with a deep need to believe in his presence and goodness and love. Perhaps God designed us that way in order that we come to believe in him and be aware of his presence. Perhaps this is how God has arranged for us to come to know him. If so, then the particular bit of the cognitive design plan governing the formation of theistic belief is indeed aimed at true belief, even if the belief in question arises from wish-fulfillment.

---

37. Adolf Grünbaum's *The Foundations of Psychoanalysis* (Berkeley: University of California Press, 1984) is a meticulous (and thoroughly unflattering) chronicle of the scientific failings of Freud and Freudianism. Some others are Malcolm Macmillan's *Freud Evaluated: The Completed Arc* (Amsterdam: North-Holland, 1991) and Allen Esterson's *Seductive Mirage: An Exploration of the Work of Sigmund Freud* (Chicago: Open Court, 1993).

Perhaps God has designed us to know that he is present and loves us by way of creating us with a strong desire for him, a desire that leads to the belief that in fact he is there. Nor is this a mere speculative possibility; something like it is embraced both by St. Augustine ("Our hearts are restless til they rest in thee, O God") and Jonathan Edwards (below, p. 305ff).

And how would Freud or a follower establish that the mechanism whereby human beings come to believe in God (come to believe that there is such a person as God) is *not* aimed at the truth? This is really the crux of the matter. Freud offers no arguments or reasons here at all. As far as I can see, he simply takes it for granted that there is no God and that theistic belief is false; he then casts about for some kind of explanation of this widespread phenomenon of mistaken belief. He hits on wish-fulfillment and apparently assumes it is obvious that this mechanism is not "reality oriented"—that is, is not aimed at the production of true belief—so that such belief lacks warrant. As we have seen, this is a safe assumption if in fact theism *is* false. But then Freud's version of the *de jure* criticism really depends on his atheism: it isn't an independent criticism at all, and it won't (or shouldn't) have any force for anyone who doesn't share that atheism. Given the results of parts II and III of this chapter, this is of course just what we should expect.

Now a believer in God, a Christian or Jew or Muslim, is unlikely to acquiesce in the F&M claim that belief in God has no warrant. (It is only a certain variety of 'liberal' theologian, crazed by the thirst for novelty and the desire to accommodate current secularity, who might agree with F&M here.) Indeed, a believer will see the shoe as on the other foot. According to St. Paul, it is *unbelief* that is a result of dysfunction, brokenness, failure to function properly, or impedance of rational faculties. Unbelief, he says, is a result of sin; it originates in an effort, as Romans 1 puts it, to "suppress the truth in unrighteousness."[38] In the next chapter, we shall begin to explore the extended A/C model, considering some of the ways in which this suppression and impedance can go.

38. Of course it isn't Paul's idea that those who don't believe are, by that very fact, seen to be more sinful than those who do. On the contrary: just a couple of chapters later he says we are *all* involved in sin, including, of course, *himself* ("Wretched man that I am! Who will rescue me from this body of death?"). Furthermore, the malfunction that lies at the root of unbelief is not necessarily that of the unbeliever herself. Some kinds of unbelief (see below, p. 215) are like blindness; upon seeing a blind man, the disciples asked Jesus, "Rabbi, who sinned, this man or his parents, that he was born blind?" (John 9:2)—to which Jesus replied that this blindness was due neither to the man's own sin nor to that of his parents.

7

Sin and Its Cognitive Consequences

The heart is deceitful above all things and desperately wicked; who can understand it?

Jeremiah 17:9

I. PRELIMINARIES

According to the Aquinas/Calvin (A/C) model, theistic belief (belief in God) has warrant, indeed, sufficient warrant for knowledge. The central feature of this model is the stipulation that God has created us human beings with a belief-producing process or source of belief, the *sensus divinitatis*; this source works under various conditions to produce beliefs about God, including, of course, beliefs that immediately entail his existence. Belief produced in this way, I said, can easily meet the conditions for warrant; given that it is true (and held sufficiently strongly), it would constitute knowledge.

So far, therefore, we have been thinking just about belief that there is such a person as God. But to go no further would be to give legitimate grounds for complaint:

> First, the beliefs that really shape and determine Christian intellectual identity and existence are much more precise and specific than belief in God. They are constituted by profound convictions about the person of Christ, about the mysterious reality of the Holy Trinity, about the presence of the Holy Spirit in one's life. . . . It is these rather than some minimalist theism which really matters to the vast

majority of religious believers. Yet until very recently these have received next to no attention on the part of philosophers interested in
the rationality of religious belief. Somehow they are taken as secondary and peripheral.[1]

Well, I doubt that these beliefs have been neglected because they
were thought secondary and peripheral; there is a more plausible explanation. Christian philosophers have been for the most part responding to various kinds of attacks on the rational justifiability of
religious belief. Those who mount such attacks typically do so by attacking belief in God, which is the heart and soul of Christian belief
as well as of the other theistic religions. This is a sensible strategy: if
the atheologian can show that *this* belief is relevantly objectionable,
he won't have to deal piecemeal with all those more specific beliefs; he
can do for them all in one fell swoop. But then Christian responses to
these objections, naturally enough, have dealt with animadversions
on belief in God. Still, Abraham is quite right; we must indeed think
about specifically Christian belief and inquire into its justification, rationality, and warrant. That is the task of the next four chapters; my
aim is to extend the model of chapter 6 to include specifically Christian belief. The extended model will bear some of the earmarks of
Reformed theology, but similar models can be constructed for other
theological traditions. This model, incidentally, will essentially involve such theological notions as *faith* and the work of the Holy
Spirit. Some may find it scandalous that theological ideas should be
taken seriously in a book on philosophy; I find it no more scandalous
than the ingression into philosophy of scientific ideas from (for example) quantum mechanics, cosmology, and evolutionary biology.

My aim is to show how it can be that Christians can be justified,
rational (both internally and externally), and warranted in holding
full-blooded Christian belief—not just 'ignorant fundamentalists',
but sophisticated, aware, educated, turn-of-the-millennium people
who have read their Freud and Nietzsche, their Hume and Mackie
(their Dennett and Dawkins). Justification and internal rationality are
easy enough: just as for theistic belief, I'll argue that many or most
Christians not only *can* be but also *are* both justified and internally rational in holding their characteristic beliefs. External rationality and
warrant are harder. The only way I can see to argue that Christian be-

---

1. William Abraham, "The Epistemological Significance of the Inner Witness of
the Holy Spirit," *Faith and Philosophy* (1990), p. 435. Abraham goes on to complain
that the "reformed epistemologists" have so far said little about the internal testimony of the Holy Spirit and haven't made explicit the relation between "talk of the
inner witness of the Holy Spirit and their epistemological proposals" (p. 446). This
is true (and the present volume aims to help repair the deficiency), but what's to prevent Abraham himself from lighting a candle (instead of cursing the darkness) and
making some of these connections explicit?

lief has *these* virtues is to argue that Christian belief is, indeed, *true*. I don't propose to offer such an argument. That is because I don't know of an argument for Christian belief that seems very likely to convince one who doesn't already accept its conclusion. That is nothing against Christian belief, however, and indeed I shall argue that if Christian beliefs are true, then the standard and most satisfactory way to hold them will not be as the conclusions of argument.

What I will do instead is extend the A/C model of chapter 6 to a model according to which specifically Christian belief (as well as theism) has both warrant and external rationality, and enough of the former to constitute knowledge. This model will include the main lines of ecumenical classic Christian belief. It also needs a certain amount of additional detail. This additional detail is broadly Reformed or Calvinist in inspiration, but I shall develop it in my own way. The point of the extended model is like the point of the A/C model itself. I shall use the model to argue three things. First, I will use it to argue that Christian belief *can* very well be both externally rational and warranted: there is a perfectly viable epistemological account of how it is that they should have these virtues, and no cogent objections to their having it. Second, I'll argue (as in chapter 6 I did with respect to theistic belief) that if Christian belief is *true*, then it *is* probably both externally rational and warranted for most Christians. Thus I'll be attacking against that stance I mentioned (above, p. x): the claim that of course we don't know whether Christian belief is, in fact, true (that's a pretty tall order, after all), but we do know that even if it happens to be true, it isn't rational or warranted. Third, I'll recommend the story or model I present as a good way, though not necessarily the only good way, for Christians to think about the epistemological status of Christian belief.

Now one important difference between bare theism and Christianity has to do essentially with *sin* and the divine remedy proposed for it; it is sin that occasions Incarnation and Atonement, redemption and renewal. The present chapter, therefore, will examine the nature of sin and its noetic effects. Chapters 8 and 9 will address faith, the Bible, and the internal instigation of the Holy Spirit; these, on the extended model, are together the central source of warrant for Christian belief. According to Calvin, whose thought I shall follow (even if at some distance), faith is "a firm and certain knowledge (*cognitio*) of God's benevolence towards us, founded upon the truth of the freely given promise in Christ, both revealed to our minds and sealed upon our hearts through the Holy Spirit."[2] Chapter 8 will show how

---

2. John Calvin, *Institutes of the Christian Religion*, ed. John T. McNeill and tr. Ford Lewis Battles (Philadelphia: Westminster Press, 1960 [originally published in 1559]), III, ii, 7, p. 551. Subsequent page references to the *Institutes* are to this edition.

Christian belief is *revealed to our minds*, thus enjoying warrant; chapter 9 will deal with its being *sealed upon our hearts*; it therefore addresses the question of religious affections and the will, asking, among other things, whether there are analogues of justification, rationality, and warrant for the affections; chapter 10 will examine actual and possible objections to the extended model.

An initial problem: the term 'Christian belief,' like most useful terms, is vague. Does Tillich count as a Christian theologian? What about Mormon beliefs: are they Christian?[3] What about people who think Jesus was a great model and moral teacher, but doubt that he was God, rose from the dead, or atoned for our sins: are their beliefs Christian? What, precisely, must a set of beliefs be in order to be Christian—that is, to be properly denominated by that term?[4]

This isn't a problem for my project. First, no doubt the term 'Christian' is vague; still, as Dr. Johnson once remarked, the existence of twilight is not a good argument against the distinction between day and night. There is such a thing as Christian belief, and there is also such a thing as non-Christian belief, even if it is difficult to say where the one begins and the other ends. Second, nothing in my project depends on a specific use of the term 'Christian'. However we propose to use that term, my project is to inquire into the epistemological status of a certain set of beliefs: the ones embodied, say, in the Apostle's Creed and the Nicene Creed. (Alternatively, we could identify the beliefs in question as belonging to the intersection of those expressed in the creeds of more specific Christian communities [the New Catholic Catechism, the Heidelberg Catechism, the Augsburg Confession, the Westminster Catechism, and so on].) Included are the affirmations that God created the heavens and the earth; that he created human beings in his own image; that human beings fell ruinously into sin, from which they require salvation; that in response God graciously sent Jesus Christ, the divine son of God, who took on our flesh (became incarnate), suffered, and died as an atonement for

---

3. See, for example, Albert Howsepian's "Are Mormons Theists?" *Religious Studies* 32 (September 1996), pp. 357ff.; for a reply, see Blake T. Ostler, "Worship-worthiness and the Mormon Conception of God," *Religious Studies* 33 (September 1997), pp. 315ff.

4. Indeed, there is vagueness with respect to theism as well: what, precisely, must you believe to be a theist? That the Ultimate or the Real is personal? Or could you be a theist if (e.g., with Carl Sagan) you proposed that the laws of nature are somehow ultimate, should be called 'God', and should be worshiped? Could you be a theist if you thought that God is really a set—perhaps the Cartesian product of the sets of possibly good actions and true propositions? (Ignore the difficulty that there probably is no such thing as the set of true propositions—or, if you refuse to ignore it, see Patrick Grim and Alvin Plantinga, "Truth, Omniscience, and Cantorian Arguments: An Exchange," *Philosophical Studies* 70 [August 1993].)

our sins, and rose from the dead, thus enabling us fallen human beings to have eternal life with God. These beliefs are ordinarily thought of as paradigmatically Christian and ordinarily referred to by the term 'Christian'. Still, nothing depends on the use of that term: my project is that of inquiring into the epistemological status of those beliefs.

II. INITIAL STATEMENT OF THE EXTENDED MODEL

Now our question is whether these beliefs are justified, rational, or warranted. But justification and internal rationality are easily dealt with. First, justification taken deontologically, in terms of intellectual rights and obligations, is no more problematic here than in the case of theism. Clearly, a person (including a highly educated, wholly with-it, twenty-first-century person who has read all the latest objections to Christian belief) *could* be justified in accepting these and other Christian beliefs and *would* be so justified if (for example) after careful and nonculpable reflection and investigation into the alleged objections and defeaters, she still found those beliefs wholly compelling. She could hardly be blamed for believing what strongly seems, after extensive investigation, to be the truth of the matter. (She's supposed to believe what seems *false* to her?)[5] As for the various analogical extensions of justification in this original sense—being responsible, doing as well as could be expected with respect to your part in belief formation, and the like—again, it is obvious, I think, both that believers *can* meet these conditions and that many believers *do* meet them.

The same goes for *internal* rationality, which is a matter of the proper function of cognitive processes downstream from experience (see above, p. 110. for explanation of this metaphor). These beliefs, we are stipulating, seem to her to be clearly true. She finds them wholly convincing, just as she does her beliefs about other persons, say, and an external world; they remain thus convincing even after she has considered the objections she has encountered. She has a powerful inclination to believe these things and hence has strong

5. It is open to someone to claim that the Christian believer enjoys only *subjective* justification, not *objective* justification; that is because (so the claim goes) the fact is there are objective epistemic duties such that one cannot accept Christian belief without violating them (above, pp. 98–99), and the believer escapes guilt only because she is not aware of them. (Thus ignorance is a protection from guilt.) Once more, however: what would those objective duties be? And is there even a suggestion of a reason for thinking there are any such duties?

doxastic evidence for them. But then there need be no cognitive malfunction, glitch, or other infelicity in her actually *believing* them; therefore, her belief is internally rational.

As we saw in the case of theistic belief, however, these observations won't or shouldn't quiet the critics. For even if Christian believers are justified and *internally* rational in their beliefs, they might still be *externally* irrational (see above, p. 112) and thus wholly without warrant. After all, even the beliefs of a madman or of a victim of a Cartesian evil demon can be both justified and internally rational. Well, then, what about external rationality and warrant? A belief is externally rational if it is produced by cognitive faculties that are functioning properly and successfully aimed at truth (i.e., aimed at the production of true belief)—as opposed, for example, to being the product of wish-fulfillment or cognitive malfunction. Now warrant, the property enough of which distinguishes knowledge from mere true belief, is a property or quantity had by a belief if and only if (so I say) that belief is produced by cognitive faculties functioning properly in a congenial epistemic environment according to a design plan successfully aimed at truth. Because rationality (in the sense of proper function of rational powers) is included in warrant, the real question, here, is whether Christian belief does or can have warrant.

According to the extended A/C model, Christian belief does indeed have warrant. In essence, the model goes like this. First, God has created us human beings *in his own image*: this centrally involves our resembling God in being *persons*—that is, beings with *intellect* and *will*. Like God, we are the sort of beings who have beliefs and understanding: we have intellect. There is also will, however: we also resemble God in having affections (loves and hates), in forming aims and intentions, and in being able to act to accomplish these aims and intentions.[6] Call this the *broad* image of God. But human beings as originally created also displayed a *narrow* image: they had extensive and intimate knowledge of God, and *sound* affections, including gratitude for God's goodness.[7] They loved and hated what was lovable and hateful; above all, they knew and loved God. Part of this image was the *sensus divinitatis* of chapter 6.

---

6. Here I am thinking of will in such a way that it includes not only decision and choice (the *executive* function of will) but also loves and hates, desire and conation (the *affective* function of will). This is a bit broader than the usual contemporary understanding of the will, but in line with older ways of thinking about it (see, e.g., Aquinas, *Summa Theologiae* I, q. 82, a. 1 and 2 and *Summa contra Gentiles* Bk. III, ch. 26).

7. Here I was helped by Derek Jeffreys.

The extended model retains this feature and adds more. First, it adds that we human beings have fallen into sin, a calamitous condition from which we require salvation—a salvation we are unable to accomplish by our own efforts. This sin alienates us from God and makes us unfit for communion with him. Our fall into sin has had cataclysmic consequences, both affective and cognitive. As to affective consequences, our affections are skewed and our hearts now harbor deep and radical evil: we love ourselves above all, rather than God. There were also ruinous *cognitive* consequences. Our original knowledge of God and of his marvelous beauty, glory, and loveliness has been severely compromised; in this way the narrow image of God in us was destroyed and the broad image damaged, distorted.[8] In particular, the *sensus divinitatis* has been damaged and deformed; because of the fall, we no longer know God in the same natural and unproblematic way in which we know each other and the world around us. Still further, sin induces in us a *resistance* to the deliverances of the *sensus divinitatis*, muted as they are by the first factor; we don't *want* to pay attention to its deliverances. We are unable by our own efforts to extricate ourselves from this quagmire; God himself, however, has provided a remedy for sin and its ruinous effects, a means of salvation from sin and restoration to his favor and fellowship. This remedy is made available in the life, atoning suffering and death, and resurrection of his divine Son, Jesus Christ. Salvation involves among other things rebirth and regeneration, a process (beginning in the present life and reaching fruition in the next) that involves a restoration and repair of the image of God in us.

So far, what we have here is the mere Christianity of which C. S. Lewis spoke;[9] we now come to a more specifically cognitive side of the model. God needed a way to inform human beings of many times and places of the scheme of salvation he has graciously made available. No doubt he could have done this in a thousand different ways; in fact he chose to do so in the following way. First, there is Scripture, the Bible, a collection of writings by human authors, but specially inspired by

---

8. As Calvin puts it, "The natural gifts in man were corrupted, but the supernatural were taken away" (II, ii, 4, p. 260). And according to Aquinas, "Man in the state of corrupted nature falls short even of what he can do by his nature, so that he is unable to fulfill all of it by his own natural power." We therefore need "a gratuitous strength superadded to natural strength" not only "to do and will supernatural good," but also, he says, to live up to our original nature as persons (*Summa Theologiae* I–II, q. 102, a. 2, *respondeo*). Here we should note an ambiguity in such terms as "our natural condition." On the one hand, the term can refer to what we human beings were like in our original and sinless condition, fresh from the hand of God, and what we would still be like if it weren't for sin; on the other, the term refers to our fallen condition, prior to regeneration and renewal.

9. *Mere Christianity* (New York: Macmillan, 1958).

God in such a way that he can be said to be its principal author. Second, he has sent the Holy Spirit, promised by Christ before his death and resurrection.[10] A principal work of the Holy Spirit with respect to us human beings is the production in us of the gift of *faith*, that "firm and certain knowledge of God's benevolence towards us, founded upon the truth of the freely given promise in Christ, both revealed to our minds and sealed upon our hearts through the Holy Spirit" of which Calvin speaks (below, p. 244). By virtue of the internal instigation of the Holy Spirit, we come to see the truth of the central Christian affirmations. Now faith is not just a cognitive affair: its being "sealed upon our hearts" is a matter of *will* and *affect*; it is a repair of the madness of the will that is at the heart of sin. Still, it is *at least* a cognitive matter. In giving us faith, the Holy Spirit enables us to see the truth of the main lines of the Christian gospel as set forth in Scripture. The internal invitation of the Holy Spirit is therefore a source of belief, a cognitive process[11] that produces in us belief in the main lines of the Christian story. Still further, according to the model, the beliefs thus produced in us meet the conditions necessary and sufficient for warrant; they are produced by cognitive processes functioning properly (in accord with their design plan) in an appropriate epistemic environment (both maxi and mini) according to a design plan successfully aimed at truth; if they are held with sufficient firmness, these beliefs qualify as *knowledge*, just as Calvin's definition of faith has it.

III. THE NATURE OF SIN

Now that we have the extended model before us in outline, we must take a more detailed look into some of its various aspects, starting with the nature of sin and its cognitive consequences. Reformed theologians used to speak of the "noetic effects of sin"; although (sadly enough) this topic has at present dropped out of favor, it will be important for our model, so after an examination of the nature of sin we'll turn in the remaining part of the chapter to its cognitive consequences.

What is sin? Whatever it is, it is both astonishingly deep and deeply elusive. According to the model, there is first the phenomenon of *sinning*: of doing what is wrong, what is contrary to God's will. This is something for which the sinner is *responsible*; he is guilty and warrants blame—but only if he recognizes that what he does *is* sin, or

10. See, e.g., John 14:26: "All this have I spoken while still with you. But the Counselor, the Holy Spirit, whom the Father will send in my name, will teach you all things and will remind you of everything I have said to you."

11. Those who raise their eyebrows at the application of this term to the work of the Holy Spirit are invited to note the explanation below, pp. 257–58.

is culpable in failing to recognize that it is. There is also the condition of *being in* sin, a state in which we human beings find ourselves from our very birth. A traditional Christian term for this condition is 'original sin'. Unlike a sinful act I perform, original sin need not be thought of as something for which I am culpable (original sin is not necessarily original guilt); insofar as I am born in this predicament, my being in it is not within my control and not up to me. (In any event there is plenty of opportunity for culpability with respect to the less original variety of sin.)

How does it happen that we human beings are mired in this desperate and deplorable condition? The traditional Christian answer: it is as a result of the sinful actions of Adam and Eve, our original parents and the first human beings. Whether this is indeed how it happened is a matter on which the model need not take a stand; what *is* part of the model is that in fact we are in the condition. G. K. Chesterton once remarked that of all the doctrines of Christianity, the doctrine of original sin has the strongest claim to "empirical verifiability," the quality that back in the palmy days of positivism was widely trumpeted as the very criterion of 'cognitive meaningfulness'; it has been verified in the wars, cruelty, and general hatefulness that have characterized human history from its very inception to the present. Indeed, no century has seen more organized hatred, contempt, and cruelty than ours, and none has seen it on as grand a scale. Our century in particular also enables us to see the *social* side of sin. We human beings are deeply communal; we learn from parents, teachers, peers, and others, both by imitation and by precept. We acquire beliefs in this way, but just as important (and perhaps less self-consciously), we acquire attitudes and affections, loves and hates. Because of our social nature, sin and its effects can be like a contagion that spreads from one to another, eventually corrupting[12] an entire society or segment of it.

Original sin involves both intellect and will; it is both cognitive and affective. On the one hand, it carries with it a sort of *blindness*, a sort of imperceptiveness, dullness, stupidity. This is a cognitive limitation that first of all prevents its victim from proper knowledge of God and his beauty, glory, and love; it also prevents him from seeing what is worth loving and what worth hating, what should be sought and what eschewed. It therefore compromises both knowledge of fact and knowledge of value.

---

12. Examples of this contagion are salient in our century (though also of course in earlier times); for an unusual fictional example, see Brian Moore's *Black Robe* (New York: E. P. Dutton, 1985).

But sin is also and perhaps primarily an *affective* disorder or malfunction. Our affections are skewed, directed to the wrong objects; we love and hate the wrong things. Instead of seeking first the kingdom of God, I am inclined to seek first my own personal glorification and aggrandizement, bending all my efforts toward making myself look good. Instead of loving God above all and my neighbor as myself, I am inclined to love myself above all and, indeed, to hate God and my neighbor.[13] Much of this hatred and hostility springs from *pride*, that aboriginal sin, and from consequent attempts at self-aggrandizement. We think of getting the world's good things as a zero-sum game: any bit of it you have is a bit I can't have—and want. I want to be better known than you, so anytime you do something noteworthy I feel a prick of envy. I may want to be rich. What counts is not how much money I have, absolutely speaking; what counts is whether I have more than you, or most people, or everybody else. But then you and others are obstacles to the fulfillment of my desires; I can thus come to resent and hate you. And God himself, the source of my very being, can also be a threat. In my prideful desire for autonomy and self-sufficiency I can come to resent the presence of someone upon whom I depend for my every breath and by comparison with whom I am small potatoes indeed. I can therefore come to hate him too. I want to be autonomous, beholden to no one. Perhaps this is the deepest root of the condition of sin.[14]

The defect here is affective, not intellectual. Our affections are disordered; they no longer work as in God's original design plan for human beings. There is a failure of proper function, an affective disorder, a sort of madness of the will. In this condition, we know (in some way and to some degree) what is to be loved (what is objectively lovable), but we nevertheless perversely turn away from what ought to be loved and instead love something else. (As the popular song has it: "My heart has a mind of its own.") We know (at some level) what is right, but find ourselves drawn to what is wrong; we know that we should love God and our neighbor, but we nonetheless prefer not to. Of course this raises an ancient question, one going back to Socrates: can a person really do what she knows or believes is wrong?[15] If she sees what is right, how can she still do what is wrong? The answer is

---

13. Question 5 of the Heidelberg Catechism: "Can you live up to all this perfectly?" Answer: "No. I have a natural tendency to hate God and my neighbor."

14. This desire for autonomy, self-definition, and self-creation can assume quite remarkable proportions: according to Richard Rorty, Martin Heidegger felt guilty about living in a world he hadn't himself created, refused to feel at home in any such world, and couldn't stand the thought that he was not his own creation (*Contingency, Irony, and Solidarity* [Cambridge: Cambridge University Press, 1989], p. 109).

15. *Meno* 77b–78a; see also *Protagoras*, 345e.

simple enough: she *sees* what is right, but *prefers* what is wrong. Socrates fails to see the possibility of *affective* disorder, as opposed to intellectual deficiency or ignorance. In the *absence* of affective disorder, perhaps, indeed, I cannot see the good but prefer the evil, knowing that it is evil. Unfortunately, however, we can't count on the absence of that disorder; sin is, in large part, precisely such disorder. Because of this affective malfunction, I desire and seek what I know or believe is bad.

There are many traditional arguments for the idea that you can't desire what on balance you see to be wrong: I don't have the space to deal with these arguments here, except to say that I don't find them at all convincing. One argument I would like to mention, though, can be put as follows: "There a serious semantic problem here. It isn't so much as coherent to suggest that a person might love and value what she knows is hateful, or hate what she knows is good. Consider Sam, who says, 'I love and propose to promote what is in fact evil': his words fail to make coherent sense. Words like 'good', 'evil', 'right', 'wrong', etc. are used to *commend* and *censure*, express approval and disapproval; hence the first part of Sam's utterance expresses his approval of the very thing of which the second part of the utterance expresses his disapproval. You can sensibly say that you are *given* to approving what is evil, that you have done so often in the past and even that you often do so; but you can't sensibly say that *right now* you approve what is evil or hate what is good. Sam hasn't contradicted himself (he hasn't asserted a proposition and its denial); what he says is nevertheless incoherent, just as if he had said 'Hooray for the red, white and blue, and furthermore execrations upon it!'"

Reply: first, there are two separate questions here: (1) Is it possible to love what one knows is evil? and (2) Is Sam's utterance coherent? These are independent: one is a question about what sorts of attitudes are possible, and the other about what sentences make coherent sense (in English). Even if Sam's utterance is incoherent, it might still be possible to love what one knows to be evil. But second, the fact is Sam's utterance makes perfect sense. When Milton's Satan says, "Evil, be thou my good," what he says is perfectly intelligible: he means to say that he prefers, and proposes to promote, what he recognizes to be evil. We can see what is going on here as follows. It is indeed true that words like 'good', 'bad', and 'evil' perform the function of expressing approval or disapproval. That is only part of their function, however: they also express properties. (It doesn't matter for present purposes precisely *what* properties they express, but perhaps the property expressed by 'good' ['bad'] is at any rate equivalent, in the broadly logical sense, to the property of being approved [disapproved] by God.) Ordinarily these two go together: one expresses approval of what one takes to have the property expressed by 'good'. The important point, however, is that the two functions can also be prized apart: either of the two components of the meaning of these terms can be canceled. When Satan says, "Evil, be thou my good," the aspect of the term 'evil' by which it ordinarily expresses disapproval gets canceled, as does the aspect of the term 'good' whereby it ordinarily expresses the property of being good. So Satan is not (of course) endorsing or proposing a condition in which what has the property of being evil shall henceforth have the property of goodness; nor is he expressing both disapproval and approval of the same thing. He is, instead, declaring, of what he knows has the property of being evil, that he approves of it, loves it, values it, and aims to promote it. His words can be used to do this just because either of the two components—property expression and attitude or affection expression—of the meaning of 'good', 'evil', and similar terms can be canceled.

As both Augustine and Pascal noted, this whole complex and confusing congeries of attitudes, affections and beliefs that constitutes the state of sin is a fertile field for ambiguity and self-deception.[16] According to the extended model, we human beings typically have at least some knowledge of God, and some grasp of what is required of us; this is so even in the state of sin and even apart from regeneration. The condition of sin involves *damage* to the *sensus divinitatis*, but not obliteration; it remains partially functional in most of us. We therefore typically have some grasp of God's presence and properties and demands, but this knowledge is covered over, impeded, suppressed. We are prone to hate God but, confusingly, in some way also inclined to love and seek him; we are prone to hate our neighbor, to see her as a competitor for scarce goods, but also, paradoxically, to prize her and love her. Perhaps I recognize, in a sort of semisubliminal way, that there is deep disorder and worse in my life. I half-recognize the selfishness and self-centeredness that characterizes most of my waking moments. Perhaps I note that even (or perhaps especially) in private soliloquy, where there is no question of influencing others, I imaginatively create, rehearse, and contemplate various situations in which I come out victorious, or heroic, or virtuously long-suffering, or anyway abundantly admirable. Perhaps I also glimpse the foolishness and corruption here, but most of the time I pay no attention. I ignore it; I hide it from myself, escaping into work, projects, family, the whole realm of the everyday. (As Pascal says, "Right now I can't be bothered; I have to return my opponent's serve."[17])

This ambiguity extends even deeper. One can't help but concur with the apostle Paul: "For what I do is not the good I want to do; no, the evil I do not want to do—this I keep on doing" (Romans 7:19). I often do what I recognize is the wrong thing, even though I don't *want* to do the wrong thing; and I don't do what's right, even though I do want to do what's right. It seems that I don't do what I want to do and, instead, do what I don't want to. Or is it instead that when I do wrong, I want to do that very thing, but don't then think it is

16. For contemporary comment, see Bas van Fraassen's "The Peculiar Effects of Love and Desire," in *Perspectives on Self-Deception*, ed. A. Rorty and B. McLaughlin (Berkeley: University of California Press), 1988. Van Fraassen offers a subtle account of some of the tangled depths of self-deception.

17. Quoted in van Fraassen, "The Peculiar Effects."

wrong (though at other times I see perfectly well that it is, and very much wish that I hadn't done it)? Or is it rather that at that time I *do* see (to at least some degree) that it's wrong, or *would* clearly see that it is if I paid attention (and I also semiknow *that* fact then), but I *don't* pay attention, because I want to do this thing? Or is it that when I do something wrong, *then* I *do* want to do that wrong thing, knowing (in a sort of muffled way) that it *is* wrong, even though I don't want to *want* to do the wrong thing? Or is it that when I am wanting to do what is wrong, I don't even raise for myself the question whether it is wrong? My second-level affections can seem typically better attuned or calibrated than my first level: I often want to do what is wrong; wanting to want to do what is wrong is much less frequent. I want to love and hate the right things—that is, what I see as the right things—even if in fact, as I sadly recognize, I do love and hate the wrong things. I don't want to love myself above all; that doesn't stop me from loving myself above all.

A traditional conundrum (or pair of conundra) asks how a person—human or otherwise—could get into this condition in the first place, and whether what is deepest here is a problem of *intellect* or a problem of *will*. According to Calvin (*Institutes* II, i, 4, p. 245), the first and primal sin is *disobedience*; he also says elsewhere that it is *failure to trust God*. According to Augustine,[18] it is *pride* that is the deepest root of sin; he also says elsewhere that *envy* occupies this unenviable position. These four conditions are clearly connected. I pridefully want to think of myself as just as good as anyone else, including God; it therefore irks me to have to obey him. And if he requires that I obey him, will I not begin to mistrust him? (I don't *want* to obey him; it is a short step to convincing myself that what he requires of me is not for my own good.) Of course I also recognize that I *don't* have divine status; hence the envy (and once again, ambiguity and self-deception). Perhaps all of these originate in that Promethean desire for autonomy, for being beholden to nothing and no one. But how can I get into the condition of desiring this autonomy in the first place? Or rather, since I am born in it, how could *Eve* have done so? She knew that God alone is the first being of the universe; she knew that she owed God obedience and love; she knew that her own interest lay in loving and serving God, and, in fact, she *did* love and serve him. So how could she get into this condition of sin? It must include an *intellectual* defect; it must be by way of somehow acquiring a false belief. Somehow she gets deceived into thinking that it would be better for

---

18. (*Psalms*, Ps. 18, ii, 15). This became a common medieval theme; compare, e.g., Peter Lombard, *II sent.*, d. 42, c. 7: "Superbia radix cuncti mali, et initium omnis peccati" ("Pride is the root of evil, and the beginning of all sin"). Luther concurred; see his *Lecture on Romans*, tr. and ed. Wilhelm Pauck (Philadelphia: Westminster Press, 1961), pp. 5ff.

her to go her own way, to be her own person. But how could she come to think a thing like that?

"Not only because he [Adam] was seized by Satan's blandishments," says Calvin, "but contemptuous of truth, he turned aside to falsehood" (II, i, 4, p. 245). So it wasn't just that he somehow non-culpably fell into false belief. He was indeed deceived, but he had a hand in it himself; it was partly a matter of self-deception. He was contemptuous of truth, and that was because at some point his affections went wrong: he was seized by pride. Still, why would his affections go wrong in this way? He must have known that this disobedience is both corrupt and contrary to his own good. So there must have been some kind of prior intellectual fault. But where could such a fault originate: how could it get started? It must be because of self-deception, turning away from what he in some sense knew was the truth. But why deceive himself ? There is a complicated many-sided, dialectical relationship between intellect and will here, one such that it isn't possible to say that either is absolutely prior to the other with respect to falling into sin. One thinks that in some way it must be pride and desire for autonomy that lie at the bottom of the whole mess. Somehow there arises a sneaking desire to be like God, indeed to be equal with him, not to have to play second fiddle (or *n*th fiddle, for very large *n*).

Of course the final mystery remains: where does this sneaking desire to be equal with God come from in the first place? How could the very idea so much as enter Adam's soul? In one way, this is easy enough for us to understand; we ourselves share in the same corruption, the same madness of the will. But Adam was made perfect; so how could it happen? That's not easy to say. God grants us an area of autonomy (we can accept or reject him), and this desire somehow arises out of that autonomy. I see what God is like, I see what I am like, and I have a choice (a choice I partly hide from myself): I can take pleasure in my condition, which is wonderfully good, or I can give in to envy. (Perhaps at first a mere prick, a small discomfort I can't even identify, a subterranean half-thought: why can't I be like that, like God, who owes no one anything and is such that what he wills determines what is good?)

> A speculation: for any free creature God creates, this falling into sin is clearly a possibility; God can't create significantly free creatures who cannot fall into sin. And perhaps a high probability of such a fall attaches to free creatures (creatures with an area of autonomy) who are created in the image of God. God sets out to create beings in his own image: they resemble him in having will and intellect, and they recognize the lustrous beauty, glory, and desirability of God's position. God is himself the center of the universe; his creatures see the splendor and wonderful desirability of that condition. Perhaps, insofar as one is free, and sees both the glory of this position and its enormous desirability, there is a powerful tendency to desire it for oneself. Perhaps there is a high prob-

ability that beings created in the image of God will also wind up resembling him in this: that they want to see and do see themselves as the center of the universe. Perhaps a substantial probability of falling into this condition is built into the very nature of free creatures who have knowledge of God's glorious status and do see it as indeed glorious and desirable. There are possible worlds in which there are free creatures with that kind of knowledge and affection who don't fall into this condition of sin, but perhaps these worlds form only a small proportion of the space of the totality of possible worlds containing free creatures. Fall isn't inevitable or necessary; nevertheless, perhaps its objective probability is very high.

IV. THE NOETIC EFFECTS OF SIN

A. The Basic Consequence

These are deep and dark (and gloomy) theological waters; fortunately the model need not take a stand on the questions how God's creatures could fall into sin, and whether it is intellect or will that is primary in sin. Suffice it to say that we human beings have indeed fallen from a pristine state into sin, a condition that involves both intellect and will. It is an affective malaise, a malfunction or madness of the will. But it is also a cognitive condition, and in what follows we will inquire a bit more closely into the cognitive consequences of sin.

According to the extended A/C model, the noetic effects of sin are concentrated with respect to our knowledge of other people, of ourselves, and of God; they are less relevant (or relevant in a different way: see below, p. 218.) to our knowledge of nature and the world. Sin affects my knowledge of others in many ways. Because of hatred or distaste for some group of human beings, I may think them inferior, of less worth than I myself and my more accomplished friends. Because of hostility and resentment, I may misestimate or entirely misunderstand someone else's attitude toward me, suspecting them of trying to do me in, when in fact there is nothing to the suggestion.[19] Due to that basic and aboriginal sin *pride*, I may unthinkingly and almost without noticing assume that I am the center of the universe (of course if you ask me, I will deny thinking any such thing), vastly exaggerating the importance of what happens to *me* as

19. There are also beliefs we think no person of good will *could* come to hold, so that holding them is *prima facie* evidence of culpability; see my "Reason and Belief in God," in *Faith and Rationality*, ed. Alvin Plantinga and Nicholas Wolterstorff (Notre Dame: University of Notre Dame Press, 1984), p. 36. According to Dietrich Bonhoeffer, certain kinds of knowledge—knowledge of how to achieve salvation or happiness—require obedience: one won't be able to acquire this sort of knowledge without obedience. ("The Call of Discipleship," in *The Cost of Discipleship* [New York: Macmillan, 1963], pp. 83ff.)

opposed to what happens to others. I may vastly overestimate my own attainments and accomplishments,[20] consequently discounting the accomplishments of others. I may also fail to perceive my own sin or see it as less distasteful than it really is; I may fail to see myself as a creature, who, if not viewed through the lens of Christ's sacrifice, would be worthy of divine punishment. (Thus among the ravages of sin is my very failure to note those ravages.) Our grasp of ourselves as image bearers of God himself, the First Being of the universe, can also be damaged or compromised or dimmed. For example, we may think the way to understand human characteristics and ventures such as love, humor, adventure, art, music, science, religion, and morality is solely in terms of our evolutionary origin, rather than in terms of our being image bearers of God.[21] By failing to know God, we can come to a vastly skewed view of what we ourselves are, what we need, what is good for us, and how to attain it.

The most serious noetic effects of sin have to do with our knowledge of God. Were it not for sin and its effects, God's presence and glory would be as obvious and uncontroversial to us all as the presence of other minds, physical objects, and the past. Like any cognitive process, however, the *sensus divinitatis* can malfunction; as a result of sin, it has indeed been damaged.[22] Our original knowledge of God and his glory is muffled and impaired; it has been replaced (by virtue

20. "'Tis inexpressible, and almost inconceivable, how strong a self-righteous, self-exalting disposition is naturally in man; and what he will not do and suffer to feed and gratify it: and what lengths have been gone in a seeming self-denial in other respects . . . ; and all to do sacrifice to this Moloch of spiritual pride or self-righteousness; and that they may have something wherein to exalt themselves before God, and above their fellow creatures," Jonathan Edwards, *Religious Affections* (New Haven: Yale University Press, 1959), p. 241.

21. Thus Herbert Simon ("A Mechanism for Social Selection and Successful Altruism," *Science* 250 [December 1990], pp. 1665ff.) believes that the *rational* way to behave is to act or try to act in such a way as to increase one's personal fitness, that is, to act so as to increase the probability that one's genes will be widely disseminated in the next and subsequent generations, thus doing well in the evolutionary derby; this, he thinks, is given by our evolutionary history. But then how do we account for the behavior of people like Mother Teresa, the Scottish missionary Eric Liddel, the Jesuit missionaries of the seventeenth century, or the Methodist missionaries of the nineteenth? Why do they devote their time and energy and indeed their entire lives to the welfare of other people, apparently not giving a fig about the fate of their genes? Two mechanisms, says Simon: "docility," whereby they are unusually likely to believe what others tell them (1666), and "limited rationality" (1667)—to speak plainly, stupidity.

22. It is no part of the model to say that damage to the *sensus divinitatis* on the part of a person is due to sin on the part of the same person. Such damage is like other disease and handicaps: due ultimately to the ravages of sin, but not necessarily sin on the part of the person with the disease. In this connection, see Jesus' remarks (John 9:1–3) about the man blind from birth.

of sin) by stupidity, dullness, blindness, inability to perceive God or to perceive him in his handiwork. Our knowledge of his character and his love toward us can be smothered: it can even be transformed into a resentful thought that God is to be feared and mistrusted; we may see him as indifferent or even malignant.

In the traditional taxonomy of the seven deadly sins, this is *sloth*. Sloth is not simple laziness, like the inclination to lie down and watch television rather than go out and get the exercise you need; it is, instead, a kind of spiritual deadness, blindness, imperceptiveness, acedia, torpor, a failure to be aware of God's presence, love, requirements.[23] And in addition to the general injury due to the condition of sin itself, there is also the possibility of special damage or disease; perhaps in some people at some times, the *sensus divinitatis* doesn't work at all. Furthermore, the deliverances of the *sensus divinitatis*, muffled as they already are, can easily be suppressed and impeded. That can happen in various ways: for example, by deliberately or semideliberately turning one's attention away from them. Perhaps I am tormented by guilt before God, or perhaps by my desire to live a way of which, as I see it, God disapproves; then I may be inclined (with Paul Tillich) to think of God as an impersonal abstract object ("the ground of being") rather than as a living person who judges me. Or I may come to think of him as unconcerned with the day-to-day behavior of his creatures. Or I may come to think of him, not as a holy God who hates sin, but more like an indulgent grandparent who smiles at the childish peccadilloes of her grandchildren.

That is just one way in which sin interferes with the deliverances of the sense of divinity. Another way in which the latter can be compromised is by way of *testimony* (which includes not only the case where someone rushes up and breathlessly tells me that my house is on fire but also the whole course of my upbringing and acculturation by parents and peers). Perhaps I am brought up to think there is no such person as God, that belief in God is a result of superstition, belonging to the infancy of the race. Perhaps I read Don Cupitt (after ingesting hallucinogens) and come to regard serious believers in God as objects of pity or figures of fun. Perhaps I am brought up to think

---

23. It is this sloth as blindness that C. S. Peirce finds in David Hume: "Lately, when I was suffering at every mouth through which a man can drink suffering, I tried to beguile it by reading three books that I hadn't read for a long time, three religious books: Bunyan's *Pilgrim's Progress*, Boethius' *Consolation of Philosophy* and Hume's *Dialogues Concerning Natural Religion*. The last one did one most good owing to the utter blindness of the man" (quoted in Edward T. Oakes, "Discovering the American Aristotle," *First Things* [December 1993], p. 27). Insofar as sloth (so thought of) is (in part) an element of original sin, it is not something for which one is wholly responsible.

of serious theistic belief as the universal obsessional neurosis of humanity and begin to look upon the rest of believing mankind with a sort of amused condescension. For these reasons or others, I ignore the promptings of the sense of divinity, a little ashamed, no doubt, to note its stirring within my heart. Ordinarily there will be a complicated interplay between *guilt* and *damage*, between what is due to my own sin (in the primary sense) and what is due to the noetic effects of sin that are beyond my control.[24]

An analogy: Thomas Reid and others point out that the idea of *truth*, as a relation between beliefs and the world, is part of our native noetic equipment. We ordinarily take it utterly for granted that there is such a thing as truth, and we ordinarily take it for granted, with respect to any given belief we hold, that it is indeed true. But the right kind of cognitive environment can squelch and smother our notion of truth, so that some people in some circumstances wind up apparently with no concept of truth at all—or, more likely, with a way of thought that displays deep and buried conflicts. One way this can happen is by way of perverse philosophizing. Following certain postmodern thinkers, I can come to see that classical foundationalism is deeply mistaken, and then (perversely) leap lightly to the conclusion that really, there is no such thing as truth. (There is only my version, your version, and so on; where these differ, there is only an issue of power, not of truth.) It can happen in other ways as well. It is said that one of the most serious results of the long Communist tyranny in eastern Europe was just such a suppression of the idea of truth. The truth was officially perverted so often and so cynically (for example, the official organ of the Communist party devoted to the dissemination of this propaganda was ironically named *Pravda*, i.e., truth) that people came to lose the very idea of truth. They were lied to at every level in utterly shameless and blatant ways; they knew they were being lied to, knew that those who lied to them knew they were lying and that those to whom they lied knew they were being lied to, and so on; the result was that the whole idea of truth tended to evaporate. One said whatever would be of advantage; the question whether it was true no longer arose. In the same sort of way, the deliverances of the *sensus divinitatis* can be compromised, skewed, or even suppressed altogether.

24. There are also those who are "always learning but never able to acknowledge the truth" (2 Timothy 3:7), despaired of by both St. Paul and Tertullian, like the theologian in C. S. Lewis's *The Great Divorce* who finds hell more interesting than heaven on the grounds that it offers more scope for lively and controversial theological inquiry and discussion. (In heaven there is that stultifying theological uniformity. . . .)

B. Sin and Knowledge

The most important cognitive consequence of sin, therefore, is failure to know God. And this failure can have further cognitive consequences. At present and especially in academia, there is widespread doubt and agnosticism with respect to the very existence of God. But if we don't know that there is such a person as God, we don't know the first thing (the most important thing) about ourselves, each other, and our world. That is because (from the point of view of the model) the most important truths about us and them is that we have been created by the Lord and utterly depend upon him for our continued existence.[25] We don't know what our happiness consists in, and we don't know how to achieve it. We don't know that we have been created in the image of God, and we don't grasp the significance of such characteristically human phenomena as love, humor, adventure, science, art, music, philosophy, history, and so on.

Can we take things a step further yet? According to John Calvin, "As soon as ever we depart from Christ, there is nothing, be it ever so gross or insignificant in itself, respecting which we are not necessarily deceived."[26] Perhaps Calvin means only what we have already noted: one who doesn't know God fails to know the most important truth about anything else. He may mean to go even further, however: perhaps he means to say that those who don't know God suffer much wider ranging cognitive deprivation and, in fact, don't really have any knowledge at all. (This view is at any rate attributed (rightly or wrongly) to some of his followers, for example, Cornelius van Til.) That seems a shade harsh, particularly because many who don't believe in God seem to know a great deal more about some topics than most believers do. (Could I sensibly claim, for example, that I know more logic than, say, Willard van Orman Quine, even if I can't do any but the simplest logic exercises, on the grounds that at any rate I know *something* about logic and he, being an unbeliever, knows nothing at all about that subject or indeed anything else?) As it stands, this suggestion is desperately wide of the mark; surely many nontheists

25. In this connection, consider the despised creationists, who believe that the world is only ten thousand years old: they are ignorant, pitifully ignorant about when God created the world. From the point of view of the model, this ignorance pales into utter insignificance compared with that of many of their cultured detractors, who foolishly believe that there is no God and thus (naturally enough) are ignorant of the vastly more important fact that the world was, indeed, created by God.

26. *Commentaries on the First Book of Moses, Called Genesis*, tr. John King (Edinburgh: Calvin Translation Society, 1847); reprinted by Baker Book House (Grand Rapids, 1979).

do know *some* things, for example, their age to the nearest year or so, to whom if anyone they are married, and which university it is that employs them. (If this weren't so, contemporary academia would display even more confusion than it does.)

1. Sin and Skepticism

A couple of less sweeping views however have a great deal to be said for them. One who is agnostic about the existence of God may also be agnostic about his origin and his place in the universe. In this section, I shall argue that one who displays a certain kind of agnosticism with respect to his origin and place in the universe, and also grasps a certain cogent argument, will not, in fact, know anything at all; nothing he believes will have warrant sufficient for knowledge. To explore this suggestion, we may begin by considering the Scottish philosopher David Hume. Thomas Reid, Hume's great contemporary and antagonist, took Hume to be a *skeptic* with respect to external objects, an enduring self, other minds, causality, the past, and so on.[27] As Reid sees him, Hume thinks that there is something *wrong* in believing the things we ordinarily do: it isn't as if Hume simply announces that as a matter of fact we don't really know all we think we know about external objects, causal relations, our own selves. Perhaps that would be bad enough, but there is something much deeper.

We can see what by considering the Hume of the conclusion of Book I of the *Treatise*.[28] Here he isn't coolly announcing, as a mildly interesting fact about us, that fewer of our beliefs constitute knowledge than we ordinarily think. Instead, he finds himself in a sort of existential crisis; he simply doesn't know what to believe. When he follows out what seem to be the promptings and leading of reason, he winds up time after time in a black coal pit, not knowing which way to turn:

> Where am I, or what? From what causes do I derive my existence, and to what condition shall I return? Whose favour shall I court, and whose anger must I dread? What beings surround me? and on whom have I any influence, or who have any influence on me? I am confounded with all these questions, and begin to fancy myself in

27. Although Reid's view has been the majority opinion with respect to Humean exegesis, there has always been a minority opinion according to which Hume really wasn't a skeptic at all. This striking divergence is testimony to the fact that Hume is a black enigma: a certain surface clarity masks a deep underlying murkiness that makes confident interpretation impossible.

28. *Treatise of Human Nature*, ed. L. A. Selby-Bigge (Oxford: Clarendon Press, 1951; first published in 1739), pp. 263ff. Subsequent page references to the *Treatise* are to this edition.

the most deplorable condition imaginable, inviron'd with the deepest darkness, and utterly depriv'd of the use of every member and faculty. (p. 269)

Of course this is Hume in his study, sometime before he emerges for that famous game of backgammon. Nature herself, fortunately, dispels these clouds of despair: she "cures me of this philosophical melancholy and delirium, either by relaxing this bent of mind, or by some avocation, and lively impression of my senses, which obliterate all these chimeras. I dine, I play a game of back-gammon, I converse, and am merry with my friends" (p. 269).

Still, the enlightened person, Hume thinks, holds the consolations of Nature at arm's length. She knows she can't help acquiescing in the common illusion, but she maintains her skepticism of "the general maxims of the world" and adopts a certain ironic distance, a wary double-mindedness: "I may, nay I must yield to the current of nature, in submitting to my senses and understanding; and in this blind submission I shew most perfectly my sceptical disposition and principles" (p. 269). This is the irony of the human condition: those who are enlightened can see that what nature inevitably leads us to believe is false, or arbitrary, or at best extremely dubious; they also see, however, that even the best of us simply don't have it in them to successfully resist her blandishments. We can't help believing those "general maxims," or if we can, it is only for brief periods of time and in artificial situations. No one can think Humean thoughts about, say, induction, when under attack by a shark or when clinging precariously to a rock face high above the valley floor. (You won't find yourself saying, "Well, I do of course believe that if this handhold breaks out, I'll hurtle down to the ground and get killed, still [fleeting sardonic, self-deprecatory smile] I also know that this thought is just a deliverance of my nature and is therefore not really to be taken seriously.") Still, in other circumstances, one can take a sort of condescending and dismissive stance with respect to these promptings of nature; in reflective moments in my study, for example, I see through them. As a rational creature, I can rise above them, recognizing that they have little or nothing to be said for them. Indeed, I see more: this skepticism is itself a *reflexive* skepticism; it arises even with respect to this very thought; this very doubt, this feeling of superiority, this seeing through what our natures impose on us, is itself a deliverance of my nature and is thus as suspect as any other. The true skeptic, says Hume, "will be diffident of his philosophical doubts, as well as of his philosophical conviction" (p. 273).[29]

---

29. And this leads to the scandal of skepticism: if I *argue* to skepticism, then of course I rely on the very cognitive faculties whose unreliability is the conclusion of my skeptical argument.

In these passages, therefore, Hume isn't shamefacedly confessing an epistemic weakness or flaw, rather as a victim of neurosis or mental disease might. ("Doctor, I often find that I simply can't bring myself to believe that induction will continue to work, or that I myself have existed for a good long time, or that there really are other people or external objects.") No; this multiply skeptical position, he thinks, is somehow the *right* one, the one that the man of sense (at least the man of philosophic sense) will adopt. The rest of us who unthinkingly acquiesce in the promptings of nature, who without a thought believe in causal connection, induction, persistent selves, external objects—the rest of us are from this perspective naive or foolish, unwitting dupes of our own nature. Hume is a sort of Presbyterian of the intellect; we are all, sage and ingenue alike, enmeshed in the toils of an original sin of the mind (and here perhaps we can see a lingering influence of the Calvinism of his youth). Of course Hume might claim that at least he has the advantage of recognizing that (ordinarily) he *is* a dupe. In this regard, he may seem like the publican in Jesus' parable, who at any rate had the grace to confess that he was indeed a sinner. But the fact is Hume is really more like the Pharisee. He isn't confessing a frailty or shortcoming, hoping for a cure; he is arguing, as he sees it, from a position of strength or at least insight; the rest of us who unthinkingly accede to the promptings of nature are the ones who suffer from intellectual shortcoming. More than that, we are irrational, in the Humean view, in that reason, carefully preserved from the corrupting influence of everyday attitudes, enjoins this skepticism upon us. To fail to accept it is to fail to follow reason, to go against its teachings, and in that sense to fall into irrationality.

Now Thomas Reid takes issue with Hume (at any rate Hume as he sees him) at just this point. He sees Hume as standing with Descartes in thinking that the deliverances of perception, memory, induction, sympathy, testimony, and any other faculty we might have must be validated before the bar of reason and consciousness. That is, none of these faculties can reasonably be trusted until it has been shown to be reliable by an argument that meets two conditions. First, the argument in question must start from premises that are either self-evident (like elementary truths of arithmetic), or else deliverances of consciousness: such propositions about my own mind as that I seem to see a horse, or am appeared to redly, or believe that the Orkney Islands are north of Aberdeen. Second, the argument must be such that each of its steps is self-evidently valid.

Now Descartes thought that in fact the other sources of belief *could* be legitimated by reason and consciousness. He thought first to establish the reliability of reason itself by giving a reasoned (rational) proof that we have been created by a benevolent God who is nondeceptive (and here we fall into that distressing Cartesian circle), but God would be a deceiver if the world weren't very much like our perceptual faculties reveal it to be. As Reid sees it, Descartes is mistaken at several points; the point of present interest, however, is Descartes's confidence that the reliability of those other sources *can* be established by reason. It took the work of modern philosophy from Descartes to Hume, so Reid thinks, to show that this is in fact a chimera, a will-o'-the-wisp; it simply can't be done. (The inevitable failure of this Cartesian project was therefore wholly evident to Reid some two hundred years or so before Rorty and Quine took this failure as a reason for proclaiming the death of epistemology [Rorty[30]] or its transmogrification into empirical psychology [Quine[31]].)

Now one reaction would be to see this condition as interesting and perhaps even mildly regrettable, but of no real importance: these other sources of belief are perfectly acceptable, whether or not we can find arguments of the above sort for their reliability. Reid's Hume, however, takes quite a different tack; he takes it to be a sign of foolishness or error or dupery (in any event, part of the deplorable human condition) to accept the testimony of any source whose veracity hasn't been (or, worse, can't be) established by way of consciousness and reason. He therefore concludes that the *rational* course is to reject these beliefs (given that we can't show in the way in question that their sources are reliable), even if because of nature's imperious edicts we can't actually follow that austere prescription.

This strikes Reid as a piece of consummate arbitrariness:

> The sceptic asks me, Why do you believe the existence of the external object which you perceive? This belief, sir, is none of my manufacture; it came from the mint of Nature; it bears her image and superscription; and, if it is not right, the fault is not mine: I ever took it upon trust, and without suspicion. Reason, says the sceptic, is the only judge of truth, and you ought to throw off every opinion and every belief that is not grounded on reason. Why, sir, should I believe the faculty of reason more than that of perception?—they came both out of the same shop, and were made by the same artist; and if he puts one piece of false ware into my hands, what should hinder him from putting another?[32]

30. See his *Philosophy and the Mirror of Nature* (Princeton: Princeton University Press, 1979).

31. As in "Epistemology Naturalized," in *Ontological Relativity and Other Essays* (New York: Columbia University Press, 1969).

32. *Thomas Reid's Inquiry and Essays*, ed. Keith Lehrer and Ronald E. Beanblossom (Indianapolis: Bobbs-Merrill, 1975), pp. 84–85.

222 *Warranted Christian Belief*

I believe that Reid is substantially right here; the Humean skeptic *is* arbitrary.[33] But this is not the place for a discussion of this point: what I want to argue instead is that Hume has a *different* reason for his skepticism, a reason shared by anyone who concurs with him in agnosticism about our origin and the origin of our cognitive faculties. Suppose, for one reason or another, you give up this idea that we have been created by a benevolent deity. Perhaps with Hume you adopt instead a thoroughgoing agnosticism: there is simply no way to know whether there is any being at all like God, no way to know whether there is a divine being who created the world, no way, indeed, to know anything about the ultimate origin of the world or of the ultimate origin of ourselves and our cognitive faculties. "Our experience," he says, "so imperfect in itself and so limited both in extent and duration, can afford us no probable conjecture concerning the whole of things."[34] *Perhaps* the world owes its existence to intelligent design: just as likely, though (at least as far as we can tell), it owes it to animal or even vegetative generation (perhaps comets are seeds and our world has arisen from one); and there are a thousand other possibilities, some of them canvassed with grace and style in the *Dialogues concerning Natural Religion*. Hume's[35] conclusion there, it seems, is that

> In such questions as the present [cosmogony, the origin of the universe], a hundred contradictory views may preserve a kind of imperfect analogy, and invention has here full scope to exert itself. Without any great effort of thought, I believe that I could, in an instant, propose other systems of cosmogony which would have some faint appearance of truth: though it is a thousand, a million to one if either yours or any one of mine be the true system. (*Dialogues*, p. 49)

He adds a bit later that on this topic, "A total suspense of judgment is here our only reasonable resource" (p. 53). Hume so understood has no idea at all how the world got here, how rational creatures such as we ourselves have arisen, and what the origin and provenance of our rational or belief-producing faculties might be.

Now turn to the question whether our cognitive faculties are reliable and do, in fact, produce for the most part true belief. Given Hume's complete agnosticism about the origins of his cognitive faculties, something like his deeply agnostic attitude to that question is no more than sensible. For suppose Hume asks himself how likely it is that our cognitive faculties are reliable, given his views (or rather lack of views) about the origin and provenance of ourselves and those

33. But perhaps not *entirely* arbitrary; see *Warrant: The Current Debate*, pp. 100ff.
34. *Dialogues concerning Natural Religion*, ed. Richard Popkin (Indianapolis: Hackett Publishing, 1980), p. 45.
35. Or at any rate Philo's; I make no pretense to settle the question of who speaks for Hume in the *Dialogues*, something Hume artfully conceals.

faculties. What is the probability that our faculties produce the considerable preponderance of true belief over false required by reliability, given his views of their origin and purpose (if any)? I should think he would have to say that this probability is either low or inscrutable—impossible to determine. From his point of view, there are innumerable scenarios, innumerable ways in which we and our cognitive faculties could have come into being: perhaps we have been created by God, but perhaps we and the world are the result of some kind of vegetative principle, or a result of copulation on the part of animals we have no knowledge of, or the result of Russell's accidental collocation of atoms, or of . . . . On many of these scenarios, our cognitive faculties wouldn't be reliable (although they might contribute to fitness or survival); perhaps on others they would be reliable; on balance, one just wouldn't know what to think about this probability.

We can see this more fully as follows. Let R be the proposition that our cognitive faculties are reliable: now what is the likelihood of R? As Reid points out, we all instinctively believe or assume that our cognitive faculties are indeed reliable; but what is the probability of that assumption, given the relevant facts? Well, what are the relevant facts? First, they would be facts about those faculties: the probability of R given (relative to) the population of China would not be relevant. And presumably the relevant facts would be facts about how these faculties originated; whether they were designed; if so, by whom and with what end in view; what constraints governed their development; and what their purpose and function is, if, indeed, they have a purpose and function. Were they, as Reid thought, created in us by a being who intends that they function reliably to give us knowledge about our environment, ourselves, and God himself—all the knowledge needed for us to attain shalom, to be the sort of beings God intended us to be? On that scenario, the purpose of our cognitive faculties would be (in part, at least) to supply us with true beliefs on those topics, and (given that they are functioning properly) there would be a high probability of their doing just that.

Did they, by contrast, arise by way of some chance mechanism, something like the mindless swerve of atoms in the Democritian void? What is the likelihood, on *that* possibility, that our cognitive faculties are reliable? Well, you might think it pretty low. More likely, you may think that you simply can't say what that probability is: perhaps it is high (though presumably not very high), perhaps it is low; you simply can't tell.[36] There will be many more such scenarios, says Hume, some involving vegetative origin, some copulative origin,

---

36. We aren't thinking here of Bayesian personal probability but of some kind of objective probability, the sort of probability Hume has in mind when he says that "it is a thousand, a million to one if either yours or any one of mine be the true system."

some still other kinds of origin; with respect to them, too, the probability that our cognitive faculties are reliable is simply inscrutable. So first, Hume thinks his grasp of the whole set of relevant scenarios is at best infirm; second, with respect to many of these scenarios, those possible origins, the probability of R is inscrutable; and finally, the probability with respect to any of these scenarios that it is in fact the truth of the matter is also, as far as Hume is concerned, quite inscrutable.

But that means that the probability of R, given Hume's agnosticism, is also inscrutable for Hume. Let F be the relevant facts about their origin, purpose, and provenance: my claim is that, for Hume, $P(R/F)$ (the probability of R on F) is inscrutable. He simply doesn't know what it is and has no opinion about its value, although presumably it wouldn't be very high. Another way to put it: the probability of R, given Hume's agnosticism, is inscrutable.

And that gives Hume a reason to be agnostic with respect to R as well; it gives him a reason to doubt that R is, in fact, true. For our cognitive faculties, our belief-producing mechanisms, are a bit like measuring instruments (more exactly, measuring instruments under an interpretation). Our faculties produce beliefs; for each belief, there is the content of that belief, the proposition believed, a proposition that is true if and only if the belief is true. Now a state of a measuring instrument (relative to a scheme of interpretation) can also be said (in an analogically extended sense) to have content. For definiteness, consider a thermometer and suppose its pointer is resting on the number 70. Given the natural scheme of interpretation, this state can be said to have the content that the ambient temperature is 70° F. And of course a thermometer is *reliable* only if the propositions it delivers in this way are for the most part true, or nearly true.

Imagine, then, that you embark on a voyage of space exploration and land on a planet revolving about a distant sun. This planet has a favorable atmosphere, but you know little more about it. You crack the hatch, step out, and immediately find something that looks a lot like a radio; it periodically emits strings of sounds that, oddly enough, form sentences in English. The sentences emitted by this instrument express propositions only about topics of which you have no knowledge: what the weather is like in Beijing at the moment, whether Caesar had eggs on toast on the morning he crossed the Rubicon, whether the first human being to cross the Bering Strait and set foot on North America was left-handed, and the like. A bit unduly impressed with your find, you initially form the opinion that this quasi radio speaks the truth: that is, the propositions expressed (in English) by those sentences are true. But then you recall that you have no idea at all as to what the purpose of this apparent instrument is, whether it *has* a purpose, or how it came to be. You see that the probability of its being reliable, given what you know about it, is for you inscrutable. Then (in the absence of investigation) you have a *de-*

feater for your initial belief that the thing does, in fact, speak the truth, a reason to reject that belief, a reason to give it up, to be agnostic with respect to it. Relative to your beliefs about the origin, purpose, and provenance of this apparent instrument, the probability that it is a reliable source of information is low or (more likely) inscrutable. And that gives you a defeater for your original and hasty belief that the thing really does speak the truth. If you don't have or get further information about its reliability, the reasonable course is agnosticism about that proposition.

The same goes, I think, in the case of Humean views (or nonviews) about our origins and the origin and purpose, if any, of our cognitive faculties. Suppose I join Hume in that agnosticism. Then P(R/F) is for me inscrutable (as for Hume); I have no idea what the probability of my faculties being reliable is, given the relevant facts about their origin and purpose. But then I have a defeater for my original belief or assumption that my faculties are in fact reliable. If I have or can get no further information about their reliability, the reasonable course for me is agnosticism with respect to R, giving it up, failing to believe it. It isn't that rationality requires that I believe its *denial*, but it does require that I not believe *it*.

Suppose, therefore, that I *am* agnostic with respect to R: I believe neither it nor its denial. And now consider any belief *B* I have: that belief, of course, will be a deliverance of my cognitive faculties. However, I don't believe that my cognitive faculties are reliable—not because I've never thought about the question, but because I *have* thought about it and seen that P(R/F) is inscrutable for me. Well, what does rationality require with respect to this belief *B*? The clear answer seems to be that I have a defeater for this belief too, a reason to withhold it, to be agnostic with respect to it. Perhaps it isn't possible, given my nature, that I *be* agnostic with respect to it, at least much of the time; as Hume says, nature may not permit this. Still, this agnosticism is what reason requires, just as Hume suggests (though for different reasons). And we can take one further step with Hume. Because *B* is just *any* belief I hold—because I have a defeater for just any belief I hold—I also have a defeater for my belief that I *have* a defeater for *B*. This universal, all-purpose defeater provided by my agnosticism is also a defeater for *itself*, a self-defeating defeater.[37] And hence this complex, confusing, multilayered, reflexive skepticism Hume describes, a skepticism in which I am skeptical of my beliefs and also of my doubts, and of the beliefs that lead to those

37. Of course this raises problems: if I have a defeater-defeater (a defeater for my defeater for R), then don't I thereby *lose* my defeater for R? Am I back where I was before I acquired the defeater for R? No; for my defeater-defeater is also a defeater for R. For explanation and detail, see part IV, section E, "The Dreaded Loop," from my "Naturalism Defeated," presently unpublished.

doubts, and of my doubts with respect to those doubts, and the beliefs leading to *them*. Thus the true skeptic will be skeptical all the way down; he "will be diffident of his philosophical doubts, as well as his philosophical conviction."

Here we can imagine the following response: "Hey, hang on a minute! You said Hume and any similarly situated agnostic has a defeater for R, a belief to which he is inclined by nature—and you added that the rational course for them therefore is to give up belief in R—*provided they have no other information* about the reliability of their faculties. But what about that strong natural inclination to believe that our faculties are in fact reliable? Doesn't *that* count as 'other information'?" According to Reid (who might object to being pressed into service in defense of Hume), this belief in the reliability of our faculties is a *first principle*:

> Another first principle is—*That the natural faculties, by which we distinguish truth from error, are not fallacious.* (275)

He goes on:

> If any truth can be said to be prior to all others in the order of nature, this seems to have the best claim; because, in every instance of assent, whether upon intuitive, demonstrative, or probable evidence, the truth of our faculties is taken for granted. . . . (277)

Surely there is truth here: this conviction is one normal human beings ordinarily have, and, as Reid gleefully points outs, even skeptics also seem to assume, in the course of ordinary daily living, to be sure, but most poignantly when proposing their skeptical arguments, that their faculties are functioning reliably. Very few skeptics, in offering their skeptical arguments, preface the argument by saying something like, "Well, here is an argument for general skepticism with respect to our cognitive faculties; of course I realize that the premises of this argument are themselves produced by cognitive faculties whose reliability the conclusion impugns, and of whose truth I am therefore extremely doubtful."

But our question is whether this belief can sensibly be pressed into service as information that can defeat the defeater provided for R by Hume's agnosticism about the origin and provenance of ourselves and our faculties. As Reid clearly sees, it cannot. If the general reliability of our cognitive faculties is under question, we can't hope to answer the question whether they *are* reliable by pointing out that these faculties themselves deliver the belief that they are, in fact, reliable. "If a man's honesty were called into question," says Reid, "it would be ridiculous to refer it to the man's own word, whether he be honest or not" (276). Concede that it is part of our nature to assume R; concede further that it is part of our nature to take R in the *basic* way, so that this conviction is not given or achieved by argument and evidence but comes with our mother's milk; concede still further, if you like, that this belief is produced by our cognitive faculties functioning properly. None of this, clearly enough, can serve to defeat the defeater for R provided by Hume's agnosticism. That is because any doubt about our cognitive faculties generally is a doubt about the specific faculty that produces this conviction; therefore we can't allay such a doubt by appealing to the deliverances of that faculty.[38]

2. Naturalism and Lack of Knowledge

Agnosticism with respect to our origins is one way to reject the theistic belief that we human beings have been created in the image of God: as we have seen, agnosticism with respect to origins destroys knowledge. There is another way to reject the belief in question: by accepting a belief incompatible with it, for example, philosophical or metaphysical naturalism. As Bas van Fraassen notes, it isn't easy to say precisely what naturalism *is*;[39] for present purposes, suppose we take it to be the view that there is no such person as God, nor anyone or anything at all like him (it isn't that you believe, for example, that there are one or more finite gods). Paradigm cases of naturalism would be the views of Daniel Dennett in *Darwin's Dangerous Idea*[40] or Bertrand Russell in "A Free Man's Worship": you think that "man is the product of causes which had no prevision of the end they were achieving, that his origin, his growth, his hopes and fears, his loves and his beliefs, are but the outcome of accidental collocations of atoms."[41] (Perhaps you even go so far as to add, with Richard Dawkins, that the very idea that there is such a person as God is really a kind of cognitive virus, an epistemic sickness or disease, distorting the cognitive stance of what would otherwise be reasonable and rational human beings.[42]) Unlike Hume, therefore, you are not agnostic as to whether there is such a person as God or any being at all like him; you think there is not.

---

38. The same goes, naturally enough, for the suggestion that we try to determine by scientific means whether our cognitive faculties are reliable; any such attempt could proceed only by reliance on the very faculties whose reliability is at issue.

39. See his "Science, Materialism, and False Consciousness," in *Warrant in Contemporary Epistemology: Essays in Honor of Plantinga's Theory of Knowledge*, ed. Jonathan Kvanvig (New York: Rowman and Littlefield, 1996).

40. New York: Simon and Schuster, 1995.

41. In *Why I Am Not a Christian* (New York: Simon and Schuster, 1957), p. 107.

42. "Viruses of the Mind," in *Dennett and His Critics: Demystifying Mind*, ed. Bo Dahlbom (Oxford: Blackwell, 1993), pp. 13ff. As evidence for the virulence and tenacity of this virus, Dawkins cites the fact that it took Sir Anthony Kenny (as learned and sapient a person as we can easily find), a very long time to fight his way clear of it. Others may wonder whether the virus is all Dawkins says it is, given that Dawkins himself apparently escaped it long ago.

There is likely to be a further difference between you and Hume. Having rejected theism, Hume had no comparable story to put in its place: he was left with no idea as to how humanity arose, under what conditions our cognitive faculties came to be, and so on. The contemporary naturalist, however, is in a different condition; for naturalism now sports a shared myth or story about ourselves and our origins, a set of shared beliefs about who we are, where we come from, and how we got here. The story is familiar; I shall be brief. We human beings have arrived on the scene after millions, indeed, billions of years of organic evolution. In the beginning, there was just inorganic matter; somehow, and by way of processes of which we currently have no grasp, life, despite its enormous and daunting complexity at even the simplest level, arose from nonliving matter, and arose just by way of the regularities studied in physics and chemistry. Once life arose, random genetic mutation and natural selection, those great twin engines of evolution, swung into action.[43] These genetic mutations are multiply random: they weren't intended by anyone, of course, but also were not directed by any sort of natural teleology and do not arise at the behest of the design plan of the organism. They are "not in a response to the needs of the organism" (Ernst Mayr); they just unaccountably appear. Occasionally, some of them yield an adaptive advantage; their possessors come to predominate in the population, and they are passed on to the next and subsequent generations. In this way, all the enormous variety of flora and fauna we behold came into being.

Including ourselves and our cognitive systems. These systems and the underlying mechanisms have also been selected for, directly or indirectly, in the course of evolution. Consider, for example, the mammalian brain in all its enormous complexity. It could have been directly selected for in the following sense: at each stage in its development, the new stage (by virtue of the structures and behaviors it helped bestow) contributed to fitness and conferred an evolutionary advantage, giving its possessors a better chance of surviving and reproducing. Alternatively, at certain stages new structures (or new modifications of old structures) arose, not because they were themselves selected for, but because they were genetically associated with something else that *was* selected for (pliotropy). Either way these structures were not selected for their penchant for producing true beliefs in us; instead, they conferred an adaptive advantage or were genetically associated with something that conferred such an advantage. And the ultimate purpose or function, if any, of these belief-producing mechanisms will not be the production of true beliefs, but *survival*—of the gene, genotype, individual, species, whatever.

---

43. Various other mechanisms (e.g., genetic drift and neutral evolution) have been proposed, but these two remain the favorites.

If you are a naturalist and also believe these things, then you are what I shall call an *ordinary* naturalist.[44] In chapter 12 of *Warrant and Proper Function* (WPF), I argued that an ordinary naturalist is like Hume in that she has a defeater for any belief she holds—including, ironically enough, ordinary naturalism itself, so that ordinary naturalism is self-defeating.[45] I shall not repeat that argument; instead, I will take this opportunity to make some corrections, simplifications, and additions.

First, a correction. In chapter 12 of WPF, there are really *two* arguments: a preliminary argument and a main argument. The main argument is for the conclusion that naturalism is self-defeating (and hence not rationally acceptable); the preliminary argument is not for that conclusion, but is, instead, a straightforward (probabilistic) argument for the *falsehood* of naturalism. The preliminary argument is also straightforwardly incorrect.[46] We can see this as follows. It began with an argument for the conclusion that P(R/N&E&C) is fairly low. Here R is the proposition that our cognitive faculties are reliable, N is metaphysical naturalism, E is the proposition that our cognitive faculties have developed by way of the mechanisms to which contemporary evolutionary theory directs our attention, and C was an unspecified proposition describing our noetic systems. In fact, C is dispensable, so in what follows I shall suppress it.

After arguing that P(R/N&E) is low, I went on:

> Suppose you do estimate these probabilities in roughly this way: suppose you concur in Darwin's Doubt, taking P(R/N&E) to be fairly low. But suppose you also think, as most of us do, that, in fact, our cognitive faculties are reliable (with the qualifications and nuances introduced above). Then you have a straightforward probabilistic argument against naturalism—and for traditional theism, if you think these two the significant alternatives. According to Bayes's Theorem,

44. Daniel Dennett's book *Darwin's Dangerous Idea* is a paradigm of ordinary naturalism as well as naturalism simpliciter; the same goes for Richard Dawkins's *The Blind Watchmaker* (London: W. W. Norton, 1986). For animadversions on *Darwin's Dangerous Idea* (and on Darwin's dangerous idea), see my "Dennett's Dangerous Idea," *Books and Culture* (May–June 1996; for a powerful animadversion on the first but not the second, see Jerry Fodor's "Deconstructing Dennett's Darwin," in *Mind and Language* 11, no. 3 (September 1996), pp. 246–62.

45. See James Beilby, ed. *Naturalism Defeated? Essays on Plantinga's Evolutionary Argument against Naturalism* (forthcoming) for fascinating objections to and critical comments on this argument, along with my reply.

46. Here I was helped by Branden Fitelson and Elliott Sober; see their paper "Plantinga's Probability Arguments against Evolutionary Naturalism," *Pacific Philosophical Quarterly* 79 (1998), pp. 115–29.

$$P(N\&E/R) = \frac{P(N\&E) \times P(R/N\&E)}{P(R)}$$

where P(N&E) is your estimate of the probability for N&E independent of the consideration of R. You believe R, so you assign it a probability of 1 (or nearly 1); and you take P(R/N&E) to be no more than 1/2. Then P(N&E/R) will be no greater than 1/2 times P(N&E), and will thus be fairly low. No doubt you will also assign a very high probability to the conditional *if naturalism is true, then our faculties have arisen by way of evolution*; if so, then you will judge that P(N/R) is also low. But you do think R is true; you therefore have evidence against N. So your belief that our cognitive faculties are reliable gives you a reason for rejecting naturalism and accepting its denial (p. 228).

A very pretty little argument: too bad it contains a serious flaw. Here is the problem: in this argument, I was confusing the absolute (logical or anyway objective) probability of R with its probability conditional on our background information B; that is, I was confusing P(R/B) with P(R) simpliciter. (For simplicity, I shall henceforth also suppress E, annexing it to N, so that henceforth N will stand for ordinary naturalism, the conjunction of naturalism simpliciter with E.) We can see this by considering the argument both ways: first, relativizing the probabilities to our background knowledge B, and second, not so relativizing them.

First interpretation: if we relativize the probabilities in question to B, then the relevant application of Bayes's Theorem will be

$$P(N/R\&B) = \frac{P(N/B) \times (R/N\&B)}{P(R/B)}$$

Here I can set P(R/B) very high, just as I say on p. 228. But I can't sensibly claim that P(R/N&B) is low. That P(R/N) is low is what I argued: I didn't argue that the probability of R is low on N plus background knowledge. In the argument that P(R/N) is low, I was abstracting from what we ordinarily think we know (for example, R itself). So I can't, without further argument, anyway, claim that the probability of R on N together with our background knowledge, is low.

Second interpretation: if we don't relativize the argument to B (or anything else), the relevant application of Bayes's will be

$$P(N/R) = \frac{P(N) \times P(R/N)}{P(R)}$$

as I said on p. 228. But if we are thinking of the *absolute* probability of R (conditioned only on necessary truths), then I can't claim (as I did) that P(R) is high: how would I know what proportion of the space of possible worlds is occupied by worlds in which R is true? In particular, the fact that R is true *in fact* is no reason for assigning it a high absolute (logical) probability. So either way the argument fails.

Fortunately, there is a repair. We are comparing theism (T) and N. So the relevant applications of Bayes's will be

$$P(N/R) = \frac{P(N) \times P(R/N)}{P(R)}$$

and

$$P(T/R) = \frac{P(T) \times P(R/T)}{P(R)}$$

where we are thinking of absolute or logical probabilities. $P(R)$ will have the same value in each expression; so the question is, how do

(a) $P(N) \times P(R/N)$

and

(b) $P(T) \times P(R/T)$

compare in value? Well, $P(R/N)$ is low, as I had argued. However, $P(R/T)$ is not; R is just what we'd expect, given T. (At any rate we've got no reason for thinking $P(R/T)$ low.) So (given that we don't assign N a considerably higher absolute probability than T) we should take the probability of T on R to be greater than that of N on R. But we do, in fact, believe R. So we have a reason to prefer T to N. Not perhaps a very *strong* reason (this doesn't tell us a whole lot about the probabilities of T and N on our total evidence) but a reason nonetheless. (It's the same sort of reason the atheologian has for preferring atheism to theism, given that he thinks it unlikely that a world created by God would display all the evil the world does, in fact, display.)

In essence, the main argument is for the conclusions that $P(R/N\&E\&C)$ (which I'll abbreviate as $P(R/N)$; see small print above) is either low or inscrutable; in either case, so I argued, one who accepts N (and also grasps the argument for a low or inscrutable value of $P(R/N)$) has a *defeater* for R. This induces a defeater, for him, for any belief produced by his cognitive faculties, including N itself; hence, ordinary naturalism is self-defeating. Now I argued that $P(R/N)$ is low or inscrutable by noting first that natural selection isn't interested in *true belief* but in *adaptive behavior* (taken broadly), so that everything turns on the relation between belief and behavior. I then presented five mutually exclusive and jointly exhaustive possibilities for the relation between belief and behavior, arguing with respect to each possibility P_i that $P(R/N\&P_i)$ is low or inscrutable, yielding the result that $P(R/N)$ is low or inscrutable.

Here we can simplify by dropping two of the five possibilities, leaving just epiphenomenalism, semantic epiphenomenalism (perhaps 'content epiphenomenalism' would be a more felicitous name), and the common sense ('folk psychological') view of the causal relation between belief and behavior. The first possibility (call it 'P_1') is epiphenomenalism, the proposition that belief (conscious belief) isn't involved in the causal chain leading to behavior at all. This view was named and suggested by T. H. Huxley ("Darwin's bulldog").[47] Although epiphenomenalism runs counter to our commonsense ways of thinking, it is nonetheless widely popular among those enthusiastic about the "scientific" study of human beings. According to *Time*, a few years ago the eminent biologist J. M. Smith "wrote that he had never understood why organisms have feelings. After all, orthodox biologists believe that behavior, however complex, is governed entirely by biochemistry and that the attendant sensations—fear, pain, wonder, love—are just shadows cast by that biochemistry, not themselves vital to the organism's behavior."[48]

And the same can be said for conscious belief: if "behavior, however complex, is governed entirely by biochemistry," there seems to be no room for conscious belief to become involved in the causal story, no way in which conscious belief can get its hand in; it will be causally inert. Furthermore, if this possibility were, in fact, actual, then evolution would not have been able to mold and shape our beliefs, or belief-producing structures, weeding out falsehood and encouraging truth; for then our beliefs would be, so to speak, *invisible* to evolution. Which beliefs (if any) an organism had, under this scenario, would be merely accidental as far as evolution is concerned. It wouldn't make any difference to behavior or fitness what beliefs our cognitive mechanisms had produced, because (under this scenario) those beliefs play no role in the production or explanation of behavior. What then is the probability of R on this scenario? That is, what is $P(R/N\&P_1)$? What reliability requires, of course, is that a large preponderance of our beliefs be true. Now most large sets of proposi-

---

47. "It may be assumed . . . that molecular changes in the brain are the causes of all the states of consciousness. . . . [But is] there any evidence that these stages of consciousness may, conversely, cause . . . molecular changes [in the brain] which give rise to muscular motion? I see no such evidence. . . . [Consciousness appears] to be . . . completely without any power of modifying [the] working of the body, just as the steam whistle . . . of a locomotive engine is without influence upon its machinery" (T. H. Huxley, "On the Hypothesis That Animals Are Automata and Its History" (1874), chapter 5 of his *Method and Results* (London: Macmillan, 1893), pp. 239–40. Later in the essay: "To the best of my judgment, the argumentation which applies to brutes holds equally good of men; and therefore . . . all states of consciousness in us, as in them, are immediately caused by molecular changes of the brain-substance. It seems to me that in men, as in brutes, there is no proof that any state of consciousness is the cause of change in the motion of the matter of the organism. . . . We are conscious automata" (243–44). (Note the occurrence here of that widely popular form of argument, *I know of no proof that not*-p; therefore, *there is no proof that not*-p; therefore, *p*.) In contrast to Huxley, I am here using the term 'epiphenomenalism' to denote *any* view according to which belief isn't involved in the causal chain leading to behavior, whether or not that view involves the dualism apparently part of Huxley's version.

48. December 28, 1992, p. 41.

tions do not meet that condition; but one large set of beliefs—at any rate, of beliefs we human beings are capable of having—would seem to be about as likely as any other on this scenario. Hence we couldn't claim with a straight face that there is a high probability, on this scenario, that most of our beliefs are true. Perhaps the verdict is that this probability is relatively low; just for definiteness, let's say it's in the neighborhood of .3 or so. Alternatively, we might think that the right attitude here is that we simply can't make a sensible estimate of this probability, so that $P(R/N\&P_1)$ is inscrutable.

The second possibility as to the relation between belief and behavior (call it P_2) is semantic epiphenomenalism. From a naturalistic point of view, the natural thing to think is that human beings are material objects.[49] Well, suppose that's what they are: then what sort of thing will a belief—perhaps the belief that Cartesian dualism is false—*be*? Presumably it will be a long-standing neural or neuronal event of some kind. This neural event will have *electrochemical* properties: the number of neurons involved; the way in which the neurons involved are connected with each other, with other neuronal events, with muscles, with sense organs, and so on; the average rate and intensity of neuronal firing in various parts of this event and the ways in which this changes over time and with respect to input from other areas. (Call these the 'syntax' of the belief.) Of course it is easy to see how *these* properties of this neuronal event should have causal influence on behavior. A given belief is neurally connected both with other beliefs and with muscles; we can see how electrical impulses coming from the belief can negotiate the usual neuronal channels and ultimately cause muscular contraction.

Now if this belief is really a *belief*, then it will also have *other* properties, properties in addition to its syntax or neurophysiological properties. In particular, it will have *content*; it will be the belief that p, for some proposition p—in this case, the proposition *Cartesian dualism is false*. But how does the *content* of this neuronal event—that *proposition* —get involved in the causal chain leading to behavior?[50] Under this scenario, it will be difficult or impossible to see how a belief can have causal influence on our behavior or action *by virtue of its content*.

---

49. Though it isn't easy to say just what a material object *is* (as Bas van Fraassen emphasizes in "Science, Materialism, and False Consciousness"; see above, footnote 39). For present purposes we need not try to address that project; we can simply narrow our focus to the claim that beliefs are neural events or processes of some sort.

50. A question just as pressing, of course, is 'How does this neuronal event *have* a content *at all*?' What is it that assigns to this neuronal event the proposition that Cartesian dualism is false, as opposed, for instance, to the proposition that it is true, or interesting, or obsolete, or vaguely obscene?

Suppose the belief had had the same electrochemical properties but some entirely different content, perhaps the proposition *Cartesian dualism is true*; would that have made any difference to its role in the causation of behavior? It is certainly hard to see how: there would have been the same electrical impulses traveling down the same channels, issuing in the same muscular contractions. The neurophysiological properties seem to have swept the field when it comes to the causation of behavior; there seems to be no way in which content can get its foot in the door. Of course, it is the *content* of my beliefs, not their electrochemical properties, that is the subject of truth and falsehood: a belief is true just if the proposition that constitutes its content is true. As in the epiphenomenalist scenario, therefore, the content of belief would be invisible to evolution. Accordingly, the fact that we have survived and evolved, that our cognitive equipment was good enough to enable our ancestors to survive and reproduce—that fact would tell us nothing at all about the *truth* of our beliefs or the reliability of our cognitive faculties. It would tell something about the *neurophysiological* properties of our beliefs; it would tell us that, by virtue of these properties, those beliefs have played a role in the production of adaptive behavior. But it would tell us nothing about the *contents* of these beliefs, and hence nothing about their truth or falsehood. On this scenario as on the last, therefore, we couldn't sensibly claim a high probability for R. As with the last scenario, the best we could say, I think, is that this probability is either low or inscrutable; $P(R/N\&P_2)$ is low or inscrutable, just as is $P(R/N\&P_1)$.

Finally, what is the probability of R, given $N\&P_3$, the commonsense (folk psychological) view as to the causal relation between behavior and belief? According to folk psychology, belief serves as a (partial) *cause* and thus *explanation* of behavior—and this explicitly holds for the content of belief. I want a beer and believe there is one in the fridge; that belief, we ordinarily think, partly explains those movements of that large lumpy object that is my body as it heaves itself out of the armchair, moves over to the fridge, opens it, and extracts the beer.

Can we mount an argument from the evolutionary origins of the processes, whatever they are, that produce these beliefs to the reliability of those processes? Could we argue, for example, that these beliefs of ours are connected with behavior in such a way that false belief would produce maladaptive behavior, behavior which would tend to reduce the probability of the believers' surviving and reproducing?[51] No. False belief doesn't by any means guarantee maladaptive action. Perhaps a primitive tribe thinks that everything is really

---

51. Thus Quine: "There is some encouragement in Darwin. If people's innate spacing of qualities is a gene-linked trait, then the spacing that has made for the most successful inductions will have tended to predominate through natural selection.

alive, or is a witch or a demon of some sort; and perhaps all or nearly all of their beliefs are of the form *this witch is F* or *that demon is G: this witch is good to eat*, or *that demon is likely to eat me if I give it a chance*. If they ascribe the right properties to the right witches, their beliefs could be adaptive while nonetheless (assuming that in fact there aren't any witches) false.[52] Also, of course, there is the fact that behavior, if it is partly produced by belief, is also partly produced by desire: it is belief and desire, along with other things, that together produce behavior. But then clearly there could be many different systems of belief and desire that yield the same bit of adaptive behavior, and in many of those systems the belief components are largely false; there are many possible belief-desire systems that yield the whole course of my behavior, where in each system most of the beliefs are false. The fact that my behavior (or that of my ancestors) has been adaptive, therefore, is at best a third-rate reason for thinking my beliefs mostly true and my cognitive faculties reliable—and that is true even given the commonsense view of the relation of belief to behavior. So we can't sensibly argue from the fact that our behavior (or that of our ancestors) has been adaptive, to the conclusion that our beliefs are mostly true and our cognitive faculties reliable. It isn't easy to estimate $P(R/N\&P_3)$; if it isn't inscrutable, perhaps it is moderately high. To concede as much as possible to the opposition, let's say that this probability is either inscrutable or in the neighborhood of .9.

Note that epiphenomenalism simpliciter and semantic epiphenomenalism unite in declaring or implying that the content of belief lacks causal efficacy with respect to behavior; the content of belief does not get involved in the causal chain leading to behavior. So perhaps we can reduce these two possibilities to one: the possibility that the content of belief has no causal efficacy. Call this possibility -C. What we have so far seen is that the probability of R on N&-C is low or in-

---

Creatures inveterately wrong in their inductions have a pathetic but praiseworthy tendency to die before reproducing their kind" ("Natural Kinds," in *Ontological Relativity and Other Essays* [New York: Columbia University Press, 1969], p. 126).

52. Objection: in any event, these tribespeople would be ascribing the right properties to the right things, so that their beliefs are, in some loose sense, accurate, even if strictly speaking false. Reply: by further gerrymandering, we can easily find schemes under which their beliefs would lead to adaptive behavior (thus being functionally equivalent with respect to behavior to the true scheme) but are not accurate even in this loose sense. There are schemes of this sort, in fact, in which the properties ascribed are logically incapable of exemplification. They think everything is a witch; perhaps, then, their analogue of property ascriptions involves ascribing certain sorts of *witches* (rather than properties). (One of these witches, for example, is such that, as *we* would put it, if a thing *has* it, then that thing is red.) Then their beliefs will not be accurate in the above sense and will indeed be necessarily false.

scrutable and that the probability of R on N&C is also inscrutable or at best moderate. Now what we are looking for is P(R/N). Because C and -C are jointly exhaustive and mutually exclusive, the calculus of probabilities tells us that

$$P(R/N) = P(R/N\&C) \times P(C/N) + P(R/N\&\text{-}C) \times P(\text{-}C/N),$$

that is, the probability of R on N is the weighted average of the probabilities of R on N&C and N&-C—weighted by the probabilities of C and -C on N.

We have already noted that the left-hand term of the first of the two products on the right side of the equality is either moderately high or inscrutable; the second is either low or inscrutable. What remains is to evaluate the weights, the right-hand terms of the two products. So what is the probability of -C, given ordinary naturalism: what is the probability that one or the other of the two epiphenomenalistic scenarios is true? Note that according to Robert Cummins, semantic epiphenomenalism is in fact the received view as to the relation between belief and behavior.[53] That is because it is extremely hard to envisage a way, given materialism, in which the content of a belief *could* get causally involved in behavior. If a belief just is a neural structure of some kind—a structure that somehow possesses content—then it is exceedingly hard to see how content can get involved in the causal chain leading to behavior: had a given such structure had a different content, its causal contribution to behavior, one thinks, would be the same. By contrast, if a belief is not a material structure at all but a nonphysical bit of consciousness, it is hard to see that there is any room for it in the causal chain leading to behavior; what causes the muscular contractions involved in behavior will be states of the nervous system, with no point at which this nonphysical bit of consciousness makes a causal contribution. So it is exceedingly hard to see, given N, how the content of a belief can have causal efficacy.

It is exceedingly hard to see, that is, how epiphenomenalism—semantic or simpliciter—can be avoided, given N. (There have been some valiant efforts, but things don't look hopeful.) So it looks as if P(-C/N) will have to be estimated as relatively high; let's say (for definiteness) .7, in which case P(C/N) will be .3. Of course we could easily be wrong—we don't really have a solid way of telling—so perhaps the conservative position here is that this probability, too, is inscrutable: one simply can't tell what it is. Given current knowledge, therefore, P(-C/N) is either high or inscrutable. And if P(-C/N) is in-

53. *Meaning and Mental Representation* (Cambridge: MIT Press, 1989), p. 130.

scrutable, then the same goes, naturally enough, for P(C/N). What does that mean for the sum of these two products, i.e., P(R/N)?

Well, we really have several possibilities. Suppose we think first about the matter from the point of view of someone who doesn't find any of the probabilities involved inscrutable. Then P(C/N) will be in the neighborhood of .3, P(-C/N) in the neighborhood of .7, and P(R/N&-C) perhaps in the neighborhood of .2. This leaves P(R/N&C), the probability that R is true, given ordinary naturalism together with the commonsense or folk-theoretical view as to the relation between belief and behavior. Given that this probability is not inscrutable, let's say that it is in the neighborhood of .9. And given these estimates, P(R/N) will be in the neighborhood of .41.[54] Suppose, however, we think the probabilities involved are inscrutable: then we will have to say the same for P(R/N). Therefore, P(R/N) is either relatively low—less than .5, at any rate—or inscrutable.

In either case, however, doesn't the ordinary naturalist—at any rate, one who sees that P(R/N) is low or inscrutable—have a defeater for R, and for the proposition that his own cognitive faculties are reliable? I say he does. To see how, we must note some analogies with clear cases. First, there are the analogies I mentioned in WPF (229–31); here are a couple more. Return (pp. 224) to that voyage of space exploration and the radio-like device that emitted sounds that constitute English sentences, sentences that express propositions of whose truth value you are ignorant. At first, you were inclined to believe these propositions, if only because of shock and astonishment. After a bit of cool reflection, however, you realize that you know nothing at all about the purpose, if any, of this instrument, or who or what constructed it. The probability that this device is reliable, given what you know about it, is low or inscrutable; and this gives you a defeater for your initial belief that the instrument indeed speaks the truth. Consider another analogy. You start thinking seriously about the possibility that you are a brain in a vat, being subjected to experiment by Alpha Centaurian cognitive scientists in such a way that your cognitive faculties are not, in fact, reliable. For one reason or another, you come to think this probability is greater than .5; then you have a defeater for your belief that your cognitive faculties are reliable. Suppose instead that you think this is a genuine possibility,

54. Of course these figures are the merest approximations; others might make the estimates somewhat differently; but they can be significantly altered without significantly altering the final result. For example, perhaps you think P(R/N&C) is higher, perhaps even 1; then (retaining the other assignments) P(R/N) will be in the neighborhood of .44. Or perhaps you reject the thought that P(-C/N) is more probable than P(C/N), thinking them about equal. Then (again, retaining the other assignments) P(R/N) will be in the neighborhood of .55.

but you can't make any estimate at all of its likelihood, so that you can't make any estimate at all of the probability that your faculties are reliable: as far as you can tell, the probability could be anywhere between 0 and 1. Then too you have a defeater for your natural belief that your cognitive faculties are reliable.

The same goes for the naturalist who realizes that P(R/N) is low or inscrutable. With respect to those factors crucially important for coming to a sensible view of the reliability of his belief-producing mechanisms—how they were formed and what their purpose is, if any—he must concede that the probability that those faculties are reliable is at best inscrutable. Unless he has some other information,[55] the right attitude would be to withhold R. But then something like Hume's attitude toward my beliefs would be the appropriate one. I recognize that I can't help forming most of the beliefs I do form; for example, it isn't within my power, just now, to withhold the belief that there are trees and grass outside my window. However, because I now do not believe that my cognitive faculties are reliable (I withhold that proposition), I also realize that these beliefs produced by my cognitive faculties are no more likely to be true than false: I therefore assume a certain skeptical distance with respect to them. And, because my doubts about my beliefs themselves depend on my beliefs, I also assume a certain skeptical distance with respect to these doubts, and with respect to the beliefs prompting those doubts, and with respect to the beliefs prompting the doubts about those doubts. . . . The ordinary naturalist, therefore, should join Hume in this same skeptical, ironic attitude toward his beliefs. This holds, of course, for N itself; for this reason, we might say that N is self-defeating, in that if it is accepted in the ordinary way, it provides a defeater for itself, a defeater that can't be defeated.[56]

> We can briefly extend this result to the case where I am *agnostic* about ordinary naturalism. I don't really believe it; either it seems to me to be about as likely as its denial, or its probability is inscrutable for me. In either case, once more, I have a defeater for R, just as in the case of the ordinary naturalist. To see this, consider once again an analogy, and just to preserve continuity, make it another instrumental analogy. You

---

55. And how could he have or get other information? Any such information would consist in beliefs that were a product of his cognitive faculties, but he has a defeater for the reliability of those faculties and hence for any belief produced by them.

56. See chapter 12 of WPF, and "Naturalism Defeated." The defeater can't be defeated because any defeater would arise from the very faculties or belief-producing processes in question. For example, the defeater might take the form of an *argument*, perhaps for the conclusion that those belief-producing processes are reliable after all. But then I would have the same defeater for each of the premises of this argument, as well as for my belief that if the premises are true, then so is the conclusion.

are confronted with a measuring instrument of some kind—a barometer, say. You believe that this barometer is in one or the other of two conditions, C1 and C2; the probability that it is in either is for you either inscrutable or about .5. The probability of its being reliable, given that it is in C1, is high, certainly high enough so that if you believed that it was in C1, you would unhesitatingly accept its deliverances. However, the likelihood that it is reliable, given that it is in condition C2 , is inscrutable so far as you are concerned: it could be high, but it could also be low; you just don't know what to think about that probability. Would it be reasonable to accept the deliverances of this instrument? I should think not. You know that if it is in C1, it is reliable; but the probability that it *is* in C1 is (for you) either about .5 or inscrutable. Either way, the rational attitude is to withhold the belief that it is reliable, accepting neither it nor its denial. And then (given that you have no other source of information) the same goes for the output of the barometer: for any proposition in its output, the rational course for you would be agnosticism with respect to that proposition. The pointer points to thirty inches; still (if you have no other information), you will not on that account believe that the ambient atmospheric pressure is thirty inches. Of course you won't form a belief inconsistent with that one either: you will withhold the proposition.

It is easy enough to make the application to agnosticism as between theism and ordinary naturalism. If I am such an agnostic, the probability of ordinary naturalism is either in the neighborhood of .5 or inscrutable for me. Suppose the former: what attitude should I take toward R? Well, there is a fifty-fifty chance that my cognitive faculties were produced in a way with respect to which the probability of R is low or inscrutable; if so, however, I have a defeater for R, good reason to withhold. Suppose the latter: then I can't rule out any probability for ordinary naturalism. Because the probability of R on ordinary naturalism is also inscrutable, I can't rule out any probability for R; in particular, I can't rule out a low probability for R. But again, that gives me a defeater for my ordinary and instinctive belief that R. In either case, therefore, I acquire a defeater for R; unless I have or can come up with a defeater-defeater for this defeater,[57] I should be agnostic with respect to R. And if I am agnostic with respect to R, then just as Hume sees, the rational attitude is to be agnostic with respect to any of the deliverances of my cognitive faculties. I may not, in fact, *be able* to be agnostic with respect to them, but agnosticism is what rationality requires. Of course I also recognize that the beliefs involved in my coming to this agnosticism— such as the belief that the relevant probabilities are inscrutable—are themselves products of my cognitive faculties, and no better off than any other such products. Hence that multilayered reflexive Humean skepticism.

---

57. And again (see footnote 56), how could I? Any such defeater-defeater would be subject to the very defeater defeating R in the first place.

By way of conclusion: the noetic effects of sin don't necessarily include failure to know anything; Calvin (if that is what, in fact, he thought) goes too far. Still, something in the same general neighborhood is true. If I reject theism in favor of ordinary naturalism, and also see that $P(R/N)$ is low or inscrutable, then I will have a defeater for any belief I hold. If so, I will not, if forming beliefs rationally, hold any belief firmly enough to constitute knowledge. The same goes if I am merely agnostic as between theism and ordinary naturalism. And the same goes if I am agnostic about my origin and the origin of my cognitive faculties. So rejection of theistic belief doesn't automatically produce skepticism: many who don't believe in God know much. But that is only because they don't accurately think through the consequences of this rejection. Once they do, they will lose their knowledge; here, therefore, is another of those cases where, by learning more, one comes to know less.

In this chapter, we have begun to explore the extended model by exploring the nature of sin and some of its cognitive consequences. These consequences extend further than one would ordinarily think; indeed, insofar as sin interferes with the *sensus divinitatis* and thus with our knowledge of God, it can easily lead to a noetic condition where what rationality demands is that complex, many-layered Humean skepticism. But here a nasty problem looms. According to the A/C model of chapter 6, knowledge requires proper function, and knowledge of God requires proper function of the *sensus divinitatis*. According to the extended model, however, this belief-producing process has been damaged because of sin, so that it no longer functions properly: how then (on this model) can we have knowledge of the existence and character of God? In the next chapter, we turn to the question how specifically Christian belief, not just generically theistic belief, can have warrant; in answering that question we will also see how the *sensus divinitatis* is repaired.

8

The Extended Aquinas/Calvin Model:
Revealed to Our Minds

The Spirit himself testifies with our spirit that we are God's children.

Romans 8:16

In chapter 6, I proposed a model—the Aquinas/Calvin (A/C) model
—according to which belief in God can have the three varieties of
positive epistemic status with which we have been concerned: justification, rationality (in both its external and internal guises), and warrant. What about specifically Christian belief, belief, not just in God,
but in trinity, incarnation, Christ's resurrection, atonement, forgiveness of sins, salvation, regeneration, eternal life? The main business
of this chapter is to extend the A/C model to cover these beliefs, to
show how they, too, can have those varieties of positive epistemic status. In chapter 7, I gave an initial statement of this extended model.
One element of the extended A/C model has to do with sin and its
epistemic consequences; most of chapter 7 was devoted to a development of this feature of the model.

In this chapter, I turn to the central elements of the model: how
can we think of the full panoply of Christian belief in all its particularity as enjoying justification, rationality in both its internal and external varieties, and warrant? How can we think of these beliefs—
some of which, as David Hume loved to point out, go entirely contrary
to ordinary human experience—as reasonable or rational, let alone
warranted, let alone having warrant sufficient for knowledge? The
materials for an answer lie close at hand. Actually, the materials have

lain close at hand for several centuries—certainly since the publication of Jonathan Edwards's *Religious Affections*[1] and John Calvin's *Institutes of the Christian Religion*.[2] As a matter of fact, they have lain close at hand for much longer than that: much of what Calvin says can be usefully seen as development of remarks of Thomas Aquinas and Bonaventura. Indeed, these materials go much further back yet, all the way back to the New Testament, in particular, the Gospel of John and the epistles of Paul.

In this chapter, I shall develop those materials and propose a model—the extended A/C model—for warranted *Christian* belief: a model in which full-blooded Christian belief in all its particularity is justified, rational, and warranted.[3] I shall argue further that Christian belief can be justified, rational, and warranted not just for ignorant fundamentalists or benighted medievals but for informed and educated twenty-first-century Christians who are entirely aware of all the artillery that has been rolled up against Christian belief since the Enlightenment. I shall argue that if Christian belief is true, then it is *rational* and *warranted* for most of those who accept it. I shall therefore be refuting the widespread idea that Christian belief is lacking in positive epistemic status, even if it happens, somehow, to be true. If I am right, the atheologian can't sensibly take the attitude, "I don't know whether Christian belief is true or not (who could know a thing like that?); still I do know that it isn't rational (or warranted, or justified, or rationally justified, or intellectually respectable or . . .)." For the sake of definiteness I shall be following one particular and traditional way of thinking about our knowledge of Christian truth. I believe that this account or something similar is, in fact, rather close to the sober truth; other models fitting other traditions can easily be constructed. My extended model will have one further feature: it will complete and deepen the previous account (chapter 6) of our knowledge of God. The central themes of this extended model are the Bible, the internal testimony of the Holy Spirit, and faith. I'll begin with a quick overview of the essential elements of the extended model.

---

1. Ed. John Smith (New Haven: Yale University Press, 1959 [first published 1746]). Subsequent page references to *Religious Affections* are to this edition.

2. Ed. John T. McNeill and tr. by Ford Lewis Battles (Philadelphia: Westminster Press, 1960 [first published in 1559]). References to the *Institutes* are to this edition.

3. Contemporary relatives and ancestors of this model can be found in Stephen Davis, *Risen Indeed* (Grand Rapids: W. B. Eerdmans Publishing, 1993); William Abraham, "The Epistemological Significance of the Inner Witness of the Holy Spirit," *Faith and Philosophy* 7, no. 4 (October 1990); C. Stephen Evans, *The Historical Christ and the Jesus of Faith* (Oxford: Clarendon Press, 1996); my *The Twin Pillars of Christian Scholarship* (Grand Rapids: Calvin College, 1989); and my "Christian Philosophy at the End of the 20th Century," in *Christian Philosophy at the Close of the Twentieth Century*, ed. Sander Griffioen and Bert Balk (Kampen: Kok, 1995), pp. 29–53.

According to the model (as we saw in chapter 7), we human beings were created in the image of God: we were created both with appropriate affections and with knowledge of God and his greatness
and glory. Because of the greatest calamity to befall the human race,
however, we fell into sin, a ruinous condition from which we require
rescue and redemption. God proposed and instituted a plan of salvation: the life, atoning suffering and death, and resurrection of
Jesus Christ, the incarnate second person of the trinity. The result
for us is the possibility of salvation from sin and renewed relationship
with God. Now (and here we come to the specifically epistemological
extension of the model) God needed a way to inform us—us human
beings of many different times and places—of the scheme of salvation he has graciously made available.[4] No doubt he could have done
this in many different ways; in fact he chose to do so by way of a
three-tiered cognitive process. First, he arranged for the production
of *Scripture*, the Bible, a library of books or writings each of which has
a human author, but each of which is also specially inspired by God
in such a way that he himself is its principal author. Thus, the whole
library has a single principal author: God himself. In this library, he
proposes much for our belief and action, but there is a central theme
and focus (and for this reason this collection of books is itself a book):
the gospel, the stunning good news of the way of salvation God has
graciously offered.[5] Correlative with Scripture and necessary to its
properly serving its purpose is the *second* element of this three-tiered
cognitive process: the presence and action of the Holy Spirit promised by Christ himself before his death and resurrection,[6] and invoked and celebrated in the epistles of the apostle Paul.[7] By virtue of

---

4. It is no part of the model to suggest that explicit beliefs about Jesus Christ are
a necessary condition of salvation: the Old Testament patriarchs, for example, are
counted as heroes of faith in the New Testament (Hebrews 11), despite the fact that
they presumably had no explicit beliefs about Jesus Christ. They trusted God to do
whatever was necessary for their salvation and shalom, but they had no particular
idea as to just what that might be. Furthermore, it is no part of the model to assert
that all who believe these things have come to believe them by way of the processes
proposed in the model: perhaps, for example, the apostles came to believe these
truths in quite a different fashion.

5. But hasn't the historical-critical Scripture scholarship of the last two hundred
years cast grave doubt on the reliability of the Bible and the claim that it is specially
inspired by God? This suggestion is a proposed *defeater* for Christian belief and is the
subject of chapter 12.

6. E.g., John 14:26: "but the Counselor, the Holy Spirit, whom the Father will
send in my name, he will teach you all things, and bring to your remembrance all
that I have said to you." See also John 14:11 and 15:26: "When the Counselor comes,
whom I will send to you from the Father, the Spirit of truth who goes out from the
Father, he will testify about me. . . ."

7. E.g., Ephesians 1:17–19: "I keep asking that the God of our Lord Jesus
Christ, the glorious Father, may give you the spirit of wisdom and revelation, so that

the work of the Holy Spirit in the hearts of those to whom faith is given, the ravages of sin (including the cognitive damage) are repaired, gradually or suddenly, to a greater or lesser extent. Furthermore, it is by virtue of the activity of the Holy Spirit that Christians come to grasp, believe, accept, endorse, and rejoice in the truth of the great things of the gospel. It is thus by virtue of this activity that the Christian believes that "in Christ, God was reconciling the world to himself, not counting men's sins against them" (2 Corinthians 5:19).

According to John Calvin, the principal work of the Holy Spirit is the production (in the hearts of Christian believers) of the third element of the process, *faith*. Like the regeneration of which it is a part, faith is a gift; it is given to anyone who is willing to accept it. Faith, says Calvin, is "a firm and certain knowledge of God's benevolence towards us, founded upon the truth of the freely given promise in Christ, both revealed to our minds and sealed upon our hearts through the Holy Spirit" (*Institutes* III, ii, 7, p. 551). Faith therefore involves an explicitly cognitive element; it is, says Calvin, *knowledge*—knowledge of the availability of redemption and salvation through the person and work of Jesus Christ—and it is revealed to our minds. To have faith, therefore, is to know and hence *believe* something or other. But (as we shall see in chapter 9) faith also involves the will: it is "sealed upon our hearts." By virtue of this sealing, the believer not only knows about the scheme of salvation God has prepared (according to the book of James [2:19], the devils also know about that, and they shudder) but is also heartily grateful to the Lord for it, and loves him on this account. Sealing, furthermore, also involves the *executive* function of the will: believers accept the proffered gift and commit themselves to the Lord, to conforming their lives to his will, to living lives of gratitude.[8]

But isn't all this just endorsing a wholly outmoded and discredited fundamentalism, that condition than which, according to many academics, none lesser can be conceived? I fully realize that the dreaded f-word will be trotted out to stigmatize any model of this kind. Before responding, however, we must first look into the use of

---

you may know him better." And 1 Corinthians 2:12–13: "We have not received the spirit of the world, but the Spirit who is from God, that we may understand what God has freely given us. This is what we speak, not in words taught us by human wisdom but in words taught by the Spirit. . . ."

8. Presented in this brief and undeveloped way, this model can seem unduly individualistic. But of course it doesn't at all preclude the importance of the Christian community and the church to the belief of the individual Christian. It is the church or community that proclaims the gospel, guides the neophyte into it, and supports, instructs, encourages, and edifies believers of all sorts and conditions.

this term 'fundamentalist'. On the most common contemporary academic use of the term, it is a term of abuse or disapprobation, rather like 'son of a bitch', more exactly 'sonovabitch', or perhaps still more exactly (at least according to those authorities who look to the Old West as normative on matters of pronunciation) 'sumbitch'. When the term is used in this way, no definition of it is ordinarily given. (If you called someone a sumbitch, would you feel obliged first to define the term?) Still, there is a bit more to the meaning of 'fundamentalist' (in this widely current use): it isn't *simply* a term of abuse. In addition to its emotive force, it does have *some* cognitive content, and ordinarily denotes relatively conservative theological views. That makes it more like '*stupid* sumbitch' (or maybe '*fascist* sumbitch'?) than 'sumbitch' simpliciter. It isn't exactly like *that* term either, however, because its cognitive content can expand and contract on demand; its content seems to depend on who is using it. In the mouths of certain liberal theologians, for example, it tends to denote any who accept traditional Christianity, including Augustine, Aquinas, Luther, Calvin, and Barth; in the mouths of devout secularists like Richard Dawkins or Daniel Dennett, it tends to denote anyone who believes there is such a person as God. The explanation is that the term has a certain indexical element: its cognitive content is given by the phrase 'considerably to the right, theologically speaking, of me and my enlightened friends.' The full meaning of the term, therefore (in this use), can be given by something like 'stupid sumbitch whose theological opinions are considerably to the right of mine'.

It is therefore hard to take seriously the charge that the views I'm suggesting are fundamentalist; more exactly, it is hard to take it seriously as a *charge*. The alleged charge means only that these views are rather more conservative than those of the objector, together with the expression of a certain distaste for the views or those who hold them. But how is *that* an objection to anything, and why should it warrant the contempt and contumely that goes with the term? An *argument* of some kind against those conservative views would be of interest, but merely pointing out that they differ from the objector's (even with the addition of that abusive emotive force) is not.

How does this model, with its excursion into theology, provide an answer to an epistemological question? How can it be a model for a way in which Christian belief has or could have justification, rationality, warrant? The answer is simplicity itself. These beliefs do not come to the Christian just by way of memory, perception, reason, testimony, the *sensus divinitatis*, or any other of the cognitive faculties with which we human beings were originally created; they come instead by way of the work of the Holy Spirit, who gets us to accept, causes us to believe, these great truths of the gospel. These beliefs don't come just by way of the normal operation of our natural faculties; they are a supernatural gift. Still, the Christian who has received this gift of faith will of course be *justified* (in the basic sense of the term) in believing as he does; there will be nothing contrary to epistemic or other duty in so believing (indeed, once he has accepted the gift, it may not be within his power to withhold belief).

Given the model, however, the beliefs in question will typically (or at least often) have the other kinds of positive epistemic status we have been considering as well. First, they will be internally rational:[9] they will be an appropriate doxastic response to what is given to the believer by way of her previous belief and current experience. That is, the believer's response is such that a properly functioning person with the same current experience and antecedent beliefs could form the same or similar beliefs, without compromising proper function. But the beliefs in question will typically also have *external* rationality. There need be no cognitive malfunction downstream from experience (see above, p. 110), in believers, but there need be none *upstream* either: all of their cognitive faculties can be functioning properly. Finally, on the model, these beliefs will also have *warrant* for believers: they will be produced in them by a belief-producing process[10] that is functioning properly in an appropriate cognitive environment (the one for which they were designed), according to a design plan successfully aimed at the production of true beliefs.

I. FAITH

> Now Faith is the substance of things hoped for, the evidence of things not seen.
>
>   Hebrews 11:1

So much for the initial account of the model; I turn now to a more detailed development of some of its aspects, beginning with *faith*. The first thing to note is that this term, like nearly any philosophically useful term, is used variously, in a number of different but analogically connected senses. According to Mark Twain, faith is "believ-

---

9. For the notion of internal rationality, see above, p. 110ff.

10. Of course *this* belief-producing process isn't exactly like the others—memory, perception, reason, and even the *sensus divinitatis*. That is because these others are all part of our original increated cognitive equipment, while (according to the model) the cognitive process here involves a special, supernatural activity on the part of the Holy Spirit. But this doesn't so much as suggest that its deliverances can't enjoy warrant, and warrant sufficient for knowledge. What it suggests, instead, is that the account of warrant of *Warrant and Proper Function* must be understood in such a way that a belief can have warrant even if it is produced by a belief-producing process of this special kind. True, such a process that consists in direct divine activity cannot fail to function properly; we may therefore say that it functions properly in a limiting sense of the term.

ing what you know ain't true"; this only slightly exaggerates a common use of the term to denote a belief that lacks warrant and, indeed, is unlikely with respect to what does have warrant for the believer. A mother who believes, in the teeth of the evidence, that her son is in fact still alive will be said to have faith that he is still alive. It is in connection with this use that one thinks of 'a leap of faith', which is rather like a leap in the dark. A second way the term is used is to denote a vague and generalized trust that has no specific object, a confidence that things will go right, a sort of Bultmannian sitting loose with respect to the future, trusting that one can deal with whatever happens. To have faith in this sense is to "accept the universe," as the nineteenth-century transcendentalist Margaret Fuller was said to have declared she did.[11]

In setting out the model, however, I am using the term in a different sense from any of those. My sense will be much closer to that which the Heidelberg Catechism (following John Calvin) ascribes to 'true faith':

> True faith is not only a knowledge and conviction that everything God reveals in his word is true; it is also a deep-rooted assurance, created in me by the Holy Spirit through the gospel, that, out of sheer grace earned for us by Christ, not only others, but I too, have had my sins forgiven, have been made forever right with God, and have been granted salvation. (Q. 21)

We can think of this account as making more explicit the content of the definition of faith offered by Calvin in the *Institutes* (above, p. 244). The first thing to see is that faith, so taken, is a *cognitive* activity. It isn't *merely* a cognitive activity; it also involves the will, both the affections and the executive function. (It is a knowledge *sealed upon our hearts*, as well as revealed to our minds.) Still, even if faith is *more* than cognitive, it is also and *at least* a cognitive activity. It is a matter of *believing* ("knowledge," Calvin says) something or other. Christians, on this account, don't merely find their identity in the Christian story, or live in it or out of it;[12] they *believe* it, take the story to be the sober truth.

---

11. To which Thomas Carlyle retorted, "Gad! She'd better!" Mark Twain, by contrast, claimed he hadn't heard it had been offered to her.

12. In this way, the model (apparently) differs from the postmodern Yale theology of Hans Frei (*The Eclipse of Biblical Narrative* [1974] and *The Identity of Jesus Christ* [1975]) and George Lindbeck (*The Nature of Doctrine: Religion and Theology in a Postliberal Age* [1984]), which emphasizes the role of the Bible in the Christian life but is a bit coy as to whether its apparent teachings—creation, sin, incarnation, atonement, Christ's resurrection—are to be taken as actually *true*. (See, for example, pp. 143–45 of *The Identity of Jesus Christ*.) This standoffishness about truth is perhaps the 'postliberal' element in Yale theology; according to the present model, however, it is also unnecessary. The model is designed to show that straightforward, downright, out-and-out *belief* in the great things of the gospel can have the epistemic virtues we are considering.

Now what one believes are propositions. To have faith, therefore, is (at least) to believe some propositions. Which ones? Not, for example, that the world is the sort of place in which human beings can flourish, or even or primarily that there is such a person as God.[13] Indeed, on this model it isn't really by *faith* that one knows that there is such a person as God. Faith is instead, says Calvin, "firm and certain knowledge of God's benevolence towards us"; that is, a firm and certain knowledge that "not only others, but I too, have had my sins forgiven, have been made forever right with God, and have been granted salvation"; that is, a firm and certain knowledge of God's plan whereby we fallen humans can attain shalom, flourishing, well-being, happiness, felicity, salvation, all of which are essentially a matter of being rightly related to God.[14] So the propositional object of faith is the whole magnificent scheme of salvation God has arranged. To have faith is to know that and how God has made it possible for us human beings to escape the ravages of sin and be restored to a right relationship with him; it is therefore a knowledge of the main lines of the Christian gospel.[15] The content of faith is just the central teachings of the gospel;[16] it is contained in the intersection of the great Christian creeds.

What is at issue, in faith, furthermore, is not just knowing that there *is* such a scheme (as we saw above, the devils believe that, and they shudder), but also and most important, that this scheme applies to and is available to *me*.[17] So what I know, in faith, is the main lines of

13. "In understanding faith," says Calvin, "it is not merely a question of knowing that God exists . . . but also—and this especially—of knowing what is his will toward us. For it is not so much our concern to know who he is in himself, as what he wills to be toward us" (549).

14. I take it this is a definition or description of faith by way of presenting a *paradigm* of it: fully formed and well-developed faith will be like this. Thus a person who (for example) believes these things, but without the firmness sufficient for *knowledge* of them, can still be said to have faith.

15. And hence not everything a typical Christian believes (as a Christian) will be, strictly speaking, part of faith. For example, she may believe that Jesus Christ performed miracles, or that God is omniscient, or that the Bible is a specially inspired word from the Lord, or that faith naturally issues in good works; none of these is, as such, part of the content of faith. (This is not in any way to downgrade the importance of these things, and certainly the content of faith may enter into her reasons for believing them.) And in thus specifying the content of faith, I am not, of course, trying to specify those beliefs which are such that accepting them is necessary for being a real Christian.

16. On the present model, therefore, faith is a bit narrower than in the account of true faith from the Heidelberg Catechism (above, p. 247), which includes a "conviction that everything God reveals in his word is true." God presumably reveals more, in his word, than the great truths of the gospel. For example, there is Jesus' turning water into wine, healing the demoniac, and raising Lazarus from the dead; these are not among the central truths of the gospel, although they are related to and illustrative of those truths.

specifically Christian teaching—together, we might say, with its universal instantiation with respect to me. Christ died for *my* sins, thus making it possible for *me* to be reconciled with God. Faith is initially and fundamentally *practical*; it is a knowledge of the good news and of its application to me, and of what I must do to receive the benefits it proclaims. Still, faith itself is a matter of belief rather than action; it is believing something rather than doing something.

II. HOW DOES FAITH WORK?

The principal answer is that faith is a work—the main work, according to Calvin—of the Holy Spirit; it is produced in us by the Holy Spirit. The suggestion that belief in the "great things of the gospel" (Jonathan Edwards's phrase) is a result of some special work of the Holy Spirit is often thought of as especially the teaching of such Calvinist thinkers as Edwards and John Calvin himself. It is, indeed, central to their teaching, and here the model follows them. On this point as on so many others, however, Calvin, despite his pugnacious noise about the pestilential papists and their colossal offenses, may be seen as following out and developing a line of thought already to be found in Thomas Aquinas. "The believer," says Aquinas, "has sufficient motive for believing, for he is moved by the authority of divine teaching confirmed by miracles and, what is more, *by the inward instigation of the divine invitation.*"[18] Here we have (embryonically, at any rate) the same trio of processes: there is *belief*, there is the *divine teaching* (as given in Scripture) which is the object of that belief, and there is also special divine activity in the production of the belief ("the inward instigation of the divine invitation").[19]

What is really involved in a believer's coming to accept the great things of the gospel, therefore, are three things: Scripture (the di-

17. See Calvin, III, ii, 16, p. 561: "Here, indeed, is the chief hinge on which faith turns: that we do not regard the promises of mercy that God offers as true only outside ourselves, but not at all in us; rather that we make them ours by inwardly embracing them." As we'll see in the next chapter, there is more that distinguishes what the devils know from what the person of faith knows: she but not they also knows the beauty, loveliness, splendor of this plan of salvation; still further, she loves it, gives it her hearty approval, is grateful for it, and commits herself to love and trust the Lord.

18. *Summa Theologiae* II-II, q.2, a.9, reply ob. 3 (my emphasis). According to Aquinas, therefore, faith is produced in human beings by God's action: "for since in assenting to the things of faith a person is raised above his own nature, he has this assent from a supernatural source influencing him; this source is God. The assent of faith, which is its principal act, therefore, has as its cause God, moving us inwardly through grace" (ST II-II, q.6, a.1, *respondeo*).

19. Calvin explicitly identifies the third person of the trinity as the divine actor

vine teaching), the internal invitation or instigation of the Holy
Spirit, and faith, the human belief that results. What sort of phenomenology is involved in this epistemic process: what does it seem
like from the inside? In the model, the beliefs constituting faith are
typically taken as basic; that is, they are not accepted by way of argument from other propositions or on the evidential basis of other
propositions. Of course they *could* be accepted on the basis of other
propositions, and perhaps in some cases are. A believer could reason
as follows: I have strong historical and archaeological evidence for
the reliability of the Bible (or the church, or my parents, or some
other authority); the Bible teaches the great things of the gospel; so
probably these things are true. A believer *could* reason in this way,
and perhaps some believers do in fact reason this way. But in the
model it goes differently.

We read Scripture, or something presenting scriptural teaching,
or hear the gospel preached, or are told of it by parents, or encounter a scriptural teaching as the conclusion of an argument (or
conceivably even as an object of ridicule), or in some other way encounter a proclamation of the Word. What is said simply seems right;
it seems compelling; one finds oneself saying, "Yes, that's right, that's
the truth of the matter; this is indeed the word of the Lord." I read,
"God was in Christ, reconciling the world to himself"; I come to
think: "Right; that's true; God really was in Christ, reconciling the
world to himself!" And I may also think something a bit different,
something *about* that proposition: that it is a divine teaching or revelation, that in Calvin's words it is "from God." What one hears or
reads seems clearly and obviously true and (at any rate in paradigm
cases) seems also to be something the Lord is intending to teach. (As
Calvin says, "the Spirit . . . is the only fit corrector and approver of
doctrine, who seals it on our hearts, so that we may certainly know

---

in question, and Aquinas does not; this is not a difference of any moment. According
to Aquinas, some of the items proposed by God for our belief can also be the objects
of *scientia*; when they are, they are not accepted by faith, for it isn't possible, he
thinks, to have both *scientia* and faith with respect to the same proposition. Because
scientia is often translated as 'knowledge', this makes it look as if Calvin contradicts
Aquinas when he says that faith is a sure and certain *knowledge* of God's benevolence
toward us. Appearances are deceiving, however, and there is no contradiction here.
Scientia for Aquinas is a very special relation between a person and a proposition; it is
one that holds when the person sees that the proposition follows from first principles
she sees to be true. Thus *'scientia'* is much narrower than our term 'knowledge'. It is
also narrower than Calvin's term *'cognitio'*, which is much closer to our contemporary
use of 'knowledge'. When Calvin says that faith is a sure and certain knowledge of
God's benevolence to us, he isn't ascribing to faith a status Aquinas denies it. On this
topic, see Arvin Vos, *Aquinas, Calvin & Contemporary Protestant Thought* (Grand Rapids:
W. B. Eerdmans, 1985), pp. 18–20.

that God speaks. For while faith ought to look to God, he alone can be a witness to himself, so as to convince our hearts that what our ears receive has come from him.") So faith may have the phenomenology that goes with suddenly seeing something to be true: "Right! Now I see that this is indeed true and what the Lord is teaching!" Or perhaps the conviction arises slowly, and only after long and hard study, thought, discussion, prayer. Or perhaps it is a matter of a belief's having been there all along (from childhood, perhaps), but now being transformed, renewed, intensified, made vivid and alive. This process can go on in a thousand ways; in each case there is presentation or proposal of central Christian teaching and, by way of response, the phenomenon of being convinced, coming to see, forming of a conviction. There is the reading or hearing, and then there is the belief or conviction that what one reads or hears is true and a teaching of the Lord.

According to the model, this conviction comes by way of the activity of the Holy Spirit. Calvin speaks here of the internal 'testimony' and (more often) 'witness' of the Holy Spirit; Aquinas, of the divine 'instigation' and 'invitation'. On the model, there is both Scripture and the divine activity leading to human belief. God himself (on the model) is the principal author of Scripture. Scripture is most importantly a message, a communication from God to humankind; Scripture is a word from the Lord.[20] But then this just is a special case of the pervasive process of testimony, by which, as a matter of fact, we learn most of what we know.[21] From this point of view, Scripture is as much a matter of testimony as is a letter you receive from a friend. What is proposed for our belief in Scripture, therefore, just *is* testimony —divine testimony. So the term 'testimony' is appropriate here. However, there is also the special work of the Holy Spirit in getting us to believe, in enabling us to see the truth of what is proposed. Here Aquinas's terms 'invitation' and 'instigation' are more appropriate. I shall therefore use the term 'inward instigation of the Holy Spirit' to denote this activity of the Holy Spirit, and (where no confusion

20. On this model (*pace* most twentieth century Christian theologians), it is not the case that revelation occurs just by way of *events*, which must then be properly interpreted. No doubt this does indeed happen, but much of Scripture is centrally a matter of God's speaking, of his telling us things we need to know, of his communicating *propositions* to us. See Nicholas Wolterstorff's *Divine Discourse* (Cambridge: Cambridge University Press, 1995) for a specific account of precisely how it could be that the Bible constitutes divine speech and a divine communication to us. For the sake of definiteness, in what follows I shall incorporate in the model the proposition that something like Wolterstorff's account is in fact correct. (Of course other accounts could also serve in the model.)

21. See *Warrant and Proper Function* (hereafter WPF), pp. 77ff.

threatens) the term 'faith' to denote both the whole tripartite process (Scripture, the inward instigation of the Holy Spirit, belief in the great things of the gospel) and the last member of that trio.

So Scripture is, indeed, testimony, even if it is testimony of a very special kind. First, the principal testifier is God. It also differs from ordinary testimony in that in this case, unlike most others, there is both a principal testifier and subordinate testifiers: the human authors.[22] There is still another difference: it is the instigation of the Holy Spirit, on this model, that gets us to see and believe that the propositions proposed for our beliefs in Scripture really *are* a word from the Lord. This case also differs from the usual run of testimony, then, in that the Holy Spirit not only writes the letter (appropriately inspires the human authors)[23] but also does something special to enable you to believe and appropriate its contents. So this testimony is not the usual run of testimony; it is testimony nonetheless. According to the model, therefore, faith is belief in the great things of the gospel that results from the internal instigation of the Holy Spirit.

III. FAITH AND POSITIVE EPISTEMIC STATUS

A. Justification

I'm proposing this model as a model of Christian belief's having the sorts of epistemic virtues or positive epistemic status with which we've been concerned: justification, rationality of both the internal and the external variety, and warrant. Justification needn't detain us for long. There should be little doubt that Christian belief can be and probably is (deontologically) *justified*, and justified even for one well acquainted with Enlightenment and postmodern demurrers. If your belief is a result of the inward instigation of the Holy Spirit, it may seem obviously true, even after reflection on the various sorts of objections that have been offered. Clearly, one is then violating no intellectual obligations in accepting it. No doubt there are intellectual obligations and duties in the neighborhood; when you note that others disagree with you, for example, perhaps there is a duty to pay attention to them and to their objections, a duty to think again, reflect more deeply, consult others, look for and consider other possible

22. *Most* others: it sometimes happens with human testimony that one person is deputized to speak for another, and in those cases there is the same principal-subordinate structure. See Wolterstorff, *Divine Discourse*, pp. 38ff.

23. According to Acts 28:25, Paul says, "The Holy Spirit spoke the truth to your forefathers when he said through Isaiah the prophet: 'Go to this people and say, You will ever . . . ' "(Isaiah 6:9, 10).

defeaters. If you have done these things and still find the belief utterly compelling, however, you are not violating duty or obligation—especially if it seems to you, after reflection, that the teaching in question comes from God himself.

Of course some writers charge that if you have faith (as on the model) and think your belief comes from God, then you are arrogant (and hence unjustified). Among the more vivid is the theologian John Macquarrie:

> The Calvinist believes that he himself, as one of the elect, has been rescued from this sea of error and that his mind has been enlightened by the Holy Spirit. However much he may insist that this is God's doing and not his own, his claim is nevertheless one of the most arrogant that has ever been made. It is this kind of thing that has rightly earned for theology the contempt of serious men.[24]

A Calvinist's first impulse might be to retort by asking whom or what Macquarrie credits with furnishing *him* with the truth, when he finds himself disagreeing with the bulk of humankind on religious matters (as, of course, he does): his own cognitive prowess and native sagacity? his own self-developed penetration and perspicacity? And is that attribution less arrogant than to attribute enlightenment to the work of the Holy Spirit? Rather than pursue this unprofitable retort, however, let's think a bit more soberly about the charge. First, note that the accusation initially seems to be brought, not necessarily against someone who actually *has* been enlightened by the Holy Spirit, but against someone who *believes* that she has. No doubt it was the Holy Spirit who was at work in the hearts of the faithful and faith-filled patriarchs and others mentioned in Hebrews 11; but presumably they didn't know about the Holy Spirit and didn't have any views to the effect that their beliefs were due to the activity of the Holy Spirit. So perhaps Macquarrie's idea is that it's all right to know something others don't, but it's not all right to *believe* that you do, attributing your knowledge to the Holy Spirit. His criticism is directed, not necessarily toward a person who accepts Christian teaching (even if in fact such a person has, as in the model, been enlightened by the Holy Spirit), but toward someone who accepts the bit of Reformed theology according to which the Holy Spirit illuminates only some of us, and thinks that she is one of those thus illuminated. And the criticism is that such a person has culpably come to think more highly of herself than she ought.

---

24. *Principles of Christian Theology* (New York: Charles Scribner, 1966, 1977), p. 50.

We'll look further into this charge of arrogance in chapter 13; for now, let me just ask this. Suppose you believe that you have been favored by the Lord in a way in which some others haven't been: does it really follow that you are arrogant? You recognize that in some respect you are better off than someone else: perhaps you have a happy marriage, or your children turn out well, or you are enjoying glowing good health while a good friend is succumbing to melanoma. And suppose you attribute at least part of the difference to God's activity. Are you then automatically arrogant? Isn't it rather that you would be arrogant if, instead, you thought the difference *wasn't* attributable to God but was a manifestation, say, of personal strength, or virtue, or wisdom on your part? Suppose you think you know something someone else doesn't—perhaps Macquarrie thinks that he, as opposed to his Calvinist friends, knows that the Calvinist view of faith is mistaken. Is he thereby arrogant? If not, is it that he fails to be arrogant because he does not attribute his good fortune to God, perhaps attributing it instead to his own native good sense? That hardly seem promising.

The fact is there isn't any arrogance involved as such in recognizing that God has given you something he hasn't (or hasn't yet) given everyone. Human beings are, indeed, tempted to arrogance, and often succumb; still, one isn't arrogant just by virtue of recognizing that God has given you a good thing he hasn't (yet, anyway) given everyone else. (You might be as puzzled as anyone else that it is *you* who are the recipient of the gift.) Arrogance would be involved, no doubt, if you thought of this gift as your *right*, so that God would be unjust if he didn't give it to you. But you're not culpable if you believe your faith is a gift from the Lord and note that not everyone has as yet received this gift. Indeed, the right attitude here, far from a crestfallen admission that you have been arrogant in thus believing, is gratitude and thanksgiving for this wonderfully great gift.[25] Hearing of Jesus Christ's resurrection, the apostle Thomas declared, "Unless I see the nail marks in his hands and put my finger where the nails were, and put my hand into his side, I will not believe it" (John 20:25). Later, Jesus shows himself to Thomas, inviting him to look at the nail marks, and put his hand into his side. Thomas then believes—upon which Jesus says to him, "Because you have seen me, you have believed; blessed are those who have not seen and yet have believed" (John 20:29). No doubt there is more than one point here; a central point, surely, is that those who have been given faith are indeed blessed. Their faith is a gift requiring joyful thanksgiving, not a moral lapse requiring shamefaced repen-

25. See my "*Ad* de Vries," *The Christian Scholar's Review* 19, no. 2 (1989), pp. 171–78.

tance. One who has faith, therefore, is (or may very well be) justified according to the model. And even apart from the model: how could you fail to be justified, within your epistemic rights, in believing what seems to you, after reflection and investigation, to be no more than the truth?

B. Internal Rationality

Internal rationality (see above, pp. 110ff.) has a dual aspect: on the one hand, it requires proper function in the part of the cognitive system that lies "downstream from experience"; on the other, it requires more generally that you have done your best or anyway well enough with respect to the formation of the belief in question.[26] You have considered how it fits in with your other beliefs, engaged in the requisite seeking for defeaters, considered the objections that you have encountered, compared notes with the right people, and so on. Clearly, on the model (and even apart from the model), someone who accepts the Christian beliefs in question can easily meet these conditions. Suppose my experience is of the sort that goes with the testimony of the Holy Spirit (and in chapter 9 we'll see more of what that experience involves), so that the great things of the gospel seem powerfully plausible and compelling to me: then (given that I have no undefeated defeaters for these propositions) there will be nothing dysfunctional or contrary to proper function in accepting the beliefs in question. Indeed, given those experiences, it would be dysfunctional *not* to form them. And suppose I carefully consider the objections people raise, consult with others, ask how the beliefs in question match the rest of my beliefs, and all the rest. Then clearly I will have done my part with respect to the formation of these beliefs. On the testimonial model, therefore, Christian belief enjoys both justification and internal rationality.[27]

26. This requirement of internal rationality may seem to overlap with justification. It does, if in fact there are intellectual duties prescribing the behavior required by rationality. Even if there are no such duties, however, internal rationality still requires the behavior in question.

27. But aren't there many different theories of (say) incarnation and atonement? Don't Christians disagree about this? So which of the many views of Incarnation and Atonement are in fact rational? The question is misplaced. There are many different theories as to how it is that people are able to think; it is still plain to many of us that some people do (sometimes) think. There are many theories about what numbers are; it is still plain that $7 + 5 = 12$. We can quite properly believe in the Atonement even if we don't see exactly how it is supposed to go and don't embrace any of the theories; it can also be that we are rational in believing in the Atonement but not in accepting some specific theory of it.

C. External Rationality and Warrant: Faith Is *Knowledge*

The part of Calvin's definition of faith that is especially striking to contemporary ears is that on his account faith is a really special case of *knowledge* ("a sure and certain knowledge"; compare also the account of true faith in the Heidelberg Catechism, above, p. 247). Faith is not to be *contrasted* with knowledge: faith (at least in paradigmatic instances) *is* knowledge, knowledge of a certain special kind. It is special in at least two ways. First, in its object: what is allegedly known is (if true) of stunning significance, certainly the most important thing a person could possibly know. But it is also unusual in the way in which that content is known; it is known by way of an extraordinary cognitive process or belief-producing mechanism. Christian belief is "revealed to our minds" by way of the Holy Spirit's inducing, in us, belief in the central message of Scripture. The belief-producing process is dual, involving both the divinely inspired Scripture (perhaps directly, or perhaps at the head of a testimonial chain) and the internal instigation of the Holy Spirit. Both involve the special activity of God.

If faith is such an extraordinary way of holding belief, why call it 'knowledge' at all? What about it makes it a case of knowledge? Here we must look a bit more deeply into the model. The believer encounters the great truths of the gospel; by virtue of the activity of the Holy Spirit, she comes to see that these things are indeed true. And the first thing to see is that, on this model, faith is a belief-producing *process* or activity, like perception or memory. It is a cognitive device, a means by which belief, and belief on a certain specific set of topics, is regularly produced in regular ways.[28] In this it resembles memory, perception, reason, sympathy, induction, and other more standard belief-producing processes. It differs from them in that it also involves the direct action of the Holy Spirit, so that the immediate cause of belief is not to be found just in her natural epistemic equipment. There is the special and supernatural activity of the Holy Spirit. Nevertheless, faith is a belief-producing process. Now as we saw in chapter 7, what is required for *knowledge* is that a belief be produced by cognitive faculties or processes that are working properly, in an appropriate epistemic environment (both maxi and mini) according to a design plan that is aimed at truth, and is furthermore *successfully* aimed at truth. But according to this model, what one believes by faith (the beliefs that constitute faith) meets these four conditions.

---

28. Although this regularity is typical of cognitive processes, it isn't really necessary; see my reply to Lehrer in *Warrant in Contemporary Epistemology*, ed. J. Kvanig (New York: Rowman and Littlefield, 1996), pp. 332ff.

First, when these beliefs are accepted by faith and result from the internal instigation of the Holy Spirit, they are produced by cognitive processes working properly;[29] they are not produced by way of some cognitive malfunction. Faith, the whole process that produces them, is specifically designed by God himself to produce this very effect — just as vision, say, is designed by God to produce a certain kind of perceptual beliefs. When it does produce this effect, therefore, it is working properly; thus the beliefs in question satisfy the external rationality condition, which is also the first condition of warrant. Second, according to the model, the maxienvironment in which we find ourselves, including the cognitive contamination produced by sin, is precisely the cognitive environment for which this process is designed. The typical minienvironment is also favorable. Third, the process is designed to produce *true* beliefs;[30] and fourth, the beliefs it produces — belief in the great things of the gospel — are in fact true; faith is a reliable belief-producing process, so that the process in question is *successfully* aimed at the production of true beliefs.

Reliability, of course, demands more than just that these beliefs be true. A thermometer stuck on 72°F is not reliable even if it is somewhere — San Diego, say — where it is always 72°F. What it would do if things were relevantly different (what it would do in appropriately nearby possible worlds) is also relevant; a process or instrument is reliable only if it would produce a true output under different conditions. On the current model, this condition is also met. The Holy Spirit doesn't work just by accident or at random, and there are a thousand ways in which, even if things had been different, the Holy Spirit would have produced the results *actually* produced. Clearly, any circumstances in which it produces this output are circumstances in which this output is true; hence, under those circumstances, it would have produced a true output. Under what conditions would the Holy Spirit have *failed*, with respect to a given person, to do this work of enabling one to see the truth of the great things of the gospel? The model need take no stand on this issue, but it is part of much traditional Christian teaching to hold that a necessary condition of my receiving the gift of faith is my acquiescing, being willing to accept the gift, being prepared to receive it. There is a contribution to this process that I myself must make, a contribution that I can withhold.

29. A *caveat*: as Andrew Dole points out in "Cognitive Processes, Cognitive Faculties, and the Holy Spirit in Plantinga's Warrant Series" (as yet unpublished), it is not obvious that one can directly transfer necessary and sufficient conditions for warrant from beliefs produced by *faculties* to beliefs produced by *processes*.

30. Though this need not be the *only* purpose involved. Perhaps the beliefs produced have other virtues in addition to truth: perhaps they enable one to stand in a personal relationship with God, to face life's vicissitudes with equanimity, to enjoy the comfort that naturally results from the belief that constitutes faith, and so on.

According to this model, faith as a belief-producing mechanism involves a supernatural element; it involves God's doing something specially and directly and quite out of the ordinary. Does that compromise the claim that the deliverances of faith constitute knowledge? I can't see how. There was no suggestion in the original account that cognitive mechanisms must all be *natural*, whatever precisely that comes to. Must the account be revised because faith doesn't go just by natural laws or regularities, working instead by way of the free cooperation of a person —God himself—whose speaking in Scripture is, of course, free, as is the action of the Holy Spirit in revealing and sealing the great truths of the gospel? Again, I can't see why. The same goes for the mechanism Thomas Reid calls 'testimony', a mechanism whereby we learn from others; this mechanism too (often) works by way of free human agency. (When you ask me how old I am, I can [freely] tell you, or in a minor fit of pique, freely refuse.)

Why, then, does faith constitute knowledge? Because what one believes by faith satisfies the conditions that are jointly sufficient and severally necessary for warrant. If the degree of warrant (which, given the satisfaction of the above conditions, is determined by the firmness or strength of belief) is high enough, then the beliefs in question will constitute knowledge.[31]

IV. PROPER BASICALITY AND THE ROLE OF SCRIPTURE

According to the model, Christian belief in the typical case is not the conclusion of an argument (which is not to say arguments cannot play an important role in its acceptance),[32] or accepted on the evidential basis of other beliefs, or accepted just because it constitutes a good explanation of phenomena of one kind or another. Specific Christian beliefs may, indeed, constitute excellent explanations of one or another phenomenon (the Christian teaching of sin leaps to mind here), but they aren't accepted because they provide such an explanation. Nor are they accepted as the conclusion of an argument from *religious experience*. According to the model, experience of a certain sort is intimately associated with the formation of warranted Christian belief, but the belief doesn't get its warrant by way of an argument from the experience. It isn't that the believer notes that she or someone else has a certain sort of experience, and somehow concludes that Christian belief must be true. It is rather that (as in the

---

31. On the account of knowledge given in WPF. I leave as homework the problem of showing how to modify the model in such a way as to accommodate the other main accounts of warrant.

32. For example, in rebutting defeaters: see below, chapter 11.

case of perception) the experience is the *occasion* for the formation of the beliefs in question, and plays a causal role (a role governed by the design plan) in their genesis.

In the typical case, therefore, Christian belief is *immediate*; it is formed in the *basic* way. It doesn't proceed by way of an argument from, for example, the reliability of Scripture or the church. As Jonathan Edwards puts it, "This evidence, that they, that are spiritually enlightened, have of the truth of the things of religion, is a kind of intuitive and immediate evidence. They believe the doctrines of God's word to be divine, because they see divinity in them."[33] Christian belief is basic; furthermore, Christian belief is *properly* basic, where the propriety in question embraces all three of the epistemic virtues we are considering. On the model, the believer is *justified* in accepting these beliefs in the basic way and is *rational* (both internally and externally) in so doing; still further, the beliefs can have warrant, enough warrant for knowledge, when they are accepted in that basic way.[34] My Christian belief can have warrant, and warrant sufficient for knowledge, even if I don't know of and cannot make a good historical case for the reliability of the biblical writers or for what they teach. I don't *need* a good historical case for the truth of the central teachings of the gospel to be warranted in accepting them. I needn't be able to find a good argument, historical or otherwise, for the resurrection of Jesus Christ, or for his being the divine Son of God, or for the Christian claim that his suffering and death constitute an atoning sacrifice whereby we can be restored to the right relationship with God. On the model, the warrant for Christian belief doesn't require that I or anyone else have this kind of historical information; the warrant floats free of such questions. It doesn't require to be validated or proved by some source of belief *other* than faith, such as historical investigation.

Instead, Scripture (through the work of the Holy Spirit) carries its own evidence with it; as Calvin says, it is 'self-authenticating':

---

33. *A Treatise concerning Religious Affections*, ed. John E. Smith (New Haven: Yale University Press, 1959 [originally published 1746]), p. 298. Subsequent references to *Religious Affections* are to this edition.

34. Of course that is not to say that a believer can properly reject proposed defeaters out of hand, without examination (see below, chapters 11–14); nor is she committed to refusing to think she could be wrong. No doubt she can be wrong: that is part of the human condition. If there were a demonstration or a powerful argument from other sources against Christian belief, an argument to which neither she nor the Christian community could see a satisfactory reply, then she might have a problem; this would be a genuine example of a clash between faith and reason. No such demonstration or argument, however, has so far reared its ugly head.

Let this point therefore stand: that those whom the Holy Spirit has inwardly taught truly rest upon Scripture, and that Scripture indeed is self-authenticated. . . .

"Therefore," he says,

illumined by his power, we believe neither by our own nor by anyone else's judgment that Scripture is from God; but above human judgment we affirm with utter certainty that it has flowed to us from the very mouth of God by the ministry of men. We seek no proofs, no marks of genuineness upon which our judgment may lean; but we subject our judgment and wit to it as to a thing far beyond any guess work! . . . Such, then, is a conviction that requires no reason; such, a knowledge with which the best reason agrees—in which the mind truly reposes more securely and constantly than in any reasons. I speak of nothing other than what each believer experiences within himself—though my words fall far beneath a just explanation of the matter.[35]

Calvin speaks here of a certainty, a knowledge that Scripture "has flowed to us from the very mouth of God," even if it is "by the ministry of men." He does not mean to say, I think (at any rate this is not how the model goes), that the Holy Spirit induces belief in the proposition *the Bible* (or the book of Job, or Paul's epistles, or the thirteenth chapter of First Corinthians) *comes to us from the very mouth of God*.[36] Rather, upon reading or hearing a given teaching—a given item from the great things of the gospel—the Holy Spirit teaches us, causes us to believe that *that* teaching is both true and comes from God. So the structure here is not: what is taught in Scripture is true; *this* (e.g., that in Christ, God was reconciling the world to himself) is taught in Scripture; therefore, this is true. It is rather that, on reading or hearing a certain teaching *t*, one forms the belief that *t*, that very teaching, is true and from God.

What is this 'self-authentication' of which Calvin speaks? Is he (or the model) claiming that the truths of the gospel are *self-evident* in something like the traditional sense in which $2 + 1 = 3$ is said to be? Not at all. Self-evident propositions are necessarily true and, at least

---

35. I, vii, 5, pp. 80–81. Here Calvin speaks of "utter certainty" and of the mind "reposing securely" in these teachings. But this is only one side of the story: elsewhere he notes that even the best and most favored of us are subject to doubt and uncertainty: "For unbelief is so deeply rooted in our hearts, and we are so inclined to it, that not without hard struggle is each one able to persuade himself of what all confess with the mouth: namely, that God is faithful" (III, ii, 15); he also says that "unbelief, in all men, is always mixed with faith" (III, ii, 4, p. 547). (What he means, of course, is not that unbelievers always have a portion of faith, but that faith always contains a portion of unbelief.) It is only in the pure and paradigmatic instances of faith that there is that 'utter certainty'.

36. As to what Calvin actually meant here, there has been considerable debate.

in the cases of maximal self-evidence, such that a properly functioning human being can't so much as grasp them without seeing that they couldn't be false.[37] But the great things of the gospel are not necessarily true (they are a result of God's free and gracious action), and it is entirely possible to grasp them without seeing that they are true (it is possible to understand them and reject them). So according to the model (and Calvin), these truths are not self-evident. The propositions *Scripture is reliable* or *God is the author of the Bible* are not self-evident; neither are such teachings as that God was reconciling the world to himself in Christ, or that this reconciliation was accomplished by virtue of Christ's atoning suffering and death.[38]

Nor does Calvin mean to say (nor is it any part of the model to assert) that Scripture is self-authenticating in the sense that it offers evidence for *itself* or somehow *proves* itself to be accurate or reliable. Suppose a question is raised with respect to a given source of belief: is this source of belief really reliable? Suppose a question is raised with respect to a particular teaching of Scripture: is this particular teaching really true? Neither the source nor the particular teaching can, by itself, give an answer that (rationally) allays that doubt. Analogy: suppose I read Hume in an unduly receptive frame of mind and become doubtful that my cognitive faculties are, in fact, reliable. I can't rationally quell or quiet that doubt by offering myself an argument for their reliability. It is the reliability of those very faculties, that very source, that is at issue; and if I have a general doubt about their reliability, I should also have the same doubt about their reliability in this specific instance; I should have the same doubt about the premises of the argument I offer myself, and about my belief that the premises imply the conclusion. Similarly for Scripture: If I am doubtful about its reliability, I can't sensibly quell or quiet that doubt by noting that, say, II Timothy 3:16 says all Scripture is God-breathed (even if I were convinced that what is taught here refers to just the books I take to be canonical). So Scripture isn't self-authenticating in *that* sense either.

<hr />

37. See WPF, 108–9.

38. According to Richard Swinburne, "Very few parts of the Bible seem to claim either 'self-evident' authority or indeed even to be the immediate 'word of the Lord' . . . much of Scripture has not seemed self-evident to so many of its readers; argument is needed to show how it is to be understood and why it is to be believed. Those to whom Scripture seems 'self-evident' are well advised to reflect on these facts before reaffirming their conviction that its truth needs no argument" (*Revelation* [Oxford: Clarendon Press, 1992], p. 118). Here two issues are conflated: (a) are these gospel truths self-evident? and (b) can they properly be believed without argument? According to the present model the answer to (b) is 'yes' but to (a) is 'no'. (There is also still a further issue: according to the model, the central truths of the gospel are self-authenticating in this way; the same does not (necessarily) go for the rest of what the Bible teaches.)

What, then, could Calvin mean when he says that Scripture is self-authenticating? We can see what he means by noting a respect in which the gospel truths resemble self-evident propositions. According to the model, these truths, like self-evident truths, are indeed evident (do indeed have warrant); and, like self-evident truths, they have their evidence *immediately*—that is—not by way of propositional evidence. They do not get their evidence or warrant by way of being believed on the evidential basis of other propositions. So from that point of view, these truths too could be said to be self-evident—in a different and analogically extended sense of that term. They are evident, but don't get their evidence from other propositions; they have their evidence in themselves (and not by way of inference from other propositions).[39] In this same extended sense, perceptual and memory beliefs too are self-evident. They too are 'evident in themselves', in that they don't get their warrant (or evidence) by way of warrant transfer from other propositions. To say that a proposition p is self-evident in this sense is just to say that p does, indeed, have warrant or evidence and does not get that warrant by way of warrant transfer (that is, by way of being believed on the basis of other propositions)—in a word (or two), p is properly basic.[40]

What Calvin means, then (and what the testimonial model endorses), is that we don't require argument from, for example, historically established premises about the authorship and reliability of the bit of Scripture in question to the conclusion that the bit in question is in fact true; that whole process gets short-circuited by way of the tripartite process producing faith. Scripture is self-authenticating in the sense that for belief in the great things of the gospel to be justified, rational, and warranted, no historical evidence and argument for the teaching in question, or for the veracity or reliability or divine character of Scripture (or the part of Scripture in which it is taught) are necessary. The process by which these beliefs have warrant for the believer swings free of those historical and other considerations; these beliefs have warrant in the basic way.

But suppose someone *does* believe these things with a degree of firmness sufficient to constitute knowledge: isn't this attitude, however it is caused, irrational, contrary to reason? Suppose I read the

---

39. Compare Jonathan Edwards: "The gospel of the blessed God don't go abroad a begging for its evidence, so much as some think; it has its highest and most proper evidence in itself" (*Religious Affections*, p. 307).

40. Faith resembles perception, memory, and rational intuition (whereby one grasps what is self-evident) in that in all three cases the beliefs in question are properly basic with respect to warrant. But faith differs from perception (though not from memory and rational intuition) in that it does not involve anything like the highly articulated and detailed sort of sensuous phenomenology that prompts perceptual belief.

gospels and come to believe, for example, that Jesus Christ is in fact the divine son of God and that by his passion, death, and resurrection we human beings, fallen and seriously flawed as we are, can be reconciled and have eternal life. Suppose I believe these things without any external evidence. Suppose, further, I pay little attention to Scripture scholarship and give no thought to the identity or credentials of the real or alleged authors of these documents. I pay little or no attention to such questions as when they were composed or redacted, by whom or how many, whether the redactor was trying to make a theological point in editing as he did, and so on.[41] Won't I be leaping to conclusions, forming belief too hastily? What am I really going on, in such a case? Where is my basis, my ground, my evidence? If I have neither propositional evidence nor the sort of ground afforded perception by perceptual experience, am I not just taking a blind leap? Isn't this leap of faith a leap in the dark? Am I not like someone whose house is on fire and blindly jumps from his third-story window, desperately hoping to catch hold of a branch of the tree he knows is somewhere outside the window? And isn't that irresponsible[42] and irrational?

Not at all. Faith, according to the model, is far indeed from being a blind leap; it isn't even remotely like a leap in the dark. Suppose you are descending a glacier at twelve thousand feet on Mount Rainier; there is a nasty whiteout and you can't see more than four feet before you. It's getting very late, the wind is rising and the temperature dropping, and you won't survive (you are wearing only jeans and a T-shirt) unless you get down before nightfall. So you decide to try to leap the crevasse before you, even though you can't see its other side and haven't the faintest idea how far it is across it. *That's* a leap in the dark. In the case of faith, however, things are wholly different. You might as well claim that a memory belief, or the belief that $3 + 1 = 4$ is a leap in the dark. What makes something a leap in the dark is that the leaper doesn't know and has no firm beliefs about what there is out there in the dark—you might succeed in jumping the crevasse and triumphantly continue your descent, but for all you know you might instead plummet two hundred feet into the icy depths of the glacier. You don't really *believe* that you can jump the crevasse (though you don't disbelieve it either); you *hope* you can, and act on what you *do* believe—namely, that if you don't jump it, you don't have a chance.

---

41. I don't mean for a moment to suggest that Scripture scholarship is unimportant or unimportant for the Christian life (see chapter 12); what I mean is only that knowledge of its results is not necessary for warranted Christian belief.

42. As is argued by, e.g., James L. Muyskens, *The Sufficiency of Hope: The Conceptual Foundations of Religion* (Philadelphia: Temple University Press, 1979), p. 113; see also pp. 134–44.

The case of faith, this sure and certain knowledge, is very different. For the person with faith (at least in the paradigmatic instances),
the great things of the gospel seem clearly true, obvious, compelling.
She finds herself convinced—just as she does in the case of clear
memory beliefs or her belief in elementary truths of arithmetic.[43]
Phenomenologically, therefore, from the inside, there is no similarity at all to a leap in the dark. Nor, of course, is there (on the model)
any similarity from the outside. This is no leap in the dark, not merely
because the person with faith is wholly convinced but also because, as
a matter of fact, the belief in question meets the conditions for rationality and warrant.

Compare belief of this sort with the *a priori* and memory beliefs I
spoke of above. In a certain sense, there isn't anything to go on in any of
the three cases. You don't accept memory and obvious *a priori* beliefs on
the basis of other beliefs; but you also lack the detailed phenomenological basis, the rich and highly articulated sensuous imagery that is involved in perception. What you do have in all three cases is another
kind of phenomenal evidence, what I have been calling *doxastic* evidence. (In WPF I called it *impulsional* evidence.) There is a certain kind
of phenomenology that distinguishes entertaining a proposition you believe from one you do not: the former simply seems right, correct, natural, approved—the experience isn't easy to describe (WPF, 190ff.). You
have this doxastic evidence in all three sorts of cases (as, indeed, in any
case of belief), and you have nothing else to go on. But you don't *need*
anything else to go on: it is not as if things would be better, from an epistemic point of view, if you believed, say, *2 + 1 = 3* or that you had oat-
meal for breakfast this morning on the evidential basis of other propositions, or on the basis of some kind of sensuous imagery more or less
like that involved in perception. (I don't mean that you can't get more
evidence, for something you believe by way of memory, but that you
would not necessarily be better off, epistemically speaking, if you believed the proposition in question on the basis of other beliefs or on the
basis of sensuous imagery.) The same goes (on the model) for the beliefs
of faith: you don't have either sensuous imagery or evidence from other
things you believe to go on; the beliefs are none the worse, epistemically
speaking, for that. In fact (on the model) they are all the better for that;
they have (or can have) much more firmness and stability than they
could sensibly have if accepted on the basis of rational argument or, as
in this case, historical investigation; they can also have much more warrant. These beliefs (on the model) are not accepted on the basis of other
beliefs; in fact, other beliefs are accepted on the basis of *them*.

---

43. Again, in the paradigmatic cases; but of course the fact is the conviction and
belief involved in faith come in all degrees of firmness. As Calvin puts it, "in the believing mind certainty is mixed with doubt" and "we are troubled on all sides by the
agitation of unbelief." In typical cases, therefore, as opposed to paradigmatic cases,
degree of belief will be less than maximal. Furthermore, degree of belief, on the part
of the person who has faith, typically varies from time to time, from circumstance to
circumstance.

You might think this model is a model of how, broadly speaking, Christian belief can have warrant by way of *religious experience*. That's not exactly right—or if it *is* right, then memory and *a priori* beliefs also get *their* warrant by way of experience. But suppose we think that (on the model) the beliefs of faith do get their warrant by way of experience— that is, by way of *doxastic* experience—and suppose we describe that experience as *religious* experience. What is crucially important to note is that we don't have here an *argument* from religious experience to the truth of these Christian beliefs. There *could* be something like that, a model according to which Christian belief got warrant by way of an argument from religious experience. This would be one in which you have religious experience (or note that others do), and then argue (perhaps by way of something roughly like the analogical argument for other minds) to the truth of these doctrines. Alternatively, it might be like the arguments some have offered from the facts of perceptual experience for the truth of perceptual beliefs. This model isn't like that. The experience in question is an *occasion* for the belief in question, not a phenomenon whose existence serves as a premise in an argument for that belief.

According to Hebrews 11, "Now faith is the substance (ὑπόστασιζ) of things hoped for and the evidence (ἐλεγχοζ) of things not seen" (King James translation). The key words 'substance' and 'evidence' are translated variously; for example, the more recent Revised Standard Version has "faith is the *assurance* of things hoped for, the *conviction* of things not seen" (my emphasis). Perhaps the former way is the better translation; in any event, it is the richer. For faith, according to Christian doctrine, is many things. It is the means or vehicle of salvation: "for it is by grace you have been saved, through faith" (Ephesians 1:8). It is also that by which we are *justified* (above, p. 87), as well as that by means of which we are *regenerated*, becoming new creatures in Christ. And it is also the foundation and substance (etymologically, that which 'stands under') of Christian hope.

But faith is also "the evidence of things not seen." By faith—the whole process, involving the internal instigation of the Holy Spirit— something becomes *evident* (i.e., acquires warrant, has what it takes to be knowledge). And what thus becomes evident or warranted is indeed not seen. This doesn't mean that it is indistinct, blurred, uncertain, or a matter of guesswork; what it means is that the belief in question isn't made evident by way of the workings of the ordinary cognitive faculties with which we were originally created. (The author refers, by way of synecdoche, to these faculties as vision.) Return to the account of Thomas's skepticism (above, pp. 254): Thomas would not believe until he saw the nail holes, put his finger where the nails were, thrust his hand into Christ's side. Jesus then says to him, "Because you have seen me, you have believed; blessed are those who have not seen and yet have believed" (John 20:29). From the present point of view, this is neither a general counsel commending credulity nor a rebuke addressed to such embryonic empiricists as Thomas. It is, instead, the observation that those who have faith have a source of knowledge that transcends our ordinary perceptual faculties and cognitive processes, a source of knowledge that is a divine gift; hence they are indeed blessed.[44]

V. COMPARISON WITH LOCKE

We can understand this testimonial model better if we compare it with a picture of a very different sort—that of John Locke, whose Enlightenment model is still dominant in some Christian circles.[45] According to Locke, all of our beliefs should be formed by "following reason." What that means, more specifically, is that epistemic duty demands "not entertaining any proposition with greater assurance than the proofs [inductive as well as deductive] it is built upon will warrant."[46] And what *that* means (as we saw in chapter 4) is that I should proportion degree of assent to the evidence; that is, I should, as far as I can, believe a proposition p with a firmness that is proportional to the degree to which p is probable with respect to what is certain for me.

All of our beliefs should be formed by following reason; but this doesn't mean, as Locke sees it, that there is no rational room for beliefs formed by faith, which he defines as "the assent to any proposition, not thus made out by the deductions of reason; but upon the credit of the proposer, as coming from God, in some extraordinary way of communication" (416). Nor does it mean that we can't properly believe an item of divine revelation, where that item itself is not more likely than not with respect to what is certain for us:

> I do not mean that we must consult reason, and examine whether a proposition revealed from God can be made out by natural principles, and if it cannot then we may reject it. . . .

---

44. Compare Aquinas: "Accordingly, if anyone would reduce the foregoing words to the form of a definition, he may say that *faith is a habit of the mind, whereby eternal life is begun in us, making the intellect assent to what is non-apparent* (ST II-II, q.4, a.i, *respondeo*).

45. Locke's cool rationalism with respect to the authority of Scripture is echoed at present by, for example, Richard Swinburne (see fn. 56), but also by those more evangelical thinkers who hold that warrant for Christian belief can only come by way of argument or evidence.

46. *An Essay concerning Human Understanding*, ed. with "Prolegomena" by Alexander Fraser (New York: Dover, 1959 [original first published in 1690]), IV, xix, 1, p. 429. Subsequent page references to Locke's essay are to this edition.

What he does mean is

> but consult it we must, and by it examine whether it be a revelation
> from God or no: and if reason finds it to be revealed from God, rea-
> son then declares for it as much as for any other truth, and makes
> it one of her dictates. (439)

Locke's claim is that before believing an allegedly revealed proposition, we must first satisfy ourselves by reason that this proposition is,
indeed, a revelation from God. What we need is a rational proof (a
proof whose premises and procedures come from reason, not from
revelation) that the proposition in question really is proposed for our
belief by God. So what we need in the case of a scriptural teaching is
a rational proof that this teaching is indeed a divine revelation; it is
that proposition which must be shown to be probable with respect to
what is certain for us. Once we have that, then we can properly believe what it teaches, although presumably with a firmness that is
proportional to the probability (with respect to what is certain for us)
that the teaching in question really does come from God.

Things are very different on the testimonial model. It isn't that
one believes, for example, that God was reconciling the world to himself in Christ, because one has first seen or shown that it is likely (with
respect to what is certain) that this particular suggestion of Paul's (or
perhaps all of II Corinthians, or perhaps the entire New Testament,
or perhaps the entire Bible) is in fact divinely inspired and hence
true. This would be vastly too tenuous and speculative. A belief that
the passage is a divine revelation, if properly formed by way of historical inquiry, could only be halting and tentative; but then the belief itself would have to be equally halting and tentative. As Calvin
puts it:

> If we desire to provide in the best way for our consciences—that
> they may not be perpetually beset by the instability of doubt or vac-
> illation, and that they may not also boggle at the smallest quibbles—
> we ought to seek our conviction in another place than human rea-
> sons, judgment, or conjectures, that is, in the secret testimony of the
> Spirit.[47]

Instead, on the present model the source of belief and knowledge
here is independent of ordinary historical investigation and of the
probability mongering, the vagaries and uncertainties to which that
line of inquiry is condemned. The belief in question is, instead, immediate and basic, an immediate response to the proclamation. Of
course this response takes place within the context of a whole inter-

---

47. *Institutes*, p. 78. Of course it doesn't follow that Scripture scholarship and
biblical commentary are not both important and necessary; Calvin himself wrote
more than twenty volumes of detailed and searching biblical commentary.

locking system of beliefs; we may add, if we like, that it obtains some of its warrant from its coherence with a coherent system. Nevertheless, the belief is still basic in that it isn't accepted on the evidential basis of these beliefs or any others. It is basic, and properly basic— with respect to warrant and rationality as well as justification. Says Calvin, no doubt with an anticipatory glance in Locke's direction,

> Since for unbelieving men religion seems to stand by opinion alone, they, in order not to believe anything foolishly or lightly, both wish and demand rational proof that Moses and the prophets spoke divinely. But I reply: the testimony of the Spirit is more excellent than all reason. For as God alone is a fit witness of himself in his Word, so also the Word will not find acceptance in men's hearts before it is sealed by the inward testimony of the Spirit. The same Spirit, therefore, who has spoken through the mouths of the prophets must penetrate into our hearts to persuade us that they faithfully proclaimed what had been divinely commanded. (79)[48]

VI. Why Necessary?

Why is this elaborate scheme necessary? Why these supernaturally inspired writings and this individually applied supernatural testimony of the Holy Spirit? Or rather (because God could have accomplished his aim of enabling human beings of many times and places to know about the possibility and means of salvation in many different ways), what might recommend this particular scheme? Wouldn't some less extravagant means suffice? Couldn't this information come to us just as well by way of ordinary *human* testimony, for example? Perhaps (as Locke thought) God could have revealed the great truths of the gospel in some direct way only to certain human beings. They could then write them down for the benefit of the rest of us, who are then supposed to be able to see in the ordinary way that these writings do, indeed, constitute divine revelation (and are accordingly both true and to be believed). Why have any truck with special faculties or supernatural belief-producing processes like faith and the internal instigation of the Holy Spirit?

Well, first of all, we have no reason to think God either specially prizes ontological economy or specially dislikes supernatural processes. But the main problem with Locke's appealingly simple device is that it wouldn't work. First, according to the extended A/C model,

---

48. Note here that the Holy Spirit plays a dual role: inspiring the human authors of Scripture (bringing it about that they say what he wants them to say) but also working in the hearts of the hearers and readers, bringing it about that they believe what they hear and read. So the inward testimony of the Holy Spirit is to what he himself has said.

we human beings, apart from God's special and gracious activity, are sunk in sin; we are prone to hate God and our neighbor; our hearts, as Jeremiah said, are deceitful above all things and desperately corrupt. In this context, that fact is of great importance: without some special activity on the part of the Lord, we wouldn't believe. As the apostle Paul says, "The man without the Spirit does not accept the things that come from the Spirit of God, for they are foolishness to him, and he cannot understand them, because they are spiritually discerned."[49] We human beings won't come to see the depth of our own sin and our need for salvation without regeneration, rebirth; according to Jesus himself, we need the testimony of the Holy Spirit to come to believe the great truths of the gospel.[50] Given our fallen nature and our natural antipathy to the message of the gospel, faith will have to be a *gift*, not in the way a glorious autumn day is a gift, but a special gift, one that wouldn't come to us in the ordinary run of things, one that requires supernatural and extraordinary activity on the part of God.[51]

Furthermore, suppose someone *did* come to believe, just by way of historical investigation that Jesus was indeed the divine son of God, that he died for our sins and rose again, and that through him we can have eternal life. *Merely* believing this—as an interesting fact about the world, rather like the fact that the universe began in a Big Bang some twelve to sixteen billion years ago—is insufficient. These truths must be sealed to the heart, as well as revealed to the mind. This sealing is the topic of the next chapter; now we note only that coming to faith includes more than a change of opinion. It also (and

49. 1 Corinthians 2:14. Compare 1 Corinthians 1:23: "We preach Christ crucified, a stumbling block to Jews and foolishness to Gentiles, but to those whom God has called, both Jews and Greeks, Christ the power of God and the wisdom of God."

50. "No one can come to me unless the Father who sent me draws him" (John 6:44); and "I will pray the Father, and he will give you another Counselor, to be with you forever, even the Spirit of truth, whom the world cannot receive, because it neither sees him nor knows him; you know him for he dwells with you, and will be in you" (John 14:16–17).

51. This, once more, is a point on which Calvin and Aquinas concur: "for since, by assenting to what belongs to faith, man is raised above his nature, this must needs come to him from some supernatural principle moving him inwardly; and this is God" (ST II-II, q.6, a.1, *respondeo*; see also article 2. When I speak of supernatural activity on the part of God, I don't mean to suggest a sort of incursion into or intervention in the natural order. The fact is, God is constantly active in the world: apart from his upholding activity, the world would disappear like a candle flame in a high wind. Supernatural activity on the part of God (as well as miracles) must be understood, instead, in terms of God's *special* activity, as opposed to the way in which he ordinarily treats the things he has created. There are depths and problems here; they will have to await another occasion.

crucially) includes a change of heart, a change in *affection*, in what one loves and hates, approves and disdains, seeks and avoids. According to the present model, faith is, indeed, a belief-producing process; it is also an affection-producing process, a process issuing in alteration of affection as well as change of opinion. Given our constitution, this alteration of affection can't be accomplished just by coming to believe, as a historical fact, the main lines of the gospel.[52]

We therefore need a change of attitude in addition to a change of opinion, and won't sustain the latter without the former. Well then, why couldn't God (supernaturally if he feels that is necessary) just arrange for a change of attitude and affections? Why do we need that supernatural source for a change in opinion? Given the right affections, wouldn't Scripture and our ordinary faculties (reason, memory, perception, sympathy, induction, etc.) be sufficient to enable us to see the truth of the message of the gospel?

I doubt it. First, what is proposed is such that by virtue of the ordinary faculties employed in historical investigation, only a few people would acquire the knowledge in question, and they only after a great deal of effort and much time; furthermore, their belief would be both uncertain and shot through with falsehood.[53] What is being taught, after all, is not something that chimes straightforwardly with our ordinary experience. It isn't like an account of an ancient war, or of the cruelty of the Athenians to the Melians, or of the overweening pride of some ancient despot. That sort of thing would be easy enough to believe. What we have instead, however, is the claim that a certain human being — Jesus of Nazareth — is also, astonishingly, the unique divine Son of God who has existed from eternity. Furthermore, this man died, which is not uncommon, but then three days later rose from the dead, which is uncommon indeed. Still further, it is by way of his atoning suffering and death and resurrection that we are justified, that our sins are forgiven, and that we may have life and have it more abundantly. *This* is heady stuff indeed, and the mere fact that some ancient authors believed it would certainly be insufficient for a sensible conviction on our part. As biblical scholars remind us, there are many ancient books with stories more or less (in my opinion, mostly less) like the biblical ones; how many of those ancient books do we in fact believe?

---

52. "If they wouldn't believe Moses and the prophets, they will not be convinced even if someone rises from the dead" (Luke 16:31).

53. As Aquinas says about the existence of God if accepted on the basis of the theistic proofs (ST I, q.1, a.1, *respondeo*; *Summa contra Gentiles*, Bk. I, ch. 4; ST II-II, q.2, a.4). It is for this reason, Aquinas says, that it was entirely appropriate for the existence of God to be proposed as an object of belief or faith, even though it could in fact be proved by reason.

Still (comes the reply), can't we discover for ourselves, without any special divine aid or assistance, that the Bible (the New Testament, say) is in fact "from God": divinely inspired in such a way that God speaks to us in it and through it,[54] and hence wholly reliable?[55] Can't we come to see this in the same way that we can learn that Herodotus and Xenophon are reasonably reliable reporters of what they hear and see? And once we see that, couldn't we then infer that the Bible's central message of incarnation and atonement is true? Can't we see and appreciate the historical case for the truth of the main lines of Christian belief without any special work of the Holy Spirit? "You must be born again" all right—your affections, aims, and intentions must be recalibrated, redirected, reversed—and that requires special divine help. But *given* that recalibration, couldn't you *then* see and appreciate the historical case for the truth of the main lines of Christianity without any special work of the Holy Spirit?

I don't think so. Even discounting the effects of sin on our apprehension of the historical case, that case isn't strong enough to produce warranted belief that the main lines of Christian teaching are true—at most, it could produce the warranted belief that the main lines of Christian teaching aren't particularly improbable. For how could such a case go?[56] First, of course, the case in question couldn't in any way rely on the thought that the Bible is in some special way inspired by God; for these purposes, we should have to treat it exactly as we would any other ancient volume. We should have to follow the example of those Scripture scholars who try to determine (for

54. Perhaps in the way proposed by Nicholas Wolterstorff's *Divine Discourse*. As I understand Wolterstorff, however, his account of how it could be that God speaks *presupposes* the main lines of Christian teaching, and hence wouldn't offer a way in which we could come to see that that teaching is in fact true (i.e., wouldn't provide the materials for an argument for the truth of that teaching).

55. This would substantially be the Locke-Swinburne model; however, it isn't clear whether they would concur with the current proposal in the suggestion that a change in affection and attitude is necessary to a proper appreciation of the historical case.

56. What follows is roughly based on Richard Swinburne's argument for a similar conclusion in his *Revelation* (Oxford: Clarendon Press, 1992), chapters 5, 7, and 8. A difference is that Swinburne thinks one believes that p if and only if one believes that p is more probable than not. (*Faith and Reason* [Oxford: Clarendon Press, 1981], p. 32); I take it that belief that p is more probable than not is nowhere nearly sufficient for belief that p. (I am about to throw an ordinary die: I believe it is more likely than not that it won't come up showing face 2 or 3, but I certainly don't *believe* that it won't; what I actually believe on this head is only that it will come up showing one of faces 1 through 6 (and not, for example, wind up delicately balanced on one of its points or edges).

example) what actually happened with Jesus—what he preached, whether he rose from the dead—without making any special theological assumptions about the reliability of the Bible or the person of Jesus.[57] They bracket any such theological beliefs they may have and then try to assess the historical case or evidence for such claims as that Jesus actually asserted that he was the divine redeemer, or the claim that he died and came back to life. Such a case for the truth of the main lines of Christianity could be at most a case for the *probability* that these teachings are true.

What would such a case be like? How could it be constructed? The conclusion of the case (or argument) would be that the central Christian claims are *probable*. Now a proposition is probable only with respect to some other proposition or propositions.[58] In this case, the relevant other propositions would be some body of background knowledge K—what we all or nearly all know or take for granted or firmly believe, or what at any rate those conducting the inquiry know or take for granted or believe.[59] And the aim would be to show that the claims of the Christian gospel are probable with respect to K—that is, probable with respect to what we know or take for granted. For simplicity, take the central Christian claims to be sin (human beings are in need of salvation), incarnation (Jesus is the incarnate second person of the trinity), atonement (by virtue of his suffering and death, he atoned for our sin and enables us to attain eternal salvation), and general availability (salvation isn't restricted to just one group of people, for example, the Jews[60]); and let's use 'G' to name their conjunction. Our aim, therefore, is to argue that G is reasonably probable on K; we can employ the usual symbolism for probability and put this by saying that $P(G/K)$ is reasonably high.

How can we construct such a case—argue that $P(G/K)$ *is* reasonably high? The usual way (and the method followed by Swinburne) is to try to find some proposition (or group of propositions) *P* which is probable with respect to K, and which is such that G is probable with respect to its conjunction with K: that is, a proposition *P* such that $P(P/K)$ and $P(G/P\&K)$ are both high. For example, you might argue first that T, the existence of God, is probable on K, our background knowledge. Then you might argue that given our background knowledge K *and* the existence of God (T), it is probable that God

---

57. See below, pp. 390ff.

58. The *absolute* or *logical* probability of a proposition would then be its probability with respect to a necessary truth.

59. These probabilities would not be Bayesian measures of degrees of belief, but something much more objective—Richard Swinburne's epistemic probability, or the objective probability of WPF (pp. 161ff.).

60. See Peter's vision in Acts 10.

would reveal certain crucial truths (truths we need to know) to humankind.[61] Call that proposition R. Then you might continue arguing in the same vein (repeating the same form of argument), finally winding up with some propositions with respect to which it is likely that God raised Jesus from the dead, thus authorizing and validating the message of the New Testament. That message could then be taken as authorized by God and hence true; and the message contains those propositions G to whose probability we are trying to argue. So you might then conclude that G is in fact probable with respect to what we know.

To illustrate and explain this procedure, suppose you are interested in the probability that Eleonore is at the party. It is very probable, on your background knowledge K, that Paul is at the party (call that proposition 'P'): $P(P/K)$ is high—for definiteness, say it's .9. It is also very likely that Eleonore is at the party (call that proposition 'E'), given that Paul is (she ordinarily goes to every party he goes to); so $P(E/P\&K)$ is also high—say it is also .9. There is a formula from the probability calculus that enables you to conclude that it is likely that Eleonore is there, too:

$P(E/K)$ equals or exceeds $P(P/K) \times P(E/P\&K)$.

Thus $P(E/K)$ will be at least .81.[62]

This sort of argument can be reiterated. Perhaps you also know that there is a pretty good probability—.8, say—that Vonnie will be there, given that Eleonore is: in that case, you can conclude that the probability of Vonnie's being there is at least .648; and perhaps you know that the probability of Jim's being there, given that Vonnie is there, is .95; then the probability that he's there will be at least .616.

Now suppose we try along these lines to construct a case for the probability of G with respect to that background knowledge K. We should first have to find the probability that T (theism) is true: what is the probability (on our background knowledge, or the totality of what we know apart from theism) that there is an omnipotent, omniscient, wholly good being who has created the world? In his book *The*

61. Thus Swinburne: "So if there is other evidence which makes it quite likely that there is a God, all powerful and all good, who made the Earth and its inhabitants, then perhaps it becomes to some extent likely that he would intervene in human history to reveal things to them" (*Revelation*, p. 70).

62. "At least": that is because there could also be some probability that Eleonore would be there even if Paul were not. The probability of Eleonore's being there (E) will be the weighted average of the probabilities of E given Paul's being there (P) and the probability of E given -P—weighted by the probabilities of P and -P. The relevant formula is

$P(E/K) = [P(E/(P\&K)) \times P(P/K)] + [P(E/(-P\&K)) \times P(-P/K)]$

63. Oxford: Clarendon Press, 1979.

Existence of God,[63] Swinburne considers this probability and concludes on the last page of the book, "On our total evidence theism is
more probable than not." The argument is complex and at many
points controversial.[64] From the present perspective, however, an
even more vexing problem is that its conclusion is only that theism is
more probable than not on the relevant body of knowledge or information K: it lies somewhere in the (half open) interval .5 to 1. Even if all
the other probabilities involved in our historical case were as high as
1, we could conclude no more than that the probability of the truth
of Christian teaching lies somewhere in that same interval.

But if my only ground for Christian teaching is its probability
with respect to K, and all I know about that probability is that it is
greater than .5, then I can't rationally *believe* that teaching. Suppose
I know that the coin you are about to toss is loaded. I don't know just
how heavily it is loaded, so I don't know what the probability is that it
will come up heads, but I do know that this probability is greater
than .5. Under those conditions I do not believe that the next toss of
this coin will come up heads. (Of course I also don't believe that it will
come up *tails*; and I *suspect* that it will come up heads.) All I know is
that it is more likely than not to come up heads; and that's not sufficient for my sensibly *believing* that it will. The same goes in this case:
if what I know is only that the probability of Christian belief (with respect to K) is greater than .5, I can't sensibly believe it.[65] I can *hope*
that it is true, and think it rather likely that it is; I can't believe it. To
give the historical case for G a run for its money, therefore, suppose
we arbitrarily assign T a much higher probability on K—let's say that
it is at least .9. Many will howl with indignation at such a high as-
signment; let us ignore them for the moment.

We must next consider the probability, given T & K, that

A God would make some kind of revelation (of himself, or perhaps of what we need to know about him) to humankind.

Well, that seems quite likely, although of course it's very hard to predict *a priori* what God would or wouldn't do. Again, let's be generous
and estimate this probability as also lying in the interval .9 to 1.

---

64. Especially, perhaps, with respect to the judgments of comparative simplicity
involved, and the judgment that simplicity is, in fact, a good guide to probability.

65. Note, of course, that we can't simply *add* theism to the relevant body of
knowledge K on the grounds that it is more probable than not on what we know; that
way lies contradiction. It is more probable than not that this die will not turn up ace;
the same, of course, for each of the other five possibilities; so if we could add each of
these propositions (it won't come up 1, it won't come up 2 . . .) to K, we wind up with
the contradiction that the die will come up showing some number between 1 and 6
(inclusive) and also that it will not.

But now we come to the hard parts. Somehow we have to make a probabilistic argument for the proposition that such a revelation would contain G, the great claims of the gospel. Of course a revelation from God would include G only if G is true; so what we really need here is a probabilistic argument for a conclusion sufficient to entail G. One common way to do this would be to argue that it is likely that Jesus taught G, and that by raising Jesus from the dead God endorsed or ratified that teaching. But just on the basis of ordinary historical scholarship, without the assumption that the Bible is, in fact, a divine revelation, it really *isn't* likely that Jesus taught anything nearly as definite as G—that is, sin, incarnation, atonement, and general availability. Scripture scholars argue at length about what precisely Jesus taught, but those who approach the matter 'from below' (i.e., without employing any special theological assumptions) for the most part are not at all prepared to assert that Jesus taught G. Indeed, even if we do accept the Bible as authoritative, it still won't be clear that *Jesus* taught G; much of our grasp of the central claims of Christian faith comes from other parts of the Bible (e.g., the Pauline epistles) and later reflection (e.g., the Nicene Creed).

Perhaps, though, it is likely just on historical grounds that the teachings of Jesus were such that by sensible interpretation and extrapolation one could arrive at G. So we must ask after the probability of

B Jesus' teachings were such that they could be sensibly interpreted and extrapolated to G

given K&T and A; that is, we must ask after the value of P(B/ (K&T&A)). B is fairly vague, but let's suppose it's rather likely, just on the basis of historical scholarship. Of course there will be many who would demur—those who think Jesus was a homosexual magician,[66] for example, not to mention those who think he was the first Christian atheist.[67] Let's say they are wrong and that this probability is high—for definiteness, in the interval .7 to .9.

But now things get harder yet. We must next consider the proposition that God endorsed Jesus' teachings by performing a great miracle and raising him from the dead. What is the probability, just on historical grounds, that

C Jesus rose from the dead?

Of course, C must be taken in a literal and bodily sense; it is not to be glossed as, for example, the mere thought that the followers of Jesus underwent some experience so impressive and revivifying that they

66. See Morton Smith, *Jesus the Magician* (New York: Harper and Row, 1978).
67. See Thomas Sheehan, *The First Coming* (New York: Random House, 1976).

acquired the energy and determination necessary to start a new religion.[68] And again, what we need to consider is the conditional probability of C on K, T, and A&B—that is, P(C/(K&T&A&B)). What is this probability? One hesitates to say much here, given the enormous controversies and disagreements among Scripture scholars. How many people are there who believe on strictly historical grounds together with theism (no help from theology, the internal instigation of the Holy Spirit, or anything like that), that Jesus Christ arose from the dead (in the strict and literal sense)? Even if you had a fine command of the vast literature and thought there *was* rather a good historical case here, you would presumably think it pretty speculative and chancy. I'd guess that it is likely that the disciples *believed* that Jesus arose from the dead, but on sheerly historical grounds (together with the assumption that there really is such a person as God, who is rather likely to make a revelation to us) it is considerably less likely that this actually did happen. Given all the controversy among the experts, we should probably declare this probability inscrutable—that is, such that we can't really say with any confidence what it is. Again, let's be generous: let's say that this proposition is more probable than not—for definiteness, say it lies in the interval .6 to .8.

Next, we must consider the probability of

D In raising Jesus from the dead, God endorsed his teachings

on the previous propositions; that is, we must consider P(D/(K&T-&A&B&C)). From C we have only that Jesus arose from the dead, not that God raised him from the dead, thereby endorsing his teaching. Given T, though, it does seem likely that *God* raised him from the dead—how else would it happen? Still, did he, in so doing, ratify what Jesus taught? Not necessarily: there are other reasons why he might have done it. Perhaps it was to endorse the teaching of the Pharisees as opposed to the Sadducees (Matthew 22:23), or perhaps as a reward for special devotion and a holy life, or perhaps for some reason of which we have no knowledge. Still, this probability should probably be pegged fairly high: let's say, for definiteness, .9.

---

68. As in much contemporary liberal and quasi-liberal theology. See, e.g., Norman Perrin, *The Resurrection according to Matthew, Mark, and Luke* (Philadelphia: Fortress Press, 1977), p. 83: of the witnesses to the resurrection appearances of Jesus, he says, "in some way they were granted a vision of Jesus which convinced them that God had vindicated Jesus out of His death and that therefore the death of Jesus was by no means the end of the impact of Jesus upon their lives."

Here we can bracket the question what sort of body Jesus had upon resurrection: was the body he had upon resurrection (whether or not it was numerically the *same* body he had before his death) a *glorified* body with supernatural powers? The latter would be still harder to establish by historical argument (see Robert Cavin's "Is There Sufficient Historical Evidence to Establish the Resurrection of Jesus?" *Faith and Philosophy* [July 1995]).

But there is still another probability to be evaluated here: the probability that in raising Jesus from the dead and endorsing his teachings, he was also endorsing their extrapolation to G, the central teaching of Christianity: we must look into the probability of

E The extension and extrapolation of Jesus' teachings to G is true

That is, we must look into P(E/(K&T&A&B&C&D)). Here the issues are more complex than they appear at first. Suppose you *were* completely convinced, on merely historical grounds, that Jesus rose from the dead: wouldn't it be an enormous further step to conclude G, that he was, in fact, the divine and unique son of God, the second person of the trinity, and that his suffering and death is a propitiatory sacrifice, whereby we can have eternal life? It isn't easy to see how a powerful historical case for all this could be made; perhaps it could go as follows. In accord with B, above, Jesus' teachings can naturally be extrapolated or extended to G; and perhaps God endorsed this extension of Jesus' teachings in raising him from the dead. But why think so? Why think *that* extrapolation (as opposed to all the other possibilities) has it right? Well, perhaps Jesus intended to (and did) found a church to interpret and preserve his teachings; God ratified that intention too; the church he founded is still extant, preserved (by the Holy Spirit, perhaps) from error, and teaches G. Here we really have five further propositions that together constitute our historical case for E; so, instead of E, we must consider the probability of the conjunction of

(1) Jesus intended to (and did) found a church to interpret and preserve his teachings,
(2) God ratified that intention in raising him from the dead,
(3) The church Jesus founded is still extant,
(4) God has preserved that church from error,

and

(5) That church teaches G

on K&T&A&B&C&D.

Now in the context of the present argument, we can take the conjunction of (1) to (5) as E. Our present project, then, is to evaluate the probability of E, so construed, on K&T&A&B&C&D. It seems sensible to estimate P((1)&(2)&(3)&(4)/(K&T&A&B&C&D)) as very

---

69. Celsus, an early critic of Christianity, apparently thought this probability fairly low, not much greater than .5 (see Origen, *Contra Celsum*, 1.68); let's suppose Celsus was wrong.

high:[69] to be generous (and keep things as simple as possible) let's say this probability is 1. That still leaves us with (5), however: what is *its* probability on K&T&A&B&C&D plus the conjunction of (1) to (4)? This is not easy to estimate. Given that there is a church that God has preserved from error, which church is it? Is it one that teaches G? At present, many mainline Protestant churches (and some Roman Catholic clergy), for example, don't seem really to *teach* G at all. These churches (and their members) display a very wide spectrum of opinion, ranging all the way from extremely liberal views, according to which very little of classical Christianity is actually true (though much of it perhaps warmly inspiring), to full-blooded classical Christian belief. Which of these opinions did Christ mean to endorse? Which of these most faithfully conforms to his intentions? Is it a group that actually teaches G?[70] That's not easy to say on historical grounds; once again, let's be generous and estimate this probability (i.e., P((5)/(K&T &A&B&C&D)) as somewhere in the interval .7 to .9. This means that P(E/(K&T&A&B&C&D)) will lie in that same interval.

Now how do we get a probability (on K) for G, given all this? Note that E entails G; so (following our present argument) to find the probability of G on K, what we need is to find the probability of E on K. How do we do that? Our argument followed the strategy of finding a series of propositions, T and A–E, such that the first is probable on K, the second on K together with the first, the third on K together with the first and second, and so on. A little arithmetic enables us to conclude that

$$P\ (E/K)$$

will be equal to or greater than

$$P(T/K) \times P(A/(K\&T)) \times P(B/(K\&T\&A)) \times P(C/(K\&T\&A\&B))$$
$$\times P(D/(K\&T\&A\&B\&C)) \times P(E/(K\&T\&A\&B\&C\&D)).$$

The little arithmetic goes as follows.
By

$$(1)\ P(X/Y) \geq P(X/Z\&Y) \times P(Z/Y)$$

we know that

$$(2)\ P(E/K) \geq P(E/K\&T\&A\&B\&C\&D) \times P(T\&A\&B\&C\&D/K).$$

---

70. Swinburne (*Revelation*, chapter 8) proposes two criteria for determining what is to count as the church: continuity of aim and continuity of organization. The first depends on continuity of doctrinal teaching; but then to apply it we would already have to know what the true church teaches. That is, we would have to know what Jesus intended his church to teach; but then we can't use this test to determine what Jesus intended his church to teach.

Consider the right multiplicand. According to the probability calculus,

(3) $P(X\&Y/Z) = P(X/Z) \times P(Y/X\&Z)$;

hence

(4) $P(T\&A\&B\&C\&D/K) = P(T\&A\&B\&C/K) \times P(D/T\&A\&B\&C\&K)$.

By substitution into (2) we have

(5) $P(E/K) \geq P(E/T\&A\&B\&C\&D\&K) \times P(T\&A\&B\&C/K) \times P(D/T\&A\&B\&C\&K)$.

Again, by (3) we know that

(6) $P(T\&A\&B\&C/K) = P(C/T\&A\&B\&K) \times P(T\&A\&B/K)$;

substituting into (5), we have

(7) $P(E/K) \geq P(E/T\&A\&B\&C\&D\&K) \times P(C/T\&A\&B\&K) \times P(T\&A\&B/K) \times P(D/A\&B\&C\&K)$.

Applying (3) and substitution a couple of more times and rearranging terms, we have

(8) $P(E/K) \geq P(T/K) \times P(A/K\&T) \times P(B/K\&T\&A) \times P(C/K\&T\&A\&B) \times P(D/K\&T\&A\&B\&C) \times P(E/K\&T\&A\&B\&C\&D)$,

which was to be demonstrated.

In some cases these values were intervals rather than real numbers, sharp probabilities. That's no problem; since we are in any event winding up with the statement that $P(G/K)$ is equal to or greater than some number, what we do is just use the lower bounds of the intervals. Doing the arithmetic, in the present case we wind up with the proposition that $P(E/K)$ is at least .21. If instead of using just the lower bounds, we use the midpoints of the intervals assigned, we find that $P(G/K)$ is at least .35. Suppose we stick with the midpoint (rather than the lower bound): then our argument entitles us to say only that the probability of G on K is at least .35. It could be higher, of course, but all we can say with confidence, given the argument, is that it is equal to or greater than .35.

Now of course it is ludicrous to assign real numbers to these probabilities: there is vagueness of many kinds here. Not only can't we sensibly assign a real number to any of these probabilities, it also seems wrong to assign them intervals with sharp boundaries; our actual reasoning must be vaguer. Perhaps the best we can really say is that these probabilities are high, or low, or fairly near .5. Still, our reasoning, even if vague, would have to be guided here roughly and vaguely by the calculus of probabilities; and the best way to let it be thus guided is to assign probabilities (and intervals of probability) that comport with the vague estimates we seriously make, and then see what the consequent probabilities would be. When we do this in the present case, in our attempt to estimate the power of a historical argument for G, an argument that doesn't rely on faith or any special theological assumptions, what we can say is only that this probability is at least high enough not to be a whole lot less likely than its denial. Of course we might quibble with the specific values I proposed. But I tried to err on the side of generosity; and even if we assigned somewhat higher probabilities, the result won't change much. The conclusion to be drawn, I think, is that K, our background knowledge, historical and otherwise (excluding what we know by way of faith or revelation), isn't anywhere nearly sufficient to support serious belief in G. If K were all we had to go on, the only sensible course would be agnosticism: "I don't know whether G is true or not: all I can say for sure is that it is not terribly unlikely." The main problem for such a historical case, as I see it, is what we can call the principle of dwindling probabilities: the fact that in giving such a historical argument, we can't simply annex the intermediate propositions to K (as I'm afraid many who employ this sort of argument actually do) but must instead *multiply* the relevant probabilities.

It is for this reason that some such scheme as proposed in the testimonial model is necessary, if we human beings are to be able to know the great truths of the gospel.

VII. Cognitive Renewal

According to Jesus Christ himself, "unless a person is born again, he cannot see the kingdom of God" (John 3:3). And according to the apostle Paul, not as high an authority but still no slouch, a Christian believer becomes a new creature in Christ. The believer enters a process whereby she is regenerated, transformed, made into a new and better person. We might say she acquires a new and better nature. This new and better nature is also a renewal, a restoration of the nature with which humankind was originally created. Sin damaged our nature; regeneration, the work of the Holy Spirit, is (among other things) a matter of setting right and repairing that damage. The ravages of sin were of two sorts. First, *affective* effects: sin induces a sort of madness of the will whereby we fail to love God above all; instead, we love *ourselves* above all. But the damage was also *cognitive*. Sin induces a blindness, dullness, stupidity, imperceptiveness, whereby we are blinded to God, cannot hear his voice, do not recognize his beauty and glory, may even go so far as to deny that he exists.

Regeneration heals the ravages of sin—embryonically in this life, and with ever greater fullness in the next. Just what are the *cognitive* benefits of regeneration? First, there is the repair of the *sensus divinitatis*, so that once again we can see God and be put in mind of him in the sorts of situations in which that belief-producing process is designed to work. The work of the Holy Spirit goes further. It gives us a much clearer view of the beauty, splendor, loveliness, attractiveness, glory of God. It enables us to see something of the spectacular depth of love revealed in the incarnation and atonement. Correlatively, it also gives me a much clearer view of the heinousness of sin, and of the degree and extent to which I am myself enmeshed in it. It gives me a better picture of my own place in the universe. Perhaps I will no longer see myself as the center of things, or see my wants, needs, and desires as more important and more worthy of fulfillment than anyone else's. I may come to see that I fit in as one of God's children, all of enormous value even if all vastly less important and valuable than God, and all equally important and valuable. There is also a certain reflexive benefit. Part of the model I am presenting is itself the main line of Christian belief, and it is part of the model that cognitive regeneration enables us to see that part of the model as indeed true.

John Calvin summarizes some of these cognitive benefits in his famous spectacles metaphor:

> Just as old or bleary-eyed men and those with weak vision, if you thrust before them a most beautiful volume, even if they recognize it to be some sort of writing, yet can scarcely construe two words, but with the aid of spectacles will begin to read distinctly; so Scripture, gathering up the otherwise confused knowledge of God in our minds, having dispersed our dullness, clearly shows us the true God. (*Institutes*, p. 70)

Here Calvin is suggesting that what we learn from Scripture and by way of faith gathers, focuses, and clarifies what we learn by way of the *sensus divinitatis*, enabling us to see God and his love, glory, beauty, and the like with much higher resolution. He could have added that it also gives us a clearer view of our world: we now see what is most important about all the furniture of heaven and earth—namely, that it has been created by God. We can even come to see, if we reflect, what is most important about numbers, propositions, properties, states of affairs, and possible worlds: namely, that they really are divine thoughts or concepts.[71]

Still further, it enables us to see what is most important about ourselves, and in so doing removes the defeater that is the Achilles' heel of naturalism. As we saw in chapter 7, one of the most far-reaching of the noetic effects of sin is that it skews belief about our

---

71. See Thomas Morris and Christopher Menzel, "Absolute Creation," *American Philosophical Quarterly* (October 1986) and Christopher Menzel, "Theism, Platonism, and the Metaphysics of Mathematics," in *Christian Theism and the Problems of Philosophy*, ed. Michael Beaty (Notre Dame: University of Notre Dame Press, 1990). This 'theistic conceptualism' is controversial, though certainly the majority opinion in the tradition of those theists who have thought about it.

origins and the origins of our cognitive systems: it prevents us from seeing that we are the creatures of a just and loving God who has created us in his own image. We may come, instead, to think that God is terrible and to be feared rather than a good and loving Father, or distant and far off, or indifferent to us and our welfare; we may come to embrace some version of austere theism, or even agnosticism or naturalism. As we saw in chapter 7, the probability that our cognitive faculties are reliable, given any of these views of God, is low or inscrutable. Now consider anyone who accepts the view in question, and who sees the epistemic relation between that view and R, the proposition that his cognitive faculties are reliable. Such a person has a defeater for R—a defeater that can't itself be defeated. And *that* means that he suffers from still another noetic deficiency: he has a defeater for any of his own beliefs and is therefore in an irrational condition. But the restoration and healing induced by the work of the Holy Spirit also counters this noetic effect of sin. It restores us to a position of seeing that we have been created in God's image; in so doing, it removes that defeater.

> A popular objection to the evolutionary argument against naturalism is a *tu quoque*—briefly, "the same to you, buddy." Perhaps the most challenging version of this objection is by Keith Lehrer. Consider theism (and call it 'T')—not austere theism, but theism itself, including the proposition that we and our cognitive faculties have been created by a just and loving God and created in his image. What is P(R/T)? Well, maybe not as high as you think. The fact that God is just and loving doesn't prevent all the ills we human beings are heir to—warfare, cruelty, starvation, earthquakes, flood, fire, and pestilence. Granted, God has his own good reasons for permitting these things; still, they do indeed occur, and so are clearly compatible with our having been created by a just and loving Father. So even if God created humankind, he might for his own good reasons permit us to suffer from cognitive malfunction of some sort, cognitive disease or disorder; and such cognitive disorder could inhibit the reliability of our cognitive faculties. Even if God is wholly good, he has or may have permitted Satan to introduce widespread natural evil into the world; but then might he not also permit Satan (that father of lies) to introduce widespread error into the world? (Indeed, hasn't he done exactly that by permitting us to fall into sin?) Lehrer develops this thought:
>
> Compare, finally,
>
> > S Satan and his cohorts produce incredible deceps of error
>
> with
>
> > E Evolutionary processes produce incredible deceps of error.
>
> I find little to choose between them. A naturalist wishing to assign a high probability to the conclusion that the proper

functioning of our faculties yields truth because they are
the result of evolution must assign a low probability to E,
while a supernaturalist wishing to assign a high probability
to the conclusion that the proper functioning of our faculties yields truth because they are designed by God must assign a low probability to S.[72]

And as a matter of fact, of course, according to Christianity precisely this
or something like it *has* happened: God has permitted us to fall into sin
with its attendant noetic effects. So what is $P(R/T)$? Wouldn't we have to
say it is low or at any rate inscrutable, just like $P(R/N\&E)$? So won't the
theist join the naturalist in having a defeater for any of his beliefs? Won't
he be in the very same leaky epistemic boat?

This is a formidable objection; there is a reply.[73] For the Christian
doesn't accept just *theism*; she also accepts the rest of the Christian story,
including fall (along with corruption of the image of God), redemption,
regeneration, and the consequent repair and restoration of that image.
She believes she knows these truths by way of divine revelation. But she
also knows, so she thinks, the truth of theism by way of divine revelation. And this delivers her (or rather R) from defeat. Consider an analogy. Suppose you tell me that

> (1) Feike is a very wealthy eccentric who loves to wear dilapidated
>   old clothes from the local Goodwill.

Acting on the principle that it is always a good idea to acquire some new
true beliefs, I infer

> (2) Feike wears dilapidated old clothes.

I have also believed for some time that

> (3) Feike is a millionaire.

But now I note that $P((3)/(2))$ is low (most people who wear dilapidated
old clothes are not millionaires); I conclude in considerable puzzlement
that (2) is a defeater, for me, of (3), and do my best to refrain from believing (3). My error is plain: (2) isn't, in fact, a defeater for (3), for me.
Why not? Well, for one thing, because I see that the warrant (2) has for
me is derivative from the warrant (1) has for me, and obviously (1) is
not, for me, a defeater for (3). But that means that (2) is not a defeater
of (3). If you would like a principle, try:

> (4) If (i) S believes A, B, and C, and (ii) S believes that the warrant B
>   has for her is derivative from the warrant A has for her, and (3)

72. In his "Proper Function vs. Systematic Coherence," in *Warrant in Contemporary Epistemology: Essays in Honor of Plantinga's Theory of Knowledge,* ed. Jonathan
Kvanvig (Lanham, Md.: Rowman and Littlefield, 1996), pp. 29–30.
73. See my "Respondeo," in *Warrant in Contemporary Epistemology,* pp. 333–38.

> *S* believes that *A* is not a defeater, for her, of *C*, then *B* is not a defeater, for *S*, of *C*.[74]

This principle, as I say, delivers R from defeat, for the Christian theist (and also delivers the evolutionary argument against naturalism from defeat by that *tu quoque*). For the Christian theist believes that she knows the whole Christian story, or that at any rate it has some considerable warrant for her. Theism is part of that story, and the warrant theism has for her is derivative from the warrant had for her of the whole Christian story. Hence by (4) theism won't be a defeater of R for her unless the whole Christian story is. But it isn't. Therefore, theism isn't a defeater of R, for her, and the objection crumbles.

To recount the essential features of the model, the internal instigation of the Holy Spirit working in concord with God's teaching in Scripture is a cognitive process or belief-producing mechanism that produces in us the beliefs constituting faith, as well as a host of other beliefs. These beliefs, of course, will seem to the believer to be true: that is part of what it is for them to be *beliefs*. They will have the internal features of belief, of seeming to be true; and they can have this to various degrees. Second, according to the model, these beliefs will be justified; they will also have at least two further kinds of virtues. In the first place, they are internally rational, in the sense that the believer's response to the experience she has (given prior belief) is within the range permitted by rationality, that is, by proper function; there is nothing pathological there. And in the second place, the beliefs in question will have warrant: they will be produced by cognitive processes functioning properly in an appropriate environment according to a design plan successfully aimed at the production of true belief. To be sure, the process in question is not like the ordinary belief-producing mechanisms we have just by virtue of creation; it will be by a special work of the Holy Spirit. Recall Hume's sarcastic gibe:

> Upon the whole, we may conclude that the *Christian Religion* not only was at first attended with miracles, but even at this day cannot be believed by any reasonable person without one. . . . Whoever is moved by *Faith* to assent to it, is conscious of a continued miracle in his own person, which subverts all the principles of his understanding, and gives him a determination to believe what is most contrary to custom and experience.[75]

---

74. Here 'derivative from' must be construed narrowly, so that the paradigm case of the warrant of p's being derivative, for me, from the warrant of q is (as in this case) where I infer p from q (explicitly or implicitly). In fact, (4) can be strengthened by weakening the antecedent in various ways.

75. *An Enquiry concerning Human Understanding* (LaSalle, Ill.: Open Court Publishing, 1956), p. 145.

According to the testimonial model, Hume (sarcasm aside) is partly right: belief in the main lines of the gospel is produced in Christians by a special work of the Holy Spirit, not by the belief-producing faculties and processes with which we were originally created. Further, some of what Christians believe (e.g., that a human being was dead and then arose from the dead) *is* as Hume says, contrary to custom and experience: it seldom happens. Of course it doesn't follow, contrary to Hume's implicit suggestion, that there is anything irrational or contrary to reason in believing it, given the internal instigation of the Holy Spirit.

What I claim for this model is that there aren't any successful philosophical objections to it (and in chapter 10 I'll look into some objections); so far as philosophical considerations go, given the truth of Christian belief, this model, or something very much like it, could be no more than the sober truth. Of course there may be philosophical objections to the truth of Christian belief itself; I shall consider some of them in part IV under the guise of defeaters. But the point here is that if Christian belief is true, then it could very well have warrant in the way proposed here. If (as I claim) the fact is there are no good philosophical objections to the model, given the *truth* of Christian belief, then any successful objection to the model will also have to be a successful objection to the truth of Christian belief.

We can take the matter a step further. If Christian belief is true, then very likely it does have warrant—if not in the way proposed in the extended A/C model, then in some other similar way. For if it is true, then, indeed, there is such a person as God, who has created us in his image; we have fallen into sin and require salvation; and the means to such restoral and renewal have been provided in the incarnation, suffering, death, and resurrection of Jesus Christ, the second person of the trinity. Furthermore, the typical way of appropriating this restoral is by way of faith, which, of course, involves belief in these things—that is, belief in the great things of the gospel. If so, however, God would intend that we be able to be aware of these truths. And if *that* is so, the natural thing to think is that the cognitive processes that do indeed produce belief in the central elements of the Christian faith are aimed by their designer at producing that belief. But then these beliefs will have warrant.

Someone who has read his Gettier[76] might object: "Isn't it possible God has created a certain process p in us for coming to know the great things of the gospel; this process p usually malfunctions, producing no belief at all; while another process p^* also (and serendipitously) malfunctions, in precisely such a way as to produce

---

76. See WPF, pp. 32ff.

in us the very beliefs *p* would have produced, had it not malfunctioned? Then the Christian story would be true, but Christian belief would have no warrant." No doubt this scenario is possible, even if a bit far-fetched. Even if it happened, however, it wouldn't follow that Christian belief, thus produced, lacks warrant. Even if Christian belief was (improbably) produced by a process *p** originally designed for some other purpose, it wouldn't follow that Christian belief does not have warrant. For perhaps God has *adopted p** and its new way of working as part of the design plan for human beings. Then, once more, Christian belief would have warrant, even if in a bit of a roundabout way.

Finally, I should like to ask how my project in this book compares with William Alston's in his magisterial *Perceiving God*.[77] There is much similarity and overlap, but also important difference. First, the central thesis of Alston's book is that "experiential awareness of God, or as I shall be saying, the *perception* of God, makes an important contribution to the grounds of religious belief " (p. 1). The religious beliefs in question are of two sorts: "beliefs to the effect that God is doing something currently *vis-à-vis* the subject—comforting, strengthening, guiding . . . —or to the effect that God has some (allegedly) perceivable property— goodness, power, lovingness" (p. 1). What kind of contribution does experiential awareness of God make to the grounds of such beliefs? "More specifically, a person can become justified in holding certain kinds of beliefs about God by virtue of perceiving God as being or doing so-and-so" (p. 1). Alston's central claim, I think, is that this experiential awareness of God (i.e., what seems to the subject to be experiential awareness of God) makes it possible for the believer to be *practically rational* in the doxastic practices in question, and practically rational to take these practices to be a source of epistemic justification. (See chapter 4 above for my evaluation of the success of this claim.)

My project differs in three ways. First, I am concerned not primarily with beliefs of the two sorts Alston mentions, but rather with the central claims or beliefs of the Christian faith. I am not limiting my attention to beliefs about God's (allegedly) perceptible properties or his current actions with respect to the believer. My aim, instead, is to examine the epistemic status of the great things of the gospel: that Jesus Christ is the second person of the trinity, that he became incarnate, suffered, died, and rose from the dead, and that by atoning for our sins he made it possible for us human beings to achieve a right relationship with God. Second, the epistemic property in which I am most interested is not justification, taken either deontologically or in the way in which Alston takes it, but warrant: does Christian belief have, can it have, the property enough of which is what distinguishes knowledge from mere

---

77. Ithaca: Cornell University Press, 1991. Subsequent page references are to this book. See above, chapter 5.

true belief? And can it (if true) have enough of that property to constitute knowledge? Third, I don't argue that these Christian beliefs have or
can have warrant by way of *perception* or experiential awareness of God
or of his presence or his properties, but by way of faith.

An Alston-like project in the neighborhood of my project would be
an effort to argue that the kinds of beliefs he mentions—that God has
some perceptible property, that he is acting a certain way *vis-à-vis* the believer—*could* have warrant by way of perception (there aren't any successful philosophical objections to the claim that they do) and that from
a Christian perspective the most satisfactory way of thinking of their
warrant is in terms of perception of God and his properties: if Christian
belief is, in fact, true, then (probably) these beliefs *do* have warrant in
these ways. What about these suggestions? First, I take it Alston has adequately (and more than adequately) disposed of the main philosophical objections to the thought that we human beings can perceive God
and perceive that he is amiable, delightful, powerful, glorious, loving,
and the like. On this point, Alston is close to Jonathan Edwards, who is
best construed, as I argued above, as holding that we do (not merely
can) perceive God and perceive these things of him.

I have just one comment to make here. There is no doubt that
human beings *seem* to experience God, and to experience him *as* being
these things. To many, it has indeed seemed that God is present to their
consciousness in something like the way in which any perceptible object
can be present to my consciousness; it is equally clear that it has seemed
to many that they experience God *as* having the properties in question.
But are these really cases of seeming to *perceive*? On the one hand, they
exhibit several salient differences from paradigm cases of perception,
such as perception of trees, horses, other people: in particular, the phenomenology is quite different. (Of course the phenomenology of the
various sensuous modalities of perception themselves also differ from
each other.) On the other hand, there is the crucial similarity that, in this
case as in the paradigm sensory cases, there is that sense of *being in the
presence* of the object in question, the powerful impression that it is *present* or *presented* to one's consciousness. The thing to say, I think, is that
these cases of putative perception of God are such that the term 'perception' applies to them either perfectly straightforwardly, or else by
way of close analogy. Which is it? Perhaps this is not a very important
question. If it isn't precisely perception, it is something closely and analogically related to it, and related in such a way that (if, in fact, things are
as they seem to the believer) it too can perfectly well be a source of warranted belief. So I have a great deal of sympathy for this Alston-like
project and would in fact be prepared to endorse it. Further, while I am
not completely clear about Alston's notion of practical rationality (see
above, pp. 119ff.), I believe it is fairly close to my *internal* rationality; I
would therefore concur with him in thinking that Christian belief does
indeed enjoy these varieties of positive epistemic status.

Where my project differs from Alston's, then, is that I am concerned
not simply with those perceptual (or 'perceptual') beliefs Alston mentions. Further (and on this point I am not, so far as I know, disputing
anything Alston says), I doubt that perception of God, in his sense, is the

central way in which Christian belief is formed. First, as Alston says, it is only the fortunate few who perceive God with any regularity.[78] Second, the sorts of beliefs with which I am centrally concerned do not ordinarily seem to come to the believers in question by way of perception. This is so even when the occasions in question are not ordinary, garden-variety occasions for the formation and sustenance of Christian belief. Thus John Wesley's famous experience:

> In the evening, I went very unwillingly to a society in Aldersgate Street, where one was reading Luther's Preface to the Epistle to the Romans. About a quarter before nine, while he was describing the change which God works in the heart through faith in Christ, I felt my heart strangely warmed. I felt I did trust in Christ, Christ alone for salvation; and an assurance was given me that he had taken away *my* sins, even *mine* and saved *me* from the law of sin and death.[79]

Here what Wesley comes to believe, or believe more profoundly, is just what the Heidelberg Catechism sees as the content of true faith: that the divine scheme of salvation applies to oneself personally. As far as one can tell, however, this wasn't a matter of *perceiving* God. There was, indeed, sensuous phenomenology ("I felt my heart strangely warmed") and an oft-noted kind of phenomenology; but it doesn't seem to be perceptual. Indeed, it isn't clear that it is *possible* to perceive, for example, that Christ has taken away my sins, or that he is the incarnate second person of the trinity or that he suffered and died, thereby enabling us to have life. Consider also the apostle Paul's vision on the way to Damascus: no doubt he then did perceive Jesus, and furthermore perceived that he said that he was indeed the Christ. So it is certainly possible to perceive Jesus the Christ and perceive that he is *saying* that he is the Christ; still, can we perceive that Jesus actually *is* the Christ? That he actually is the second person of the trinity? I'm inclined to doubt it. And the more ordinary cases where someone's belief in the great things of the gospel comes by way of faith (i.e., Scripture/internal instigation of the Holy Spirit/faith) seem even less properly thought of as cases of perception.

Accordingly, there is indeed such a thing as perceiving God; furthermore, perceiving God plays an important role in the religious and spiritual lives of many Christians, in particular, Christians who have been blessed with considerable progress in the spiritual life. Indeed, we might think, following Edwards, that perceiving God—perceiving that he is lovely, amiable, holy, glorious, and the like—is an essential element in the full-blown, well-rounded Christian life. I agree, furthermore, that these perceptual beliefs can have warrant. The central Christian beliefs, however, are not perceptual beliefs; they come, not by way of perception

---

78. "The experiential awareness of God is a rare phenomenon except for a very few souls" (*Perceiving God*, p. 36).

79. *John Wesley*, ed. Albert Outler (New York: Oxford University Press, 1964), p. 66.

of God, but by way of faith. The warrant those beliefs have is not perceptual warrant; it comes rather by way of faith. In sum, perception of God is an important part of the mature Christian life, but maturity in the Christian life isn't attained by most of us; and even for the fortunate few who do achieve maturity, the warrant their central Christian beliefs enjoy does not come by way of perception. I therefore see Alston's project here as covering only part of the relevant epistemological territory—an important part, but only a part, and not the part by way of which the central beliefs of the Christian faith have warrant.

9

The Testimonial Model:
Sealed upon Our Hearts

Love the Lord your God with all your heart and with all your soul
and with all your mind and with all your strength.

Jesus Christ

If I have the gift of prophecy and can fathom all mysteries and all
knowledge, and if I have a faith that can move mountains, but have
not love, I am nothing.

St. Paul

He that has doctrinal knowledge and speculation only, without
affection, never is engaged in the business of religion.

Jonathan Edwards

I. BELIEF AND AFFECTION

In chapter 8, I proposed a model to show how Christian belief can
have warrant. On this model, Christian belief is produced in the believer by the internal instigation of the Holy Spirit, endorsing the
teachings of Scripture, which is itself divinely inspired by the Holy
Spirit. The result of the work of the Holy Spirit is *faith*—which,
according to both John Calvin and the model, is "a firm and certain
knowledge of God's benevolence towards us, founded upon the truth
of the freely given promise in Christ, both revealed to our minds and
sealed upon our hearts through the Holy Spirit." According to the
model, these beliefs enjoy justification, rationality, and warrant. We

may therefore say with Calvin that they are "revealed to our minds." There is more, however; they are also "sealed upon our hearts." What could this latter mean, and how does it figure into the model? Given that these truths are revealed to our minds, what more could we need? Why must they also be sealed upon our hearts? To answer, suppose we ask whether one could hold the beliefs in question but nonetheless fail to have faith. The traditional Christian answer is, "Well yes: the demons believe and they shudder" (James 2:19);[1] but the demons do not have faith. So what is the difference? What more is there to faith than belief? What distinguishes the Christian believer from the demons?

According to the model,[2] the shape of the answer is given in the text just mentioned: the demons *shudder*. They *believe* these things, but *hate* them; and they also hate God. Perhaps they also hope against hope that these things aren't really so, or perhaps they believe them in a self-deceived way. They know of God's power and know that they have no hope of winning any contest of power with him; nevertheless, they engage in just such a contest, perhaps in that familiar self-deceived condition of really knowing, in one sense, that they couldn't possibly win such a contest, while at some other level nevertheless refusing to accept this truth, or hiding it from themselves.[3] Or perhaps the problem here is not merely cognitive but *affective*: knowing that they couldn't possibly win, they insist on fighting anyway, thinking of themselves as courageously Promethean, as heroically contending against nearly insuperable odds, a condition, they point out, in which God never finds himself, and hence a way in which they can think of themselves as his moral superior. The devils also know of God's wonderful scheme for the salvation of human beings, but they find this scheme—with its mercy and suffering love— offensive and unworthy. No doubt they endorse Nietzsche's notion that Christian love (including the love displayed in incarnation and atonement) is weak, whining, resentful, servile, duplicitous, pusillanimous, tergiversatory, and in general unappealing.

1. Perhaps this needs qualification. The content of faith is plausibly *indexical*: a person *x* has faith only if *x* believes or knows that God is benevolent toward *x herself*. But perhaps the devils do not believe that God is benevolent toward *them*. They know that God is all-powerful, all-knowing, and perfectly good, and that he has arranged a way of salvation for human beings; but perhaps they reject the belief that God is benevolent toward them. (Note, incidentally, that the author of *James* sometimes (in chapter 2, e.g.) seems to use the term 'faith' to mean mere cognitive or intellectual assent.)

2. And perhaps also according to Calvin. He sees this sealing, as in the first instance, a matter of God's putting his mark, imprint, seal upon the believer; but perhaps this seal consists in the believer's having the appropriate affections.

3. See Milton's *Paradise Lost*, books 5 and 6.

The person with faith, however, not only believes the central claims of the Christian faith; she also (paradigmatically) finds the whole scheme of salvation enormously attractive, delightful, moving, a source of amazed wonderment. She is deeply grateful to the Lord for his great goodness and responds to his sacrificial love with love of her own. The difference between believer and devil, therefore, lies in the area of *affections*: of love and hate, attraction and repulsion, desire and detestation. In traditional categories, the difference lies in the orientation of the *will*. Not primarily in the *executive* function of the will (the function of making decisions, of seeking and avoiding various states of affairs), though of course that is also involved, but in its *affective* function, its function of loving and hating, finding attractive or repellent, approving or disapproving. And the believer, the person with faith, has the right beliefs, but also the right affections. Conversion and regeneration alters affection as well as belief.

According to Calvin, it is the Holy Spirit who is responsible for this sealing upon our hearts of that firm and certain knowledge of God's benevolence toward us; it is the Holy Spirit who is responsible for this renewal and redirection of affections. Calvin is sometimes portrayed as spiritually cold, aloof, bloodless, rationalistic—a person in whom intellect unduly predominates. These charges may (or may not) have some validity with respect to the Reformed scholasticism of a century later; even a cursory examination of Calvin's work, however, reveals that with respect to him they are wildly inaccurate.[4] Calvin's emblem was a flaming heart on an outstretched hand; it bore the motto: *Cor meum quasi immolatum tibi offero, Domine*.[5] Of the Holy Spirit, he says that "persistently boiling away and burning up our vicious and inordinate desires, he enflames our hearts with the love of God and with zealous devotion."[6] The *Institutes* are throughout aimed

---

4. See, e.g., Dennis Tamburello, *Union with Christ: John Calvin and the Mysticism of St. Bernard* (Louisville, Ky: Westminster John Knox Press, 1994), chapters 1–3.

5. "My heart, as if aflame, I offer to you, Oh Lord." This particular phenomenology—a phenomenology that is naturally expressed in terms of one's heart being warmed or even aflame—goes back in the Christian tradition at least to the disciples who met the risen Christ on the road to Emmaus: "Then their eyes were opened and they recognized him, and he disappeared from their sight. They asked each other 'Were not our hearts burning within us while he talked with us on the road and opened the Scriptures to us?'" (Luke 24:31–32). There are parallel passages in Aquinas; and in *Preface to the Epistle to the Romans* (1522), Luther says that faith "sets the heart aflame." John Wesley reports, "As one was reading Luther's *Preface to Romans* . . . I felt my heart strangely warmed." In the Orthodox tradition, St. Seraphim of Sarov reports something similar (see William Abraham, "The Epistemological Significance of the Inner Witness of the Holy Spirit," *Faith and Philosophy* 7, no. 4, p. 440).

6. John Calvin, *Institutes of the Christian Religion*, ed. John T. McNeill and tr. Ford Lewis Battles (Philadelphia: Westminster Press, 1960 [originally published in 1559]), III, i, 3, p. 540.

at the *practice* of the Christian life (which essentially involves the affections), not at theological theory; the latter enters only in the service of the former.

So the initial difference between believer and demon is a matter of affections: the former is inspired to gratitude and love, the latter to fear, hatred, and contempt. The Holy Spirit produces knowledge, in the believer; in sealing this knowledge to our hearts, however, it also produces the right affections. Chief among these right affections is love of God—desire for God, desire to know him, to have a personal relationship with him, desire to achieve a certain kind of unity with him, as well as delight in him, relishing his beauty, greatness, holiness, and the like. There is also trust, approval, gratitude, intending to please, expecting good things, and much more. Faith, therefore, isn't just a matter of believing certain propositions—not even the momentous propositions of the gospel. Faith is more than belief; in producing faith, the Holy Spirit does more than produce in us the belief that this or that proposition is indeed true. As Aquinas repeats four times in five pages, "the Holy Spirit makes us lovers of God."[7] And according to Martin Luther,

> there are two ways of believing. In the first place I may have faith *concerning* God. This is the case when I hold to be true what is said concerning God. Such faith is on the same level with the assent I give to statements concerning the Turk, the devil and hell. A faith of this kind should be called knowledge or information rather than faith. In the second place there is faith *in*. Such faith is mine when I not only hold to be true what is said concerning God, but when I put my trust in him in such a way as to enter into personal relations with him, believing firmly that I shall find him to be and to do as I have been taught. . . . The word *in* is well chosen and deserving of due attention. We do not say, I believe God the Father or concerning God the Father, but *in* God the Father, *in* Jesus Christ, and *in* the Holy Spirit.[8]

Following Luther, we may distinguish *believing in God* from believing *that God exists*. The latter itself comes in two varieties: theism, and believing *de re* of God that he exists. A theist is one who believes a certain proposition: that there is an all-powerful, all-knowing, wholly good person who has created and sustains the world. Where God is indeed the unique being meeting this condition, the theist believes that there is such a being, but also, no doubt, believes of God, the being who in fact

---

7. *Summa contra Gentiles*, tr. Charles J. O'Neil (Notre Dame: University of Notre Dame Press, 1975), Bk. 4, ch. 21, 22 (pp. 122, 125, 126).

8. *Luther's Catechetical Writings*, tr. J. N. Lenker, 2 vols. (Minneapolis: Lutheran Press, 1907), 1:203, quoted in H. R. Niebuhr, *Faith on Earth* (New Haven: Yale University Press, 1989), p. 9. Consider also Pascal: "So those to whom God has imparted religion through the feeling of the heart are very fortunate and justly convinced" (*Pensées*, tr. M. Turnell [London: Harvill Press, 1962], p. 282).

meets this description, that he exists. It isn't necessary, however, that he does the latter; perhaps he forms the *de dicto* belief but never performs the *de re* act of believing something or other *of* the being in question. It is even clearer that one can believe of God that he exists without being a theist: one can believe of God that he exists even if one is (from the theist's point of view) confused and mistaken about what properties God has. Perhaps I encounter God in experience, believing that he loves me, or perhaps I pick him out as the being that my parents worship. Then I will believe of God that he exists, even if I fail (for example) to believe that God created the world. (Perhaps, like some Mormons, I think God himself was created, and add that the world has always existed and was not created.) It is even possible to believe of God that he exists and be an atheist: I encounter God in experience, believe of the thing that I encounter that it exists, but fail to believe that this thing I encounter is all-powerful or all-knowing or wholly good, or has created the world; and I also believe that there is nothing that has those properties. Believing *in* God, of course, is different from either believing of God that he exists or being a theist. The demons, no doubt, are theists and also believe of God that he exists; the demons do not believe in God, because they do not trust and love God and do not make his purposes their own.

II. JONATHAN EDWARDS

Our topic, therefore, essentially involves the affections. In trying to understand the religious affections, we can obviously do no better than to consult Jonathan Edwards, one of the great masters of the interior life and a peerless student of the religious affections. Edwards, of course, concurs with Calvin that true religion is more than just right belief. Indeed, according to him, true religion is first a matter of having the right affections: "True religion, in great part, consists in holy affections."[9] "The Holy Scriptures do everywhere place religion very much in the affections; such as fear, hope, love, hatred, desire, joy, sorrow, gratitude, compassion and zeal" (p. 102). Mere knowledge isn't enough for true religion:

> There is a distinction to be made between a mere notional understanding, wherein the mind only beholds things in the exercise of a speculative faculty; and the sense of the heart, wherein the mind don't only speculate and behold, but relishes and feels. That sort of knowledge, by which a man has a sensible perception of amiableness and loathsomeness, or of sweetness and nauseousness, is not just the same sort of knowledge with that, by which he knows what a triangle is, and what a square is. The one is mere speculative knowledge; the other sensible knowledge, in which more than the mere

9. *A Treatise concerning Religious Affections*, ed. John E. Smith (New Haven: Yale University Press, 1959 [first published 1746]), p. 95. Page references to *Religious Affections* are to this edition.

intellect is concerned; the heart is the proper subject of it, or the soul as a being that not only beholds, but has inclination, and is pleased or displeased. (p. 272)

Of course he doesn't think true religion is *just* a matter of affections, of loves and hates, as if belief and understanding had no role to play: "Holy affections are not heat without light; but evermore arise from some information of the understanding, some spiritual instruction that the mind receives, some light or actual knowledge" (p. 266). Still, true religion *primarily* involves (so he seems to say) the affections, in particular love: "all true religion summarily consists in the love of divine things" (p. 271). And love brings other affections in its train: "love to God," he says, "causes a man to delight in the thoughts of God, and to delight in the presence of God and to desire conformity to God, and the enjoyment of God" (p. 208); elsewhere, he adds that one who loves God will also delight in contemplating the great things of the gospel, taking pleasure in them, finding them attractive, marvelous, winsome (p. 250). Further, one who thus delights in the great truths of the gospel may find himself disgusted by various attempts (see chapter 2) to trade that splendidly rich and powerful gospel for cheap and trivial substitutes. Still further, acquiring the right affections enables one to see the true heinousness of sin: "he who sees the beauty of holiness, must necessarily see the hatefulness of sin, its contrary" (p. 274); and he who *sees* the hatefulness of sin (in himself and others) will also (given proper function) *hate* it.

A. Intellect and Will: Which Is Prior?

But how exactly is this supposed to work? What is the relation between affection and belief here, between will and intellect? Which, if either, is primary? Is it that first one sees (i.e., comes to know or believe) that the great things of the gospel and God himself are lovely and amiable, and then comes to love them? Or is it rather that first one comes to love them, thus coming to see that the things in question are, indeed, worthy of love? In working in our hearts, does the Holy Spirit first and supernaturally get us to see the truths of the great things of the gospel, our affections naturally following suit (so that we come to love and delight in them)? Or is it rather that the Holy Spirit first corrects our affections, cures the madness of our wills, so that we begin to love God above all rather than ourselves, as a result of which we come to believe the great things of the gospel? Or is neither prior, so that will and intellect are cured simultaneously? This question, of course, is connected with a correlative question we examined in chapter 7: is sin primarily a matter of intellect, of blindness, of failing to see or believe the right things, thus leading to wrong affection and wrong action? Or is it primarily a matter of the wrong affections, of loving and hating the wrong things?

Although Edwards emphasizes the centrality of the affections, he also seems to endorse the position that intellect is prior to will. He seems to suggest that the believer first *sees* the beauty, amiability, loveliness of God and the great things of the gospel, her affections then naturally following:

> [The saints] first see that God is lovely, and that Christ is excellent and glorious, and their hearts are first captivated with this view, and the exercises of their love are wont from time to time to begin here, and to arise primarily from these views; and then, consequentially, they see God's love; and great favor to them. (p. 246)

Here the focus of his attention isn't the question whether it is intellect or will that is prior (but whether the saints first see that God loves them and then come themselves to love God, or the other way around). Nevertheless, there is the clear suggestion that what happens first is that the saint sees that God is lovely and Christ excellent and glorious; this vision is captivating, delightful, winsome; the result is love for God. Elsewhere he is more explicit: "Knowledge is the key that first opens the hard heart and enlarges the affections, and so opens the way for men into the kingdom of heaven" (p. 266); "Gracious affections do arise from the mind's being enlightened, rightly and spiritually to understand or apprehend divine things." Furthermore,

> Truly spiritual and gracious affections . . . arise from the enlightening of the understanding to understand the things that are taught of God and Christ, in a new manner, the coming to a new understanding of the excellent nature of God, and his wonderful perfections, some new view of Christ in his spiritual excellencies and fullness, or things opened to him in a new manner, that appertain to the way of salvation by Christ, whereby he now sees how it is, and understands those divine and spiritual doctrines which once were foolishness to him. . . . That all gracious affections do arise from some instruction or enlightening of the understanding, is therefore a further proof. (pp. 267, 268)

This apparently fits less than perfectly well with another of Edwards's characteristic doctrines: that what lies at the bottom of sin is *hardness of heart*—which, he says, is a matter of having the wrong affections, or (less disastrously) at any rate lacking the right affections:

> Divines are generally agreed, that sin radically and fundamentally consists in what is negative, or privative, having its root and foundation in a privation or want of holiness. And therefore undoubtedly, if it be so that sin does very much consist in hardness of heart, and so in the want of pious affections of heart; holiness does consist very much in those pious affections. (p. 118)

Now by a hard heart, is plainly meant an unaffected heart, or a heart not easy to be moved with virtuous affections, like a stone, insensible, stupid, unmoved and hard to be impressed. Hence the hard heart is called [in Scripture] a stony heart, and is opposed to an heart of flesh, that has feeling, and is sensibly touched and moved. (p. 117)

These passages suggest (as I argued in chapter 7) that sin is fundamentally a matter of failing to have the right affections and having the wrong ones; it isn't (in the first instance, anyway) a failure of knowledge. It is less a failure to *see* something than to *feel* something.[10] The hard-hearted person fails to love the right things; he lacks the virtuous affections of love for the Lord and neighbor and for the great truths of the gospel; he also lacks the hatred and sorrow for sin, gratitude for salvation, joy, peace, and all the rest that flow from a proper love of God. And *that* suggests that on receiving the gift of faith and the rebirth (regeneration) that goes with it, what happens is that the affections are redirected, so that one makes at least the first halting steps in the direction of loving God above all.

Somehow consequent upon that is a new knowledge of the loveliness and gloriousness of God and of the Christian story as well. Still, this suggestion is compatible with the thought that in acquiring faith it is a kind of knowledge or enlightenment that is prior. Perhaps sin is, indeed, a malfunction of the will (a misdirection of affection); perhaps this malfunction is, indeed, what is repaired with regeneration; but perhaps the way this repair is effected is by way of being granted a certain kind of knowledge or enlightenment. It can be both that sin is fundamentally malfunction or dysfunction of the will, and that what comes first in regeneration is a certain understanding or insight. Then revealing would be prior to sealing, with respect to faith, even though what needs repair is, at bottom, will rather than intellect.

Sometimes Edwards seems to suggest that neither intellect nor will is prior:

Spiritual understanding consists primarily in a sense of heart of that spiritual beauty. I say, a sense of heart; for it is not speculation merely that is concerned in this kind of understanding: nor can there be a clear distinction made between the two faculties of understanding and will, as acting distinctly and separately, in this matter. When the mind is sensible of the sweet beauty and amiableness of a thing, that implies a sensibleness of sweetness and delight in the

---

10. Though of course I don't mean to suggest for a moment that an affection is simply a *feeling* of some sort, as if it had no intentional component.

presence of the idea of it; and this sensibleness of the amiableness or delightfulness of beauty, carries in the very nature of it, the sense of the heart; or an effect and impression the soul is the subject of, as a substance possessed of taste, inclination and will. (p. 272)

If there is no clear distinction between the two, then clearly neither is prior to the other. Even in this passage, however, it looks as if, according to Edwards, intellect really is prior. He speaks here of "a sense of heart"; that *sounds* like affection, but I think appearances are deceiving. To see how, we must note one further characteristic Edwardsian idea: that upon conversion and regeneration the believer acquires a "new simple idea." She thus acquires the ability to perceive something she wasn't able to perceive before. She can now perceive the beauty and amiability of the Lord, something she was unable to do prior to conversion. This ability involves a new phenomenology, one not available to "natural men":

For if there be in the saints a kind of apprehension or perception, which is in its nature, perfectly diverse from all that natural men have, or that it is possible they should have, till they have a new nature; it must consist in their having a certain kind of ideas or sensations of mind, which are simply diverse from all that is or can be in the minds of natural men. And that is the same thing as to say, that it consists in the sensations of a new spiritual sense. (p. 271)

Here Edwards speaks the epistemological language of the mid-eighteenth century. Knowledge or cognition involves mental entities Locke calls 'ideas' and Hume 'impressions and ideas'. These are on the order of mental images, like bits of visual or auditory imagery or other sensuous imagery. The details of the process, as the British empiricists thought of it, need not concern us now (and in any event are incoherent). But (to take an Edwardsian example) think of the taste of honey. You know what honey tastes like, and that knowledge crucially involves a certain kind of phenomenology. You wouldn't know what honey tastes like unless you actually tasted it (or in some other way experienced that taste). You can't have knowledge (more exactly, sensible knowledge) of the taste of honey or of its sweetness, without undergoing that phenomenology—without having that simple idea (as Edwards would think of it). There is a certain kind of experience that normally goes with seeing something red, and there is a certain kind of knowledge, namely, knowledge of what it's like to see something red, that you aren't able to have unless you have that experience. (Maybe this experience is a little like hearing the sound of a trumpet; still, that kind of analogy can take us only so far.) One who has never tasted sweetness or perceived red can know a good deal about the sweetness of honey and the look of something red (e.g., that both are experienced by many people, that people find the first pleasant and the second mildly exciting); there is also something she doesn't know, namely, what honey tastes like and what a sunset looks like.

Now according to Edwards, one kind of experiential knowledge is spiritual knowledge; more exactly, there is such a thing as spiritual knowledge, and spiritual knowledge *is* experiential knowledge. This is knowledge of God's 'moral' qualities, as Edwards puts it—knowledge of his holiness, loveliness, beauty, glory, and amiability. Like knowledge of the taste and sweetness of honey, this knowledge requires that one have a certain characteristic phenomenal imagery, "a certain kind of ideas or sensations of mind," as he puts it. This is a *new* idea and a new *simple* idea. It is simple, first, because (unlike the image of a house, say) it is not compounded out of other ideas. And it is new in the sense that it is not available to "natural men"; it is available only to those in whom the process of regeneration has begun. In the fall into sin, Edwards thinks, we human beings lost a certain cognitive ability: the ability to apprehend God's moral qualities. With conversion comes regeneration; part of the latter is the regeneration (to a greater or lesser extent) of this cognitive ability to grasp or apprehend the beauty, sweetness, amiability of the Lord himself and of the whole scheme of salvation. And it is just this cognitive ability that involves that new simple idea. There is little to say by way of describing this new experience except to say that it is the experience of God's moral qualities; and one who doesn't have this new simple idea—one in whom the cognitive process in question has not been regenerated—doesn't have spiritual knowledge of God's beauty and loveliness.[11] Such a person may know, in a way, that God *is* beautiful and lovely (perhaps she takes this on the authority of someone else), but there is a kind of knowledge of this loveliness she doesn't have (experiential knowledge), and it is precisely this kind of knowledge that is the spiritual knowledge of which Edwards speaks. Spiritual knowledge is experiential knowledge, and a necessary condition of having the latter is having the right phenomenology, the right imagery, the new simple idea.

I spoke of a cognitive ability, the ability to grasp and apprehend the beauty and sweetness and amiability of the Lord and of the great things of the gospel. Edwards constantly uses more specific language, the language of *perception*. One in whom the process of regeneration

11. According to Edwards, those who have the requisite experience and enjoy the requisite phenomenology note that previous to this experience they hadn't really understood such phrases as 'a spiritual sight of Christ'; these terms had not conveyed "those special and distinct ideas to their minds which they were intended to signify; in some respects no more than the names of colors are to convey the ideas to one that is blind from birth" (*The Great Awakening*, ed. C. C. Goen [New Haven: Yale University Press, 1972], p. 174).

has reached a certain point can *see* the beauty of the Lord, *taste* his sweetness, *feel* his presence. I believe Edwards thinks these uses of the terms 'see', 'taste', and 'feel' are figurative or (better) analogical. On the other hand he thinks the term 'perceive' is being used perfectly literally, and in the same sense in which it is used when we speak of sight and hearing, taste and touch as perception. This ability to apprehend the beauty and glory of the Lord is in fact a *perceptual* ability. One may know that the Lord is, indeed, beautiful and glorious; there is also the different condition of *perceiving* that the Lord is beautiful and glorious. Here Edwards appeals to the language of Scripture, which often represents regeneration as a matter of giving eyes to see, ears to hear, unstopping the ears of the deaf, opening the eyes of the blind. It is important to see that Edwards thinks of these properties—beauty, glory, holiness, as well as love and benevolence —as genuine and objective properties, genuinely inhering in God. It isn't that beauty is really a subjective reaction on our part to something or other; rather, there is the property the Lord has of being beautiful; we grasp or apprehend that property and that the Lord has it; and a necessary condition of so doing is undergoing a certain kind of phenomenology. And of course this precisely mirrors the situation with respect to sensory perception.[12]

Edwards believes we perceive these moral qualities of God; and I believe that Edwards's views here are, at the least, plausible. I don't propose to canvass the objections to perception of God, however, or defend its plausibility. That is because this has already been done in fine style by William Alston.[13] Alston shows that none of the objections to perception of God—that only material objects can be perceived (and God isn't a material object), that there aren't the right kinds of tests and measurements, that we can't demonstrate that the alleged perception is veridical and hence really perception, that not everyone has this alleged ability, that people disagree as to what it is that they (as they take it) perceive of God, and all the rest—Alston clearly shows that none of these objections is anywhere nearly cogent. He also develops a powerful generic account of perception according to which perception of God is perfectly possible. If indeed there is such a person as God, there is no reason why he couldn't have endowed us, his creation and his children, with the ability to perceive him and to perceive that he has certain properties.

12. For an insightful account of Edwards's sense of the heart (with extensive and useful quotations from Edwards's works), see William Wainwright's "Jonathan Edwards and the Sense of the Heart," *Faith and Philosophy* 7, no. 1 (January 1990).

13. *Perceiving God* (Ithaca: Cornell University Press, 1991). See also my reply in chapter 10 to Richard Gale's suggestion that perception of God is not possible.

We can now return to the question that occasioned this detour: according to Edwards, which comes first, affection or intellection? Love for God or knowledge of God? I think Edwards's answer is that it is knowledge. I think he thinks that one first perceives the beauty and loveliness of the Lord, first comes to this experiential knowledge, and then comes to develop the right loves and hates: love for the Lord, for the great truths of the gospel, hatred for sin: "all gracious affections do arise from some instruction or enlightening of the understanding"; "Gracious affections do arise from the mind's being enlightened, rightly and spiritually to understand or apprehend divine things." What he means here, I think, is that this experiential knowledge of God and his qualities comes first; then there is a consequent raising of affections. "Truly spiritual and gracious affections . . . arise from . . . some new view of Christ in his spiritual excellencies and fullness." His idea, I think, is that the regenerated person perceives the beauty and loveliness of the Lord and of the great things of the gospel and then, naturally enough, comes to love them. It is the perceiving that comes first; in this respect, therefore, intellect is prior to will.

Is Edwards right? Is it really true that intellect precedes will, that knowledge precedes love in this case? The question divides itself. We may think of the structure of intellect and will as follows. There are various dependency relations among the acts of intellect and will, of such a sort that certain intellectual acts (acts of cognition) are necessary conditions for certain acts of will. Any given act of will could be *basic* in the sense that it doesn't depend on any prior act of intellect, and any given act of intellect could be basic in the sense that it doesn't depend on any prior act of will. Perhaps one can't love God without first seeing that he is, indeed, lovely and attractive; if so, then no act of loving God will be basic in the present sense. On the other hand, perhaps certain affective acts do not depend on any prior acts of intellection; if so, those acts will be basic. What is the relevant sense of *dependency* involved? I suggest that it is a matter of design plan: an act of will is dependent, for a creature S, on a certain act of intellect if and only if S's design plan specifies that S will engage in the act of will in question only consequent upon engaging in the kind of act of intellect in question.[14]

14. Of course there are other kinds of dependency; we could call the variety currently under discussion 'design plan dependency'. For present purposes I'm thinking of design plan dependency as including logical and causal dependency; thus, if a given act of will's (intellect's) occurring entails or causally necessitates a given act of intellect's (will's) occurring, the latter act will be design-plan-dependent on the former.

Given these preliminaries, it is evident that there are several different ways to take the claim that intellect precedes will here. It might be claimed only that

(1) For any affective act of will, there is at least one kind of act of intellect upon which it is dependent, and some acts of intellect are not dependent on any act of will.

By way of illustration, perhaps no one who is functioning properly comes to love God without first seeing, knowing, that God is indeed lovely and attractive (and perhaps that latter cognitive act must involve Edwards's experiential knowledge); but perhaps that cognitive, intellective act of knowing that God is lovely and attractive is not dependent on any (affective) act of will. One comes to see that God is lovely and then (and therefore) loves him. This is quite compatible with there being *some* acts of intellect that are dependent on acts of will; it requires only that there also be some that are not. So it might be held, more strenuously, that

(2) For every (affective) act of will, there is a prior act of intellect on which it is dependent, and for no act of intellect is there a prior act of will on which it is dependent.

It isn't easy to see which (if either) of these Edwards means to assert. And perhaps, indeed, he means to assert neither; perhaps he is thinking just of *religious* affections and the characteristic acts of intellect associated with them. Perhaps he means to claim only that the religious affections depend on a preceding (or concomitant) grasp or perception of some of the qualities of God, although it is not the case that perception of God's moral qualities is dependent on a prior affection. Perhaps he means to say that, in the process of regeneration, what happens first is that the Holy Spirit enables one to perceive something of God's moral qualities; this then (according to the normal working of the design plan) raises one's religious affections. He is committed to this much, but perhaps to nothing stronger.

Still, even this much is too strong. In the state of sin, we are inclined to be indisposed to God and neighbor; this is the essence of our sinful condition. The real problem, then, is a matter of will. It isn't merely that we fail to see the beauty of the Lord and the lovableness of our brothers and sisters, thus failing to love them. Mere absence of the right affections is only part of the problem; there is also the fact that we are inclined to be resentful and dismissive toward the Lord and competitive and self-serving with respect to other people. What is required here isn't, first of all, more knowledge. Given our sinful inclinations to hate God and neighbor, we might perceive God's moral qualities and nonetheless continue to hold him at arm's length, refusing to love him—perhaps thus being in an even worse condition than when his presence was obscured by the smoke of our wrongdoing (Anselm) and we hated him, as it were, from afar.

Edwards might retort that one simply can't perceive the moral qualities of God and fail to love him, to be attracted by him, to find him marvelously delightful and fascinating. This is dubious at best. No doubt one whose affective capacities or faculties are *functioning properly* will love the Lord on perceiving his loveliness, glory, and beauty; no doubt such a person will find him delightful. Conversely, consider someone who did perceive God's beauty and glory but was nonetheless put off by him: such a person would be malfunctioning in some way. (A person who saw God's beauty but didn't love him wouldn't, perhaps, *describe* God as beautiful (although he might describe him as terrible and fascinating, as a bird, transfixed by terror, might describe a snake, or a mariner the horrifying beauty and power of a storm that threatens his life); it doesn't follow that he doesn't, in fact, perceive that beauty.) When intellect and will function properly and are appropriately tuned to each other, we will delight in what we see to be delightful, love what we see to be amiable.[15] A chief component of sin, however, just is dysfunction of the affections; and there is no good reason to think someone suffering from a mad misdirection of affection couldn't be put off by what he saw to be beautiful. Curing the cognitive effects of sin doesn't automatically cure the affective madness. The gift of faith and consequent regeneration isn't just a matter of restoring the intellect to a pristine condition in which we can once again perceive God and his glories and beauties; it also, and essentially, requires curing that madness of the will.

So which is primary in faith and regeneration: intellect or will? I say neither. Sin is a malfunction of the will, a skewing of affections; it is loving and hating the wrong things. Still, it also involves blindness, an inability to see the glory and beauty of the Lord. The answer to the question 'which is prior?' is 'neither' or 'there's no saying'. Regeneration is a matter of curing both intellectual and affective disorders. The structure of will and intellect here is perhaps a spiral, dialectical process: heightened affections enable us to see more of God's beauty and glory; being able to see more of God's beauty and glory and majesty in turn leads to heightened affections. There are certain things you won't know unless you love, have the right affections; there are certain affections you won't have without perceiving some of God's moral qualities; neither perceiving nor affection can be said

---

15. As I see it, therefore, there are such properties as being delightful, desirable, beautiful, and the like; there is also the *cognitive* condition of noting that something is delightful, desirable, or beautiful; in addition, there is the *affective* condition of delighting in the thing in question, or desiring it, or admiring and being drawn to its beauty. I believe Edwards concurs.

to be prior to the other. Regeneration consists in curing the will, so that we at least begin to love and hate the right things; it also includes cognitive renewal, so that we come to perceive the beauty, holiness, and delightfulness of the Lord and of the scheme of salvation he has devised.

B. The Affirmations of Faith

So far we have been speaking of perception of God, religious affections, and relations between them. Now we turn to a different though related question: how is it, according to Edwards, that we come to believe what he calls the great things of the gospel—trinity, incarnation, atonement, and so on? It is one thing to perceive the glory and beauty of the Lord and something quite different to know that Jesus Christ was, in fact, the divine son of God who took on human flesh, and suffered and died, thereby atoning for human sin. Do we also perceive the latter? No. Edwards doesn't believe that we perceive the great truths of the gospel; we do not perceive such qualities of the Lord as that he loved us so much that he sent his only begotten son to suffer and die, thus enabling us to have life. A certain sort of perception may be *involved* in our coming to know these things, but we don't perceive these things themselves:

> A view of this divine glory directly convinces the mind of the divinity of these things, as this glory is in itself a direct, clear and all-conquering evidence of it. . . . He that has his judgment thus directly convinced and assured of the divinity of the things of the gospel, by a clear view of their divine glory, has a reasonable conviction; his belief and assurance is altogether agreeable to reason; because the divine glory and beauty of divine things is in itself, real evidence of their divinity, and the most direct and strong evidence. He that truly sees the divine, transcendent, supreme glory of these things which are divine, does as it were know their divinity intuitively; he not only argues that they are divine, but he sees that they are divine; he sees that in them wherein divinity chiefly consists. (p. 298)

There are two ways of understanding this and similar passages. On the one hand, Edwards might think the believer perceives the divine glory and beauty of the things of the gospel, and then infers from that, in a quick argument, that they are indeed divine, from God, and hence are to be believed. On the other hand, the account could be that the believer sees the loveliness and beauty—divine beauty—of the things of the gospel, and consequently and *immediately* forms the beliefs that these things are true and that they are from God. The difference would be that, in the first case, there is an *inference*, perhaps so quick and inexplicit that one scarcely notices it, but an inference nonetheless. Then the internal instigation of the Holy Spirit would work as follows: the Holy Spirit enables the believer to see the glory and beauty of the gospel, whereupon she infers that they are in fact divine and hence to be believed. The "real evidence" Edwards mentions would be *propositional* evidence: it would be such propositions as *this* (one of the gospel teachings) *is glorious and beautiful*; and the conclusion would be *this teaching is from God (and hence true)*.

On the second construal, a perception of the glory and beauty of the teaching in question would be an *occasion* of the formation of the belief that the teaching is, indeed, from God (and is true), but the transition from the one to the other would not be by way of an inference. The belief in question would be held in the basic way, although occasioned by the perception of something else (the beauty and glory of the teaching in question). This second way would resemble the way in which (as I see it) Calvin thinks the *sensus divinitatis* operates. It isn't that on beholding the glory of the mountains or the majesty of the ocean one *infers* that there is such a person as God who has created it; rather, the perception of the mountains or ocean (or one's own sin, or danger, or . . .) is the occasion of the formation of the belief about God in question. On this construal, the "real evidence" in question wouldn't be propositional evidence functioning as premise for an inference. It would rather be something else that makes the belief in question evident—that is, something else that plays the appropriate role in the belief's having warrant for one. It would be like the role played by perception of someone else's facial expression in coming to the warranted belief that she is angry or depressed or delighted: again, even if I don't infer the latter from the former, the former is still my evidence for the latter in the sense that the former is (part of) what makes the latter evident (warranted) for me.

Under the second construal, there are again two ways things could go. It could be that perception of the beauty and delightfulness of the great things of the gospel directly and without intermediary occasions the formation of the relevant belief. Then again, it could be that the Holy Spirit enables the believer to perceive that beauty and delightfulness and also enables her to make the right affective response of delight, admiration, and love: and it is that affective response which is the immediate occasion of the belief in question. You see that the great things of the gospel are glorious and beautiful; you find them winsome, delightful, and attractive; so you believe them. If things went this second way, then with respect to the formation of belief in the great things of the gospel, will (affection) would precede intellect.

Which of these is the truth of the matter? What does Edwards think: is there or isn't there a quick inference involved? It's not easy to tell, and indeed perhaps he thinks the belief is formed both ways at once: "he not only argues that they are divine, but he sees that they are divine." I think the second position (according to which perception of the beauty of one of the great things of the gospel is a direct or indirect *occasion* of the formation of the belief that it is indeed true, not a premise of an inference whose conclusion is that belief) is the stronger. That is because the alleged inference in question seems dubious, questionable—just as would be an inference to the proposition that the sun is shining on the oaks from propositions reporting how I am now being appeared to. On the other hand, there need be nothing dubious or questionable about a process in which perception of the beauty and glory of that teaching is an *occasion* (direct or indirect) for the belief that it is true.

Or *is* there something dubious here? Would it be somehow irrational to form a belief *B* as a response just to the perception that *B* is attractive and beautiful, or to the fact that you delight in the thought that *B*, that you have a certain affective response to *B*? Wouldn't this be like the cases we noted earlier on (above, pp. 149ff.) in which noncognitive or nonintellectual features of a cognitive situation can influence belief formation, thus impeding cognitive proper function? I don't think so. It needn't be the case that wherever there is influence of this sort—that is, from nonintellectual factors—what you have is impedance: perhaps the design plan calls for just this sort of belief formation, and perhaps the relevant part of the design plan is successfully aimed at true belief. According to the physicist Steven Weinberg, scientists often accept a view or a theory not (or not only) because there is good evidence for it, but because it is *beautiful*:

> Nevertheless, despite the weakness of the early experimental evidence for general relativity, Einstein's theory became the standard textbook theory of gravitation in the 1920s and retained that position from then on, even while the various eclipse expeditions of the 1920s and 1930s were reporting at best equivocal evidence for the theory. I remember that, when I learned general relativity in the 1950s, before modern radar and radio astronomy began to give impressive new evidence for the theory, I took it for granted that general relativity was more or less correct. Perhaps all of us were just gullible and lucky, but I do not think that is the real explanation. I believe that the general acceptance of general relativity was due in large part to the attractions of the theory itself—in short, to its beauty.[16]

16. *Dreams of a Final Theory* (New York: Pantheon, 1992), p. 98. See also P. Dirac, *The Development of Quantum Theory* (New York: Gordon and Breach, 1971), pp. 30–37; speaking of some of De Broglie's work, he says, "This connection of De Broglie's was very beautiful mathematically and was in agreement with the theory of relativity. It was very mysterious, but because of its mathematical beauty one felt that there must be some deep connection between the waves and the particles illustrated by this mathematics."

Here we have the same three possibilities: (a) Weinberg argued to the truth of general relativity, employing as a premise the proposition that the theory is beautiful (more exactly, displays a certain hard-to-specify *kind* of beauty or aesthetic appeal), or (b) Weinberg's perception of the beauty of the theory was the direct occasion of his belief that it is true, or (c) Weinberg's perception of the beauty was the direct occasion of an affective response of admiration, attraction, and delight, that affective response then occasioning belief.[17] There need be nothing irrational here, and won't be, if in fact this sort of belief formation is in accord with a part of our cognitive design plan, which is successfully aimed at the formation of true belief. Similarly with the great things of the gospel.

We can also compare the second Edwardsian construal with Augustine's famous dictum: "Our hearts are restless till they rest in you, O Lord."[18] Perhaps this restlessness without God leads to belief in God; and perhaps God has designed us in this way to impel us to try to get in touch with him. If either Edwards or Augustine is right, the process by which belief (in God, or in the great things of the gospel) arises in us would be a little like the way in which Freud thinks theistic belief arises. According to Freud (see above, chapter 5), religious belief arises out of wishful thinking: we see that the world is cold, cruel, heedless of us and our needs and desires, hostile, unthinking, and all the rest; we respond by forming a belief in a heavenly father who loves us and is actually in control of the world. The difference would be, of course, that according to Freud this process of belief formation does not have the production of true belief as its purpose, but rather the production of belief with some other property—that of enabling us to cope with the cold, cruel world into which, as our continental cousins say, we have been *geworfen*. If Augustine or Edwards is right, however, the processes leading to the formation of the beliefs in question are directed to the truth: the relevant module of the design plan has as its purpose the production of true belief, even if it goes by way of perception of beauty or wish-fulfillment.

> Indeed, there is a connection between belief and perception of beauty (and similar qualities) that goes much deeper than Weinberg suggests. As Leibniz and many since have noted, there are ordinarily

17. Ironically enough, Weinberg also argues (more exactly, asserts) that religious beliefs arrived at by way of experience are really formed by wishful thinking, completely failing to note the parallel with his idea that scientific beliefs are sometimes accepted because of their beauty.

18. *Confessions*. See here George Herbert's poem "The Pulley" in *The Poetical Works of George Herbert*, with life, critical dissertation, and explanatory notes by the Rev. George Gilfillan (Edinburgh: James Nichol, 1853), p. 167.

many different theories or beliefs compatible with our evidence. If we plot our data on Cartesian coordinates, we will be able to draw as many lines as we please through the points we plot, and we could project any of the appropriately related hypotheses. All emeralds so far examined have been green; if so, however, they have also all been grue, where an emerald is grue if either it is examined before 2050 A.D. (bringing Goodman up to date) and is found to be green, or is not so examined and is blue.[19] So (instead of projecting that all emeralds are green) we could project that all emeralds are grue, thus concluding that emeralds not observed before 2050 are blue. The sun has come up every morning so far; we form the belief that it comes up every day and will also come up tomorrow. We could have formed quite a different belief, however: where T is today, we could have formed the belief that the sun comes up every day prior to T and never after T. Why do we accept the hypotheses we do; why do we project green rather than grue, and the hypothesis that the sun will continue to come up rather than the one according to which it won't? Why do we project simple hypotheses rather than complex ones? Not because we have evidence that simpler hypotheses are more likely to be correct than complex ones; for, for any alleged evidence for this conclusion, there will be a more complex inference from the same data for the denial of this conclusion. So why do we do it?

Because we find simple beliefs (whatever precisely simplicity is) more natural and more attractive than complex beliefs. Only a madman would project grue or its partner in crime, bleen.[20] Messy, complex beliefs are ugly, disgusting, weird, repellent: we dislike them and therefore reject them. We may hope that the world is in fact such that simplicity (at least simplicity of a certain sort and in certain areas) is a mark of truth; but we have no hope whatever of establishing that in a way that doesn't already rely upon simplicity. For suppose we note that in the last one thousand cases the simplest hypothesis has turned out to be true. Where t is the present, say that a belief is 'simplex' if it is formed before t and simple, or after t and complex; what we will have observed, so far, is that simplex beliefs tend to be true. But that means that from now on we should go for complex beliefs.

How shall we think of these things in the model? There are the three Edwardsian possibilities: it could be that there is a quick inference from the beauty and glory of the gospel to its truth; it could be

19. See Nelson Goodman, *Fact, Fiction and Forecast* (Cambridge: Harvard University Press, 1955; reprint, Indianapolis: Bobbs-Merrill, 1973), p. 74 in the 1973 edition; and see the corrected version of the paradox in *Problems and Projects* (Indianapolis: Bobbs-Merrill, 1972), p. 359. See also *Warrant and Proper Function*, pp. 128ff.

20. Where, as you expect, x is bleen if either it is examined before 2050 A.D. and is found to be blue, or is not so examined and green.

that such belief is uninferred, but directly consequent, according to the design plan, upon perception of the beauty and glory of the gospel; and it could be that perception of the beauty of the gospel induces admiration and delight, which induces belief. We need not choose among them. There is that affective response, there is the perception of beauty and glory, and there is the belief; it is no part of the model to say which, if any, is prior to which.

III. ANALOGUE OF WARRANT

We should note the deep analogies between will and intellect, affection and belief here. Intellect is the province of belief; will, the province of affection. Now when our cognitive faculties function properly, we won't believe just any propositions; we will (ordinarily) believe true propositions.[21] To put the matter in an older terminology, intellect is ordered to truth. Like intellect, however, affection also has an appropriate object—or, rather, the various affections have appropriate objects. When the sources of affection function properly, we will love what is lovable, take delight in what is delightful, and desire what is desirable. We will love God above all and our neighbor as ourselves; we will delight in his beauty and glory, and in created reflections of that beauty and glory; we will desire what is in fact good for us. Here I am assuming the unfashionable view that some individuals and some states of affairs are genuinely and objectively lovable, delightful, and desirable; others are genuinely and objectively hateful, disgusting, and undesirable; still others are none of the above. Delightfulness is not or not just the dispositional property a thing or state of affairs has of tending to produce delight in us; it is, rather, an objective property of an object or state of affairs, one that in no way depends upon human reactions to it. The beauty and delightfulness of a Mozart sonata are objective properties of (tokens of) the pattern of sounds; they aren't just subjective reactions on the part of the listener (or the dispositional properties of being apt for the production of such subjective reactions), although of course if things are going right, there will be such a reaction. (It may be that a thing's delightfulness depends on *God's* attitude toward it, but that is a very different matter.)

---

21. And, of course, not just any true propositions, but ones appropriate to the circumstances. I meet you at a party; you tell me you live in Omaha; I form the belief that you live there, rather than, say, the true belief that you were born in Cleveland or that Caesar crossed the Rubicon.

Like beliefs, affections can be justified or unjustified—or, rather, I can be justified or unjustified in having a certain affection.[22] Furthermore, affections, like beliefs, can be rational or irrational: if I react to disaster with an amused smile, or love myself above all, or disdain someone because her relatives are poorer than mine, there is lack of proper function. There can also be proper and improper function with respect to the *degree* of affection, just as with degree of belief. I value a silly little ditty from a cigar commercial ("Man to man with a RoiTan! Man to man with a RoiTan cigar!") as much as Bach's B Minor Mass: that's a case of affective malfunction. Similarly if you value my good opinion more than God's.

Still further, there is an analogue of *warrant* for affections. A belief has warrant when it is formed by cognitive faculties functioning properly in a congenial epistemic environment (both maxi and mini) according to a design plan successfully aimed at truth. An affection can have an analogous property. As we have already seen, it can be produced by faculties functioning properly or not. The environmental condition is equally obvious. On some distant planet, there could be a gas that causes human beings to react to disaster with a silly giggle or an indifferent shrug, or to become furiously angry for no reason at all. The right kind of affective environment (for us) will be one where, given our design plan, we will form the right affective responses. What about the last two conditions for warrant: (1) the faculty in question being such that it is aimed at the production of true beliefs, and (2) the design plan's being a good one? As to the first, again, there are clear analogues. It could be that a specific form of affection is aimed, not at our valuing something that is genuinely valuable, but at something else—at the continuation of the species, or survival, or whatever. An affection (or an instance of an affection) has the analogue of warrant only if it is produced by a process that isn't aimed at the production of affections with any of *those* properties, but instead at the production of affection that is appropriate to its object: valuing or loving or desiring what is valuable or lovable or desirable. The last condition for warrant is that the production of the belief be governed by a design plan that is good in the sense that there is a high objective probability that a belief formed in such a way as to satisfy the first three conditions will be true. Again, there is a clear ana-

---

22. Furthermore, affection, like belief, is not within our direct control; for example, I can't just by willing to do so, take the right attitude toward someone who has wronged or offended me. But also affection, again like belief, is to some extent within our indirect control; one can train oneself not to be so sensitive to slights, to see (and feel) them as unimportant. One can fight against pride and self-centeredness, and sometimes achieve partial success.

logue in the case of affection: the design plan governing the production of the affections is a good one just if, for example, it is objectively likely that a given instance of desire will be for something desirable and a given instance of hate will be of something hateful (given the satisfaction of the other three conditions).[23]

IV. EROS

Conversion, therefore, is fundamentally a turning of the will, a healing of the disorder of affection that afflicts us. It is a turning away from love of self, from thinking of oneself as the chief being of the universe, to love of God. But what is this love of God like, and how shall we understand it? William James, that cultured, sophisticated New England Victorian gentleman, notes the throbbing elements of longing, yearning, desire, eros in the writings of Teresa of Avila, looks down his cultivated nose, and finds all that a bit, well, *tasteless*, a bit *déclassé*. Sniffs James, "in the main her idea of religion seems to have been that of an endless amatory flirtation . . . between the devotee and the deity."[24] Here the joke is on James. There is an intimate and long-standing connection between eros and developed spirituality. The Bible is full of expressions of that longing, yearning, *Sehnsucht*, desire; the Hebrew word for knowledge, as in knowledge of God, is also a word for sexual intercourse;[25] and when the children of Israel are unfaithful, turning aside to false gods, this is represented as adultery. The Psalms are particularly rich in such expressions of eros:

> My soul yearns, even faints for the courts of the Lord; my heart and my flesh cry out for the living God. (Psalm 84:2)
>
> Oh God, you are my God, earnestly I seek you; my soul thirsts for you, my body longs for you. (Psalm 63:1)
>
> One thing have I desired of the Lord, that I will seek after; that I . . . behold the beauty of the Lord. (Psalm 27:4)

---

23. Is there an analogue of the Gettier problem for affections? I leave this problem for homework, only reminding the reader that the essence of Gettier situations is the "resolution problem": the fact that cognitive minienvironments can be misleading, even if embedded in maxienvironments apt for our style of cognitive faculties (above, pp. 158ff.).

24. *The Varieties of Religious Experience* (New York: Longmans, Green, 1902), p. 340.

25. A feature that is retained in the King James translation: "And Adam knew his wife Eve and she conceived and bare Cain" (Genesis 4:1).

> As the deer pants for streams of water, so my soul pants for you, O God. My soul thirsts for God, for the living God. (Psalm 42:1–2)

> I open my mouth and pant, longing for your commands. (Psalm 119:131)

This love for God isn't like, say, an inclination to spend the afternoon organizing your stamp collection. It is longing, filled with desire and yearning; and it is physical as well as spiritual: "my body longs for you, my soul pants for you." It is erotic; and one of the closest analogues would be with sexual eros. There is a powerful desire for *union* with God, the oneness Christ refers to in John 17. Another perhaps equally close analogue would be love between parent and small child; and this kind of love too is often employed in Scripture as a figure for love of God—both God's love for us and ours for him. Here too, of course, there is longing, yearning, desire for closeness, though not *sexual* longing; think of the longing in the homesickness of an eight-year-old or in the love of a mother for her hurt and suffering child.

Of course expressions of this eros are not found only in the Psalms. In Isaiah, we read, "I will rejoice over Jerusalem and take delight in my people" (65:19); "As a bridegroom rejoices over his bride, so will your God rejoice over you" (62:5b). This implies, I take it, not merely that God will rejoice over his people the way a bridegroom rejoices over his bride, but that the bride will return this love; when things go properly, God's people love him the way a bride loves her new husband, with a similar sort of erotic desire. Then there is the Song of Songs, with its intensely erotic imagery, imagery the church has all along taken to be a picture of the love between Christ and his church:

> I belong to my lover, and his desire is for me. Come, my lover, let us go to the countryside, let us spend the night in the villages. Let us go early to the vineyards to see if the vines have budded, if their blossoms have opened, and if the pomegranates are in bloom—there I will give you my love. (7:10-12)

In the New Testament, the relationship between Christ and his church is repeatedly compared to that between husband and wife:

> He who loves his wife loves himself. For no man ever hates his own flesh, but nourishes and cherishes it, as Christ does the church, because we are members of his body. "For this reason a man shall leave his father and mother and be joined to his wife, and the two shall become one flesh" [Genesis 2:24]. This mystery is a profound one, and I am saying that it refers to Christ and the church. (Ephesians 5:28b–32)

Christians over the centuries have echoed these expressions. Thus Augustine:

Late it was that I loved you, beauty so ancient and so new, late I loved you! . . . You called, you cried out, you shattered my deafness: you flashed, you shone, you scattered my blindness: you breathed perfume, and I drew in my breath and I pant for you: I tasted, and I am hungry and thirsty: you touched me, and I burned for your peace.[26]

The great mystical masters of the spiritual life, furthermore, speak in similarly erotic terms:

And although the attractions by which God draws us be admirably pleasing, sweet and delicious, yet on account of the force which the divine beauty and goodness have to draw unto them the attention and application of the spirit, it seems that it not only raises us but that it ravishes and bears us away. As, on the contrary, by reason of the most free consent and ardent motion, by which the ravished soul goes out after the divine attractions, she seems not only to mount and rise, but also to break out of herself and cast herself into the very divinity.[27]

It isn't only the great mystics who have this sort of experience:

as I turned and was about to take a seat by the fire, I received a mighty baptism of the Holy Ghost . . . the Holy Spirit descended upon me in a manner that seemed to go through me, body and soul. I could feel the impression, like a wave of electricity, going through and through me. Indeed, it seemed to come in waves and waves of liquid love; for I could not express it in any other way.[28]

Even (and perhaps especially) the Puritans, dour and emotionally pinched as they are often represented, are full of expressions of erotic love of God. There is of course Jonathan Edwards; but he was by no means alone. Thus Henry Scougal:

when once the soul is fixed on that supreme and all sufficient good, it finds so much perfection and goodness as does not only answer and satisfy its affection, but master and overpower it too: it finds all its love to be too faint and languid for such a noble objection, and is only sorry that it can command no more. It . . . longs for the time when it shall be wholly melted and dissolved into love.[29]

26. *Confessions*, tr. Rex Warner (New York: New American Library, 1963), X, 27, p. 235.

27. Francis of Sales, *Treatise on the Love of God*, Library of St. Francis de Sales, tr. Henry B. Mackey (London: Burnes and Oates, 1884) Bk. VII, chap. iv, p. 294. See also, for another example among many, Fr. Nouet Conduite de l'homme d'Oraison, Bk. VI in Anton Poulain, *The Graces of Interior Prayer*, tr. Leonora York Smith (London: Routledge and Kegan Paul, 1950), p. 111, quoted in William Alston's *Perceiving God*, p. 54.

28. Quoted (anonymously) in William James, *Varieties of Religious Experience*, p. 350.

29. *The Life of God in the Soul of Man, or, the Nature and Excellency of the Christian Religion* (Philadelphia: G. M. and W. Snider, 1827 [first published 1677]), p. 62.

What an infinite pleasure must it needs be, thus, as it were, to lose ourselves in him, and being swallowed up in the overcoming sense of his goodness, to offer ourselves a living sacrifice always ascending unto him in flames of love.[30]

Amy Plantinga Pauw notes that

The joy between Christ and the saints is described by such a staid figure as Samuel Willard in frankly erotic terms: "We shall then dwell at the Fountain of his Love, and the reciprocal ardours of Affection between him and us, shall break over all Banks and Bounds, and we shall be entirely satisfied, both in Soul and in Body."[31]

What is to be made of this erotic love of God, this yearning, longing, desire, and its apparent fulfillment in some kind of ardent union between "the devotee and the deity"? This phenomenon comes in all grades of intensity: there is the full-blown, breathtaking, overpowering scenario de Sales points to, but also the much quieter and more restrained movement of the heart toward God on the part of one who gives thanks for a glorious June morning, or who for one brief moment sees the glory and beauty of the Christian story and feels a pang of attraction deeper than gratitude; and there is every degree

30. Ibid., p. 66.
31. "Edwards on Heaven and the Trinity," *Calvin Theological Journal* 30, no. 2 (November 1995), pp. 392ff. The quotation from Willard is from *A Compleat Body of Divinity* (Boston, 1726), sermon 146. See also Abraham Kuyper, *To Be near unto God*, tr. John Hendrik de Vries (Grand Rapids: W. B. Eerdmans, 1918, 1925), p. 675: "The homesickness goes out after God Himself, until in your soul's transport of love you feel the warmth of his father heart in your own heart. It is not the Name of God, but God Himself Whom your soul desires, and can not do without, God Himself in the outshining of His life; and it is this outshining of His life that must penetrate you and must be assimilated in the blood of your soul."

We should also note here some of John Donne's "Holy Sonnets," for example, 14:

Batter my heart, three person'd God; for, you
As yet but knocke, breathe, shine and seek to mend;
That I may rise, and stand, o'erthrow mee, and bend
Your force, to breake, blowe, burn and make me new.
I, like an usurpt towne, to another due,
Labour to admit you, but Oh, to no end,
Reason your viceroy in mee, mee should defend,
But is captiv'd, and proves weake or untrue.
Yet dearly 'I love you,' and would be loved faine,
But am betrothed unto your enemie:
Divorce mee, untie, or break that knot againe,
Take mee to you, imprison mee, for
Except you enthrall mee, shall never be free,
Nor ever chast, except you ravish mee.

between these two. What is to be made of this phenomenon? Most psychiatric literature has tended to follow Freud in understanding religion as a kind of neurosis, the "universal obsessional neurosis of humanity."[32] From this point of view, religious eros is to be understood as a kind of analogue, displacement, or sublimation of (broadly) sexual energy (presumably on the part of those who have little by way of the more conventional sexual outlets).

What is it for sexual energy to be sublimated in art, or poetry, or love of God? The idea is that there is some finite store of energy whose 'natural' use or outlet is sexual; this energy can somehow be diverted into other channels, perhaps especially if the natural channels aren't available. (There is also the suggestion that these other channels are socially somehow more respectable.) The person in whom the sublimation occurs, of course, is not aware of this origin of what he thinks of as his higher feelings and desires. (Here there is more of that unmasking for which Freud is famous.) We might stop to try to understand this claim more fully: what is this 'energy' like, and what does it mean to say that it gets pointed in some other direction, and why would energy be diverted in this fashion? And isn't the whole claim really metaphorical ('sublimation', 'energy', 'diversion', etc., are all used metaphorically here), and, if so, what is it a metaphor for? Is there any way to give a literal statement of the theory? Let's not tarry over those questions, however, and pretend we have a reasonably good grasp of the alleged theory: is there any reason to *believe* it?

Here I think things stand as with Freud's account of religious belief as wish-fulfillment (chapter 5). We are confronted with a question: how is it that some people display this ardent desire and love for God? One sort of answer would be: "Well, God himself, according to Scripture and Christian belief, is essentially love; union with him is also the chief end of us human beings; it is therefore no surprise that he would create us in such a way that we have a deep desire for union with him, even if that desire has been partly suppressed and effaced by sin." But suppose you think there is no God and that Christian (and other) theism is an illusion (and delusion) of some kind: *then* how does it happen that many of us display this love for God? I take it Freud's suggestion is an answer to *that* question, or to that question with that presupposition. The answer is supposed to help us understand what would otherwise be (from that atheistic perspective) a

---

32. See above, chapter 5, pp. 137ff. See also *Comprehensive Textbook of Psychiatry*, vol. 2, ed. A. M. Freedman, H. I. Kaplan, and B. J. Sadock (Baltimore: Williams and Wilkins, 1975), in particular, the article by Mortimer Ostow, "Religion and Psychiatry."

puzzling phenomenon. The proposed explanation is that there is the natural, unsurprising, well-established phenomenon of sexual energy; we then imagine that this energy (for one reason or another) gets 'diverted' (in those deprived of the natural outlets) into another direction, a direction that may have some psychological function. In this way, we come to understand erotic love for God.

Like his account of theistic belief as wish-fulfillment, this account (assuming we can make real sense of it) is of the sort that is vastly more likely to be true if theism is false than if it is true. It is, of course, *possible* that something like it *is* true, even if theism is true too. Even if theism is true, it is possible that (due, e.g., to sin) there is something like a drying up of the natural sources of love of God, and a sort of makeshift interim arrangement whereby sexual energy is commandeered for this purpose. Perhaps it is even possible that we were originally designed, in the unfallen state, in such a way that it was sexual energy that was somehow diverted and used in this other fashion— that is, for love of God (although, if that was part of the original human design plan, why call the energy in question 'sexual'?). These things are possible, though not likely (given theism or Christianity). Even if they were true, however, there would remain an important difference: from the Christian or theistic perspective, this system or set of systems would have been designed or redesigned with love of God as its aim or end: that is what it would be *for*. Not so, of course, from Freud's perspective.

From a Christian perspective, then, here (as often) Freud has things just backwards. It isn't that religious eros, love for God, is really sexual eros gone astray or rechanneled, and it isn't sexual eros (important as it is) that is basic or fundamental, with religious eros somehow derivative from it. The fact is things are just the other way around. It is *sexual* desire and longing that is a sign of something deeper: it is a sign of this longing, yearning for God that we human beings achieve when we are graciously enabled to reach a certain level of the Christian life. It is love for God that is fundamental or basic, and sexual eros that is the sign or symbol or pointer to something else and something deeper. (Of course I don't mean to say that the importance and worth of sexual eros is *exhausted* in its being a sign of love of God.)

In fact sexual eros points to two deeper realities. First, it points to human love for God, which is a passionate desire for the central condition for which God has designed us. According to the Westminster Catechism, the chief end of man is to glorify God and enjoy him forever. What is this "glorifying God and enjoying him forever"? The first is not fundamentally a matter of telling God how great he is, paying him effusive compliments, metaphysical or otherwise. God is, indeed, great, magnificent, and awe-inspiring beyond description; but he already knows that, and doesn't need to hear it from us, as with someone who is insecure, or whose swollen ego needs constant feeding of this type. More likely, it is a matter of *perceiving, noting, appreciating, delighting in, relishing*, God's glory and loveliness, his amiability and sweetness—the whole list of divine properties so often mentioned by Jonathan Edwards— and a natural expression of that perception and delight.[33] And the second—"enjoying him forever"—is some kind of *union* with God, a being united to, at one with him. To quote Samuel Willard again, "We shall then dwell at the Fountain of his Love, and the reciprocal ardours of Affection between him and us, shall break over all Banks and Bounds, and we shall be entirely satisfied, both in Soul and in Body."[34] Sexual eros with its longing and yearning is a sign and foreshadowing of the longing and yearning for God that will characterize us in our healed and renewed state in heaven; and sexual satisfaction and union, with its transports and ecstasy, is a sign and foreshadowing of the deeper reality of union with God— a union that is at present for the most part obscure to us. Bernard Williams seems to believe that heaven would be a bit boring for a person of taste and sensibility;[35] and Michael Levine suggests that friendship with God could be fairly interesting, but doubts that it would be "supremely worthwhile."[36] Perhaps these reactions are as spiritually immature as those of a nine-year-old child on first hearing of the pleasures of sex: could it really match marbles, or chocolate?[37]

Of course it isn't only sexual eros that is in this way a sign or symbol of love for God. Sexual eros and love for God are both passionate desires for union, a passionate desire to be united with the object of desire. And there are other manifestations of the same kind of desire for union. Think of the haunting, supernal beauty of

33. As Ronald Feenstra reminded me, it is also, no doubt, a matter of developing the image of God in us, both individually and corporately.

34. Compare Edwards, "I thought with myself, how excellent a Being that was; and how happy I should be, if I might enjoy that God, and be wrapped up to God in heaven, and be as it were swallowed up in him" ("A Personal Narrative," in *A Jonathan Edwards Reader*, ed. John Smith, Harry Stout, and Kenneth Minkema [New Haven: Yale University Press, 1995], p. 284).

35. "The Macropoulos Case" in *Problems of the Self* (Cambridge: Cambridge University Press, 1973), pp. 94–95.

36. "Swinburne's Heaven: One Hell of a Place," *Religious Studies* 4 (1993), p. 521.

37. Compare C. S. Lewis: such a person is "like an ignorant child who wants to go on making mud pies in a slum because he cannot imagine what is meant by the offer of a holiday at the sea" ("The Weight of Glory," in *The Weight of Glory and Other Addresses*, ed. with Introduction by Walter Hooper [New York: Macmillan, 1980], p. 4).

the prairie on an early morning in June, or the glorious but slightly menacing aspect of the Cathedral group in the Grand Tetons, or the gleaming splendor of Mount Shuksan and Mount Baker from Skyline Ridge, or the timeless crash and roar of the surf, or the melting sweetness of Mozart's "Dona Nobis Pacem" that can bring hot tears to your eyes, or the incredible grace, beauty, and power of an ice-skating routine or a kickoff returned for ninety-eight yards. In each, there is a kind of yearning, something perhaps a little like nostalgia, or perhaps homesickness,[38] a longing for one knows not what. This longing is different from sexual eros, though no doubt connected with it at a deep level (which is perhaps one of the things Freud *did* see). In these cases it isn't easy to say with any precision what the longing is a longing *for*, but it can seem to be for a sort of union: it's as if you want to be absorbed into the music, to become part of the ocean, to be at one with the landscape. You would love to climb that mountain, certainly, but that isn't enough; you also somehow want to become one with it, to become part of it, or to have it, or its beauty, or this particular aspect of it, somehow become part of your very soul.[39] Of course you can't; you remain unsatisfied. Jean-Paul Sartre says that man (and I doubt that he meant to single out just males) is too much, "de trop"; perhaps the truth is more like "not enough." He also says that man is a "useless passion." What he should have said is that man is an *unfulfilled* passion. When confronted with beauty, it is never enough; we are never really satisfied; there is more beyond, a more that we yearn for, but can only dimly conceive. We are limited to mere fleeting glimpses of the real satisfaction—unfulfilled until filled with the love of God. These longings too are types of longing for God; and the brief but joyous partial fulfillments are a type and foretaste of the fulfillment enjoyed by those who "glorify God and enjoy him forever."

Sexual eros points to something deeper in a second way. As we have just seen, it is a sign or type of a deeper reality, a kind of love for God of which we now just have hints and intimations. It is also a sign, symbol, or type of *God's* love—not just of the love God's children will someday have for *him* but of the love he also has for *them*. As we noted above (p. 312), Scripture regularly compares God's love for his people and Christ's love for his church to the love

---

38. Kuyper, *To Be near unto God*, pp. 674–75.
39. Compare C. S. Lewis again: our "inconsolable secret" is that "We do not want merely to *see* beauty, though, God knows, even that is bounty enough. We want something else which can hardly be put into words—to be united with the beauty we see, to pass into it, to receive it into ourselves, to bathe in it, to become part of it" (*The Weight of Glory*, p. 126).

of a groom for his new bride. Now a widely shared traditional view of God has been that he is impassible, without desire or feeling or passion, unable to feel sorrow at the sad condition of his world and the suffering of his children, and equally unable to feel joy, delight, longing, or yearning. The reason for so thinking, roughly, is that in the tradition originating in Greek philosophy, passions were thought of (naturally enough) as *passive*, something that *happens* to you, something you undergo, rather than something you actively *do*. You are *subject to* anger, love, joy, and all the rest. God, however, is pure act; he doesn't 'undergo' anything at all; he acts, and is never merely passive; and he isn't subject to anything. As far as eros is concerned, furthermore, there is an additional reason for thinking that it isn't part of God's life: longing and yearning signify need and *incompleteness*. One who yearns for something doesn't yet have it, and needs it, or at any rate thinks he needs it; God is of course paradigmatically complete and needs nothing beyond himself. How, then, could he be subject to eros? God's love, according to this tradition, is exclusively *agape*, benevolence,[40] a completely other-regarding, magnanimous love in which there is mercy but no element of desire. God loves us, but there is nothing we can do for him; he wishes nothing from us.

On this particular point I think we must take leave of the tradition; this is one of those places where it has paid too much attention to Greek philosophy and too little to the Bible. I believe God can and does suffer; his capacity for suffering exceeds ours in the same measure that his knowledge exceeds ours. Christ's suffering was no charade; he was prepared to endure the agonies of the cross and of hell itself ("My God, my God, why have you forsaken me?").[41] God the Father was prepared to endure the anguish of seeing his Son, the second person of the trinity, consigned to the bitterly cruel and shameful death of the cross.[42] And isn't the same true for other passions?

40. See Anders Nygren, *Agape and Eros*, tr. Philip S. Watson (New York: Macmillan, 1939).

41. Can we say that Christ qua human being (according to his human nature) suffered while Christ qua divine (according to his divine nature) did not? This is hardly the place to try to address a question as ancient and deep as this one, but I'm inclined to think this suggestion incoherent. There is this person, the second person of the divine trinity who became incarnate. It is this person who suffers; if there really were *two* centers of consciousness here, one suffering and the other not, there would be two persons here (one human and one divine) rather than the one person who is both human and divine. See my "On Heresy, Mind, and Truth," *Faith and Philosophy*, 16, no. 2 (April 1999), p. 182.

42. He no doubt also suffers at the sufferings and defections of all his children: "this bitter grief is inflicted upon God, when a soul falls away from Him" (Kuyper, *To Be near unto God*, p. 30).

"There is more rejoicing in heaven over one sinner who repents than over ninety-nine righteous persons who do not need to repent" (Luke 15:7); is God himself to be excluded from this rejoicing?

Similarly for eros: "As a bridegroom rejoices over his bride, so will your God rejoice over you" (Isaiah 62:5). The bridegroom rejoicing over his bride doesn't love her with a merely agapeic love. He isn't like her benevolent elder brother (although Christ is also said to be our elder brother). He desires and longs for something outside himself, namely union with his beloved. The church is the *bride* of Christ, not his little sister. He is not her benevolent elder brother, but her husband, lover. These scriptural images imply that God isn't impassive, and that his love for us is not exclusively agapeic. They suggest that God's love for his people involves an erotic element of desire: he desires the right kind of response from us, and union with us, just as we desire union with him.

We can take this one step further (and here we may be crossing the boundary into groundless speculation). According to Jonathan Edwards, "The infinite happiness of the Father consists in the enjoyment of His Son."[43] This presumably isn't agape. It doesn't involve an element of mercy, as in his love for us. It is, instead, a matter of God's taking enormous pleasure, enjoyment, delight, happiness, delectation in the Son. Given the necessary existence of the Father and the Son, and their having their most important properties essentially, there is no way in which God could be deprived of the Son;[44] but if (*per impossible*) he were, it would occasion inconceivable sadness. The love in question is eros, not agape.[45] It is a desire for union that is continually, eternally, and joyfully satisfied. And our being created in his image involves our capacity for eros and for love of what is genuinely lovable, as well as knowledge and agenthood.

43. "An Essay on the Trinity," in *Treatise on Grace and Other Posthumously Published Writings*, ed. Paul Helm (Cambridge: James Clarke, 1971), p. 105.

44. And this is the answer to one of the traditional arguments for the conclusion that God has no passions: the Father and the Son do indeed *need* each other, but it is a need that is necessarily and eternally fulfilled.

45. "So when we say that God loves his Son, we are not talking about a love that is self-denying, sacrificial, or merciful. We are talking about a love of delight and pleasure. . . . He is well-pleased with his Son. His soul delights in the Son! When he looks at his Son he enjoys and admires and cherishes and prizes and relishes what he sees" (John Piper, *The Pleasures of God* [Portland: Multnomah Press, 1991], p. 31).

46. The thought that God is trinitarian distinguishes Christianity from other theistic religions; here we see a way in which this doctrine makes a real difference, in that it recognizes eros and love for others at the most fundamental level of reality. Does this suggest that we should lean toward a *social* conception of the trinity, the conception of Gregory and the Cappadocian fathers, rather than the Augustinian conception, which flirts with modalism? See Cornelius Plantinga Jr., "Social Trinity & Tritheism," in *Trinity, Incarnation, and Atonement*, ed. Ronald Feenstra and Cornelius Plantinga Jr. (Notre Dame: University of Notre Dame Press, 1989).

Accordingly, the eros in our lives is a sign or a symbol of God's erotic love as well. Human erotic love is a sign of something deeper, something so deep that it is uncreated, an original and permanent and necessarily present feature of the universe. Eros undoubtedly characterizes many creatures other than human beings; no doubt much of the living universe shares this characteristic. More important, all of us creatures with eros reflect and partake in this profound divine property. So the most fundamental reality here is the love displayed by and in God: love within the trinity.[46] This love is erotic. It is a matter of perceiving and desiring and enjoying union with something valuable, in this case, Someone of supreme value. And God's love for us is manifested in his generously inviting us into this charmed circle (though not, of course, to ontological equality), thus satisfying the deepest longings of our souls. Within this circle, there is mercy, self-sacrifice, overflowing agape; there is also that longing and delight, that yearning and joy that make up eros.[47]

> Suppose we use the term 'human eros' to refer to sexual eros and also to the kinds of longing involved in our experience of beauty, nostalgia, and the like. I say that human eros is a *sign*, a *symbol*, a *type*, a *figure*,[48] a *foreshadowing*, both of God's love, and also of spiritually mature human love for God: but exactly what does that mean, and why can't I settle on just one of those five words? To take the easier question first, let's settle on the word 'type'; human eros is a type of God's love and of love for God. Of course this is just to give it a name: what *is* that relationship? This is a large and nontrivial question; here I can only try to mention a few of the surface essentials. First, the relation is not symmetrical: human eros is a type of God's love, but God's love is not a type of human eros. Second, the relationship in question is not, of course, the familiar type-token relationship. A horse is a token of the type *the horse*; an inscription of the word 'fish' is a token of that word. But sexual eros is not a token of divine love, and divine love is not a token of sexual eros; hence, neither is a token of the other.
>
> Third, like the type-token relation and unlike the relation between a word and what it denotes, the type-relationship here is not *conventional*. The word 'fish' stands for fish; the relationship between 'fish' and fish is conventional in the sense that this relationship holds by virtue of the existence of a certain linguistic convention. (Perhaps this relationship goes by way of the convention's establishing a relationship between the word 'fish' and the property of being a fish, the former expressing the latter.) The relationship between 'fish' and fish depends on us

47. For a more poetic account of connections between human romantic love and divine love, see Charles Williams, *Religion and Love in Dante: The Theology of Romantic Love* (Westminster: Dacre Press, 1941). (See also, of course, Dante's *Divine Comedy*, the Paradiso.) Williams argues (p. 11) that being in love (that more or less ordinary but also utterly extraordinary way in which most of us are at one time or another) is a way of participating in the divine Love himself.

48. See Erich Auerbach's powerful "*Figura*" in *Scenes from the Drama of European Literature* (New York: Meridian Books, 1959).

human beings and what we do; it holds because we (or some of us) have done what it takes to establish the convention whereby the former is a word for the latter. The fish (the type) is also a symbol for Jesus Christ. The connection between the fish and Jesus Christ is also conventional, though in a slightly different way. The former was adopted as a symbol for the latter because of a relation between the Greek word for fish (*icthus*) and a certain Greek phrase: Ἰησοῦζ χριζτόζ θεοῦ Υιόζ Σωτήρ. The letters of the word, taken in order, are the first letters of the words of that phrase, taken in order. *That* relationship isn't itself merely conventional; but the relation between the fish and Jesus Christ is, in that it depends essentially upon our treating that type and some of its tokens in a certain conventional way. Not so for the way in which human eros is a type of divine love: this relationship doesn't depend on the establishment of any human conventions.

Still, none of this tells us what this relationship *is*. Perhaps we can make a little progress by considering a biblical example. In Hebrews 8:5, we read that the high priest "serves at a sanctuary that is a copy and shadow of what is in heaven"; and in the next chapter, "It was necessary, then, for the copies of the heavenly things to be purified with these sacrifices, but the heavenly things themselves with better sacrifices than these" (9:23). What is meant here, I take it, is that the earthly sanctuary, the temple, is a type of what is in heaven, whatever exactly it is. The sacrifice of an animal, furthermore, is a type of the sacrifice of Christ, and the animals themselves types of Christ. The relationship here is that there is a certain kind of (sometimes functional) *resemblance* between the earthly copy and the heavenly exemplar, a relationship that is independent of any human convention. Of course that isn't saying much: any two things resemble each other in indefinitely many ways (and indefinitely many ways independent of human convention); what's at issue here is a *relevant* relationship, where it is easy to give examples but hard to say what relevance consists in.

Perhaps the answer lies in the following area. There are features or properties of God that are very good—that is, features or properties such that exemplifications of them are good. These features would include his love, power, knowledge, mercy, justice, beauty, glory, and the like, and it is by exemplifying these features to the maximal degree that God is supremely good.[49] In creating creatures who are also good, God intends to make them in such a way that they *resemble* him by virtue of displaying some of these same features. They reflect and recapitulate the features of God in question. Of course there will be enormous differences; God's creatures are finite, created, and conditional, while he himself is infinite, uncreated, and unconditional; the theme in question is, so to say, transposed into another key.[50] Where *b* is a type of *a*, therefore, *a*

---

49. Of course I don't mean to suggest that God somehow depends on these features, or is ontologically subsequent to them (whatever exactly that means); these features themselves, as well as other properties, can perhaps best be thought of as divine concepts. See my *Does God Have a Nature?* (Milwaukee: Marquette University Press, 1980).

50. C. S. Lewis, "Transposition," in *Transposition and Other Addresses* (London: G. Bles, 1949).

will be of great value in some respect; *b* will resemble *a* in that respect, though *b* will be of less value than *a* (hence the asymmetry). Still further, part of what it is for human eros to be a type, a sign, or an analogue of divine love is God's *intending* to create something that resembles him in the relevant respect, and intending to create it just because it *does* resemble him in that respect. (The sound made by a deer drinking at a water hole may vaguely resemble the sound made by a very small mountain stream; neither stream nor deer, one thinks, is created because of that relationship.) These things are (I think) necessary; are they also sufficient? I doubt it. but do not know what further condition to add.

The fact that human eros is a type of divine love means that this feature of our lives can be *explained* or *understood* a certain way. We understand it better, see what it is all about, see what is most important about it, when we see that it is a type or sign of divine love. We see how it fits in with the rest of reality, and how it is connected with what is most real. There are, of course, various evolutionary accounts of erotic love; they center, naturally enough, in the connection of eros with reproduction or, more broadly, with the mechanisms of survival and reproduction. Why do human beings display eros, and what is its significance? From an evolutionary or sociobiological point of view, the answer has to do with how this feature of our nature came to be, bit by bit, in small stages, each stage proving to be fitness inducing (or genetically connected with something fitness inducing). From a Christian perspective, however, things look quite different. The significance of this feature of our lives lies in the fact that displaying it is part of what it is to be created in the image of God; in this way, we human beings share in one of the fundamental properties of the First Being of the universe. The questions 'Why is it there?' and 'What's most significant about it?' are to be answered in terms of its being a type of divine love.

In sum, then: according to the model, faith is a matter of a sure and certain knowledge, both revealed to the mind and sealed to the heart. This sealing, according to the model, consists in the having of the right sorts of affections; in essence, it consists in loving God above all and one's neighbor as oneself. There is an intimate relation between revealing and sealing, knowledge and affection, intellect and will; they cooperate in a deep and complex and intimate way in the person of faith. And the love involved is, in part, erotic; it involves that longing and yearning with which we are all familiar. Finally, love between human beings—between men and women, between parents and children, among friends—is a sign or type of something deeper: mature human love for God, on the one hand, and, on the other, the love of God displayed both among the members of the trinity and in God's love for his children.

10

Objections

It is often taken for granted by the wise of this world, believers and
unbelievers alike, that "religious experience" is a purely subjective
phenomenon. Although it may have various psychosocial functions
to play, any claims to its cognitive value can be safely dismissed without a hearing.

William P. Alston

Or, as we shall see, with at best a perfunctory hearing. In this chapter, we shall note and evaluate some alleged results of those perfunctory hearings.

The extended Aquinas/Calvin (A/C) model of the last three chapters is intended to show how specifically Christian belief can have justification, internal and external rationality, and warrant. According to
the model, we human beings have fallen into sin, a grievous condition from which we cannot extricate ourselves. Jesus Christ, both a
human being and the divine son of God, made atonement for our sin
by way of his suffering and death, thus making it possible for us to
stand in the right relationship to God. The Bible is (among other
things) a written communication from God to us human beings, proclaiming this good news. Because of our sinful condition, however,
we need more than this information: we also need a change of heart.
This is provided by the internal instigation of the Holy Spirit (IIHS);
he both turns our affections in the right direction and enables us to
see the truth of the great things of the gospel. The process whereby
we come to believe those things, therefore, satisfies the conditions for
warrant (and also the conditions for the affective analogue of warrant). But it is obvious that the beliefs in question are also such that
they can be and often are both justified and internally rational.

324

In this chapter, I shall do two things. First, I wish to consider some of the arguments for the conclusion that theistic and/or Christian belief lacks warrant; second, I want to consider objections to my arguments and claims about the way in which Christian belief *can* have warrant. What I have argued so far, in order of ascending strength, is that (1) the extended A/C model depicts a way in which Christian belief could have warrant; (2) given the truth of Christian belief, there are no cogent objections to its having warrant in the way suggested by the A/C model; and (3) given the truth of Christian belief, it very likely does have warrant, if not by way of the extended A/C model, then by way of a closely similar model. (3) is stronger than (2). (2) says that, given the assumption that Christian belief is true, there aren't any cogent objections to the A/C model and hence none to Christian belief's having warrant; but of course there might be no cogent objections to a proposition *p*, even if *p* is, as it turns out, false. (3) adds that in fact Christian belief very likely *has* warrant, given its truth. A successful argument for the conclusion that Christian or theistic belief lacks warrant, therefore, will be a successful argument against both (2) and (3)—provided, of course, that it doesn't assume (or argue for) the falsehood of Christian belief. Such an objection, therefore, will have to be independent of the question of the *truth* or *falsehood* of Christian belief; it will have to be cogent even on the supposition that Christian belief is *true*. Our question is really this: are there general epistemological reasons, independent of doubts about the *truth* of Christian or theistic belief, to think that it lacks warrant? If any of the objections is successful, therefore, it will remain successful even if we assume that indeed there is such a person as God and that Christian belief is, as a matter of fact, true.

There is also an initial difficulty. Those who raise the *de jure* question about Christian or theistic belief typically complain that it is "irrational," or "unjustified," or "unreasonable," or "rationally unjustified," or "rationally indefensible" or the like; they seldom make a serious attempt to explain what they mean by these terms. Instead, they typically take it for granted that we know perfectly well what these terms mean; then they argue that theistic belief has the unflattering properties expressed by them. But these terms and their associated concepts have had an enormously checkered career in modern and contemporary epistemology; to assume that their meanings are perfectly clear is excessively naive. It is also confusing, making it hard to construe the objector's complaints with any exactitude. We have seen that the relevant *de jure* question is really the question whether Christian belief does or can have warrant: the property or quantity, enough of which is what distinguishes knowledge from mere true belief; I shall therefore handle this problem by construing the objections as arguments for the claim that Christian belief has no warrant. This course has the added attraction that, in at least some cases, it is likely that this is what the objector intended.

A number of thinkers consider the question whether Christian belief can be justified or warranted by way of *religious experience*, and go on to argue that it cannot. Now I argued in chapter 6 that it isn't clear what it means to say that a belief is warranted by way of experience, and so didn't propose to say whether or not, on the model, theistic and Christian belief gets its warrant from or by way of religious experience. Technically speaking, therefore, these objections wouldn't apply to my claims about how it can be that such belief has warrant. For the purpose of considering these objections, however, let's concede what may well be false—namely that (on the model) these beliefs *do* get their warrant from experience. Then at any rate we can see the objections as initially relevant.

I. WARRANT AND THE ARGUMENT FROM RELIGIOUS EXPERIENCE

The first objection is really less an objection, so it seems to me, than a confusion, a failure to make an important distinction. Anthony O'Hear considers the idea that theistic belief might be justified or receive warrant (it is hard to tell which he is thinking of) in a *direct* way, not by way of argument or inference. (In my terms, the question is whether theistic belief might be *properly basic*, either with respect to warrant or with respect to justification.) Referring to William James, John Baillie, and others, he notes that one suggestion as to how this might go would be by way of *religious experience*, broadly conceived. He then goes on to say:

> It is the idea of direct personal contact with a non-sensory reality that non-believers will find hard to grasp. In order to bring out the nature of the difficulty, I will consider the extent to which religious experience can provide evidence for the existence of a reality beyond the experience itself. Presumably people who are convinced that they are in personal contact with some super-reality will not often attempt to argue or prove their conviction at all, nor will their conviction be arrived at inferentially, any more than we naturally infer from statements about our sensations to statements about physical objects. Nevertheless the question of the extent to which the conviction can be justified by the experience naturally arises.[1]

Here there are several questions. First, note that this quotation illustrates that initial difficulty I mentioned above: is O'Hear talking about *justification*, or *rationality*, or *warrant*, or what? This isn't clear

---

1. *Experience, Explanation and Faith* (London: Routledge and Kegan Paul, 1984), p. 27. Page references to O'Hear are to this work.

from what he says here or elsewhere. Despite the occurrence of 'justified' in the last line of the quotation, I don't think he's really speaking of justification—and in any event, as we have already seen
(above, pp. 99ff.), the question of justification is too easily answered
to be interesting. Although O'Hear speaks of "personal contact," perhaps his question is best construed in the present context as the question whether religious experience could put us in *epistemic contact*
with a nonsensory reality (i.e., one that can't, ordinarily, be seen,
heard, touched, etc.) such as God; and *that* question, I take it, is the
question of whether beliefs about such a nonsensory reality could acquire warrant by way of religious experience.

Now his initial suggestion is that there is something problematic
about the very *idea* of a human person's being in cognitive contact
(the kind required by warrant) with a nonsensory reality such as God.
Why is this problematic? O'Hear doesn't directly answer that question, but proposes to "bring out the difficulty" by turning to the question whether "religious experience can provide evidence for the existence of a reality beyond the experience itself." This *sounds* like he
thinks the way to answer the question

> Does religious experience make it possible for us to have the
> right sort of cognitive connection with God?

is to ask

> Is there a *good argument* from the *existence of the experience* in ques
> tion to the existence of God: an argument whose premises report
> the experience in question and whose conclusion is that there is
> such a person as God?

That this is what he has in mind is confirmed by what he says a bit
later:

> Christians, for example, tend to explain this unpredictability [of re
> ligious experience of the relevant sort] by saying that these experi
> ences are a gift of God. This may be so, but saying it certainly weak
> ens attempts to argue from the experience to the reality. (p. 44)

This clearly suggests that what is at issue, here, with respect to the
question whether theistic belief can have warrant by virtue of religious experience, is whether there is a good argument from premises
reporting that experience to the existence of God. O'Hear goes on to
say that what we are really asking for is

> grounds on which the religious experiences we have . . . could be
> regarded as experiences of an objective sort. (p. 45)

the answer, he says,

> will have to be in terms of the explanatory power of the hypothesis
> that religious experiences are due at least in part to the existence

and operation of an objective religious reality, rather than due to merely worldly factors, such as features of a person's psychology, chemistry or upbringing. (p. 45)

His thought, then, as far as I can make it out, is twofold:

(a) theistic belief can have warrant by virtue of religious experience only if there is a good (noncircular) argument from
premises reporting the occurrence of such experiences to the
existence of God

and

(b) such an argument will have to involve as a premise the proposition that the existence of God is the best explanation of
religious experiences.

(Of course such an argument would also have to provide reasons for thinking that premise true.)

I say (a) is part of O'Hear's thought; perhaps 'assumption' would be a better term because he doesn't explicitly make this claim but rather just takes it for granted. Another way to put the assumption: theistic belief can have warrant by way of religious experience only if some theistic argument from religious experience is successful. This assumption is widely shared and seldom argued; as I shall maintain, however, it has the substantial disadvantage of being false. In fact, one of the main points to see here is that the question whether theis-tic belief can receive warrant by way of religious experience (and thus in the basic way) is a wholly *different* question from the question whether there is a good argument from the existence of religious ex-perience to the existence of God. (Not only are these different ques-tions: an affirmative answer to the first does not require an affirma-tive answer to the second.) I shall argue that (a) is false. (a)'s being false doesn't distinguish religious experience and theistic or Christian belief from other kinds of experience and belief: perceptual experi-ence and belief, memorial experience and belief, *a priori* experience and belief, and the like, all resemble Christian belief in this respect. In each of these cases, it is entirely possible that the beliefs in question have warrant even if there is no good argument from the existence of the experience in question to the truth of those beliefs.[2]

This is one of the most important things to see here; before ar-guing this claim, however, I want to note another writer who also simply assumes that (a) is true, without so much as raising the ques-tion whether it is. According to the late J. L. Mackie,

---

2. See *Warrant and Proper Function* (hereafter WPF), pp. 61ff. and 93ff.

an experience may have a real object: we ordinarily suppose our normal perceptual experience to be or to include awareness of independently existing material spatio-temporal things. The question then is whether specifically religious experiences should be taken to have real objects, to give us genuine information about independently existing supernatural entities or spiritual beings.[3]

So far so good: this is the question whether religious experience can or does provide warrant for belief in "independently existing supernatural entities or spiritual beings" such as God. But Mackie goes on:

> Whether their content [i.e., the content of religious experiences] has any objective truth is the crucial further question. . . . The issue is whether the hypothesis that there objectively is a something more gives a better explanation of the whole range of phenomena than can be given without it. (p. 183)

Mackie concludes his examination of the possible warrant conferred by religious experience with these words:

> if the religious experiences do not yield any argument for a further supernatural reality, and if, as we have seen in previous chapters, there is no other good argument for such a conclusion, then these experiences include in their content beliefs that are probably false and in any case unjustified. [I take it 'unjustified', here, means 'without warrant'.] (p. 186)

Here we see the very same assumption at work as in O'Hear. Like the latter, Mackie assumes that theistic (or other religious) belief could get warrant by way of religious experience only if there is a good argument from the existence and character of that experience to the existence of God (or "something more"). (And like O'Hear, he also seems to endorse (b).) Neither Mackie nor O'Hear *argues* for this claim, simply taking it utterly for granted that the only way a belief (or at any rate a religious or theistic belief) could *possibly* receive warrant from experience would be by way of an implicit argument from the existence and properties of that experience to the truth of the belief in question. But why think a thing like that? It certainly isn't self-evident. In fact, once we explicitly raise the question whether it is true, (a) looks extremely problematic. Presumably one wouldn't want to say that perceptual beliefs get warrant from experience only if there is a good (noncircular) argument from the existence of perceptual experience to the truth of perceptual beliefs; if not, however, what is the reason for saying it in the case of theistic or Christian belief ?

Mackie makes this assumption, I believe, because he makes another: that theistic and Christian belief is or is relevantly like a *scien-*

---

3. *The Miracle of Theism* (Oxford: Clarendon Press, 1982), p. 178. Page references to Mackie are to this work.

tific hypothesis—something like special relativity, for example, or quantum mechanics, or the theory of evolution. Still speaking of whether theistic belief can receive warrant by way of religious experience, he (characteristically) remarks: "Here, as elsewhere, the supernaturalist hypothesis fails because there is an adequate and much more economical naturalistic alternative" (p. 198). This remark is relevant only if we think of belief in God as or as like a sort of scientific *hypothesis*, a *theory* designed to explain some body of evidence, and acceptable or warranted to the degree that it explains that evidence. On this way of looking at the matter, there is a relevant body of evidence shared by believer and unbeliever alike; theism is one hypothesis designed to explain that body of evidence, and naturalism is another; and theism has warrant only to the extent that it is a good explanation thereof, or at any rate a better explanation than naturalism.

But why should we think of theism like this? Why should we think of it as a kind of hypothesis, a sort of incipient science? Consider the extended A/C model of chapters 8 and 9. On that model, it is not that one notes the experiences, whatever exactly they are, connected with the operation of the *sensus divinitatis*, and then makes a quick inference to the existence of God. One doesn't argue thus: I am aware of the beauty and majesty of the heavens (or of my own guilt, or that I am in danger, or of the glorious beauty of the morning, or of my good circumstances): therefore there is such a person as God. The Christian doesn't argue: "I find myself loving and delighting in the great things of the gospel and inclined to believe them; therefore they are true." Those would be silly arguments; fortunately they are neither invoked nor needed. The experiences and beliefs involved in the operation of the *sensus divinitatis* and IIHS serve as *occasions* for theistic belief, not *premises* for an argument to it.

The same holds for, say, memory beliefs. Obviously one could take a Mackie-like view here as well. One could hold that our beliefs about the past are really like scientific hypotheses, designed to explain such present phenomena as (among other things) apparent memories, and if there were a more "economical" explanation of these phenomena that did not postulate past facts, then our usual beliefs in the past would have no warrant. But of course this is merely fantastic; we don't in fact accept memory beliefs as hypotheses to explain present experience at all. Everyone, even small children and others with no interest in explaining anything, accepts memory beliefs. We all remember such things as what we had for breakfast, and we never or almost never propose such beliefs as good explanations of present experience and phenomena. And the same holds for theism and Christian belief in the suggested model.

So Mackie apparently believes that

(c) theistic belief is or is relevantly like a quasi-scientific hypothesis, designed to explain religious experience (perhaps among other things).

This explains why he believes (a), that is, that theistic belief can get no warrant from religious experience unless there is a good argument from premises reporting the experiences to the existence of God. As we have seen, however, (c) is false.

Well, perhaps Mackie would insist on (a) even if it is clear that Christians do *not* take belief in God or Christian belief generally as hypotheses; perhaps he would nonetheless insist that the only way in which such belief could *possibly* get warrant would be by being successful quasi-scientific hypotheses. But precisely this is what is refuted by the A/C model of chapter 6 and the extended A/C model of chapters 8 and 9. These models show that it is clearly possible that theistic and Christian belief have warrant, but not by way of being hypotheses that nicely explain a certain range of data. For if Christian belief is, in fact, true, then obviously there could be such cognitive processes as the *sensus divinitatis* and IIHS or faith. As we saw, beliefs produced by these processes would meet the conditions necessary and sufficient for having warrant: they would be the result of cognitive faculties functioning properly in a congenial epistemic environment according to a design plan successfully aimed at truth. Hence (a) is plainly false. It is plainly false that Christian belief has warrant (and could constitute knowledge) only if there is *also* a good argument from the existence of the experiences involved in the operation of IIHS to the truth of Christian belief; and the same point holds for theistic belief and the *sensus divinitatis*. Why suppose that if God proposes to enable us to have knowledge of a certain sort, he must arrange things in such a way that we can see an argumentative connection between the experiences involved in the cognitive processes he selects and the truth of the beliefs these processes produce? That requirement is both entirely gratuitous and also false, since it doesn't hold for such splendid examples of sources of knowledge as perception, memory, and *a priori* intuition.

II. WHAT CAN EXPERIENCE SHOW?

A second objection is that Christian and theistic belief could never receive warrant from religious experience because religious experience could never indicate or show anything as *specific* as that there is such a person as God—let alone such beliefs as that in Christ God was reconciling the world to himself. How could experience of any sort reveal the existence of a being who is omniscient, omnipotent, wholly good, and a fitting object of worship? How could it reveal that there is only *one* being like that? How could experience carry that kind of information? John Mackie is a spokesman for this objection too:

> Religious experience is also essentially incapable of supporting any argument for the traditional central doctrines of theism. Nothing in an experience as such could reveal a creator of the world, or omnipotence, or omniscience, or perfect goodness, or eternity, or even that there is just one god. (182)

Now why would Mackie say a thing like that? And what precisely does he mean? For present purposes, suppose we restrict ourselves to the experience involved in the operation of the *sensus divinitatis*. I *think* what Mackie means is this: given any course of experience, religious or otherwise—that is, given any course of sensuous imagery, affective experience, and inclinations to believe I might have—that experience could be exactly as it is and there be no omnipotent being, or omniscient being, or perfectly good or eternal being. My experience could be precisely what it is, and there be no such person as God or anyone or anything at all like God. I could feel the very way I do feel, and there be no God.[4]

I *think* this is what he means; I can't be sure. That is because it seems of only dubious relevance. Perhaps it is true that my experience could be just as it is and there be no such person as God; perhaps the existence and character of my experience don't entail the existence of God. What follows? Why should it follow that my experience cannot reveal a creator of the world or an omnipotent or omniscient being? Consider an analogy: in WPF (pp. 50ff.), I noted that we all ordinarily think we have existed for many years (or, in the case of you younger readers, many months). It is logically possible, however, that I should have existed for only a microsecond or two, displaying all the temporally specific properties I do in fact display. Then I wouldn't have such properties as being more than sixty years old or being responsible for something that happened ten minutes ago, although I would have such properties as *thinking* that I am more than sixty years old and that I am responsible for something that happened ten minutes ago.

Not only is this logically possible, it is also compatible with the existence and character of all of my present experience. It is not compatible with my *beliefs*, of course (in that I believe I've existed for

---

4. Conceding for purposes of argument that God is not a necessary being. Of course if God *is* a necessary being, as most of the Christian tradition has thought, then his existence is *entailed* by the existence of my experience, because entailed by the existence of anything at all.

quite a while); still, it is compatible with the *existence* of those beliefs. It is possible that I should have precisely the beliefs and experiences I now have, despite my having come into existence just a second or less ago. (In fact [see WPF, pp. 50ff.], that is precisely what happens, according to those who think the word 'I', as I use it, denotes something like a momentary person stage.) For any course of experience and any set of beliefs I might have at this very moment, it is possible that I have that experience and hold those beliefs but nonetheless have existed for only a second or less.

Does it follow that nothing in my experience can reveal that I have existed for more than the last second or so? Certainly not. To assume that it *does* follow is to assume something more general and vastly stronger than O'Hear's (a) (above, p. 328) — which, as we have already seen, is itself too strong to be true. There isn't the slightest reason to believe that if experience can reveal p, then the existence of that experience (or the proposition that it occurs) must entail the truth of p. There is no reason to think that if experience can reveal a proposition p, then that experience must be such that it (logically) cannot so much as exist if p is false. For consider perception, and consider your experience — the sensuous imagery, the affective experience, the doxastic experience — on an occasion when you see a horse. It is compatible with those experiences that there be no horse there then, that there be no horses at all, that there be no material objects that exist when I am not undergoing those experiences, and, indeed, that there be no material objects at all. Does it follow that perceptual experience doesn't reveal an external world? Does it follow that I can't tell from my experience that there is a horse in my backyard? Or that the lilacs are not in bloom? Surely not; that would be a leap of magnificent (if grotesque) proportions.

Well then, how *does* perceptual experience reveal an external world — a horse, say? When I perceive a horse, I am the subject of experiences of various kinds: sensuous imagery (I am appeared to in a certain complicated and hard-to-describe fashion) and also, ordinarily, affective experience (perhaps I am frightened by the horse, or feel a certain admiration for it, or delight in its speed and strength or whatever). There is also doxastic experience. When I perceive a horse, there is that sensuous and affective experience, but also the feeling, experience, intimation with respect to a certain proposition (that I see a horse) that *that* proposition is *true*, *right*, to be believed, the way things really are. This doxastic experience plays a crucial role in perception. How *does* perceptual experience teach me that there is a horse in my backyard? By way of this belief's being occasioned (in part) by the experience, and by way of the belief's having warrant — being produced by properly functioning cognitive faculties in an appropriate epistemic environment (both mini and maxi), according to a design plan successfully aimed at truth. So can I tell from my experience that there is a horse there? Certainly. Telling such a thing from one's experience is forming the belief that a horse is there in response to the sensuous and doxastic experience, the belief's being formed under the conditions that confer warrant. The fact is, this happens all the time.

My point here is not that, in fact, people *do* tell from their experience such things as that there is a horse in the backyard, but rather that this is *possible*. More exactly, my point is that your seeing a horse in your backyard (thus determining by experience that there is a horse there) is not precluded by the fact that your experience is logically compatible with there being no horse there (or anywhere else). Your experience is logically compatible with there being no horse there: fair enough; but it simply doesn't follow that you can't tell by experience that there is a horse there. (How else would you tell? Deduce it from first principles and self-evident truths?) That's the way it is with *horses*; can I also tell from my experience that *I* have existed for more than a microsecond or so? Certainly. I do this by remembering, for example, that I had breakfast much more than a microsecond ago and that I went to college embarrassingly long ago. True, my experience here (in particular, my doxastic experience) is compatible with its being the case that I have existed for only a microsecond; it simply doesn't follow that I can't tell by experience that I have existed for at least a good hour, say. I determine by experience that I have existed for more than a microsecond if the belief that I did something more than a microsecond ago is occasioned by my experience (doxastic and otherwise) and if that belief is formed under conditions that confer warrant upon it. This happens often: so we often tell (by experience) that we have existed for more than a microsecond.

And of course the same goes for religious experience and theistic belief. True: the existence of the experiences that go with the operation of the *sensus divinitatis* (or IIHS) are compatible with there being no omnipotent, omniscient, wholly good creator of the universe. It doesn't follow from that, however, that we can't tell—and tell, broadly speaking, by experience—that there is such a person. For here, as elsewhere, there is doxastic experience: the belief that there is an almighty person to whom I owe allegiance and obedience just seems right, proper, true, the way things are. And one tells by experience that there is such a person if (1) the beliefs in question are formed in response to the experience (doxastic and otherwise) that go with the operation of the *sensus divinitatis* and (2) those beliefs are formed under the conditions of warrant. That these conditions should be met is, of course, entirely compatible with the fact that the existence of the experience, doxastic and otherwise, accompanying the operation of the *sensus divinitatis* is compatible with the falsehood of its deliverances. These beliefs can have warrant, and enough warrant to constitute knowledge, even if the existence of those experiences is compatible with the denials of those beliefs.[5] The same goes for belief in the great things of the gospel: they too can have warrant (and warrant sufficient for knowledge), even if, in fact, the existence of the experiences accompanying the IIHS is compatible with the falsehood of those beliefs.

Could it be that Mackie's point lies in a different direction? Perhaps he's thinking like this: an experience could reveal a *blue* object, all right, but not an *omnipotent* object. The claim is not that experience can't reveal any objects at all; the claim is rather that there are *some* properties such that experience could not reveal that there is an object with *those* properties. Examples would be such properties as omniscience, omnipotence, being divine, being the son of God, and the like. Here Mackie would presumably be relying on the analogy with sensuous experience: sensuous experience can perhaps reveal the existence of objects with color and shape properties (it can reveal the existence of blue and square objects) but not the existence of objects with properties like omnipotence.

By way of response: this is perhaps true of *sensuous experience* and of *perception*. It is not true of experience generally, however; in particular, it isn't true of *doxastic* experience. Memory and *a priori* belief formation involve doxastic experience; and the deliverances of memory and reason are not limited to the existence of things with perceptible properties. The same goes for the *sensus divinitatis* and the IIHS. Should we therefore conclude that what one learns, if anything, by way of these sources of belief is not really something learned by *experience*? Perhaps. If we do, however, then the claim that one can't learn by experience that there is, for example, an omnipotent being is no longer relevant to the model's stipulation that one can learn these things by way of the *sensus divinitatis* or the IIHS. Maybe one can't learn that sort of thing by experience; it will not follow that one cannot learn that sort of thing by way of the *sensus divinitatis* and the IIHS.

III. A KILLER ARGUMENT?

Richard Gale asks whether religious experience is 'cognitive', as he puts it.[6] What precisely does he mean? I think he means to ask whether religious experience is or could be part of a cognitive process that puts us in epistemic touch with God. The question is

---

5. I point out that this is so on *my* account of warrant, but the same goes for the other main accounts. Clearly beliefs produced by IIHS could be coherent with the appropriate body of belief, or formed by a reliable belief-producing mechanism, or justified, even if, as Mackie points out, the existence of the relevant experiences is compatible with the falsehood of the beliefs in question.

6. *On the Nature and Existence of God* (Cambridge: Cambridge University Press, 1991), pp. 285ff. In the remainder of this section page, references are to this work.

whether religious experience resembles sense experience in being part of a cognitive process that issues in *knowledge* of or *warranted belief* about an independent reality: God, for example. Gale argues that in fact religious experience is *not* cognitive, in this sense. He gives this argument in the course of addressing what he calls "the analogical argument for cognitivity," which he associates with William Alston, Gary Gutting, Richard Swinburne, and William Wainwright. Their argument, he says, has two premises:

1. Religious experiences are analogous to sense experiences.
2. Sense experiences are cognitive.

Therefore:

3. Religious experiences are cognitive. (p. 288)

Gale directs most of his fire at the first premise.

Here we must issue a couple of *caveats*. First, strictly speaking, Gale is objecting to this argument by objecting to premise 1; so, strictly speaking, his conclusion would not be that religious experience or belief is *not* cognitive, but only that this particular argument for its cognitivity fails. For present purposes, this doesn't matter: in fact Gale does much more than merely object to premise 1. What he really offers and what I want to consider is an argument for the conclusion that religious experience and belief are necessarily not cognitive. This argument, if successful, would show that it isn't possible that we should have anything like a perceptual awareness of God. Second, he also seems to believe or assume that any *experiential* awareness of God would have to be or be like *perceptual* awareness of God (that any experience of God that was part of a cognitive process yielding knowledge of or warranted belief about God would have to play the same role, in that process, as perceptual experience plays in perception); he therefore concludes, I think, that it is not possible to have knowledge of God by way of experience—that is, that religious experience is not cognitive.

Now it isn't entirely clear just how Gale's argument bears on my argument for the conclusion that theistic and Christian belief can have warrant by way of the *sensus divinitatis* and the IIHS (that, given the truth of these beliefs, there are no cogent objections to their having warrant in that way, so that any objection to these beliefs will have to be to their *truth* rather than to their rationality or reasonability). First of all, Gale didn't have my argument in mind, an omission that is entirely excusable, given that he proposed *his* argument well before I proposed *mine*. But second, the bearing of his argument on mine isn't clear because it isn't clear whether knowledge by way of the *sensus divinitatis* and the IIHS is properly thought of as knowledge by way of *experience*. It would be a shame, however, to pass up the chance to consider an argument as engaging as Gale's; so suppose we assume, for purposes of argument, that if there *is* any such thing as knowledge by way of these processes, that knowledge is knowledge by way of experience. Then we can consider Gale's argument as an argument against my conclusion. (Of course it could turn out that his argument is only dubiously relevant to mine precisely because it is dubious that knowledge by way of the *sensus divinitatis* and the IIHS, if there is any such knowledge, should be thought of as knowledge by experience.)

So how does the argument go? It begins with a playful threat directed at those who, as Gale thinks, accept the analogical argument for the cognitivity of religious experience:

> We have yet to unearth a deep disanalogy between sense and religious experience that will totally destroy the analogical premise of its analogical argument. This "big disanalogy" will prove to be the shipwreck of this defense of cognitivity, a time for Alston, Gutting, Swinburne, and Wainwright to join their fellow analogical arguers on the deck for a few heart-felt choruses of "Nearer My God to Thee." (p. 326)

Brave words! Does Gale speak with the tongue of an angel, or is he only a clanging cymbal? Precisely what *is* this killer argument?

> Necessarily, any cognitive perception is a veridical perception of an objective reality. It now will be argued that it is conceptually impossible for there to be a veridical perception of God . . . from which it follows by modus tollens that it is impossible that there be a cognitive religious experience. . . . A veridical sense perception must have an object that is able to exist when not actually perceived and be the common object of different sense perceptions. For this to be possible, the object must be housed in a space and time that includes both the object and perceiver. It then is shown that there is no religious experience analogue to this concept of objective existence, there being no analogous dimensions to space and time in which God, along with the perceiver, is housed and which can be invoked to make sense of God existing when not actually perceived and being the common object of different religious experiences. Because of this big disanalogy, God is categoreally unsuited to serve as the object of a veridical perception, whether sensory or nonsensory. (pp. 326–27)

Note first the implied claim in the second sentence: if it is conceptually impossible that there be a veridical *perception* of God, then it follows that it is impossible that there be "a cognitive religious experience"; Gale seems to believe that any variety of religious experience would be cognitive only if it were a part of a veridical perception of God. This seems wrong: as I argued in chapters 6 and 8, we can appropriately think of the *sensus divinitatis* and IIHS, on the extended A/C model, as providing knowledge of God that is knowledge by way of experience, but not *perceptual* knowledge. Consider the *sensus*

divinitatis: you are in grave danger and form the belief that God is
able to help; there needn't be anything here we can sensibly refer to
as *perception*. You suddenly realize that what you did was despicable;
you form the belief that God disapproves, acknowledging to him that
you did it; again, there need be nothing present that is properly
called perception. On the model, there is knowledge of God here,
and experience plays a crucial role—both the doxastic experience
and also the experience that goes with feeling afraid or guilty or
ashamed. This experience is closely associated with the operation of
the *sensus divinitatis*, and perhaps triggers the production of the relevant belief. But the result is not, I should think, a *perceptual* belief.
Furthermore, it is if anything clearer yet that knowledge of God and
of the great things of the gospel by the IIHS is not perceptual knowledge (above, p. 288). If we don't think of the *sensus divinitatis* and
IIHS as issuing in perceptual knowledge, however, then Gale's objection would be irrelevant.

   For present purposes then, suppose we also temporarily concede
that knowledge of God by way of *sensus divinitatis* or IIHS would be
perceptual knowledge of God, at least in an appropriately analogical
sense. Alternatively, suppose we consider Gale's objection to perceptual knowledge of God, bracketing, for the moment, the question of
its bearing on the extended A/C model. How does this objection go?
"A veridical sense perception," he says, "must have an object that is
able to exist when not actually perceived and be the common object
of different sense perceptions." That seems right, or at any rate plausible; and if there is such a thing as experience of God, God will, of
course, be able to exist when[7] not being experienced by any human
cognizer (even if in fact his presence is always experienced by some
human being or other). Furthermore, God himself, the very same
being, would be grasped, cognized, or apprehended by many different persons. So what exactly is supposed to be the problem with supposing that you and I are both aware of God, and that God continues
to exist when neither of us is aware of him? The problem, he thinks,
is that if an object can exist when unperceived, and can be perceived
by different perceivers, then "the object must be housed in a space
and time that includes both the object and perceiver." Why so? Gale's
strongest argument here is contained in the following passages:

> Another invidious consequence of their nondimensionality is that
> no analogous explanation can be given of how they can exist un-
> perceived and be common objects of different perceptions to that

---

   7. At any rate, if God is indeed in time. And even if he isn't, someone who says,
at a given time when (*per impossible*) no one is experiencing God, that God exists,
speaks the truth. See my "On Ockham's Way Out," *Faith and Philosophy* (July 1986).

which was previously given for empirical particulars. Whereas we could explain our failure to perceive an empirical particular, as well as our perceiving numerically one and the same empirical particular, in terms of our relationship to it in some nonempirical dimension, no such analogous explanation can be offered for our failure to perceive God and the like, or our perceiving numerically one and the same God. . . .

Similarly, how is Gutting going to decide when two religious experiences of a very powerful and loving nonhuman person had by two people at one time or by one person at two different times are of numerically one and the same being or only qualitatively similar ones? (pp. 341–42)

The alleged problem, therefore, seems to be twofold: it concerns (a) perceiving God at one time but not at another and (b) two different people's both perceiving God—that is, perceiving the very same all-powerful, all-knowing, and loving nonhuman person. It isn't as easy to see, however, just what Gale is claiming about (a) and (b). Two possibilities present themselves for (a) and three for (b). With respect to (a), Gale could be claiming that (1) if God is not in time and space, then *no explanation could be given* of our perceiving him at one time but not at another, and (2) if God is not in time and space, then it *would not be possible* that we experience him at one time but not at another. With respect to (b), the same two possibilities present themselves, and in addition there is the possibility that (3) if God is not in time and space, then *we couldn't decide* (*tell*) when two people are both perceiving God—that is, both perceiving the very same divine person.

Well, consider (1) with respect to (a). Strictly speaking, I suppose, it wouldn't damage the *sensus divinitatis* model or the claim that it is possible to perceive God if there were no *explanation* of our perceiving God at one time but not at another. All the model says is that such knowledge occurs; it doesn't go on to add that there is an explanation of it, unless the model itself is an explanation. Still, I believe Gale is really claiming, in this first possibility, that we can't see any way in which it could happen that we should perceive God at one time but not at another. More strongly, I think he means to claim that we *can* see that a person could perceive God at one time and not at another only if he and we were in the same time and space. We can see that this is the only condition under which such a thing could happen. So really, (1) and (2) with respect to (a) come to the same claim: it would be possible for us to perceive or experience God at one time but not at another only if he were in the same space and time (spacetime) as we.

So says Gale; is he right? I think not. Even with respect to things that *are* in space and time, there are a wide variety of explanations for my perceiving a thing at one time and not at another. I might perceive the thing at t_1, but then at t_2 have my eyes closed, or be asleep, or thinking of something else, or have lost my glasses, or have a brown paper bag over my head, or be under water, or be suffering from cognitive malfunction. Similarly for perceiving or cognizing God. God is, of course, always existent; furthermore, because (as we may assume for purposes of argument) he isn't in space, he is never related to me spatially in different ways at different times. Still, why should that mean that I couldn't perceive him or experience him at one time and not at another? I might perceive or experience him at t_1 but not at t_2 because at the latter I am asleep, or my attention might be elsewhere (I have just hit my thumb with a hammer or shot myself in the foot), or I might be suffering from cognitive malfunction, or I might be angry with God because of my friend's suffering and thus not in the right frame of mind. There are plenty of ways in which I might perceive him at one time but not at another, even if it's not possible that I be spatially related to him in different ways at different times.

Even if I am wide awake and eager to feel his presence, eager to receive an answer to prayer, or guidance, or a sense of his love, or a perception of his beauty and grace, I still might not get what I am hoping for. This might be because at that time, and for reasons of his own, God doesn't propose to communicate with me in those ways. Even if I am properly related to you both spatially and temporally and ask you a question, I might not get an answer. I ask you why you are smiling in that enigmatic way: you make no reply, perhaps because you think the question is an impertinence, or not worth answering, or because answering would interfere with your desire to remain enigmatic. When it comes to knowing and knowing about other persons, their cooperation is often required. Naturally enough, the same would be true of God, and perhaps on many or most occasions he chooses not to be perceived. As I argued in chapter 6, it isn't easy to say just what the necessary and sufficient conditions for perception are; whatever they are, however, they involve a certain sort of experience, an experience in which the perceived object seems to be *present to* or *given to* the percipient. Clearly, this experience could be absent at one time and present at another, whether or not God is in space.

This argument, then—the argument for the claim that if God is not in space and time, then we couldn't experience or perceive him at one time but not at another—seems to me to be entirely without promise. But what about Gale's claims with respect to (b)? Here he makes a double assertion: if God is not in time and space, then there could be no *explanation* of two people's both perceiving or experiencing him (we can't conceive of any way in which this could happen), and furthermore there couldn't be any way of telling that it was *God*, the very same person, that I experienced on two different occasions. Is there any reason to accept either of the suggestions? How could it happen that two different people should both perceive or experience God? Suppose both had the right kind of experience, including that sense of God's being present, being given. Suppose, furthermore, both formed the right kind of true belief about God—for example, that he is indeed present, given to them. And suppose, finally, the conditions of warrant are met: this belief is produced in them by cognitive faculties functioning properly in a congenial epistemic environment according to a design plan successfully aimed at truth. Then they would both be perceiving God, despite the fact that God is not in space. Is there really a problem here? If so, it is well concealed. Gale or someone else might claim that there is a problem with the very idea of our forming beliefs about God: what would make it *God* the belief was about? But this is a wholly different kind of objection and is really the objection dealt with in chapters 1 and 2; it is as inconclusive here as it was there.

Similarly for the other part of the suggestion: that it would be impossible to tell whether it was the same divine person one experienced on two different occasions. Because God is not in space, so the claim goes, we could never tell whether we encountered the same divine being on occasion *B* that we had encountered on occasion *A*. But is there any reason for thinking this true? This argument, I think, is as fatally flawed as the last. The idea seems to be that with objects not in space, one can't, in principle, tell when one has encountered the same one again, or only encountered another thing that is appropriately *like* the first thing. But is this in fact true? What exactly is the problem? Suppose your experience is related to God in the right way and you form beliefs about him on two subsequent occasions, t_1 and t_2; at t_2 you form the true belief that the being about whom you are then forming a belief is the same being about whom you formed a belief at t_1: if this belief is formed under warrant-conferring conditions, then you would have told that the being about whom you formed a belief at t_2 is the very same being as the one about whom you formed the belief at t_1. Indeed, that's just what it *is* to tell that the t_2 belief is about the same being as the t_1 belief. Well, perhaps the claim is that one can never tell that a t_2 belief *is* about the same being as a t_1 belief, if both beliefs are about a *nonspatial* object. This also seems quite wrong. At t_1 I think of the null set, or the proposition that all men are mortal; I then read Gale's book or watch a football game on TV, and at t_2 think again about the null set (or that proposition). Is there really a problem with my telling or knowing that it is the same thing I think about at t_2 as at t_1? Should I be in doubt as to whether the set I think of at t_2 really is the same set as that I thought of at t_1?

Could it be that Gale's suggestion is that if a *dispute* arose over whether what I experience on a given occasion is the same being as you experience on a given occasion, the dispute might turn out to be intractable? Alternatively, might I not (like Teresa of Avila and others) be uncertain, on a given occasion, whether it was *God* I was in contact with, as opposed to Satan, who appears as an angel of light and is out to deceive me? Couldn't this happen? Of course it could. But it doesn't show I could *never* tell that I am experiencing God; what it shows is only that perhaps on *those* occasions I can't tell whether it is God with whom I am in contact. True: it is possible that appearances be just what they are and I *not* experience God. As we have already seen, however, nothing follows from this: the same is true with respect to perception, memory, and my knowledge that I have existed for a substantial length of time. It is clearly possible that I have the experience that goes with perceiving a horse and yet no horse is there.[8] So it could be that on *some* occasion I really can't tell: still, this hardly shows that I can *never* tell. And once more: the way I tell whether it is God, that very person, whom I perceive or experience on two different occasions, is by forming (under warrant-conferring conditions) the true belief that indeed I encountered God on both occasions.

I think it is clear, therefore, that these arguments don't even begin to show that perception of God is impossible, or that religious experience is never cognitive, or that there couldn't be knowledge of God by way of the *sensus divinitatis* and IIHS. Gale's arguments depend upon a lot of assumptions that have little or no claim to assent: that if you sometimes can't tell whether *p*, for example, then you can never tell whether *p*; or that if God is not in space and time, then you could never tell that it was he with whom you were in contact on successive occasions; or that if God is not in space and time, it couldn't be that you should experience him on one occasion and not on another. All of these assumptions seem monumentally dubious at best.[9]

IV. SON OF GREAT PUMPKIN?

Now according to the extended A/C model, belief in God and belief in the central tenets of the Christian faith can be rational and have warrant when they are not accepted on the evidential basis of other beliefs. On this model, they can have warrant that they don't get by way of being believed on the evidential basis of other beliefs; they can

---

8. But aren't there checks and tests for telling whether you really perceive a horse? Indeed there are; but consider the experiences that go with checking to see whether you perceive a horse and determining that you *did* see a horse: it is also logically possible that you have all *those* experiences when, in fact, there is no horse there.

9. And, of course, there remains the point that the extended A/C model does not, strictly speaking, require that one *perceive* God at all.

have warrant that they don't get by way of warrant transfer from other beliefs. In this respect, they are like memory beliefs, perceptual beliefs, some *a priori* beliefs, and so on. The beliefs of the Christian faith, on the suggestion in question, are a proper *starting point* for thought. Another way to put this: these beliefs are *properly basic*, and properly basic with respect to warrant. What I mean to consider next is a nest of objections to the thought that these beliefs *could* receive warrant in the basic way. Now objections of this sort have so far been centered on the claim that belief in God (as opposed to specifically Christian belief) is or can be properly basic; that is because for the most part it is belief in God, not specifically Christian belief, that has so far been claimed to be or possibly to be properly basic. To simplify matters, I will confine discussion to the *sensus divinitatis* and belief in God; what I say, however, will apply equally well to the IIHS and the beliefs produced by it.

First, there is the claim that if belief in God is really properly basic with respect to warrant, then arguments and objections will not be relevant to it; it will be beyond rational scrutiny and will be insulated from objections and defeaters. But obviously objection and argument *are* relevant to theistic belief: therefore, it isn't warrant-basic. Thus Michael Martin: "Plantinga's foundationalism is radically relativistic and puts any belief beyond rational appraisal once it is declared basic."[10]

Why think a thing like that? Theistic belief would certainly *not* be immune to argument and defeat just by virtue of being basic. In this, theistic belief only resembles other kinds of beliefs accepted in the basic way. You tell me that you went to the Grand Tetons this summer; I acquire the belief that you did so and hold it in the basic way.[11] But then your wife tells me that the fact is you went to the Wind Rivers, which, she says, you always confuse with the Tetons. Furthermore, the next time I see you, you go on at great length about the glories of Gannett Peak (which is in the Wind Rivers). Then I will no longer believe you went to the Tetons, despite the fact that I originally formed that belief in the basic way. Another example: I see what looks like a sheep in the field across the road, and I form in the basic way the belief that there is a sheep there; you, the owner of the field, tell me that there aren't any sheep in it, although there is a dog in the neighborhood that looks just like a sheep from this distance. Then I will no longer believe that I see a sheep, despite the fact that the

10. *Atheism: A Philosophical Justification* (Philadelphia: Temple University Press, 1990), p. 276.

11. I don't hold it on the evidential basis of such an argument as *George says he went to the Tetons last summer; most of what George says is true; so probably this is.* I *could* accept testimony on the basis of such an argument, and perhaps in certain special circumstances (a murder trial, for example) I *would* do so; but in the typical case I don't.

belief is accepted in the basic way. Still another example: Gottlob Frege formed in the basic way the belief that for every property or condition, there exists the set of just those things that have the property or satisfy the condition; he learned to his sorrow that this is not so (Bertrand Russell pointed out that it leads to paradox[12]), and this despite the fact that the original belief had been basic.

So it is not true, in general, that if a belief is held in the basic way, then it is immune to argument or rational evaluation; why, therefore, think it must hold for theistic belief? The fact, if it is a fact, that belief in God is properly basic doesn't for a moment imply that it is immune to argument, objection, or defeat; it is surely no consequence of my foundationalism or of the A/C model (*simpliciter* or extended) that basic beliefs are beyond rational appraisal.[13] I wouldn't so much as mention this, except that there seems to be a fairly widespread impression to the contrary.

A related complaint: according to the Great Pumpkin Objection,[14] if belief in God can be properly basic, then so can any other belief, no matter how bizarre: if belief in God can be properly basic, then all bets are off, and anything goes. You might as well claim that belief in the Great Pumpkin (who returns every Halloween to the most sincere pumpkin patch) is properly basic with respect to warrant. You might as well make the same claim for atheism, voodoo, astrology, witchcraft, and anything else you can think of. According to Dostoevski, if God does not exist, everything is possible; according to this objection, if belief in God is properly basic, everything is warranted. This objection, of course, is plainly false. To recognize that *some* kinds of belief are properly basic with respect to warrant doesn't for a moment commit one to thinking all *other* kinds are; even if the extended A/C model is correct, it doesn't follow that these other beliefs are properly basic with respect to warrant. Descartes and Locke thought *some* beliefs were properly basic with respect to warrant; should we object that they were therefore committed to thinking just *any* belief is properly basic?

12. One condition is that of being nonselfmembered; so, if Frege's belief were true, there would be a set of nonselfmembered sets—which would have to be both a member of itself and not a member of itself. Hence Frege's belief was false.

13. In "Reason and Belief in God," in *Faith and Rationality* (Notre Dame: University of Notre Dame Press, 1983), a paper Martin quotes several times in his book, I said, "Suppose someone accepts belief in God as basic. Does it not follow that he will hold this belief in such a way that no argument could move him or cause him to give it up? . . . Does he not thereby adopt a posture in which argument and other rational methods of settling disagreement are implicitly declared irrelevant? Surely not." See pp. 82ff., "Is Argument Irrelevant to Basic Belief?"

14. See "Reason and Belief in God," pp. 74ff.

So the Great Pumpkin Objection as it stands is obviously a non-starter. Michael Martin recognizes this,[15] but raises a related objection; it is this objection, I think, that underlies his claim that my views are "radically relativistic":

> Although reformed epistemologists would not have to accept voodoo beliefs as rational, voodoo followers would be able to claim that insofar as they are basic in the voodoo community they are rational and, moreover, that reformed thought was irrational in this community. Indeed, Plantinga's proposal would generate many different communities that could *legitimately* claim that their basic beliefs are rational. . . . Among the communities generated might be devil worshipers, flat earthers, and believers in fairies, just so long as belief in the devil, the flatness of the earth, and fairies was basic in the respective communities. (p. 272)

Call this objection 'Son of Great Pumpkin' (SGP). How exactly does it go? The first thing to see here is that SGP has moved up a level from the Great Pumpkin Objection itself. The latter complains that, on the view I've been presenting, just any proposition, no matter how fantastic, would have to be accepted as properly basic; this complaint, as Martin sees, is obviously false. SGP, therefore, moves up a level: according to SGP, someone who took any proposition p in the basic way could *legitimately claim* that p was properly basic—properly basic with respect to *rationality*, says Martin—that is, such that it can be both rationally accepted and accepted in the basic way. Take any possible community and any beliefs accepted as basic in that community: the epistemologists of that community could legitimately claim that these beliefs are rationally accepted in the basic way. Could, if *what*? What does Martin mean? There is more than one possibility, but I think he means this: could, if the 'Reformed epistemologist' can legitimately claim that theistic belief is properly basic. So the structure of the objection would have to be this:

(1) If Reformed epistemologists can legitimately claim that belief in God is rationally acceptable in the basic way, then for any other belief accepted in some community, the epistemologists of that community could legitimately claim that *it* was properly basic, no matter how bizarre the belief.

But

(2) The consequent of this conditional is false.

So

(3) The Reformed epistemologist can't legitimately claim that belief in God is rationally acceptable in the basic way.

15. *Atheism*, p. 272.

Is this a good argument? One initial problem is that the argument is pretty loosely stated; Martin doesn't tell us what he means by 'rational', and he doesn't tell us what he means by 'legitimately'. As to the first, perhaps the best candidates would be rationality as justification (deontological justification), internal rationality, and rationality in the sense of warrant. We needn't linger long over rationality as justification: obviously the voodooists could be within their intellectual rights in thinking what they do think (if only by virtue of cognitive malfunction); hence they could be justified. But then, presumably someone (the voodoo epistemologists, e.g.) could legitimately *claim* that those voodooists were justified, no matter what, precisely, Martin means by 'legitimately'. Premise (2) of the argument, specified with respect to justification, is thus clearly false.

Well, suppose we specify the argument to internal rationality; take 'rationally acceptable' to mean 'internally rational'. Then again the answer is pretty easy. A belief is internally rational if it is produced by faculties functioning properly 'downstream from experience' (see above, p. 110)—if, given your experience (including doxastic experience) at the time in question, it is compatible with proper function that you accept the belief in question. That could certainly be so for the voodooists. Perhaps they have always been taught that these voodoo beliefs are true, and all alleged contrary evidence is cleverly explained away by the priests; or perhaps they are all in the grip of some cognitive malfunction upstream from experience, one that skews their doxastic experience. If that could be so for the voodoists, then the voodoo epistemologists could no doubt know that the voodoists *are* internally rational in these judgments, and hence (one supposes, legitimately) report this fact. Premise (2) fails for internal rationality, just as for justification.

Accordingly, if we are to have something worth considering here, the argument must presumably be specified to rationality in the sense of warrant. The question is whether, if I can legitimately claim that belief in God is properly basic with respect to warrant, the epistemologists of the voodoo community can legitimately claim that those voodoo beliefs are properly basic with respect to warrant. But now we do need to know what is meant, here, by 'legitimately claim'. There seem to be three salient possibilities: claim *truthfully*, claim *justifiably*, and claim *warrantedly*. First, therefore, Martin could mean that if belief in God can *truthfully* be said to be warrant basic, then the same goes for voodoo belief. We have already seen, however, that this is false. It is entirely possible that belief in God have warrant in the basic way and voodoo belief *not* have it in the basic way; this state of affairs would obtain, for example, if the A/C model is true, but voodoo belief originates in some kind of cognitive error. So premise (1) of the argument would fail.

Second, Martin might mean that if belief in God can *justifiably* be said to be warrant basic, then the same goes for voodoo belief: it too can justifiably be said to be warrant basic. Again, this is too easy: obviously those epistemologists might be *justified* in thinking that voodoo belief was warrant basic: it might seem just obvious to them, after protracted reflection and after considering objections, that, indeed, voodoo belief is warrant basic. So taken, premise (2) fails.

If we are to locate a respectable objection, then, it looks as if we must specify 'legitimately' to 'warrantedly'. Take both 'rationally acceptable' and 'legitimately' as 'warrantedly': then is the argument a good one? Martin's claim, so construed, would be that (1) if the claim made by the Reformed epistemologist—namely, that belief in God is properly basic with respect to warrant—has warrant, then for any proposition *p* (no matter how bizarre) accepted by some community, if the epistemologists of that community were to claim that *p* is properly basic with respect to warrant, their claim would itself have warrant; (2) the consequent of (1) is false; the conclusion of the argument would be that the Reformed epistemologist's claim does not enjoy warrant. A problem with evaluating this version of the argument is that the Reformed epistemologist (*this* Reformed epistemologist, anyway) doesn't claim as part of his philosophical position that belief in God and the deliverances of IIHS *do* have warrant. That is because (above, p. 186ff.) in all likelihood they have warrant only if they are true, and I am not arguing that these beliefs are in fact true. No doubt the Reformed epistemologist does believe that they *are* true, and is prepared to *claim* that they are, even if he doesn't propose to argue for that claim. So for the nonce, suppose we think of the Reformed epistemologists as actually claiming that belief in God and the deliverances of the IIHS enjoy warrant in the basic way; suppose further that they claim this 'legitimately'—that is, under the current interpretation, suppose this claim itself has warrant for them. Would it follow that for any proposition *p*, if there were a community who endorsed *p*, these people (or the epistemologists of their community) would be warranted in believing that *p* is properly basic with respect to warrant for those in this community?

It would not follow. Suppose the extended A/C model is true (not just possible); then (a) the central claims of the Christian faith are, in fact, true, (b) there really are such cognitive processes as the *sensus divinitatis* and IIHS, and (c) their deliverances do meet the conditions for warrant. Suppose a Reformed epistemologist believes the great things of the gospel on the basis of the *sensus divinitatis* and IIHS; suppose he notes, further, that his belief and that of many others is accepted in the basic way (where, of course, accepting *p* on the basis of testimony is one way to believe *p* in the basic way). Suppose he further comes to see or believe that God intends his children to know about him and to know the great things of the gospel, but also that it isn't possible for enough of us to know enough about him by way of inference from other beliefs; he therefore concludes (correctly) that God has instituted cognitive processes by virtue of which we human beings can form these true beliefs in the basic way. He concludes still further that the cognitive processes or mechanisms by way of which we form these beliefs are functioning properly when it delivers them, and are also functioning in an epistemically congenial environment according to a design plan successfully aimed at truth: that is, he concludes that Christian belief, taken in this basic way, has warrant. He thus concludes that these beliefs are properly basic with respect to warrant, drawing this conclusion from beliefs that themselves have warrant; but forming a belief in that way itself meets the conditions for warrant; hence, his view that theistic belief is properly basic with respect to warrant is itself warranted.

It doesn't follow, of course, that the voodoo epistemologist is also warranted in claiming that voodoo belief is properly basic with respect to warrant. For suppose voodoo belief is in fact false, and suppose further that it arose originally in some kind of mistake or confusion, or out of a fearful reaction to natural phenomena of one sort or another, or in the mind of some group hoping to gain or perpetuate personal political power. If so, then those original voodoo beliefs did not possess warrant. Suppose still further that these voodoo beliefs were passed on to subsequent generations by way of testimony and teaching. Now if a testifier testifies to some belief p that has no warrant for her, then p will also have no warrant for anyone believing it on just the basis of her testimony. If p has no warrant for the testifier, then it has none for the testifiee either—even if the latter's faculties are working perfectly properly.[16] I am taught a lot of garbage by my parents (out of profound ignorance, they teach me that the stars are really pinholes in a giant canvass stretched over the earth each night in order to give humankind a good night's sleep, or that Frisians are politically inferior and should not be allowed to vote); then, even if my own cognitive faculties are functioning properly in the conditions propitious for warrant, my beliefs acquired by way of this testimony lack warrant.

So consider the voodoo epistemologist, and suppose he accepts those voodoo views on the basis of testimony and (analogous to the Reformed epistemologist) reasons from their truth together with other premises to their being properly basic with respect to warrant. Then his conclusion that voodoo beliefs are warrant-basic will not itself be warranted, because it is accepted on the basis of an argument at least one premise of which has no warrant for him. That is because

16. See WPF, p. 83.

inference exhibits the same sort of warrant-dependent structure as testimony. I believe *p* and *q*; these together yield (deductively, or in some other way) *r*; *r* will have warrant for me if *p* and *q* do (and perhaps we must add if *p and q*, the conjunction of *p* and *q* does); but if either *p* or *q* lacks warrant for me, the same will go for *r*. (Clearly I can't come to know some proposition by inferring it from propositions some of which I don't know.[17]) The voodoo philosophers are mistaken in holding their voodoo views; furthermore, their claim that voodoo views are properly basic with respect to warrant is both false and not itself warranted.

It could certainly happen, therefore, that the views of the Reformed epistemologist are legitimate in the sense of being warranted, and those of the voodoo epistemologist, who arrives at his views in structurally the same way as the Reformed epistemologist, are not. That could be if, for example, the central claims of the Christian faith are true and voodoo belief is false. It is therefore not the case that if the claim that belief in God and in the great things of the gospel is properly basic with respect to warrant is itself warranted, then by the same token the claim that voodoo belief is properly basic with respect to warrant is itself warranted. Martin's argument, construed as we are currently construing it, therefore fails; its first premise is false.

By way of summary: Martin's complaint, apparently, is that if the Reformed epistemologist can legitimately claim that Christian belief is properly basic with respect to rationality, then the philosophers of a community with clearly crazy beliefs could, with equal legitimacy, claim that those crazy beliefs are properly basic with respect to rationality; but clearly they couldn't claim this; so the Reformed epistemologist can't legitimately make his claim. This complaint is multiply ambiguous, inheriting the multiple ambiguity of 'legitimately' and 'rationality'. Most of the disambiguations, however, show no promise at all. The last disambiguation, where 'legitimately' and 'rationality' are both understood as referring to warrant, is at least interesting; the argument so construed, however, suffers from the annoying defect of having a false premise. Son of Great Pumpkin does no better than Great Pumpkin.[18]

Now in the spirit of Son of Great Pumpkin, we might raise a slightly more general question here. I propose the extended A/C model as a way in which Christian belief can have warrant in the

---

17. Here I ignore such carping criticisms as that I might deduce *r* from *p* and *q* by deducing it from *p* alone, which does in fact have warrant for me.

18. Note, in particular, that Son of Great Pumpkin doesn't furnish the objector with a criticism of Christian belief that is independent of its truth—that is, can be thought to hold even if Christian belief is in fact true. It therefore does not provide a *de jure* criticism.

basic way and argue three things: (a) this model is possible, both logically and epistemically; (b) given the truth of Christian belief, there
are no philosophical objections to this model's also being not merely
possible but true; and (c) if Christian belief is indeed true, then very
probably it does have warrant, and has it in some way similar to the
extended A/C model. Now couldn't this be argued with equal cogency with respect to any set of beliefs, no matter how weird? And
wouldn't that at any rate reduce the interest of my claim?

Certainly not. Many propositions are not such that, if they are
true, then very likely they have warrant: the proposition *No beliefs
have warrant* comes to mind. But, you say, isn't this just a bit of logical
legerdemain; are there any systems of beliefs seriously analogous to
Christian belief for which these claims cannot be made? For any such
set of beliefs, couldn't we find a model under which the beliefs in
question have warrant, and such that, given the truth of those beliefs,
there are no philosophical objections to the truth of the model? Well,
probably something like that *is* true for the other theistic religions:
Judaism, Islam, some forms of Hinduism, some forms of Buddhism,
some forms of American Indian religion. Perhaps these religions are
like Christianity in that they are subject to no *de jure* objections that
are independent of *de facto* objections. Still, that isn't true for just *any*
such set of beliefs. It isn't true, for example, for voodooism, or the belief that the earth is flat, or Humean skepticism, or philosophical naturalism.

For consider the set of beliefs involved in Hume's skepticism with
respect to his origins and the origins of his cognitive faculties (above,
p. 218). Hume—at any rate, as we understood him in chapter 7—
holds that we ought to be skeptical of the reliability of our belief-
forming processes. He thinks he can see that what nature inevitably
leads us to believe is unlikely, or arbitrary, or at best extremely dubious; hence the right cognitive attitude with respect to the beliefs induced in us by nature is that attitude of ironic detachment. We recognize that we can't help holding these beliefs; we also recognize that
they are not to be relied upon. But if we are skeptical of the reliability of our cognitive processes, then we also have reason to be skeptical of any particular deliverances of those processes, including the
beliefs that lead us to be skeptical of them—hence the reflexive, self-
referential character of the irony. Now: can we find a possible model
in which these beliefs—including the beliefs that what nature leads
us to believe is arbitrary, or not to be relied upon—are warranted?
More poignantly, can we find a model such that if this belief is true,
then very likely it is warranted? Clearly not.

Perhaps someone will think that Hume's skepticism about his origins and the origins of his cognitive faculties is not much like Christian belief; no doubt this is true. So consider instead philosophical
naturalism: the view that there is no such person as God or anyone
(or anything) at all like him. (Contemporary naturalists ordinarily

add that the only things there are, are the entities hypothesized or acknowledged by contemporary science.) Such naturalists also add that we and our cognitive faculties have arisen by way of the processes pointed to in contemporary evolutionary theory—principally random genetic mutation and natural selection. This is, of course, a great deal more like Christian belief. For many, perhaps particularly many academics, it plays some of the same roles as those played by religious belief: it tells us where we come from, where we are going, and what the fundamental explanations are for the main features of our own nature. But if I am right in the argument I gave in chapter 12 of WPF (and corrected in this volume, pp. 227ff.), this set of beliefs is not such that if it is true, then very likely it has warrant. For what the argument shows is that if these beliefs are true, then it is not likely that our belief-producing processes and mechanisms are, in fact, reliable, in which case the beliefs that they produce, including the belief that naturalism is true, do not have warrant. So it is false that what I argue for Christian belief is true for just any set of beliefs; indeed, it isn't true for what (in the Western academic world, at any rate) is perhaps the main alternative to Christian belief.

V. CIRCULARITY?

Still, isn't there something circular in my argument? According to Paul Noble, Jonathan Edwards's "theistic defense of passional reason raises the spectre of epistemic circularity: the theistic metaphysics grounds one's belief in the legitimacy of 'spiritual perception', and yet Edwards also appeals to such perceptions as vindicating the truth of theism."[19] Wouldn't something like the same be true of my model? Isn't it true that my own proposal has warrant for me (or anyone who accepts it) only if theistic belief is in fact true and, indeed, warranted? I propose the extended A/C model as a model for the way in which Christian and theistic belief can have warrant, but won't it be the case that I am warranted in proposing this model only if, in fact, the model or something like it is correct, and Christian belief does have warrant? No. What I claim for the model is only that it is (1) possible, (2) subject to no philosophical objections that do not assume that Christian belief is false, and (3) such that if Christian belief is true, the model is at least close to the truth. But obviously it is not the case that my assertion of or belief in the truth of (1), (2), or (3) has warrant only if the model is true or Christian belief is warranted.

Now suppose I proposed the model as indeed the truth (or close to the truth) about the way Christian belief has warrant: *then,* would my proposal be in some way circular? Well, why should we think so? Perhaps the idea is something like this: because central Christian beliefs are included in or entailed by the model, I am warranted in thinking the model true only if I am warranted in accepting Christian belief; those central Christian beliefs must already have warrant, for me, if my belief that the model is true is to have warrant. But then am I not involved in some kind of objectionable circle?

I can't see how. It is indeed true that I will have to be warranted in accepting Christian belief if I am to be warranted in accepting the extended A/C model as true; that is because the former is included in the latter. It is not the case, however, that if Christian belief has warrant for me, then the model must also have warrant for me. That would be true if I *argued* for Christian belief by way of an argument one premise of which was the extended A/C model. More exactly, that would be true if such an argument were the only source of warrant, for me, of Christian belief. For then any warrant enjoyed by my Christian belief would accrue to it by way of warrant transfer from the premises of that argument; but one premise of that argument would be a conjunction, one conjunct of which was itself part of Christian belief. There would therefore be a vicious circle in the *receives-its-warrant-from* relation.

So if the source of the warrant of my Christian belief were this argument, then indeed the project would suffer from vicious circularity. But it isn't, and it doesn't. The source of warrant for Christian belief, according to the model, is not argument of any sort; in particular, its warrant does not arise from some argument about how Christian belief can have warrant. To show that there is circularity here, the objector would have to show that any warrant enjoyed by Christian belief *must,* somehow, have come from argument of some sort; and this, as we have seen, can't be done. This objection, then, is no more successful than the others.

No doubt there are other objections, perhaps even other sensible objections. I don't know of any, however, and am therefore obliged to refrain from responding to them until I hear about them. In the meantime, I shall provisionally take it that there aren't any such objections.

Now the objections considered in this chapter are objections to the claim that Christian belief can have warrant in the basic way. They are therefore philosophical objections to a philosophical claim. Now of course it is possible that Christian belief *could* have warrant in this way, even if *in fact* it has little or no warrant. For perhaps there is a source of warrant, for Christian belief, but the warrant in question is *defeated.* No doubt the belief that the earth is flat once had warrant for many. But then people encountered *defeaters* for this belief: for example, there is the peculiar way in which ships disappear over the horizon, along with the other arguments that led people to give up this belief. (Even if you are skeptical with respect to *those* arguments, you may be swayed by pictures of the earth taken from a satellite and by eyewitness reports as to what the earth looks like from three hundred miles away.) Might not the same be true for Christian belief? Aren't there serious defeaters for it—defeaters that are prominent now, even if they weren't available 250 years ago? That is the topic of the next (and last) section of this book.

PART IV

DEFEATERS?

11

Defeaters and Defeat

> The philosophical case against theism is rather easily dealt with.
> There is no philosophical case against theism.
>
> G. K. Chesterton

I've argued that Christian belief—the full panoply of Christian belief, including trinity, incarnation, atonement, resurrection—can, if true, have warrant, can indeed have sufficient warrant for knowledge, and can have that warrant in the basic way. There are no cogent philosophical objections to the notion that these beliefs can have warrant in this way. It is easily possible to work out an account—for example, the extended Aquinas/Calvin (A/C) model—of how it is that beliefs of these sorts do indeed have warrant. This way does not involve arguments from other beliefs. Rather, the fundamental idea is that God provides us human beings with faculties or belief-producing processes that yield these beliefs and are successfully aimed at the truth; when they work the way they were designed to in the sort of environment for which they were designed, the result is warranted belief. Indeed, if these beliefs are true and the degree of their warrant sufficiently high, they constitute knowledge.

Of course this hardly settles the issue as to whether Christian belief (even if true) has or can have warrant in the circumstances in which most of us actually find ourselves. Someone might put it like this: "Well, perhaps these beliefs can have warrant, and perhaps (if they are true) even warrant sufficient for knowledge: there are circumstances in which this can happen. Most of us, however—for example, most of those who read this book—are not in those circumstances. What you have really argued so far is only that theistic and Christian belief (taken in the basic way) can have warrant, *absent defeaters*. But defeaters are not absent." The claim is that there are serious defeaters for Christian belief: propositions we know or believe that make Christian belief—at any rate, Christian belief held in the basic way and with anything like sufficient firmness to constitute knowledge—*irrational* and hence unwarranted. Philip Quinn, for example, believes that for "intellectually sophisticated adults in our culture" there are important defeaters for belief in God—at least if, as in the extended A/C model, held in the basic way. As a result, belief in God held in the basic way, as in the model, is for the most part irrational: "I conclude that many, perhaps most, intellectually sophisticated adults in our culture are seldom if ever in conditions which are right for [theistic beliefs] to be properly basic for them."[1] The defeaters that particularly impress Quinn are, first, natural evil (evil that is not due to human free will) and, second, projective theories of theistic belief, such as those of Freud, Marx, and Durkheim.

In this and the next chapters, I'll deal with four proposed defeaters for Christian belief. In this chapter, after a brief investigation of the nature of defeaters, I'll argue that the projective theories Quinn mentions do not in fact constitute a defeater for Christian belief. In chapter 12, I'll argue that contemporary historical biblical criticism ('higher criticism') doesn't serve as a defeater for Christian belief, even when its alleged results do not support Christian belief and, indeed, even when they go counter to it. In chapter 13 I'll examine the claim that the facts of religious pluralism constitute a defeater for Christian belief; I'll also look into the idea that the development of postmodern thought is, in some way, a defeater for such belief. I'll argue that neither offers such a defeater. Finally, in chapter 14 I'll consider what has often been seen as the most formidable challenge of all to Christian belief: the facts of suffering and evil. This challenge too, I'll argue, does not as such constitute a defeater for Christian belief.

---

1. "On Finding the Foundations of Theism," *Faith and Philosophy* 2, no. 4 (1985), p. 481. See my "The Foundations of Theism: A Reply," *Faith and Philosophy* 3, no. 3 (1986) pp. 298ff.; and Quinn's rejoinder, "The Foundations of Theism Again," in *Rational Faith: Catholic Responses to Reformed Epistemology*, ed. Linda Zagzebski (Notre Dame: University of Notre Dame Press, 1993), pp. 14ff.

I. THE NATURE OF DEFEATERS

Now what we need initially is some account of what a defeater, for a belief, is. The fact is there is a great deal to be said about defeaters.[2] First, however, we need some examples. As in the last chapter I see (at a hundred yards) what I take to be a sheep in a field and form the belief that there is a sheep in the field; I know that you are the owner of the field; the next day you tell me that there are no sheep in that field, although you own a dog who looks like a sheep at a hundred yards and who frequents the field. Then (in the absence of special circumstances) I have a defeater for the belief that there was a sheep in that field and will, if rational, no longer hold that belief. This is a *rebutting* defeater—what you learn (that there are no sheep in that field) is inconsistent with the defeated belief. But there are also *undercutting* defeaters. Here is an example due to John Pollock. You enter a factory and see an assembly line on which there are a number of widgets, all of which look red. You form the belief that indeed they are red. Then along comes the shop superintendent, who informs you that the widgets are being irradiated by red and infrared light, a process that makes it possible to detect otherwise undetectable hairline cracks. You then have a defeater for your belief that the widget you are looking at is red. In this case, what you learn is not something incompatible with the defeated belief (you aren't told that this widget isn't red); what you learn, rather, is something that undercuts your grounds or reasons for thinking it red. (You realize that it would look red even if it weren't.) Defeaters are reasons for giving up a belief *b* you hold; if they are rebutting defeaters, they are also reasons for accepting a belief incompatible with *b*. Acquiring a defeater for a belief puts you in a position in which you can't rationally continue to hold the belief.

Defeaters of this kind are *rationality* defeaters; given belief in the defeating proposition, you can retain belief in the defeated proposition only at the cost of irrationality. There are also *warrant* defeaters that are not rationality defeaters. Thus in Carl Ginet's fake barn example, as you are driving through southern Wisconsin, you seem to see many fine barns. Fixing on a particular one, you say to yourself, "That is a splendid barn!" What you don't know, however, is that the local Wisconsinites have erected many clever barn facades (from the road indistinguishable from real barns) to make themselves look more prosperous. What you are actually looking at, however, is a real

---

2. Some of which is to be found in Michael Bergmann's *Internalism, Externalism, and Epistemic Defeat* (University of Notre Dame Ph.D. dissertation, 1997). See also John Pollock's *Contemporary Theories of Knowledge* (Totowa, N.J.: Rowman Littlefield, 1986), pp. 37ff.; and my unpublished paper "Naturalism Defeated."

barn, not a barn facade. Still, you don't *know* that it is a barn; it is only by sheer serendipitous good fortune that the belief you form is true. (You might just as well have been looking at a barn facade—indeed, you might *better* have been looking at a barn facade, because the ratio of barn facades to barns in this area is 3:1.) To put the matter in the terminology of chapter 5 (above, pp. 158ff.), you are in an unfavorable cognitive minienvironment, and it is those barn facades that make the minienvironment unfavorable. The presence of the fake barns is a *warrant* defeater for you: given the presence of the fake barns there, you don't know that the thing you are looking at is, indeed, a barn—even though it is and you believe that it is. The existence of the fake barns is not a rationality defeater, however, for there is nothing irrational, in your circumstances, in believing that what you see is a barn.

Defeaters depend on and are relative to the rest of your noetic structure, the rest of what you know and believe. Whether a belief *A* is a defeater for a belief *B* doesn't depend merely on my current experience; it also depends on what other beliefs I have, how firmly I hold them, and the like. Consider, for example, the above case, where your saying that there are no sheep in the field is a defeater for my belief that I see a sheep there; this depends on my assuming you to be trustworthy, at least on this occasion and on this topic. By contrast, if I know you are a notorious practical joker especially given to misleading people about sheep, what you say will not constitute a defeater; neither will it if I am inspecting the sheep through powerful binoculars and clearly see that it is a sheep, or if there is someone I trust standing right in front of the sheep, who tells me by cell phone that it is indeed a sheep.

As a result of this relativity to noetic structure, it can happen that you and I both learn a given proposition *p*, that it constitutes a defeater for another belief *q* for me, but does not do so for you. For example, you and I both believe that the University of Aberdeen was founded in 1495; you but not I know that the current guidebook to Aberdeen contains an egregious error on this very matter. We both win a copy of the guidebook in the Scottish national lottery; we both read it; sadly enough, it contains the wholly mistaken affirmation that the university was founded in 1595. Given my noetic structure (which includes the belief that guidebooks are ordinarily to be trusted on matters like this), I thereby acquire a defeater for my belief that the university was founded in 1495; you, however, knowing about this improbable error, do not. The difference, of course, is with respect to the rest of what we know or believe: given the rest of what *I* believe, I now have a reason to reject the belief that the university was founded in 1495; the same does not hold for you. You already know that the current guidebook contains an error on the matter of the date of the university's foundation; this neutralizes in advance (as we might put it) the defeating potential of the newly acquired bit of knowledge, that is, that the current guidebook to Aberdeen says the university was founded in 1595. So this new bit of knowledge is a defeater for that belief with respect to my noetic structure but not with respect to yours.

A defeater for a belief *b*, then, is another belief *d* such that, given my noetic structure, I cannot rationally hold *b*, given that I believe *d*. In the typical case of defeat, I will first believe *b* and then later come to believe the defeater *d*: I believe that there is a sheep in the pasture before me; then you come along with that information about the sheep dog. I believe that the widget I'm looking at is red; then the shop superintendent tells me about the irradiation by red light. Sometimes, however, I already believe the defeater (or, strictly speaking, part of the defeater), but do not initially realize its bearing on the defeatee. I believe that you were at the basketball game last night at 9:30; I also believe that you are never at a game without your husband, that Sam, whom I trust, reported seeing either Tom or your husband at a bar at that time, and that George, whom I also trust, reports that Tom was not at the bar then. This is sufficiently complicated that I might not initially see the connection between these propositions and my belief that you were at the game then. As long as I haven't noticed the connection, I don't have a defeater, although I do have what we might call a potential defeater. Once I see the connection, *then* I have a defeater: the defeater is the conjunction of those propositions, together with the proposition that if that conjunction is true, then you weren't at the game at 9:30.

A famous similar kind of case: Frege once believed that

(F) For every condition or property *P*, there exists the set of just those things that have *P*.

Bertrand Russell wrote him a letter, pointing out that (F) has very serious problems. If it is true, then there exists the set of non-self-membered sets (because there is the property or condition of being non-self-membered). This set, however, inconsiderately fails to exist. That is because if it did exist, it would exemplify itself if and only if it did not exemplify itself; that is, it would both exemplify itself and fail to exemplify itself, which is wholly unacceptable behavior for a set. Before he realized this problem with (F), Frege did not have a defeater for it. Once he understood Russell's letter, however, he did; and the defeater was just the fact that (F), together with the truth that there is such a condition as being non-self-membered, entails a contradiction.

We might initially try explaining the notion of a defeater as follows:

(D) *D* is a defeater of *B* for *S* at *t* if and only if (1) *S*'s noetic structure *N* (i.e., *S*'s beliefs and experiences and salient relations
among them) at *t* includes *B,* and *S* comes to believe *D* at *t* ,
and (2) any person (a) whose cognitive faculties are functioning properly in the relevant respects, (b) whose noetic
structure is *N* and includes *B,* and (c) who comes at *t* to believe *D* but nothing else independent of or stronger than *D*
would withhold *B* (or believe it less strongly[3]).

The idea, roughly speaking, is that belief *D* is a defeater of *B* for you
if proper function requires giving up belief *B* when you acquire *D.*
This fits the above examples of defeaters rather well; still, it is nonetheless not quite what we want. To see the problem, imagine a canny
Freudian replying as follows:

> Consider the 'optimistic overrider'. You are suffering from what
> you know to be a really serious disease; nonetheless, you believe
> that you will recover within six months. You then learn some statis-
> tics that accurately fit your case—statistics according to which the
> probability that you will recover is very low. Does your belief in
> these statistics give you a defeater for the belief that you will re-
> cover? One would think so; but it need not on (D). For perhaps
> there is a kind of mechanism that operates in these cases to main-
> tain optimism about your chances of recovery, just because such op-
> timism enhances the chances of recovery. That is, what proper func-
> tion requires in a case like this is believing that you will recover,
> despite your knowledge of the statistics. What proper function re-
> quires in this case, then, is (a) the belief that those statistics are in
> fact accurate, but also (b) the belief that you will nevertheless re-
> cover. So the definition is incorrect. It fails to take account of the
> fact that not all cognitive processes are aimed at the production of
> true belief. Furthermore, this is directly relevant to the case of belief
> in God. For, as Freud pointed out, belief in God arises from *wish-
> fulfillment,* not from belief-producing processes or faculties aimed at
> the truth. The function of the processes that produce theistic belief
> is psychological health, enabling us to carry on in this otherwise
> grim and threatening world. The function of these processes is not
> to provide us with true beliefs. So suppose you are a believer in

---

3. We could use the term 'partial defeater' for defeaters that don't require
withholding *B* but do require holding it less firmly. A full treatment would explain
degrees of belief (which are not to be thought of as probability judgments; see
Warrant: The Current Debate, p. 118) and show how partial and full defeat are related. Here there is no space for that, but note that full defeat is really a special case
of partial defeat, at least if we stipulate that coming to withhold *B* is a special case
of coming to believe *B* less strongly. For the sake of brevity I'll henceforth suppress
mention of partial defeaters, although the application of what I say to them should
be routine.

God, and someone provides you with a powerful argument against the existence of God—some version of the problem of evil, for example. Suppose, indeed, someone shows you that the existence of God is logically incompatible with the existence of evil. What does proper function require in that case? Well, conceivably it requires that you continue to believe in God. Even if it did, however, you would have a defeater. So the definition is faulty.

Agreed, the definition is indeed faulty.[4] Here we need a distinction. Say that (D) above defines the notion of a defeater *simpliciter*. We also need the notion of a *purely epistemic* defeater:

(D*) D is a purely epistemic defeater of B for S at t if and only if (1) S's noetic structure N at t includes B and S comes to believe D at t, and (2) any person S* (a) whose cognitive faculties are functioning properly in the relevant respects, (b) who is such that the bit of the design plan governing the sustaining of B in her noetic structure is successfully aimed at truth (i.e., at the maximization of true belief and minimization of false belief) and nothing more, (c) whose noetic structure is N and includes B, and (d) who comes to believe D but nothing else independent of or stronger than D, would withhold B (or believe it less strongly).

A couple of comments. First, it is of course the addition of clause (b) that distinguishes (D*) from (D); very roughly speaking, the idea is that a purely epistemic defeater for B is a belief D that would be a defeater *simpliciter* for B if the only processes governing the sustaining of B were processes aimed at truth (and not, for example, at survival, or psychological comfort). The point is then that D could be a purely epistemic defeater of B even if proper function requires the maintenance of B, in S's noetic structure, despite the formation of D; that can occur if the processes maintaining B are not aimed at truth. Second, with respect to clause (a), it is not required, of course, that *all* of S*'s faculties are functioning properly in *every* respect. For example, the fact that S*'s memory for names is defective need not be relevant. Further, it isn't required that D itself arise rationally or by way of proper function; as I'll argue below, it is possible for a belief that is irrationally acquired to be a defeater, even for a belief that is rationally acquired. Perhaps (D*) is a bit unwieldy; still, in practice there shouldn't be any difficulty in applying it to the cases of interest. The above canny Freudian, therefore, will presumably hold that the theist does have a purely epistemic defeater in the facts of evil (once she reflects on the facts of evil and sees how they are related to the existence of a perfectly good God), even if she does not have a defeater *simpliciter*.

4. Here I was greatly helped by a series of communications from William Talbott.

And she may go on to make one final claim: once you see that belief in God is not sustained by truth-aimed processes (arising, instead,
from wishful thinking), then you will also have a defeater *simpliciter*
for theistic belief. You will have this defeater in two different ways.
First, once you see that the cognitive processes responsible for a
given belief you hold are not aimed at the truth, and also clearly see
the facts of evil, then, she claims, you will be in a situation where the
rational response is to give up belief in God. For, she says, you see
that you really have evidence against the existence of God, while on
the other side your belief in God is without evidence and without
warrant. She adds that even if we ignore evil altogether, the theist
who sees that her theistic belief issues from wish-fulfillment (or any
other cognitive process that is not aimed at the truth) has a defeater
for that belief. Merely seeing that the sources of a given belief are not
aimed at truth (but at some other desideratum such as survival, psychological welfare, or the ability to carry on in this hostile and indifferent world) is sufficient (in the absence of other evidence), she says,
to give you a defeater *simpliciter* for that belief. The rational response,
once you see the source of such a belief, is to give up the belief.

What further conditions (if any) must a defeater belief meet? In
particular, must such a belief itself be warranted or rationally formed?
Suppose I hold a belief *B*, but then come to accept a belief *D* that goes
against *B* in some way, where this belief *D* I accept has no warrant. Can
it still be a defeater for *B*? I should think so. I've believed for years that
you were born in Yankton, South Dakota; this belief has a good deal of
warrant for me. (I was told this by your uncle, whom I know to be a generally reliable person.) One day, however, you tell me in all seriousness
that you were born not in Yankton, but in New Haven (and you add
some story as to why your uncle thinks you were born in Yankton).
Then (under normal circumstances) I have a rationality defeater for my
belief that you were born in Yankton. If there are no special circumstances (if I have no reason to think you were joking, or trying to deceive me, or are misinformed about where you were born, or the like),
the rational response would be to give up the belief that you were born
in Yankton. Suppose, however, the fact is you yourself were misinformed by your parents; you actually were born in Yankton, but for reasons having to do with academic prestige your parents tell you that you
were born in New Haven. Then *your* belief that you were born in New
Haven has little or no warrant. That is because (as I argued in *Warrant
and Proper Function*, pp. 83ff.) a belief acquired by way of testimony has
warrant for the testifiee only if it has warrant for the testifier; because
your parents don't even hold this belief, it is not among their warranted
beliefs. Hence *my* newly acquired belief that you were born in New
Haven also lacks warrant. Nevertheless, this belief still gives me a defeater for my old belief that you were born in Yankton. So it is quite possible for a belief *A* to serve as a defeater for another belief *B* even if *A* has
little or no warrant, and even when *B* has more warrant than *A*.

But what if the potential defeating belief is acquired *irrationally*? Can it still be a defeater? Suppose I've always thought you a genial sort who is rather well disposed to me. Unhappily, I start sinking into a paranoid condition; because of cognitive malfunction, it comes to seem to me that you are, in fact, trying to harm me by destroying my academic reputation. Because of the cognitive malfunction, this just seems wholly obvious to me; it has a great deal of what I have been calling 'doxastic evidence'. Can my belief *D* that you are trying to destroy my reputation serve as a defeater for my belief *B* that you are favorably disposed toward me?

Here we must recall the distinction between internal and external rationality. *Internal* rationality is a matter of proper function 'downstream from experience' (including doxastic experience: see above, pp. 110ff.). Given my experience, I am internally rational just if I form the right beliefs in response to that experience. What internal rationality requires, therefore, is the appropriate doxastic response to experience, including doxastic experience. For present purposes, we may think of internal rationality as also including *epistemic justification*, being within one's epistemic rights, having flouted no epistemic duties or obligations. *External* rationality, by contrast, is a matter of the proper function of the *sources* of experience, including, in particular, the sources of *doxastic* experience. External irrationality can arise in several ways. For example, it can happen by way of impedance. I write a book on topic X; because of pride and egoism, I think it easily the best book on X, even though your book on X is better, and even though I would have recognized that fact had it not been for the way in which my pride has impeded the proper function of the relevant rational faculties. This is a case of external irrationality: the problem is that, because of my pride and arrogance, my book just seems to me much better than yours; the proposition that it is better has, for me, a great deal of doxastic evidence. In a case like this, therefore, my irrationally formed belief can give me a defeater, I think, for my previous and rationally formed belief that your book is the best book on X.

Return now to the case of paranoia: I think we see a similar situation. My belief that you are out to get me is externally irrational; it arises from sources of doxastic experience that are not functioning properly. By virtue of their malfunction, however, my experience is such that I am powerfully impelled to believe *D*, that you are trying to ruin me. This now seems to me much more obvious than that you are favorably disposed toward me: the doxastic evidence for *D* is much stronger than that for *B*. What internal rationality calls for, under those circumstances, therefore, is my giving up *B*; I have a defeater for it in *D*, even though *D* is arrived at irrationally. I can therefore have a defeater *D* for a belief *B*, even where *B* is rationally held and *D* is irrationally acquired.

There is still another way in which I can acquire a defeater by way of irrationality. Suppose I believe *B*, but by virtue of cognitive malfunction do not believe it nearly as strongly as rationality requires; it isn't nearly as resistant to the challenge of other beliefs as it should be. For example, due to cognitive malfunction (a brain lesion, perhaps) I am arithmetically challenged: like everyone else, I believe that $2 + 1 = 3$, but no more strongly than I believe, for example, that my wife's social security number is n. You, a mathematics professor whom I trust, tell me that as a matter of fact it is false that $2 + 1 = 3$. I take your word for it, just as I might believe the government expert who informs me that my wife's social security number really isn't n (there was some kind of mix-up when she lost her card and applied for a new one). This then gives me a defeater for my belief that $2 + 1 = 3$. I have this defeater for this belief, however, only because of failure of cognitive proper function, only because the doxastic evidence for me for $2 + 1 = 3$ isn't nearly as strong as proper function requires.

II. DEFEATERS FOR CHRISTIAN OR THEISTIC BELIEF

What we've seen so far is that you have a defeater for one of your beliefs *B* just if you acquire another belief *D* such that, given that you hold that belief, the rational response is to reject *B* (or hold it less firmly). What we want to know, however, is (for example) whether the suffering and evil the world displays or the facts of pluralism provide a defeater for Christian belief. Of course they might for some people, but not for others; there is that relativity to noetic structures. So what are we really asking when we ask whether these things constitute defeaters? There are various directions we could go here; suppose we follow Philip Quinn (above, p. 358) in thinking about the noetic structures of "intellectually sophisticated adults in our culture." We are asking whether these proposed defeaters would in fact constitute defeaters for Quinn's sophisticated believers. Of course they will constitute defeaters, for a given person *S*, only if *S* believes them. And not just any proposition which is such that, if I believed it, I would have a defeater for Christian or theistic belief will do the trick. As we have seen, an irrationally acquired belief can serve as a defeater; but clearly you don't give me a defeater in the relevant sense for Christian belief by causing me to come to believe something in an irrational way—by hypnosis say, or by injecting mind-altering drugs. You give me a defeater in the relevant sense only if you propose to me a belief which is such that a *rational* sophisticated believer (rational both internally and externally) would accept it upon being presented with it. Hence you don't necessarily provide a defeater for theistic belief just by asserting, even loudly or slowly, that belief in God is false, or stupid, or that God is dead, or that, given electricity and the wireless (below, p. 403), we now know better. Although these propositions, if I accepted them, might provide me with defeaters for Christian belief, they are not, just by themselves, such that rationality would require a sophisticated believer to accept them. Something further is required.

What? One way that could be relevant would be to give an *argument* for the falsehood of the relevant proposition from premises a sophisticated believer accepts. Of course there are subtleties here. It might be that the rational thing to do, once I see the inconsistency between those premises and B, is to hang on to B and give up instead (the conjunction of) those premises. I believe $p_1, \ldots p_n$; you show me that $p_1, \ldots p_n$ entail that there aren't any persisting selves; once I see this, perhaps the rational thing to do is to give up (one or more of) the p_i rather than the belief that there are persisting selves. So merely giving an argument with premises a sophisticate accepts is not sufficient for providing a defeater; the premises must also be such that once I see the conflict, rationality requires that I give up the prospective defeatee rather than the premises. Still, argument is one way to give me a defeater.

Is there any other way? Yes; you can put me in a position where I have *experiences* such that, given those experiences (and given my noetic structure), the rational thing to do is to give up the purported defeatee. I claim that there are no prickly pear cacti in the upper peninsula of Michigan; you take me into the woods up there and show me a particularly luxuriant specimen; rationality requires that I drop my now discredited belief. So another way to provide a defeater for Christian or theistic belief would be to point to or provide a kind of experience such that a sophisticate who underwent that experience would be rationally required to give up the belief in question.

III. PROJECTIVE THEORIES A DEFEATER FOR CHRISTIAN BELIEF?

Now we can turn to the projective theories of religious—in particular, theistic—belief Quinn mentions. These theories propose to explain theistic belief and other religious belief in terms of our projecting into the heavens something like an idealized father. Freud proposes such a theory, as do Marx, Durkheim, and others; according to Quinn, such projective theories, along with natural evil, constitute defeaters for theistic and hence Christian belief. I'll deal with evil in the last chapter; but what about Freud and Marx? Aren't their theories, as Quinn says, reasons for responsible and informed contemporary Christian believers to give up belief in God, or at any rate accept it less firmly?

I don't think so; allow me to explain. The fact is I've already given some of my reasons in chapter 6, pp. 192ff. As I argued there, the heart and soul of the F&M (Freud-and-Marx) complaint is that theistic belief lacks warrant: it is not produced by cognitive faculties functioning properly according to a design plan successfully aimed at truth. According to Marx, such belief arises from a sort of cognitive disorder produced by a disordered society; according to Freud, it is produced by cognitive processes that are aimed at psychological comfort or survival rather than truth. Now if I *believed* these things, then perhaps I would have a reason to give up theistic belief.[5] But why should I believe them? Is there a rationally compelling argument for one or another of them? Freud and Marx certainly give no reasons for thinking these theories true; they simply announce them. More important, as I argued in chapter 6, their attack on the warrant of theistic belief really presupposes that theistic belief is false; it presupposes atheism. If I am aware of that, however, how can their attack constitute a defeater, for me, of theistic belief? If theistic belief is false, then perhaps the F&M thesis would be a good way to think of it; but, of course, I do not believe that theistic belief *is* false. Freud and Marx's declarations, therefore, do not give me a defeater for theistic belief; what they announce might be a defeater, if I came to believe it, but they provide no reason at all for my coming to believe it. A person can easily be apprised of Freud's views, here, and continue to accept theistic belief in complete rationality.

Projective theories like Freud's *could* be a defeater for theistic belief (and hence for Christianity) for *some* people. Suppose I believe very firmly that if theism is true, there couldn't be any coherent projective theories of religious or theistic belief; suppose I also accept theism, though not particularly firmly. Now suppose I then come to believe that

(F) Freud's theory (or some other projective theory) is indeed coherent.

Then (F) will be a defeater—perhaps a partial defeater—for my theistic belief; as long as I accept it and continue to accept the rest of my noetic structure (including the idea that theism is true only if there are no coherent projective theories of theistic belief), I can't rationally also accept theism. Of course that idea is false; but a false belief can nonetheless serve as a defeater. Or suppose I don't realize either that Freud's theory really presupposes atheism, or that he gives no argument either for atheism or for his theory. Then too I might have a defeater, at least a partial defeater, for my theistic belief. So I *could* acquire a defeater in learning about these theories. However, the point is that rationality does not *require* that I acquire such a defeater under those conditions. The point is that a rational person could perfectly well be a theist, learn about and be well acquainted with Freud's (and others') projective theories, and rationally remain a theist—in particular, if she sees that Freud's views are unargued and in any event really presuppose atheism. Alternatively, a theist for whom Freud's views did constitute a defeater could acquire a defeater for that defeater (a defeater-defeater) by coming to be apprised of these or other epistemological truths. Here is a

---

5. Although, as I argued above (p. 197), it is possible that theistic belief originates in something like wishful thinking, but nonetheless has warrant. If I also believe this, then coming to think that belief in God is a product of wish-fulfillment would not automatically give me a defeater for such belief.

place, then, where the philosopher can be of service to the Christian community by pointing out truths which, when added to a Christian noetic structure, can preserve Christian or theistic belief from defeat or provide a defeater-defeater for a defeater of such belief.

Now Quinn argues that projective theories of theistic belief are defeaters for such belief if they successfully *explain* theistic belief:

> I believe it is useful to think of projection theories of religious belief as constituting a research program in the human sciences. . . . The unifying idea of the research program is that there is in us a mechanism of belief formation and maintenance that involves projecting attributes of individual humans or their societies outwards and postulating entities in which the projected attributes are instantiated. . . . The existence of the postulated entities is supposed to play no role in explaining the formation or persistence of belief in the postulates. If such hypotheses can explain religious beliefs in a wide variety of circumstances, leaving unexplained no more anomalies than other good theories, then appeal to some principle of economy such as Ockham's razor can be made to justify the conclusion that the entities whose existence is postulated as a result of the operation of the projection mechanism do not exist because they are explanatorily idle.[6]

If I understand Quinn's suggestion as specified to theistic belief, it is that:

(Q1) the existence of God is not needed in order to explain theistic belief;

hence

(Q2) the existence of God is explanatorily idle;

and

(Q3) that is a good reason for holding that there is no such person as God.

It's not clear that Quinn *accepts* (Q1) through (Q3); perhaps he is only proposing them as possibilities. (And even if he did accept them, he might also hold that there are also good reasons *for* theistic belief.) In any event, I believe there are several serious problems with these suggestions. First, according to the theory in question, believers in God *postulate* the existence of God ("there is in us a mechanism of belief formation and maintenance that involves projecting attributes of individual humans or their societies outwards and postulating enti-

---

6. "The Foundations of Theism Again," in *Rational Faith: Catholic Responses to Reformed Theology* (Notre Dame: University of Notre Dame Press, 1993), pp. 41–42.

ties in which the projected attributes are instantiated.") Belief in God, however, is clearly not a result of *postulation*; believers in God do not ordinarily postulate that there is such a person, just as believers in other persons or material objects do not ordinarily postulate that there are such things. Postulation is a process that goes with scientific theories; one postulates entities of a certain sort (e.g., quarks or gluons) as part of an explanatory theory. Christians, however, do not ordinarily propose the existence of God as an *explanation* of anything at all (see above, pp. 330ff.). Still, perhaps this is not a central point. It shouldn't be essential to the theories in question that belief in God be formed by way of postulation; indeed, the theories would work as well or better if what they claimed was that believers in God came to believe as they do by way of unconscious mechanisms of one sort or another.

Second, even if the existence of theistic belief can be 'explained' (whatever exactly that amounts to) without postulating the existence of God, it might still be that theism itself explains lots of *other* things. Theistic belief is only *one* of the things that theism can be invoked to explain. Theism has also been used to explain the fine-tuning of the universe; the existence of propositions, properties, and other abstract entities; the origin of life; the nature and existence of morality; the reliability of our epistemic faculties; and much else besides. Hence the fact that it is explanatorily idle with respect to *theistic belief* doesn't by itself show that it is explanatorily idle *tout court*; there is no reason, so far, to infer (Q2) from (Q1).

Third, given (Q2), why infer (Q3)? According to Ockham's famous razor, *entia non multiplicandum sunt praetor necessitatem*; "entities ought not to be multiplied beyond necessity."[7] Taken as the suggestion that one ought not postulate entities of a certain kind unless required to in some way, the razor manifests a certain robust common sense. (Perhaps one can explain certain phenomena by way of postulating the existence of mice in the garage; then it would be multiplying entities beyond necessity if one were to postulate both mice and fairies to explain the phenomena.) But theism isn't ordinarily accepted as an explanatory hypothesis. So suppose theistic belief is indeed explanatorily idle: why should that compromise it, or suggest that it has low epistemic status? If theistic belief is not proposed as an explanatory hypothesis in the first place, why should its being explanatorily idle, if indeed it is, be held against it? Beliefs such as that I had an orange for breakfast are not (ordinarily) accepted as hypotheses; should we take the fact that they don't explain much of

---

7. As the razor is ordinarily understood. There is apparently some doubt as to whether Ockham himself ever put it just this way.

anything as a point against them, a defeater for them? So it is hard to see why theistic belief's being explanatorily idle (if it is) is a point against it. Indeed, (Q3) actually says something much stronger: explanatory idleness, it says, is a reason for taking theistic belief to be, not just epistemically suspect, but *false*. But why think *that*? Suppose (contrary to fact, as I see it) explanatory idleness *is* something against theistic belief. Why go on to infer that it gives one a reason for *denying* the existence of God? Wouldn't agnosticism, withholding belief, be sufficient? Maybe I don't know of any phenomena that I can explain only by supposing there is intelligent life on other planets. Should I then deny that there is any such life? Wouldn't simple agnosticism be sufficient?

The crucial point, here, is that on the model (and in actuality as well) theistic belief is not ordinarily accepted as an *explanation*. It is not that the theist sizes up what the world appears to be like (including the existence of theistic belief itself) and then proposes the existence of God as the best explanation of these phenomena. If that *were* how she was thinking, then the fact that theistic belief is explanatorily idle (if it is) with respect to some range of data might be relevant. But it isn't. On the model, the believer in God ordinarily believes in the basic way, not on the evidential basis of other propositions, and not by way of proposing belief in God as an explanation of something or other. Hence the fact that there are better explanations of some range of phenomena (if there are) does not so far cast any doubt on belief in God.

Allow me to return to an analogy I have used elsewhere. I apply for a National Endowment for the Humanities fellowship; realizing I am not really qualified, I offer you five hundred dollars to write a glowing if inaccurate letter of recommendation. Perhaps, as they say, everyone has a price; as it turns out, yours is definitely more than five hundred dollars. You indignantly refuse, and write a blistering letter to the chair of my department. The letter mysteriously disappears from her office. One of the most respected members of the department, however, reports having seen me apparently trying to enter her office through a second-story window. I have means, motive, and opportunity. Further, I am known to have done this sort of thing before. But *I* clearly remember being on a solitary hike in the mountains the entire afternoon during which the letter disappeared. I believe that I did not remove that letter, and that belief has warrant for me. But I do not propose my belief that I am innocent, or that I took a walk in the woods, as an *explanation* of the facts pointing to my guilt. I don't propose my innocence or my going for a hike as an explanation of anything at all: these beliefs enter my noetic structure in quite a different way. Suppose, then, that these beliefs are, in fact, explanatorily idle; and add, if you like, that there *is* a good (if false) explanation of x's claiming to have seen me trying to gain entrance to the office: namely, that I took the letter in order to avoid further embarrassment. Does the explanatory idleness of my beliefs constitute a defeater for them? Of course not. They aren't proposed as explanations.[8] Similarly for theistic belief.

Taken as they stand, therefore, Quinn's claims do not seem to show that projective hypotheses furnish a defeater for Christian or theistic belief. Could it be that a stronger argument of the same sort is lurking in the neighborhood? As Quinn states the objection, the fact that theistic belief is *explanatorily idle* gives us reason to believe that there is no such person as God, so that the theist who realizes that this belief is indeed explanatorily idle has a rebutting defeater. But there may be another and possibly stronger way to put the objection. Perhaps the problem is not just that belief in the existence of God is explanatorily idle (if it is); after all, many of our beliefs do not function as explanations, or at least don't function primarily as explanations. Perhaps the idea, instead, is that

(Q4) If S can give an explanation of a certain range of her beliefs without assuming the existence of the entities whose existence those beliefs affirm, then S has an undercutting defeater for those beliefs.

The idea would then be that when the theist learns of these projective theories, she sees that the existence of her theistic belief can be explained without assuming the existence of God; *that*, according to (Q4), provides her with a rebutting defeater for her belief in the existence of God. This way of putting the objection differs from Quinn's in two ways. First, what provides a defeater for belief in the existence of God is not the fact that this belief is explanatorily idle (if it is), but rather the fact that there is an explanation of belief in God available that does not presuppose the truth of that belief—that is, does not presuppose the existence of God. Second, the kind of defeater allegedly provided is undercutting, not rebutting.

Still, is (Q4) really true? There are at least two versions of (Q4). On the one hand, (Q4) could require that the proposed explanation must involve only entities whose existence S already accepts; on the other, the explanation could involve either entities whose existence she already accepts or entities whose existence she does not already accept. Because the first version is the weaker and hence more plausible, suppose we confine our attention to it. So imagine that I can give an explanation of

8. Granted: if the evidence for my having taken the letter continues to mount (the letter turns up in my back pocket; my fingerprints are all over the file it was kept in; the mountain I thought I was hiking on that afternoon was destroyed by a volcanic eruption the preceding morning), I may eventually have to conclude that my memory is playing me tricks. The point is only that the explanatory idleness of my belief does not constitute any kind of defeater for it—because it isn't accepted as an explanation.

a certain range of my beliefs without assuming the existence of the entities E those beliefs affirm; suppose further I can give the explanation in terms of entities I already do accept. Does that give me a defeater for belief in the existence of those entities E? I don't think so. Consider my belief in the external objects of perception (trees, houses, horses, other people): perhaps I could explain these beliefs as implanted in me by God, for reasons of his own. This explanation does not presuppose the existence of those objects, and it is in terms of entities (God) whose existence I already accept. Would the availability of this explanation give me a defeater for those perceptual beliefs? I doubt it. Another possibility: perhaps I could also explain them (in accordance with the projection theories we are considering) as projections I myself unconsciously make: I am appeared to in various ways and, as a result, project beliefs to the effect that there are material objects that persist even when I am not having any experience. Would that explanation of such beliefs give me a defeater for them? Again, I doubt it. Perhaps there is also a projective explanation of my belief in the existence of other people: I see these bodies around me; I project the belief that they are, or are the bodies of other thinking, feeling creatures like myself (the alternative is pretty lonely); does that give me a defeater for my belief that there are other persons? Again, I don't think so. The fact is there is little reason to accept (Q4), at least if taken with complete generality. This means, I believe, that we have no good reason to think one acquires a defeater for theistic belief in learning of these alleged projective explanations of it.

Of course even if alleged projective explanations of theistic belief do not give me a defeater for such belief, there are many more candidates for that post. In the next chapters, we will move on to a consideration of some of those other alleged defeaters: contemporary historical biblical criticism, pluralism and postmodernism, and the facts of evil.

12

Two (or More) Kinds of Scripture Scholarship

In chapter 8, I presented a model for the way Christian belief has or can have warrant. According to the model, Scripture is *perspicuous*: the main lines of its teaching—creation, sin, incarnation, atonement, resurrection, eternal life—can be understood and grasped and properly accepted by anyone of normal intelligence and ordinary training. As Jonathan Edwards said, the Housatonic Indians can easily grasp and properly appropriate this message; a Ph.D. in theology or history or biblical studies is not necessary. Underlying this point is a second: there is available a source of warranted true belief, a way of coming to see the truth of these teachings, that is quite independent of historical study: Scripture/the internal instigation of the Holy Spirit/faith (IIHS for short). By virtue of this process, an ordinary Christian, one quite innocent of historical studies, the ancient languages, the intricacies of textual criticism, the depths of theology, and all the rest can nevertheless come to know that these things are, indeed, true; furthermore, his knowledge need not trace back (by way of testimony, for example) to knowledge on the part of someone who *does* have this specialized training. Neither the Christian community nor the ordinary Christian is at the mercy of the expert here; they can know these truths directly.

Nevertheless, of course, the serious and scholarly study of the Bible is of first importance for Christians. The roll call of those who have pursued this project is maximally impressive: Chrysostom, Augustine, Aquinas, Calvin, Jonathan Edwards, and Karl Barth, just for starters. These people and their successors begin from the idea that Scripture is divinely inspired in such a way that the Bible constitutes (among other things) a divine revelation, a special message from God to humankind; they then try to ascertain the Lord's teaching in the whole of Scripture or (more likely) a given bit. Since the Enlightenment, however, another kind of scripture scholarship has also come into view. Variously called 'higher criticism', 'historical criticism', 'biblical criticism', or 'historical critical scholarship', this variety of scripture scholarship brackets or prescinds from what is known by faith and aims to proceed 'scientifically', strictly on the basis of reason; I shall call it 'historical biblical criticism'—HBC for short. Scripture scholarship of this sort brackets the belief that the Bible is a special word from the Lord, as well as any other belief accepted on the basis of faith rather than reason. Now it often happens that the declarations of those who pursue this latter kind are in apparent conflict with the main lines of Christian thought; one who pursues this sort of scholarship is quite unlikely to conclude, for example, that Jesus was really the preexistent second person of the divine trinity who was crucified, died, and then literally rose from the dead the third day. As Van Harvey says, "So far as the biblical historian is concerned . . . there is scarcely a popularly held traditional belief about Jesus that is not regarded with considerable skepticism."[1] I shall try to describe both of these kinds of scripture scholarship. Then I shall ask the following question: how should a classical Christian, one who accepts "the great things of the gospel," respond to the deflationary aspect of HBC? How should he think about its apparently corrosive results with respect to traditional Christian belief? Given the extended Aquinas/Calvin (A/C) model, I shall argue that he need not be disturbed by the conflict between alleged results of HBC and traditional Christian belief.[2] That conflict does not offer a defeater for his acceptance of the great things of the gospel—nor, to the degree that those alleged results rest on epistemological assumptions he doesn't share, of anything else he accepts on the basis of biblical teaching.

I. SCRIPTURE DIVINELY INSPIRED

Now according to the A/C model, Scripture or the Bible figures importantly into the process whereby the believer comes to believe the great things of the gospel, and also into the process whereby these beliefs have warrant for him. Roughly speaking, he reads or hears

---

1. "New Testament Scholarship and Christian Belief" (hereafter NTS), in *Jesus in History and Myth*, ed. R. Joseph Hoffman and Gerald A. Larue (Buffalo: Prometheus Books, 1986), p. 193.

2. I therefore concur (for the most part) both with C. Stephen Evans in his *The Historical Christ and the Jesus of Faith: The Incarnational Narrative as History* (Oxford: Clarendon Press, 1996) and with Peter van Inwagen in "Critical Studies of the New Testament and the User of the New Testament," in *God, Knowledge, and Mystery* (Ithaca: Cornell University Press, 1995).

the central message of Scripture; moved by the invitation or instigation of the Holy Spirit, he comes to believe. The Bible also figures into the intellectual economy of traditional Christians in quite another way. By way of the above process, perhaps I come to believe that a specific teaching—say, that in Christ, God was reconciling the world to himself—is true and is a divine revelation. But a traditional Christian also believes, for example, that the Gospel of John and Paul's epistle to the Romans and the book of Acts are divinely inspired and hence authoritative for Christian belief and practice. Indeed, he will believe this of the entire Bible. The whole Bible is a message from the Lord to humankind; this entire book is authoritative for Christian belief and practice.

Now that belief *itself* is not one of the great things of the gospel—it is not an essential element of Christian belief. It wasn't accepted by the earliest Christians and isn't to be found in the ecumenical creeds. This is partly because there were Christians before these books were written, and, barring divine revelation to them that the books were indeed soon to *be* written and would indeed be authoritative, they wouldn't have known about them. The apostle Paul himself, for example, was certainly a Christian believer before he wrote his first epistles; he was a person of faith and held the essentials of Christian belief. Still, he no doubt didn't believe that the Bible—the Bible as we now have it, in Protestant or Catholic (or Orthodox) version—was divinely inspired. So the belief that God has inspired, say, the New Testament in such a way that it is a communication from God to us human beings—that belief is not itself an essential element of Christian belief. Strictly speaking, therefore, giving an account of how it is that this belief about the Bible has warrant for the Christian, if it does, lies outside the scope of my project, which concerns the way in which traditional Christian belief has warrant. Yet that belief does figure heavily into Christian practice; at millions of worship services every week, Christians all over the world hear passages of Scripture and respond by saying, "This is the Word of the Lord."

I shall therefore begin this chapter by inquiring into the epistemology of the belief that the Bible is divinely inspired in a special way, and in such a way as to constitute divine discourse—the belief that the Lord speaks in a special way to us human beings in and through this book. How *does* a Christian come to believe that the Gospel of Mark, the book of Acts, or the entire New Testament is authoritative because divinely inspired? What (if anything) is the source of warrant for this belief? There are several possibilities. For many of us it will be by way of ordinary teaching and testimony. Perhaps I am brought up to believe that the Bible is, indeed, the Word of God (just as I am brought up thinking that thousands perished in the American Civil War), and I've never encountered any reason to doubt this.

But an important feature of warrant is that if I accept a belief *B* just on testimony, then *B* has warrant for me only if it had warrant for the testifier as well. The warrant a belief has for the testifiee is derivative from the warrant it has for the testifier.[3] Our question, therefore, becomes this: what is the epistemological status of this belief for those members of the community who don't accept it on the testimony of other members? What is the source of the warrant (if any) this belief has for the Christian community? Well, perhaps a Christian might come to think something like the following:

> Suppose the apostles were commissioned by God through Jesus Christ to be witnesses and representatives (deputies) of Jesus. Suppose that what emerged from their carrying out this commission was a body of apostolic teaching which incorporated what Jesus taught them and what they remembered of the goings-on surrounding Jesus, shaped under the guidance of the Spirit. And suppose that the New Testament books are all either apostolic writings, or formulations of apostolic teaching composed by close associates of one or another apostle. Then it would be correct to construe each book as a medium of divine discourse. And an eminently plausible construal of the process whereby these books found their way into a single canonical text, would be that by way of that process of canonization, God was authorizing these books as together constituting a single volume of divine discourse.[4]

So a Christian might come to think something like the above: she believes

(1) that the apostles were commissioned by God through Jesus Christ to be witnesses and deputies,

(2) that they produced a body of apostolic teaching that incorporated what Jesus taught,

and

(3) that the New Testament books are all either apostolic writings or formulations of apostolic teaching composed by close associates of one or another apostle.

She also believes

(4) that the process whereby these books found their way into a single canon is a matter of God's authorizing these books as constituting a single volume of divine discourse.

---

3. See *Warrant and Proper Function*, pp. 34–35.

4. Nicholas Wolterstorff, *Divine Discourse: Philosophical Reflections on the Claim That God Speaks* (Cambridge: Cambridge University Press, 1995), p. 295.

She then concludes that indeed

(5) the New Testament is a single volume of divine discourse.

But our question then would be: how does she know, why does she believe each of (1) through (4)? What is the source of *these* beliefs?

Could it be, perhaps, by way of ordinary historical investigation? I doubt it. The problem, once more, is the principle of dwindling probabilities. In chapter 8 (pp. 271ff.), we saw that this principle is a real obstacle for those who think that Christians might come to know the great things of the gospel by way of ordinary historical investigation —by coming to know, in this way, that the Bible is indeed the Word of God and that God does indeed teach these things. Of course the problem isn't as severe in the present case. We are imagining the Christian as already convinced of the great things of the gospel; her knowledge of them does not depend on her beliefs about the authority or divine inspiration of the Bible. According to the model, she doesn't reason thus: the Bible is the Word of God; it says that in Christ, God was reconciling the world to himself; therefore, in Christ, God was reconciling the world to himself. It is rather that upon hearing the gospel preached, reading the Bible, or in some other way encountering its message, she comes to believe these things *immediately* (i.e., not by way of inference), as a result of the work of the Holy Spirit in her heart. So suppose a Christian proposes to give a historical argument for the divine inspiration and consequent authority of the New Testament, say: we are to think of her as already knowing the central truths of Christianity. She already knows that there is such a person as God, that the man Jesus is also the divine son of God, and that through his ministry, passion, death, and resurrection we sinners can have life. These constitute part of her background information and can be employed in the historical argument in question. Her body of background information with respect to which she estimates the probability of (1) through (4), therefore, includes the main lines of Christian teaching. And of course she also knows that the books of the New Testament—some of them, anyway—apparently teach or presuppose these things. So her epistemic condition is much more favorable to (1) through (4) than it would be if she didn't already know these things. With respect to her background information B, therefore, perhaps each of (1) through (4) could be considered at least quite plausible and perhaps even likely to be true.

Still, each is only probable. Perhaps, indeed, each is *very* likely and has a probability as high as .9 with respect to that body of belief B; more exactly, perhaps the probability of (1) on B is as high as .9, the probability of (2) on (1)&B as high as .9, and the same for $P((3)/(B\&(1)\&(2)))$ and $P((4)/(B\&(1)\&(2)\&(3)))$ (see above, pp. 272ff.). Even so, we can conclude only that the probability of their conjunction, on B, is at least somewhat more than .5. In that case, *belief* that the New Testament is the Word of God would not be appropriate; what would be appropriate is the belief that it is rather *likely* that the New Testament is the Word of God. (The probability that the next throw of this die won't come up either 1 or 2 is greater than .5; that is nowhere nearly sufficient for my *believing* that it won't come up 1 or 2.[5]) We could quibble about these probabilities: no doubt they could sensibly be thought to be greater than I suggested. No doubt; but they could also sensibly be thought to be less than I suggested. The historical argument for (1) to (4) will at best yield probabilities, and at best only a fairly insubstantial probability of (5) itself. The estimates of the probabilities involved, furthermore, will be vague, variable, and not really well-founded. If the belief in question is to have *warrant* for Christians, its epistemic status for them must be something different from that of a conclusion of ordinary historical investigation.

Now most Christian communities have taught that the warrant enjoyed by this belief is *not* conferred on it just by way of ordinary historical investigation. For example, the Belgic Confession, one of the most important confessions of the Reformed churches, gives a list (the Protestant list) of the canonical books of the Bible; it then goes on:

> And we believe without a doubt all things contained in them—not so much because the church receives them and approves them as such, but above all because the Holy Spirit testifies in our hearts that they are from God, and also because they prove themselves to be from God.

There is a possible ambiguity here: "we believe all things contained in them not so much because the church receives them"—to what does this last 'them' refer? The teachings contained in the books, or the books themselves? If the former, then what we have here is another example of what we've already noted: the Holy Spirit leading us to see, not that a given *book* is from God, but that some *teaching*—for example, in Christ, God was reconciling the world to himself—is true. If the latter, however, what we would be led to believe is such propo-

---

5. If I *believe* whatever is quite likely with respect to my background information or what I know, I will wind up believing contradictions: for each number n between 1 and 6, it is likely that the die won't come up n; but, of course, it is also likely that the die will come up n for one of those numbers. I do not mean to say that historical investigation can *never* furnish enough evidence so that the appropriate attitude is that of belief (rather than just believing probable). That there was a Holocaust, an American Civil War, a French Revolution, a war between the Athenians and Spartans, and a Roman conquest of the Jews are all to be believed, not just believed probable. But the same doesn't go for (1) through (4). We don't have anywhere near that level of evidence for, for example, the claim that the apostles were commissioned by God, or that God authorized the books of the New Testament as constituting a volume of divine discourse.

sitions as *the Gospel of John is from God*. I think it is at least fairly clear that the latter is what the confession intends. According to the confession, then, there are two sources for the belief that (e.g.) the Gospel of John is from God. The first is that the Holy Spirit testifies in our hearts that this book is indeed from God; the Holy Spirit doesn't merely impel us to believe, with respect to a given teaching of this book, that it is from God but impels us as well to believe that the Gospel of John itself is from God. The second is that the book "proves itself" to be from God. Perhaps here the idea is that the believer first comes to think, with respect to many of the specific teachings of that book, that they are, indeed, from God; that is, the Holy Spirit causes her to believe this with respect to many of the teachings of the book. She then infers (with the help of other premises) that the whole book has that same status.[6]

This is only *one* way in which this belief could have warrant; there are other possibilities. Perhaps the believer knows by way of the IIHS that the Holy Spirit has guided and preserved the Christian church, making sure that its teachings on important matters are, in fact, true; then the believer would be warranted in believing, at any rate of those books of the Bible endorsed by all or nearly all traditional Christian communities, that they are from God. Or perhaps, guided by the Holy Spirit, she recapitulates the process whereby the canon was originally formed, paying attention to the original criteria of apostolic authorship, consistency with apostolic teaching, and the like, and relying on testimony for the propositions that such and such books were composed by apostles. There are also combinations of these ways. All (and still others besides) are consistent with the extended A/C model; the model need not choose among them. However precisely this belief receives its warrant, traditional Christians have accepted the belief that the Bible is the Word of God and that in it the Lord intends to teach us truths.[7]

---

6. Jonathan Edwards, *The Religious Affections* (New Haven: Yale University Press, 1959), p. 303: "And the opening to view with such clearness, such a world of wonderful and glorious truth in the gospel, that before was unknown, being quite above the view of a natural eye, but appearing so clear and bright, has a powerful and invincible influence on the soul to persuade of the divinity of the gospel."

7. I don't for a moment mean to suggest that teaching us truths is *all* that the Lord intends in Scripture: there is also raising affection, teaching us how to praise, how to pray, how to see the depth of our own sin, how marvelous the gift of salvation is, and a thousand other things.

II. TRADITIONAL CHRISTIAN BIBLICAL COMMENTARY

Of course it isn't always easy to tell what the Lord *is* teaching us in a given passage: what he teaches is indeed true; still, sometimes it isn't clear just what his teaching is. Part of the problem is the fact that the Bible contains material of so many different sorts; it isn't in this respect like a contemporary book on theology or philosophy. It isn't a book full of declarative sentences, with proper analysis and logical development and all the accoutrements academics have come to know and love and demand. The Bible does, indeed, contain sober assertion, but there is also exhortation, expression of praise, poetry, the telling of stories and parables, songs, devotional material, history, genealogies, lamentations, confession, prophecy, apocalyptic material, and much else besides. Some of these (apocalyptic, for example) present real problems of interpretation (for us, at present): what exactly is the Lord teaching in Daniel, or Revelation? That's not easy to say. What are we to learn from the imprecatory psalms? Again, not easy to say.

Even if we stick to straightforward assertion, there are a thousand questions of interpretation. Just a couple of examples. In Matthew 5:17-20, Jesus declares that not a jot or a tittle of the law shall pass away and that "unless your righteousness surpasses that of the Pharisees and the teachers of the law, you will certainly not enter the kingdom of heaven," but in Galatians Paul seems to say that observance of the law doesn't count for much; how can we put these together? How do we understand Colossians 1:24: "Now I rejoice in what was suffered for you, and I fill up in my flesh what is still lacking in regard to Christ's afflictions, for the sake of his body which is the church"? Is Paul suggesting that Christ's sacrifice is incomplete, insufficient, that it requires additional suffering on the part of Paul or the rest of us? That seems unlikely. Is it that our suffering can be a *type* of Christ's, thus standing to the latter in the relation in which a type stands to the reality it typifies? Or shall we understand it like this: we must distinguish between two kinds of Christ's suffering, the redemptive suffering, the expiatory and vicarious Atonement to which nothing can be added or taken away, on the one hand, and, on the other hand, another kind, also "for the sake of his body," in which we human beings can genuinely participate? Perhaps suffering which can build up, edify the body of Christ, even as our response to Christ can be deepened by our meditating on Christ's sacrifice for us and the amazing selfless love displayed in it? Or what? Do Paul and James contradict each other on the relation between faith and works? Or rather, since God is the author of Scripture, is he proposing an inconsistent or self-contradictory teaching for our belief? Well no, surely not, but then how shall we understand the two in relation to each other? More generally, given that God is the principal author of

Scripture, how shall we think about the apparent tensions the latter displays? 1 John seems to say that Christians don't sin; in Paul's epistle to the Romans, he says that everyone sins; shall we draw the conclusion that there are no Christians? There are also problems about how to take the parables of Jesus. In Luke 18:1–8, for example, is Jesus suggesting that God will hear us just from sheer perseverance on our part, perhaps finally answering just because he's finally had enough? That doesn't sound right, but then how do we take the parable?

Some of these issues are important to the way the church conducts its day-to-day business: how shall we understand the Eucharist? Should infants be baptized? What is the proper structure of authority in the church? Although these issues are important, the scriptural teaching on them isn't very clear—which is why Christians of wisdom and good will disagree about them. There are other issues—for example, whether a conversion experience is necessary for salvation, how important glossolalia is to a proper Christian life, the extent to which Christians should live in the world and accommodate to contemporary culture (how to be in but not of the world), what the structure of a worship service should be—on which the scriptural teaching is even less plain. And there are still others—whether it is infralapsarianism or supralapsarianism or neither that is the truth, whether Christ died for everyone or only for the elect, just what and when the millennium will be—on which scriptural teaching is less plain yet.

And here we must pause to note a serious blemish on the face of Christendom. Christians have been at each other's throats and fought enormously destructive battles over all of these matters. In some cases, of course, the battles were literal battles; and the sight of Christians (with their teachings about peace and love and turning the other cheek) at each other's throats must surely have been an important cause of modern and Enlightenment apostasy.[8] Nowadays, per-

---

8. And perhaps also of contemporary apostasy. In explaining why "contemporary theologians" are not interested in the topics contemporary philosophers of religion discuss, the theologian Gordon Kaufman proposes that

> it now seems that the Christian faith, Christian ways of understanding the world and the human place within the world, a powerful Christian sense of divine authorization and thus superiority over other religions, Christian imperialism, Christian racism and sexism, and other characteristics of the Christian religion and of "Christian civilization," bear some significant responsibility for most of the evils I have just mentioned . . . two horrible world wars, the Nazi holocaust and other instances of genocide, the ecological crisis, the use of atomic bombs in World War II and the ever-present possibility of nuclear obliteration of the human race. . . . Christian theologians today have thus been driven, in a way unprecedented historically, to ask some hard questions about Christian faith, practices and institutions, questions that force close examination of the very symbols and ideas that

haps, we don't engage in literal battles;[9] nevertheless, serious Christians still spend an enormous amount of time and energy in disputes over these matters. Isn't it obvious, however, that the path of wisdom for Christians is to proportion willingness to fight, here, both to the degree to which it is clear that the item in question is, indeed, proposed for our belief by God and also to its importance for the Christian life? Christians will have much to answer for, along these lines, and it is not going to be pleasant.

Scripture, therefore, is inspired: what it teaches is true; yet it isn't always trivial to tell what it *does* teach. Indeed, many of the sermons and homilies preached in a million churches every Sunday morning are devoted in part to bringing out what might otherwise be obscure in scriptural teaching. Given that the Bible is a communication from God to humankind, a divine revelation, there is much about it that requires deep and perceptive reflection, much that taxes our best scholarly and spiritual resources to the utmost. This fact wasn't lost on Augustine, Aquinas, Calvin, and the others I mentioned above; between them they wrote an impressively large number of volumes devoted to powerful reflection on the meaning and teachings of Scripture. (Calvin's commentaries alone run to some twenty-two volumes.) Their aim was to determine as accurately as possible just what the Lord proposes to teach us in the Bible. Call this enterprise 'traditional biblical commentary' and note that it displays at least the following three features.

First, Scripture itself is taken to be a wholly authoritative and trustworthy guide to faith and morals; it is authoritative and trustworthy, because it is a revelation from God, a matter of God's speaking to us. Once it is clear, therefore, what the teaching of a given bit of Scripture is, the question of the truth and acceptability of that teaching is settled. In a commentary on Plato, we might decide that what Plato really meant to say was XYZ; we might then go on to consider and evaluate XYZ in various ways, asking whether it is true, or

---

Zhave traditionally informed this faith. ("Evidentialism: A Theologian's Response," *Faith and Philosophy* [January 1989], pp. 41–42)

Kaufman's essential position here, I think, is that contemporary philosophy of religion still (or again) takes seriously traditional Christianity, with its belief in God, incarnation, atonement, and so on, while contemporary theologians, paying attention to the factors he mentions, have "gone beyond" all that. See above, chapter 2. (Of course, as Kaufman acknowledges, he speaks for only *some* contemporary theologians.)

9. But I won't easily forget the sight (in Belfast) of a Protestant preacher shaking his jowls and roaring about "the God-cursed blasphemy of the idolatrous whore of Rome!" and looking for all the world as if there is nothing he would like better than to sink his sword into the breast of some hapless Roman Catholic.

close to the truth, or true in principle, or superseded by things we have learned since Plato wrote, and the like; we might also ask whether Plato's grounds or arguments for XYZ are slight, or acceptable, or substantial or compelling. These questions are out of place in the kind of scripture scholarship under consideration. Once convinced that God *is* proposing XYZ for our belief, we do not go on to ask whether it is true, or whether God has made a good case for it. God is not required to make a case.

Second, an assumption of the enterprise is that the principal author of the Bible—the entire Bible—is God himself (according to Calvin, God the Holy Spirit). Of course each of the books of the Bible has a human author or authors as well; still, the principal author is God. This impels us to treat the whole more like a unified communication than a miscellany of ancient books. Scripture isn't so much a library of independent books as itself a book with many subdivisions but a central theme: the message of the gospel. By virtue of this unity, furthermore (by virtue of the fact that there is just one principal author), it is possible to "interpret Scripture with Scripture." If a given passage from one of Paul's epistles is puzzling, it is perfectly proper to try to come to clarity as to what God's teaching is in this passage by appealing not only to what Paul himself says elsewhere in other epistles but also to what is taught elsewhere in Scripture (for example, the Gospel of John[10]). Passages in Psalms or Isaiah can be interpreted in terms of the fuller, more explicit disclosure in the New Testament; the serpent elevated on a pole to save the Israelites from disaster can be seen as a type of Christ (and thus as getting some of its significance by way of an implicit reference to Christ, whose being raised on the cross averted a greater disaster for the whole human race). A further consequence is that we can quite properly accept propositions that are inferred from premises coming from different parts of the Bible: once we see what God intends to teach in a given passage *A* and what he intends to teach in a given passage *B*, we can put the two together, and treat consequences of these propositions as themselves divine teaching.[11]

---

10. See, for example, Richard Swinburne (*Revelation* [Oxford: Clarendon Press, 1992], p. 192), who suggests that Paul's Christology at Romans 1:4 should be understood in terms of the 'high' Christology of the first chapter of John's Gospel. We could say the same for Paul's Christology in his speech in Acts 13, where he seems to suggest that a special status was *conferred* on Jesus, as opposed to John 1, according to which Jesus is the incarnation of the preexistent Word. See also Raymond Brown, *New Testament Christology* (New York: Paulist Press, 1994), pp. 133ff.

11. Of course this procedure, like most others, can be and has been abused; that possibility in itself, however, is nothing against it, though it should serve as a salutary caution.

Third (and connected with the second point), the fact that the principal author of the Bible is God himself means that one can't always determine the meaning of a given passage by discovering what the human author had in mind. Of course various postmodern hermeneuticists aim to amuse by telling us that, in this case as in all others, the author's intentions have nothing whatever to do with the meaning of a passage, that the reader herself confers on the passage whatever meaning it has, or perhaps that even entertaining the idea of a text's having meaning is to fall into "hermeneutical innocence"— adding, with a certain air of insouciant bravado, that such innocence is ineradicably sullied by its inevitable association with homophobic, sexist, racist, oppressive, and other unacceptable modes of thought. This is, indeed, amusing. Returning to serious business, however, it is obvious (given that the principal author of the Bible is God) that the meaning of a biblical passage will be given by what it is that the Lord intends to teach in that passage, and it is precisely this that biblical commentary tries to discern. But we can't just assume that what the Lord intends to teach us is identical with what the human author had in mind;[12] the latter may not so much as have thought of what is, in fact, the teaching of the passage in question. Thus, for example, Christians take the suffering servant passages in Isaiah to be references to Jesus; Jesus himself says (Luke 4:18–21) that the prophecy in Isaiah 61:1–2 is fulfilled in him; John (19:28–37) takes passages from Exodus, Numbers, Psalms, and Zechariah to be references to Jesus and the events of his life and death; Matthew (21:5) and John (12:15) take it that Zechariah 9:9 is a reference to Jesus' triumphal entry into Jerusalem; Hebrews 10 takes passages from Psalms, Jeremiah, and Habakkuk to be references to Christ and events in his career, as does Paul for passages from Psalms and Isaiah in his speech in Acts 13. Indeed, Paul refers to the Old Testament on nearly every page of Romans and both Corinthian epistles, and frequently in other epistles. There is no reason to suppose the human authors of Exodus, Numbers, Psalms, Isaiah, Jeremiah, or Habakkuk had in mind Jesus' triumphal entry, his incarnation, or other events of Jesus' life and death—or, indeed, anything else explicitly about Jesus. But the fact that it is God who is the principal author here makes it quite possible that what we are to learn from the text in question is something rather different from what the human author proposed to teach.

12. A further complication: we can't simply assume that there is some one thing, the same for everyone, that the Lord intends to teach in a given passage; perhaps what he intends to teach me or my relevant sociological group is not the same as what he intended to teach a fifth-century Christian.

III. HISTORICAL BIBLICAL CRITICISM

For at least the last couple of hundred years, there has also been a quite different kind of scripture scholarship: historical biblical criticism (HBC). There is much to be grateful for with respect to HBC; it has enabled us to learn a great deal about the Bible we otherwise might not have known. Furthermore, some of the methods it has developed (form criticism, source criticism, others) can be and have been employed to excellent effect in traditional biblical commentary. It differs importantly from the latter, however. HBC is fundamentally an Enlightenment project; it is an effort to look at and understand biblical books from a standpoint that relies on reason alone; that is, it is an effort to determine from the standpoint of reason alone what the scriptural teachings are and whether they are true. Thus HBC eschews the authority and guidance of tradition, magisterium, creed, or any kind of ecclesial or "external" epistemic authority. The idea is to see what can be established (or at least made plausible) using only the light of what we could call "natural, empirical reason." The faculties or sources of belief invoked, therefore, would be those that are employed in ordinary history: perception, testimony, reason taken in the sense of *a priori* intuition together with deductive and probabilistic reasoning, Reid's sympathy, by which we discern the thoughts and feelings of another, and so on—but bracketing any proposition one knows by faith or by way of the authority of the church. Spinoza (1632–77) already lays down the charter for this enterprise: "The rule for [biblical] interpretation should be nothing but the natural light of reason which is common to all—not any supernatural light nor any external authority."[13]

> This doesn't preclude, of course, a rational argument (an argument from reason alone) for the proposition that indeed there has been a divine revelation, and that the Bible (or some part of it) is precisely that revelation: exactly this is the Lockean project (see above, pp. 79ff.). Nor does it preclude a direct argument, one that proceeds independently of any claim to revelation, for the central claims of Christianity. Indeed, many critics of the Christian faith seem to take it for granted that if Christian belief were to be rationally acceptable, it would have to be held on the basis of just such argument. Christian belief would have to be or be like a scientific explanation (as they think of it): any rational justification or warrant it enjoyed would have to be by way of its being a good explanation of the observed phenomena.[14] From this point of view, a

13. *Tractatus Theologico-politicus*, 14.

14. See, e.g., John Mackie, *The Miracle of Theism* (Oxford: Oxford University Press, 1982, pp. 186ff.), and Daniel Dennett, *Darwin's Dangerous Idea* (New York: Simon and Schuster, 1995), pp. 152ff.; see also my "Is Theism Really a Miracle?" *Faith and Philosophy* (1986), and "Dennett's Dangerous Idea: Darwin, Mind and Meaning," *Books and Culture* (May–June 1996); and see above, pp. 329ff.

Christian must presumably be thinking along the following lines: "What is the best explanation for all that organized complexity in the natural world and the characteristic features of human life and all the rest of what we see about us? Well, let's see, perhaps there is an omniscient, omnipotent, wholly good being who created the world. Yes that's it; and perhaps this being is one of three persons, the other two being his divine son and a third person proceeding from the first two (or maybe just the first), yet there are not three gods but one; the second person became incarnate, suffered, was crucified, and died, thus atoning for our sins and making it possible for us to have life and have it more abundantly. Right; that's got to be it; that's a dandy explanation of the facts." The critics then conclude, naturally enough, that Christian belief leaves a good bit to be desired.

This project or enterprise is often thought of as part and parcel of the development of modern empirical science, and indeed practitioners of HBC like to drape about their shoulders the mantle of modern science. The attraction is not just that HBC can perhaps share in the prestige of modern science, but also that it can share in the obvious epistemic power and excellence of the latter.[15] It is common to think of science itself as our best shot at getting to know what the world is really like; HBC is, among other things, an attempt to apply these widely approved methods to the study of Scripture and the origins of Christianity. Thus Raymond Brown, a scripture scholar than whom none is more highly respected, believes that HBC is "scientific biblical criticism";[16] it yields "factual results" (p. 9); he intends his own contributions to be "scientifically respectable" (p. 11); and practitioners of HBC investigate the Scriptures with "scientific exactitude" (pp. 18–19).[17]

What *is* it, exactly, to study the Bible scientifically? That's not so clear; as we'll see below, there is more than one answer to this question. One theme that seems to command nearly universal assent, however, is that in working at this scientific project (however exactly it is to be understood) one doesn't invoke or employ any theological assumptions or presuppositions. You don't assume, for example, that

15. To understand historical criticism and its dominance properly, says David Yeago, one must understand "the historic coupling of historical criticism with a 'project of the Enlightenment' aimed at liberating mind and heart from the shackles of ecclesiastical tradition. In the modern context, claims to 'Enlightenment' must be backed up with the claim to have achieved a proper *method*, capable of producing real knowledge to replace the pre-critical confusion and arbitrariness of tradition" ("The New Testament and the Nicene Dogma," *Pro Ecclesia* 3, no. 2 (Spring 1994), p. 162.)

16. *The Virginal Conception and Bodily Resurrection of Jesus* (New York: Paulist Press, 1973), p. 6.

17. See also John Meier, *A Marginal Jew: Rethinking the Historical Jesus* (New York: Doubleday, 1991), vol. 1, p. 1.

the Bible is inspired by God in any special way, or contains anything like specifically divine discourse. You don't assume that Jesus is the divine son of God, or that he arose from the dead, or that his suffering and death are in some way a propitiatory atonement for human sin, making it possible for us to get into the right relationship to God. You don't assume any of these things because, in pursuing science, you don't assume or employ any proposition which you know by faith.[18] (As a consequence, the meaning of a text will be what the human author intended to assert [if it is assertive discourse]; divine intentions and teaching don't enter into the meaning.[19]) The idea, says E. P. Sanders, is to rely only on "evidence on which everyone can agree."[20] According to Jon Levenson,

> Historical critics thus rightly insist that the tribunal before which interpretations are argued cannot be confessional or "dogmatic"; the arguments offered must be historically valid, able, that is, to compel the assent of *historians* whatever their religion or lack thereof, whatever their backgrounds, spiritual experiences, or personal beliefs, and without privileging any claim of revelation.[21]

18. Nor can you employ a proposition which is such that the warrant it has for you comes from some proposition you know or believe by faith; we might put this by saying that in doing science you can't employ any proposition whose epistemic provenance, for you, includes a proposition you know or believe by faith.

But is this really true? Why should we believe it? What is the status of the claim that if what you are doing is science, then you can't employ, in your work, any proposition you believe or know by faith? Is it supposed to be true by definition? If so, whose definition? Is there a good argument for it? Or what? See my "Methodological Naturalism?" in *Facets of Faith and Science*, ed. J. van der Meer (Lanham, Md.: University Press of America, 1995).

19. Thus Benjamin Jowett (the nineteenth-century master of Balliol College and eminent translator of Plato): "Scripture has one meaning—the meaning which it had to the mind of the prophet or evangelist who first uttered or wrote, to the hearers or readers who first received it" ("On the Interpretation of Scripture," in *The Interpretation of Scripture and Other Essays* [London: George Routledge, 1906], p. 36; quoted in Jon D. Levenson, *The Hebrew Bible, the Old Testament, and Historical Criticism* [Louisville, Ky.: Westminster/John Knox Press, 1993], p. 78). Jowett was not a paragon of intellectual modesty, which may explain a poem composed and circulated by undergraduates at Balliol:

> First come I, my name is Jowett.
> There's no knowledge but I know it.
> I am the master of the college.
> What I don't know isn't knowledge.

20. *Jesus and Judaism* (Philadelphia: Fortress Press, 1985), p. 5.

21. "The Hebrew Bible, the Old Testament, and Historical Criticism," in *The Hebrew Bible, the Old Testament, and Historical Criticism*, p. 109. (An earlier version of this essay was published under the same title in *Hebrew Bible or Old Testament? Studying the Bible in Judaism and Christianity*, ed. John Collins and Roger Brooks [Notre Dame: University of Notre Dame Press, 1990].)

Barnabas Lindars explains that

> There are in fact two reasons why many scholars are very cautious
> about miracle stories. . . . The second reason is historical. The reli-
> gious literature of the ancient world is full of miracle stories, and we
> cannot believe them all. It is not open to a scholar to decide that,
> just because he is a believing Christian, he will accept all the Gospel
> miracles at their face value, but at the same time he will repudiate
> miracles attributed to Isis. All such accounts have to be scrutinized
> with equal detachment.[22]

And even Luke Timothy Johnson, who is in general astutely critical
of HBC:

> It is obviously important to study Christian origins historically. And
> in such historical inquiry, faith commitments should play no role.
> Christianity is no more privileged for the historian than any other
> human phenomenon.[23]

In practice, this emphasis means that HBC tends to deal especially with questions of *composition* and *authorship*, these being the
questions most easily addressed by the methods employed. When
was the document in question composed—or, more exactly, since we
can't assume that we are dealing with a single unified document here,
when were its various parts composed? How was the Gospel of Luke,
for example, composed? Was it written by one person, relying on his
memory of Jesus and his words and deeds, or was it assembled from
various reports, alleged quotations, songs, poems, and the like in the
oral tradition? Was it dependent on one or more earlier written or
oral sources? Why did the editor or redactor put the book together in
just the way he did? Was it perhaps to make a theological point in a
then-current controversy? Where traditional biblical commentary assumes that the entire Bible is really one book with a single principal
author, HBC tends to give us a collection of books by many authors.
And even within the confines of a single book, it may give us a collection of discontinuous sayings and episodes (pericopes), stitched together by one or more redactors. How much of what is reported as
the sayings and discourse of Jesus really was said by Jesus? Can we

---

22. *Theology* 89, no. 728 (March 1986), p. 91.

23. *The Real Jesus* (San Francisco: Harper San Francisco, 1996), p. 172. (The target of much of Johnson's criticism is the notorious 'Jesus Seminar'.) Here Johnson
speaks specifically of *history*; he holds that the historian as such cannot properly employ what he knows by faith. In personal communication he informs me that, in his
opinion, history is by its nature limited in this way. Proper biblical scholarship, however, is not; hence the sort of project in which one brackets what one knows by faith
is not epistemically superior but, in fact, epistemically inferior to biblical scholarship
informed by faith. His view, therefore, resembles the one outlined below, pp. 401ff.

discern various strata in the book—perhaps a bottom stratum including the actual sayings of Jesus himself, and then successive overlaying strata? As Robert Alter says, scholarship of this kind tends to be "excavative"; the idea is to dig behind the document as we actually have it to see what can be determined of its history.[24]

Of course the idea is also to see, as far as this is possible, whether the events reported—in the Gospels, for example—really happened, and whether the picture they give of Jesus is accurate. Did he say the things they say he said, and do the things they say he did? Here the assumption is that we can't simply take at face value the Gospels as we now have them. There may have been all sorts of additions and subtractions and alterations made in the interest of advancing theological points. Further, the New Testament books are written from the standpoint of faith—faith that Jesus really was the Christ, did indeed suffer and die and rise from the dead, and did accomplish our salvation. From the standpoint of reason alone, however, this faith must be bracketed; hence (from that standpoint) the hermeneutics of suspicion is appropriate here. (This suspicion is sometimes carried so far that it reminds one of the way in which the CIA's denial that Mr. X is a spy is taken as powerful evidence that Mr. X is a spy.)

A. Varieties of Historical Biblical Criticism

Those who practice HBC, therefore, propose to proceed without employing theological assumptions or anything one knows by faith (if indeed there is anything one knows by faith); these things are to be bracketed. Instead, one proceeds scientifically, on the basis of reason alone. Beyond this, however, there is vastly less concord. What is to count as reason? Precisely what premises can be employed in an argument from reason alone? What exactly does it mean to proceed scientifically? Here I think we find at least three distinct positions.

1. Troeltschian Historical Biblical Criticism

Many contemporary biblical critics appeal to the thought and teaching of Ernst Troeltsch.[25] Thus John Collins:

---

24. I don't mean to suggest that the traditional biblical commentator cannot also investigate these questions; if she does, however, it will be in the ultimate service of an effort to discern what the Lord is teaching in the passages in question.

25. See especially his "Über historische und dogmatische Methode in der Theologie" in his *Gesammelte Schriften* (Tübingen: Mohr, 1913), vol. 2, pp. 729–53, and his article "Historiography" in James Hastings, *Encyclopedia of Religion and Ethics* (New York: Scribner's, 1967 [reprint of 1909 edition]).

Among theologians these principles received their classic formulation from Ernst Troeltsch in 1898. Troeltsch sets out three principles . . . (1) The principle of criticism or methodological doubt: since any conclusion is subject to revision, historical inquiry can never attain absolute certainty but only relative degrees of probability. (2) The principle of analogy: historical knowledge is possible because all events are similar in principle. We must assume that the laws of nature in biblical times were the same as now. Troeltsch referred to this as "the almighty power of analogy." (3) The principle of correlation: the phenomena of history are inter-related and interdependent and no event can be isolated from the sequence of historical cause and effect.[26]

Collins adds a fourth principle, this one taken from Van Harvey's *The Historian and the Believer*,[27] a more recent *locus classicus* for the proper method of historical criticism:

To these should be added the principle of autonomy, which is indispensable for any critical study. Neither church nor state can prescribe for the scholar which conclusions should be reached. (p. 2)

Now the first thing to note is that each of these principles is multiply ambiguous. In particular, each (except perhaps the second) has a noncontroversial, indeed, platitudinous interpretation. The first principle seems to be a *comment on* historical inquiry rather than a principle for its practice: historical inquiry can never attain absolutely certain results. (Perhaps the implied methodological principle is that in doing historical criticism, you should avoid claiming absolute certainty for your results.) Fair enough. I suppose nearly everyone would agree that few historical results of any significance are as certain as, say, that $2 + 1 = 3$; if so, however, they don't achieve absolute certainty. (The only reasonably plausible candidates for historical results that *are* absolutely certain, I suppose, would be such 'historical' claims as that either Caesar crossed the Rubicon or else he didn't.)

The third also has a platitudinous interpretation. Troeltsch puts the principle like this: "The sole task of history in its specifically theoretical aspect is to explain every movement, process, state and nexus of things by reference to the web of its causal relations."[28] This too can be seen as toothless if not platitudinous. Every event is to be explained by reference to the web of its causal relations—which, of course, would also include the intentions and actions of persons. Well then, consider even such an event as the resurrection of Jesus from

26. "Is Critical Biblical Theology Possible?" in *The Hebrew Bible and Its Interpreters*, ed. William Henry Propp, Baruch Halpern, and David Freedman (Winona Lake, Ind.: Eisenbrauns, 1990), p. 2.

27. Subtitled *The Morality of Historical Knowledge and Christian Belief* (New York: Macmillan, 1966).

28. "Historiography," p. 718.

the dead: according to the principle at hand, this event too would have to be explained by reference to the web of its causal relations. No problem; on the traditional view, this event was caused by God himself, who caused it in order to achieve certain of his aims and ends, in particular making it possible for human beings to be reconciled with him. So taken, this principle would exclude very little.

I say the second principle is perhaps the exception to the claim that each has a banal, uncontroversial interpretation: that is because on any plausible interpretation the second principle seems to entail the existence of *natural laws*. That there *are* such things as natural laws was a staple of seventeenth- and eighteenth-century science and philosophy of science;[29] what science discovers (so they thought) is just these laws of nature.[30] Empiricists have always been dubious about natural laws, however, and at present the claim that there are any such things is, at best, extremely controversial.[31]

Among the main problems is the alleged *necessity* of these laws. A natural law is supposed to be a universal generalization. Consider, for example, Newton's first law: "Every body continues in its state of rest, or of uniform motion in a straight line, unless it is compelled to change that state by forces impressed on it." The idea is that this universal generalization is in some sense *necessarily* true. The alleged kind of necessity ('natural' or 'physical' necessity) is supposed to be weaker than the broadly logical necessity enjoyed by truths of logic, arithmetic, and the like (natural laws are ordinarily thought to be contingent in the broadly logical sense) but necessary in some sense nonetheless. In *what* sense? That's not easy to say, but here is a picture. Think of natural necessity in terms of the ordinary semantics for counterfactuals: we imagine the possible worlds as constituting a space—for simplicity, a three-dimensional space; we somehow settle on or at any rate postulate the existence of a distance measure on this space of possible worlds; and the larger the sphere of possible worlds (centered on the actual world[32]) in which a

---

29. Thus Descartes, *Principles of Philosophy*, part 2:

xxvii. The first law of nature: that each thing as far as in it lies, continues always in the same state; and that which is once moved always continues so to move.

xxxix. The second law of nature: that all motion is of itself in a straight line.

30. An opinion preserved among such contemporary philosophers as David Armstrong (see his *What Is a Law of Nature?* [Cambridge: Cambridge University Press, 1984]) and David Lewis (see, e.g., his "New Work for a Theory of Universals," *Australasian Journal of Philosophy* [1983], pp. 343ff.).

31. See, in particular, Bas van Fraassen's *Laws and Symmetry* (Oxford: Clarendon Press, 1989) for an extended and powerful argument against the existence of natural laws.

32. Of course a natural law could be 'more necessary' in some other possible world than it is in the actual world. Therefore, although a natural law will be true throughout some sphere centered on the actual world, that sphere may be included in a larger sphere whose center is not the actual world.

given proposition is true, the more necessary that proposition is. Then the idea would be that natural laws are propositions true in very large spheres (centered on the actual world); they remain true as we proceed outward from the actual world for a very long ways.

This is a pretty little picture (though both metaphorical and highly speculative); still, why saddle the historian or scripture scholar with an opinion on this topic? It is hard to see that the practice of HBC actually requires allegiance to the view that there is such a thing as natural necessity or, that there are such things as natural laws, explained in this way or in any other. Why must the historian take a hand in this philosophical dispute? But perhaps Troeltsch and Collins don't really mean to insist that the critical historian has to believe in natural *laws*; perhaps they could put their claims just as well by saying the same empirical generalizations or *physical regularities* obtained in the past as obtain now. Newtonian physics (at least approximately, and for middle-sized objects traveling at moderate speed) held then as now; special and general relativity were true then just as now (if indeed they are true now); quantum electrodynamics applied at earlier times (at any rate times not too close to the Big Bang) just as at present. And this whether we think of these as statements of natural law, with that peculiar sort of necessity, or as statements of exceptionless regularities, or as regularities holding for the vast majority of cases, or (as in the case of some quantum mechanical regularities) probabilistic.

So Troeltsch's principles have platitudinous interpretations; but these are not, in fact, the interpretations given to them in the community of HBC. Within that community, those principles are understood in such a way as to preclude *direct divine action* in the world. Not that all in this community *accept* Troeltsch's principles in their nonplatitudinous interpretation; rather, those who think of themselves as accepting (or rejecting) those principles think of themselves as accepting (or rejecting) their nonplatitudinous versions. (Presumably *everyone* accepts them taken platitudinously.) So taken, these principles imply that God has not, in fact, specially inspired any human authors in such a way that what they write is really divine speech addressed to us; nor has he raised Jesus from the dead, turned water into wine, or performed miracles of any other sorts. Thus Rudolf Bultmann:

> The historical method includes the presupposition that history is a unity in the sense of a closed continuum of effects in which individual events are connected by the succession of cause and effect.

This continuum, furthermore,

> cannot be rent by the interference of supernatural, transcendent powers.[33]

---

33. *Existence and Faith*, ed. Schubert Ogden (New York: Meridian Books, 1960), pp. 291–92. Writing fifty years before Troeltsch, David Strauss concurs: "all things

Many other theologians, oddly enough, chime in with agreement: God cannot or at any rate would not and will not act directly in the world. Thus John Macquarrie:

> The way of understanding miracles that appeals to breaks in the natural order and to supernatural interventions belongs to the mythological outlook and cannot commend itself in a post-mythological climate of thought. . . .
> The traditional conception of miracle is irreconcilable with our modern understanding of both science and history. Science proceeds on the assumption that whatever events occur in the world can be accounted for in terms of other events that also belong within the world; and if on some occasions we are unable to give a complete account of some happening . . . the scientific conviction is that further research will bring to light further factors in the situation, but factors that will turn out to be just as immanent and this-worldly as those already known.[34]

And Langdon Gilkey:

> contemporary theology does not expect, nor does it speak of, wondrous divine events on the surface of natural and historical life. The causal nexus in space and time which the Enlightenment science and philosophy introduced into the Western mind . . . is also assumed by modern theologians and scholars; since they participate in the modern world of science both intellectually and existentially, they can scarcely do anything else. Now this assumption of a causal order among phenomenal events, and therefore of the authority of the scientific interpretation of observable events, makes a great difference to the validity one assigns to biblical narratives and so to the way one understands their meaning. Suddenly a vast panoply of divine deeds and events recorded in scripture are no longer regarded as having actually happened. . . . Whatever the Hebrews believed, *we* believe that the biblical people lived in the same causal continuum of space and time in which we live, and so one in which no divine wonders transpired and no divine voices were heard.[35]

Gilkey says no divine wonders have transpired and no divine voices have been heard; Macquarrie adds that, in this postmythological age, we can't brook the idea of "breaks in the natural order and supernatural intervention." Each, therefore, is ruling out the possi-

---

are linked together by a chain of causes and effects, which suffers no interruption" *Life of Jesus Critically Examined* [Philadelphia: Fortress Press, 1972], sec. 14; quoted in Harvey, *The Historian and the Believer*, p. 15.)

34. *Principles of Christian Theology*, 2d ed. (New York: Charles Scribner's Sons, 1977), p. 248.

35. "Cosmology, Ontology, and the Travail of Biblical Language," in *God's Activity in the World: The Contemporary Problem*, ed. Owen C. Thomas (Chico, Calif.: Scholars Press, 1983), p. 31.

bility of miracle, including the possibility of special divine action in inspiring human authors in such a way that what they write constitutes an authoritative communication from God. Now it is far from easy to say just what a miracle is; this topic is connected with deep and thorny questions about occasionalism, natural law, natural potentialities, and so on. We needn't get into all that, however. The Troeltschian idea is that there is a certain way in which things ordinarily go; there are certain regularities, whether or not due to natural law, and God can be counted on to act in such a way as not to abrogate those regularities. Of course God *could*, if he chose, abrogate those regularities (after all, even those natural laws, if there are any, are his creatures); but we can be sure, somehow, that he will not. Troeltschian scripture scholarship, therefore, will proceed on the basis of the assumption that God never does anything specially; in particular, he neither raised Jesus from the dead nor specially inspired the biblical authors.

> A thousand questions arise about these regularities: what sort are we thinking of? Suppose there has never been and never will be a combination of three dimes and two nickels in my pocket, or a freshwater lake the size of Lake Baikal surrounded by mainly Japanese speakers, or heavily glaciated mountains in Australia contemporaneous with a Dutch-speaking population, or dinosaurs and humans at the same time: are these the sorts of regularities in question? Presumably not. What about the fact that none of the Great Lakes has ever been or ever will be filled with single-malt Scotch whiskey? Or that there has never been or ever will be a sphere of gold a mile in diameter? Probably not. How about the fact that there has never been a sphere of plutonium a mile in diameter? Probably so: such a sphere would contain a quantity of plutonium greater than the critical mass and would therefore have exploded. How, precisely, do we characterize the regularities we are talking about? That's very difficult. At any rate the idea is that there *are* such regularities; and among them would be that human beings, once they are dead, do not come back to life, that water doesn't change into wine, and that human beings are not specially inspired by God in such a way that what they write is properly regarded as divine speech and revelation.

2. Duhemian Historical Biblical Criticism

Not all who accept and practice HBC accept Troeltsch's principles, and we can see another variety of HBC by thinking about an important suggestion made by Pierre Duhem. Duhem was both a serious Catholic and a serious scientist; he was accused (as he thought) by Abel Rey[36] of allowing his religious and metaphysical views as a

---

36. "La Philosophie scientifique de M. Duhem," *Revue de Métaphysique et de Morale* 12 (July 1904), pp. 699ff.

Christian to enter his physics in an improper way. Duhem repudiated this suggestion, claiming that his Christianity didn't enter his physics in any way at all and *a fortiori* didn't enter it in an improper way.[37] Furthermore, the *correct* or *proper* way to pursue physical theory, he said, was the way in which he had in fact done it; physical theory should be completely independent of religious or metaphysical views or commitments.

Why did he think so? What did he have against metaphysics? Here he strikes a characteristic Enlightenment note: if you think of metaphysics as ingressing into physics, he says, then your estimate of the worth of a physical theory will depend on the metaphysics you adopt. Physical theory will be dependent on metaphysics in such a way that someone who doesn't accept the metaphysics involved in a given physical theory can't accept the physical theory either. And the problem with *that* is that the disagreements that run riot in metaphysics will ingress into physics, so that the latter cannot be an activity we can all work at together, regardless of our metaphysical views:

> Now to make physical theories depend on metaphysics is surely not the way to let them enjoy the privilege of universal consent. . . . If theoretical physics is subordinated to metaphysics, the divisions separating the diverse metaphysical systems will extend into the domain of physics. A physical theory reputed to be satisfactory by the sectarians of one metaphysical school will be rejected by the partisans of another school. (p. 10)

Duhem's main point, I think, is that if a physical theorist employs metaphysical assumptions or other notions that are not accepted by other workers in the field, and employs them in such a way that those who don't accept them can't accept his physical theory, then to that extent his work cannot be accepted by those others; to that extent, furthermore, the cooperation important to science will be compromised. He therefore proposes a conception of science (of physics in particular) according to which the latter is independent of metaphysics:

> I have denied metaphysical doctrines the right to testify for or against any physical theory. . . . Whatever I have said of the method by which physics proceeds, or the nature and scope that we must attribute to the theories it constructs, does not in any way prejudice either the metaphysical doctrines or religious beliefs of anyone who

37. See the appendix to Duhem's *The Aim and Structure of Physical Theory*, tr. Philip P. Wiener, foreword by Prince Louis de Broglie (Princeton: Princeton University Press, 1954; first published in 1906). The appendix is entitled "Physics of a Believer" and is a reprint of Duhem's reply to Rey; it was originally published in the *Annales de Philosophie chrétienne* 1 (October–November 1905), pp. 44ff. and 133ff.

accepts my words. The believer and the nonbeliever may both work in common accord for the progress of physical science such as I have tried to define it. (pp. 274–75)

Duhem's proposal, reduced to essentials, is that physicists shouldn't make essential use of religious or metaphysical assumptions in doing their physics: that way lies chaos and cacophony, as each of the warring sects does things its own way. If we want to have the sort of commonality and genuine dialogue that promote progress in physics, we should avoid assumptions, metaphysical, religious, or otherwise, that are not accepted by all parties to the discussion.[38]

This is an interesting suggestion. Although Duhem himself didn't do so, it can obviously be applied far beyond the confines of physical theory: for example, to scripture scholarship. Suppose we say that *Duhemian* scripture scholarship is scripture scholarship that doesn't involve any theological, religious, or metaphysical assumptions that aren't accepted by everyone in the relevant community.[39] Thus the Duhemian scripture scholar wouldn't take for granted either that God is the principal author of the Bible or that the main lines of the Christian story are in fact true; these are not accepted by all who are party to the discussion. She wouldn't take for granted that Jesus rose from the dead, or that any other miracle has occurred; she couldn't so much as take it for granted that miracles are possible because these claims are rejected by many who are party to the discussion. On the other hand, of course, Duhemian scripture scholarship can't take it for granted that Christ did *not* rise from the dead or that *no* miracles have occurred, or that miracles are *im*possible. Nor can it employ Troeltsch's principles (taken nonplatitudinously); not everyone accepts them. Duhemian scripture scholarship fits well with Sanders's suggestion that "what is needed is more secure evidence, evidence on

38. Of course this proposal must be qualified, nuanced, sophisticated. It makes perfect sense for me to continue to work on a hypothesis after others have decided it is a dead end; science has often benefited from such disagreements. But in these cases there is ordinarily a deeper agreement as to what the aims of science are, what counts as genuine science, and what the proper methods to be employed might be. Furthermore, the disputes can often be settled on the basis of this deeper agreement; it is possible for one of the disputants to turn out to be right in a way that is recognized by all the disputants.

39. It may be difficult to specify the relevant community. Suppose I am a scripture scholar at a denominational seminary: what is my relevant community? Scripture scholars of any sort, all over the world? Scripture scholars in my own denomination? In Western academia? The people, academics or not, in my denomination? Christians generally? The first thing to see here is that our scripture scholar clearly belongs to many different communities and may accordingly be involved in several different scholarly projects.

which everyone can agree" (above, p. 388). It also fits well with John Meier's fantasy of "an unpapal conclave" of Jewish, Catholic, Protestant, and agnostic scholars, locked in the basement of the Harvard Divinity School library until they come to consensus on what historical methods can show about the life and mission of Jesus.[40] Among the proposed benefits of Duhemian HBC, obviously, are just the benefits Duhem cites: people of very different religious and theological beliefs can cooperate in this enterprise. Of course this is not a reason for thinking the results of Duhemian scholarship are more likely to be true or closer to the truth than, say, traditional biblical commentary; still, although in principle the traditional biblical commentator and the Troeltschian biblical scholar could discover whatever is unearthed by Duhemian means, it is, in fact, likely that much will be learned in this cooperative enterprise that would not be learned by either group working alone.

3. Spinozistic Historical Biblical Criticism

Troeltschian and Duhemian HBC do not exhaust HBC; one can be a practitioner of HBC and accept neither. You might propose to follow reason alone in scripture scholarship, but think that the Troeltschian principles, taken in the strong version in which they imply that God never acts specially in the world, are not, in fact, deliverances of reason. Reason alone, you say, certainly can't demonstrate that God never acts specially in the world, or that no miracles have ever occurred. If so, you wouldn't be a Troeltschian. But you might reject Duhemianism as well: you might think that, as a matter of fact, there are deliverances of reason not accepted by everyone party to the project of scripture scholarship. (The deliverances of reason are indeed *open* to all; nevertheless, impeding factors of one kind or another can sometimes prevent someone from seeing the truth of one or another of them.) Then you might yourself employ those deliverances of reason in pursuing scripture scholarship, thereby employing assumptions not accepted by everyone involved in the project, and thereby rejecting Duhemianism. You might therefore propose to follow reason alone, but be neither Troeltschian nor Duhemian. Suppose we use the term 'Spinozistic HBC'[41] to denote this last variety of HBC. The Spinozist concurs with the Troeltschian and Duhemian that no theological assumptions or beliefs are to be employed in HBC. She differs from the Troeltschian in paying the same compliment to Troeltsch's principles: they too are not deliverances of

---

40. *A Marginal Jew: Rethinking the Historical Jesus*, vol. 1, pp. 1–2.

41. According to Spinoza, as we saw, "The rule for [biblical] interpretation should be nothing but the natural light of reason" (above, p. 386).

reason and hence are not to be employed in HBC. And she differs from the Duhemian in holding that there are some deliverances of reason not accepted by all who are party to the project of scripture scholarship; hence she proposes to employ some propositions or beliefs rejected by the Duhemian.

A final point: It is clearly inaccurate to suppose that every scripture scholar falls neatly into one or another of these four categories. Not every work of scripture scholarship is either a clear example of traditional biblical commentary or else a clear example of HBC. Not every work of HBC is a clear example of just one of Troeltschian, Duhemian, or Spinozistic HBC. There are all sorts of halfway houses, lots of haltings between two opinions, many who fall partly into one and partly into another, and many who have never clearly seen that there *are* these categories. A real live scripture scholar is unlikely to have spent a great deal of thought on the epistemological foundations of the discipline and is likely to straddle one or more of the categories I mention.

B. Tensions with Traditional Christianity

There has been a history of substantial tension between HBC and traditional Christians. Thus David Strauss in 1835: "Nay, if we would be candid with ourselves, that which was once sacred history for the Christian believer is, for the enlightened portion of our contemporaries, only fable." Of course the unenlightened faithful were not so unenlightened that they failed to notice this feature of biblical criticism. Writing ten years after the publication of Strauss's book, William Pringle complains, "In Germany, Biblical criticism is almost a national pursuit. . . . Unhappily, [the critics] were but too frequently employed in maintaining the most dangerous errors, in opposing every inspired statement which the mind of man is unable fully to comprehend, in divesting religion of its spiritual and heavenly character, and in undermining the whole fabric of revealed truth."[42]

Perhaps among Pringle's complaints were the following. First, practitioners of HBC tend to treat the Bible as a set of separate books rather than a unified communication from God. Thus they tend to reject the idea that Old Testament passages can be properly understood as making reference to Jesus Christ or to events in his life: "Critical scholars rule out clairvoyance as an explanation axiomatically. Instead of holding that the Old Testament predicts events in the life of Jesus, critical scholars of the New Testament say that each

---

42. "Translator's Preface," *Calvin's Commentaries*, vol. 16, tr. William Pringle (Grand Rapids: Baker Book House, 1979), p. vi. Pringle's preface is dated at Auchterarder, January 4, 1845.

Gospel writer sought to exploit Old Testament passages in order to bolster his case for the messianic and dominical claims of Jesus or of the church on his behalf."[43] More generally, Brevard Childs: "For many decades the usual way of initiating entering students in the Bible was slowly to dismantle the church's traditional teachings regarding scripture by applying the acids of criticism."[44]

Second, following Ernst Troeltsch, HBC tends to discount miracle stories, taking it as axiomatic that miracles don't and didn't really happen or, at any rate, claiming that the proper method for HBC can't admit miracles as either evidence or conclusions. Perhaps Jesus effected cures of some psychosomatic disorders, but nothing that modern medical science can't explain. Many employing this method propose that Jesus never thought of himself as divine, or as the (or a) Messiah, or as capable of forgiving sin[45]—let alone as having died and then risen from the dead. "The Historical Jesus researchers," says Luke Timothy Johnson, "insist that the 'real Jesus' must be found in the facts of his life before his death. The resurrection is, when considered at all, seen in terms of visionary experience, or as a continuation of an 'empowerment' that began before Jesus' death. Whether made explicit or not, the operative premise is that there is no 'real Jesus' after his death."[46]

Those who follow these methods sometimes produce quite remarkable accounts—and accounts remarkably different from traditional Christian understanding. According to Barbara Thiering's *Jesus and the Riddle of the Dead Sea Scrolls*,[47] for example, Jesus was buried in a cave; he didn't actually die and was revived by the magician Simon Magus, whereupon he married Mary Magdalene, settled down, fathered three children, was divorced, and finally died in Rome. According to Morton Smith, Jesus was a practicing homosexual and conjurer.[48] According to German scripture scholar Gerd

---

43. Levenson, *The Hebrew Bible, the Old Testament, and Historical Criticism*, p. 9. Of course *clairvoyance* isn't at issue at all: the question is really whether the Scripture has one principal author, namely, God. If it does, then it doesn't require clairvoyance on the part of a human author for a passage from a given time to refer to something that happens much later. All that is required is God's omniscience.

44. *The New Testament as Canon: An Introduction* (Valley Forge, Pa.: Trinity Press International, 1994), p. xvii.

45. "The crisis grows out of the fact now freely admitted by both Protestant and Catholic theologians and exegetes: that as far as can be discerned from the available historical data, Jesus of Nazareth did not think he was divine [and] did not assert any of the messianic claims that the New Testament attributes to him" (Thomas Sheehan, *The First Coming* [New York: Random House, 1986], p. 9).

46. *The Real Jesus*, p. 144.

47. San Francisco: Harper San Francisco, 1992.

48. *Jesus the Magician* (New York: Harper and Row, 1978).

Lüdemann, the resurrection is "an empty formula that must be rejected by anyone holding a scientific world view."[49] G. A. Wells goes so far as to claim that our name 'Jesus', as it turns up in the Bible, is empty; like 'Santa Claus', it doesn't trace back to or denote anyone at all.[50] John Allegro apparently thinks there was no such person as Jesus of Nazareth; Christianity began as a hoax designed to fool the Romans and preserve the cult of a certain hallucinogenic mushroom (*Amanita muscaria*). Still, the name 'Christ' isn't empty: it is really a name of that mushroom.[51] As engaging a claim as any is that Jesus, while neither merely legendary, nor actually a mushroom, was, in fact, an atheist, the first Christian atheist.[52] And even if we set aside the lunatic fringe, Van Harvey is correct: "So far as the biblical historian is concerned . . . there is scarcely a popularly held traditional belief about Jesus that is not regarded with considerable skepticism."[53]

IV. WHY AREN'T MOST CHRISTIANS MORE CONCERNED?

So HBC has not in general been sympathetic to traditional Christian belief; it has hardly been an encouragement to the faithful. The faithful, however, seem relatively unconcerned; they find traditional biblical commentary of great interest and importance, but the beliefs and attitudes of HBC have not seemed to filter down to them, despite its dominance in mainline seminaries. According to Van Harvey, "Despite decades of research, the average person tends to think of the life of Jesus in much the same terms as Christians did three centuries ago."[54] Harvey finds this puzzling: "Why is it that, in a culture so dominated by experts in every field, the opinion of New Testament historians has had so little influence on the public?"[55] Are traditional Christians just ignoring inconvenient evidence? In what follows, I'll try to answer these questions. Obviously HBC has contributed greatly to our knowledge of the Bible, in particular the circumstances and conditions of its composition; it has given us new alternatives as to how to understand the human authors, and this has also given us new ideas about how to understand the divine Author. Nevertheless, there are in fact excellent reasons for tending to ignore that "considerable skepticism" of which Harvey speaks. I don't mean

49. *What Really Happened to Jesus: A Historical Approach to the Resurrection* (Louisville, Ky.: Westminster/John Knox Press, 1995).

50. "The Historicity of Jesus," in *Jesus in History and Myth*, ed. R. Joseph Hoffman and Gerald A. Larue (Buffalo: Prometheus Books, 1986), pp. 27ff.

51. *The Sacred Mushroom and the Cross* (Garden City, N.Y.: Doubleday, 1970).

52. Sheehan, *The First Coming*.

53. NTS, p. 193.

to claim that the ordinary person in the pew ignores it because she has these reasons clearly in mind; no doubt she doesn't. I say only that these reasons are *good* reasons for a traditional Christian to ignore the deflationary results of HBC.

What might these reasons be? Well, one reason might be that skeptical scripture scholars display vast disagreement among themselves.[56] There is also the fact that quite a number of the arguments they propose seem at best wholly inconclusive.[57] Perhaps the endemic vice or at any rate the perennial temptation of HBC is what we might call "the fallacy of creeping certitude," which is committed by those who ignore the principle of dwindling probabilities. To practice this fallacy, you note that some proposition A is probable (to .9, say) with respect to your background knowledge k; you therefore annex A to k. Then you note that a proposition B is probable with respect to k&A; you therefore add it too to k. Then you note that C is probable to .9 with respect to A&B&k, and also annex it to k; similarly for (say) D, E, F, and G. You then pronounce A&B&C&D&E&F&G highly probable with respect to k, our evidence or background information. But the fact is (as we learn from the probability calculus) that these probabilities must be *multiplied*: so that in fact the probability of A&B&C&D&E&F&G is .9 to the seventh power, that is, less than .5![58]

Suppose we look into reasons or arguments for preferring the results of HBC to those of traditional commentary. Why should we suppose that the former take us closer to the truth than the latter? Troeltsch's principles are particularly important here. As understood

---

54. NTS, p. 194.

55. Ibid.

56. This lack of accord is especially well documented by Stephen Evans, *The Historical Christ and the Jesus of Faith*, pp. 322ff.

57. For example, John Dominick Crosson argues that Jesus' body was eaten by dogs; hence he did not rise from the dead. What is the evidence for the proposition that his body *was* eaten by dogs? Just that this is what ordinarily happened to criminals executed by crucifixion. But then Crosson could have made a much briefer argument: Jesus didn't rise from the dead, because most people don't.

58. Eleonore Stump criticizes another very good illustration of this procedure in chapter 3, "Historical Biblical Studies: Practices," of her *The Knowledge of Suffering* (not yet published). In "Biblical Criticism and the Resurrection" (not yet published), William Alston suggests his own version of the fallacy of creeping certitude, and he also mentions the widespread use of the argument from silence, which, so to say, promotes the failure to assert p to the assertion of not-p. (For example, Thomas Sheehan says that according to Matthew, "He [Christ] does not ascend into heaven" [*The First Coming*, p. 97], giving as a reference Matthew 28:16–20. Matthew 28:16–20, however, does not say that Jesus did not ascend into heaven; it simply doesn't say that he did.) Stump and Alston argue (with great cogency, in my opinion) that a good bit of negative HBC doesn't satisfy ordinary canons of proper scholarship; I shall argue that even if the scholarship were impeccable, the epistemological assumptions I have been mentioning make the work of dubious relevance to traditional Christian belief.

in the interpretative community of HBC, they preclude special divine action, including special divine inspiration of Scripture and the occurrence of miracles. As Gilkey says, "Suddenly a vast panoply of divine deeds and events recorded in scripture are no longer regarded as having actually happened." Many academic theologians and scripture scholars appear to believe that Troeltschian HBC is *de rigueur*; it is often regarded as the only intellectually respectable variety of scripture scholarship, or the only variety that has any claim to the mantle of science. (And many who arrive at relatively traditional conclusions in scripture scholarship nevertheless pay at least lip service to the Troeltschian ideal, somehow feeling in a semiconfused way that this is the epistemically respectable or privileged way of proceeding.) Still, why think scripture scholarship should proceed in this specific way—as opposed both to traditional biblical commentary and varieties of HBC that do not accept Troeltsch's principles? Are there any reasons or arguments for those principles?

A. *Force Majeure*

If so, they are extraordinarily well hidden. One common suggestion, however, seems to be a sort of appeal to *force majeure*: we simply can't help it. Given our historical position, there is nothing else we can do; we are all in the grip of historical forces beyond our control (this thing is bigger than either one of us). This reaction is typified by those who (like Harvey, Macquarrie, and Gilkey) claim that nowadays, given our cultural situation, we just don't have any options. There are potent historical forces that impose these ways of thinking on us; like it or not, we are blown about by these powerful winds of doctrine; we can't help ourselves. "The causal nexus in space and time which the Enlightenment science and philosophy introduced into the Western mind . . . is also assumed by modern theologians and scholars; since they participate in the modern world of science both intellectually and existentially, they can scarcely do anything else," says Gilkey (above, p. 394); another example is Bultmann's famous remark to the effect that "it is impossible to use electrical light and the wireless and to avail ourselves of modern medical and surgical discoveries, and at the same time to believe in the New Testament world of spirits and miracles."[59]

59. *Kerygma and Myth* (New York: Harper and Row, 1961), p. 5. Compare Marcus Borg's (Jesus Seminar major domo) more recent comment: "to a large extent, the defining characteristic of biblical scholarship in the modern period is the attempt to understand Scripture without reference to another world because in this period the visible world of space and time is the world we think of as 'real' " ("Root Images and the Way We See," in *Fragments of Infinity* [Dorset, England, and Lindfield,

But isn't this view—that we are all compelled by contemporary historical forces to hold the sort of view in question—historically naive? First, why think we proceed together in lockstep through history, all at any given time perforce holding the same views and making the same assumptions? Clearly we don't do any such thing. The contemporary intellectual world is much more like a horse race (or perhaps a demolition derby) than a triumphal procession,[60] more like a battleground than a Democratic party fund-raiser, where everyone can be counted on to support the same slate. At present, for example, there are many like Macquarrie, Harvey, and Gilkey who accept the semideistic view that God (if there is any such person) couldn't or wouldn't act miraculously in history. Of course this is not the view of nearly everyone at present; hundreds of millions would reject it. Far more people reject this view than accept it. (So even if Gilkey and the others were right about the inevitable dance of history, they would be wrong in their elitist notion to the effect that what *they* do is the current step.)

The utter obviousness of this fact suggests a second interpretation of this particular justification of Troeltschian HBC. Perhaps what the apologists really mean is not that *everyone* nowadays accepts this semideism (that is trivially false); it's rather that everyone *in the know* does. Everyone who is properly educated and has read his Kant and Hume (and Troeltsch) and reflected on the meaning of the wireless and electric light knows these things; as for the rest of humanity (including, I suppose, those of us who have read our Kant and Hume but are unimpressed), their problem is simple ignorance. Perhaps people generally don't march lockstep through history; still, those in the know do; and right now they all or nearly all reject special divine action.

Even if we chauvinistically stick to educated Westerners, this is still doubtful *in excelsis*. "The traditional conception of miracle," Macquarrie says, "is irreconcilable with *our* modern understanding of both science and history": to whom does this 'our', here, refer? To those who have gone to university, are well-educated, know at least a little science, and have thought about the bearing of these matters on

---

Australia, 1991], p. 38; quoted in Huston Smith's "Doing Theology in the Global Village," *Religious Studies and Theology*, 13–14, nos. 2 and 3 [December 1995], p. 12). On the other side, note Abraham Kuyper, *To Be near unto God*, tr. John Hendrik de Vries (Grand Rapids: Eerdman's, 1918). Writing not long after the invention of the "wireless," he saw it (along with the telephone) not as an *obstacle* to traditional faith but as an *aid* to it: "This now comes to the help of our weak faith" (p. 50); and "There is now a telegraph without wire, which in its wondrous working has become a beautiful symbol for our prayer. Fellowship with God without any middle-means" (p. 341).

60. To adapt a remark of Jerry Fodor's.

the possibility of miracles? If so, the claim is once more whoppingly false. Very many well-educated people (including even some theologians) understand science and history in a way that is entirely compatible both with the possibility and with the actuality of miracles. Many physicists and engineers, for example, understand "electrical light and the wireless" vastly better than Bultmann or his contemporary followers, but nonetheless hold precisely those New Testament beliefs Bultmann thinks incompatible with using electric lights and radios. There are large numbers of educated contemporaries (including even some with Ph.D's!) who believe Jesus really and literally arose from the dead, that God performs miracles in the contemporary world, and even that there are both demons and spirits who are active in the contemporary world. As a matter of historical fact, there are any number of contemporaries, and contemporary intellectuals very well acquainted with science, who don't feel any problem at all in pursuing science and also believing in miracles, angels, Christ's resurrection, the lot.

Once more, however, Macquarrie and the others must know this as well as anyone else; so what do he and his friends really mean? How can they make these claims about what 'we'[61]—we who use the products of science and know a bit about it—can and can't believe? How can they blithely exclude or ignore the thousands, indeed, millions of contemporary Christians who don't think as they do? The answer must be that they think those Christians somehow don't count. What they really mean to say, I fear, is that they and their friends think this way, and anyone who demurs is so ignorant as to be properly ignored. But that's at best a bit slim as a *reason* for accepting the Troeltschian view; it is more like a nasty little piece of arrogance. Nor is it any better for being tucked away in the suggestion that somehow we just can't help ourselves. Of course it is possible that Gilkey and his friends *can't* help themselves; in that case, they can hardly be blamed for accepting the view in question.[62] This incapacity on their parts, however, is no recommendation of Troeltsch's principles.

So this is at best a poor reason for thinking serious biblical scholarship must be Troeltschian. Is there a better reason? A second suggestion, perhaps connected with the plea of inability to do otherwise, is given by the idea that the very practice of science presupposes rejection of the idea of miracle or special divine action in the world.

---

61. We might call this the *preemptive* 'we': those who don't agree with us on the point in question are (by comparison with us) so unenlightened that we can properly speak as if they do not so much as exist. Of course claiming royalty at the font does not automatically guarantee legitimacy.

62. Some, however, might see here little more than an effort to gain standing and respectability in a largely secular academia by adopting a stance that is, so to say, more Catholic than the pope.

"Science proceeds on the assumption that whatever events occur in the world can be accounted for in terms of other events that also belong within the world," says Macquarrie; perhaps he means to suggest that the very practice of science requires that one reject the idea (e.g.) of God's raising someone from the dead. Of course the argument form

> If X were true, it would be inconvenient for science; therefore, X is false

is at best moderately compelling. We aren't just given that the Lord has arranged the universe for the comfort and convenience of the National Academy of Science. To think otherwise is to be like the drunk who insisted on looking for his lost car keys under the streetlight, on the grounds that the light was better there. (In fact it would go the drunk one better: it would be to insist that because the keys would be hard to find in the dark, they must be under the light.)

But why think in the first place that we would have to embrace this semideism in order to do science?[63] Many contemporary physicists, for example, believe that Jesus was raised from the dead; this belief seems to do little damage to their physics. To be sure, that's physics; perhaps the problem would be (as Bultmann suggests) with *medicine*. Is the idea that one couldn't do medical research or prescribe medications if one thought that God has done miracles in the past and might even occasionally do some nowadays? To put the suggestion explicitly is to refute it; there isn't the faintest reason why I couldn't sensibly believe that God raised Jesus from the dead and also engage in medical research into, say, Usher's syndrome or multiple sclerosis, or into ways of staving off the ravages of coronary disease. What would be the problem? That it is always *possible* that God should do something different, thus spoiling my experiment? But that *is* possible: God is omnipotent. (Or do we have here a new antitheistic argument? If God exists, he could spoil my experiment; nothing can spoil my experiment; therefore. . . .) No doubt if I thought God *often* or *usually* did things in an idiosyncratic way, so that there really aren't much by way discoverable regularities to be found, *then* perhaps I couldn't sensibly engage in scientific research; the latter presupposes a certain regularity, predictability, stability in the world. But that is an entirely different matter. What I must assume to

---

63. Here I can be brief; William Alston has already proposed a compelling argument for the claim I support—namely, that one can perfectly well do science even if one thinks God has done and even sometimes still does miracles. See his "Divine Action: Shadow or Substance?" in *The God Who Acts: Philosophical and Theological Explorations*, ed. Thomas F. Tracy (University Park: Pennsylvania State University Press, 1994), pp. 49–50.

do science, is only that *ordinarily* and for the *most* part these regularities hold.[64] This reason, too, then, is monumentally insufficient as a reason for holding that we are somehow obliged to accept the principles underlying Troeltschian biblical scholarship.

It is therefore difficult to see any reason for supposing that Troeltschian scripture scholarship is somehow *de rigueur* or somehow forced on us by our history.

B. A Moral Imperative?

Van Harvey proposes another reason for pursuing Troeltschian scholarship and preferring it to traditional biblical commentary;[65] his reason is broadly *moral* or *ethical*. He begins[66] by referring to a fascinating episode in Victorian intellectual history[67] in which certain Victorian intellectuals found themselves wrestling with a problem of intellectual integrity. As Harvey sees it, they "believed that it was morally reprehensible to insist that these claims [Christian claims about the activities and teachings of Jesus] were true on faith while at the same time arguing that they were also the legitimate objects of historical inquiry" (NTS, 195). Now I think this is a tendentious account of the problem these intellectuals faced—tendentious, because it makes it look as if these intellectuals were endorsing, with unerring prescience, precisely the position Harvey himself proposes to argue for. The fact is, I think, their position was both less idiosyncratic and far more plausible. After all, why should anyone think it was immoral to believe by faith what could also be investigated by other sources of belief or knowledge? I am curious about your whereabouts last Friday night: were you perhaps at the Linebacker's Bar? Perhaps I could find out in three different ways: by asking you, by asking your wife, and by examining the bar for your fingerprints (fortunately, the bar is never washed.) Would there be something immoral in using one of these methods when, in fact, the others were available? That's not easy to believe.

It wasn't just *that* that troubled the Victorians. Had they been confident that both faith and historical investigation were reliable avenues to the truths in question, they surely wouldn't have thought it

64. As Alston argues.

65. I *think* the argument is intended to support Troeltschian HBC; it could also be used, however, to support Spinozistic or (less plausibly) Duhemian HBC.

66. NTS pp. 194ff.; a fuller (if older) and influential presentation of his views is to be found in his *The Historian and the Believer* (above, fn. 27).

67. Described with insight and verve in James C. Livingston's monograph *The Ethics of Belief: An Essay on the Victorian Religious Conscience* in the American Academy of Religion's *Studies in Religion* (Tallahassee: Scholars Press, 1978). I thank Martin Cook for calling my attention to this monograph.

immoral to believe on the basis of one of these as opposed to the other or both. Their problem was deeper. They were troubled (among other things) by the German scripture scholarship, about which they knew relatively little; still, they did know enough to think (rightly or wrongly) that it posed a real threat to the Christian beliefs that for many of them were, in any event, already shaky. They suspected or feared that this scripture scholarship could show or would show or already had shown that essential elements of the Christian faith were just false. They were also troubled by what many saw as the antisupernaturalistic and antitheistic bent of science: could one really believe in the New Testament world of spirits and miracles in the era of the steam engine and ocean liner? They were troubled by the advent of Darwinism, which seemed to many to contradict the Christian picture of human origins. They were convinced, following Locke and the whole classical foundationalist tradition, that the right way to hold beliefs on these topics is by following the (propositional) evidence wherever it leads; and they were deeply worried about where this evidence was, in fact, leading. They were troubled, in short, by a variety of factors, all of which seemed to suggest that traditional Christian belief was really no more than a beautiful story: inspiring, uplifting, perhaps necessary to public morality, but just a story. Given our scientific coming of age, they feared, informed people would regretfully have to jettison traditional Christian belief, perhaps (especially on ceremonial occasions) with an occasional nostalgic backward look.

On the other hand, many of them also longed for the comfort and security of serious Christian belief; to lose it was like being thrown out of our Father's house into a hostile or indifferent world. And of course many of the Victorians had strong moral opinions and a highly developed moral sense. They thought it weak, spineless, cowardly to refuse to face these specters, to hide them from oneself, to engage in self-deception and double-think. All this, they thought, is unworthy of a serious and upright person. They abhorred the weakness and moral softness of the sort of stance in which you suspect the bitter truth, but refuse to investigate the matter, preferring to hide the truth from yourself, perhaps hoping it will somehow go away. Many of them thought this was precisely what some of the clergy and other educators were doing, and despised them for it. Far better to face the sad truth with intellectual honesty, manly courage, and a stiff upper lip. So it wasn't just that they thought it reprehensible to believe on faith what can also be addressed by reason or historical investigation. It was rather that they suspected and deeply feared that the latter (together with the other factors I mentioned) would undermine the former. And they scorned and detested a sort of willful head-in-the-sand attitude in which, out of timidity or fear or a desire for comfort, one refuses to face the facts. Reasons such as these account for the moral fervor (indeed, stridency) of W. K. Clifford's oft-anthologized "The Ethics of Belief."[68]

However things may have stood with the Victorians, Harvey proposes the following bit of moral dogma:

> The gulf separating the conservative Christian believer and the New Testament scholar can be seen as the conflict between two antithetical ethics of belief. . . . New Testament scholarship is now so specialized and requires so much preparation that the layperson has simply been disqualified from having any right to a judgment regarding the truth or falsity of certain historical claims. Insofar as the conservative Christian believer is a layperson who has no knowledge of the New Testament scholarship, he or she is simply not entitled to certain historical beliefs at all. Just as the average layperson is scarcely in a position to have an informed judgment about the seventh letter of Plato, the relationship of Montezuma to Cortez, or the authorship of the Donation of Constantine, so the average layperson has no right to an opinion about the authorship of the Fourth Gospel or the trustworthiness of the synoptics. (NTS, p. 197)

"The layperson has simply been disqualified from having any right to a judgment regarding the truth or falsity of certain historical claims": strong words! In an earlier age, priests and ministers, often the only educated members of their congregations, would exercise a certain intellectual and spiritual leadership, hoping the flock would come to see, appreciate, and believe the truth. On Harvey's showing, the flock doesn't so much as have a right to an opinion on these points—not even an opinion purveyed by the experts! Harvey complains (p. 193) that many students seem unreceptive to the results of scripture scholarship. If he's right, however, the students don't have a right to believe the results of scripture scholarship; they are therefore doing no more than their simple duty in refusing to believe them. One hopes Harvey remembers, when teaching his classes, not to put his views on these matters in an attractive and winsome fashion; after all, if he did so, some of the students might *believe* them, in which case they would be sinning and he himself would be giving offense in the Pauline sense (Romans 14, not to mention 1 Corinthians 8:9).

Suppose we sadly avert our gaze from this elitism run amok: why does Harvey think that only the historian has a right to hold an opinion on these matters? Clearly enough, because he thinks the only way to achieve accurate and reliable information on these matters is by way of Troeltschian scholarship. And *that* opinion, obviously, presupposes the philosophical and theological opinion that there isn't any

---

68. First published in *The Contemporary Review* 29 (1877); reprinted in Clifford's *Lectures and Essays* (London: Macmillan, 1879), pp. 345ff.

other epistemic avenue to these matters; it presupposes that, for example, faith (and the internal instigation of the Holy Spirit) is not a source of warranted belief or knowledge on these topics. If the latter *were* a source of warranted belief, and if the "average layperson" had access to this source, then presumably there would be nothing whatever wrong with her holding views on these matters on this basis. "Just as the average layperson is scarcely in a position to have an informed judgment about the seventh letter of Plato, the relationship of Montezuma to Cortez, or the authorship of the Donation of Constantine, so the average layperson has no right to an opinion about the authorship of the Fourth Gospel or the trustworthiness of the synoptics," says Harvey. The only way to determine the truth about the seventh letter of Plato is by way of ordinary historical investigation; the same goes, Harvey assumes, for questions about the life and ministry of Christ, whether he rose from the dead, whether he thought of himself as a messiah, and the like. What lies at the bottom of this moral claim is really a philosophical-theological judgment: that traditional Christian belief is completely mistaken in taking it that faith is, in fact, a reliable source of true and warranted belief on these topics.[69]

This view is not, of course, a result of historical scholarship, Troeltschian or otherwise; nor is it supported by arguments that will appeal to anyone who doesn't already agree with him—or, indeed, by any arguments at all. Harvey's view is rather a *presupposition*, a methodological prescription of the pursuit of Troeltschian historical criticism and proscription of traditional biblical commentary. So it can hardly be thought of as an independent good reason for preferring the former to the latter. What we have are different philosophical-theological positions that dictate different ways of pursuing scripture scholarship. A way to show that the one really *is* superior to the other would be to give a good argument either for the one philosophical-theological position or against the other. Harvey does neither, simply assuming (uncritically, and without so much as mentioning the fact) the one position and rejecting the other. He assumes there is no source of warrant or knowledge in addition to reason. This is not self-evident; millions, maybe billions of Christians and others reject it. Is it sensible, then, just to *assume* it, without so much as acknowledging this contrary opinion, without so much as a feeble gesture in the direction of argument or reason?

---

69. As he says in *The Historian and the Believer*, "Faith has no function in the justification of historical arguments respecting fact" (p. 112), and "Believers have no distinctively Christian justificatory warrants for ascertaining whether Hitler was mad . . . whether Jesus was raised from the dead" (p. 242).

C. Historical Biblical Criticism More Inclusive?

John Collins recognizes that Troeltschian scholarship involves theological assumptions not nearly universally shared. He doesn't argue for the truth of these assumptions, but recommends them on a quite different basis. Criticizing Brevard Childs's proposal for a 'canonical' approach to scripture scholarship,[70] he claims that the problem is that Childs's approach doesn't provide an *inclusive context* for the latter:

> If biblical theology is to retain a place in serious scholarship, it must be . . . conceived broadly enough to provide a context for debate between different viewpoints. Otherwise it is likely to become a sectarian reservation, of interest only to those who hold certain confessional tenets that are not shared by the discipline at large. Childs's dogmatic conception of the canon provides no basis for advancing dialogue. In my opinion historical criticism still provides the most satisfactory framework for discussion.[71]

He adds that

> One criterion for the adequacy of presuppositions is the degree to which they allow dialogue between differing viewpoints and accommodate new insights. . . . Perhaps the outstanding achievement of historical criticism in this century is that it has provided a framework within which scholars of different prejudices and commitments have been able to debate in a constructive manner.[72]

So why should we prefer Troeltschian scripture scholarship over traditional Bible commentary? Because it offers a wider context, one in which people with conflicting theological opinions can all take part. We may be conservative Christians, theological liberals, or people with no theological views whatever: we can all take part in Troeltschian scripture scholarship, provided we acquiesce in its fundamental assumptions. This is why it is to be preferred to the more traditional sort.

Now this would perhaps be a reason for practicing *Duhemian* scripture scholarship, but of course Troeltschian scripture scholarship is not Duhemian: the principles on which it proceeds are not accepted by nearly everyone. They would be accepted by only a tiny minority of contemporary Christians, for example. And this shows a fundamental confusion, so it seems to me, in Collins's defense of

---

70. See, e.g., Childs's *The New Testament as Canon*, pp. 3–53.

71. "Is a Critical Biblical Theology Possible?" in *The Hebrew Bible and Its Interpreters*, pp. 6–7. Collins speaks here not of Troeltschian HBC but of HBC *simpliciter*; just a couple of pages earlier, however, he identifies HBC with Troeltschian HBC.

72. Ibid., p. 8.

Troeltschian scholarship. The defense he offers is appropriate for *Duhemian* scholarship; it isn't at all appropriate for *Troeltschian* scholarship. The principles of Troeltschian historical scholarship, so interpreted as to preclude miracle, direct divine action, and special divine inspiration of the Bible, are extremely controversial philosophical and theological assumptions. Those who do not accept these controversial assumptions will not be inclined to take part in Troeltschian HBC, just as those who don't accept traditional Christian philosophical and theological views will not be likely to engage in traditional biblical commentary. (If you don't think the Lord speaks in Scripture, you will be unlikely to spend a great deal of your time trying to figure out what it is he says there.) As Jon Levenson puts it, historical criticism "does not facilitate communication with those outside its boundaries: it requires fundamentalists, for example, to be born again as liberals—or to stay out of the conversation altogether."[73] He adds that "if inclusiveness is to be gauged quantitatively, then [Brevard] Childs would win the match hands down, for far more people with biblical interests share Christian faith than a thoroughgoing historicism. Were we historical critics to be classed as a religious body we should have to be judged a most minuscule sect indeed—and one with a pronounced difficulty relating to groups that do not accept our beliefs."

V. NOTHING TO BE CONCERNED *ABOUT*

We are now prepared to return to Harvey's original question: why is it that the person in the pew pays little attention to contemporary HBC and, despite those decades of research, retains rather a traditional picture of the life and ministry of Jesus? As to why *in actual historical fact* this is the case, this is a job for an intellectual historian. What we have seen so far, however, is that there is no compelling or even reasonably decent argument for supposing that the procedures and assumptions of HBC are to be preferred to those of traditional biblical commentary. A little epistemological reflection enables us to see something further: the traditional Christian (whether in the pew or not) has good reason to reject the skeptical claims of HBC and continue to hold traditional Christian belief despite the allegedly corrosive acids of HBC.

A. Troeltschian Historical Biblical Criticism Again

As we have seen, there are substantially three types of HBC. For present purposes, however, we can consider Duhemian and Spinozistic

---

73. *The Hebrew Bible, the Old Testament, and Historical Criticism*, p. 120.

HBC together. Let's say, therefore, that we have both Troeltschian and non-Troeltschian HBC. Consider the first. The Troeltschian scripture scholar accepts Troeltsch's principles for historical research, under an interpretation according to which they rule out the occurrence of miracles and the divine inspiration of the Bible (along with the corollary that the latter enjoys the sort of unity accruing to a book that has one principal author). But then it is not at all surprising that the Troeltschian tends to come up with conclusions wildly at variance with those accepted by the traditional Christian. As Gilkey says, "Suddenly a vast panoply of divine deeds and events recorded in scripture are no longer regarded as having actually happened." Now if (instead of tendentious claims about our inability to do otherwise) the Troeltschian offered some good reasons to think that, in fact, these Troeltschian principles are *true*, then traditional Christians would have to pay attention; then they might be obliged to take the skeptical claims of historical critics seriously. Troeltschians, however, apparently don't offer any such good reasons. They simply declare that nowadays we can't think in any other way, or (following Harvey) that it is immoral to believe in, for example, Christ's resurrection on other than historical grounds.

Neither of these is remotely persuasive as a reason for modifying traditional Christian belief in the light of Troeltschian results. As for the first, of course, the traditional Christian knows that it is quite false: she herself and many of her friends nowadays (and hundreds of millions of others) do think in precisely that proscribed way. And as far as the implicit claims for the superiority of these Troeltschian ways of thinking go, she won't be impressed by them unless some decent arguments of one sort or another are forthcoming, or some other good reason for adopting that opinion is presented. The mere claim that this is what many contemporary experts think will not and should not intimidate her. And the second proposed reason (Harvey's reason) seems to be itself dependent on the very claim at issue. Why does the critic think it immoral to form beliefs about historical facts on grounds other than historical research? Because he believes that the only reliable ground for beliefs of the former type is research of the latter type. Again, however, he offers no argument for this assumption, merely announcing it as what those in the know believe, and perhaps also adopting an air of injured puzzlement about the fact that people in the pews don't seem to pay much attention.

To see the point here, consider an analogy: suppose your friend is accused and convicted of stealing an ancient and valuable Frisian vase from the museum in Franeker. As it happens, you remember clearly that at the time this vase was stolen, your friend was in your office, defending his eccentric views about the Gospel of John. You have testified to this in court, but to no avail. I come along and offer to do a really scientific investigation to see whether your view here is, in fact, correct. You are delighted, knowing as you think you do that your friend is innocent. When I explain my methods to you, however, your delight turns to dismay. I refuse to accept the testimony of memory; I propose to ignore completely the fact that you *remember* your friend's being in your office. Further, my method precludes from the start the conclusion that your friend is innocent, even if he *is* innocent. Could I blame you for losing interest in my 'scientific' investigation? I think the traditional Christian ought to view Troeltschian HBC with the same suspicion: it refuses to admit a source of warranted belief (faith and divine revelation, both of which the traditional Christian takes to be sources of warrant) the traditional Christian accepts, and it is precluded in advance from coming to such conclusions as that Jesus really did arise from the dead and really is the divine son of God.

B. Non-Troeltschian Historical Biblical Criticism

Troeltschian HBC, therefore, has no claim on serious Christians; it is wholly reasonable for them to form and maintain their beliefs quite independently of it. How about non-Troeltschian (Duhemian and Spinozistic) HBC? This is a very different kettle of fish. The non-Troeltschian proposes to employ only assumptions that are clearly deliverances of reason (or accepted by everyone party to the project). She doesn't (for purposes of scholarship) accept the traditional Christian's views about the Bible or the life of Christ, but she also doesn't accept Troeltsch's principles. She doesn't assume that miracles did or could happen; but that is quite different from assuming that they didn't or couldn't, and she doesn't assume that either. She doesn't assume that the Bible is, in fact, a word from the Lord and hence authoritative and reliable; but she also doesn't assume that it isn't.

Of course that may not leave her a lot to go on. The non-Troeltschian is handicapped in this area in a way in which she isn't in such areas as physics or chemistry. In the latter (apart, perhaps, from a bit of controversy about the anthropic principle and the principle of indifference[74]), there is little by way of theological controversy that seems relevant to the pursuit of the subject. Not so for scripture scholarship; here the very foundations of the subject are deeply disputed. Does the Bible have one principal author, namely God himself? If not, then perhaps Jowett ("Scripture has one meaning—the meaning which it had to the mind of the prophet or evangelist who

74. See Ernan McMullin's "Indifference Principle and Anthropic Principle in Cosmology," *Studies in the History and Philosophy of Science* 24, no. 3 (1993), and my "Methodological Naturalism?" in *Facets of Faith and Science*, vol 1, ed. J. van der Meer (Lanham, Md.: University Press of America, 1996).

first uttered or wrote, to the hearers or readers who first received it") is right; otherwise, he is wrong.[75] Is it divinely inspired, so that what it teaches is both true and to be accepted? If it reports miraculous happenings—risings from the dead, a virgin birth, the changing of water into wine, healings of people blind or lame from birth—are these to be taken more or less at face value, or dismissed as contrary to "what we now know"? Is there an entry into the truth about these matters—faith or divine testimony by way of Scripture, for example —quite different from ordinary historical investigation? If we prescind from all these matters and proceed responsibly (remembering to pay attention to the law of dwindling probabilities), what we come up with is likely to be pretty slender.

A. E. Harvey, for example, proposes the following as beyond reasonable doubt from everyone's point of view (i.e., Duhemianly): "that Jesus was known in both Galilee and Jerusalem, that he was a teacher, that he carried out cures of various illnesses, particularly demon-possession and that these were widely regarded as miraculous; that he was involved in controversy with fellow Jews over questions of the law of Moses: and that he was crucified in the governorship of Pontius Pilate."[76] It isn't even clear whether Harvey means that the *conjunction* of these propositions is beyond reasonable doubt, or only each of the conjuncts;[77] in either case what we have is pretty slim.

Or consider John Meier's monumental *A Marginal Jew: Rethinking the Historical Jesus.* (The first volume has 484 pages; the second has 1,055 pages; a third volume is expected soon.) Meier aims to be Duhemian, or anyway Spinozistic: "My method follows a simple rule: it prescinds from what Christian faith or later Church teaching says about Jesus, without either affirming or denying such claims" (p. 1). (I think he also means to eschew assumptions incompatible with traditional Christian belief.) Meier's fantasy of "an unpapal conclave" of Jewish, Catholic, Protestant, and agnostic scholars, locked in the basement of the Harvard Divinity School library until they come to consensus on what historical methods can show about the life and mission of Jesus, is thoroughly Duhemian. This conclave he says, would yield "a rough draft of what that will-o'-the-wisp 'all reasonable people' could say about the historical Jesus" (p. 2). Meier sets

---

75. See note 19 above.

76. *Jesus and the Constraints of History* (Philadelphia: Westminster Press, 1982), p. 6.

77. It could be that each of the conjuncts is beyond reasonable doubt but that their conjunction is not. Suppose (just to arbitrarily choose a number) what is probable to degree .95 or higher is beyond reasonable doubt. Then if each of the above is beyond reasonable doubt, their conjunction might still be little more than twice as probable as its denial.

out, judiciously, objectively, carefully, to establish that consensus.[78] What is striking about his conclusions, however, is how slender they are, and how tentative—and this despite the fact that, on occasion, he cannot himself resist building towers of probability. About all that emerges from Meier's painstaking work is that Jesus was a prophet, a proclaimer" of an eschatological message from God, someone who performed powerful deeds, signs, and wonders that announce God's kingdom and also ratify his message.[79] As Duhemian or Spinozist, of course, we can't add that these signs and miracles involve special or direct divine action; nor can we say that they don't. We can't say that Jesus rose from the dead, or that he did not; we can't conclude that scripture is specially inspired, or that it isn't.

Now what is characteristic of non-Troeltschian HBC is just that it doesn't involve those Troeltschian principles: but it also rejects any alleged source of warranted belief in addition to reason (Spinozistic) and any theological assumptions not shared by everyone party to the discussion.[80] Traditional Christians, rightly or wrongly, think they do have sources of warranted belief in addition to reason: divine testimony in Scripture and also faith and the work of the Holy Spirit, or testimony of the Spirit-led church. They may be *mistaken* about that; but until someone gives a decent argument for the conclusion that they *are* mistaken, they need not be impressed by the result of scholarship that ignores this further source of belief. If you want to learn the truth about a given area, you shouldn't restrict yourself to only *some* of the sources of warranted belief (as does the Spinozist) or only to beliefs accepted by everyone else (with the Duhemian); maybe you know something some of the others don't. Perhaps you remember that your friend was in your office expostulating about the errors of postmodernism at the very time he is supposed to have been stealing that Frisian vase; if no one else was there, then you know something the rest don't.

So the traditional Christian needn't be fazed by the fact that non-Troeltschian HBC doesn't support his views about what Jesus did and said. He thinks he knows some things by faith and the IIHS— that Jesus arose from the dead, for example. He may concede that if you leave out of account all that he knows in this way, then with re-

78. "Meier's treatment, in short, is as solid and moderate and pious as Historical Jesus scholarship is ever likely to be. More important, Meier is a careful scholar. There is nothing hasty or slipshod in his analysis: he considers every opinion, weighs every option" (Luke Timothy Johnson, *The Real Jesus*, p. 128).

79. Johnson, *The Real Jesus*, pp. 130–31?

80. Of course one might in fact accept those additional sources of warranted belief, but be interested in seeing just how much can be argued from a strictly Duhemian or Spinozistic point of view; to pursue a Duhemian or Spinozistic project is not necessarily to believe that there are no such additional sources. It is only to bracket them for the project in question.

spect to the remaining body of knowledge or belief the resurrection isn't particularly probable. Still, that hardly presents him with an intellectual or spiritual crisis. We can imagine a renegade group of whimsical physicists proposing to reconstruct physics by refusing to use belief that comes from memory, say, or perhaps memory of anything more than one minute ago. Perhaps something could be done along these lines, but it would be a poor, paltry, truncated, trifling thing. And now suppose that, say, Newton's laws or special relativity turned out to be dubious and unconfirmed from this point of view: that would presumably give little pause to more traditional physicists. This truncated physics could hardly call into question physics of the fuller variety.

Similarly here. The traditional Christian thinks he knows *by faith* that Jesus was divine and that he rose from the dead. Hence, he will be unmoved by the fact that these truths are not especially probable on the evidence to which non-Troeltschian HBC limits itself—that is, evidence that explicitly excludes what one knows by faith. Why should that matter to him? So this is the rest of the answer to Harvey's question: if the HBC in question is non-Troeltschian, then the fact that it doesn't verify traditional Christian beliefs is due to its limiting itself in the way it does, to its refusing to use all the data or evidence the Christian thinks he has in his possession. For a Christian to confine himself to the results of non-Troeltschian HBC would be a little like trying to mow your lawn with a nail scissors or paint your house with a toothbrush; it might be an interesting experiment if you have time on your hands, but otherwise why limit yourself in this way?

As we saw above (pp. 388–89) E. P. Sanders, Barnabas Lindars, Jon Levenson, and many others all declare that what one knows by faith or theological assumptions not endorsed by all should play no role in proper scripture scholarship; and perhaps we can think of this as a sort of unspecific endorsement of Duhemian scholarship. *Why* should they play no role? We must rely only on "evidence on which everyone can agree," says Sanders. "The arguments offered must be historically valid, able, that is, to compel the assent of *historians* whatever their religion or lack thereof, whatever their backgrounds, spiritual experiences, or personal beliefs, and without privileging any claim of revelation," says Levenson. "It is not open to a scholar to decide that, just because he is a believing Christian, he will accept all the Gospel miracles at their face value, but at the same time he will repudiate miracles attributed to Isis. All such accounts have to be scrutinized with equal detachment," says Lindars. Construed as endorsement of non-Troeltschian HBC, the claim here, I think, is that only such scholarship is properly *objective*.

Is this true, and is objectivity required or desirable in this enterprise? Here we must go back to a distinction outlined in chapter 1. Objectivity can be thought of as a matter of being oriented toward or paying attention to the *object* of knowledge or opinion, as opposed to the subject; what is objective may be thought of as coming from the object rather than from myself as subject. It is thus an objective fact that Amsterdam is larger than Aberdeen. But the term is also used to denote an opinion that is shared by nearly everyone; it is then contrasted with 'subjective', taken as in the phrase, "Well, that's only my subjective opinion." My own subjective opinions are the ones that are peculiar to me (and perhaps my friends). In which of these senses is it claimed that non-Troeltschian scholarship is objective? In the second, clearly enough; everyone will accept (with the Duhemian) those assumptions no one party to the project rejects; and presumably nearly everyone will accept the deliverances of reason. Of course it is far from obvious that if you want to learn the truth about a given area, the reasonable thing to do is to employ only assumptions accepted by everyone party to the dispute. Maybe you know something some of the others don't.

More generally, then, HBC is either Troeltschian or non-Troeltschian. If the former, then it begins from assumptions entailing that much of what the traditional Christian believes is false; it comes as no surprise, then, that its conclusions are at odds with traditional belief. It is also of little direct concern to the classical Christian. It offers her no reason at all for rejecting or modifying her beliefs; it also offers little promise of enabling her to achieve better or deeper insight into what actually happened. As for non-Troeltschian HBC, however, this variety of historical criticism omits a great deal of what she sees as relevant evidence and relevant considerations. It is therefore left with little to go on. Again, the fact that it fails to support traditional belief need not be upsetting to the traditional believer; given those limitations, that is only to be expected, and it casts no doubt at all on Christian belief. Either way, therefore, the traditional Christian can rest easy with the claims of HBC; she need feel no obligation, intellectual or otherwise, to modify her belief in the light of its claims and alleged results.[81]

81. *Alleged* results: because of the enormous controversy and disagreement among followers of HBC, it is very difficult to find anything one could sensibly call 'results' of this scholarship. Thus Harold Attridge (in "Calling Jesus Christ," in *Hermes and Athena*, ed. Eleonore Stump and Thomas Flint [Notre Dame: University of Notre Dame Press, 1993], p. 211):

> There remains enormous diversity among those who attempt to describe what Jesus really did, taught, and thought about himself. For some contemporary scholars he was a Hellenistic magician; for others, a Galilean charismatic or rabbi; for yet others, a prophetic reformer; for others, a sly teller of wry and engaging tales; for some he had grandiose ideas; for others he eschewed them. In general, the inquirer finds the Jesus that her historical method allows her to see. It is as true today as it was at the end of the liberal quest for the historical Jesus catalogued by Albert Schweitzer that we moderns tend to make Jesus in our own image and likeness.

The Schweitzer reference is to his *Von Reimarus zu Wrede* (1906), tr. W. Montgomery as *The Quest of the Historical Jesus: A Critical Study of Its Progress from Reimarus to Wrede* (New York: Macmillan, 1956).

C. Conditionalization

Still, she *may* perfectly properly pay attention to it, and may even join in the game. Perhaps, for example, she is convinced (mistakenly, in my opinion) that any enterprise (like traditional biblical commentary) that makes religious or theological assumptions isn't really science; and perhaps she thinks it is important to engage in science in this area. Perhaps she likes to pursue scripture scholarship in conjunction with her friends who don't make the assumptions she does; or perhaps she thinks much of interest may emerge from a venture pursued by people of very different assumptions. Perhaps she concurs with the Thomist of Etienne Gilson's *The Spirit of Medieval Philosophy*[82] in thinking that science and philosophy are purely *rational* pursuits; they involve no assumptions that are not deliverances of reason alone. Then she might think it important to engage in Spinozistic or Duhemian science, even if the results are pretty slim.[83] So she might sensibly take part in Duhemian scripture scholarship.

Can traditional biblical commentary also be pursued in Duhemian fashion? The traditional Christian wants to know the answer to various questions about the Bible, among others, the questions to which traditional biblical commentary addresses itself. Now the sensible thing to do, in pursuing the answer to a question, is to use all that you believe or think you know (insofar as it is relevant); that will give you the best shot at reaching the correct answer. But suppose you are also convinced that it is important to investigate these matters *scientifically*, and that if you employ beliefs you accept by faith, the resulting inquiry will not be science. Suppose you decide you want to do science, but also want to work on these questions. What can you do?

You can *conditionalize*.[84] Instead of addressing a given question, 'What is the best way to think about *x*, employing all that you know including what you know by faith?' you address instead the question 'What would be the best way to think about *x*, if in fact the deliverances of faith were true?' *This* question can then be approached Duhemianly (or Spinozistically), using only beliefs that are among the deliverances of reason; no theological assumptions or deliverances of faith need be involved. In pursuing this enterprise you are doing Duhemian scholarship. Your results can be displayed as a conditional *if F, then P*; where *F* represents the deliverances of faith. When you work at this conditional, you are doing Duhemian science. Of course when you affirm the antecedent of the conditional and detach its consequent, then you have left Duhemian (and Spinozistic) science for theology; but that's no problem. You have the dual aim of working Duhemianly while also trying to dis-

---

82. (New York: Charles Scribner's Sons, 1940; republished, Notre Dame: University of Notre Dame Press, 1991), the first couple of chapters.

83. But see my *The Twin Pillars of Christian Scholarship* (Grand Rapids: Calvin College, 1990); I argue that a common Thomistic reason for so thinking is not, in fact, a good reason.

84. To borrow a term from Bayesian epistemologists, who use it to mean something quite different. See *Warrant: The Current Debate*, p. 122.

cover the best way to think about the topic at issue from the perspective of Christian faith: in this way you can accomplish both. Indeed, this will be a project in which people who don't share your faith can sensibly co-operate, just as a Christian might engage (questions of frivolity aside), in this conditional fashion, in Troeltschian HBC.[85]

VI. CONCLUDING CODA

But isn't all of this just a bit too sunny? Isn't it a recipe for avoiding hard questions, for hanging onto belief no matter what, for guaranteeing that you will never have to face negative results, even if there *are* some? "HBC is either Troeltschian or non-Troeltschian: in the first case, it proceeds from assumptions I reject; in the second, it fails to take account of all of what I take to be the evidence; either way, therefore, I needn't pay attention to it." Couldn't I say this *a priori*, without even examining the results of HBC? But then there must be something defective in the line of thought in question. Isn't it clearly *possible* that historians should discover facts that put Christian belief into serious question, count heavily against it? Well, maybe so. How could this happen? As follows: HBC limits itself to the deliverances of reason; it is possible, at any rate in the broadly logical sense, that just by following ordinary historical reason, using the methods of historical investigation endorsed or enjoined by the deliverances of reason, someone should find powerful evidence against central elements of the Christian faith;[86] if this happened, Christians would face a genuine faith-reason clash. A series of letters could be discovered, letters circulated among Peter, James, John, and Paul, in which the necessity for the hoax and the means of its perpetration are carefully and seriously discussed; these letters might direct workers to archaeological sites in which still more material of the same sort is discovered. . . .[87] The Christian faith is a *historical* faith, in the sense that it essentially depends upon what did in fact happen: "And if Christ has not been raised, your faith is futile" (1 Corinthians 15:17). It could certainly happen that by the exercise of reason we come up with powerful

85. For more on conditionalization, see my "On Christian Scholarship," in *The Challenge and Promise of a Catholic University* (Notre Dame: University of Notre Dame Press, 1994). I hope to go into greater detail on these matters in a book on Christian philosophy.

86. Or, less crucially, evidence against what appears to be the teaching of Scripture. For example, archaeological evidence could undermine the traditional belief that there was such a city as Jericho.

87. The example is Bas van Fraassen's; see his "Three-Sided Scholarship: Comments on the Paper of John R. Donahue, S. J.," in *Hermes and Athena*, p. 322. "Finish it yourself, if you have the heart to do it," says van Fraassen.

evidence[88] against something we take or took to be a deliverance of the faith. It is conceivable that the assured results of HBC should include such evidence. Then Christians would have a problem, a sort of conflict between faith and reason.

However, nothing at all like this has emerged from HBC, whether Troeltschian or non-Troeltschian; indeed, there is little of any kind that can be considered 'assured results', if only because of the wide-ranging disagreement among those who practice HBC. We don't have anything like assured results (or even reasonably well-attested results) that conflict with traditional Christian belief in such a way that belief of that sort can continue to be accepted only at considerable cost; nothing at all like this has happened. What would be the appropriate response if it *did* happen or, rather, if I came to be convinced that it had happened? Would I have to give up Christian faith, or else give up the life of the mind? What would be the appropriate response? Well, what would be the appropriate response if I came to be convinced that someone had given a wholly rigorous, ineluctable disproof of the existence of God, perhaps something along the lines of J. N. Findlay's alleged ontological disproof?[89] Or what if, with Reid's Hume (above, pp. 218–19), I come to think that my cognitive faculties are probably not reliable, and go on to note that I form this very belief on the basis of the very faculties whose reliability this belief impugns? If I did, what would or should I do—stop thinking about these things, immerse myself in practical activity (maybe play a lot of backgammon, maybe volunteer to help build houses for Habitat for Humanity), commit intellectual suicide? I don't know the answer to any of these questions. There is no need to borrow trouble, however: we can think about crossing these bridges when (more likely, if) we come to them.

---

88. Or *think* we come up with it; even if we are mistaken about the evidence in question, it could still precipitate this sort of problem for us.

89. "Can God's Existence Be Disproved?" *Mind* (April 1948).

13

Postmodernism and Pluralism

What is truth?

Pontius Pilate

To say of what is that it is not, or of what is not that it is, is false; while to say of what is that it is, and of what is not that it is not, is true.

Aristotle

You shall know the truth and the truth shall set you free.

Jesus

I was planning to title this chapter "Postmodernism and Pluralism"; in fact that is what I *did* title the chapter. But the title may be a misnomer. Our project, in this fourth and last part of the book, is to evaluate various possible defeaters for Christian belief. The problem with postmodernism, though, is that it is extremely hard to find in it anything that is a sensible candidate for being a defeater for Christian belief. Religious pluralism, perhaps, can be thought with some show of reason to be such a defeater; it's much harder to find a likely candidate in postmodernism. Permit me to explain.

I. POSTMODERNISM

Postmodernism, of course, is variously characterized. Among the views that go under this rubric are to be found a rejection of classical foundationalism; the declaration that there are no foundations of any sort, classical or otherwise; the claim that there is no such thing as objectivity (and it's a good thing too); deconstruction ('the deconstruction company'); the claim that there is no such thing as truth, or that if there is, it is something totally different from what we thought (perhaps it is a social construction, "what our peers will let us get away with saying," or something else of that sort); the claim that truths are made, not discovered; the claim that there aren't any objective normative standards and that we somehow make whatever standards there are; and the claim that all that really matters is power. There is opposition to 'metanarratives', there is the insistence that God is dead (which is ordinarily intended to imply, I believe, that there is no such person as God), and there are patronizing references to God ("good old God," as Jacques Lacan refers to him[1]). There is also a kind of exultation or apotheosis of autonomy, so that (as with Heidegger[2]) one feels guilty for not having created the world (along with the suggestion that God should be ashamed for having the temerity to interfere with one's autonomy[3]). There is a sort of recrudescence of the nineteenth-century romantic exultation of the self, self-deification and its rejection of all things bourgeois. There is historicism, the idea that our historical and cultural setting determines what we can think, so that we can't but think what we do think (and right now we can't accept serious Christian belief); there is warmed-over Nietzschean and Sartrian bombast, lots of *Sturm und Drang* (or "sturm und drang und tenure," as Ernest Gellner says[4]), and much else besides.

A. Is Postmodernism Inconsistent with Christian Belief?

Now many of these claims are not sensible candidates for the post of being defeaters of Christian belief, and indeed some of them are entirely congenial to it. For example, postmoderns typically reject classical foundationalism, which has also been rejected by such doughty spokespersons for Christian belief as Abraham Kuyper, William Alston, and Nicholas Wolterstorff and, for that matter, in anticipatory fashion by Augustine, Aquinas, Calvin, and Edwards. (Its rejection is also a central motif of this book.) Many other themes of postmodernism can elicit only enthusiastic applause from a Christian

1. Cited in Grace M. Jantzen, "What's the Difference? Knowledge and Gender in (Post)modern Philosophy of Religion," *Religious Studies* 32 (December 1996), p. 446.

2. At least according to Richard Rorty; see his *Contingency, Irony and Solidarity* (Cambridge: Cambridge University Press, 1989), p. 109.

3. "God is thus the proper name of that which deprives us of our nature, of our own birth; consequently he will always have spoken before us, on the sly. He is the difference which insinuates itself between myself and myself as death" (Jacques Derrida, *Writing and Difference*, tr. A. Bass [Chicago: University of Chicago Press, 1978], p. 181).

4. *Postmodernism, Reason, and Religion* (London: Routledge, 1992).

perspective: one thinks of sympathy and compassion for the poor and oppressed, the strong sense of outrage at some of the injustices our world displays, celebration of diversity, and the 'unmasking' of prejudice, oppression, and power-seeking masquerading as self-evident moral principle and the dictates of sweet reason. Another theme on which Christian and postmodern can heartily agree is the way in which, even in the best of us, our vision of what is right and wrong, true or false, is often clouded and covered over by self-interest. True, postmoderns tend to see these beams in the eyes of others, not in their own; but in this they don't differ from the rest of us, including Christians.

Other postmodern claims, however, do appear to be incompatible with Christian belief: for example, the claims that God is dead, that there are no 'objective' moral standards, and perhaps also the claim that there isn't any such thing as *truth*, at least as commonsensically thought of. With respect to rejection of truth, there is an initial problem: what, precisely, *is* it to reject truth? To do that, must you assert that there simply *isn't* any such thing as truth, or is it sufficient to say that there is such a thing, all right, but it is very different from what we thought (and there is nothing else at all like what we thought truth was)?[5] According to Aristotle's marvelously monosyllabic account of truth quoted in the epigraph, "To say of what is that it is, or of what is not that it is not, is true," if someone claims there is no such thing as truth, is he committed to denying, for example, that *snow is white* is true if and only if snow is white? Do postmoderns propose to deny that? These are tough questions. Still, there is one common postmodern sort of view of truth according to which what is true depends on what we human beings say or think, and that *does* seem incompatible with Christian belief. At any rate it does if we accept the plausible proposition that

(1) Necessarily, there is such a person as God if and only if it is true that there is such a person as God.

For the postmodern claim about truth implies that whether it is true that there is such a person as God depends upon us and what we do or think. But if the truth of this proposition depends on us, then, given (1) so does the very existence of God. According to (1) there is such a person as God if and only if it is *true* that there is; hence if its being *true* that there is such a person as God depends on us and what

---

5. Compare the claim (a) there are no elephants, with the claim (b) there are elephants, but they are really a variety of prime numbers (and there is nothing at all like what we thought elephants were like). Compare the claim (a) that there are no universals with the claim (b) that there are some, but as it turns out they are merely names, *nomina*.

we do and think, then so does there *being* such a person as God; God depends on us for his existence. From a Christian perspective, that is wholly absurd. This way of thinking about truth, therefore, is incompatible given (1) with Christian belief.

The same goes for the idea that there simply *is* no such thing as truth. One of our most fundamental and basic ideas is that there is such a thing as *the way things are*. Things could have been very different from the way they are; there are many ways things could have been, but among them is the way they actually are. There actually are horses; there aren't any unicorns, although (perhaps) there could have been; there being horses, then, is part of the way things are. Now the existence of truth is intimately connected with there being a way things really are, a way the world is. For it is *true* that there are horses if and only if there being horses is part of the way things are. Of course a postmodernist might reply, "Well, obviously there is such a thing as the way things are—who could deny that? But when I say there is no such thing as truth, I don't mean to deny that at all. I only mean to say that there is no such thing as truth *understood a certain way*. There is no such thing as truth understood, for example, as requiring a sort of detailed structural correspondence between the way the world is and English (or German or Swahili or Chinese) sentences." This latter would be harmless enough; it would also be uninteresting. Postmoderns sometimes seem to oscillate between a momentous but clearly false claim (there simply is no such thing as truth at all) and a sensible but rather boring claim (there is no such thing as truth, conceived in some particular and implausible way). Taken the strong way, however, as the suggestion there really is no such thing as the way the world is, and hence no such thing as truth, the postmodern claim is incompatible with Christian belief. For it is certainly crucial to Christian belief to suppose that there *is* a way things are, and that it includes the great things of the gospel; it is crucial to Christian belief to suppose that such propositions as *God created the world* and *Christ's suffering and death are an atonement for human sin* are true.

B. Do These Claims Defeat Christian Belief?

Various claims plausibly labeled 'postmodern' do indeed conflict with Christian belief. As we saw in chapter 11 (above, p. 366), however, this is not yet to say that these claims or the making of them constitute *defeaters* for Christian belief. One often hears that this or that element of Christian belief has been "called into question" by postmodernism or postmodern ways of thinking, or that postmodernism has "destroyed" this or that traditional way of looking at the world. But you don't automatically produce a defeater for Christian belief just by standing on your roof and proclaiming (even loudly and slowly), "God is dead!" (Not even if you add: "And everybody I know says so too.") Nor can you call Christian belief (or anything else) into question just by declaring, "I hereby call *that* into question!" You can't destroy a way of thinking just by announcing, "I hereby destroy that way of thinking!" This will not do the job, not even if it is embodied in writing of coruscating wit and style, and not even if you adopt a superior air and elegant gestures while intoning it. Something further is required. What? Well, as we saw in chapter 11, to provide me with a defeater for my belief B, you have to do or say something such that (given that I am aware of it and have heard and understood it) I can no longer rationally continue to believe B, or continue to believe it as firmly as before. In the typical case, you will do this either by putting me into a position where I can see that my belief is to be rejected (e.g., by arranging for me to have the right sorts of experience) or by giving me an argument of some kind.

Here someone will point out that many postmoderns would not agree. They typically don't think arguments are either necessary or sufficient for anything of importance; they may be unsure that there is any such thing as rationality; indeed, they may even reject the whole warrant-and-defeaters structure of our discussion. If so, wouldn't it be a waste of time to inquire whether postmodern thought does provide a defeater for Christian belief? Not necessarily. Their rejection of the notion of defeaters does not imply that, in fact, they have not provided a defeater. They could certainly provide a defeater even if they (mistakenly) rejected the whole line of thought presupposed by the idea that there are or could be defeaters for Christian belief. You are a card-carrying postmodern and reject all talk about defeaters; I am not. I believe there are no cacti in the Upper Peninsula; you show me one. The fact that you don't yourself think much of defeaters doesn't for a minute imply that you haven't given me one, anymore than the fact that I don't believe in viruses means that I can't give you a cold. If I am *right* about viruses, *then* I can't; but I'm wrong. The same goes for the postmodern who doesn't believe in defeaters: if she's right about there being no such things, then no doubt she can't give me one; but perhaps she's wrong. In adopting the warrant-and-defeaters framework, we are, of course, presupposing that she *is* wrong. If so, she might be able to produce a defeater for Christian belief, even if she doesn't think she can.

Still, she can't do it by bare assertion, no matter how impassioned or confident. Must it be by way of argument then? We saw in chapter 11 that you can give me a nonargumentative defeater for certain kinds of beliefs; but could she give me a defeater *for an element of Christian belief* without giving me an argument? Here is a possibility: perhaps she can give me a defeater by citing the trajectory of her own intellectual and spiritual life. Perhaps she was raised as a traditional believer; in her sophomore year in college, she is introduced to Freud, Marx, and Nietzsche; the next year she advances to Heidegger, Derrida, and Rorty. She is captivated by Nietzsche's brilliant, sparkling style, by Heidegger's air of Teutonic profundity, by Derrida's mischievous and playful spirit, and by the brave, 'making-the-best-of-a-really-lousy-situation' attitude of Rorty. She tells me about these authors and their ideas, presenting them in an attractive and favorable light. Does that give me a defeater? Not automatically. Nor do I automatically get a defeater by retracing her steps and reading these authors myself: where she finds profound insight, I may find posturing obscurantism. Reading these authors is unlike perceiving a cactus (realizing that it is a cactus one sees) in the Upper Peninsula. One can't see the cactus and rationally continue to believe that there are no cacti there. On the other hand, one can sensibly read these authors and—despite verbal pyrotechnics and airs of profundity—remain unmoved, rationally continuing to accept Christian belief.

Are there other possibilities for nonargumentative defeaters here? Postmoderns sometimes point out the involvement of Christians in the injustice and oppression our sad world displays. As I'll argue in the next chapter, however, the suffering and evil our world contains don't automatically give me a defeater for Christian belief. Neither does the fact that Christians are responsible for a good bit of it; after all, it is part of Christian belief to see human beings, Christians included, as deeply flawed and sinful. Are there still other possibilities? Perhaps, but it is hard to see what they could be. So it seems that something like an argument is needed. Postmoderns, however, don't ordinarily give arguments for claims inconsistent with Christian belief. Indeed, they don't ordinarily give arguments for anything at all, perhaps because they think the whole frame of mind that makes argument seem useful is something we should 'get beyond'. Still, there are at least a couple of postmodern arguments worth considering here, although neither is such that its relevance to Christian belief is completely obvious.

1. The Argument from Historical Conditionedness

The first argument appeals to historicist consideration: we are all of us heavily constrained and conditioned by the society within which we live and within which we have been socialized. Had I been born at a different time and place, I would have failed to believe many of the things I do in fact believe—among them being, perhaps, some of the things I take most seriously. Perhaps, for example, I wouldn't have been a Christian or even a theist; perhaps I would have thought of those outside my tribe or clan as subhuman; perhaps I would have thought slavery was entirely acceptable, and so on. So the claim is that in my doxastic life I can't transcend my cultural setting—at any rate with respect to religious and philosophical belief.[6] But then those beliefs are somehow substandard, unwarranted, irrational, or in some other way not up to par. Christian belief, therefore, is irrational or at any rate unwarranted. Now what we have here so far is not a purported defeater for Christian belief itself, but for the different belief that Christian belief is warranted. Still, if I come to see or believe that Christian belief is not warranted for me, then perhaps I thereby acquire a defeater for it.

Why should we accept the argument? There are powerful reasons not to. First, like many such skeptical arguments, it discredits itself if it discredits anything; it falls into the very snare it sets for others. For consider its central premise:

(CP) Suppose a person S holds a religious or philosophical belief B: if B is such that if S had been born elsewhere or elsewhen, she would not have accepted B, then B is not warranted for S.

But suppose I accept (CP), which is itself a religious or philosophical belief. Isn't it clear that there are times and places such that if I had been born there and then, I would not have accepted it? If I'd been born in nineteenth-century New Guinea, or medieval France, or seventeenth-century Japan, I would (very likely) not have accepted (CP); so according to (CP), (CP) is not warranted for me; and once I see that it isn't warranted, I have a defeater for it; so I shouldn't believe it. Perhaps you think that this argument is just a nasty little dialectical trick, not worth taking seriously. Well, I disagree: if you see that a belief really does defeat itself, then you can't sensibly hold that belief.

No matter what you think of that argument, however, why can't it be that we know more at some times than at others? Had Einstein been born in the eighteenth century, he would not have believed special relativity; nothing follows about special relativity. Many now think it is wrong to treat someone with hatred or contempt or indifference on the mere grounds that they are of a different race: their views are not automatically unwarranted just because they might have believed otherwise if they had been brought up in Nazi Germany or ancient Sparta. Perhaps we should think, instead, that if they had been brought up in Nazi Germany or ancient Sparta, they wouldn't have known something they *do* know. I argued in *Warrant and Proper Function* that warrant is relative to circumstances; some circumstances are warrant conferring and others are not. I could therefore have been in other circumstances, circumstances that

6. See John Hick, *An Interpretation of Religion* (New Haven: Yale University Press, 1989), p. 2.

would not have conferred warrant on some belief *B* I actually have. Indeed, some of those circumstances are such that if I had been in them, I would not have held *B* at all. At present, for example, I believe I hear a crow cawing in the woods behind my house; had I been out of town, I would not have believed that. That fact, however, does nothing at all to suggest that my present belief lacks warrant. As it stands, therefore, (CP) is clearly too strong. No doubt the partisan of (CP) will say that he didn't intend (CP) to apply to *all* beliefs; it is to apply only to religious and philosophical beliefs. But why think it is true even thus restricted? You believe there aren't any things that do not exist; the philosopher Alexius Meinong, notoriously, did not. Now suppose you had been his student; given his charismatic personality and powerful intellect, perhaps you would have been misled into thinking there are some things—unicorns and golden mountains, for example—that do not exist. How would that so much as slyly suggest that you don't in fact, as things stand, know that there aren't any things that do not exist? This argument therefore fails. No doubt there are various ways in which to complicate the argument and make it subtler; none of these is successful, I think, because the basic idea of the argument is just a mistake.

2. Do Human Beings Construct the Truth?

There is a second argument I wish to consider briefly. Richard Rorty is widely credited (some might say "debited") with the view that "truth is what our peers will let us get away with saying."[7] Now this is a bit vague, but if taken seriously, it does, indeed, seem to be incompatible with Christian belief. That is because if a proposition is true (true 'for me', I suppose) if and only if my peers will let me get away with saying it, then, given proposition (1) on p. 424, God is dependent ('for me', if that makes sense) for his very existence on my peers. For if they were to let me get away with saying that there is no such person as God, then it would be *true* that there is no such person, in which case there would be no such person. So whether there is such

---

7. What he actually says is:

> For philosophers like Chisholm and Bergmann, such explanations *must* be attempted if the realism of common sense is to be preserved. The aim of all such explanations is to make truth something more than what Dewey called 'Warranted assertability': more than what our peers will, *ceteris paribus*, let us get away with saying. (*Philosophy and the Mirror of Nature* [Princeton: Princeton University Press, 1979], pp. 175–76)

It is clear from the context here (and elsewhere) that Rorty sides with Dewey against Chisholm and Bergmann.

a person as God depends upon the behavior of my peers.[8] Not easy to believe. The view in question has still other peculiar consequences. For example, it promises an auspicious way of dealing with war, poverty, disease, and the other ills our flesh is heir to. Take AIDS: if we all let each other get away with saying that there just isn't any such thing as AIDS, then on this Rortyesque view it would be *true* that there isn't any such thing as AIDS; and if it were *true* that there is no such thing as AIDS, then there would *be* no such thing. So all we have to do to get rid of AIDS, or cancer, or poverty is let each other get away with saying there is no such thing. That seems much easier than the more conventional methods, which involve all that time, energy, and money.

Similarly, consider the Chinese authorities who murdered those students at Tiananmen Square and then compounded their wickedness with bald-faced lies, claiming they'd done no such thing. From the present point of view, this is a most uncharitable way to think about the matter. For in denying that it ever happened, the authorities were merely trying to bring it about that their peers would let them get away with saying it had never happened, in which case it would have been *true* that it had never happened, in which case it would never have happened. So the charitable thought here, from a Rortian point of view, is that the Chinese authorities were only trying to bring it about that this terrible thing had never happened: and who can fault them for a thing like that? The same goes for those Nazi skinhead types who claim there was no Holocaust and that Hitler and his cohorts were as gentle as lambs and never harmed a soul; they too should charitably be seen as trying to see to it that those terrible things never did happen. And in your own personal life, if you have done something wrong, no problem: lie about it, get your peers to let you get away with saying you didn't do it. If you succeed, then in fact you won't have done it; furthermore, as an added bonus, you won't have lied about it either!

Now you will no doubt say that all this is belaboring a straw man; Rorty couldn't mean to assert, as the sober truth, that truth is what your peers will let you get away with saying. That is just a rough-and-ready, informal, and conversational way of conveying his real opinion. Putting it thus informally accords with his idea that philosophy is best thought of as a sort of conversation, and with his scorn for the analytic philosopher's panoply of definitions, principles, necessary and sufficient conditions, attempts at rigor, and all the rest. (If you and a friend were having a conversation, would you begin a sentence by saying, "Necessarily, a proposition P is true if and only if?" Well, maybe it depends on the friend.)

8. And what if my peers are an unusually tolerant bunch who will also let me get away with saying that there *is* such a person? Would it then be true ('for me') that there is such a person, and also true that there isn't?

Perhaps that's right; unfortunately it does complicate matters. My aim is to ask whether Rortian thought offers a defeater for Christian belief; one of the most prominent strands in Rorty's thought is what he has to say about truth; but then I need to know whether what he means to say about truth is or isn't incompatible with Christian belief. For that, it would be nice to have a relatively serious way of stating what this strand of thought might be. What could he mean? Well, presumably Rorty's claim is that the truth of a belief or proposition depends in some important way on social reality of one sort or another; truth is in some way a function of society and what it does or would do. What is true 'for us', then, will depend somehow on our own society. For any proposed truth B, there is some property P—some property a society can have—such that B is true ('for us') if and only if our society displays P.[9] Of course Rorty might regard that way of putting the matter as a bit gradgrindian if not outright silly (perhaps on a par with that obsessive concern with quotation marks which Derrida playfully ascribes to Oxford philosophers[10]); but life is too short to worry about a thing like that.

So our problem is that one can't easily tell, without further elucidation, whether Rorty's view of truth is or is not incompatible with Christian belief. This problem about determining what Rorty intends here is not trivial. Gary Gutting, for example, suggests that Rorty doesn't really intend to say anything at all shocking or paradoxical about truth, or anything out of accord with robust common sense. He doesn't really mean to say that what is true depends in some way upon properties of society; instead, he is only rejecting certain eminently rejectable *theories* of truth. "The key point," says Gutting, "is that our 'discourse on truth' should be limited to an assertion, without philosophical commentary or elaboration, of the baseline commonplaces about truth; and a review of the arbitrariness and/or incoherence of efforts to criticize (i.e., analyze, modify, or justify) the baseline truths."[11] The basic idea is that there are a number of commonplace and commonsense truths about truth: that beliefs are true or false but not both, that you can't ordinarily make a belief true just by wishing it to be true, that it is possible that we all hold false beliefs (just as we think people once held false beliefs about the shape of the earth), that the belief that all men are mortal is true if and only if all

9. And of course we aren't thinking of 'Cambridge' properties like *being such that* B *is true*. But then precisely what properties *are* we thinking of ? It would be entirely out of the spirit of a Rortian inquiry to answer that question, so I won't try.

10. *The Post Card from Socrates to Freud and Beyond*, tr. Alan Bass (Chicago: University of Chicago Press, 1987), p. 98.

11. "Richard Rorty: The Rudiments of Pragmatic Liberalism," in *Pragmatic Liberalism and the Critique of Modernity* (New York: Cambridge University Press, 1999).

men are mortal, and so on. These platitudes are all true and are all to be accepted; furthermore, any philosophical criticism of them, or elaboration of them, or modification of them, or rejection of them is bound to wind up in "arbitrariness or incoherence." Gutting proposes this as an interpretation of Rorty, at least of Rorty "by his own best lights."

So construed, Rorty seems a bit like Thomas Reid transposed into a conversational key, perhaps seasoned with a dash of Wittgenstein. If this is what Rorty means, then he is certainly not vulnerable to those charges of dissolute antirealism and relativism often flung his way. Thus taken, his views aren't so much as mildly shocking; they certainly don't constitute defeaters for Christian belief. But could this really be what he meant when, for example, he sided with Dewey in suggesting that truth is what our peers will let us get away with saying? If so, he has expressed himself a little carelessly. And even making all due allowances for the license conferred by his intent to be conversational and not pedantic, wouldn't it be a bit of a stretch to think that what he intends here is only a rejection of some philosophical criticism of those baseline platitudes? And isn't it also a little hard to swallow the suggestion that Rorty is ambiguous as between rejecting truth itself, on the one hand, and some particular theory of truth, on the other? This would be a little like being ambiguous between rejecting some theory of kangaroos and rejecting kangaroos themselves. This suggestion, it seems to me, implausibly emasculates Rorty.

What Rorty really opposes, according to Gutting, is a view ordinarily associated with realism with respect to truth—that is, *representationalism*. This is the idea that we (or our minds) possess and think by way of representations, which are true just if they "correspond to reality." The problem with this view, according to Rorty (according to Gutting), is that it inevitably encounters the question how we know and whether we know that our representations do, in fact, correspond to reality. Here further problems arise. According to Gutting, Rorty endorses all the commonsense, baseline platitudes about truth and our relation to it; but don't these platitudes themselves include this very representationalism? Isn't representationalism—at any rate the basic version of it—itself platitudinous? It is a baseline platitude that beliefs are *about* things of one kind or another; for example, some of my beliefs are about the moon. It is another baseline platitude that beliefs can *represent things as being one way or another*; for example, one of my beliefs about the moon represents it as a satellite of the earth. And it is still another baseline platitude that this belief is true if and only if, in fact, the moon is a satellite of the earth—that is, if and only if the way that belief represents the moon as being, is the way the moon really is—i.e., if and only if the belief about the moon corresponds to what the moon is like. Representationalism itself seems to be included in that stock of baseline platitudes; at any rate, there is a platitudinous version of it. So Rorty really can't both reject representationalism and accept all those baseline platitudes.[12]

On Gutting's semi-interpretation, then, Rorty isn't open to those charges of irresponsible antirealism and relativism; on the other hand, his views do turn out to be a bit pedestrian, and of course taken this way they don't constitute a defeater for Christian belief (or much of anything else). So suppose we take Rorty the more robust way, as making substantive and controversial claims about truth. Let's take him as claiming that truth is a human construction and that a belief or other candidate for truth is true ('for us') just if it stands in a certain relationship to (our) society. As I suggested above, this does indeed seem incompatible with Christian belief. First, it seems to make the truth about God (if only the truth about God 'for us') dependent on what we do or think. This is clearly incompatible with Christian views about God, according to which God is not dependent on anything at all. And second, this Rortian doctrine implies that there is some contingent property (some non-Cambridge contingent property) P such that it is true ('for us') that there is such a person as God if and only if our society has P. Now presumably our society can have a property only if our society exists; hence it looks as if the existence of God entails the existence of our society, so that if our society had not existed, God would not have existed either. Again, this is clearly incompatible with Christian theism.

Of course this claim on Rorty's part will constitute a defeater only if he also makes us aware of some reason why we should believe it; the mere fact that he or someone else merely makes the claim doesn't provide a defeater. Now in general, Rorty is a bit standoffish about arguments; still, he does present something that could perhaps be construed as an argument for the conclusion that truth relevantly depends on us as a society. He begins his book *Contingency, Irony, and Solidarity* (hereafter CIS) by claiming, "About two hundred years ago, the idea that truth was made rather than found began to take hold of the imagination of Europe," thus apparently contradicting one of those platitudes, the one according to which (in the general case, anyway) truth is discovered or found rather than made. This certainly *sounds* like the nonplatitudinous suggestion that truth is a social

12. Could it be that what Rorty is rejecting is not representationalism as such, but some more specific and detailed version of it—one, perhaps, in which the correspondence in question involves some kind of isomorphism between elements of the representer (thought or sentence) and the represented? Perhaps; but then (as with truth) Rorty's rejection of representationalism isn't nearly as interesting as it looks at first sight.

construction, and that a given candidate for truth depends for its being true, if it is, on something we human beings do. In any event, here is Rorty's argument:

> To say that truth is not out there is simply to say that where there are no sentences there is no truth, that sentences are elements of human languages, and that human languages are human creations.
>
> Truth cannot be out there—cannot exist independently of the human mind—because sentences cannot so exist, or be out there. (CIS, p. 5)

How exactly shall we understand this? It is hard to be sure, but here is a possibility: truths are sentences, sentences are elements of language, and languages are human creations; therefore truths are human creations, and if there weren't any human beings (or other language-using creatures), there wouldn't be any truths. According to this thought, we human beings create truths. The way we do this is perhaps not within anyone's direct control (just as the stock market isn't within anyone's direct control), but still we somehow do it. I *think* this is what Rorty intends to assert; what he actually says, of course, is terse and enigmatic (as befits a conversational contribution). If it is what he means, however, there are two sorts of objections to the argument, one serious and the other fatal.

First, the serious objection. Sentences are indeed true or false, but they aren't the only things that are. *Beliefs* are also true or false, as are assertions, claims, suggestions, and the like. Rorty's argument seems to presuppose that beliefs, assertions, claims, suggestions, and so on are all themselves sentences. Alternatively, perhaps his idea is that it is sentences that are true or false in the *primary* sense, with other things (beliefs and assertions, for example) being true in a secondary way. (Thus he might say that an assertion is true if it is the assertion of a true sentence.)

This is at best dubious. Here is a reason for thinking that at least some things true in the fundamental sense are not sentences. Suppose we use the term 'proposition' to denote the things that are true or false in the primary sense, leaving open just what they are and, in particular, whether or not they are all sentences. Consider, then, the proposition (the truth) that $2 + 1 = 3$. Now this truth, as we ordinarily think, is *necessarily* true; that means, among other things, that it couldn't have failed to be true; there are no possible circumstances in which it is not true. But the *sentence* '$2 + 1 = 3$' could have failed to be true. That is because it is a sentence, and is true, on Rorty's view, because of something we do with it. Furthermore, what we do with it is something *we* could have failed to do. Therefore, on Rorty's view, things could have been such that this sentence would not have been true; indeed, before there were human beings, Rorty thinks, there was no such thing as the sentence '$2 + 1 = 3$'; under those conditions, that sentence would not have been true. Hence the sentence could have failed to be true. The *proposition* $2 + 1 = 3$, therefore, has a property that the *sentence* '$2 + 1 = 3$' does not have: being necessarily true—that is, being such that it could not have failed to be true. The proposition (truth) that $2 + 1 = 3$, therefore, is not the sentence '$2 + 1 = 3$'.[13] The same will go, naturally enough, for any other necessary truth. This is an argument for the conclusion that some truths—*necessary* truths—are not sentences; but we can make a similar if slightly more complicated argument for the same conclusion with respect to contingent truths. In the interests of brevity (whose interest you may already think has been shamefully slighted in this book) I shall omit that argument.

That was the serious objection: at least some of the things that are true or false in the primary sense are not, contra Rorty's assumption, sentences. I turn now to the fatal objection. Suppose for the moment that sentences *were* the only things that are true (or false) in the primary sense. Then perhaps we could say that truths are made by us human beings: for we make it the case that a given sequence of sounds or marks is, indeed, a *sentence* and thus capable of being true or false. (What we make to be sentences, I take it, are *types* as opposed to tokens.) For take any given truth: it is a sequence of shapes or sounds, and is also a sentence. We don't make the string of shapes or sounds; perhaps we create *tokens* of those types, but the types would be there whatever we did or didn't do. Still, that string of shapes or sounds owes its being a sentence to what we, the users of language, do with it. And perhaps we could express this by saying that truths are made.

Of course it wouldn't follow that we make a given sentence *true*, or that it is by virtue of something we do that a given sentence is in fact true. We make it the case that the sequence of marks 'There once were dinosaurs' is a sentence and thus capable of being true or false. It doesn't follow that we make it true that there once were dinosaurs. By virtue of our language-making activity, we bring it about that a certain string of marks—'there once were dinosaurs'—is true if and only if there once were dinosaurs. But that is not sufficient for making that sentence true. For the sentence to be true, there must once have been dinosaurs; and that, presumably, is not something we have made to be the case, by our language-making activities or in any other way. Taken one way, therefore, the conclusion of Rorty's argument is that we human beings are responsible for the existence of *sentences* (for the fact that certain strings of marks or sounds are sentences) and thus for the existence of the things that are true or false; so taken, the conclusion is unobjectionable, platitudinous, and certainly not a candidate for a defeater of Christian belief. Taken the

---

13. Or, indeed, any other contingently existing object: see *Warrant and Proper Function* (hereafter WPF), pp. 117ff.

other way, as the nonplatitudinous claim that we human beings are responsible, not just (for example) for the sentencehood of 'God created the world', but for God's having created the world, the conclusion of the argument is, indeed, incompatible with Christian belief; taken that way, however, there is not the slightest reason (beyond a certain confusion) for thinking that conclusion true. It certainly doesn't follow from the premises. Either way, therefore, there is no defeater here.

C. Postmodernism a Failure of Nerve

One final note. Postmodernists nearly all reject classical foundationalism; in this they concur with most Christian thinkers and most contemporary philosophers. Momentously enough, however, many postmodernists apparently believe that the demise of classical foundationalism implies something far more startling: that there is no such thing as truth at all, no way things really are. Why make that leap, when as a matter of logic it clearly doesn't follow? For various reasons, no doubt. Prominent among those reasons is a sort of Promethean desire not to live in a world we have not ourselves constituted or structured. With the early Heidegger, a postmodern may refuse to feel at home in any world he hasn't himself created.[14] Now some of this may be a bit hard to take seriously (it may seem less Promethean defiance than foolish posturing); so here is another possible reason. As I pointed out (above, p. 73), classical foundationalism arose out of uncertainty, conflict, and clamorous (and rancorous) disagreement; it emerged at a time when everyone did what was right (epistemically speaking) in his own eyes. Now life without sure and secure foundations is frightening and unnerving; hence Descartes's fateful effort to find a sure and solid footing for the beliefs with which he found himself. (Hence also Kant's similar effort to find an irrefragable foundation for science.)

Such Christian thinkers as Pascal, Kierkegaard, and Kuyper, however, recognize that there aren't any certain foundations of the sort Descartes sought—or, if there are, they are exceedingly slim, and there is no way to transfer their certainty to our important nonfoundational beliefs about material objects, the past, other persons, and the like. This is a stance that requires a certain epistemic hardihood: there is, indeed, such a thing as truth; the stakes are, indeed, very high (it matters greatly whether you believe the truth); but there is no way to be sure that you have the truth; there is no sure and certain method of attaining truth by starting from beliefs about which

14. See CIS, p. 109.

you can't be mistaken and moving infallibly to the rest of your beliefs. Furthermore, many others reject what seems to you to be most important. This is life under uncertainty, life under epistemic risk and fallibility. I believe a thousand things, and many of them are things others—others of great acuity and seriousness—do not believe. Indeed, many of the beliefs that mean the most to me are of that sort. I realize I can be seriously, dreadfully, fatally wrong, and wrong about what it is enormously important to be right. That is simply the human condition: my response must be finally, "Here I stand; this is the way the world looks to me."

There is, however, another sort of reaction possible here. If it is painful to live at risk, under the gun, with uncertainty but high stakes, maybe the thing to do is just reduce or reject the stakes. If, for example, there just isn't any such thing as truth, then clearly one can't go wrong by believing what is false or failing to believe what is true. If we reject the very idea of truth, we needn't feel anxious about whether we've got it. So the thing to do is dispense with the search for truth and retreat into projects of some other sort: self-creation and self-redefinition as with Nietzsche and Heidegger, or Rortian irony,[15] or perhaps playful mockery, as with Derrida.[16] So taken, postmodernism is a kind of failure of epistemic nerve.

II. PLURALISM

Postmodernism, therefore, doesn't offer anything that can sensibly be thought a defeater for Christian belief. But what about the facts of religious pluralism, the fact that the world displays a bewildering and kaleidoscopic variety of religious and antireligious ways of thinking, all pursued by people of great intelligence and seriousness? There are theistic religions, but also at least some nontheistic religions (or perhaps nontheistic strands of religion) among the enormous variety

15. Although here as elsewhere Rorty is ambiguous. Note that his ironist thinks there is no intrinsically final vocabulary; she believes that no way of thinking is intrinsically closer to the truth than any other ("The difficulty faced by a philosopher who, like myself, is sympathetic to this suggestion—one who thinks of himself as auxiliary to the poet rather than to the physicist—is to avoid hinting that this suggestion gets something right, that any sort of philosophy corresponds to the way things really are" [CIS, p. 8]). Paradoxically, however, the ironist is also nervous about her own final vocabulary, thinking she may somehow have it wrong: "The ironist spends her time worrying about the possibility that she has been initiated into the wrong tribe, taught to play the wrong language game. She worries that the process of socialization which turned her into a human being by giving her a language, may have given her the wrong language, and so turned her into the wrong kind of human being" (CIS, p. 75).

16. See Rorty on Derrida, CIS, pp. 122ff.

of religions going under the names 'Hinduism' and 'Buddhism'. Among the theistic religions, there are Christianity, Islam, Judaism, strands of Hinduism and Buddhism, American Indian religions, some African religions, and still others. All of these differ significantly from each other. Furthermore, there are those who reject all religions. Given that I know of this enormous diversity, isn't it somehow arbitrary, or irrational, or unjustified, or unwarranted (or maybe even oppressive and imperialistic) to endorse one of them as opposed to all the others? How can it be right to select and accept just one system of religious belief from all this blooming, buzzing confusion? Won't that be in some way irrational? And don't we therefore have a defeater for Christian belief? As the sixteenth-century writer Jean Bodin put it, "each is refuted by all."[17] According to John Hick: "In the light of our accumulated knowledge of the other great world faiths, [Christian exclusivism] has become unacceptable to all except a minority of dogmatic diehards."[18]

This is the problem of pluralism, and our question is whether a knowledge of the facts of pluralism constitutes a defeater for Christian belief. The specific problem I mean to discuss can be thought of as follows. To put it in an internal and personal way, I find myself with religious beliefs, and religious beliefs that I realize aren't shared by nearly everyone else. For example, I believe both

> (1) The world was created by God, an almighty, all-knowing and perfectly good personal being (the sort of being who holds beliefs, has aims and intentions, and can act to accomplish these aims)

and

> (2) Human beings require salvation, and God has provided a unique way of salvation through the incarnation, life, sacrificial death, and resurrection of his divine son.[19]

---

17. *Colloquium Heptaplomeres de rerum sublimium arcanis abditis*, written by 1593 but first published in 1857. English translation by Marion Kuntz (Princeton: Princeton University Press, 1975), p. 256.

18. *God Has Many Names*, p. 27. It is no doubt true that Christian exclusivism (see below for a definition of that term) is a minority opinion in the world at large: I suppose there are no more than a couple of billion or so Christian exclusivists, with the world's population perhaps approaching three times that figure. Of course, these matters are not really settled by counting heads. If they were, however, it would be of some interest to note that there are perhaps a million times more of those "dogmatic diehards" than people who accept anything like Hick's pluralism.

19. Note that it is no part of (2) to add that those—the Old Testament patriarchs, for example, as well as countless others—who haven't encountered this way of salvation cannot share in it.

Now I realize there are many who do not believe these things. First, there are those who agree with me on (1) but not (2): there are non-Christian theistic religions. Second, there are those who don't accept either (1) or (2), but nonetheless do believe that there is something beyond the natural world, a something such that human well-being and salvation depend on standing in a right relation to it. And third, in the West and since the Enlightenment, anyway, there are people—*naturalists*, we may call them—who don't believe any of these three things. Some speak here of a *new* awareness of religious diversity, and speak of this new awareness as constituting (for us in the West) a crisis, a revolution, an intellectual development of the same magnitude as the Copernican revolution of the sixteenth century and the alleged discovery of evolution and our animal origins in the nineteenth.[20] No doubt there is at least some truth to this. Of course the fact is all along many Western Christians and Jews have known that there are other religions, and that not nearly everyone shares *their* religion. The ancient Israelites—some of the prophets, say—were clearly aware of Canaanite religion; and the apostle Paul said that he preached "Christ crucified, a stumbling block to Jews and folly to the Greeks" (1 Corinthians 1:23). Other early Christians, the Christian martyrs, say, must have suspected that not everyone believed as they did. The church fathers, in offering defenses of Christianity, were certainly apprised of this fact; Origen, indeed, wrote an eight-volume reply to Celsus, who urged an argument very similar to those urged by contemporary pluralists.[21] Aquinas, again, was clearly aware of those to whom he addressed the *Summa contra Gentiles*; and the fact that there are non-Christian religions would have come as no surprise to the Jesuit missionaries of the sixteenth and seventeenth centuries or to the Methodist missionaries of the nineteenth. Still, in recent years probably *more* Western Christians have become aware of the world's religious diversity; we have probably learned more about people of other religious persuasions, and we have come to see more clearly that they display what looks like real piety, devoutness, and spirituality. What is new, perhaps, is a more widespread sympathy for other religions, a tendency to see them as more valuable, as contain-

20. Thus Joseph Runzo: "Today, the impressive piety and evident rationality of the belief systems of other religious traditions, inescapably confronts Christians with a crisis—and a potential revolution" ("God, Commitment, and Other Faiths: Pluralism vs. Relativism," *Faith and Philosophy* 5, no. 4 (October 1988), pp. 343ff.

21. See Robert Wilken's paper "Religious Pluralism and Early Christian Thought", so far unpublished. Wilken focuses on the third century; he explores Origen's response to Celsus, and concludes that there are striking parallels between Origen's historical situation and ours. "What is different today, I suspect, is not that Christianity has to confront other religions," he says, "but that we now call this situation 'religious pluralism'."

ing more by way of truth, and a new feeling of solidarity with their practitioners.

Now one way to react to these other religious responses to the world is to continue to believe what I have all along believed; I learn about this diversity, but continue to believe (i.e., take to be true), such propositions as (1) and (2) above, consequently taking to be false any beliefs, religious or otherwise, that are incompatible with (1) and (2). Following current practice, I shall call this *exclusivism*; the exclusivist holds that the tenets or some of the tenets of *one* religion— Christianity, let's say—are in fact true; he adds, naturally enough, that any propositions, including other religious beliefs, that are incompatible with those tenets are false. Here we need a couple of initial qualifications. First, I shall use the term 'exclusivism' in such a way that you don't count as an exclusivist unless you are rather fully aware of other faiths, have had their existence and their claims called to your attention with some force and perhaps fairly frequently, have noted that the adherents of other religions sometimes appear to display great intelligence, moral excellence, and spiritual insight, and have to some degree reflected on the problem of pluralism, asking yourself such questions as whether it is or could be really true that the Lord has revealed himself and his programs to Christians, say, in a way in which he hasn't revealed himself to those of other faiths. And second, suppose I am an exclusivist with respect to (1), for example, but reasonably believe, like Thomas Aquinas, say, that I have a knockdown, drag-out argument, a demonstration or conclusive proof of the proposition that there is such a person as God; and suppose I think further that if those who don't believe (1) were to be apprised of this argument (and had the ability and training necessary to grasp it, and were to think about the argument fairly and reflectively), they too would come to believe (1). Then, obviously, the facts of religious pluralism would not furnish me with a defeater for (1). My condition would be like that of Kurt Gödel, upon his recognition that he had a proof for the incompleteness of arithmetic. True, many of his colleagues and peers didn't believe that arithmetic was incomplete, and some believed that it *was* complete; these facts did not give Gödel a defeater for his belief; he had his proof, after all. Furthermore, he wouldn't have had a defeater in these facts even if he were *mistaken* in thinking he had a proof.

Accordingly, I shall use the term 'exclusivist' in such a way that you don't count as an exclusivist if you rationally think you know of a demonstration or conclusive argument for the belief with respect to which you are an exclusivist, or even if you rationally think you know of an argument that would convince all or most intelligent and honest people of the truth of that proposition. And our question is whether it is possible to be a rational exclusivist in the above sense; our question, that is, is whether I have a defeater for my Christian belief in my knowledge of the facts of religious pluralism, coupled with my belief that I do not have a proof or argument that can be counted on to convince those who disagree with me. Must I recognize that the existence of these other ways of thinking gives me a defeater for my own?

A. A Probabilistic Defeater?

Precisely how would such a defeater work? Suppose we begin by considering a *probabilistic* antitheistic argument from pluralism. J. L. Schellenberg asks us to "Consider first the case of one who supposes there to be a number of mutually exclusive religious alternatives to a certain religious belief r having probabilities equal to the probability of r."[22] He then suggests that such a person ought to suppose that r is improbable (less likely than its denial)—at any rate if she thinks there is more than one alternative having a probability equal to that of r; hence she ought not believe it. Schellenberg then concedes that the typical believer will not suppose that what she believes is no more probable than alternatives to it (if she did, why would she be *believing* it?); but he thinks his argument can nonetheless be restated as follows:

> Summarizing (and allowing for a non-uniform assignment of probabilities to alternatives), we can say quite generally that the following may be held by the critic to be a sufficient condition for the improbability of any religious belief r with an epistemic status superior to that of each of its alternatives: r is improbable if the number of times by which its probability exceeds that of each of the available mutually exclusive alternatives (or the average of their probabilities) is exceeded by the number of those alternatives.

By way of example:

> Even if a Christian were to suppose her trinitarian belief to be significantly *more* likely to be true than each of the various Jewish, Hindu, Buddhist . . . alternatives, the application of the approach here described could still yield the conclusion that her belief was probably false. For it might upon reflection seem intuitively obvious or at any rate very likely to the Christian that the degree of superiour probability she could credibly claim would not be sufficient to prevent the combined probability of the relevant alternatives from outweighing that of the beliefs she holds. (p. 148)

The basic idea, therefore, is that reflection on the facts of pluralism should lead the believer to think that the probability of her belief is relatively low, perhaps even less than .5. But here is the crucial question: probability with respect to *what*? What is the body of evi-

22. "Pluralism and Probability," *Religious Studies*, 33 no. 2 (June 1997), p. 147.

dence with respect to which Schellenberg thinks the Christian's belief must be more probable than not, if she is not to be irrational? If it is the set of beliefs *actually accepted* by the believer, then, of course, the probability of her beliefs will be 1. After all, the believer doesn't just think it *likely* that, for example, Jesus Christ is the divine son of God; she *believes* it; it is a member of the set of propositions she believes; hence its probability with respect to that set is 1. If *that* set isn't the one Schellenberg has in mind, however, which one is it? What is the body of beliefs Christian belief must be probable with respect to in order to be reasonable? Schellenberg's approach (like so many others) seems to make sense only if the believer, to be rational, must hold her Christian beliefs on the basis of their relation to *other* beliefs she has—or, at any rate, only if those Christian beliefs *are* probable with respect to those other beliefs. One of the main burdens of this book, however, is that the believer can be perfectly rational in accepting some of her beliefs in the *basic* way—not on the basis (probabilistic or otherwise) of other beliefs.

No doubt there are subsets *S* of her total set of beliefs with respect to which Christian belief is indeed improbable; perhaps, in fact, it is improbable with respect to the rest of what she believes (supposing, for the moment, that there is some neat way to segregate her Christian belief from her other beliefs). But how is that relevant? The same will be true, no doubt, with respect to many other beliefs she holds in perfect rationality. She is playing bridge and is dealt all the sevens and eights. The odds against this are pretty formidable; there are many alternatives that are at least equally probable; does that mean that her belief that she was dealt all the sevens and eights is irrational? Of course not. The reason, clearly, is that this belief has a source of warrant independent of any it gets by way of its probabilistic relations to her other beliefs. The same goes for Christian belief. If there is a source of warrant for Christian belief that is independent of any it acquires by way of probabilistic relations to other beliefs, then the fact (if it is a fact) that Christian belief isn't particularly likely with respect to those others doesn't show anything of much interest. It certainly doesn't provide a defeater for Christian belief.

B. The Charge of Moral Arbitrariness

This approach, therefore, appears to be a nonstarter. Is there something else in the nearby bushes that could produce a defeater? Perhaps the most important suggestion in the neighborhood is that there is something *arbitrary* about accepting Christian belief. This arbitrariness is thought to have both a moral and an intellectual component: it is thought to be both unjustified (contrary to doxastic duty) and irrational. The moral charge is that there is a sort of egoism, perhaps pride or hubris, in accepting beliefs when one realizes both that others do not accept them and that in all likelihood one possesses no arguments that would convince those dissenters. The epistemic charge also focuses on arbitrariness: here the claim is that the exclusivist is treating similar things differently, thus falling into intellectual arbitrariness. And the idea would be that in either case, when the believer comes to see these things, then she has a defeater for her belief, a reason for giving it up or, at the least, holding it with less firmness. I shall focus on the moral charge, dealing with the charge of epistemic arbitrariness *ambulando*.

1. The Abstract Case

The moral charge is that there is a sort of self-serving arbitrariness, an arrogance or egoism, in accepting such propositions as (1) or (2); one who accepts them is guilty of some serious moral fault or flaw. According to Wilfred Cantwell Smith, "except at the cost of insensitivity or delinquency, it is morally not possible actually to go out into the world and say to devout, intelligent, fellow human beings: '. . . we believe that we know God and we are right; you believe that you know God, and you are totally wrong'."[23] So what can the believer say for herself? Well, it must be conceded immediately that if she believes (1) or (2), then she must also think that those who believe something incompatible with them are mistaken and believe what is false; that's just logic. Furthermore, she must also believe that those who do not believe as she does—those who believe neither (1) nor (2), whether or not they believe their negations—*fail* to believe something that is true, deep, and important. Of course she

---

23. *Religious Diversity* (New York: Harper and Row, 1976), p. 14. A similar statement from John Hick:

> Nor can we reasonably claim that our own form of religious experience, together with that of the tradition of which we are a part, is veridical whilst others are not. We can of course claim this; and indeed virtually every religious tradition has done so, regarding alternative forms of religion either as false or as confused and inferior versions of itself. . . . Persons living within other traditions, then, are equally justified in trusting their own distinctive religious experience and in forming their beliefs on the basis of it. . . . let us avoid the implausibly arbitrary dogma that religious experience is all delusory with the single exception of the particular form enjoyed by the one who is speaking. (*An Interpretation of Religion*, p. 235).

On the topic of epistemic arrogance, see also Paul De Vries "The 'Hermeneutics' of Alvin Plantinga," *Christian Scholar's Review* (June 1989), pp. 363ff.; Lee Hardy, "The Interpretations of Alvin Plantinga," *Christian Scholar's Review* (December 1991), pp. 163ff.; my reply "*Ad* De Vries," *Christian Scholar's Review* (December 1991), pp. 171ff.; and De Vries's reply to Hardy and myself, "Intellectual Humility and Courage: An Essential Epistemic Tension," *Christian Scholar's Review* (December 1991), pp. 179ff.

does believe this truth; hence she must see herself as *privileged* with respect to those others—those others of both kinds. There is something of great value, she must think, that *she* has and *they* lack. They are ignorant of something—something of great importance—of which she has knowledge. But does this make her properly subject to the above censure?

I think the answer must be no. Or if the answer is yes, then I think we have here a genuine moral dilemma, a situation in which no matter what you do, you are wrong. Given the pluralistic facts of the matter, there is no real alternative; there is no reflective attitude that is not open to the same strictures. These charges of arrogance are a philosophical tar baby: get close enough to them to use them against the Christian believer, and you are likely to find them stuck fast to yourself. How so? As follows: as an exclusivist, while I realize that I can't convince others that they should believe as I do, I nonetheless continue to believe as I do. And the charge is that I am, as a result, arrogant or egoistical, arbitrarily preferring my way of doing things to other ways.[24] But what are my alternatives with respect to a proposition like (1) or (2)? There are three choices.[25] I can continue to hold it; I can withhold it, in Roderick Chisholm's sense, believing neither it nor its denial; or I can accept its denial. Consider the third way, a way taken by those pluralists who, like John Hick, hold that such propositions as (1) and (2) and their colleagues from other faiths are literally false, although in some way still valid responses to the Real. This seems to me to be no advance at all with respect to the arrogance or egoism problem; this is not a way out. If I do this I will then be in the very same condition as I am now: I will believe many propositions others don't believe, realizing that I have no argument that will necessarily convince those others. For I will then believe the denials of (1) and (2) (as well as the denials of many other propositions explicitly accepted by those of other faiths). Many others, of course, do not believe the denials of (1) and (2), and in fact believe (1) and (2). I am therefore in the condition of believing propositions that many others do not believe; I also realize I have no demonstrations of what I believe. If, in the case of those who believe (1) and (2), that

24. "The only reason for treating one's tradition differently from others is the very human but not very cogent reason that it is one's own!" (John Hick, *An Interpretation of Religion*, p. 235).

25. To speak of choice here suggests that I can simply *choose* which of these three attitudes to adopt, which is wholly unrealistic. Perhaps we have very little control over our beliefs; then the moral critic of belief can't properly accuse the believer of dereliction of moral duty, but he could still argue that her stance is unhappy, regrettable, a miserable state of affairs. Even if I can't help it that I am overbearing and conceited, my being that way is a bad state of affairs.

is sufficient for intellectual arrogance or egoism, the same goes for those who believe their denials. This third alternative, therefore, is no help at all with respect to the arrogance-egoism-arbitrariness problem.

So consider the second option: I can instead *withhold* the proposition in question. I can say to myself: "The right course here, given that I can't or couldn't convince these others of what *I* believe, is to believe neither these propositions nor their denials." The pluralist objector can say that the right course is to *abstain* from believing the offending proposition, and also abstain from believing its denial; call him, therefore, 'the abstemious pluralist'. Does he thus really avoid the condition that, on the part of the exclusivist, leads to the charges of egoism and arrogance? Not really. Think, for a moment, about disagreement. Disagreement, fundamentally, is a matter of adopting conflicting attitudes with respect to a given proposition. In the simplest and most familiar case, I disagree with you if there is some proposition *p* such that I believe *p* and you believe *-p*. That's just the simplest case, however; there are also others. The one that is presently of interest is this: you believe *p* and I withhold it, fail to believe it. Call the first kind of disagreement 'contradicting'; call the second 'dissenting'.

My claim is that if *contradicting* others is arrogant and egoistical, so is *dissenting*. For suppose you believe some proposition *p* that I don't believe: perhaps you believe that it is wrong to discriminate against people simply on the grounds of race, while I, recognizing that there are many people who disagree with you, do not believe this proposition. I don't disbelieve it either, of course; but in the circumstances I think the right thing to do is to abstain from belief. Then am I not implicitly condemning your attitude, your *believing* the proposition, as somehow improper—naive, perhaps, or unjustified, or unfounded, or in some other way less than optimal? I am implicitly saying that my attitude is the superior one; I think my course of action here is the right one and yours somehow wrong, inadequate, improper, in the circumstances at best second-rate. I realize that there is no question, here, of *showing* you that your attitude is wrong or improper or naive; so am I not guilty of intellectual arrogance? Of a sort of egoism, thinking I know better than you, arrogating to myself a privileged status with respect to you? The problem for the believer was that she was obliged to think she possessed a truth missed by many others; the problem for the abstemious pluralist is that he is obliged to think that he possesses a virtue others don't, or acts rightly where others don't. If one is arrogant by way of believing a proposition others don't, isn't one equally arrogant by way of withholding a proposition others don't?

Perhaps you will respond by saying that the abstemious pluralist gets into trouble, falls into arrogance, by way of implicitly saying or believing that his way of proceeding is *better* or *wiser* than other ways pursued by other people; and perhaps he can escape by abstaining from *that* view as well. Can't he escape the problem by refraining from believing that racial bigotry is wrong, and also refraining from holding the view that it is *better*, under the conditions that obtain, to withhold that proposition than to assert and believe it? Well, yes, he can; then he has no *reason* for his abstention; he doesn't believe that abstention is better or more appropriate; he simply does abstain. Does this get him off the egoistical hook? Perhaps. Of course he can't, in consistency, also hold that there is something wrong with *not* abstaining, with coming right out and *believing* that bigotry is wrong; he loses his objection to the exclusivist. Accordingly, this way out is not available for the abstemious pluralist who accuses the exclusivist of arrogance and egoism.

Indeed, I think we can see that the abstemious pluralist who brings charges of intellectual arrogance against the believer is in a familiar but perilous dialectical situation; he shoots himself in the foot, is hoist with his own petard, holds a position that in a certain way is self-referentially inconsistent in the circumstances. For he believes

(3) If S knows that others don't believe p (and, let's add, knows that he can't find arguments that will persuade them of p), then S should not believe p;

this or something like it is the ground of the charges he brings against the believer. The abstemious pluralist realizes, no doubt, that many do not accept (3); and I suppose he also realizes that it is unlikely that he can find arguments for (3) that will convince them. Given his acceptance of (3), therefore, the right course for him is to abstain from believing (3), to withhold or disbelieve it. Under the conditions that do in fact obtain—namely, his knowledge that others don't accept it—he can't properly accept it. So if (3) is true, nobody can believe it without being arrogant. (3) is either true or false; if the first, I fall into arrogance if I believe it; if the second, I fall into falsehood if I believe it; so I shouldn't believe it.

I am therefore inclined to think that one can't, in the circumstances, properly hold (3) or any other proposition that will do the job the objector wants done. One can't find here some principle on the basis of which to hold that the believer is doing the wrong thing, suffers from some moral fault—that is, one can't find such a principle that doesn't, as we might put it, fall victim to itself.

The abstemious pluralist is therefore self-referentially inconsistent; but even apart from this dialectical argument (which in any event some will think unduly cute), aren't the charges against the exclusivist unconvincing and implausible? I must concede that there are a variety of ways in which I can be and have been intellectually arrogant and egoistic; I have certainly fallen into this vice in the past, will no doubt fall into it in the future, and am not free of it now. Still, am I really arrogant and egoistic just by virtue of believing something I know others don't believe, where I can't show them that I am right? Suppose I think the matter over, consider the objections as carefully as I can, realize that I am finite and furthermore a sinner, certainly no better than those with whom I disagree, and indeed inferior both morally and intellectually to many who do not believe what I do. But suppose it *still* seems clear to me that the proposition in question is true: am I really immoral in continuing to believe it? I am dead sure that it is wrong to try to advance my career by telling lies about my colleagues. I realize there are those who disagree (even if they would never so much as consider lying about their colleagues, they think nothing is really right or wrong); some of these are people whom I deeply respect. I also realize that in all likelihood there is no way I can show them that they are wrong. Nonetheless, I think they *are* wrong. If I think this after careful reflection—if I consider the claims of those who disagree as sympathetically as I can, if I try my level best to ascertain the truth here—and it *still* seems to me sleazy, despicable, *wrong* to lie about my colleagues to advance my career, could I really be doing something immoral in continuing to believe as before? I can't see how. If, after careful reflection and thought, you find yourself convinced that the right propositional attitude to take to (1) and (2), in the face of the facts of religious pluralism, is abstention from belief, how could you properly be taxed with egoism for so abstaining? Even if you knew others did not agree with you? And won't the same hold for believing them? So I can't see how the moral charge against exclusivism can be sustained, and if it can't, this charge does not provide a defeater for Christian belief.

2. *A Concrete Case: Gutting*

So far we have been considering this charge of moral arbitrariness in abstraction from any actual presentation of a pluralistic case for the arbitrariness or egoism of accepting Christian belief. To remedy that defect, I propose to consider the argument Gary Gutting[26] gives for this conclusion. As we saw above, the classical foundationalist holds that there is a duty or obligation to accept only what one sees to be at least probable with respect to foundational certainties. Gutting accepts the deontology of the classical picture, but proposes a different duty. Because of "the modern phenomenon of religious disagreement," he says, Christian and theistic belief requires justification (p. 11). Gutting means to investigate the question whether someone

---

26. *Religious Belief and Religious Skepticism* (Notre Dame: University of Notre Dame Press, 1982); page references to Gutting's work are to this book.

can justifiably, dutifully accept Christian belief, *given that there is dis-agreement about it* (and presumably given that she is aware of the disagreement). The question is not (as with the classical picture) whether being justified in accepting Christian belief requires evidence just as such; the question is whether being justified requires evidence or argument *once you know that others disagree with you.*

His conclusion, in brief, goes as follows. (1) We must begin by distinguishing "decisive assent" from "interim assent." When I give decisive assent to *p*:

> I view the present case for *p* as allowing me to end the *search* for reasons for or against believing *p*. Interim assent, on the other hand, accepts *p* but without terminating inquiry into the truth of *p*. Its effect is to put me on the side of *p* in disputes about its truth. However, my endorsement of *p* is combined with a commitment to the epistemic need for continuing discussions of *p*'s truth. (105)

That is, I believe that "further discussion is needed for the project of determining the truth of *p*." (2) A person has a right to give *decisive* assent to a proposition that she knows others don't assent to only if she has a good argument for that proposition. (3) She has a right to give *interim* assent to a proposition which others reject, even if she doesn't have good arguments for it. (4) Since there is a good argument (one from religious experience) for the existence of God, taken vaguely as "a good and powerful being, concerned about us, who has revealed himself to human beings" (p. 171), we have a right to give this proposition decisive assent. Finally, (5) there is no argument of this sort for specific Christian doctrines (for the belief, e.g., that in Christ, God was reconciling the world to himself) or for more specific beliefs about God, such as that he is all-powerful, or wholly good, or all-knowing, or the creator of the heavens and the earth.

Clearly there is much to discuss here, and much to question. I shall restrict myself to the following. (1) What does Gutting mean by 'justification'? And (2) *why* am I not justified in giving decisive assent to a proposition for which I don't have a good argument and about which I know people disagree? As to the first, he clearly thinks of justification in deontological terms, in terms of right and wrong, duty and obligation, being within one's epistemic rights. Someone who accepts traditional Christian belief in the face of disagreement and without having an argument for her beliefs, he charges, is not satisfying her intellectual obligations. What duty, specifically, is it that she violates? The duty to avoid epistemological egoism. *That's* the duty that is violated by the Christian who is aware of disagreement but has no good arguments:

> First believing *p* [when I don't have an argument and know that others disagree] is arbitrary in the sense that there is no reason to

think that my intuition (i.e., what seems obviously true to me) is more likely to be correct than that of those who disagree with me. Believing *p* because its truth is supported by *my* intuition is thus an *epistemological egoism* just as arbitrary and unjustifiable as ethical egoism is generally regarded to be. (p. 86, Gutting's emphasis)

[A] neutral epistemic observer has no intuitions pro or con about *p* and has not thought about *p* to an extent sufficient to make his not having any intuitions significant. From the point of view of such an observer, the facts are simply these (taking for simplicity the case of disagreement between two peers): (1) person A has an intuition that *p* is true; (2) person B has an intuition that *p* is false; (3) there is no reason to think that either A or B is more likely to be correct in his intuition. Surely the only proper attitude for such an observer is to withhold judgment on *p*. But even if I am A or B, should I not judge the situation in the same way as the neutral observer? Surely it is wrong to prefer my intuition simply because it is mine. (p. 87)

So there is a moral problem with the believer who knows others disagree with her but does not have an argument for her own views: she is being epistemically arrogant, egoistic, and self-centered in thus arbitrarily preferring the way *she* thinks things are to the way others think they are. (And perhaps, once she sees this, she will have a defeater for those beliefs.)

Here we must ask some questions. First, is it really true that if I am such a person, then I "prefer my intuition simply because it is mine"? Not really. I think it is wrong to discriminate against someone just because he's of a different race (even though I know others disagree). I am not aware of any *arguments* for my belief here, or at any rate any arguments that would convince those dissenters; the view just seems *right* to me. Still, it isn't the case that I accept this belief on the grounds that it is *my* belief or *my* intuition: that makes no sense. I don't accept it as the conclusion of an argument, the premise of which is that this is my intuition; I am not reasoning as follows: *p seems to me to be right*, therefore *p*. I don't accept it on the basis of other propositions at all. It is true that I accept it because, when I think about it, it seems right; the 'because', however, doesn't mean that the latter is my *reason*, or *argument* or *evidence* for the former.

If Gutting's position is to have real bite, he must tell us more about those arguments the possession of which protects me from epistemological egoism when I believe something others do not believe. What kind of an argument is required? Well, such an argument, he says, must be a *good* argument. Fair enough; bad arguments won't do the job; but what is goodness, for an argument? In the chapter on Rorty to which I referred above (p. 431), Gutting apparently agrees with Rorty that a good argument (good 'for me') consists in reasons that are accepted by my epistemic community. If that is how the wind blows, however, there will be little problem for the Christian; after all, the Christian epistemic community may be quite prepared to accept reasons for Christian belief (e.g., that Scripture affirms it) that those outside that community will not accept. So taken, Gutting's requirement is easy to meet—trivially easy to meet.

So let's suppose he has something more stringent in mind. A good argument, presumably, will be valid, and must also have some nonformal virtues: it must not be circular or beg the question against those with whom I disagree. But then what about its premises? If my argument is valid, won't the same disagreement break out with respect to the premises? If they are also propositions that wouldn't be accepted by those who disagree with me, then presumably I won't have a right to accept *them* either, unless I have a further argument for them. Of course the premises of that further argument will have to meet the same conditions: if others don't accept them, then I can't give them decisive assent unless I have a further good argument for them. The result seems to be that my duty precludes my being party to any *ultimate* disagreements, at least any *ultimate* disagreements of which I am aware, and at least as far as decisive assent goes. Can that be right? Perhaps there is no way you can find much moral common ground with a member of the Ku Klux Klan. Perhaps you can't find any premises you both accept that will serve in a good argument for your views and against his. Would it really follow that you don't have a right to give decisive assent to the proposition that racial bigotry is wrong? Hardly.

Well, perhaps it is Gutting's idea that if I don't have an argument for *p* and know that others don't believe it, then I am being egoistical, even if I don't reason in the above fashion—that is, don't believe or accept the intuition just because it is mine. But is this really true? Certainly not just as it stands. We can see this by going back to an earlier example. The police haul me in, accusing me of a serious crime: stealing your Frisian flag again. At the police station, I learn that the mayor claims to have seen me lurking around your back door at the time (yesterday midafternoon) the crime occurred; I am known to resent you (in part because I am peeved about your article in *The National Enquirer* according to which I am really an alien from outer space). I had means, motive, and opportunity; furthermore there have been other such sordid episodes in my past. However, *I* recall very clearly spending the entire afternoon on a solitary hike near Mount Baker. My belief that I was hiking there then isn't based on argument. (I don't note, e.g., that I feel a little tired, that my hiking boots are muddy, and that there is a topographical map of Mount Baker in my parka pocket, and then conclude that the best explanation of these phenomena is that I was hiking there.) Furthermore, I can't think of any argument or any other way to convince the police that I was at Mount Baker (sixty miles from the crime scene) when the theft took place. Nevertheless, I believe that's where I was. So I hold a belief for which I can't give an argument and which I know is disputed by others. Am I therefore guilty of epistemological egoism? Surely not.

Why not? Because I *remember* where I was, and *that* puts me within my rights in believing that I was off hiking, even if others disagree with me. Well, not quite; strictly speaking, it is, I suppose, my *believing* that I remember, rather than my *actually* remembering, that puts me in the right, morally speaking. I am justified, am not going contrary to duty or obligation here, because I believe, and nonculpably believe, that I have a source of knowledge or information about my movements that the police don't have: my memory. If I thought that I knew no more than they knew, and *still* held firmly to the belief that I was innocent, then, perhaps, I would be epistemically egoistical. But I think I know something they don't, and know it by way of a means to knowledge they don't have. (They know about where *they* were by memory, not about where *I* was.) It is because of this that I am not flouting any duties or obligations; this is what confers justification on me. It is because of this that I can't properly be accused of arbitrariness or egoism in preferring my view to theirs.

Because this is the crucial point here, let's look into it a bit further. Both rationality and epistemic duty, says the critic, requires that one treat similar cases similarly. The Christian believer, however (she says), violates this duty by arbitrarily believing (1) and (2) (above, p. 438) in the face of the plurality of conflicting religious beliefs the world presents. Well, let's suppose that rationality and epistemic duty do, indeed, require treating similar cases similarly. Clearly you do not violate this requirement if the beliefs in question are *not* on a par. And the Christian believer thinks they are *not* on a par: she thinks (1) and (2) *true* and those incompatible with either of them *false*. So they aren't relevantly similar, as she sees it, and she isn't treating similar cases differently. To make his case, therefore, the critic would have to argue that Christian belief is, in fact, false; but presumably he doesn't intend his charge of arbitrariness to depend on the assumption that Christian belief is false.

The rejoinder, of course, will be that it is not *alethic* parity (their having the same truth value) that is at issue: it is *epistemic* parity that counts. What kind of epistemic parity? Well, perhaps the critic is thinking initially of *internal* epistemic parity: parity with respect to what is internally available to the believer. What is internally available includes, for example, detectable relationships between the belief in question and other beliefs you hold; so internal parity would include parity of propositional evidence. What is internally available to the believer also includes the *phenomenology* that goes with the belief in question: the *sensuous* phenomenology, and also the nonsensuous phenomenology involved, in doxastic evidence, in the belief's just having the feel of being *right*. Once more, then, (1) and (2) are not on an internal par, for the Christian believer, with beliefs that are incompatible with them. After all, (1) and (2) *do* seem to her to be true; they do have for her the phenomenology that accompanies that seeming, and they do have doxastic evidence for her; the same cannot be said for propositions incompatible with them.

The next rejoinder: isn't it likely that those who reject (1) and (2) in favor of other beliefs have propositional evidence for their beliefs that is on a par with that of the Christian for her beliefs; and isn't it also probably true that the same or similar phenomenology accompanies their beliefs as accompanies hers? So that those beliefs really are epistemically and internally on a par with (1) and (2), and the believer is still treating like cases differently? I don't think so: I think there really are arguments available for (1), at least, that are not available for its competitors. As for similar phenomenology, this is not easy to say; it is not easy to look within the breast of another; it is hard indeed to discover this sort of thing, even with respect to someone you know really well. Still, I am prepared to stipulate both sorts of parity. Let's agree for the purpose of argument that these beliefs are on an epistemic par in the sense that those of a different religious tradition have the same sort of internally available markers—evidence, phenomenology, and the like—for their beliefs as the Christian has for (1) and (2). What follows?

Return to the case of moral belief. King David saw the beautiful Bathsheba, was smitten, sent for her, slept with her, and made her pregnant. After the failure of various stratagems to get her husband, Uriah, to think he was the father of the baby, David arranged for Uriah to be killed by telling his commander to "put Uriah in the front line where the fighting is fiercest; then withdraw from him so he will be struck down and die" (2 Samuel 11:15). Then the prophet Nathan came to David and told him a story about a rich man and a poor man. The rich man had many flocks and herds; the poor man had only a single ewe lamb, which grew up with his children, "ate at his table, drank from his cup, lay in his bosom, and was like a daughter to him." The rich man had unexpected guests. Instead of slaughtering one of his own sheep, he took the poor man's single ewe lamb, slaughtered it, and served it to his guests. David exploded in anger: "The man who did this deserves to die!" Then, in one of the most riveting passages in all the Bible, Nathan turns to David, stretches out his arm, points to him, and declares, "*You are that man!*" And then David sees what he has done.

My interest here is in David's reaction to the story. I agree with David: such injustice is utterly and despicably wrong; there are scarcely words for it. I believe that such an action is wrong, and I believe that the proposition that it *isn't* wrong—either because really *nothing* is wrong, or because even if *some* things are wrong, *this* isn't—is false. As a matter of fact, there isn't a lot I believe more strongly. I recognize, however, that plenty of people disagree with me; many believe that some actions are *better*, in one way or another, than others, but that none is really right or wrong in the full-blooded sense in which I think *this* action is. Once more, I doubt that I could find an argument to show them that I am correct and they incorrect. Further, for all I know, their conflicting beliefs have for them the same internally available epistemic markers, the same phenomenology, *mutatis mutandis*, as mine have for me; perhaps they have the same degree of doxastic evidence. Am I then being arbitrary, treating similar cases differently in continuing to hold, as I do, that in fact that kind of behavior *is* dreadfully wrong? I don't think so. Am I wrong in thinking racial bigotry despicable, even though I know that others disagree, and even if I think they have the same internal markers for their beliefs as I have for mine? Again, I don't think so. I believe in serious actualism, the view that no objects have properties in worlds in which they do not exist, not even nonexistence. Others do not believe this; I am unable to convince them; and perhaps the internal markers of their dissenting views have for them the same qualities as mine have for me. Am I being arbitrary in continuing to think as I do? I can't see how.

And the reason here is this: in each of these cases, the believer in question doesn't really think the beliefs in question *are* on a relevant epistemic par. She may agree that she and those who dissent are equally convinced of the truth of their belief, and even that they are internally on a par, that the internally available markers are similar, or relevantly similar. Still, she must think that there is an important epistemic difference: she thinks that somehow the other person has made a mistake, or has a blind spot, or hasn't been wholly attentive, or hasn't received some grace she has, or is blinded by ambition or pride or mother love or something else; she must think that she has access to a source of warranted belief the other lacks.[27] If the believer concedes that she *doesn't* have any special source of knowledge or true belief with respect to Christian belief—no *sensus divinitatis*, no internal instigation of the Holy Spirit, no teaching by a church inspired and protected from error by the Holy Spirit, nothing not available to those who disagree with her—*then*, perhaps, she can properly be charged with an arbitrary egoism, and *then*, perhaps, she will have a defeater for her Christian belief. But why should she concede these things? She will ordinarily think (or at least *should* ordinarily think) that there are indeed sources of warranted belief that issue in these

---

27. And of course the pluralist critic must think the same sort of thing. He thinks the thing to do when there is internal epistemic parity is to withhold judgment; he knows that there are others who don't think so (and won't be convinced by any argument he can muster), and, for all he knows, that belief has internal parity with his. If he continues in that belief, therefore, he will be in the same condition as the person he criticizes; but if he doesn't continue in this belief, he no longer has an objection.

beliefs. (And here we have a way in which the epistemologist can be of use to the believer.)

She believes, for example, that in Christ, God was reconciling the world to himself; she may believe this on the basis of what the Bible or church teaches. She knows that others don't believe this and furthermore don't accept the Bible's (or church's) authority on this or any other point. She has an explanation: there is the testimony of the Holy Spirit (or of the divinely founded and guided church); the testimony of the Holy Spirit enables us to accept what the Scriptures teach. It is the Holy Spirit who "seals it upon our hearts, so that we may certainly know that God speaks"; it is the work of the Spirit "to convince our hearts that what our ears receive has come from him."[28] She therefore thinks she is in a better epistemic position with respect to this proposition than those who do not share her convictions; for she believes she has the witness of the divinely guided church, or the internal testimony of the Holy Spirit, or perhaps still another source for this knowledge. She may be *mistaken*, in so thinking, deluded, in serious and debilitating error, but she needn't be *culpable* in holding this belief. In this case, as in the Frisian flag episode, the believer nonculpably believes that she has a source of knowledge or true belief denied those who disagree with her. This protects her from epistemic egoism, as well as from the defeater that might accompany awareness of it.[29]

As a result, of course, the serious believer will not take it that we are all, believers and unbelievers alike, epistemic peers on the topic of Christian belief. She will probably feel considerable sympathy for Cardinal Newman:

> in the schools of the world, the ways towards Truth are considered high roads open to all men, however disposed, at all times. Truth is to be approached without homage. Everyone is considered on a level with his neighbor, or rather, the powers of the intellect, acuteness, sagacity, subtlety and depth, are thought the guides into Truth. Men consider that they have as full a right to discuss reli-

28. Calvin, *Commentaries on the Catholic Epistles*, tr. and ed. John Owen (Grand Rapids: Baker Book House, 1979), commentary on 1 John 2:27, p. 200.

29. Even if she isn't egoistic in accepting Christian belief, won't she nevertheless have a defeater, here, if, in fact, Christian belief *is* on an epistemic par with its denial? Not if she doesn't believe that it is. She could perhaps be *given* such a defeater, if Gutting or someone could produce a powerful argument for the claim that there is epistemic parity here. As we saw in chapter 8, however, it is likely that Christian belief is such that if it is true, then it is warranted for those who accept it. This means that an argument for the conclusion that Christian belief is on an epistemic par with unbelief would require a previous argument that Christian belief is false. But if the critic already has an argument for the falsehood of Christian belief, why is he bothering with this charge of arbitrariness?

gious subjects, as if they were themselves religious. They will enter upon the most sacred points of Faith at the moment, at their pleasure—if it so happen, in a careless frame of mind, in their hours of recreation, over the wine cup.[30]

Newman's idea is that there is something in addition to "the powers of the intellect, acuteness, sagacity, subtlety and depth" that is needed for a proper discussion of religious subjects, or at least for a proper grasp of the truth with respect to them. Here he is echoing Jesus: "I praise you, Father, Lord of heaven and earth, because you have hidden these things from the wise and learned, and revealed them to little children" (Luke 10:21). If these things are hidden from the wise and learned, it won't be relevant to complain that the wise and learned don't accept them (adding that it is epistemically egoistic to accept what the wise and learned do not unless you have a good argument). The Christian believer will therefore think there is an important source of knowledge, here, in addition to the powers of intellect mentioned. So on this point he believes, presumably nonculpably, that those who disagree with him are really not his epistemic peers on *this* topic, even though he might be vastly inferior to them, epistemically speaking, on other topics.

The central question here, therefore, is whether the Christian's beliefs are or are not on an epistemic par with the beliefs of those who disagree with her. This is the crucial issue. If something like the extended Aquinas/Calvin (A/C) model presented in chapter 8 is in fact correct, then there is a significant difference between the epistemic situation of those who accept Christian belief and those who do not; the objector is therefore assuming, unjustifiably and without argument, that neither that model nor any other according to which there is a source of warranted Christian belief is in fact correct and that there is no such source for Christian belief. That assumption has nothing to be said for it; the arbitrariness charge therefore disintegrates.

Now Gary Gutting, to be sure, claims (p. 84) that the believer does not have a right, in this context, to the view that he is better off, epistemically speaking, than the unbeliever. He gives two reasons.[31] First, the believer's view that he is the beneficiary of the *sensus divinitatis* or the internal instigation of the Holy Spirit, or the teaching of a church inspired and protected from error by the Holy Spirit or "derives from

---

30. *Sermons, Chiefly on the Theory of Religious Belief, Preached before the University of Oxford* (London, Rivington, 1844), pp. 190–91.

31. As Marie Pannier pointed out in discussion, perhaps Gutting should really have given a third, which would be to reapply his principle that one can justifiably give only interim assent to any proposition she knows is not accepted by others; for presumably the believer knows that others, such as the objector, won't agree that the believer is better off, epistemically speaking, than the unbeliever.

theological doctrines that presuppose theism and so cannot be legitimately called upon in a defense of the believer's epistemic right to accept theism"; and second, "there are at least some believers who themselves do not see 'God exists' as obviously properly basic; it is very hard to see how the believer can nonarbitrarily apply Calvin's views to deny that they are his epistemic peers."

These arguments seem mistaken. Gutting's second reason for thinking the Christian doesn't have a right to think there are such sources of warranted belief seems irrelevant: the fact that some believers do not think belief in God is properly basic does not so much as slyly suggest that there are no such sources. What about the first reason, the claim that the believer is involved in some objectionable form of *circularity* if she thinks that she is the beneficiary of one of those sources of belief? But how can she be involved in circularity? She isn't putting forward an *argument* for anything; nor is she proposing a *definition*: so how does circularity so much as rear its ugly head? If she were giving an argument for theism and then proposed as a premise that she enjoyed the benefits of one of those special sources of belief, *then* her argument might be circular. But she isn't arguing for that; nor need she be arguing for anything else. Am I engaged in objectionable circularity if I appeal to physics to help explain how it is that I can perceive trees and grass— even if my knowledge of physics rests in part on observation? Not if I am not arguing for the conclusion that perception is a source of warranted belief.

But don't the realities of religious pluralism count for *anything*? Is there nothing at all to the claims of the pluralists?[32] Could that really be right? Of course not. For at least some Christian believers, an awareness of the enormous variety of human religious responses does seem to reduce the level of confidence in their own Christian belief. It doesn't or needn't do so by way of an *argument*. Indeed, there aren't any respectable arguments from the proposition that many apparently devout people around the world dissent from (1) and (2) to the conclusion that (1) and (2) are false or can be accepted only at the cost of moral or epistemic deficiency. Nevertheless, knowledge of others who think differently can reduce one's degree of belief in Christian teaching. From a Christian perspective, this situation of religious pluralism is itself a manifestation of our miserable human condition; and it may indeed deprive Christians of some of the comfort and peace the Lord has promised his followers. It can also deprive the believer of the *knowledge* that (1) and (2) are true, even if they *are* true and he *believes* that they are. Since degree of warrant depends in part on degree of belief, it is possible, though not necessary, that knowledge of the facts of religious pluralism should reduce his

32. See W. P. Alston, "Religious Diversity and Perceptual Knowledge of God," *Faith and Philosophy* 5, no. 4 (October 1988), pp. 433ff.

degree of belief and hence the degree of warrant (1) and (2) enjoy for him; it can therefore deprive him of knowledge of (1) and (2). He might be such that if he *hadn't* known the facts of pluralism, then he would have known (1) and (2), but now that he *does* know those facts, he doesn't know (1) and (2). In this way he may come to know less by knowing more.

Things *could* go this way, with the exclusivist. On the other hand, they *needn't* go this way. Consider once more the moral parallel. Perhaps you have always believed it deeply wrong for a counselor to use his position of trust to seduce a client. Perhaps you discover that others disagree; they think it more like a minor peccadillo, like running a red light when there's no traffic; and you realize that possibly these people have the same internal markers for their beliefs that you have for yours. You think the matter over more fully, imaginatively re-create and rehearse such situations, become more aware of just what is involved in such a situation (the breach of trust, the injustice and unfairness, the nasty irony of a situation in which someone comes to a counselor seeking help but receives only hurt), and come to believe even more firmly that such an action is wrong. In this way, this belief could acquire more warrant for you by virtue of your learning and reflecting on the fact that some people do not see the matter your way. Something similar can happen in the case of religious beliefs. A fresh or heightened awareness of the facts of religious pluralism could bring about a reappraisal of one's religious life, a reawakening, a new or renewed and deepened grasp and apprehension of (1) and (2). From the perspective of the extended A/C model, it could serve as an occasion for a renewed and more powerful working of the belief-producing processes by which we come to apprehend (1) and (2). In this way knowledge of the facts of pluralism could initially serve as a defeater; in the long run, however, it can have precisely the opposite effect. The facts of religious pluralism, therefore, like historical biblical criticism and the facts of evil, do not or need not constitute a defeater for Christian belief.

14

Suffering and Evil

Why do you make me look at injustice?
   Why then do you tolerate the treacherous? Why are you silent
while the wicked swallow up those more righteous than themselves?

Habakkuk

Our world contains an appalling amount and variety both of suffering and of evil; perhaps no century rivals ours for the magnitude of either. I'm thinking of *suffering* as encompassing any kind of pain or discomfort: pain or discomfort that results from disease or injury, or oppression, or overwork, or old age, but also disappointment with oneself or with one's lot in life (or that of people close to one), the pain of loneliness, isolation, betrayal, unrequited love; and there is also suffering that results from awareness of others' suffering. I'm thinking of *evil*, fundamentally, as a matter of free creatures' doing what is wrong, including particularly the way we human beings mistreat and savage each other. Often pain and suffering result from evil, as in some of the events for which our century will be remembered—the Holocaust, the horrifying seventy-year-long Marxist experiment in eastern Europe with its millions of victims, the villainy of Pol Pot and his followers, genocide in Bosnia and Africa. Of course much suffering and evil are banal and everyday, and are none the better for that.

Now the evil and suffering in our world have, indeed, baffled and perplexed Christians and other believers in God. This bafflement and perplexity are widely represented in Christian and Hebrew Scriptures, especially, though by no means exclusively, in Psalms and the book of Job. Faced with the shocking concreteness of a particularly horrifying example of suffering or evil in his own life or the life of someone close to him, a believer can find himself tempted to take toward God an attitude he himself deplores—an attitude of mistrust, or suspicion, or bitterness, or rebellion. Such a problem, broadly speaking, is a spiritual or pastoral problem. A person in its grip may not be much tempted to doubt the existence or even the goodness of God; nevertheless he may resent God, fail to trust him, be wary of him, be unable to think of him as a loving father, think of him as if he were far off and unconcerned.

Now many philosophers and others have argued that knowledge of the amount, variety, and distribution of suffering and evil ("the facts of evil," for short) confronts the believer with a problem of quite another sort.[1] These facts, they argue, can serve as the premise of a powerful argument against the very existence of God—against the existence, that is, of an all-powerful, all-knowing, and wholly good person who has created the world and loves the creatures he has created. Call such an argument 'atheological'; atheological arguments go all the way back to the ancient world, to Epicurus, whose argument is repeated in the eighteenth century by Hume:

> Epicurus' old questions are yet unanswered.
> Is he willing to prevent evil, but not able? then he is impotent.
> Is he able, but not willing? then he is malevolent. Is he both able
> and willing? whence then is evil?[2]

And the claim is that this argument (more exactly, knowledge of this argument) constitutes a defeater for theistic belief—and if for theistic belief, then also for Christian belief.

Our question in this chapter, therefore, is whether knowledge of the facts of evil *does* constitute a defeater for theistic and Christian belief. Does knowledge of the facts of evil, together with the rest of what I know, give me a reason to give up belief in God? Does this knowledge make it the case that I cannot continue to hold Christian belief *rationally*? Note that this is not the traditional problem of theodicy: I will not be making any attempt to "justify the ways of God to man" or

---

1. It is worth noting that many *different* problems, questions, and topics fall under the rubric of the problem of evil. There are, for example, the problems of *preventing* suffering and evil, those of *alleviating* it (knowing how to comfort and help those who suffer from it), those of maintaining the right attitude toward those who suffer, the pastoral or spiritual problem I mentioned above, and more; and, of course, a proper response to one of these problems might be totally inappropriate as a response to another.

2. *Dialogues concerning Natural Religion*, ed. Richard Popkin (Indianapolis: Hackett Publishing, 1980), p. 63. Hume puts the argument in the mouth of Philo, widely thought to represent Hume's own views.

to give an answer to the question why God permits evil generally or why he permits some specially heinous forms of evil. Our question is, instead, *epistemological*: given that theistic and Christian belief can have warrant in the way suggested in chapters 6 through 8, does knowledge of the facts of evil provide a defeater for this belief?

Of course the answer need not be the same for all Christians: perhaps the facts of suffering and evil, in our sad world, do not constitute such a defeater for very young Christians, or for culturally insulated Christians, or for Christians who know little about the suffering and evil our world contains, or for those who don't have an adequate appreciation of the seriousness of what they do know about. Our question, however, is about Philip Quinn's "intellectually sophisticated adults in our culture" (above, p. 358); can I be mature, both intellectually and spiritually, be aware of the enormous and impressive amounts and depths of suffering and evil in our world, be aware also of the best atheological arguments starting from the facts of evil, and still be such that Christian belief is rational and warranted for me? Could it still have warrant sufficient for knowledge, for me? I shall argue that the right response is, "Yes indeed." And it isn't that this can be so just for an exceptional few, perhaps the Mother Teresas of the world. I shall argue that for any serious Christian with a little epistemology, the facts of evil, appalling as they are, offer no obstacle to warranted Christian belief.

Now until twenty or twenty-five years ago, the favored sort of atheological argument from evil was for the conclusion that there is a *logical inconsistency* in what Christians believe. They believe both that there is such a person as God (a person who is omnipotent, omniscient, and wholly good), and also that there is evil in the world; it isn't logically possible (so went the claim) that both of these beliefs be true. Thus the late John Mackie:

> I think, however, that a more telling criticism can be made by way of the traditional problem of evil. Here it can be shown, not merely that religious beliefs lack rational support, but that they are positively irrational, that the several parts of the essential theological doctrine are inconsistent with one another.[3]

3. "Evil and Omnipotence," *Mind* (1955). The article has been widely reprinted. For difficulties with Mackie's argument, see my *God, Freedom, and Evil* (New York: Harper and Row, 1974; and Grand Rapids: W. B. Eerdmans, 1977), pp. 12ff. In Mackie's posthumous *The Miracle of Theism* (Oxford: Oxford University Press, 1982), he wavers between his earlier claim that the existence of God is straightforwardly inconsistent with that of evil, and the claim that the existence of evil is powerful but logically inconclusive evidence against the existence of God. See pp. 150–75, and see my "Is Theism Really a Miracle?" *Faith and Philosophy* (April 1986). The claim that the

Mackie goes on to argue that the existence of God is logically incompatible with the existence of evil; he concludes that since the theist is committed to both, theistic belief is clearly irrational.

At present, however, it is widely conceded that there is nothing like straightforward contradiction or necessary falsehood in the joint affirmation of God and evil; the existence of evil is not logically incompatible (even in the broadly logical sense) with the existence of an all-powerful, all-knowing, and perfectly good God.[4] An important line of thought in the demise of the traditional claim of contradiction has involved the notion of *free will*: although it is logically possible that there be free creatures (creatures whose actions are not antecedently determined, e.g., by God, or by natural law and antecedent conditions) who always do only what is right, it is not within

---

believer in God (the God of theism) is committed to a contradiction goes back to some of the French encyclopedists, F. H. Bradley, J. McTaggart, and J. S. Mill. More recently (in addition to Mackie), see, for example, H. J. McCloskey, "God and Evil," *Philosophical Quarterly* 10 (1960), p. 97; and Henry David Aiken, "God and Evil," *Ethics* 48 (1957–58), p. 79.

4. For argument for this conclusion, see my *God, Freedom, and Evil*, pp. 7ff. For a fuller and more accurate account, see my *The Nature of Necessity* (Oxford: Clarendon Press, 1974), chapter 9; and *Alvin Plantinga* (Profiles series), ed. James Tomberlin and Peter van Inwagen (Dordrecht: D. Reidel, 1985), pp. 36–55. Many fascinating problems and questions have emerged from the discussion of the free will defense over the last twenty-five years. In particular, there are arguments against the existence of (true and nontrivial) counterfactuals of freedom by Robert Adams ("Middle Knowledge and the Problem of Evil," *American Philosophical Quarterly* [1977]) and by William Hasker ("A Refutation of Middle Knowledge," *Noûs* [December 1986]). One particularly interesting strand here is the "grounding and founding" objection (according to which counterfactuals of freedom with false antecedents couldn't be true because they are incapable of being properly grounded or founded). This objection goes all the way back to the Jesuit-Dominican controversy in the sixteenth century, a dispute whose increasing rancor finally induced the pope to forbid the disputants to vilify one another in public (although he apparently didn't object to vilification among consenting adults in the privacy of their own quarters). The grounding and founding objection has been dealt with in magisterial fashion in my colleague Thomas Flint's *Divine Providence: The Molinist Account* (Ithaca: Cornell University Press, 1998).

Another issue of great interest is the question of "selective freedom" (David Lewis's term) (See G. Stanley Kane, "The Free-Will Defense Defended," *New Scholasticism* 50, no. 4 [1976], and David Lewis, "Evil for Freedom's Sake?" *Philosophical Papers* [November 1993]): couldn't God have let go forward those creaturely free choices he foresaw would be right, and cut off those he foresaw would be wrong? This question is connected with another fascinating issue, that of *backtracking counterfactuals* (see David Lewis, "Counterfactual Dependence and Time's Arrow," *Noûs* 13, no. 4 [November 1979], p. 455). It is extremely tempting to go into these issues here, but doing so would take us from epistemology deep into metaphysics (some would say *abstruse and arcane* metaphysics, but of course they would be mistaken); self-restraint must be the order of the day.

God's power to create free creatures and cause them to do only what is right. (If he *causes* someone to do what is right, then that person does not do what is right *freely*.) Of course that doesn't necessarily suffice to get the theist off the hook. There is also no logical contradiction in the thought that the earth is flat, or that it rests on the back of a turtle, which rests on the back of another turtle, and so on, so that it's turtles all the way down; nevertheless these views (given what we now think we know) are irrational. (You would be distressed if your grown children adopted them.) Those who offer atheological arguments from evil have accordingly turned from the claim that the existence of God is flatly incompatible with that of evil to *evidential* or *probabilistic* arguments of one sort or another. Here the claim is not that Christian belief is logically inconsistent, but rather that the facts of evil offer *powerful evidence against* the existence of God. These evidential arguments are also typically probabilistic: in the simplest cases, they claim that the existence of God is unlikely or improbable with respect to the facts of evil together with the rest of our background knowledge—that is, what we all know, or perhaps what all reasonable and well-informed people now believe. So the typical atheological claim at present is not that the existence of God is *incompatible* with that of evil; it is rather that the latter offers the resources for a strong evidential or probabilistic argument against the former.

Now from an atheological point of view, the old argument for inconsistency in Christian belief had a lot to be said for it. It was short and sweet; if there is a contradiction in Christian belief, then Christian belief is false, and that's all there is to it. It doesn't matter what else is or isn't true, and it doesn't matter whether there are any good arguments or evidence of other kinds *for* Christian belief: if it is inconsistent, it's false, and that settles the matter. Furthermore, once you see that a proposition is false, you can't rationally continue to believe it; so such an argument would show at one stroke that Christian belief is *false* and that it is *irrational*, at least for those apprised of the argument. But things are very different with contemporary evidential arguments from evil. First, suppose evil does constitute evidence, of some kind, against theism: what follows from that? Not much. There are many propositions I believe that are true and rationally accepted, and such that there is evidence against them. The fact that Peter is only three months old is evidence against his weighing nineteen pounds; nevertheless I might rationally (and truly) believe that's how much he weighs. Is the idea, instead, that the existence of God is improbable with respect to our *total evidence*, all the rest of what we know or believe? To show this, the atheologian would have to look into all the evidence *for* the existence of God—the traditional ontological, cosmological, and teleological arguments, as well as many others;[5] he would be obliged to weigh the relative merits of all of these arguments, and weigh them against the evidential argument from evil in order to reach the indicated conclusion. This is vastly messier and more problematic than a terse and elegant demonstration of a contradiction *à la* Mackie.

Another problem for this atheological argument can be brought out by considering responses to the most popular contemporary version of the argument from design—the so-called fine-tuning argument. This argument begins from the apparent fact that the fundamental constants of physics—the speed of light, the gravitational constant, the strength of the weak and strong nuclear forces—must apparently have values that fall within an exquisitely narrow range for life to be so much as possible. If these values had been even minutely different (if, for example, the gravitational constant had been different in even the most minuscule degree), habitable planets would not have developed and life (at least life at all like ours) would not have been possible. And this suggests or makes plausible the thought that the world was designed or created by a Designer who intended the existence of living creatures and eventually rational, intelligent, morally significant creatures. One contemporary response is that *possibly* "there has been an evolution of worlds (in the sense of whole universes) and the world we find ourselves in is simply one among countless others that have existed throughout all eternity."[6] And given infinitely many universes, Daniel Dennett thinks, all the possible distributions of values over the cosmological constants would have been tried out (p. 179); as it happens, we find ourselves, naturally enough, in one of those universes where the constants are such as to allow the development of intelligent life. But then the probability of theism, given the whole array of worlds, isn't particularly high.

In the same way, then, a theist might agree that it is unlikely, given just what we know about *our* world, that there is such a person as God. But perhaps God has created countless worlds, in fact, all the worlds (all the universes) in which there is a substantial overall balance of good over evil. In some of these worlds there is no suffering and evil; in some a good deal; as it happens, we find ourselves in one of the worlds where there is a good deal. But the probability of theism, given the whole ensemble of worlds, isn't particularly low.[7]

---

5. See my "Two Dozen or So Good Theistic Arguments," not yet published.

6. Daniel Dennett, *Darwin's Dangerous Idea* (New York: Simon and Schuster, 1995), p. 177.

7. For a development of this idea, see Donald Turner's Ph.D. dissertation, *God and the Best of All Possible Worlds* (University of Pittsburgh, 1994).

Still further, suppose theism *were* improbable with respect to the rest of what I believe; alternatively, suppose the rest of what I believe offered evidence *against* theism and none *for* it. What would follow from that? Again, not much. There are many true beliefs I hold (and hold in complete rationality) such that they are unlikely given the rest of what I believe. I am playing poker; it is improbable on the rest of what I know or believe that I have just drawn to an inside straight; it doesn't follow that there is even the slightest irrationality in my belief that I have just drawn to an inside straight. The reason, of course, is that this belief doesn't depend, for its warrant, on its being appropriately probable on the rest of what I believe; it has a quite different source of warrant, namely, perception. Similarly for theism: everything really turns, here, on the question whether, as I have been arguing, theism has or may have some source of warrant—perception of God, or the *sensus divinitatis*, or faith and the internal instigation of the Holy Spirit (see above, chapters 8 and 9)—distinct from its probability on other propositions I believe.

The important questions with respect to these atheological evidential arguments, therefore, are of the following sort: precisely what are they supposed to prove? That theism is false? Or that it is irrational for any thoughtful person apprised of the facts of evil to accept it? Or that the facts of evil and those probabilistic considerations together constitute a defeater for it? Or for at least *some* reflective theists, even if not for all? Or that the facts of suffering and evil make it more rational to reject belief in God than to accept it? Or what? One of the main problems here is to make out the proposed bearing of the atheological arguments from evil: precisely what are they supposed to accomplish? We'll have to bear this question in mind as we look at some of these arguments. Twenty-five years ago, there were no developed atheological evidential arguments from evil; that is understandable because (apparently) nearly all atheologians were of the opinion that the existence of God is flatly inconsistent with that of evil. Since then, however, there have been several attempts to state and develop evidential arguments from evil. Some of these efforts are ingenious and indeed revealing; I shall argue, however, that they are no more successful than the older argument for inconsistency. Indeed, what is most surprising, here, is the *weakness* of these arguments. I shall then go on to suggest that there is a wholly different (and more promising) way in which the atheologian could claim that the facts of evil constitute a defeater for theistic belief. Promising as it is, however, this claim, in my opinion, also fails.

I. EVIDENTIAL ATHEOLOGICAL ARGUMENTS

The last twenty-five years or so have seen the development of several different versions of the evidential argument from evil. In this section I examine a couple of the best.

A. Rowe's Arguments

I turn first to an argument William Rowe has been proposing and developing for the past twenty years.[8] Consider some particularly horrifying cases of evil or suffering: a five-year-old girl's rape and murder (E_1) or a fawn's lingering and painful death in a forest fire (E_2). Rowe's argument goes as follows:

> P: No good we know of is such that we know that it justifies an omnipotent, omniscient, perfectly good being [a *perfect being*, for short] in permitting E_1 and E_2;[9]

8. See his "The Problem of Evil and Some Varieties of Atheism," *American Philosophical Quarterly* (1979), pp. 335–41, reprinted in *The Evidential Argument from Evil*, ed. Daniel Howard-Snyder (Bloomington: Indiana University Press, 1996), pp. 1–11; "Evil and the Theistic Hypothesis: A Response to S. J. Wykstra," *International Journal for Philosophy of Religion* 16 (1984), pp. 95–100; "The Empirical Argument from Evil," in *Rationality, Religious Belief, and Moral Commitment*, ed. Robert Audi and William J. Wainwright (Ithaca: Cornell University Press, 1986); "Evil and Theodicy," *Philosophical Topics* 16 (1988), pp. 119–32; "Ruminations about Evil," *Philosophical Perspectives* 5 (1991), pp. 69–88; "William Alston on the Problem of Evil," in *The Rationality of Belief and the Plurality of Faith*, ed. Thomas D. Senor (Ithaca: Cornell University Press, 1994); and "The Evidential Argument from Evil: A Second Look," in Howard-Snyder, *The Evidential Argument from Evil* (hereafter EAESL).

9. Rowe actually states P as "No good we know of justifies an omnipotent, omniscient, perfectly good being in permitting E_1 and E_2"; neither the theist nor the neutral bystander, however, can be expected to accept this premise because it could be that some good we know of does justify a perfect being in permitting E_1 and E_2, even though we don't know that it does. Indeed, Rowe countenances conjunctive goods such as G, the conjunction of all the goods there are. But G (one supposes) is a good state of affairs; and if theism is true, G justifies a perfect being in permitting E_1 and E_2. Alternatively, the theist might think that the unthinkably great good of incarnation and atonement—a good that we know of—justifies E_1 and E_2. This could happen as follows: God selects for actualization one of the best worlds; but all the best worlds include incarnation and atonement (see below, p. 489), and hence also a great deal of evil—if not specifically E_1 and E_2, then others just as bad. The most the atheologian can sensibly claim, therefore (if he is hoping for agreement from theist and neutral bystander) is that no good we know of is such that *we know* that it justifies a perfect being in permitting E_1 and E_2. If Rowe insists on his premise as originally stated, then, it seems to me, the theist should respond that there is no reason to think it true and good reason to think it false.

Therefore, probably

 Q: No good at all justifies a perfect being in permitting E_1 and
     E_2;

Therefore probably

 not-G: There is no perfect being.

Here we are thinking of goods and evils as *states of affairs*. A state of affairs can be *actual* or *nonactual*; only an actual good, says Rowe, could
justify a perfect being in permitting E_1 and E_2 (or, indeed, any other
evil). So the idea behind P is that we do not know of any good that is
actual and is such that we know that it suffices to justify a perfect
being in permitting E_1 and E_2.

   There are several problems with this argument. At the simplest
level, however, the main problem, once the others are straightened
out or ignored, is with the inference from P to Q. I look inside my
tent: I don't see a St. Bernard; it is then probable that there is no St.
Bernard in my tent. That is because if there were one there, I would
very likely have seen it; it's not easy for a St. Bernard to avoid detec-
tion in a small tent. Again, I look inside my tent: I don't see any
noseeums (very small midges with a bite out of all proportion to their
size); this time it is not particularly probable that there are no
noseeums in my tent—at least it isn't any more probable than before
I looked. The reason, of course, is that even if there were noseeums
there, I wouldn't see 'em; they're too small to see. And now the question is whether God's reasons, if any, for permitting such evils as E_1
and E_2 are more like St. Bernards or more like noseeums. Suppose
the fact is God has a reason for permitting a particular evil like E_1 or
E_2, and suppose we try to figure out what that reason might be: is it
likely that we would come up with the right answer? Is it even likely
that we would wind up with plausible candidates for God's reason?
A series of important recent papers by Stephen Wykstra, William
Alston, and Peter van Inwagen argue (among other things) that it is
not.[10] The main reason is the epistemic distance between us and

---

10. Wykstra: "Difficulties in Rowe's Argument for Atheism, and in One of
Plantinga's Fustigations against It," read on the *Queen Mary* at the Pacific Division
Meeting of the American Philosophical Association, 1983; "The Humean Obstacle to
Evidential Arguments from Suffering: On Avoiding the Evils of 'Appearance',"
International Journal for Philosophy of Religion 16 (1984), pp. 73–94; "The 'Inductive'
Argument from Evil: A Dialogue" (co-authored with Bruce Russell), *Philosophical
Topics* 16, pp. 133–60; Alston: "The Inductive Argument from Evil and the Human
Cognitive Condition," *Philosophical Perspectives* 5, pp. 29–67; van Inwagen: "The
Place of Chance in a World Sustained by God," in *Divine and Human Action*, ed. T. Morris
(Ithaca: Cornell University Press, 1988); "The Magnitude, Duration, and Distri-

God: given that God *does* have a reason for permitting these evils, why think we would be the first to know? Given that he is omniscient and given our very substantial epistemic limitations, it isn't at all surprising that his reasons for some of what he does or permits completely escape us. But then from the fact that no goods we know of are such that we know that they justify God in (serve as his reasons for) permitting E_1 or E_2, it simply doesn't follow that it is probable, with respect to what we know, that there aren't any such goods, or that God has no reason for permitting those evils. The arguments in these papers seem to me to be conclusive; I shall not repeat them here.

More recently (and partly under the pressure of some of the works mentioned in footnote 10), Rowe has himself come to view this argument with a jaundiced eye: "I now think this argument is, at best, a weak argument."[11] He therefore sets this argument aside in favor of one whose prospects he thinks are brighter: "I propose to abandon this argument altogether and give what I believe is a better argument for thinking that P makes Q more likely than not" (p. 267). After giving *that* argument, Rowe goes on to say that "we can simplify the argument considerably by bypassing Q altogether and proceeding directly from P to -G" (p. 270). This new argument goes as follows. First, we must note that Rowe intends P in such a way that it is entailed by not-G; P is equivalent to

P' There is no perfect being and known good such that the latter justifies the former in permitting E_1 and E_2.

Rowe then assumes that P(G/k) and P(P/G&k) both equal .5 (where k is our background information—what all or most of us know or believe.) It then follows by the probability calculus that P(G/P&k) is considerably less than P(G/k); hence P disconfirms G. The argument thus simplified is Rowe's *new* evidential argument from evil. I regret to say, however, that this new argument is, if anything, weaker than the old. That is because an analysis of purely formal features of the argument shows that it is counterbalanced by other arguments of the same structure and strength for a conclusion inconsistent with Rowe's conclusion (and hence for the denial of Rowe's conclusion).[12] In essence, the problem is twofold.

---

bution of Evil: A Theodicy," *Philosophical Topics* (1988); "The Problem of Evil, the Problem of Air, and the Problem of Silence," *Philosophical Topics* (1991). One hopes these pieces will put the final quietus to the "I can't see what reason God could have for *p*; therefore, probably God doesn't have a reason for *p*" form of argument. (But of course they won't.)

11. See EAESL, p. 270.

12. For details, please consult my "Degenerate Evidence and Rowe's New Evidential Argument from Evil," *Noûs* 32, no. 4 (Dec. 1998); see also Rowe's reply in "Reply to Plantinga," *Noûs* 32, no. 4 (Dec. 1998).

First, Rowe's argument really depends on the fact (as already noted) that the conclusion he proposes to support, i.e.,

not-G There is no perfect being

entails P, the premise of his argument. Now the probability calculus tells us that if a proposition A entails a proposition B, then B confirms A in the sense that the probability of A on B conjoined with our background information k will exceed that of A on k *simpliciter* (unless either A or B has an absolute probability of 1). Thus any contingent consequence C of not-G will confirm not-G with respect to any body of background information k (k, of course, cannot include or entail C).

But then by the same token, any contingent consequence of G will confirm G with respect to any body of background information k. This means that Rowe's argument will be counterbalanced by other arguments—for example, one that takes as its premise any of the following propositions:

P* Neither E_1 nor E_2 is such that we know that no good justifies a perfect being in permitting it.

P** No evil we know of is such that we know that no perfect being is justified by some good in permitting it.

P*** No evil we know of is such that we know that no perfect being would permit it.

Presumably there will be as many arguments of this sort *for* G as there are arguments of Rowe's sort *against* G.

The second problem is like unto the first. Rowe's argument is really an "argument from degenerate evidence"—an argument in which you take as your new evidence, not the new proposition you learn, but a weaker consequence of it. We can see this as follows. Rowe's premise P is equivalent to

P' Either not-G or no good we know of is such that we know that it justifies E_1 and E_2,

where a good g justifies an evil e iff if there were a perfect being b, and g and e were actual, then b would be justified by g in permitting e.[13] (For example, perhaps a certain kind of moral growth on my part requires a certain amount of suffering; and perhaps we can see that a perfect being would be justified by that moral growth in permitting the suffering in question.) Now what we learn by reflecting on E_1 and E_2 (and other evils) and their relation to a perfect being is really

-J No good we know of is such that we know that it justifies E_1 and E_2.

Clearly enough, -J entails and is stronger than P', the premise of Rowe's argument. And the problem with arguments of this sort is that, once again, there will be other arguments of the same structure and strength for an incompatible conclusion. For example, suppose I win the Indiana

13. For the argument, see "Degenerate Evidence."

lottery (W). The probability of W with respect to k is very low, say one in a million. Now suppose I take as my new evidence not W, but

W or -G.

By an argument just like Rowe's,[14] we can show that the probability of -G on this premise together with the relevant background information is very high indeed—something like .999999. Of course there is a similar argument for G; here the premise will be

W or G.

Clearly, neither of these arguments makes any real advance, and that is because they counterbalance each other.

Rowe's argument from P to -G displays the same structure as this lottery argument. He proposes to argue for -G; our "new evidence" is really -J; but to get his premise P he weakens this new evidence by adding the conclusion of his argument, -G, as a disjunct, so that P is or is equivalent to the proposition -*J or -G*. That makes this an argument from degenerate evidence. To construct the counterbalancing argument we simply weaken -J by adding as a disjunct G, the proposition that there is a perfect being, rather than -G; this counterbalancing argument will be for the denial of Rowe's conclusion and will be as strong as his. Arguments from degenerate evidence, clearly enough, do not serve to advance the discussion.

B. Draper's Argument

Paul Draper presents an argument of quite a different sort.[15] He asks us to consider the pattern of pain and pleasure in the world: the amount and distribution of each and the sorts of conditions under which each is found. Draper then claims two things: first, this pattern of pain and pleasure is much less probable on theism than on a certain other hypothesis *h* inconsistent with theism; and second, this fact poses a serious problem for theistic belief. A way in which Draper's argument is superior to the Rowe variety is that it doesn't require that we be in a position to judge, with respect to any kinds of evils, the likelihood that an omniscient, omnipotent, and wholly good being would permit them. Nevertheless, he says, "Our knowledge about pain and pleasure creates an epistemic problem for theists" (p. 12). Why so, exactly?

14. Again, for details see "Degenerate Evidence."

15. See his "Pain and Pleasure: An Evidential Problem for Theists," *Noûs* 23 (1989), pp. 331 ff. (This work is reprinted in EAESL page references in the text are to this work). See also his "Evil and the Proper Basicality of Belief in God," *Faith and Philosophy* 8 (April 1991), pp. 135 ff.; "Probabilistic Arguments from Evil," *Religious Studies* 28, no. 3 (September 1992), pp. 285ff.; and "Evolution and the Problem of Evil," in Louis Pojman, ed., *Philosophy of Religion*, 3d ed. (Belmont, Calif.: Wadsworth, 1997).

1. Draper's Argument Initially Stated

The problem is not that some proposition about pain and pleasure can be shown to be both true and logically inconsistent with theism. Rather, the problem is evidential. A statement reporting the observations and testimony upon which our knowledge about pain and pleasure is based bears a certain significant negative evidential relation to theism. And because of this, we have a *prima facie* good epistemic reason to reject theism—that is, a reason that is sufficient for rejecting theism unless overridden by other reasons for not rejecting theism. (p. 12)

What is that statement, and what is the significant negative evidential relation it bears to theism? As for the statement:

Now let "O" stand for a statement reporting both the observations one has made of humans and animals experiencing pain or pleasure and the testimony one has encountered concerning the observations others have made of sentient beings experiencing pain and pleasure. By "pain" I mean physical or mental suffering of any sort. (pp. 13–14)

So O is the statement that bears a "significant negative evidential relation to theism." Note that O is person relative: each of us will have her own O, and my O may differ from yours. My O, we might say, sets out the facts about the magnitude, variety, distribution, duration, and the like (for short, the 'disposition') of pleasure and pain as *I* know them; yours does the same for *you*.

But what is this significant negative evidential relation in which O stands to theism? Here Draper bows in the direction of David Hume: most contemporary philosophers of religion (unlike Hume) "fail to recognize that one cannot determine what facts about evil theism needs to explain or how well it needs to explain them without considering alternatives to theism" (p. 13). The important question is "whether or not any serious hypothesis that is logically inconsistent with theism explains some significant set of facts about evil or about good and evil much better than theism does" (p. 13). And the answer to this important question, says Draper, is that indeed there is such a serious hypothesis, one that is both inconsistent with theism and explains some significant facts about good and evil much better than theism does. This is the "hypothesis of indifference" (HI, for short):

HI: Neither the nature nor the condition of sentient beings on earth is the result of benevolent or malevolent actions performed by non-human persons. (p. 13)[16]

---

16. In "Evolution and the Problem of Evil," he takes metaphysical naturalism—

HI, of course, is inconsistent with theism (taking the latter to entail that the world has been created by a person who is wholly good as well as omnipotent and omniscient). Draper's claim is that:

> C: HI explains the facts O reports much better than theism does. (p. 14)

He claims furthermore that if one could show that there is a serious hypothesis that is incompatible with theism and explains O much better than theism does, then "one would have a *prima facie* good reason to believe that this alternative hypothesis is more probable than theism and hence that theism is probably false."[17] What is it for a proposition to 'explain' something like the facts that O reports?

> I will reformulate C as the claim that the facts O reports are much more surprising on theism than they are on HI, or, more precisely, that the antecedent probability of O is much greater on the assumption that HI is true than on the assumption that theism is true. (p. 14)

I take it the more precise formulation is the operative one here; we aren't really talking about *explanation*[18] but just about the antecedent probabilities of O on theism and HI. Accordingly, we must ask what this 'antecedent probability' is. "By the 'antecedent' probability of O," says Draper, "I mean O's probability, independent of (rather than prior to) the observations and testimony it reports" (p. 14). So the antecedent probability of O is the probability of O on something like the rest of what I know.[19]

Finally, the probability in question is *epistemic* probability, not (for example) logical, statistical, or physical probability. And what is epistemic probability?

---

substantially, the view that there is no such person as God or anything much like God—to be the serious alternative hypothesis. My evaluation of Draper's approach does not depend on a choice between these two candidates for the post of serious alternative hypothesis.

17. "The Skeptical Theist" in EAESL, p. 178.

18. See William Alston's reply to Draper in "Some (Temporarily) Final Thoughts on Evidential Arguments from Evil," in EAESL, pp. 328–30.

19. Or perhaps on a noetic structure as similar as possible to mine that does not contain or entail O. This still isn't quite right: the noetic structure in question also can't contain or entail some proposition *almost as strong as* O. Perhaps we should think, then, of a noetic structure that contains no propositions about the distribution of pain and pleasure and is otherwise as similar as possible to mine. For possible difficulties with this notion, see Peter van Inwagen, "Reflections on the Chapters by Draper, Russell, and Gale" in EAESL, p. 222.

The concept of epistemic probability is an ordinary concept of probability for which no adequate philosophical analysis has, in my opinion, been proposed. As a first approximation, however, perhaps the following analysis will do:

> Relative to K, p is epistemically more probable than q, where K is an epistemic situation and p and q are propositions, just in case any fully rational person in K would have a higher degree of belief in p than in q. (p. 27, footnote 2)

As Draper says, epistemic probability is an ordinary concept that is difficult to analyze or explain; suppose we provisionally accept his proposed first approximation.[20] (I take it there is an implicit restriction to *human* persons; how things might go with other rational creatures is not our present concern.) What does K include? What goes into an epistemic situation? We shall have to return to this question later; for now, let's say initially that K, for a given person *S*, would include at least some of the other propositions *S* believes, as well as the experiences *S* is undergoing and perhaps has undergone; it would also include what *S* remembers, possibly a specification of *S*'s epistemic environment, and no doubt more besides.

Now we see the general shape of the argument: the first premise is C, the claim that the antecedent epistemic probability of O given HI is much greater than the antecedent probability of O given theism. And second, if C is true, says Draper, then "we have a *prima facie* good epistemic reason to reject theism—that is, a reason that is sufficient for rejecting theism unless overridden by other reasons for not rejecting theism" (p. 12). Here he is apparently relying on a general principle, perhaps something like

(1) For any propositions *P* and *Q* and person *S*, if *S* believes *P* and *Q* and there is a serious hypothesis *R* that is incompatible with *P* and such that the antecedent epistemic probability of *Q* with respect to *R* for *S* is much greater than the antecedent epistemic probability of *Q* with respect to *P* for *S*, then *S* has a *prima facie* good epistemic reason to reject *P*.

Draper's claim is that the antecedent epistemic probability of O on HI is much greater than on theism, and because HI is a serious hypothesis and is inconsistent with theism, we have a *prima facie* good reason for rejecting theism:

> Now suppose I succeed in showing that C is true (relative to our own and my reader's epistemic situations.) Then the truth of C is (for us) a *prima facie* good (epistemic) reason to believe that theism is less probable than HI. Thus, since the denial of theism is obvi-

---

20. For a fuller account of a closely related notion (epistemic conditional probability), see chapters 8 and 9 of *Warrant and Proper Function* (hereafter WPF).

ously entailed by HI and so is at least as probable as HI, the truth of C is a *prima facie* good reason to believe that theism is less probable than not. And since it is epistemically irrational to believe both that theism is true and that it is less probable than not, the truth of C is also a *prima facie* good reason to reject (i.e., to cease or refrain from believing) theism. (p. 14)

The claim, then, is that the truth of C gives me a *"prima facie* good reason to believe that theism is less probable than not"—that is, that its probability is less than .5. Less probable than not with respect to *what*? The answer must be K. The idea is that the truth of C gives me a *prima facie* good reason for thinking that theism is improbable with respect to my noetic situation; hence, unless I can find some reasons *for* theism, the rational thing to do is to give it up.[21] We could put this by saying that, according to Draper, my knowledge of the truth of C gives me a defeater for theism, unless I can find some reasons for it; alternatively, it gives me a potential defeater for theism, a potential defeater that will be *actual* unless I can find those reasons for theism.

2. On Being Evidentially Challenged

This is a subtle challenge and a fascinating new entry into the lists; Draper deploys it with power and sophistication. Nevertheless I think the argument utterly fails to show that traditional Christian theism is threatened by a defeater or epistemologically threatened in some other way. Suppose we take a closer look. Now Draper's argument really has two premises, C and (1). I have argued elsewhere[22] that in fact C is false: it is not the case that the amount, duration, and distribution of pain and pleasure, as I understand it, are more probable on HI than on theism. Here I want to focus on the other premise, the claim that if, in fact, O is much more likely on a serious alternative hypothesis like HI than on theism, then the theist has a *prima facie* reason to reject theism. Why think a thing like that? Suppose (contrary to fact, as I see it) C were true: what kind and how much of a challenge to theistic belief would this be? How widespread

21. In "Evolution and the Problem of Evil," Draper puts the same thought slightly differently; speaking of a similar argument, he says, "This is why my case against theism is a *prima facie* one. I am entitled to conclude only that *other evidence held equal* . . . it is highly probable that theism is false." What is it to hold other evidence equal? Here's a suggestion: it would be to consider the probability of theism with respect to an evidential situation that was as similar as possible to mine, given that it contained no evidence for or against theistic belief, or given that the evidence it contained for theistic belief was precisely balanced by the evidence it contained against theistic belief.

22. "On Being Evidentially Challenged," EAESL, pp. 250ff.

is this alleged evidential disability? Before we can answer this question, however, we must ask another: what, exactly, is a *serious* alternative hypothesis? Draper's answer: "Specifically, one hypothesis is a 'serious' alternative to another only if (i) it is not *ad hoc*—the facts to be explained are not arbitrarily built into it—and (ii) it is at least as plausible initially as the other hypothesis."[23] Condition (i) requires no present comment; what about condition (ii)? How are we to understand 'plausibility' here? I think Draper means to abstract from specific epistemic situations: we are to think of the plausibility of a hypothesis as depending not on considerations such as the specific evidence (propositional and nonpropositional) I may have for or against it, but on more general considerations such as its scope and specificity, and perhaps how it fits in with what is generally known (a hypothesis entailing that the world is flat wouldn't be plausible). Thus, for example, he defends the plausibility of HI as follows:

> And it [HI] is at least as plausible initially as G [i.e., theism]. After all, G is a very specific supernaturalist hypothesis with strong ontological commitments. If, on the other hand, we take the Indifference Hypothesis to be the hypothesis that the first causes of the universe, *if there are any*, are neither benevolent nor malevolent, then the Indifference Hypothesis is consistent with naturalism as well as with many supernaturalist hypotheses and its ontological commitments are much weaker than G's.[24]

So what counts for plausibility are these general facts about relative scope and strength. Still further, if I had to consider the *specific* evidence I have (propositional or otherwise) for HI to evaluate its plausibility, I would have to take any reasons I have *for* theism as evidence *against* HI; HI might then be very implausible for me. So plausibility must abstract from such specific evidence.

Suppose we say that a proposition P is *evidentially challenged* for S if it satisfies the antecedent of (1): P is evidentially challenged for a person S if and only if S believes P and there are propositions Q and R such that S believes Q, R is a serious hypothesis incompatible with P, and Q is much more probable with respect to R than with respect to P. What (1) claims, therefore, is that if a proposition P is evidentially challenged for S, then S has a *prima facie* good epistemic reason for rejecting P—for being agnostic with respect to it or believing its denial. Is this really true? Is being evidentially challenged a serious handicap?

Well, how widespread is it? How many of my beliefs *are* evidentially challenged, for me? More, perhaps, than we might initially think. For example, here are three more propositions related, for me, as are theism, O and HI:

---

23. "Probabilistic Arguments from Evil," pp. 315–16.
24. Ibid., p. 316.

(2) George is a non-Catholic academic,

(3) George is a professor at Notre Dame,

and

(4) George is a Catholic academic.

First, I believe both (2) and (3). Second, (3) is vastly more likely on (4) (relative to K) than it is on (2). (After all, the proportion of Catholic academics who are professors at Notre Dame is many times greater than that of non-Catholic academics who are professors there.) Further, (4) is incompatible with (2). Still further, (4) is a serious hypothesis: it is not *ad hoc*, and it is as plausible as (2). (True, I have a lot of evidence for (2) — the fact, e.g., that George is an elder in the Christian Reformed Church, which is non-Catholic, the fact that George has always claimed to be a Protestant, and so on — but as we saw above, this specific evidence isn't relevant to the plausibility of (4).) So (2) is evidentially challenged for me. Does this fact give me a good reason to reject it? (Should I reconsider: George *is* a professor at Notre Dame, after all, and that is much more likely on (4) than on (2); so maybe he's really a Catholic?) Not clearly.

A similar trio of propositions:

(2*) I am in my study,

(3*) I am within four feet of a dog,

and

(4*) I am at the dog pound.

Again, I believe (2*) and (3*); (4*) is a serious (in Draper's sense) alternative to (2*), and (3*) is much more likely on (4*) than it is on (2*) (usually there aren't any dogs in my study); therefore (2*) is evidentially challenged for me. So, incidentally, is (3*) itself:

(3*) I am within four feet of a dog,

(5) I hear no doggie sounds such as barking, growling, panting, or jingling of tags,

and

(6) I am not within earshot of any dogs.

Again, (6) is a serious alternative hypothesis to (3*), and (5) is much more likely with respect to (6) than it is with respect to (3*). (3*), therefore, is evidentially challenged for me. A couple of more examples: my friend has a cat named Maynard; I believe that Maynard is a cat and also (as my friend reports) that Maynard likes cooked green beans; the latter, however, is much more likely on the serious (in Draper's sense) alternative hypothesis that Maynard is a Frisian, or possibly a Frenchman; so the belief that Maynard is a cat is evidentially challenged for me. I believe (naturally enough) that you are a human being; you and I are on a walk in the woods, however, so I also believe that you are in a forest; of course that proposition is vastly more likely on the serious alternative hypothesis that you are a tree; so the belief that you are a human being is evidentially challenged for me. (As far as that goes, so is the belief that *I* am a human being.)

I think you get the picture. It seems likely that most of what we believe—at any rate for propositions that are contingent in the broadly logical sense—is also evidentially challenged. I don't know how to give a *proof* of this claim (it probably isn't worth spending a whole lot of time trying to find a proof); but it certainly seems likely to be the case. And this suggests that a challenge of this sort is not very significant *by itself* or *in the general case*. If most of the propositions I believe face an evidential challenge, then I don't learn much of interest about theism by learning that it, too, faces such a challenge.

Under what conditions (if any) would a challenge of this sort *be* significant? What sorts of beliefs are such that their being subject to an evidential challenge gives us serious reason to doubt them? Here we think first of scientific hypotheses. I propose a hypothesis H^* to explain the behavior of gases: you point out that certain data are more probable with respect to another hypothesis H' incompatible with mine; that certainly seems to be a strong *prima facie* reason to doubt my hypothesis. Of course the data must be *relevant* data, the sort of data H^* is in the business of explaining. Suppose Sam presently feels a mild pain in his left knee. That is much less probable with respect to H^* than with respect to the hypothesis H': *Overcome by astonishment at learning that H^* is false, Sam fell and injured his knee*; still, that is nothing whatever against H^*. For the typical scientific hypothesis H, there will be a body of relevant data (past and future as well as present) such that the success of H depends on how well it explains that data; and many scientific hypotheses (at least on the most usual stories) get all or nearly all of their warrant from the fact that they account for the relevant data.[25] A proposition of that sort is seriously threatened by a relevant evidential challenge. If I discover that a belief of *this* sort is subject to an evidential challenge, then I do have substantial evidence against it and a strong *prima facie* reason to give it up.

---

25. At any rate nearly all of its *original* warrant. Special relativity, for example, gets its warrant *for me*, not from the fact that it properly accounts for those data, but from the fact that I have been *told* and *believe* that it does (in such a way as to satisfy the conditions for warrant). But if those conditions are indeed satisfied, then there must be someone at the other end of the testimonial chain for whom these beliefs have warrant in some way other than by testimony. See WPF, chapter 4.

As I have argued throughout this book, however, it is an enormous assumption to think that belief in God or, more broadly, the larger set of Christian (or Jewish or Muslim) beliefs of which belief in God is a part, is in this respect like a scientific hypothesis. Not only is this assumption enormous: it is also false. The warrant for these beliefs, if they have warrant, does not derive from the fact (if it is a fact) that they properly explain some body of data. For most believers, theistic belief is part of a larger whole (a Christian or Muslim or Jewish whole); it is accepted as part of that larger whole and is not ordinarily accepted because it is an *explanation* of anything; hence its rationality or warrant, if it has some, does not depend on its nicely explaining some body of data.[26]

Still, does this fact, crucially important as it is, deliver theism from Draper's evidential challenge? Is it *only* scientific hypotheses for which (relevant) evidential challenges are serious? No. Suppose you are under the impression that your friend Paul has been vacationing on Cape Cod for the last couple of weeks (you have a rather weak memory that this is where he said he was going), but the postcards you get from him were mailed from Grand Teton National Park; he doesn't say in the postcards where he is, but he does note the remarkably dry air, as well as the great differences between day and night temperatures. Then I think your belief that he is vacationing at Cape Cod is seriously challenged (a relevant alternative hypothesis being that he is vacationing in the Tetons). And this is true even though the warrant for your belief that he was vacationing on the cape didn't arise as a result of its properly explaining data of one kind or another. So it isn't just scientific hypotheses that can be called into question by virtue of facing a relevant evidential challenge.

Suppose we look a bit deeper here. That I am in my study (and not at the dog pound), that Maynard is a cat, that you are a human being—these are all subject to an evidential challenge; of course that doesn't suggest for a moment that there is something irrational or problematic in these beliefs, or that they are improbable with respect to our epistemic situations. Why not? Because each of these propositions has a good deal of warrant for me, warrant that is independent of its probabilistic relationships to the beliefs involved in the evidential challenges. In cases like this, being evidentially challenged comes to very little. And it isn't even necessary that the belief in question have a *high* degree of warrant. I believe rather infirmly (I have a relatively weak memory belief here) that the population of greater New York City is more than 17 million; I also believe that the area of

26. See my "Is Theism Really a Miracle?" and see above, pp. 330ff. I don't mean to deny, of course, that Christian or theistic belief can get more warrant by nicely explaining something else one believes.

greater New York City is 1,384 square miles; that proposition is many times more likely with respect to the serious alternative hypothesis that the population of New York City is less than 10 million. My belief that the population of New York City is more than 17 million is therefore subject to an evidential challenge; that fact doesn't provide me with a *prima facie* defeater for it, even though it doesn't have a high degree of warrant. Perhaps most of what I believe faces an evidential challenge, but most of what I believe (so one thinks) also has warrant of one kind or another; and when it does, an evidential challenge doesn't amount to much. With respect to most of what I believe, being evidentially challenged does not threaten to serve as a defeater for the proposition in question, and neither does my knowing, if I do, that it is evidentially challenged. Neither the challenge nor the knowledge, in the case of the propositions mentioned, puts me in a condition where, if I continue to believe the challenged proposition, I am irrational or in some other way out of line, epistemically speaking. And that is because the propositions in question get warrant from such sources as perception, memory, sympathy, testimony, *a priori* intuition, and the like; they do not depend, for their warrant, on their relation to such propositions as those furnishing the evidential challenge.

Well then, how does it stand with theism? According to Draper, "Establishing the truth of H [that theistic belief faces an evidential challenge] would be insignificant if the typical theist could rationally continue to believe that God exists after learning that H is true."[27] What I propose to argue here is that the typical theist *can* rationally continue to believe that God exists after learning that theism faces an evidential challenge. Suppose I accept traditional Christian belief, including, of course, theistic belief. Now suppose I come to believe that in fact theistic belief is subject to an evidential challenge. I don't as a matter of fact believe that the pattern of pain and pleasure in the world does provide such a challenge—at any rate I don't think Draper's argument for this conclusion is successful—but suppose I come to believe that there is an evidential challenge of this or some other kind for Christian or theistic belief. Would that give me a defeater for my theistic belief? Would it make it irrational for me to continue believing?

Not if that belief has any significant degree of warrant for me. Suppose Christian and theistic belief has a good deal of warrant for me by way of faith and the internal instigation of the Holy Spirit (IIHS) (see above pp. 249ff.); then the fact that theism is evidentially challenged doesn't give me a defeater and doesn't bring it about that

---

27. "Evil and the Proper Basicality of Belief in God," p. 138.

my theistic belief is irrational. Compare the case of Maynard and my belief that he is a cat. You point out that this belief suffers from an evidential challenge: that he likes cooked green beans is much less likely on his being a cat than on his being a Frisian. I agree, but am undeterred, continuing in full rationality to believe that he is indeed a cat. This belief is rational for me in these circumstances because it has warrant for me quite independent of its relationship to the proposition that Maynard likes cooked green beans. There is of course no cognitive malfunction involved in my continuing to hold a belief with significant warrant from such sources as memory, perception, IIHS, and the like, even when I learn that the belief is subject to an evidential challenge. Our cognitive design plan permits, indeed, requires maintaining such a belief in the face of such a "challenge." And clearly the same goes for my theistic belief, if, in fact, it has warrant in the way proposed in chapter 8.

And this is true even if I don't myself *believe* that theistic belief has warrant for me. Perhaps I have never thought much about epistemology, have at best a hazy idea as to what warrant is, and have never considered such questions as whether a proposition's being evidentially challenged gives me a reason for rejecting it. You point out that my belief that Maynard is a cat is evidentially challenged; I continue (in my epistemological innocence) to believe as firmly as before that Maynard is a cat; neither the rationality nor the warrant of that belief is diminished. Again, the same goes for theistic belief, if it has significant warrant for me. You point out that theism is evidentially challenged for me: I agree that that is so and continue to believe as firmly as before; if Christian belief and hence theism *do* have significant warrant for me, my continuing so to believe is wholly rational and remains warranted. It is perfectly rational, internally, because it still seems obviously true to me; it is perfectly rational, externally, because the belief in question is held under the conditions of warrant. If it had sufficient warrant for knowledge before you made your point about its being evidentially challenged, it still has sufficient warrant.

So if theistic belief has significant warrant for me, then (in the typical case and provided I do not believe that it lacks warrant) my coming to believe that it faces an evidential challenge does not provide me with a defeater for it. Here we see a special case of a pattern we have seen before. I argued in chapters 6 and 8 that if theistic and Christian belief is true, then very likely it has warrant. A consequence is that if Christian belief is true, then very likely (in the typical case) an evidential challenge to theism is an insignificant challenge.

But even if theism has little or no warrant, it could still be (and in the typical case would still be) that an evidential challenge doesn't provide a real challenge or a *prima facie* defeater. Analogy: perhaps I am once more told by my friend that she has a pet named Maynard who is a cat but nonetheless loves cooked green beans; having never met this Maynard, I believe on the basis of my friend's testimony that Maynard is a cat. As it turns out, my friend is indulging (unbeknownst to me) her penchant for telling whimsical (and false) stories. Then my belief that Maynard is a cat has little by way of warrant: the epistemic minienvironment (see above, pp. 158ff.) isn't right, being polluted by my friend's thus lying to me, so that the environmental condition for warrant is not met. Still, my belief that Maynard is a cat is (all else being equal) entirely rational (even if not warranted), both internally and externally; and that holds even though I am quite aware that it is evidentially challenged. The same can be true for theistic belief. Perhaps I mistakenly but rationally believe that it has warrant; I rationally believe that some of the theistic arguments, for example, are very strong, or I believe, mistakenly, in some story like the one told in chapters 6 and 8, according to which theistic belief does indeed have warrant. Under those conditions, my theistic belief does not, in fact, have warrant; nevertheless, my learning that it is subject to an evidential challenge does not compromise its rationality and does not give me a defeater for it.

So when *could* a belief's being evidentially challenged (more exactly, my knowledge that it is evidentially challenged) actually offer me a defeater for a belief and make it irrational for me to continue to hold it? I can see two sorts of cases in which learning that theism is subject to an evidential challenge could be a defeater for it. First, suppose I am a theist, am rational in accepting this belief, but hold it with little firmness and furthermore think my reasons for it are absolutely minimal—barely sufficient for holding the belief rationally. Then if I learn that theism is subject to an evidential challenge, perhaps I have a defeater for it. I say 'perhaps' advisedly; the situation isn't really clear.

The second sort of situation is clearer. Consider a belief *B* I accept because I think it the best explanation of a certain range of data *D*; *B* has no warrant apart from its properly explaining *D*, and I am aware of this fact. Finding that *B* is subject to an evidential challenge, one thinks, gives me a defeater for it—provided that the belief that is more probable with respect to the alternative hypothesis is one that *B* is supposed to explain. I believe the butler did it: my only reason for so believing is that this hypothesis best explains all the facts and circumstances of the crime. Now I come to see that the hypothesis that Lady Fauntleroy did the deed better explains some of those facts and circumstances.[28] Then my belief that the butler did it faces a relevant evidential challenge, a challenge which is *prima facie* a defeater

---

28. And in this context perhaps we can gloss 'explanation' in terms of probability.

for that belief. (Of course it doesn't matter if some alternative hypothesis better explains the fact that Beijing is a large city.) So suppose I accept theism as a hypothesis; I accept it because I think it the best explanation of some range of phenomena including the origin of the universe, the reality and objectivity of right and wrong, and also the distribution of pain and pleasure. Suppose, furthermore, I rightly believe that I have no other sort of reason for theistic belief—no promptings from the IIHS, or from the *sensus divinitatis*, or from the testimony of others. I believe that I have no other source and am correct in that belief. Now suppose I come to think that the Indifference Hypothesis, or naturalism, or something else does a better job of explaining the magnitude, duration, and distribution of pain and pleasure; then my theistic belief would be subject to an evidential challenge, a challenge that is *prima facie* a defeater for theistic belief and a reason for giving it up. (Even then, however, I might conclude that theism did a better job of explaining some *other* relevant phenomena.)

So there are some situations in which an evidential challenge—not just any old evidential challenge, but a relevant one—does furnish a defeater: cases where someone believes that the warrant enjoyed by his theistic belief is minimal, and cases where he believes that the warrant theism has for him depends just on its explaining a certain range of phenomena. Most theists, however, are not in either of these conditions. Are there other conditions in which theists often find themselves, conditions in which coming to see that theism faces an evidential challenge really does provide a defeater or a *prima facie* defeater for theistic belief? I doubt very much that the typical theist is in any such condition. I therefore think Draper's challenge, subtle and sophisticated as it is, fails; in his own words, "the typical theist could rationally continue to believe that God exists after learning that H [that theism is evidentially challenged] is true."

II. NONARGUMENTATIVE DEFEATERS?[29]

These new arguments by Rowe and Draper are subtle and sophisticated; many deep and interesting topics come up in considering them. Upon close examination, however, they fail, and fail resoundingly. They fail to provide a defeater for theistic belief and, indeed, give the person on the fence little if any reason to prefer atheism to theism. They are not much of an improvement over the older "if I can't see any reason God might have for permitting that evil E, then

29. In writing this section I am indebted to John Cooper (sermon in South Bend Christian Reformed Church, 2/28/92), John Haas (sermon in SBCRC, 5/5/97), and Leonard Vander Zee (sermon in SBCRC, 1/5/97).

probably he doesn't have any" kind of argument. If the facts of evil really do provide a substantial challenge to Christian or theistic belief, it must be by a wholly different route; the probabilistic relationships to which Rowe and Draper point do not carry sufficient epistemic clout. And indeed the fact is most defeaters do not proceed by way of the subject's becoming aware of probabilistic relationships. I have always thought your name was Sam: you tell me that Sam is only your nickname and that your name is really Ahab; I then give up the belief that your name is Sam. But I don't do so because I think that your name's being Sam is unlikely, given that you say it is Ahab, or that it is more probable that you would say your name is Ahab on the hypothesis that it is Ahab than on the hypothesis that it is Sam. The defeat doesn't seem to go via probabilistic argumentation. I see what I take to be a patch of snow on a distant crag; as I approach a bit closer, however, the patch apparently moves; I no longer believe it is a patch of snow—perhaps it's a mountain goat? Again, I don't engage in probabilistic reasoning. I thought your zip code was 49506; then I get a letter from you with a return address that includes zip code 49508; I no longer believe that it is 49506, but not because of probabilistic reasoning. In most actual cases of defeat, probabilistic reasoning apparently doesn't enter in.

And perhaps something similar holds with respect to evil. There is no cogent argument for the conclusion that the existence of evil is incompatible with the existence of God; there is also no serious evidential or probabilistic argument from evil; fair enough. It doesn't follow that suffering and evil do not constitute a serious obstacle to Christian belief or theistic belief, and it doesn't follow that they do not constitute a defeater for it. I have argued throughout that belief in God can be properly basic; rational belief in God does not depend on one's having or there being good arguments for the existence of God. Should something analogous be said for the facts of evil, thought of as a potential defeater for theistic belief? Perhaps the defeating power of these facts in no way depends on the existence of a good antitheistic argument (deductive, inductive, abductive, probabilistic, whatever) from the facts of evil.

Clearly enough, suffering and evil do constitute *some* kind of problem for at least *some* believers in God; the Old Testament (in particular Job and Psalms) is full of examples. Indeed, there is the agonized cry uttered by Jesus Christ himself: "My God, my God, why have you forsaken me?"—a cry in which he is echoing the words of Psalm 22. In the book of Job, a searching and powerful exploration of the facts of evil and human responses to them, Job thinks God is unfair to him; he is incensed, and challenges God to explain and justify himself. Countless others, in the grip of their own cruel suffering or the suffering of someone close to them, have found themselves angry with God; one can become resentful, mistrusting, antagonistic, hostile. Still, these situations don't typically produce a defeater for theistic belief. It isn't as if Jesus, or the psalmist, or Job is at all inclined to give up theistic belief. The problem is of a different order; it is a spiritual or pastoral problem rather than a defeater for theistic belief. Perhaps God permits my father, or my daughter, or my friend, or me to suffer in the most appalling way. I may then find myself thinking as follows: "No doubt he has all those dandy divine qualities and no doubt he has a fine reason for permitting this abomination—after all, I am no match for him with respect to coming up with reasons, reasons that are utterly beyond me—but what he permits is appalling, and I hate it!" I may want to tell him off face to face: "You may be wonderful, and magnificent, and omniscient and omnipotent (and even wholly good) and all that exalted stuff, but I utterly detest what you are doing!" A problem of this kind is not really an evidential problem at all, and it isn't a defeater for theism.

Still, perhaps that's not the only realistic reaction here: perhaps I *could* react in this way, but aren't there other reactions in which I would have a defeater? Couldn't suffering and evil, under some circumstances, at any rate, actually serve as a defeater for belief in God? Think of some of the horrifying examples of evil our sad world displays. Dostoevski's classic depiction is fictional, but no less convincing and no less disturbing:

> "A Bulgarian I met lately in Moscow," Ivan went on, seeming not to hear his brothers words, "told me about the crimes committed by Turks and Circassians in all parts of Bulgaria through fear of a general rising of the Slavs. They burn villages, murder, outrage women and children, they nail their prisoners by the ears to the fences, leave them so till morning, and in the morning they hang them— all sorts of things you can't imagine. People talk sometimes of bestial cruelty, but that's a great injustice and insult to the beasts: a beast can never be so cruel as a man, so artistically cruel. The tiger only tears and gnaws, that's all he can do. He would never think of nailing people by the ears, even if he were able to do it. These Turks took a pleasure in torturing children, too; cutting the unborn child from the mother's womb, and tossing babies up in the air and catching them on the points of their bayonets before their mother's eyes. Doing it before the mother's eyes was what gave zest to the amusement."[30]

The list of atrocities human beings commit against others is horrifying and hideous; it is also so long, so repetitious, that it is finally wearying. Occasionally, though, new depths are reached:

---

30. *The Brothers Karamazov*, tr. Constance Garnett (New York: Random House, 1933), pp. 245–46.

A young Muslim mother in Bosnia was repeatedly raped in front of her husband and father, with her baby screaming on the floor beside her. When her tormentors seemed finally tired of her, she begged permission to nurse the child. In response, one of the rapists swiftly decapitated the baby and threw the head in the mother's lap.[31]

These things are absolutely horrifying; it is painful even to consider them, to bring them squarely before the mind. To introduce them into cool philosophical discussion like this is distressing and can seem inappropriate, even callous. And now the question: wouldn't a rational person think, in the face of this kind of appalling evil, that there just couldn't be an omnipotent, omniscient, and wholly good person superintending our world? Perhaps he can't give a demonstration that no perfect person could permit these things; perhaps there isn't a good probabilistic or evidential atheological argument either: but so what? Isn't it just apparent, just evident that a being living up to God's reputation couldn't permit things like that? Don't I have a defeater here, even if there is no good antitheistic argument from evil? Perhaps I don't in fact give up belief in God in the face of the facts of evil: might that not be because I simply can't bear the thought of living in a Godless universe? Because of some psychological mechanism not aimed at the truth, perhaps the sort of wish-fulfillment Freud suggests? If so, then suffering and evil (or rather, my apprehension of it) would or could be a defeater,[32] for me, for Christian belief, even though it doesn't eventuate in my giving up such belief.

Something like this, I think, is the best version of the atheological case from evil. The claim is essentially that one who is properly sensitive and properly aware of the sheer horror of the evil displayed in our somber and unhappy world will simply see that no being of the sort God is alleged to be could possibly permit it. This is a sort of inverse *sensus divinitatis*: perhaps there is no good antitheistic argument from evil; but no argument is needed. An appeal of this sort will proceed, not by rehearsing arguments, but by putting the interlocutor in the sort of situation in which the full horror of the world's suffering and evil stands out clearly in all its loathsomeness. Indeed, from the atheological point of view, giving an argument is counterproductive here: it permits the believer in God to turn his attention away, to avert his eyes from the abomination of suffering, to take refuge in antiseptic discussions of possible worlds, probability functions, and other arcana. It diverts attention from the situations that in fact constitute a defeater for belief in God.

---

31. Eleonore Stump, "The Mirror of Evil," in *God and the Philosophers*, ed. Thomas Morris (New York: Oxford University Press, 1994), p. 239.
32. A "purely epistemic" defeater; see above, p. 363.

Suppose we look into this claim. Recall first that a defeater for a belief is *relative to a noetic structure*; whether my new belief *B* is a defeater for an old belief *B** depends upon what else I believe and what my experience is like. I believe that tree is a maple; you tell me it's really an elm; that will defeat my belief that it's a maple if I think you know what you are talking about and aim to tell the truth, but not if I think you are even less arboreally informed than I, or that there is only a fifty-fifty chance that you are telling what you take to be the truth. Coming to see the full horror of the evil the world displays might be a defeater for theistic belief with respect to *some* noetic structure and not with respect to *others*.

What I want to argue first is that if classical Christianity is true, then the perception of evil is not a defeater for belief in God with respect to *fully rational* noetic structures—any noetic structure with no cognitive dysfunction, one in which all cognitive faculties and processes are functioning properly. From the point of view of classical Christianity (at any rate according to the model of chapters 6 and 8), this includes also the proper function of the *sensus divinitatis*. Someone in whom this process was functioning properly would have an intimate, detailed, vivid, and explicit knowledge of God; she would have an intense awareness of his presence, glory, goodness, power, perfection, wonderful attractiveness, and sweetness; and she would be as convinced of God's existence as of her own. She might therefore be *perplexed* by the existence of this evil in God's world—for God, she knows, hates evil with a holy and burning passion—but the idea that perhaps there just *wasn't* any such person as God would no doubt not so much as cross her mind. Confronted with evil and suffering, such a person might ask herself why God permits it; the facts of evil may be a spur to inquiry as well as to action. If she finds no answer, she will no doubt conclude that God has a reason that is beyond her ken; she won't be in the least inclined to doubt that there *is* such a person as God. For someone fully rational, therefore, the existence of evil doesn't so much as begin to constitute a defeater for belief in God.

In an earlier piece of work I explained epistemic conditional probability (roughly, and ignoring complications and qualifications) as follows:

> The conditional epistemic probability of *A* on *B*, then, initially and to a first approximation, is the degree to which a rational person, a person whose faculties are functioning properly, would accept *A* given that she was certain of *B*, knew that she accepted *B*, reflectively considered *A* in the light of *B*, and had no other source of warrant or positive epistemic status for *A* or for its denial.[33]

33. "Epistemic Probability and Evil," in *Archivo di Filosofia*, ed. Marco Olivetti (Rome: Cedam, 1988), p. 574.

Then (no doubt because of youth, inexperience, and epistemic innocence) I went on to say that perhaps the existence of God *was* in this
sense epistemically improbable on the existence of certain sorts of evil
(p. 576).

But first, that account of epistemic probability doesn't have this result—more exactly, it doesn't clearly apply in this case, or any case
where a belief has positive epistemic status or warrant for a person S just
by virtue of S's being rational in the sense in question.[34] On the extended Aquinas/Calvin (A/C) model, the *sensus divinitatis* is among our
cognitive faculties or processes; if it is functioning properly in S, then
the belief that there is such a person as God will automatically have warrant for S. Applied to the existence of God taken as A and that of any
sort of evil as B, the definition will not yield the consequence that the
former is improbable on the latter; that is because the condition expressed by the last clause in the definition, "and had no other source of
warrant or positive epistemic status for A or for its denial," will not be
satisfied by belief in the existence of God, if the believer's cognitive faculties are functioning properly.

Further: consider a person S in whom the *sensus divinitatis* does not,
in fact, function properly; S has only a sort of weak and *pro forma* resid-
ual belief in God, left over from the religion of his childhood. Add that
S suffers just from *that* cognitive malfunction (and no other). Now suppose S becomes seriously aware of the facts of evil and thinks about
them in connection with the existence of God: perhaps, given these conditions, S will give up belief in God, or come to think it improbable with
respect to his evidence. Would it follow that the facts of evil are in some
sense negative evidence with respect to the existence of God, evidence
that is counterbalanced and outweighed in a fully rational noetic structure by the positive evidence provided by a properly functioning *sensus
divinitatis*? No. For perhaps various modules of the cognitive establishment are designed to work together. If so, the deliverances of one module m that isn't itself subject to dysfunction might still have no epistemic
standing, given the failure of *another* module m^*. m's functioning in this
way—that is, the way it functions when there is malfunction of m^* but
no malfunction in m, given the malfunction of m^*—might not be part of
the design plan at all. When the electric current is fluctuating because of
a problem in the wiring, the air raid siren emits a weak and pathetic
squeak; it doesn't follow that the vibrating disk that produces the sound
is designed to produce that squeak under those conditions. True, it is
designed in such a way that in fact it *will* produce that squeak then; but
its doing so is not part of the design plan. Its functioning in this way
under those conditions will of course be part of its *maxi*plan (WPF, pp.
22ff.). It does not follow that its behaving in this way is part of its design
plan; that behavior might be, instead, an unintended by-product rather
than part of the design plan itself. And the same goes for the *sensus
divinitatis* and the other processes actually involved in the production or

---

34. Here I am deeply indebted to Richard Otte.

suppression of theistic belief. Perhaps the *sensus divinitatis* and the '*sensus probabilitatis*' are designed to work together as a unit; if so, the deliverances of one in the presence of the malfunction of the other need not enjoy any degree of rationality or warrant at all. Hence the sort of situation envisaged doesn't show that the facts of evil are any kind of evidence against the existence of God.

On the A/C model, therefore, the facts of evil do not constitute any sort of defeater for theistic belief for a fully *rational* person, one all of whose cognitive faculties are functioning properly. Nevertheless (so the wily atheologian will claim), that fact is at best of dubious relevance with respect to the question whether Christian believers in God—the ones there actually are—have a defeater for theism in the world's ills. For according to Christian doctrine itself, none of us human beings enjoys this pristine condition of complete rationality. The *sensus divinitatis* has been heavily damaged by sin; for most of us most of the time the presence of God is not evident. For many of us (much of the time, anyway) both God's existence and his goodness are a bit shadowy and evanescent, nowhere nearly as evident as the existence of other people or the trees in the backyard. Relative to a fully rational noetic structure (one of an unfallen human being, say), knowledge of the facts of evil may constitute no defeater for theism; relative to the sorts of noetic structures we human beings actually have, however (so the claim goes), they do. Given the noetic results of sin (see chapter 7), the typical believer in God does have a defeater in the facts of evil.

To pursue this line, however, would be to neglect still another feature of Christian belief: that the damage to the *sensus divinitatis* is in principle and increasingly repaired in the process of faith (see chapter 8) and regeneration. The person of faith may be once more such that, at least on some occasions, the presence of God is completely evident to her. In addition, she knows of the divine love revealed in the incarnation, the unthinkable splendor of the suffering and death of Jesus Christ, himself the divine and unique son of God, on our behalf. Of course this knowledge does not provide an answer to the question, Why does God permit evil? It is nonetheless of crucial importance here.[35] I read of one more massive atrocity and am perhaps

35. As Albert Camus (hardly an unambiguous defender of Christian belief) clearly recognized. Christ, says Camus, is the solution to the problems of evil and death:

His solution consisted, first, in experiencing them. The god-man suffers too, with patience. Evil and death can no longer be entirely imputed to him

shaken. But then I think of the inconceivably great love displayed in Christ's suffering and death, his willingness to empty himself and take on the nature of a servant, his willingness to suffer and die so that we sinful human beings can achieve redemption; and my faith may be restored. I still can't imagine why God permits this suffering, or why he permits people to torture and kill each other, or why he permits gigantic and horrifying social experiments such as Nazism and communism, or why he permits a Holocaust; nevertheless I see that he is willing to share in our suffering, to undergo enormous suffering himself, and to undergo it for our sakes. Confronted with a particularly loathsome example of evil, therefore, I may find myself inclined to question God, perhaps even to be angry and resentful: "Why should I or my family suffer to promote his (no doubt exalted) ends, when I don't have even a glimmer of an idea as to how my suffering contributes to some good?" But then I think of the divine willingness to endure greater suffering on my behalf and am comforted or, at any rate, quieted. And here is a respect in which Christian theism has a resource for dealing with evil that is not available to other forms of theism.[36] Note that probabilities have little to do with the matter. Such a person doesn't reason thus: it's not very likely that an omnipotent, omniscient, and wholly good person would permit such atrocities— but it's more likely that such a being who was himself willing to undergo suffering on our behalf would permit them. The comfort involved here doesn't go by way of probabilistic reasoning.

There is much to be said about the Christian meaning of suffering,[37] and much of it provides further epistemic resources for dealing with evil. Perhaps our suffering is deeply connected with the possibility of salvation for human beings;[38] perhaps we share in Christ's suffering in such a way that our suffering too is salvific, and perhaps

---

since he suffers and dies. The night on Golgotha is so important in the history of man only because, in its shadows, the divinity, ostensibly abandoning its traditional privileges, lived through to the end, despair included, the agony of death. Thus is explained the *Lama sabachthani* and the frightful doubt of Christ in agony. (*Essais* [Paris: Gallimard, 1965], p. 444. Quoted in Bruce Ward, "Prometheus or Cain? Albert Camus's Account of the Western Quest for Justice," *Faith and Philosophy* [April 1991], p. 213; this passage is translated by Ward)

36. Another such resource has to do with the fact that from the point of view of Christian trinitarian doctrine, personal relationships such as love are to be found at the deepest levels of reality; see above, pp. 320ff.

37. Some of which is said in *Salvifici Doloris*, Apostolic Letter of John Paul II (Boston: Pauline Books and Media), pp. 30ff., a profound meditation on suffering and a powerful effort to discern its meaning from a Christian perspective.

38. *Salvifici Doloris*, pp. 30ff.

even essential to the plan of salvation.[39] Someone who suffers may then look forward to receiving the divine gratitude for taking part in this project of salvation,[40] and to enjoying forever the love and approval of God; she may then concur with Paul: "We are fellow heirs with Christ, provided we suffer with him in order that we may also be glorified with him."[41] She may thus reflect that human suffering is in a way an occasion of gratitude. There is another way in which it is perhaps an occasion for gratitude. It is plausible to think that the best possible worlds God could have actualized contain the unthinkably great good of divine incarnation and redemption—but then, of course, also sin and suffering. God chooses one of these worlds to be actual—and in it, humankind suffers. Still, in this world there is also the marvelous opportunity for redemption and for eternal fellowship with God, an inconceivably great good that vastly outweighs the suffering we are called upon to endure.[42] Still further, in being offered eternal fellowship with God, we human beings are invited to join the charmed circle of the trinity itself; and perhaps that invitation can be issued only to creatures who have fallen, suffered, and been redeemed.[43] If so, the condition of humankind is vastly better than it would have been, had there been no sin and no suffering. *O Felix Culpa*, indeed!

Accordingly, those who have faith (those in whom the process of regeneration has taken or is taking place) will also be such that the presence and goodness of God is to some degree evident to them; so for them the belief that there is such a person as God will have considerable warrant. They too, then, like someone in whom the *sensus*

39. As is suggested by Paul's enigmatic remark: "Now I rejoice in what was suffered for you, and I fill up in my flesh what is still lacking in regard to Christ's afflictions" (Colossians 1:24).

40. "According to Julian of Norwich, before the elect have a chance to thank God for all He has done for them, God will say, 'Thank you for all your suffering, the suffering of your youth' " (Marilyn Adams, "Horrendous Evils and the Goodness of God," *Proceedings of the Aristotelian Society*, supplementary vol. 63 (1989), reprinted with emendations in *The Problem of Evil*, ed. Marilyn Adams and Robert Adams (New York: Oxford University Press, 1990), p. 219. The passage Adams cites is from *Revelations of Divine Love*, chapter 14).

41. Romans 8:17. Compare 2 Corinthians 4:17: "For this slight momentary affliction is preparing us for an eternal weight of glory beyond all comparison."

42. Paul continues in Romans 8:18: "For I consider that the sufferings of this present time are not worth comparing with the glory that is to be revealed in us."

43. Thus Abraham Kuyper: "The angels of God have no knowledge of sin, hence also they have no knowledge of forgiveness, hence again they have no knowledge of that tender love that is formed from forgiveness. Nor have they that richer knowledge of God which springs from this tenderer affection. They stand as strangers in the face of it, and therefore says the Apostle that, with respect to this mystery, the angels are, as it were, jealously desirous 'to look into it' " (*To Be near unto God*, p. 307).

divinitatis had never been damaged, will feel little or no inclination to atheism or agnosticism when confronted with cases of horrifying evil. They may be perplexed; they may be shocked; they may be spurred both to action and to inquiry by the presence of appalling evil in God's world; but ceasing to believe will not be an option. If the salient suffering is their own, they may concur with the author of Psalm 119: 75–76: "I know, O Lord, that your laws are righteous, and in faithfulness you have afflicted me. May your unfailing love be my comfort, according to your promise to your servant."

They may also enjoy a blessed contentment. Consider, for example, this letter from Guido de Bres to his wife, written shortly before he was hanged:

> Your grief and anguish, troubling me in the midst of my joy and gladness, are the cause of my writing you this present letter. I most earnestly pray you not to be grieved beyond measure. . . . If the Lord had wished us to live together longer, He could easily have caused it to be so. . . . Let His good will be done, then, and let that suffice for all reason. . . . I pray you, my dear and faithful companion, to be glad with me, and to thank the good God for what He is doing, for He does nothing but what is altogether right and good. . . .
>
> I am shut up in the strongest and wretchedest of dungeons, so dark and gloomy that it goes by the name of the Black Hole. I can get but little air, and that of the foulest. I have on my hands and feet heavy irons which are a constant torture, galling the flesh even to my poor bones. But, notwithstanding all, my God fails not to make good His promise, and to comfort my heart, and to give me a most blessed content.[44]

De Bres suffered greatly; yet he enjoyed a most blessed content. The furthest thing from his mind, no doubt, was the thought that maybe there wasn't any such person as God, that maybe he had been deceived all along. And this continuing to believe, given the model of chapter 8, betrays no irrationality at all: it isn't as if he had a defeater for theistic belief in his suffering, but somehow suppressed it and (perhaps by way of wishful thinking) continued to believe anyway. No, his belief was instead a result of the proper function of the cognitive processes—a rejuvenated *sensus divinitatis*, the internal instigation of the Holy Spirit—that produce belief in God.

Of course most of us are not in the spiritual condition of Guido de Bres. Not nearly all of us enjoy that comfort and content in the face of suffering. As Calvin points out (*Institutes*, III, ii, 15, p. 560), most of us sometimes have difficulty thinking that God is, indeed,

---

44. Quoted in Cornelius Plantinga Jr., *A Place to Stand* (Grand Rapids: Board of Publications of the Christian Reformed Church, 1981), p. 35. De Bres (1522–67) was the author of the Belgic Confession.

benevolent toward us; and even the great masters of the spiritual life sometimes find themselves in spiritual darkness.[45] Christians must concede that their epistemic and spiritual situation differs widely from person to person, and within a given person from time to time. Aren't there any conditions at all, then, in which the facts of evil constitute a defeater for Christian belief?

Well, I should think the right answer is "Probably not." Consider a person in whom the *sensus divinitatis* doesn't work at all well, a person who believes in God in a thoughtless and merely formal way, a person for whom the belief has no real vivacity or liveliness — perhaps such a person, on coming to a deep appreciation of the facts of evil, will ordinarily give up theistic belief. As I argued above, however (pp. 485ff.), that doesn't show that this person has a defeater for theistic belief. She has such a defeater only if it is part of our cognitive design plan to give up theistic belief in those circumstances; and we have no reason to think that it is. The design plan includes the proper function of the *sensus divinitatis*; how things actually go when that process does not function properly *could* be part of the design plan; more likely, though, it is an unintended by-product rather than a part of the design plan.

Nevertheless, let's suppose, just for purposes of argument, that as a matter of fact such a person really *does* have a defeater for theistic belief. What it is important to see, here, is that if she does have a defeater, it is only because of a failure of rationality somewhere in her noetic structure (perhaps there is dysfunction with respect to the *sensus divinitatis*). And now suppose we return to our original question: does a person *S* who believes that there is such a person as God have a defeater in the facts of evil? We can now see that there is no reason to think so. The very fact that *S* continues in theistic belief is evidence that the *sensus divinitatis* is functioning properly to at least some degree in her, and in such a way that knowledge of the facts of evil does not constitute a defeater. It is perhaps *possible* (if failure to believe in these circumstances *is* part of the design plan) that she has a defeater; but there is no reason to think so. I conclude, therefore, that in all likelihood believers in God do not have defeaters for theistic belief in knowledge of the facts of evil.

45. Thus Teresa of Liseaux:

> I get tired of this darkness all around me. . . . It is worse torment than ever; the darkness itself seems to borrow, from the sinners who live in it, the gift of speech. I hear its mocking accents: "It's all a dream, this talk of a heavenly country bathed in light, scented with delicious perfumes, and of a God who made it all, who is to be your possession in eternity! . . . Death will make nonsense of your hopes; it will only mean a night darker than before, the night of mere non-existence." . . . And all of the time it isn't just a veil, it's a great wall which reaches up to the sky and blots out the stars.

Of course all this is from the perspective of Christian theism. If Christian theism is true, then the existence of the sin and evil and suffering we see does not, in the typical case, constitute a defeater for belief in God. In particular, it doesn't constitute a defeater for Quinn's "intellectually sophisticated adult in our culture" (above, p. 358), at least if she has given a little thought to the epistemology of the matter. Now someone who doesn't accept Christian theism may be unmoved by this fact; he may concede that from the standpoint of Christian theism, suffering and evil do not constitute a defeater for Christian belief; but (so he says) Christian theism is *false*. Hence this fact—that if it were true, evil would not constitute a defeater for Christian belief—cuts no ice with respect to his claim that, as a matter of fact, evil *does* constitute such a defeater. But if he is thinking of an *internal* defeater for theistic belief, then he is mistaken; knowledge of the facts of evil does not constitute an internal defeater, at least for those believers for whom it seems very clear that there is such a person as God and that, indeed, the whole Christian story is true. For such a person, this will seem clear even after he is fully aware of the evils the world contains and has thought hard about them. Therefore there is nothing *internally* irrational in his believing these things; it is not that he somehow fails to believe what seems to him clearly true or somehow mismanages epistemic matters downstream from experience. So if there is irrationality here, it must be *external*; it must be that this inclination to believe, this doxastic evidence, is itself a product of cognitive dysfunction, or else of cognitive processes not directed at truth. The Christian or theistic believer, naturally enough, won't agree: she will see her belief as the product of cognitive faculties functioning properly, functioning in the way God intended them to (and aimed at producing true beliefs).

What we see here is another instance of a general pattern: once more it appears that questions about the rationality of belief in God (and in the whole Christian story) aren't merely epistemological. What a rational person will do when confronted with suffering and evil depends on what the cognitive design plan for human beings is; but from a filled-out Christian perspective, that design plan will be such that someone who (like Mother Teresa, e.g.) continues to accept Christian belief in the face of the world's suffering and evil displays no irrationality whatever. Indeed, it is the person who gives up belief in God under these circumstances who displays cognitive dysfunction; for such a person, the *sensus divinitatis* must be at least partly disordered. The atheologian can properly claim that evil constitutes a defeater for Christian belief, therefore, only if he already assumes that Christian belief is false. But then a Christian believer can't sensibly be expected to concede that she *does* have a defeater for Christian belief—at least until the atheologian produces a good reason or two for supposing Christian belief is false. Because she is a Christian believer, she will think, naturally enough, that her Christian belief is true, in which case the facts of evil do not defeat it.

This chapter has been devoted to the question whether knowledge of the facts of evil constitutes a defeater for Christian belief. Of course there are many related projects lurking in the neighborhood. One of particular interest is that of employing the resources of the Christian faith in thinking about sin and evil—not in order to defend the epistemic status of Christian belief but as part of a larger project of Christian scholarship, of discerning the ways in which Christian belief illuminates many of the important areas of human concern. This is an extremely important task that hasn't received nearly the attention it deserves from Christian philosophers.[46] Here is one issue that arises in this area. According to Christian belief, God is wholly good, but also perfectly loving, loves each of his creatures with a perfect love. If so, could it be that he would permit a person S to suffer for the good of someone *else* (or, more abstractly, permit S to suffer because S's suffering is an element in the best world God can actualize)? If he is perfectly loving, wouldn't he permit S to suffer only in the interests of securing an outweighing good for S herself? This is a fascinating and complex issue; I don't have the space to deal with it properly. It is clear, however, that we need some distinctions. First, God (assuming that he is perfectly loving) could certainly permit someone to suffer for the good of someone else if, as in Christ's case, this suffering is voluntarily assumed. Suppose, therefore, my suffering is not voluntarily assumed: I am not able, for one reason or another, to make the decision whether to accept suffering (just as someone in a coma might not be able to make an important decision affecting her life). Suppose also God knew that if I *were* able to make that decision, I would accept the suffering: then too, so far as I can see, his being perfectly good wouldn't at all preclude his permitting me to suffer for the benefit of others. Alternatively, suppose I am able to make the decision and in fact would *not* accept the suffering; God knows that this unwillingness on my part would be due only to ignorance: if I knew the relevant facts, then I would accept the suffering. In that case too God's perfect goodness would not preclude his permitting me to suffer; and this would be true even if I were myself innocent of wrongdoing. Indeed, suppose what God knows is that if I knew enough and also had the right affections, *then* I would accept the suffering: in that case, too, as far as I can see, his being perfectly loving would not preclude his allowing me to suffer.

There is another distinction that must be made. Perhaps God's reason for permitting me to suffer is not that by undergoing this suffering *I* can thus achieve a greater good (the good of enjoying his gratitude, for example: see footnote 40) but because he can thus achieve a better

---

46. For interesting and seminal work in this area, I should like to recommend *Salvifici Doloris* (see fn. 37), Marilyn Adams's "Horrendous Evils and the Goodness of God" (see fn. 40), Diogenes Allen's *The Traces of God in a Frequently Hostile World* (Cowley Publications, 1980), and Eleonore Stump's "The Mirror of Evil" (see fn. 31).

world overall. Nevertheless, perhaps it is also true that he would not permit me to suffer for that end, an end outside my own good, unless he could also bring good *for me* out of the evil. Then his reason for permitting me to suffer would not be that this suffering contributes to my own improvement; nevertheless, he would not permit me to suffer unless the suffering could somehow be turned to my own good. A constraint on God's *reasons* (induced, perhaps, by his being perfectly loving) is one thing; a constraint on the conditions under which he would permit involuntary and innocent suffering is another. To return to an earlier example (above, p. 489), perhaps God sees that the best worlds he can actualize are ones that include the unthinkably great good of divine incarnation and atonement. Suppose he therefore actualizes a world α in which human beings fall into sin and evil, salvation from which is accomplished by incarnation and atonement. And suppose still further that the final condition of human beings, in α, is better than it is in the worlds in which there is no fall into sin but also no incarnation and redemption. Then God's actualizing α involves suffering for many human beings; his reason for permitting that suffering is not that thereby the suffering individuals will be benefited (his reason is that he wishes to actualize a very good world, one with the great good of incarnation, atonement, and redemption). Nevertheless his perfect goodness perhaps mandates that he actualize a world in which those who suffer are benefited in such a way that their condition is better than it is in those worlds in which they do not suffer.

The book of Job gives splendid expression to some of the themes of this chapter.[47] As the story opens, Satan challenges God: his servant Job, he says, is a toady, a sycophantic timeserver who will turn on God and curse him to his face if things don't go his way. God disagrees, and then permits Satan to afflict Job, whose friends Eliphaz the Temanite, Bildad the Shuhite, and Zophar the Naamathite come to comfort and console him. After seven days and nights of silence (one pictures them hunkered down around a campfire), they tell him repeatedly and at great length that the righteous always prosper and the wicked always come to grief:

> Consider now: Who, being innocent, has ever perished? Where were the upright ever destroyed? As I have observed, those who plow evil and those who sow trouble reap it. (4:7–8)

> All his days the wicked man suffers torment, the ruthless through all the years stored up for him. Terrifying sounds fill his ear; when all seems well, marauders attack him. He despairs of escaping the darkness; he is marked for the sword. He wanders about—food for vultures. . . . Distress and anguish fill him with terror. . . . (15:20–24)

47. For profoundly insightful comment on the main themes of Job, see Eleonore Stump's "Second-Person Accounts and the Problem of Evil," Stob Lecture at Calvin College, January 1999 (Grand Rapids: Calvin College, 1999).

So Job must be wicked indeed to warrant such great suffering:

> Is it for your piety that he rebukes you and brings charges against you? Is not your wickedness great? Are not your sins endless? . . . you stripped men of their clothing, leaving them naked. You gave no water to the weary and you withheld food from the hungry, though you were a powerful man, owning land, an honored man, living on it. And you sent widows away empty-handed and broke the strength of the fatherless. That is why snares are all around you, why sudden peril terrifies you, why it is so dark you cannot see and why a flood of water covers you. (22:4–11)

Job must repent and mend his ways:

> But if you will look to God and plead with the Almighty, if you are pure and upright, even now he will rouse himself on your behalf and restore you to your rightful place. (8:5–6)

Job is understandably nettled:

> Doubtless you are the people, and wisdom will die with you! But I have a mind as well as you. . . . (12:1–3)

> Miserable comforters are you all! Will your long-winded speeches never end? (16:2–3)

He knows that the rain falls on the just and on the unjust, that the wicked often prosper:

> Why do the wicked live on, growing old and increasing in power? They see their children established around them, their offspring before their eyes. Their homes are safe and free from fear; the rod of God is not upon them. Their bulls never fail to breed; their cows calve and do not miscarry. They send forth their children as a flock; their little ones dance about. . . . They spend their years in prosperity and go down to the grave in peace. (21:7–13)

Job also knows he has done nothing unusually heinous or wicked: "my hands have been free of violence and my prayer is pure" (16:17). No doubt "no one does good, no, not one"; but Job is described in the prologue as "blameless and upright"; he knows that he isn't being singled out because he is so much more wicked than the rest of humanity (in particular, he is no greater sinner than Eliphaz, Bildad, or Zophar). So he begins to accuse God of treating him unfairly in permitting him to suffer in this way:

> then know that God has wronged me and drawn his net around me. (19:6)

> As surely as God lives, who has denied me justice. . . . (27:2)

He doesn't fear to speak his mind to the Lord. Indeed, a certain suggestion of sarcasm sometimes creeps in: "Does it please you to oppress me, to spurn the work of your hands, while you smile on the schemes of the wicked?" (10:3), as well as a certain self-righteousness: "So these three men stopped answering Job, because he was righteous in his own eyes" (32:1), and even a touch of defiance: "I will never admit you are in the right; till I die, I will not deny my integrity. I will maintain my righteousness and never let go of it . . . " (27:5–6). He believes that he is innocent of all wrongdoing and wants to go to court with God to get this thing straightened out:

> Oh that I had someone to hear me! I sign now my defense [after a lengthy recital of his virtues]—let the Almighty answer me; let my accuser put his indictment in writing. Surely I would wear it on my shoulder, I would put it on like a crown." (31:35–36).

(Again, that note of sarcasm.) But when he ruefully recalls that God would be prosecuting attorney, judge, jury, and executioner, he isn't sanguine about the outcome:

> If I say, "I will forget my complaint, I will change my expression, and smile," I still dread all my sufferings, for I know you will not hold me innocent. (9:27–28)

There are at least two ways we can understand Job here. In the first way, Job's problem is really intellectual; he can't see any reason at all why God should allow him to be afflicted as he is; and he is inclined to conclude, unthinkingly, that probably God doesn't *have* a good reason. The point here is that the reason for Job's sufferings is something entirely beyond his knowledge or awareness; but then the fact that he can't see what sort of reason God might have for permitting his suffering doesn't even tend to suggest that God has no reason. And when God replies to Job, he doesn't tell him what his reason is for permitting these sufferings (perhaps Job couldn't so much as grasp or comprehend it). Instead, he attacks the implicit inference from Job's not being able to see what God's reason is to the notion that probably he has none; he does this by pointing out how vast is the gulf between Job's knowledge and God's:

> Then the Lord answered Job out of the tempest: Who is this whose ignorant words darken counsel? Brace yourself and stand up like a man; I will ask questions and you shall answer. Where were you when I laid the earth's foundations? Tell me, if you know and understand! Who settled its dimensions? Surely you should know! Who stretched his measuring-line over it? On what do its supporting pillars rest? Who set its corner-stone in place, when the morning stars sang together and all the sons of God shouted for joy? . . . . Have you descended to the springs of the sea or walked in the unfathomable deep? Have the gates of death been revealed to you? Have you ever seen the door-keepers of the place of darkness? Have you comprehended the vast expanse of the world? Come, tell me all this, if you know! Which is the way to the home of light and

where does darkness dwell? And can you then take each to its ap-
pointed bound and escort it on its homeward path? Doubtless you
know all this; for you were born already, so long is the span of your
life! (38:1–7, 16–21)

Job complains that God apparently has no good reason for permitting the evil that befalls him. He suspects that God doesn't have a
good reason because he, Job, can't imagine what that reason might
be. In reply, God does not tell him what the reason is; instead, he attacks Job's unthinking assumption that if he, Job, can't imagine what
reason God might have, then probably God doesn't have a reason at
all. And God attacks this assumption by pointing out how limited
Job's knowledge is along these lines.[48] No doubt he can't see what
God's reason might be, but nothing of interest follows from this: in
particular it doesn't follow that probably God doesn't *have* a reason.
"All right, Job, if you're so smart, if you know so much, tell me about
it! Tell me how the universe was created; tell me about the sons of
God who shouted with joy upon its creation! No doubt you were
there!" And Job sees the point: "I have spoken of great things which
I have not understood, things too wonderful for me to know" (42:3).

There is quite another way to understand Job—a way that can be
combined with the first. Taken this second way, the idea is not that
Job suspects or is inclined to think probably God doesn't have a reason for allowing his afflictions. It is rather that Job just becomes
angry with God, hates and abhors what God is doing (or not doing),
and is expressing his displeasure—and all of this quite independent
of whether or not he thinks God has a reason. "Sure, maybe God has
a reason—being God, he naturally would, wouldn't he? But *I* can't
see the slightest suggestion as to what his reason may be; and why do
I have to suffer so that he can attain these no doubt dandy ends of
his—without so much as being consulted? without so much as a by-
your-leave? I hate it! And I'm angry with him! These 'reasons' of his,
whatever they are, are wholly inscrutable; and why should I suffer
for these things beyond my ken? I don't give a fig for those reasons,
and I detest what he is doing!" Here there isn't the suggestion that
God maybe doesn't have reasons and is perhaps even *unjust*; this
thought doesn't really enter, or at least isn't center stage. There is, instead, mistrust of God, wariness of him and his alleged magnificent
ends, hatred of what this does to Job and requires of him, a hint or
more than a hint of rebellion. And then when God comes to Job in
the whirlwind, it is not to convince him that God really does have reasons (although it may, in fact, do this); it is instead to still the tempest
in his soul, to quiet him, to restore his trust for God. The Lord gives

48. Thus inviting Job to consider the possibility that God's reasons for permitting evil are more like noseeums than St. Bernards; see above, p. 466.

Job a glimpse of his greatness, his beauty, his splendid goodness; the
doubts and turmoil disappear and are replaced, once more, by love
and trust, a state of mind expressed in all its Christian completeness
by the apostle Paul:

> No, in all these things we are more than conquerors through him
> who loved us. For I am convinced that neither death nor life, nei-
> ther angels nor demons, neither the present nor the future, nor any
> powers, neither height nor depth, nor anything else in all creation,
> will be able to separate us from the love of God that is in Christ
> Jesus our Lord.[49]

It is time, and past time, to bring this book and this trilogy to a
close. In *Warrant: The Current Debate* and *Warrant and Proper Function*,
what I argued, essentially, is that the only viable answer to the question 'What is knowledge?' lies in the neighborhood of proper function: a belief has warrant if and only if it is produced by cognitive faculties functioning properly in a congenial epistemic environment
according to a design plan successfully aimed at the production of
true belief. (This is the basic idea; there is a good bit of fine-tuning required, including some in chapter 6 of the present book.)

In this, the final member of the trilogy, I argued first in part I
(chapters 1 and 2) that there really is such a thing as Christian belief
and that (contra Kaufman, Hick, and Kant under one interpretation)
we can, in fact, talk and think about God. In part II, the next three
chapters, I distinguished *de jure* from *de facto* objections to Christian
belief; the former are to the effect that such belief is intellectually or
rationally questionable, even if true. Although *de jure* objections have
been very common ever since the Enlightenment, it isn't easy to tell
what the objections are supposed to be. I argued that no viable *de jure*
objection lies in the neighborhood either of justification or of internal rationality. The only initially promising candidate for a viable *de
jure* objection to Christian belief, I said, can be approached by way of
Freud's claim that Christian belief does not have warrant, or at any
rate warrant sufficient for knowledge. Freud, however, simply presupposes that theistic and hence Christian belief is false; therefore
this alleged *de jure* objection fails to be independent of the *truth* of
Christian belief. If Christian belief were false, perhaps Freud would
be right; but the *de jure* objection was supposed to be *independent* of its
truth or falsehood; hence this is not a successful *de jure* objection. I argued further that the same fate will befall any alleged *de jure* objection formulated in terms of warrant. That is because if Christian belief is true, it very likely does have warrant; hence any objection to its
having warrant will have to be an objection to its being true; but in

49. Romans 8:16–19.

that case the alleged *de jure* objection either becomes or presupposes a *de facto* objection. Accordingly, a common agnostic attitude—I have no idea whether Christian belief is true, but I do know that it is irrational (or unjustified, or . . .) cannot be defended.

In part III, chapter 6, I presented the Aquinas/Calvin model of how it is that belief in God can have warrant, and even warrant sufficient for knowledge. In the next chapter, I considered the noetic effects of sin, and the way in which the existence of sin throws a monkey wrench into the A/C model. In chapters 8 and 9, I extended the A/C model in such a way as to deal both with sin and with the full panoply of Christian belief: trinity, incarnation, atonement, resurrection. Chapter 10 dealt with objections to this model. Finally, in part IV, I turned to potential or actual *defeaters* for Christian belief—possible reasons to give it up or hold it less firmly. There were projection theories (chapter 11), contemporary historical biblical criticism (chapter 12), postmodernism and pluralism (chapter 13), and the age-old problem of evil (chapter 14). None of these, I argued, presents a serious challenge to the warrant Christian belief can enjoy if the model, and indeed Christian belief, is, in fact, true.

But *is* it true? This is the really important question. And here we pass beyond the competence of philosophy, whose main competence, in this area, is to clear away certain objections, impedances, and obstacles to Christian belief. Speaking for myself and of course not in the name of philosophy, I can say only that it does, indeed, seem to me to be true, and to be the maximally important truth.

Index